Index to

The Modern Theatre

Orig Vol., Page

Anonymous	He's Much To Blame	IV,	163
Anonymous	Matilda	VIII,	1
Anonymous	The School for Wives	IX,	233
Anonymous	What Is She?	X,	217
Cobb, James	Ramah Droog	VI,	139
Cobb, James	The Wife of Two Husbands	VI,	75
Colman, George	The English Merchant	IX,	165
Colman, George	Who Wants a Guinea?	III,	207
Cowley, Mrs.	Which Is The Man?	X,	149
Cumberland, Richard	False Impressions	V,	1
Cumberland, Richard	The Box-Lobby Challenge	V,	137
Cumberland, Richard	The Carmelite	V,	283
Cumberland, Richard	The Imposters	VI,	1
Cumberland, Richard	The Mysterious Husband	V,	69
Cumberland, Richard	The Natural Son	V,	215
Dibdin, Thomas	The School for Prejudice	IV,	331
Holcroft, Thomas	Duplicity	IV,	1
Holcroft, Thomas	Seduction	IV,	253
Holcroft, Thomas	The School for Arrogance	IV,	75
Holman, J. G.	The Votary of Wealth	III,	1
Hull, Thomas	Henry The Second, or The Fall of Rosamond	IX,	337
Inchbald, Mrs.	I'll Tell You What	VII,	1
Inchbald, Mrs.	Next Door Neighbours	VII,	68
Inchbald, Mrs.	The Wise Man of the East	VII,	116
Jephson, Robert	Braganza	VI,	263
Jephson, Robert	The Law of Lombardy	VI,	193
Lee, Miss	The Chapter of Accidents	IX,	81
Macready, William	The Bank Note	IX,	1
Macnally, Leonard	Fashionable Levities	X,	1
More, Hannah	Percy	VII,	181
Morton, Thomas	Secrets Worth Knowing	III,	141
Morton, Thomas	Zorinski	III,	85
O'Keeffe, John	Lie of a Day	X,	299
Philon, Frederic	He Would Be A Soldier	VIII,	225
Reynolds, Frederick	Folly As It Flies	II,	287
Reynolds, Frederick	Fortune's Fool	II,	219
Reynolds, Frederick	How To Grow Rich	I,	217
Reynolds, Frederick	Laugh When You Can	II,	145
Reynolds, Frederick	Life	I,	143
Reynolds, Frederick	Notoriety	I,	279
Reynolds, Frederick	Speculation	II,	1
Reynolds, Frederick	The Delinquent	II,	75
Reynolds, Frederick	The Rage	I,	67
Reynolds, Frederick	Werter	III,	291
Reynolds, Frederick	The Will	I,	1
Reynolds, Frederick	The Fugitive	VIII,	133
Sheridan, Richard B.	A Trip to Scarborough	VII,	237
Siddon, Henry	Time's A Tell-Tale	X,	81
St. John, John	Mary Queen of Scots	VIII,	67
Watson, George	England Preserved	VIII,	309

THE MODERN THEATRE

A collection of plays

selected by

MRS. ELIZABETH INCHBALD

First published London, 1811

in ten volumes

Reissued in 1968
in five volumes
by Benjamin Blom, Inc.

Benjamin Blom, Inc.

New York

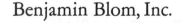

THE

MODERN THEATRE;

A COLLECTION OF

SUCCESSFUL MODERN PLAYS,

AS ACTED AT

THE THEATRES ROYAL, LONDON.

PRINTED FROM THE PROMPT BOOKS UNDER THE AU-
THORITY OF THE MANAGERS.

SELECTED BY

MRS INCHBALD.

———

IN TEN VOLUMES.

VOL. III.

VOTARY OF WEALTH.   SECRETS WORTH KNOWING.
ZORINSKI.   WHO WANTS A GUINEA.
                    WERTER.

LONDON:

PRINTED FOR LONGMAN, HURST, REES, ORME, AND BROWN,
PATERNOSTER-ROW.

1811.

First published London, 1811
Reissued 1968,
by Benjamin Blom, Inc. Bx 10452

Library of Congress Catalog Card No. 67-13004

Manufactured in the United States of America

THE

VOTARY OF WEALTH,

A

COMEDY,

IN FIVE ACTS.

AS PERFORMED AT THE

THEATRE-ROYAL, COVENT-GARDEN.

BY

J. G. HOLMAN.

VOL. III.　　　　A

DRAMATIS PERSONÆ.

OLD VISORLY,	Mr Emery.
LEONARD VISORLY,	Mr Pope.
DROOPLY,	Mr Lewis.
SHARPSET,	Mr Fawcett.
OAKWORTH,	Mr Munden.
CLEVELAND,	Mr Murray.
HENRY MELVILLE,	Mr H. Johnston.
MASTER OF HOTEL,	Mr Thompson.
BAILIFF,	Mr Abbot.
SIMPSON,	Mr Blurton.
SERVANT,	Mr Curtis.
LADY JEMIMA VISORLY,	Mrs Davenport.
CAROLINE,	Miss Betterton.
MRS CLEVELAND,	Miss Chapman.
JULIA CLEVELAND,	Mrs Pope.
GANGICA, a Gentoo,	Mrs H. Johnston.

SCENE—London.

THE

VOTARY OF WEALTH.

ACT THE FIRST.

SCENE I.

An Apartment in OLD VISORLY'S *House.* OLD
VISORLY *and* LADY JEMIMA *at breakfast.* OLD
VISORLY *reading Newspapers.*

Lady Jem. A very pleasant, sociable companion,
indeed, Mr Visorly! Can you pore over newspapers
at no other time? You compliment me most highly,
in letting me see that while you are in my company
you need other entertainment.

Old Vis. My dear, I beg your pardon. One is
anxious, you know, for the good of one's country.

Lady Jem. You are anxious, Mr Visorly, for any
thing that is to shew disrespect to me.

Old Vis. Lord! how you talk.---I shew disrespect to you! (*Still reading.*)

Lady Jem. There! are you not still inattentive to me and my remonstrances? Ah! I might have known what I had to expect. This is the consequence of losing sight of what was due to my birth and rank, and marrying a commoner.

Old Vis. My dear Lady Jemima, why should you urge that so often? I am sensible of the honour, and of my own unworthiness.

Lady Jem. Still you pay no attention to what I am complaining of. Any thing, I find, is preferable to my conversation.

Old Vis. Never spoke a truer word in her life. (*Aside.*) My dear, I shall have done in a moment--- I am among the deaths.

Lady Jem. I wish to the Lord you were.

Old Vis. Oh fie, fie, Lady Jemima!

Lady Jem. You would provoke the patience of a saint (OLD VISORLY *starts up; he has been still reading*) What is the matter?

Old Vis. Tol lol de rol! (*Singing and capering.*)

Lady Jem. The man is mad.

Old Vis. Tol lol de rol!

Lady Jem. What frenzy has seized you?

Old Vis. Frenzy, my dear! only the frenzy that arises from good news.

Lady Jem. Can't you give utterance to your good news without such absurdity?

Old Vis. Well, well, I will, my dear. (*Reads.*) " On Thursday, the 14th of last March, died, at an advanced age, at Calcutta, in Bengal"---Tol lol de rol!

Lady Jem. Oh, mad, mad!

Old Vis " John Cleveland, Esq.---His immense wealth devolves on his only son, who is shortly expected in England."—There is a fortune for our dear son Leonard!

Lady Jem. How do you mean for our Leonard?

Old Vis. Mr Cleveland, the son and heir of the deceased, is my first cousin---I'm his nearest of kin. ----The old fellow who is dead was such a capricious sort of animal, that he might have left every shilling of it away from his own son; but now it is come into his possession, it is in the fair road to our family.

Lady Jem. This, indeed, is welcome news—and here comes our dear Leonard to partake it.

Enter LEONARD.

Old Vis. Ah, my dear boy!

Lady Jem. Ah, my dear son!

Leo. Good morning—How do you do?

Lady Jem Here is news!

Old Vis. Ah, my boy, we have news for you!

Leo. Well, let me have it.

Old Vis. Why, then——

Lady Jem. No, no, Mr Visorly—I'll tell it him.

Leo. I'll save you the trouble.—Old Cleveland is dead at Calcutta—his son inherits all his fortune—and the good news is, that their bulses and lacks may eventually come to our family.

Old Vis. Ay, my boy!

Lady Jem. Yes, Leonard!

Leo. I would not give five guineas for the chance of inheritance.

Old Vis. No!

Leo. No. I know a little more of the circumstances than you do.—Mr Cleveland has a daughter.

Old Vis. Poh, poh! some—some—you understand me.

Lady Jem. Mr Visorly, I am shocked at your indelicate allusions.

Leo. I wish they were well grounded; but 'tis a melancholy fact, that the daughter is legitimate, and her mother, Cleveland's wife, is living.

Old Vis. Dear me, dear me!

Lady Jem. How do you know all this?

Leo. From the most positive information—Cleveland's own acknowledgment:——He has written to me.

Old Vis. Really!

Leo. Yes—Stating, that as we were the nearest and only male relations he had, to us he has taken the liberty of consigning his remittances—with directions how he wishes them to be invested. Understanding that your residence in London was only casual, and also thinking the trouble of business more suited to my time of life, he thought it better to address his letter to me. In it he explains all the particulars of his marriage, and recommends his wife and daughter to our attention.

Lady Jem. How—are they not with him?

Leo. No. His daughter we may hourly expect.— Not being able to settle his affairs immediately on the death of his father, he sent her before him, unwilling to detain her from her mother.

Lady Jem. Why, is the mother in England?

Leo. Yes—and has been for several years. His marriage was without the consent of his father, and for some time unknown to him.—Enraged when he discovered it, he insisted on a separation.—To avoid ruin, which would have been the consequence of his father's resentment, he was forced to comply. The child was suffered to remain with him—the wife was doom'd to return to England, where, for these fifteen years, she has lived in retirement.

Old Vis. Well, what is to be done?

Lady Jem. They are recommended, it seems, to our attention; but, really, I don't well see how I can reconcile to myself taking notice of, and introducing to my acquaintances, people, one doesn't know who —and that have been living one doesn't know where.

Leo. What do you talk of? Are they not the wife and daughter of a nabob? Your high-bred friends

will worship you for the introduction.   Think what
will be the magnificence of their house, the splendour
of their equipage, the brilliancy of their entertain-
ments.   Such suppers as theirs will be, the fashionable world would scramble for a seat at, even if they
were given by a personage from a hotter place than
Bengal.

Old Vis. Leonard says very truly.   We shall get
credit by shewing such gold pheasants to our friends.

Leo. Certainly; for all will be charmed with the
splendour of their plumage—even those who are so
little fashionable as not to attempt plucking the feathers.

Old Vis. Well, we must prepare to shew them all
possible civility.

Leo. Ay, ay, pray let us ; for I have something in
view that will pay us for our trouble.

Lady Jem. What is that, son ?

Leo. The hope of making the young lady a part of
our family.

Old Vis. What an excellent thought ! Ah, Leonard, Leonard, you are a cunning rogue !

Lady Jem. You amaze me, child, that you don't
extend your views.—My son, the grandson of the
earl of Castlegreat, ought to aspire to the proudest
heiresses of the noblest peers —not stoop to a thing
of mushroom growth.

Leo. Consider, mother, *this* mushroom is the
growth of a golden soil.

Lady Jem. Well, son, pursue your own inclinations ; my affection for you will always make me yield
to your wishes.

Leo. Then this glorious fortune may be mine.   Invite them to your house.   The mother having long
experienced a constrained seclusion from society,
will, doubtless, be gratified with attentions from a
woman of your rank—the daughter is young--I
don't despair of success with her ; and the preference

the father has shewn, in the trust consigned to me, makes me hope every thing from him. So all seems fair for my success; and half a million, at least, is the prize. Think of that—think of that.

Enter Servant.

Serv. A person below desires to speak with you, sir. (*To* LEONARD.)

Leo. What is his name?

Serv. He says his own name is immaterial; but he desired me to mention the name of Cleveland.

Leo. Shew him up directly.

[*Exit Servant, and enter* OAKWORTH.

Leo. You are welcome, sir.

Oak. Thank you, sir; thank you. So I, be got to you at last. You great folks take a plaguy time coming at.—Ma'am, your humble servant. Mayhap, I should say your ladyship—Pray excuse all faults.

Leo. Never mind: Lady Jemima doesn't stand on ceremony.

Oak. Don't she? Why, then, Lady Jemima is a lady just after my own heart.

Old Vis. Well, sir—you come concerning Mr Cleveland.

Oak. Why, yes, sir; yes. You must know, sir, that I am an old fellow that remember Mrs Cleveland (Heaven bless her!) when she was not the height of my knee. Often and often is the time that I have danced her o'top of it. Well, that is neither here nor there. When her father died—Ah! I shall never forget it—he has not left a better man behind him—there was not a dry eye in the village except the undertaker's, and folks do say he cried a bit. Well, her father, good soul, had met with so many losses and crosses, that there was little enough left for his daughter to live like a lady on; so she was persuaded by her friends to take a voyage to India

with a cousin of hers, who had married, and was going to settle there.

Leo. Mr Cleveland has acquainted me with the
rest.   There he married her, and from thence, by
the severity of his father, he was forced to send her.

Oak. Ah, poor dear! Home she came again, miserable enough, to be sure. Well, mayhap, all for the
best. Now she will be as happy as the day is long. But
for this many a year she has led but a lonesome sort
of a life; for you may think my dame and I, though
we love her like a child of our own, can't have been
company good enough for her: but she was as kind
to us, and made as much of us, as though we had been
the best people in the land.

Lady Jem. We shall soon, I hope, have the pleasure of receiving her in this house. She must not
think of seeing any other habitation.

Leo. Oh, certainly not. She must make this her
abode.

Old Vis. Oh, to be sure; to be sure.

Oak. Why, do you know, now, this is the very
thing that came into my head, and that I told her of.
—Says I, as sure as I am a sinner, if those relations
of Mr Cleveland's have the least bit of kind-hearted-
ness about them, they'll never let you live in any
house but their own.

Leo. Certainly!—How right you were!

Oak. And I am glad to find such friendly, good
souls in this great town of London—for, do you
know, I had got a notion of its being but a bad sort
of a place.

Leo. I trust you will find it otherwise.

Oak. Why, I hope I shall.

Lady Jem. When did Mrs Cleveland arrive?

Oak. But last night.

Lady Jem. And where is she?

Oak. Why, she is at a—at a—What the plague do

you call it ? It is the like of an inn, only it goes by
a finer name.

Leo. Oh, an hotel.

Oak. Ay, ay, an hotel.

Leo. But what hotel ?

Oak. Od rabbit it, I forget the name of it ; but I
can ask the man who shewed me the way here ; for,
as I never was in London before, I can't travel without a guide. He waits below, to take me back again
—he will tell me. (*Going.*)

Lady Jem. Stay, sir, he shall direct us both. The
carriage is waiting, and I will not lose a moment in
paying my respects to Mrs Cleveland.

Oak. Well, now, that is kind of you indeed, my
lady. I will leave the direction below stairs, and go
on before.

Leo. By no means. Lady Jemima will take you
in the carriage with her.

Oak. Why, you are joking sure !

Lady Jem. (*Aside to* Leo.) My dear Leonard,
think if I should meet any of my friends, with this
bumpkin for my Cicisbeo !

Leo. Oh, mother, to oblige me. (*Aside.*) My mother is ready to attend you, sir.

Oak. Psha, psha ! No tricks upon travellers. Her
ladyship ride with such a lout as *me !*

Lady Jem. It may well surprise you. (*Aside.*)—
Oh, sir, I shall be proud of the honour.

Oak. The honour ! That is a good one. Come
then, my lady. Lord, how my dame would laugh to
see me seated in a coach with a Lady Jemima !

[*Exeunt* OAKWORTH *and* LADY JEMIMA.

Leo. Won't you accompany my mother, sir ? I
have business which must detain me.

Old Vis. Yes, yes, I will go with you, Lady Jemima (*Calling after her.*)—I say, Leonard, where
will her ladyship wish the rustic if she meets any of

her noble relatives? Ha! ha! 'Tis a good joke.—
Ah, Leonard, you are a droll dog!   [*Exit.*

Manet LEONARD.

If my designs succeed, on what a pinnacle of fortune shall I be placed! The independence bequeathed me by my grandfather I have turned to good
account. What though it has been the means of
effecting the ruin of a few thoughtless profligates?
Their vices were incurable, and they would have been
as completely beggared by the skilful operations of
others, if all my thoughts had been engaged in the
exercise of devotion, and my guineas appropriated
to charitable donations—Nay, to preserve my estimation with the world, I have raised from the earth
those whom others, less mindful of opinion, would
have left grovelling in misery.—Psha! when I scru-
tinize my conduct with an eye half inclined to con-
demnation, I find matter for praise instead of cen-
sure.   Dupes will be dupes—knaves will make their
prey of them—and lucky is the dupe that becomes
the prey of a knave with some conscience, and a
great regard for a good reputation.—Whom have we
here?

Enter SHARPSET, *dressed as a Methodist Preacher.*

Sharp. Peace be unto this house!

Leo. Who is this? With what hedge divine have I
the honour of an acquaintance?

Sharp. Thy name is Leonard Visorly.

Leo. Well, sir, what is your business?

Sharp. To discourse with thee on the state of thy
conscience.

Leo. I request you will save yourself that trouble:
my conscience is a charge of which I choose to have
the sole guardianship.

Sharp. But it is my duty to inquire whether thou
hast treated that precious charge like unto a faithful

guardian—whether thou hast not stained with guilt
that which was consigned to thy care spotless and
pure, and which now goads thee with complainings
for thy iniquity.   Therefore, I say—

Leo. You shall say no more in this house.   Out
with you directly. (*Offering to push him out.*)

Sharp. Oh, Leonard, Leonard, is this the way you
treat an old friend, after so long an absence?

Leo. An old friend!—What do you mean? Who
are you?

Sharp. And so my reverend appearance has concealed from your recognition your friend, and brother in iniquity, Jeremy Sharpset!

Leo. Sharpset!

Sharp. The very same.

Leo. But what is the meaning of this transforma-
tion?

Sharp. The restlessness of my disposition, and inclination for any pursuit, in preference to laudable
exertion, and honest industry.

Leo. You always had a propensity to confess your
faults.

Sharp. Yes, but not much propensity to amend
them.   To be sure I shewed a little disposition towards it, by quitting you.

Leo. Your most humble servant.

Sharp. I am afraid you felt the loss of me.

Leo. Yes, I confess it—You were very serviceable.

Sharp. Yes, I was: I did the roguery, and you received the profits.

Leo. Come, come—You were not ill paid.

Sharp. Oh no—I don't complain.—How is poor
Drooply?

Leo. Still the creature of my bounty.

Sharp. Well, that is kind of you—A generous
weakness in your character—You swindled him out
of two thousand a-year, and are good enough to al-

low him a hundred. Ah, you are a model of philanthropy!

Leo. Come, a truce with your sarcasm.

Sharp. Ah, bless your honest tender heart! He is as grateful to you as ever, I conclude.

Leo. Yes, he esteems me his friend and preserver.

Sharp. Poor fellow! He was wont to set the table in a roar, now quite chop-fallen. I declare I never think of him but with a heart-ache.

Leo. Well, well—but what have you been doing since we parted?

Sharp. All sorts of things I ought not to do. To confess the truth, the reason I quitted you was, I was tired of the work you chalked out for me—You wanted to push me a little farther in roguery than I liked. I am but a petty larceny villain.—That ruin of poor Drooply, in which I was the chief engine for you—that hit me hard. I am foolish enough to have qualms. I know you despise me for it; but we all have our weaknesses.

Leo. Well, well—but what became of you?

Sharp. I'll tell you. I had unluckily, once in my life, dined at a lord-mayor's feast.—I shall never forget it.—Talk of earls and dukes entertaining!—Psha! a rivulet to the ocean.—Ever after I panted for city honours: So all my *honest* earnings I was determined to deposit in trade. An opportunity soon offered. I was to become a sleeping partner in a great house. I paid down my cash to the last guinea. A docket was struck against the firm the very next week: So the poor sleeping partner had nothing but the open air for his slumbers; and, instead of being in the road to claim a seat at a Guildhall dinner, I had scarcely enough to purchase one in Porridge Island.

Leo. So all your hopes of a gold chain vanished?

Sharp. Yes; and I was in a very likely way to be adorned with an iron one—but I was resolved to take myself out of the reach of temptation and danger, by leaving London.

Leo. In what capacity did you travel?

Sharp. Still I had a taste for partnership. I engaged with a very respectable gentleman, to divide with him the attention and profits of——

Leo. Of what?

Sharp. A collection of wild beasts.

Leo. I guess you were not a sleeping partner here.

Sharp. No; my companions were rather hostile to repose.—Not much liking such uncivilized society, and being a little apprehensive that my fellow-travellers might, one time or other, make a supper of me, I soon cut this connection; and, instead of exhibiting the merits of others, I got a taste for displaying my own.

Leo. How, pray?

Sharp. I joined a party of strolling players.

Leo. Indeed!

Sharp I know you must be shocked at my descending so damned low as to turn actor.—But I did not disgrace myself long.

Leo. How happened that?

Sharp. The audience would not let me.

Leo. How so?

Sharp. I came out in Richard the Third. I thought it devilish fine; but the good folks in the front thought otherwise.—I ranted—they hooted.—However, I out-roared them, and pushed on till I got into Bosworth Field.—" A horse! a horse! my kingdom for a horse!"—When a drunken, fox-hunting squire, (I shall never lose the sound of his damned voice,) bawled out of the boxes, that I should have the best horse in his stable, if I would ride away directly, and never come back again.

Leo. Ha! ha! ha!

Sharp. The actors warned me it would not do.

I thought it envy in them, and have some reason to
think they sent in a party to hiss me.   However, by
way of comfort, they told me, though I should never act tragedy, they thought I should succeed in
low comedy.—Low comedy! only think of their impudence! Is this a face for low comedy? No, no,
damn it! I could not stoop to that.

Leo. Well, your next resource?

Sharp. Oh, then I got a call, and mounted the
habiliments in which you see me: This was lucra-
tive; but my conscience would not suffer me any
longer to drain from the pockets of the poor the
earnings of their industry; nay, what is worse, embitter their innocent minds with groundless terrors,
and inspire them with prejudice against their fellow-
creatures.

Leo. So then you deign at last to return to me?

Sharp. Yes; for I had rather cheat the rich than
delude the poor.

Leo. Well, well, I'll endeavour to find you employment.

Sharp. That I don't doubt, as long as there is a
pigeon to be plucked, and as I am disposed to be a
rook, at your service.

Leo. No; I have honester objects in view, to at-
tain which I may need your assistance.

Sharp. Well, I'm glad of that; for, upon my soul,
I am tired of being a rogue.

Leo. If I reach the point of my present aim, I
may myself relinquish that character. I shall then
have wealth enough to gratify even *my* ambition. I
am no further a knave than as it forwards my grand
pursuit, the attainment of wealth. And who would
not use any means to gain that, which covers vice
with the garb of respect, and without which virtue
meets but pity or derision?

Sharp. Well observed: and never was observation
more patly illustrated. You are a glorious instance

of the first part of your sentiment, and here comes
a proof of the latter.

[SHARPSET *walks up the Stage.*

Enter DROOPLY.

Leo. Ah, Drooply, how do you do ?

Dro. How do you do, my dear fellow ?

Leo. Where have you hid yourself ? Nobody has
seen you of late.

Dro. I have been striving to follow the example
of my acquaintances, and learning to be as shy of
them as they are of me.

Leo. Why, what an altered being you are ! You
used to be a merry fellow.

Dro. Yes ; for I used to be a rich fellow.

Leo. Come, come, cheer up. Good spirits are a
man's best friends.

Dro. Ay ; but, like the rest of his friends, when
his money leaves him, they leave him too.

Leo. Nay, nay, your friends have not all deserted you.

Dro. All but you : There is not another man in
the world who would care a straw if the devil had
one.

Leo. If you are so despondent, I must recommend
you a spiritual comforter.—Can your reverence administer consolation to this afflicted being ? (*To*
SHARPSET.)

Sharp. No ; for I can't return him the money I
won of him.

Dro. Whom have we here ?

Sharp. What ! not remember me ? If I had done
you a kindness, I might expect to be forgotten ; but
I thought every one remembered an ill turn.

Leo. In this pious pastor you behold a quondam
acquaintance—Mr Sharpset.

Dro. What ! Sharpset turned methodist ?

Sharp. Yes; but don't wrong my understanding —Only from necessity.

Leo. You might triumph now, if you were disposed to indulge spleen; for the man who was the chief gainer by your losses at play is now as low in the world as yourself.

Sharp. No; I am so completely without gratification, I have not even the comfort a malicious disposition would afford me.   It is far from a relief to me to see another unfortunate.

Leo. You are mutually distressed; yet how differently you bear your misfortunes.

Sharp. That is easily accounted for.   I have a thousand resources—Drooply has none.   Born to no other inheritance, I have learned to turn to account what I inherit from nature; so that, though my acquisitions have been squandered, I am still in possession of my original patrimony.

Dro. Ah, you lucky dog! you have an estate in every corner of your brain, and a pretty income at the end of every finger.   Now, the whole produce of my skull would not get me change for sixpence; and as for my hands, curse them! they are fit for nothing but to dangle by my sides, or stuff out my coat-pockets.

Leo. Why, I am afraid they will never fill your pockets with any thing but themselves.

Dro. Oh! I wish I had been a Turk.

Leo. A Turk!

Dro. Yes, a Turk: They are the only wise people on earth: They teach all their great men some honest employment.

Leo. Do they?—I know some great men I wish they would give a lesson to.

Dro. Oh! if we had that good Mussulman custom among us, how many a rich man would be of more use to society when his estate was gone, than while he possessed it! as a good cobler is a more va-

luable character than a rich man who does not employ his wealth properly.

Leo. Why, you are turning moralist.

Dro. Yes; the loss of wealth seldom lessens a
man's morality.—While I am creeping about, such
a piece of moving lumber, what respect I feel for
every reputable tinker that comes in my way!—
This very morning, how I did envy a merry rogue
of a shoe-black! With what glee he put the polish
of an artist on the boot he was blacking! how merrily he brushed and sung; and how conceitedly and
happily he looked at his work when he had done it!
—Oh, you jolly dog, thought I, what a happy man
had been spoiled, if you had been born to two thousand a-year! You would never have enjoyed the
luxury of polishing a shoe, or the independent ex-
ultation of existing by your own industry.

Leo. We must endeavour to dispel your melancholy. You are a martyr to *ennui.* I must find you
employment.

Dro. You must do something beside—find me capacity.

Leo. That you don't want. Your talents have
been only slumbering.

Dro. Hav'n't they? They have had a pretty long
nap, and a sound one too. I'm afraid it will be a
hard matter to wake them.

Leo. I don't despair, especially when I shall set
the loud voice of friendship to rouse them.

Dro. If they don't wake at that call, you may take
your oath their slumber is everlasting. But though
I am master of this poor tenement, I really am so ignorant of the state of the *upper story,* as not to know
whether the inhabitants have perished by neglect, or
are only dozing from want of employment; but this
I do know, there is a lively fellow in the *first floor,*
(*Pointing to his heart,*) who would dance with joy to

do you the slightest service, and lose every drop of blood to prove his friendship and gratitude. [*Exeunt.*

ACT THE SECOND.

SCENE I.

An Apartment in VISORLY'S *House.*

Enter LEONARD *and* CAROLINE.

Car. Yes, I have not been in town above half an hour.

Leo. Have you brought with you from the country house the box which I told you contains the writings of your property?

Car. Yes—Shall I give it to you?

Leo. No; I am too busy at present—only take care of it.

Car. Well, my dear brother, I am so glad we are to have our house full of company—Oh, that is delightful! How I do love a racketting, noisy scene! In a morning the fashionable bustle of Bond Street, the musical thunder of a footman's rap, the dealing out tickets to the whole *ton* world—and then at night driving to twenty different assemblies—seeing the whole world in the course of an evening.—Oh dear, dear, what a charming age to live in! We see more of life in one day, than our ancestors did in their whole existence.

Leo. Yes; but I doubt whether we are the happier for it.

Car. To be sure we are. What is all this but happiness? Care can never reach us; for in all this hurry nobody has time to think, and you know it is thinking makes one unhappy.

Leo. Well, I'm not cynic enough to attempt to reason people out of their notions of happiness; for as it exists in imagination, the idea is the reality. But, my dear Caroline, I have told you my wish to be thought well of by this young East Indian. From living in the same house, and being nearly of an age, you will most likely contract a friendship.

Car. Yes; and her taking my brother for her lover will be the best security for that friendship; for then we can't be rivals—and nothing is so apt to make young ladies disagree, as being both of the same mind.

Old Vis. (*Without.*) This way, Mrs Cleveland.

Leo. Here comes the mother.

Enter MRS CLEVELAND, LADY JEMIMA, *and* OLD VISORLY.

Old Vis. Believe me, madam, we experience the greatest pleasure in welcoming you to this house.— My daughter, madam—my son Leonard.

Leo. I feel extreme happiness in the event of this moment, which makes me known to you, madam. Suffer me to assure you, that if I can be the humble instrument of rendering you a service, I shall esteem it the greatest bliss of my life.

Mrs Clev. Sir, I thank you.

Lady Jem. I hope, madam, we shall be able to make your residence here not entirely disagreeable to you. Our friends and connections, among whom, I am proud to say, are some of the first rank, will, I am sure, do their *possible* to second our poor endeavours.

Mrs Clev. Your kindness, madam, merits my warmest return of gratitude. The endearing attentions with which you honour me will tend to soothe the terrors of a mind, anxious for the safety of the dear objects on which all its future happiness depends.

Leo. With what sincere joy, madam, I consider how short will be the continuance of your apprehensions, and how complete the happiness you will so soon possess.

Mrs Clev. Heaven grant it! I have passed many a tedious year with no other solace than the hope of what now appears so near me. Fifteen years absence from the husband of my affections, and from my dear child, has been a period, you may well conceive, barren of comfort:—And even now I have much to dread—a long and dangerous voyage.—But I will hope the best, and not wrong Providence, by doubting its goodness.

Enter OAKWORTH.

Oak. I am out of breath—quite out of breath——and I am almost out of my wits.—She is arrived! she is arrived!

Mrs Clev. My daughter!

Oak. Yes—I have seen her, I have seen her!

Mrs Clev. O good Heaven!

Oak. I have—Ah, the sweet little dear! and not so little either—She is quite a woman. Ah, bless her! I've had a kiss, and I'll have another.—I beg pardon, gentlefolks:——If I'm unmannerly, 'tis joy makes me so.

Mrs Clev. Where is she?

Oak. In this very house by this time.—Oh, here she comes! here she comes!

Enter JULIA.

Mrs Clev. My child! Oh, my sweet child!
Jul. My mother!

Mrs Clev. How have I longed for this blest moment!—But your dear father—did you leave him well?

Jul. Yes, quite well, and eager for the happiness which I feel now.

Mrs Clev. My sweet, sweet Julia! How well am I repaid for my past years of misery!—Oh, height of bliss! The mother clasps once more in her fond arms her long lost, only child.—(*To the company.*) Pardon these transports—Joy like mine will keep no limits.

Leo. We all participate too much in your felicity to wish repressed such exquisite emotions.

Old Vis. Yes, madam, we all feel boundless joy. —What a pretty little creature it is, Leonard.—Oh, you will be a happy rogue!   [*Aside to* LEONARD.

Mrs Clev. My Julia, to these generous friends we owe the utmost gratitude: Their kindness grants us an asylum while your father shall remain from us.

Car. 'Tis for us to be grateful for your kind compliance with our wishes.—(*Crossing to* JULIA.) Tho' we can't rival the splendour of Calcutta, I hope London will have some charms for you.

Jul. Oh yes; I find already it has every charm; for I'm with my mother, and with friends who look as if they loved me.

Oak. And who that sets eyes on you can help loving you, you dear, pretty creature?—I beg pardon, gentlefolks.

Jul. Who is that good old gentleman? You can't think how glad he was to see me: He kissed me as fondly as if I had been his own daughter.

Mrs Clev. He is one, my Julia, who has made my comfort, for these fifteen years, the chief business of his life.

Jul. What, has he been so kind to my dear mother?—Oh! then I must kiss him again.

[*Runs and kisses him.*

Oak. I am too happy—I am too happy!

Jul. Tho' my new friends are so kind to me, I must not forget those who have loved me before. —Where is Gangica?

Enter GANGICA.

Gan. Here, my dear mistress.

Jul. Mother, you must love Gangica for my sake : she has left her country and all her relations, because she would not part with me : therefore I must love her better than ever ; and every body that loves me, must love Gangica.

Mrs Clev. Her affection for my dear child makes her certain of my love.—But I feel exhausted with excess of joy.—We should not lament that there are few incidents in life which waken such extreme delight; for were they frequent, how shortly would our weak frames yield to the tumults of ecstacy !

Lady Jem. Let me conduct you, madam, to your apartments.

Mrs Clev. You are all goodness.—Come, my dear child. [*Exeunt* LADY JEMIMA, MRS CLEVELAND, JULIA, CAROLINE, *and* GANGICA.

Manet LEONARD, OLD VISORLY, *and* OAKWORTH.

Oak. (*Looking after them, then wiping his eyes.*) I can't tell how it is.—I be no whimperer, gentlemen ; but, somehow, my eyes do nothing but moisten to-day.

Old Vis. I feel the tear of sensibility bedew *my* cheek.—Ah ! Leonard, my boy, if you can but get her.—(*Aside to* LEONARD.)

Leo. Hush, sir, hush !—(*To* OAKWORTH.) What delight, sir, you must feel at the happiness of this family, to whom you have shewn so much attachment ! What gratitude do they not owe you !

Oak. Gratitude to me ! That is a great mistake of yours, and it behoves me to set you right.—Mrs

Cleveland's father saved me once from ruin—me and my family from beggary; and I think he must have but a bad notion of the value of a kindness done him, who, if he could live long enough, would not strive to repay it down to the fiftieth generation.

Leo. What a noble heart!

Oak. Noble heart! Psha, psha! sure the world is not so bad that a man need be praised for not being a monster.

Leo. I am proud of the happiness of being known to you.

Old Vis. And so am I, most sincerely.

Oak. Why, to be sure, a mighty matter to be proud of, gentlemen—being known to an old, stupid, country bumpkin. Surely you be jeering a body—but if you be, I can't find in my heart to be angry; for as long as you are so good and so kind to the dear creatures I love, you may flout and jeer at me as much as you please.

Leo. You mistake us extremely: It is the farthest from our thoughts to be deficient in any particle of respect.

Old Vis. Oh dear! we never dreamed of such a thing.

Oak. Well, I suppose I shall be able in time to understand your London speechifying; but, in truth, your fine civil sayings are so like making game, that, for a little while, I shall be deucedly puzzled.

Leo. You never can be at a loss for our meaning. —We feel the value of such integrity as yours; and, be assured, we shall always say less of your merits than we think you deserve.

Old Vis. Always less than you deserve.

Oak. Do you know, I shall take that very kind of you; for if you are so good as to fancy I have any deserts at all, you must in conscience think they be very little.—And if so be you keep your word, and say less than you think, I shall be mighty happy; because then you will just say nothing at all.—So, gen-

tlemen, as in duty bound, I am your most humble
servant.   [*Exit.*

Old Vis. Poor old fellow.—Age begins to make
havoc—the upper works are giving way.

Leo. Ah, sir! how few, like you, enjoy, in advanced life, robustness of form, vigour of intellect—in
short, all the advantages of youth, without its inexperience.

Old Vis. Very few, indeed, Leonard.—I am one
out of five thousand.

Leo. Years in you, sir, have only just slackened
the blazing fire of youth.

Old Vis. Yes—slackened—not extinguished it.

Leo. This old rustic, sir, appears to stand vastly
well with the mother : I must endeavour to gain his
good graces; for the sentiments of a man she has
known so long, and esteems so highly, must have
great weight with her.

Old Vis. Very true.—I'll take care to pay him vast
attention.—I'll do your business with him—I'll cajole
the old fool.

Leo. Yes, sir; but be cautious lest your partial
affection for me should make you too lavish in my
panegyric.

Old Vis. Do you think I don't know how to get
round such a silly old bumpkin?——Leave me to
wheedle him—I'll do it cunningly, shrewdly, Leonard—wisely, my boy.   [*Exit* OLD VISORLY.

Leo. Now the game is started, I must set my whole
pack full cry for the chace.—Here comes my prime
agent in knavery, Sharpset.—Having used him so
essentially in the plunder of Drooply, and that business completed, I could have dispensed with his return; for no intercourse is so grating as that which
subsists with a confederate in villainy.—However, to
keep him in my power, I have still contrived to keep
him in my debt—so that I need not fear him ; and
he has talents to render him still useful to me.

Enter SHARPSET.

I am glad to find you return'd to the laity.—I would rather see knavery wear any garb than that of religion.

Sharp. Your reason for which is, that then only you are afraid of its being an overmatch for you.

Leo. Not so; but that I have not ceased to respect, though I have dared to violate.

Sharp. Hey-day! I believe you congratulate me on laying down the trade of preaching, because you mean to take it up.—But it tells well for morality, that even some knaves can admire the cause which honest men are risking their lives to defend. But a truce to this style; for it sits awkwardly upon us.— Your visitors, I find, are arrived.

Leo. Yes; and the girl is beautiful as an angel.

Sharp. Oh, a divinity!

Leo. Why, have you seen her?

Sharp. No.

Leo. Then whence these raptures?

Sharp. Did not you tell me she was heiress to half a million?

Leo. Oh! your servant:—But, I assure you, her intrinsic worth—

Sharp. Can be nothing to her *sterling* worth.

Leo. I am convinced—I feel something like love.

Sharp. To be sure you do.—I should adore a twentieth part of the sum, if it were in the pocket of the ugliest old harridan that ever was ducked for a witch.

Leo. You seem to hold beauty very cheap.

Sharp. Oh no—I only value money very highly.

Leo. But when they are combined—

Sharp. That is always possible.—Whoever has the money need not be long without the beauty.

Leo. In one object I hope to possess the ultimatum of my wishes in both.—It must now be my care to

have all around her impressed with esteem for me—
My eulogium, wafted to her on every breath, cannot
fail of infusing a favourable prepossession.—Be you
mindful, that, on all occasions, your report of me
may swell the gale of approbation. I need not tell
you that your interest will be no sufferer by your
panegyric.

Sharp. And, I assure you, I am so good natur'd
a fellow, that, make it equally profitable to me, and
I would rather speak in a man's praise than against
him—So much am I unlike the greater part of my
acquaintance.

Leo. The chief personage I wish to enlist in my
favour is an old rustic, much devoted to the family,
and ranking high in the mother's esteem—His name
is Oakworth.

Sharp. What?

Leo. Oakworth.

Sharp. Oak—Oak—worth.—Where does he come
from?

Leo. With Mrs Cleveland, from Warwickshire.—
What surprises you?

Sharp. Oh nothing—Only it strikes me I have
heard that name before.

Leo. Be earnest to throw yourself in his way; and
remember, by discreetly applied praise, to pave my
passage to the esteem I desire. To merit esteem is,
at best, a tedious method of obtaining it—The *purchased* diploma equally gives the title, and saves the
labour of deserving it.   [*Exit.*

Manet SHARPSET.

Sharp. So I am to throw myself in the way of
this old rustic, Oakworth.—You little guess, my very
worthy friend, what you are directing.—To throw
myself in the way of no less interesting a personage to
me than my identical dad—my own natural father.—
It is now a long while since I saw the good old boy—

I was but fourteen, I think, when it entered my mad
head to scamper away from him—A project well
worthy of so experienced an age.—That frolic has
thrown me into many a situation which would be whimsical to relate—Yes, and many a situation it would
not be prudent to relate.—I long to have a glimpse
of the old buck.—I wonder whether he would know
me.—Whom have we got here? Oh! this is one of
the Asiatic importations.

Enter GANGICA, *looking about with curiosity.—On
seeing* SHARPSET, *she starts back.*

Don't be frighten'd, my dear—I am very tame.

Gan. You not hurt me?

Sharp. Lord love you, not I.—I suppose she
thought I should dart at her like one of her native
tygers.—I assure you, my dear, I sha'n't bite.

Gan. No, no; but you may do great deal mischief, and not bite.

Sharp. But I wont do any mischief at all.

Gan. Dat's good man. You not wonder I am
afraid—I am stranger.

Sharp. 'Tis a sign so, by your being afraid; for
were you not a stranger, you would know that nobody in this country has the power of wronging a-
nother with impunity.—Beside, your being a stranger is a sure title to protection.

Gan. O den, dis be very good country.—Glad
I come here.

Sharp. And so am I glad you are come here, my
little marigold.

Gan. What for you glad I come here?

Sharp. Because I like the look of you.

Gan. Oh, you mock—You not like my copper
face.

Sharp. Why not, my dear?—In my mind, a lady
looks better with a face of copper than of brass—
And that is all the fashion.

Gan. Oh., if my face were like my dear Miss Julia's! Oh, she so pretty!—she so good!

Sharp. And you love her very much?

Gan. Ay, dat I do—I would die for her.—Oh, I would do great deal more.—I would live to bear pain in my limbs, and sorrow in my heart, to make her happy.

Sharp. Well said, my little disciple of Brama!—If the hallowed waves of the Ganges had any share in infusing this gratitude, I wish its stream lay near enough to be resorted to as a fashionable bathing place.—This little sun-burnt favourite may do Leonard service—I'll try to retain her in his cause.— (*Aside.*) I know who loves your young lady very much.

Gan. So do I.

Sharp. Ay!—who?

Gan. Every body.

Sharp. Yes, yes.—But there is a gentleman here, in this house—a young handsome gentleman.

Gan. Yes. (*With a little titter.*)

Sharp. Very handsome.

Gan. Yes—very handsome.

Sharp. What—you have seen him?

Gan. Yes—I see him now.

Sharp. (*Looking about.*) Who?

Gan. Why, handsome—very handsome gentleman. (*Looking in his face.*)

Sharp. Meaning me!—This girl's simplicity has done more than all the bronze of her sex could ever accomplish—Wonderful to relate—made me blush.— I had no notion, though, that these natives of Indostan had so much taste. But, my dear, I am not the only handsome gentleman in this house—I mean another, who has conceived a great esteem for your young lady; and your good opinion of him will, I know, give him great satisfaction—and so—But I had better have done with talking, and appeal to the rhetoric of all times, and all nations. (*Taking out a purse.*) You must know, my dear, that this gentleman is very generous—and I am sure he will be highly pleased at my making you a present from him of this little purse. (*Gives her the purse.*)

Gan. But what for you give me dis?

Sharp. Why, that—that you may speak well of this young gentleman.

Gan. How I speak well of him I not know?

Sharp. Um—But when you do know him—

Gan. Den, if he good man, I speak well of him widout dis—if he bad man, I not speak well of him for whole shipfull of money. (*Returns the purse.*)

Sharp. So, so—my friend Leonard will not be able to *buy* his diploma here. There is something mighty fascinating in this dusky piece of disinterestedness. Since I find we are not likely to come to right understanding as agents, I'll try how we can agree as principals.—Pray, my dear, have you left your heart in India?

Gan. No—my heart in de right place. (*Pointing to it.*)

Sharp. I'll answer for that—'Tis in the right place, I am sure. But you have not resolved never to love any body?

Gan. No—I love great many.

Sharp. The deuce you do!

Gan. Yes; my young lady I love dearly, dearly: And I love every body dat love her.

Sharp. Oh, is that all? But all your love seems to belong to your lady. Can't you love a little on your own account?

Gan. What you say?

Sharp. Why, you have not made a vow to die a maid.

Gan. I never make vows—it is wicked.

Sharp. Very well.—Why, then, if I were to be very fond of you.

Gan. Yes.

Sharp. Would you be fond of me?

Gan. I not know.

Sharp. Why not?

Gan. Because, though your face white and pretty, I not know if your mind so.

Sharp. Why, that's true, my love—But you may take my word for it.

Gan. No, no—not take man's word when he praise himself.

Sharp. Well, how are you to know?

Gan. Why, in great long time—if I find you do all good—not one bit of bad.

Sharp. Oh Lord! Oh Lord! Oh Lord! here is a trial of gallantry! here is a test for a lover!

Gan. Well, good bye—I stay too long while with you—My lady want me, may be. I see you again some time.

Sharp. Yes, my dear, I hope so.

Gan. Good bye, good bye.   [*Exit* GANGICA.

Manet SHARPSET.

Sharp. I am afraid I stand but a poor chance of success here. It is not very likely that my little Gentoo's system for choosing a lover should come into fashion—But if it should, Lord, Lord, what a different class of beings the favourites of the ladies would be!—No—yes—'tis he—my papa, by all that's miraculous!—Oh, the deuce!—what a business here will be!

Enter OAKWORTH.

Oak. Whew, whew—plague take it! I never was so tired with riding a whole day after the fox, as I am now with half an hour's plaguy palaver from this old master of the house. He may be a very good sort of a man—which I don't doubt; but he be cursed tiresome.—Who be this fine spark?—Servant, sir.

5

Sharp. How do you do—how do you do? (*Hiding his face with his handkerchief.*)

Oak. Pretty well, at your service.—Poor gentleman, he have got the tooth-ache, I believe.—I am afraid you feel uncomfortable, sir.

Sharp. I do, upon my soul, sir.

Oak. Are you often attacked in this way?

Sharp. No, sir, I have not been attacked in this way for a great many years.

Oak. Dear, dear! What! you be quite taken by surprise?

Sharp. Never more so in my life, sir.

Oak. Well, sir, but I hope you will soon get rid of so troublesome a companion.

Sharp. I hope I shall, sir.

Oak. And as you seem to be very uneasy, it will be but kind in me to keep you company a bit.

Sharp. If you stay with me, how the devil am I to get rid of my troublesome companion? (*Aside.*) Oh Lord!—Oh Lord!

Oak. You seem to be in huge great pain. I would not be plagued in this way. I would get somebody to lug him out.

Sharp. Oh how I wish somebody would be so kind!

Oak. If I could borrow a pair of *pinchers*, I would do it for you in a moment—I have drawn fifty so in our village.

Sharp. Oh! I could not think of troubling you.

Oak. It will be a pleasure.

Sharp. No, by no means—I think I am rather better.

Oak. Ah! the fear of the tug always makes it leave off aching. But you'd better have him out—he'll plague you again.

Sharp. I am afraid he will, but I must bear it.—He doesn't know my voice, and my face and person must be still more altered.—Hang it, I'll e'en try.

(*Takes his handkerchief from his face by degrees.*) I begin to feel easier, sir.

Oak. Heartily glad to hear it.

Sharp. (*Takes it quite away.*) My face is rather enlarged, sir. (*Feeling it, as though it were swelled.*)

Oak. Um! I see no swelling at all.—Ah! you were more frightened than hurt.

Sharp. So it turns out, sir—for he has not the slightest remembrance of me. (*Aside.*) Upon my soul, it was very kind of you to offer to operate—and for an entire stranger too.

Oak. One should be ready to lend every body a lift.

Sharp. Yes—and a pretty lift you would have given to my poor grinders.—But how came you to understand drawing teeth?

Oak. Oh, in a little village, a man that means to do good to his neighbours, must turn his hand to every thing.—Why, I have bled folks afore-now.

Sharp. That has run in the family. I have bled 'em a little too. (*Aside.*) Well, sir, and I dare say you have a good dame at home, who is as ready to assist her neighbours as you are?

Oak. Why, yes; my old girl don't grudge stirring her stumps when there is any good to be done.

Sharp. I'm glad to hear the good old dame is alive. Now I'll venture to touch on a tender subject. (*Aside.*) Any—any sons and daughters?

Oak. No—no; they be all gone. (*Sighing.*)

Sharp. What!—none left?

Oak. No, no—Yes—one, mayhap—one may be alive—one ungracious boy.—No, no; it be hardly possible, though there is a chance, a little chance—I have always kept a watch on the Old Bailey sessions papers, and the county assize lists—and to be sure I never found his name down in them; but there is little certainty or comfort in that—for you know,

my poor wicked boy may have been hanged, or sent
to Botany Bay under some other name.

Sharp. Hanged, or sent to Botany Bay !

Oak. Ah ! sir, it grieves my heart to think it—but
he had such little sharping tricks about him when he
was but a child, that I were forced to lash, and lash,
every day of my life.   I dare say, if he be alive, he
have got my well-meant marks on his back to this
day.

Sharp. Really ! It aches at the recollection. (*Aside.*)

Oak. Yes—you must suppose I had his well-doing
at heart—and so I never spared him.   I did hope, by
good advice, and good example, and a good horse-
whip, all together, to have made an honest man of
him—But the rogue scampered away when he was
but a younker, and so got loose into the wide wicked
world, with a bad disposition, and necessity to whet
it.   You must needs think as I do, about what is become of him.

Sharp. I really think, sir, you judge too severely
of your son, Je—What is your son's name, sir ?

Oak. Jeremy.

Sharp. O, sir, take comfort—Many a lad with as
bad a beginning has turned out a great man.

Oak. Ay, a *great* man, mayhap—But I am afraid
nobody with so bad a beginning has turned out a
good one.

Sharp. Upon my soul, you can't think how it
shocks me that you should judge so harshly of a child
of your own.   I dare swear no more harm has happened to Jerry than there has to me.

Oak. O dear, O dear ! it be quite a different case.

Sharp. Not at all—not at all—A case very much
in point, I assure you.

Oak. How be that ?   Why, were you a bit of a
rogue when you were a younker ?

Sharp. To own the truth to you, my dear sir, (but
don't mention it,) I was.

Oak. Ah! but you never ran away from your home.

Sharp. I did.

Oak. You don't say so?

Sharp. Honour.

Oak. Yes, yes; but you soon saw your error, and went back to your father?

Sharp. So far from it, my good sir, that it was many years before we met.

Oak. Indeed!

Sharp. And then quite by accident.

Oak. Really!

Sharp. Yes; and the best joke was, he did not know me.

Oak. Not know you! Oh, the old fool!—Beg pardon, sir, for making so free with your father.

Sharp. No apology. Pray make as free with him as you please.—Was it not droll?

Oak. Devilish droll—Ha, ha, ha! I can't help laughing.—So you met him, and he did not know you?

Sharp. No—he did not know me.

Oak. Well, and what did he say when he did know you?

Sharp. Why, that, my dear sir, I must defer telling you till another opportunity.

Oak. Well, sir, whenever you please—I long to hear the rest.

Sharp. Depend upon it, sir, it won't be concealed from you.—Good day to you, sir.

Oak. Good bye, sir.—Ha, ha, ha! Only think of your own father's not knowing you! Ha, ha ,ha!

Sharp. Ha, ha, ha! [*Exeunt on different sides.*

ACT THE THIRD.

Old Visorly's *House.*

Enter Julia *and* Caroline.

Car. But you surely won't stay at home this evening too?

Jul. Yes, indeed I had rather.

Car. You have the most unaccountable domestic propensity. Has novelty no pleasure for you?

Jul. Yes, 'tis novelty makes me domestic; a dear novelty—the novelty of a mother. Now I have gained her sweet society, should I resign it for frivolous amusements I can command at all times?

Car. Well, you are a dear, good girl.

Jul. But where are you going this evening?

Car. That I cannot tell without referring to my engagement list; but, as near as I can guess, to about a dozen assemblies, the opera, a concert, and a masqued ball.

Jul. My dear Caroline, you'll be fatigued to death.

Car. Oh no: I am never weary with pleasure.

Jul. And do you often make these laborious exertions for your amusement?

Car. Oh yes; all through the season—And I don't think that half long enough.

Jul. Well, to be equal to such efforts, a woman of

fashion must be endued with more strength than any creature in the universe.

Car. To be sure. Your elephant is nothing to her; for grovelling instinct restrains him from exceeding the paltry limits of mere corporeal exertion; but the elevated spirits and glowing imagination of a woman of fashion make her a being all essence—She is like the wind—light, fleet, and invincible.

Jul. And is she not sometimes like the wind in my native country, which now breathes all gentleness, yet, in a few hours will whirl a whole fortune to destruction?

Car. Why, yes, I am afraid there have been instances of the tornado kind. I really don't know whether many men may not be better pleased with your quiet stay-at-home notions than with more dash and spirit; but perhaps you never yet examined your inclinations with an eye to how a husband would approve them. Ah, Julia, you blush, my dear: I believe this scrutiny has not been unattended to.

Jul. How you talk!

Car. Yes. I *talk,* and you *think;* but both on the same subject. My dear girl, have I yet claim enough on your confidence to ask if the being I allude to has stolen into your dreams, and been admitted into your waking reveries, in the form of a beautiful accomplished youth, whose exact likeness you have never yet realized, or have you already assigned him " a local habitation and a name ?"

Jul. Heigho!

Car. Oh, then I lay my life Mr Heigho has a name and place of abode. Am I not right?

Jul. Yes.

Car. And in what quarter of the globe does he exist?

Jul. Nay, where should he? I have not been long enough in this country to have found him here. I must have met him before.

Car. (*Aside.*) So, my poor brother, your chance is gone.—What is his name?

Jul. Henry Melville.

Car. And you expect him here, no doubt.

Jul. Oh yes, in the same vessel with my father.

Car. And does he know your partiality?

Jul. Yes, and I know his for me, and my father approves.

Car. Oh, you happy girl! Now, the man I love neither knows my partiality for him, nor do I know whether he cares at all for me—And if we did know that we cared for each other, I am sure my father would let us care on till both our hearts broke, before he would give his consent.

Jul. Why so?

Car. Because the poor dear fellow has lost all his fortune; but luckily my father's consent is not essential, as I have a fortune independent of him.

Jul. Then you are not in a very hopeless state?

Car. Oh yes, I am: for my lover (my love I should say) lost all self-importance with his fortune; and I very much fear I shall never be able to make him comprehend that a young woman with a good estate is ready to let him be master of it.

Jul. How strange!

Car. Hints won't do—And if I could bring myself to say to him plainly, " Dear sir, I adore you!" he would only think I was making a jest of him.

Enter a Servant.

Serv. Mr Drooply to wait on you, ma'am. (*To* CAROLINE.)   [*Exit.*

Car. Lord, how my heart beats! Julia, my dear girl, this is the very man.

Jul. Then, my sweet Caroline, you can very well dispense with me.

Car. Oh no—Pray don't go.

Jul. You would be very angry if I took you at your word. Adieu! [*Exit* JULIA.

Car. Will this provoking creature for ever give me the trouble of making love to him without understanding me?

Enter DROOPLY.

So, sir, you are come.

Dro. Yes: but I will go away again if I intrude.

Car. Nay! Did not I send for you?

Dro. So I understood.

Car. And why do you give me the trouble? You made your visits formerly without being sent for.

Dro. Did I? Yes. I dare say I was a very troublesome fellow.

Car. Nay, you found those visits always received with pleasure: therefore it is strange you need be reminded to continue them.

Dro. My visits received with pleasure! Ah, this is the way in which you always used to banter me.

Car. Banter you! Stupidity!

Dro. Yes, yes. I know you are at your old tricks. You were always cutting your jokes at me.

Car. I?

Dro. Yes, you; and I remember I used to laugh at them; but that was when my pockets were full. Upon my soul, I can't now. No, no, you must excuse me. I defy a man to laugh at a joke when he has lost all his money.

Car. You strange creature! Do you know that I have been thinking of you a great deal lately?

Dro. Yes, I don't doubt it—to play me some trick or other.

Car. Silly animal! (*Aside.*) I have been even dreaming of you—Do you ever dream of me?

Dro. I could not think of taking such a liberty.

Car. Provoking! Oh, I had almost forgot—I knew I had something particular to tell you. It was whis-

pered to me, t'other night, at Lady Blab's, that you——
(now mind, if it is true, I sha'n't be angry,) that you
had told some friend in confidence (now mind, I
have promised not to be angry) that you were in love.

Dro. I told some friend?

Car. Yes; and that delicacy, occasioned by the
loss of your fortune, had prevented you from declaring your passion to the object of it.

Dro. I never——

Car. Now do stop a moment; but that if you
thought it would be favourably received (——now remember I have promised not to be angry——) you
would overcome your diffidence, and reveal it.

Dro. I assure you that——

Car. A moment's patience, pray.——At last, by great
entreaty, I learnt the lady's name.

Dro. And what was it?

Car. Need you be told——it was——Caroline Visorly.

Dro. Upon my soul it is a trumped-up story from
beginning to end.

Car. Incorrigible stupidity!

Enter GANGICA.

Gan. Beg pardon——did not know company was
here. (*Going.*)

Car. If you want any thing, you need not run
away, child. (GANGICA *goes up to a table where some
work lies.*) Well, sir, I have no more to say——only
don't entirely relinquish the society of one to whom
yours ever was, and ever will be a pleasure. Adieu!
[*Exit.*

Dro. Now who the devil can have told such a
cursed pack of lies of me——All done to ruin me in
her good opinion.   That I, a poor undone dog, with
not a sixpence in the world but what I receive from
her brother's friendship——I might say his——charity,
should presume to cherish hopes of Caroline Visorly.
No, no——all my hopes of her vanished with my for-

tune. I love her—I do love her ; and what a good-
natured soul it is, not to have flown into a rage at
supposing I could be guilty of such vanity—such
presumption—such folly.—Ay, that—that saved me :
—Knowing the folly, she pardoned the presumption.

[GANGICA *has been at the table getting her work,*
and comes forward with it in her hand.

Gan. You happy, very happy man.

Dro. Oh yes, my dear, very, very—(*Hardly attending to her.*)

Gan. Bless me—but you not look, you not speak
like happy man.

Dro. And pray, my little dear, what should make
you suppose I am a happy man?

Gan. Because pretty lady love you.

Dro. Pretty lady love me !—Why, even little Tawny
must cut a joke at me.

Gan. Yes, pretty lady dat went out just now love
you.

Dro. Oh, I am known for a *butt* by instinct. I
have not a doubt but it would be the same all the
world over. If I were to land at Otaheite, the natives would begin quizzing me directly in their damn'd
gibberish.—Why, you are a comical little rogue. So
that lady loves me, does she?

Gan. Yes.

Dro. You'd find it hard to make me believe that.

Gan. And you find it much more great deal harder
make me believe she not love you.

Dro. Indeed!

Gan. Yes : she not make me believe herself, if she
say she not love you.

Dro. No?

Gan. No ;—because dey tell me dat always tell true.

Dro. They? Who are they?

Gan. Dese—(*Pointing to her eyes.*)   Truth not
always come from here ; (*The mouth ;*) always from
here ; (*Her eyes.*)

Dro. Hey!

Gan. You tink, because I stranger, I not understand. Oh, language of love is the same in my country, your country, all country.   [*Exit.*

Dro. Hey! What! No, it can't be. Let me think.
—Um! Faith, it begins to dawn—now it glares! Oh,
what a blind dolt have I been! Ha! ha! Huzza! I
hear myself laugh again, and think I could cut a caper—Tol lol de rol! Whew! A fine girl loves me,
and so—Fortune, go hang.   [*Exit.*

Scene changes to another Apartment in VISORLY'S
House.

Enter LEONARD, *with a letter in his hand, followed
by a Servant.*

Leo. Is my father at home?

Serv. Yes, sir.

Leo. Tell him I wish to see him directly. [*Exit
Servant.*] (*Reads.*) " Sir, knowing you to have the
management of Mr Cleveland's concerns, I write to
inform you that the ship in which he came passenger
from India was wrecked off Portland, the 29th ult.,
and every soul perished."

Enter OLD VISORLY.

Old Vis. Well, my dear boy, what news—what
news?

Leo. Very important, sir :—Cleveland is no more.

Old Vis. Dear me—dear me!

Leo. By this I learn that the vessel that brought
him from Bengal is wrecked, and he has perished.

Old Vis. Poor man! poor man! Alack! He was
a good twenty years younger than I am—Only to
think that I should outlive him! Ah, there is no

knowing who is to go to the grave first—Mayhap I may outlive you, Leonard. (*Weeping.*)

Leo. Oh, sir, don't indulge such melancholy ideas. His death, though, to be sure, very dreadful, and likely to awaken sensibility in the breasts of his relations, yet carries with it to us a kind of consolation.

Old Vis. How do you mean, Leonard?

Leo. You know my wish to be united to his daughter—and perhaps he might have had in his mind a different alliance for her.

Old Vis. Very true.

Leo. Now my attainment of that object is infinitely more secure, the mother and the girl being both under our own roof, and likely now to continue so.

Old Vis. Very true. Lord, what a blockhead was I, to fall a blubbering, and for a man too, who, though he was my first cousin, I should not have known from Adam! But I have a very tender heart.

Leo. Yes, and a very soft head. (*Aside.*) But now, sir, to break these dismal tidings to his wife and daughter—that must be my mother's business.

Old Vis. Yes, we will go and prepare her to make the melancholy discovery. You have the way, my dear Leonard, of placing things in a right point of view. It is really quite a weakness my being so tender-hearted.   [*Exeunt,*

SCENE II.

Another Apartment.

Mrs Cleveland *and* Julia.

Mrs Clev. My dear, dear Julia, what happiness has Heaven allotted me, to compensate for my past

13

wretchedness! To have my lovely child restored to
me, adorned with every grace, endowed with each
perfection a mother's fondest wishes could desire—
Oh, none but a mother can know the happiness I feel.

Jul. May increasing joy be ever my dear mother's
portion—It must—goodness like her's must be the
object of Heaven's choicest blessings.

Mrs Clev. When your dear father, and the happy
youth to whom my Julia has assigned her heart have
passed the perils of the ocean, and tread secure on
English ground, then shall I have no wish on earth
ungratified ; but till those joyful tidings reach me,
my heart will beat with apprehension.

Jul. Nay, do not be alarmed with needless terrors.
I feel confident of their safety.

Mrs Clev Ah, my dear girl, yours is the age of
sweet delusion, when Hope, as yet unknown for a
deceiver, promises each wish acquaintance with reality

Jul. I have escaped the perils which you dread,
and reached your arms in safety.   Why not be confident the same good fate attends on them ?

Mrs Clev. Ah, my Julia—but winds and waves are
treacherous—besides, the foe—nay, that's a silly terror.—The ocean is our own, and our extended fleets,
rich with the commerce of the world, sail as securely
to their native ports, as if peace universal reigned.

Jul. Then free from apprehension let us await the
speedy completion of our happiness.

Enter GANGICA.

Gan. Oh, madam ! Oh, my young lady ! Oh me,
unhappy me !

Both. What is the matter ?

Gan. Oh, I can't speak—I can't tell you what I
know, cut your dear hearts, and make dem bleed a
mine do.

Mrs Clev. Speak, child, for Heaven's sake!

Jul. Tell us, Gangica, tell us all.

Gan You will know—you must know—but spare poor Gangica—don't bid her tell you, for fear you hate her for making you so wretched.

Jul. Speak, Gangica, directly.

Gan. Your dear, dear father dead—dead—dead.

[MRS CLEVELAND *transfixed with horror;* JULIA *sinks on the sofa.*

Enter OAKWORTH.

Mrs Clev. (*Recovering.*) Where is my child?

[OAKWORTH *points to her.*

Oh, Julia! Julia!

[*Bursts into tears, and takes* JULIA *in her arms;* GANGICA *goes to the sofa, and leans over* JULIA.

Enter LADY JEMIMA.

Lady Jem. I find the dismal tidings are already known:—Madam, be comforted.

Mrs Clev. Alas!

Oak. This be a woeful day.—Alack, alack, that ever I lived to see it.

Lady Jem. A letter has been just now brought, directed for Miss Cleveland. (*Shewing the letter.*) It may contain something important, and I hope—

Mrs Clev. Pray, give it me—I grasp at any hope. —Julia, 'tis from Henry Melville. (*Reads.*) " Snatched by Providence from a wat'ry grave, I haste to acquaint my dearest Julia with my safety—As my situation was infinitely more perilous than her dear father's, I rely on his deliverance, and conclude he will have embraced his lovely daughter before this reaches her."—No, no, he has not embraced his lovely daughter—he never will embrace her.

Lady Jem. Take comfort, madam. You have new strong reason to hope the best.

Jul. Yes, dearest mother, be assured the same protecting angel has preserved my father too.

Oak. Do, do hope it. Heaven will not forsake the good.

Mrs Clev. Come, my child—in Heaven I trust.

[*Exeunt* MRS CLEVELAND, JULIA, *and* LADY JEMIMA.

[GANGICA, *oppressed with grief, remains leaning on the sofa.*

Oak. Oh dear, Oh dear, Oh dear! This world be full of troubles. But a little bit ago we were so happy as nothing was ever like it—and now it is all weeping and misery. Oh, those devildom hard-blowing gales and cursed craggy rocks, they have brought cruel sorrow to many a family. Poor little Gangica, she takes on as dismally as any on us. It is a tender-hearted little creature. Gangica, come, dear, don't you droop, you may see your young lady's father again, alive and well.

Gan. No, no, no—I never see him more—He be sunk down—deep down—roaring waves roll over him—I never see him more.

Oak. Yes, yes; Heaven will let him live, to comfort his wife, his child, ay, and to reward your fidelity.

Gan. Oh, if he live—if I see him again, dat be my reward.

Enter SHARPSET.

Sharp. Sir, how do you do?—Ah, my little dear, you here. Why, you have been crying, and you look gloomy too, sir.

Oak. Yes, sir; we have neither much cause to look cheerfully.

Sharp. I am sorry for that—I heard indeed that ill news had arrived, which concerns the ladies.

Oak. Then, when you know that we belong to

those ladies, you can't expect us to be gay when those we love are in affliction.

Sharp. Very true, sir. But, poor thing, (*To* GAN-GICA,) come, do cheer up a little—don't be so very dismal—do let me see you smile again.

Gan. Smile! when i full of sorrow—Why, you wish my face mock my heart.

Oak. Come, sir, leave her as nature made her—don't teach her any of your damn'd fashionable tricks, making the face look one thing while the heart means another. Go, my good girl, and comfort yourself with the hope that we may soon have reason to smile again. (*Exit* GANGICA.) There is a creature that will make me expect in future to find the fairest mind in a dark-coloured case. I hope I may live to see her as happy as she deserves to be. If I had but a son of my own—but what signifies wishing?

Sharp. Ah, what indeed! For have you not a son of your own, sir?

Oak. If I have, I love her too well to wish she had him. No, no—if I had a son such as I could wish—

Sharp. I am afraid you are very hard to please, sir.

Oak. I should take great pains to get him this girl for a wife.

Sharp. And I am so much of your way of thinking, that if you were my father, I should be highly grateful for your kind endeavours.

Oak. Would you? Then only let me find out that you are worthy of her, and though you are a stranger to me, I'll do all I can for you. (*Going.*)

Sharp. That is very kind of you indeed, sir.

Oak. But hold, hold—Are you sure your father would approve of it?

Sharp. Quite sure, sir.

Oak. How do you know?

Sharp. He has already signified his approbation.

Oak. Indeed! When?

Sharp. Just now, sir.

Oak. Why, has he ever seen the girl?

Sharp. Oh Lord, yes, sir.

Oak. Well, well, but I should like to have a little conversation with the old gentleman.

Sharp. Ah, sir, you have had a great deal in your time.

Oak. What, then I know him?

Sharp. Nobody half so well, sir.

Oak. Really! What, an old acquaintance?

Sharp. A very old one, sir—You knew him long before I did.

Oak. Bless my soul! And pray, sir, what is your name?

Sharp. I am called Sharpset, sir.

Oak. Then you must be mistaken, sir—I have no acquaintance of that name.

Sharp. My dear sir, that is not the family name; that is not my father's name.

Oak. Well, what is your father's name?

Sharp. The very reason, sir, which made me adopt another name still prevents me from just at present avowing my real one; but depend upon it, you shall know, sir.

Oak. Well, sir, whenever it is proper to tell me, I shall be glad to know, (*Going :*) but give me your hand, for your father's sake.

Sharp. And I grasp yours with affection—for my father's sake.   [*Exeunt severally.*

SCENE III.

The Street.

Enter HENRY MELVILLE.

Hen. That, I find, is the house of Mr Visorly. There I shall learn my Julia's residence. This is but a sorry garb for a lover to seek his mistress in; but if I know my Julia's heart, her joy at finding me preserved from death will make her little heed, or scarcely see the poorness of my raiment. Her father's safety, though I little doubt it, I long to be assured of. Now, then, to be resolved on that important point, and meet my Julia. [*Exit.*

SCENE IV.

An Apartment in VISORLY'S House.

Enter HENRY.

Hen. To find she is in this house is more good fortune than I could hope.

Enter JULIA.

My Julia!
Jul. Oh, Henry! To behold you again, after such danger—But where is my father?
Hen. Have you not seen him yet?

Jul. Oh no, no—Tell me, does he live?

Hen. I hope so, Julia.

Jul. Oh, is it only hope?

Hen. Be comforted—he *may* be safe, he surely *must.* Soon as our vessel bulged on the rock, and the impetuous torrent rushed at the dreadful chasm to o'erwhelm us, the boats were instantly hauled out, and in a moment throng'd. In one, least crowded, was your father: he call'd to me, and earnestly conjured me to come into it— As I was going to comply, I saw a poor old man kneeling to Heaven to save him from the fate his feeble age denied him to contend against. The boat could safely hold but one—I placed him in it, seized on a friendly coop, and with it trusted to the waves.

Jul. My generous Henry! But my father—

Hen. The sea was very boisterous, and often washed over me; yet at intervals I snatched a short view, and still saw his boat riding in safety. At length the bursting billows showering so frequently their torrents on me, deluged my senses. When I recovered them, I found myself in a small vessel, whose crew had humanely rescued me from death.

Jul. Oh my poor father!

Hen. Nay, droop not, Julia.—This vessel was a sloop of war sailing for the Downs. Before I recovered, it was under weigh; I was therefore forced to remain in it till it gained its station.—Landed at Deal, I could of course hear no tidings of your father, whose boat, no doubt, safely reached the nearest shore. His not being yet arrived argues nothing against his safety.

Jul. But would he not have written to acquaint us with it?—News of the wreck could reach us, but no intelligence from him—No, he is gone! My father is gone for ever.

Hen. My Julia's grief distracts me—Still let me hope 'tis without cause; but as no moment should be

lost to prove it groundless, I will this instant fly to
know the truth.   Farewell, my Julia! When next
we meet, I trust all grief will vanish.

[*Exeunt severally.*

ACT THE FOURTH.

SCENE I.

VISORLY'S *House.*

Enter LEONARD *and* SHARPSET.

Leo. Where have you been? I never wanted your
assistance more, and I have been hunting after you
of late in vain.

Sharp. Whew! you seem in a blessed humour.
What has produced such an amiable tone of temper?

Leo. All my scheme is likely to be ruined. There
is a lover, a favoured lover come to light.

Sharp. Oh, the deuce!

Leo. Yes, saved from the wreck.——Damnation! But
there is still one consolation——he brings no tidings
of the father——the waves have not spared him.

Sharp. Poor man!

Leo. Amiable tenderness!

Sharp. Mock as you will, I cannot, like you, steel
my heart against the common feelings of humanity.

Leo. Psha! he's dead——Will your preaching re-

animate him? No. Then to the purpose of doing
service to the living, of aiding your friend.

Sharp. How?

Leo. This girl, now the rightful inheritor of her
father's immense fortune, must be mine.

Sharp. But you tell me of a lover.

Leo. Yes, and there is not time for endeavouring
to undermine his hold on her heart—Measures must
be adopted, sudden and forcible.

Sharp. How do you mean?

Leo. To bear her away. Once in my possession,
all may go smoothly: at her age, nay, at any age, a
transfer of affection is no uncommon incident.

Sharp. But the difficulty—See how she is surrounded.

Leo. Difficulty! Every difficulty yields to the en-
terprising. Her lover is gone, like a true hero of
romance, to conjure up the dead. 'Tis easy to get
the rest out of the way.—First, I'll remove the main
obstacle, her rustic protector.

Sharp. Remove him! How do you mean, remove
him?

Leo. We must lack invention, indeed, not to effect that.—By an hundred stratagems we can keep
him out of the way long enough to answer my purpose.

Sharp. But I have a trifling objection to his being
put to the slightest inconvenience.

Leo. Objection? What?

Sharp. He only happens to be my father.

Leo. What do you say? Your father?

Sharp. My father.

Leo. You astonish me. Well, well, this may turn
to account. Then you may have influence to bring
him over to my interest.

Sharp. Not I, nor all the world would be able to
influence him to a dishonest action—Beside, friend
Leonard, to let you into a secret, I neither like your

scheme, nor wish to forward it. After a long absence, I have had the happiness to meet my father, and when I behold in him what a glow of youth an honest heart infuses into an aged face, I am determined to abandon my roguery, and try to make the rosy honours of honesty hereditary.

Leo. You mean, then, to defeat my purposes?

Sharp. I certainly mean not to aid them.

Leo. But am I to expect your opposition?

Sharp. I hope, Leonard, your own reflections will render that needless. Could you have fairly gained the girl's affections, I should have rejoiced at your success, and thought the society of an amiable woman the likeliest school for forming an honest man; but force—to use force against a lovely, helpless female, none but a devil could inspire the thought, and none but devils could be found to execute it.

Leo. Bravo! One might judge by your energy that you were a new-made proselyte. Apostates are always the maddest enthusiasts.—But, fool! do you think I am to be preached out of my intentions?

Sharp. And do you think I am to be bullied out of mine?

Leo. Well, sir, take your course, but be cautious that you do not thwart me—Dare not to breathe a word of my designs, unless your devotion to your new tenets is warm enough to make you welcome a prison in their defence. Mark me—a prison. You may remember there are certain bonds of yours in my possession, that give me as entire a power over your person, as though you were my purchased slave. Remember this, and act accordingly.   [*Exit.*

Sharp. How my blood boils at the villain! Too true he has me in his power; but I'll keep him in view—I'll watch his motions. I've deserved a prison before now, and have escaped it: Well, then, if I am brought to one at last for a good deed, all's square again, and I begin the world a fresh man.

Enter DROOPLY, *repeating, as he enters,*

" Come, thou goddess, fair and free,
    In heav'n yclep'd Euphrosyne."

Sharp. Why, Drooply—Surprising ! so sprightly—
so gay !

Dro. Gay as a lark, my boy.

" Haste thee, nymph, and bring with the.
    Jest and youthful jollity."

Sharp. What ! have you found your estate again ?

Dro. No ; but I have found myself again : I've re-
gained my spirits, and they are worth all the estates
in the universe.

Sharp. But what has effected this wonderful change?

Dro. What ! Need you ask ? What can breathe ani-
mation into a cloud of despondency but woman, dear,
lovely, angelic woman.

Sharp. So you have gained your spirits by losing
your heart.

Dro. Yes ; and a man hardly knows he has a heart
till he loses it. But huzza ! I am in love, and, what
is more, I am beloved.—Damn my estate, and give
me your hand, my boy, though you won it.

Sharp. I won it ! yes, and won it fairly too.

Dro. Who doubts it ? Not I, I'm sure.

Sharp. Why, then, may be you ought.

Dro. You are a comical dog.

Sharp. I say, perhaps you ought to doubt it.

Dro. Hey-day—the oddest kind of quizzing this :—
The man who won my estate wanting to make me believe I was cheated of it. You are a devilish droll
dog ; but I have something else to do than to mind
your waggery. (*Going.*)

Sharp. Stay ! You are an honest fellow, and have
been damn'd unlucky in your acquaintance.

Dro. Poh, poh, poh!

Sharp. Drooply, when a man assures you of his honesty, I'll give you leave to doubt him ; but when he

insists on his knavery, don't be so stupidly incredu-
lous.

Dro. What are you driving at ?

Sharp. Plainly to tell you, you have been duped—
cheated—robbed.

Dro. By you ?

Sharp. Yes—but I have been only second in command. Do you remember by whose kindness you
were first made happy with my acquaintance ?

Dro. Hum ! Yes : by my friend Leonard Visorly.

Sharp. He is my commanding officer.

Dro. Leonard ! my friend ! my patron !

Sharp. Your plunderer.—He laid plans which I only executed—he received the booty, while I was paid
but a subaltern's share.

Dro. I am petrified.

Sharp. But be silent—be prudent ! for I've but
shewn you your malady, without being able to pre-
scribe a remedy. He has played the politician so
well, that his villainy is known only to me—the minor agents were all of my employing—So remember,
don't break out ; for you have nothing but my testimony to support an accusation, and he has wound his
snares so well, that he has me in his toils. Adieu.
Be cautious, and trust that the day of retribution will
come.   [*Exit* SHARP.

Dro. Here is a damper to my gaiety ! Not even
love can support a man's spirits against ingratitude.
I lost my fortune, but still I thought I had a friend
left. To find that friend my—Oh, damn it, I can't
bear the thought. I'll go instantly and seek Caroline:
But how to tell her of her brother's villainy ? I hope
I may not meet him—I should not know how to——

Enter LEONARD.

Leo. Drooply ! (*Holding out his hand.*)

Dro. How do you do ? How do you do ?

Leo. What ! Won't you shake hands with me ?

Dro. Won't I shake hands with you! that is a good
joke. (*Holding out his hand, and then drawing it back.*)
Not but I think shaking hands a cursed foolish habit.

Leo. Why?

Dro. Because, in this damn'd hypocritical world,
one often gives the gripe of friendship to a scoundrel.

Leo. Very true; one is often mistaken.

Dro. Yes, miserably.

Leo. But when we come to the knowledge of a
friend's real worth—

Dro. It sometimes teaches us to consider him a
friend no longer.

Leo. Your gloom, I find, has taken the general
course, and led you to misanthropy. When men have
been unfortunate, they generally grow unjust.

Dro. Yes; and for that there is some excuse—
But when men are unjust and fortunate too, what
black souls they must have.

Leo. Very true: But have you had experience of
such?

Dro. Haven't I lost a fortune?

Leo. Yes—by play, not knavery.

Dro. Why, play and knavery are so much con-
nected, that I can't separate them for the soul of
me.

Leo. You appear to have suspicions.

Dro. No, no *suspicions* at all.

Leo. You surely talk as if you had doubts.

Dro. You mistake—I have not a *doubt* on the subject. Good bye! I am very miserable, and of course
very bad company for you.

Leo. When we meet again, I shall be glad to see
you more cheerful.

Dro. Why, when we meet again, Leonard—Farewel.   [*Exit.*

Leo. Um! All is not as it should be! Can that villain Sharpset have dared reveal to him—I fear it—
and if he have betrayed me to him, he will not stop

there. His malice then must have a check—he shall instantly be taken care of: I have the power to secure him.   The old rustic, whom he calls his father, I have been forced to entrap somewhat illegally; but he will be safe till my scheme is executed; and then the fellow that I have bribed to swear a debt against him may, by flight, secure himself from the vengeance of the violated law. All is well arranged; and this very night shall put me securely in possession of my eastern beauty, and her eastern riches.   [*Exit.*

SCENE II.

A House of Confinement.

OAKWORTH *and Bailiff.*

Oak. But what right, I say, have you to keep me here against my will?

Bail. Lord love your heart, I don't vant to keep any gemman in my house against his vill.

Oak. Then let me out directly.

Bail. You may go farther, and fare vorse. Vhere do you think to go?

Oak. Why, home, to be sure.

Bail. That is a devilish good one. You are a comical kind of a gemman; but a great many comical gemmen wisits me—I sees most of the vits one time or other.

Oak. Have done with your nonsense, and let me go home—and damme but I'll trounce you and the rascals who brought me here.

Bail. Vy, as for your trouncing, I laughs at that. —I does nothing but vat I can justify.

Oak. What! Can you justify kidnapping a man in

the streets?—I am too old to go for a soldier. If I
were not, and my country wanted me, I should not
need be dragged to my duty.

Bail. Vat do you talk about kidnapping for?—You
knows as vell as I can tell you vy you came here.

Oak. I'll be cursed if I do.

Bail. Vy, you know if you paid your debts, you
could not be brought into trouble.

Oak. Pay my debts! I don't owe a farthing to
mortal man.

Bail. Come, come, do behave a little genteelly.—
There is nothing unlike a gemman in not *paying* your
debts; but it's damn'd shabby to *deny* 'em.

Oak. Well, sir, since you insist upon it, pray, whom
may I be indebted to?

Bail. (*Looking at the writ.*) " To Thomas Testify
von hundred pounds."

Oak. I never heard of such a man.—I am not the
person. It is a mistake.

Bail. Come, come, old one, that's too bad.

Oak. I tell you it's all a mistake—Let me out, I
say.

Bail. Yes, yes, to take you to Newgate, if you
like.—(*Noise without.*)

SHARPSET, (*entering.*)

Ay, ay, it is all right.—I owe the money—that can't
be denied.

Bail. Only mind this honest gemman, he doesn't
pretend to humbug people as you do.

Sharp. What!—(*Seeing* OAKWORTH.) You here,
sir!

Oak. Bless my soul!

Bail. Oh, they know von another—Both of a kid-
ney, I varrant.—Oh, that old one is a deep one.

[*Exit.*

Sharp. How came you here, sir!

Oak. Dragged here—dragged by main force.

Sharp. On what pretence?

Oak. Because they want to persuade me I owe a hundred pounds to a Mr Thomas Testify.

Sharp. Whom you know nothing of?

Oak. No more than the man in the moon.

Sharp. Sir, there is rank villainy going forward.

Oak. Yes, that is pretty clear.

Sharp. You must send directly for Mrs Cleveland —Every thing dear to herself depends on it—Therefore send to her immediately, and tell her not to leave her daughter.

Mrs Cleveland, (*entering.*)

Let me see him instantly; and, Gangica, do you stay under the care of the servants.—My good friend, do I find you in a place like this?

Oak. And are you so very good as to seek me in a place like this?—How came you to know of my being here?

Mrs Clev. You sent for me, did you not?

Oak. No.

Mrs Clev. Amazing! A messenger came to me, acquainting me with your situation, and directing me where to find you—on which, you may conclude, I lost no time in hastening to you.

Oak. Dear good creature!

Mrs Clev. But who can have been so kind to inform me where?

Sharp. The kindness, madam, was the kindness of the devil, who often puts on the semblance of goodness only to betray.—Quit this place, and return home instantly—There is a villainous design against your daughter—Your absence and his has been artfully caused, to effect her ruin.

Mrs Clev. Oh, horrible!

Sharp. Lose not a moment in questioning, or all is lost—Though the debt alleged be a false one, give

your draft for it, and take him with you. Haste,
madam, haste ; and Heaven prosper you ! [*Exeunt.*

SCENE III.

The Garden belonging to OLD VISORLY'S *House.*

Enter LEONARD.

Leo. The evening is as dark as I could wish—
the moon has civilly withdrawn her intrusive rays—
the mother and Oakworth are admirably disposed
of—my own family, too, conveniently from home ;
for though I am not sure they would thwart a design so greatly for my advantage, yet I had rather
be without needless confidants.—Simpson ! Simpson !

Enter SIMPSON.

Sim. Sir ?
Leo. Is the carriage at the garden gate, and every
thing in readiness ?
Sim. Yes, sir.
Leo. Very well.—Wait hereabout, or be at the
garden gate.——(*Exit* SIMPSON.) Now then to my
young lady.   [*Exit.*

SCENE *changes to an apartment in* VISORLY'S *House.*

JULIA, *alone.*

I wish my mother would return, and bring me
news of poor Oakworth.—'Tis hard that he, so good
and friendly to others, should himself experience
cruel treatment.—Alas ! my spirits quite sink under
the pressure of misfortune.—Oh, my dear father, may I
hope ever again to be blessed with thy fond embrace ?

Enter LEONARD.

Jul. Ha!—Who is there?—(*Finding it to be* LEO-
NARD.) I beg your pardon, sir, for my childish alarm
—but I am really so weak, that I am agitated by the
slightest circumstance.—Indeed I beg your pardon.

Leo. Madam, my situation is a most unfortunate
one. I hoped, by years of attention to your every
wish, to have convinced you, that for you alone I
cherished existence.

Jul. Sir!

Leo. But I have the misery to find your hand is
not unpromised, nor, I fear, your mind uninfluenced.

Jul. Sir, my hand and heart are both most solemnly affianced.

Leo. Then all my cherished hopes are vanished.—
I thought to have convinced you by every action
that my soul was yours, before my lips should venture
the confession.—I indulged the gay dream, that by
my tender assiduity you might be won to sympathy,
and have heard me breathe the vows of love with
looks that spoke a language—Ah! how remote from
what they now convey.—Yet even those looks, so ad-
verse to my wishes; those eyes, could they dart death,
should not impede me from declaring this heart, to
you devoted, never will forego its claim.

Jul. Sir!—What mean you?

Leo. Listed under Love's banner, never to desert
his cause.—You must—you shall be mine.

Jul. Horrible!

Leo. A whole life of tenderness shall atone for
what has now the look of violence. (*Approaches her.*)

Jul. Violence!—Oh, Heaven! help! help!—Oh!
—(*She faints ; he catches her in his arms.*)

Leo. She is mine!   [*Exit, bearing her off.*

SCENE IV.

The Garden.

Enter DROOPLY.

Dro. Well, I have found no great difficulty in scampering over the garden wall.—If any of the family should find me here though, I should be strangely suspected of either an intrigue or a burglary.— It was an excellent thought of Caroline's to let me know when we should next meet, by leaving a letter for me in a sly corner of the pavilion; for there is no trusting servants.—I'll e'en get my dear little packet, and over the wall again.—(*Going towards the pavilion.*) Ha!—I hear somebody coming.—(*In his hurry to get to the pavilion, he stumbles over a garden-chair.*)

Enter LEONARD, *with* JULIA *in his arms.*

Leo. Oh, you are there, Simpson!—Here, take the lady in your arms.—A fortunate fainting-fit has prevented out-cry.—Place her in the carriage, while I return for an instant; for I have forgot to provide myself with the most material companion for long journies.—Here, take one of my pistols, and defend your prize at the hazard of your life.

[*Exit, leaving* JULIA *in* DROOPLY's *arms.*
Dro. What the devil shall I do? And what prize have I got here?—(*The moon bursting by degrees from a cloud.*) My sweet, pretty moon, do enlighten me a little more, that I may see who I am hugging so lovingly.—(*It grows lighter.*) Thank you kindly, my dear Lady Luna.—What, the young East Indian!

—Oh, that villain!—She revives!—Don't be alarm'd, madam.

Jul. Where am I?—Who are you?

Dro. No agent of villainy, but one who will protect you.

Jul. Oh, where is that wretch: Am I in his power?

Dro. No, madam, nor ever shall be.—Ha! he is coming.

Jul. Let me fly from his sight.

Dro. There, madam, into that pavilion. (*He goes with her, enters it, and brings out* CAROLINE's *letter in his hand.*) She is safe, and I have got my dear Caroline's letter—So now, Mr Leonard, have at you! (LEONARD *enters, and is crossing the stage—* DROOPLY *meets him—*DROOPLY *has put the pistol in his pocket.*)

Leo. (*Starting.*) Drooply!——What do you do here?

Dro. I am only engaged in a little affair of gallantry.

Leo. What, here!—Do you disgrace my father's house with your gallantries?

Dro. Do you never disgrace your father's house with your gallantries?

Leo. Insolent!

Dro. No, no; I must do you the justice to own, you carry your gallantries *out of your* father's house.

Leo. What do you mean?

Dro. Mean! Sure you forget Simpson is in the secret.

Leo. What of Simpson?

Dro. An't I Simpson?—You did me the honour to salute me so just now.

Leo. Damnation!—Well, sir, then where is your charge.

Dro. Here, you villain. (*Presents his pistol.*)

Leo. Drooply, I am in your power—command any

thing—do but this instant restore me Julia, and you
shall again glitter in gaiety, again be the rich, the
courted Drooply.

Dro. Yes, to be pillaged again, you conclude, by
the well-laid schemes of the friendly Mr Visorly.

Leo. Ha!

Dro. Yes; I know your baseness.—This heart,
which once felt only gratitude and friendship towards
you, now despises and abhors you—This tongue,
once lavish in your praise, and prodigal of thanks,
now execrates your infamy.

Leo. This is no time to prove my innocence.—I
am traduced, vilely slandered—All this I can clear
up, and will; but the moments are most precious to
me.—Where is the lady?—Restore me Julia, and
make your own terms.

Dro. What terms do you think would bribe me to
restore a lovely innocent to a villain's power?—I am
poor, I am wretchedly poor.—But would you return
my fortune, would you add your own, your father's,
nay, all the wealth of this rich city, it should not bribe
me to an act of villainy.

Leo. Be prudent, and attend to what I say.

Dro. I'll attend to one thing you said most strictly.—You charged me to defend my prize at the hazard of my life—That I do most willingly.

Leo. Drooply, urge me no further—I am desperate—Julia must be mine.—Be wise: accept the offers of my friendship—don't risk my vengeance.

Dro. Your vengeance!—Poh!—What! because
you found me gentle, nay, humble, to the man I
thought my friend and patron, do you think I want
spirit to oppose a robber and a ravisher?—Leonard,
be assured, it is a vast pleasure for me to have a pop
at you on my own account; but had I no wrongs,
sooner than be your accomplice in the ruin of an unprotected woman, damme, but I would march up to

you if you held a lighted match to the touch-hole of a nine-pounder. (*Goes up close to him.*)

OAKWORTH (*without.*)

Oak. She must have been taken this way.

Enter OAKWORTH, MRS CLEVELAND, *and* GANGICA.—*The moment* OAKWORTH *sees* LEONARD *and* DROOPLY *he runs down the stage and collars them both.*

Oak. Give her up, give her up this instant, or I'll throttle you both.

Mrs Clev. Where is my daughter?

Oak. Ay, where is the lady? Give her up directly.—Curse your pistols; I don't mind your pistols.—Give her up, I say.

Mrs Clev. (*To* LEONARD.) Heavens! is it you?—you concerned in this villainy?——Where is my daughter, sir?

Leo. Ask that gentleman—He has conveyed her hence.

Mrs Clev. You, then, that I have accused, are her defender :—I ask your pardon.

Dro. May I perish if he isn't making his bow for the mother's civility!

Mrs Clev. Where is my daughter, sir? (*To* DROOPLY.)

Leo. There is one hope left. If he conveyed her to the carriage—and where else could he—they have doubtless driven off with her.——Where is the lady, villain?

Dro. Damme, if his impudence does not petrify me!

Oak. (*Rushing up to him.*) Ay, where is the lady, villain?

Dro. A little patience; you shall know the whole.

Leo. No, sir, no fabrications, no fictions.—Where is the lady?

Dro. Should you be pleased to see her?

Leo. Doubtless.

Dro. Oh, I'll do any thing to oblige you.—(*Goes to the pavilion, and leads her out.*) Now, sir, why don't you appeal to the lady to proclaim your innocence?—What, dumb!—Ah, I know your modesty of old.—Then I will speak for you.—From which of us, madam, have you experienced this outrage?

Jul. Oh, from him, from him. (*Pointing to* LEONARD.—MRS CLEVELAND *and* OAKWORTH *express astonishment, and* LEONARD *rushes out.*)

Dro. That is right, Leonard—move off; but run as fast as you will, the devil must overtake you.

Mrs Clev. Then to you I owe my daughter's preservation.—Oh, sir, accept a mother's thanks!

Dro. Offer them, madam, to Providence only, which made me the humble instrument to preserve an angel, and expose a fiend.—Where, madam, shall I have the honour of conducting you?

Mrs Clev. Any where, so I avoid that hated habitation.

Oak. Let us go, madam, to the hotel where we first arrived.

Mrs Clev. And where, would to Heaven, we had remained.—Come, dearest Julia.   [*Exeunt.*

ACT THE FIFTH.

SCENE I.

VISORLY'S *House.*

Enter OLD VISORLY *and* LEONARD.

Old Vis. Oh, Leonard, Leonard, it is a bad business, a very bad business.

Leo. So is every thing unsuccessful, sir. Were I now in possession of the girl and her fortune, you might probably not be condemning the means by which I accomplished it.

Old Vis. Yes, I should—I should condemn such means.—Oh fie! against her will.

Leo. Seemingly, sir, only seemingly.—The man who would deal successfully with the sex must often force them to follow their own inclinations.

Old Vis. I don't know that; but I have found that the man who would deal quietly with the sex is always forced to let them follow their own inclinations.

Leo. It was a desperate effort, but the only chance left for obtaining her.—That foiled, she is lost most certainly, perhaps her fortune too.

Old Vis. Perhaps!—Why, to be sure it is. If she is lost, her fortune must be lost—You can't contrive to marry the fortune without marrying the girl, can you?

Leo. No, sir :—But with your aid the fortune may be ours without the encumbrance.

Old Vis. The fortune ours—Eh! how?

Leo. Had Cleveland died unmarried, you were his heir.

Old Vis. Yes—What of that?

Leo Are we sure he did not die unmarried?

Old Vis. We should be pretty sure, I think, when he has left a wife and child behind to convince us.

Leo. Is she his wife?—Can she prove herself such?

Old Vis. Eh!

Leo. By his own account, the marriage was a private one; a private marriage in the East Indies!— Reflect first on the probability of its being no marriage, and next consider the difficulty of proving it, if it were one.

Old Vis. Yes, yes, very true.—But you surely do not doubt the marriage; therefore, to claim a property, because, perhaps, legal proof can't be obtained—

Leo. Is, you think, not strictly within the pale of moral rectitude.

Old Vis. I can't say but I am of that opinion.

Leo. Oh, sir, despise all abstract refinement, and be assured that you fulfil every moral obligation when your conduct is sanctioned by the laws of your country.

Old Vis. There is something in that; but yet justice, you know, can only be guided by appearances; and one's conscience will not always acquiesce.

Leo. My dear sir, when your conscience opposes a legal decree, you should consider it as acting contumaciously, and that it ought to be silenced for contempt of the court.

Old Vis. If I could be satisfied that they were really not married.

Leo. There is strong presumption.—Would Cleveland's father, think you, have endeavoured to dissolve the sacred ties of marriage—have insisted on his son's abruptly dismissing—a wife?—No, no, sir— depend on it, the father, anxious for his son's respec-

tability, demanded only his parting with a favourite
mistress.

Old Vis. Very likely—very likely—I always said
you had the way of placing things in a right point
of view. Oh, my scruples are gone—Should I be robbed of my right by a mistress, and a——

Leo. Certainly not, sir. Now then you are convinced of the rectitude of your cause, let me urge a
strong motive for proceeding with vigour.—I have
this morning received the unwelcome tidings of the
failure of a speculation in which I had embarked the
entire amount of my own fortune, so that I am now
compelled to become a burden to you.

Old Vis. O Lord, Lord! Dear me, how sorry I am
to hear it; for, my dear boy, to let you into the true
state of my affairs—Lady Jemima's cursed fashionable style of living has made such a miserable hole in
my property, that it is not clear to me but I may die
in a jail.

Leo. You amaze me, sir.—Then this is our only
resource, and, at all hazards, we must accomplish it.

Enter a Servant.

Serv. Mr Oakworth desires to see both you and
my young master directly, sir.

Old Vis. Very well.   [*Exit Servant.*

Leo. I'll keep out of his way.—He is a passionate
old fellow, and I am sure he would lose his temper
with me.—Do you see him, sir, and let him be the
bearer of your determination.   [*Exeunt severally.*

SCENE II.

The Hotel.

Mrs CLEVELAND *and* JULIA.

Mrs Clev. How is my dear child now?

Jul. Better—much better—thanks to your tender care.

Mrs Clev. Oh, the wretch that could alarm my angel thus, and aim by violence to tear my precious treasure from her mother's arms! Heaven's vengeance will await him.

Jul. My spirits would, I think, soon recover this rude shock, but for the dread that overpowers me for the fate of my dear father.

Mrs Clev. Ah, my child, I fear—(*Seeing* JULIA *much depressed.*) Yet still, my love, there is hope: that hope we will cherish.—Come, my child, take comfort—take comfort, dearest Julia.

Jul. Oh, what are all the riches we possess without my father!

Mrs Clev. Poor indeed!—but we will trust he yet survives, to bestow a value on the gifts of fortune.

Enter OAKWORTH.

Oak. Oh Lord! Oh Lord! Oh Lord! what will this world come to!

Mrs Clev. What is the matter?

Oak. Roguery! Villainy! Infamy!

Mrs Clev. Where?—From what quarter?

Oak. From the devil's nest—the house of the Visorlys.

Mrs Clev. Pray, let me know the worst?

Oak. I will—I will.—As you desired me, I demanded that all the property remitted by Mr Cleveland should be consigned to you.

Mrs Clev. Well, could they refuse it?

Oak. They did—they did.—I mean the old one did; for the young rascal took care to keep out of my way. He was wise—he was wise there.

Mrs Clev. But on what plea, on what pretence were you refused?

Oak. A wicked pretence, a damnable pretence— a pretence they ought to swing for.

Mrs Clev. What—what?

Oak. That they did not believe—they did not believe——

Mrs Clev. What?

Oak. Must I tell you?

Mrs Clev. Yes, pray do.

Oak. That you were—Mr Cleveland's wife.

Mrs Clev. Gracious Heaven!

Oak. Yes; and he said that he was heir-at-law, and should not part with a sixpence of what was his right.

Mrs Clev. Oh, Julia!

Jul. Dear mother, can this man's preposterous claim give you a moment's concern?

Mrs Clev. My child, we are lost—we are ruined.

Oak. What do you say?

Mrs Clev. Never till this moment did I reflect that I have no legal testimony in my possession to prove myself a wife. Married in India, in private too—my husband dead—my child without a proof of—Oh God! Oh God!

Oak. Compose yourself, dear madam.

Mrs Clev. Hard as my lot is, were I alone concerned I might feel resignation; but my dear girl, my lovely Julia—heiress of thousands—is—the child of poverty.

Jul. Dear mother, do not let me add to your af-

fliction.—With you, with such a mother, I can bear
poverty—I can indeed.

Oak. Poverty.—No, no, not so bad as poverty.—
You know I have a home—'tis but an humble one, to
be sure—and I am a tough old fellow; I can work
like a horse.—Poverty—not so bad as poverty either.

Enter HENRY.

Jul. Oh, Henry!

Hen. Julia—dearest Julia, you are in tears, and
you have cause.—I hoped to dry them, but alas!—

Mrs Clev. Then my dear husband is no more.—
(HENRY *holds down his head despondently, assenting
in silence.*)—My cup of misery is full. (*After a pause.*)
Sir, you were to have been united to my daughter;
her father sanctioned your affections: I am informed
he loved your merits, and thought them, though un-
combined with fortune, sufficient to entitle you to
the heiress of his wealth. I now must tell you that
wealth is lost to her.

Hen. For her sake I lament it, not for my own.—
To her generous father's bounty I owe almost existence—He found me only grateful, and his goodness
called mere gratitude desert; for I fear I have no
merit but an honest heart—yet, while that shall
beat within my breast, I'll press my Julia to it, nor
would I resign my dear, my destined bride, to be the
husband of an empress.

Mrs Clev. Oh, little do the vicious know how precious are the sweets of virtue! That alone can elevate
the soul amidst calamity and poverty.

(*Exeunt* MRS CLEVELAND, JULIA, *and* HENRY.—
*The Master of the Hotel enters as she is finishing
the last speech.*)

Mas. of Hot. (*To* OAKWORTH, *as he is going out.*)
Sir, sir, a word with you, if you please.

Oak. What do you want?

Mas. of Hot. This hotel of mine, sir, stands at a very great rent.

Oak. So I suppose.

Mas. of Hot. Taxes come very high.

Oak. Well.

Mas. of Hot. A great many servants.

Oak. So I see—and what the devil is all this to me?

Mas. of Hot. It ought to make people consider.

Oak. Don't plague me about what people ought to consider.

Mas. of Hot. To cut the matter short, sir, you know that one of the ladies, as I came into the room, was owning her poverty.

Oak. Eh! What?

Mas. of Hot. Yes, sir; and as I can't afford to lose my money, I beg leave to hint that I shall look to you to see my bill fairly discharged.

Oak. Impudent scoundrel!

Mas. of Hot. Sir, I shall teach you to use better language to a man in his own house.

Enter a Gentleman, followed by a Waiter.

Gent. Hey-day! nothing but bustle and upr)ar!

Wait. I hope you are not hurt, sir.

Gent. Not at all; but no thanks for that to the careless dog of a postillion who overturned me. I have been quarrelling with him outside of the house, and I find you are at the same employment within.—Get me a coach directly. (*To the Waiter.*)

Wait. Yes, sir.   [*Exit.*

Gent. Well, what is the matter here?

Oak. Only this worthy master of the house insulting his customers.

Gent. That is an odd way of recommending himself.

Oak. (*To Landlord.*) Away with you, and be careful that you let none of your insolence break out

before the ladies, or I'll be the death of you, you
dog.   [*Exit Master of the Hotel.*

Gent. Sir, give me leave to ask, that is, if there
be no offence in the question, are the ladies you mention under any pecuniary embarrassment; for it
would be a sad thing to have ladies liable to the rudeness of this unfeeling fellow?

Oak. No, sir, thank Heaven! Even my poor pocket could satisfy his paltry demands. No, no—
though they are unfortunate, they are not in the power
of such a pitiful scoundrel as that.

Gent. I am glad of it; but still you say they are
unfortunate.

Oak. Yes; misery be the lot of the villains who
made them so!

Gent. Who are those villains?

Oak. Their own relations.

Gent. Heav'ns, what depravity! But can't this
villainy be in any way redressed?

Oak. Only one way, if at all; and there the remedy would be as bad as the disease.

Gent. What is the remedy?

Oak. Going to law.

Gent. If law can give the remedy, redress is certain: in this country the way to justice is not through
blind mazes and crooked paths—No, 'tis a public
road, open to all, obvious to all.

Oak. That is very true; but, like other public roads,
you would get on a very little way, without money
to pay the tolls.

Gent. The warm interest you take in the cause of
your friends convinces me that they are worthy of
it. I have a fortune, an ample fortune, and I can
no way employ it so satisfactorily as in rescuing the
virtuous from the machinations of villainy.

Oak. Sir, sir, let me rightly understand you. I
beg your pardon; but do you indeed mean to em-

12

ploy your fortune to relieve the distress of strangers,
utter strangers to you?

Gent. Certainly, or how should I relieve distress
at all? for all that belong to me, thank Heaven, are
above the power of fortune's malice.

Oak. Bless you! bless you! The widow's blessing
—the orphan's—

Gent. Nay, nay, good old man, I were blest enough
for all that I can do, in seeing how happy I have
made you. But a widow—an orphan, say you? Those
are sacred names. The husband gone, who is protector to the widow?—Heaven.—The parent lost,
who is the orphan's father?—Heaven. The man, then,
who will not assert their rights, is not uncharitable
only, for he is impious.—Good man, why do you
tremble thus?

Oak. I am old—I feel now I am an old man; and
though my nerves, I think, would bear me stoutly
up under adversity, yet, somehow, this sudden turn
of good fortune has *shook* me, has *shook* me a good
deal.

Gent. Compose yourself——then tell the ladies
that I shall see them very soon, for I now must go.

Oak. Don't go, don't go yet. Let them hear, sir,
from your own lips your goodness.

Gent. My business hence is nothing trivial; and
only a case of misfortune could have detained me
here an instant; therefore assure your friends—But
why not debar myself a few moments longer of my
own gratification, to convince them of my certain protection? (*Aside.*) My good old friend, tell the ladies I
wait to see them. (*Exit* OAKWORTH.) Ay, ay,
'twill make but a few minutes difference, and the
dear good creatures I so long to behold will forgive
me when I tell them that the cause of my delay was
to dry the tear of affliction.

Enter MRS CLEVELAND, *led in by* OAKWORTH, JU-
LIA *following with* HENRY.

Mrs Clev. Sir, your goodness——
Jul. My father!
Clev. My wife! my child! Oh, heavenly powers!
[*The scene closes upon them.*

SCENE III.

Another Apartment in the Hotel.

Enter DROOPLY *and* CAROLINE, *a Waiter following,*
with a Portmanteau, and a small iron Box.

Dro. Put the things carefully into a chamber, and
be sure take care of that little box.
Wait. Yes, sir.   [*Exit.*
Dro. And here we are, my dearest Caroline, with
the parson's blessing upon us. I hardly durst raise
my hopes to this happiness, even before your worthy
brother contrived to make me an estate out of pocket;
but, my generous girl, when I reflect that you take a
beggar to your arms—
Car. Nay, nay, I am only doing an act of common honesty, in paying the debts of my family; and
I am to consider you a very gentle creditor, to be
satisfied with less than a third of your demand, and
to take charge of me into the bargain.
Dro. My dearest girl!
Car. But, amidst our happiness, let us not forget the melancholy situation of the dear Clevelands
—Let us instantly try to see them.
Dro. Here comes the little Gentoo full of glee.
Oh, this looks well!

Enter GANGICA.

Car. Gangica!

Gan. Ah, you here! Oh, I glad of dat—I so happy.

Car. What has happened to make you so?

Gan. (*Pointing to her heart.*) Dis too full of joy to let me talk.   I can't tell you—but come—come wid me—you know all—den you be too happy to talk.—Come, come.   [*Exeunt.*

SCENE *changes.*

CLEVELAND, MRS CLEVELAND, JULIA, *and* HENRY.

Clev. The villains! ample shall be their punishment.

Mrs Clev. It will be ample, be assured; but do not you wrest vengeance from that Power who best knows how to deal it; that Power which never withholds its succour from the innocent, nor lets the guilty 'scape its awful indignation.

Jul. But say, my father, by what miracle are you restored to us?

Clev. Henry, no doubt, has told you that he saw me in the boat, which his humanity declined a place in.—We laboured for the nearest shore, but found that an attempt to land would whelm us in the raging surf—Thus were we compelled to trust our little skiff to the wide ocean, and for many hours were driven at random by its fury—At length we gained the land, but far from the coast on which we left our wreck.

Jul. But why did you not, the instant that you landed, acquaint us with your safety?

Clev. Alas! I had lost the power of doing so. Enfeebled by fatigue, when I reached the shore, I scarce had sense or motion : a fever followed, from which reason and health returned together—So on the instant I set out to be myself the herald of my safety.

Hen. I sought you on the coast near Portland.

Clev. Well might you hear no tidings of me; for we made our landing at the Isle of Wight, to the humanity of whose inhabitants myself and poor companions owe our lives. Think you those wretches the Visorlys will venture to you?

Mrs Clev. Convinced that you are no longer living, I have no doubt but the instructions we have given to Oakworth to communicate will bring them here.

Clev. The young one has never seen me, and Old Visorly not since I was quite a child; so it is impossible I should be known.

Mrs Clev. But promise to preserve your temper.

Clev. Depend on me.

Oak. (*Without.*) This way.

Mrs Clev. I hear Oakworth's voice. We will retire.

[*Exeunt* MRS CLEVELAND, JULIA, *and* HENRY.

Enter OAKWORTH, OLD VISORLY, *and* LEONARD.

Oak. This is the stranger I told you of. I leave you with the gentleman, begging his pardon for introducing him to such damn'd bad company.

(*Exit* OAKWORTH.

Leo. We understand that you have volunteered to defend the cause of Mrs Cleveland. Are we rightly informed, sir?

Clev. You are.

Leo. I thought the days of chivalry were over.

Clev. So did I; but since monsters still exist— 'tis fit that they revive again.

Leo. You have begun your career of enterprise, most illustrious knight, with rather a hopeless adventure.

Clev. It may not be found so.

Leo. You seem an intelligent man. A little conversation will, I have no doubt, bring us to the same opinion, and all errors will be rectified before we part.

Clev. You need not doubt it, sir.

Old Vis. Now, my boy Leonard will talk him over in a grand style. Oh, he is a blessing to my old age! (*Aside.*)

Leo. This woman has the power of influencing persons very much in her favour.

Clev. Innocence always has that power.

Leo. Innocence! Sir, sir, you are duped, deceived.

Clev. How, sir?

Leo. Nay, sir, if you fly off in this way, you are not the man of sense I take you for.

Clev. Well, sir, go on.

Leo. You are led to believe this lady to have been Mr Cleveland's wife.

Clev. Yes, sir, I am.

Leo. Grossly imposed on.—We have the most convincing reasons to believe the contrary.

Clev. Indeed!

Leo. Sir, sir, what do you think of us? Should we be so lost to the common feelings of human nature, as to proceed as we have done, but upon just ground?

Old Vis. Oh, I assure you, sir, before I consented, Leonard thoroughly convinced me.

Clev. He did?

Leo. Yes, and you shall be convinced. Oh, sir, let me appeal to your respectability. You are a man who must, I am certain, rank high in the world's estimation. How would that be injured by your present interference! How would the world despise, abhor the man who could support the claims of mere pretenders against a rightful heir! (*Pointing to* Old Visorly.)

Clev. How the world will despise, will abhor such wretch, will very soon be known.

Leo. You, perhaps, are not aware that she has no proofs of her marriage.

Clev. Proofs may be found.

Leo. In India, you think. Will you go thither for them?

Clev. I have been.

Leo. What?

Clev. I have been.

Leo. You knew Cleveland, perhaps?

Clev. Yes.

Leo. Do you know, then, of his marriage?

Clev. I was present at it.

Leo. You surprise me!

Clev. Will this satisfy you?

Leo. A witness may be suborned. The law will scarcely be content with one person's testimony.

Clev. With mine it clearly will.

Leo. You may be mistaken, sir. It will be rash to risk it. I will make an offer, a handsome offer:—We will resign our claim to half the fortune. Manage the business with the ladies as you please; you may depend on our secrecy. We tender to *you*, mind, to *yourself*, half the fortune.

Clev. It is a handsome offer.

Old Vis. Very, indeed! May be you think a third would be enough.

Clev. No, no, far from it; for though the bribe sounds handsomely, it would be want of policy in me to take it.

Leo. How?

Clev. For this plain reason, that, tho' I admit these ladies to be Cleveland's wife and daughter, still Cleveland's fortune is the right of—

Leo. Whom?

Clev. Me.

Leo. You! By what title?

Clev. The clearest in the world—founded on the simple principle, that while a man can prove himself alive, his heirs are not allowed to take possession of his property.

Leo. Alive !

Clev. Why, gentlemen, you are very hard to be convinced. Surely you should admit a man alive, when he is able himself to tell you so.

Leo. Confusion !

Old Vis. Oh dear, oh dear, oh dear !

Clev. And how do you now feel yourselves, my very worthy cousins ? *(Goes to the door.)* Come, come in, and thank your kinsmen for all their kindness.

Enter MRS CLEVELAND *and* JULIA.

Old Vis. Oh, Leonard, Leonard, did I ever think you would have brought me into such disgrace !

Clev. Sensible rebuke of age to youth ! You should have led your son into the path of honesty, not been seduced by him into the road of villainy.

Old Vis. I'll go home, and if I continue in my present mind, I think it very likely I shall hang myself before to-morrow morning.—Oh, Leonard, Leonard ! [*Exit.*

Clev. With your company, sir, (*To* LEONARD,) I cannot dispense till I receive assurance that my property remitted to you is vested as I directed.

Enter DROOPLY, CAROLINE, HENRY, *and* OAKWORTH.

Dro. My worthy brother, give me joy.

Leo. Your brother !

Car. Even so, sir.

Leo. You are well paired. I wish you all the happiness that mutual poverty can give you.

Car. Poverty ! Nay, we need not starve. My estate is surely sufficient to prevent that.

Leo. Your estate! You must first persuade me to resign the writings of it.

Car. Thank you, dear brother; but you happen to forget you have already done that.

Leo. I? How—when?

Car. By your direction I brought the box to town with me, which, you said, contained the writings.

Leo. Yes—ay—that box.—Hey! Let me see it—I have got the key of it.

Dro. The key, my dear fellow! Do you think I do things so cursed mechanically as to want keys? A man just come into possession of an estate, and not break open the box that contained his claim to it!

Leo. What, broke open!

Dro. Yes, with a kitchen poker. Lord, how alarmed you are! Yes, I broke it open, and found I had killed two birds with one stone : for, instead of only getting the writings of one estate, I found the writings of two—this lady's and my own.

A Person enters, and converses apart with CLEVE-
LAND, *and then exit.*

Leo. Curses fall on me!

Dro. That they will, fast enough; never fear. What a shrewd guesser you must be! You had the wisdom to foresee, that, some time or other, there would be a junction of the properties, and you therefore commodiously packed up the writings together. Ah, you are a considerate fellow!

Clev. (*To* LEONARD.) Sir, we need your presence here no longer. My property I find is vested as I appointed. Now, sir, depart, loaded, not with my reproaches, not with my malediction ; for the whole world's contempt, and the heaviest curses of the injured, would add but a feather's weight to the mountain of remorse which conscious guilt will heap upon thy wretched bosom. When I reflect on the severity of suffering conscience can inflict, I could almost forget my injuries, and pity thee.

Leo. To palliate my guilt I do not seek—yet, in justice, let me declare, the erroneous judgment of the world made me a villain. I beheld the eye of observance and respect ever directed to the wealthy; were he fool or knave, no matter ; while all that is truly amiable or great in genius or in virtue, when linked with poverty, was heeded with the stare of disavowal, or the scowl of contempt. To be a golden idol for the world's worship was my aim. I have lost my fortune, character, and happiness in the attempt, and now must meet in penury mankind's abhorrence, and feel too I deserve it. [*Exit.*

Mrs Clev. (*To* CAROLINE.) I grieve to think how much you must be afflicted.

Car. I am indeed ; for with all his unworthiness, I cannot forget he is my brother.

Clev. Such remembrance honours you ; for never should the principles of justice absorb the feelings of nature.

Enter SHARPSET *and* GANGICA.

Oak. Ah, my good friend, you at liberty !

Sharp. Yes, sir, I found bail.

Oak. I am very glad to see you.

Mrs Clev. Sir, I shall ever feel myself your debtor.

Sharp. Oh, madam !

Oak. I know a way to repay him, madam.

Mrs Clev. How ?

Oak. By making him rightful possessor of the treasure he holds in his hand.

Jul. Gangica, do you consent to——

Gan. I do all as you please, ma'am.

Jul. I am sure it will please me that you make yourself happy.

Oak. Now I have performed my promise, you must renew my acquaintance with your father.

Sharp. You and my father, sir, have never been asunder.

Oak. Hey! What do you mean?

Sharp To restore you a truant son, sir, who, till he had atoned as far as lay in his power for his former errors, could not hope to be acknowledged by such a father.

Oak. What, my own boy turned out an honest man?

Sharp. Yes, sir; and who, now knowing the precious value of that first of titles, will never forfeit it.

Oak. Now, then, I can say I am completely happy.

Mrs Clev. Ever, ever may you remain so!—You will; for benevolence like yours makes the human heart a heaven.

Clev. The gratitude I owe to all who have befriended these dear objects of my love, I hope to shew by something more than words. What a prospect of happiness opens to our view! Blest with friends, proved such in the trying moments of affliction— with fortune to command profusely every luxury, and, I trust, with minds to employ it only in pursuit of one—the luxury of doing good.   [*Exeunt.*

ZORINSKI,

A

PLAY,

IN THREE ACTS.

AS PERFORMED AT THE

THEATRE-ROYAL, HAY-MARKET.

BY

THOMAS MORTON.

DRAMATIS PERSONÆ.

CASIMIR, *King of Poland,*	*Mr Aickin.*
ZORINSKI,	*Mr Barrymore.*
RODOMSKO,	*Mr Bensley.*
RADZANO,	*Mr C. Kemble.*
ZARNO,	*Mr Bannister, jun.*
O'CURRAGH,	*Mr Johnstone.*
AMALEKITE,	*Mr Suett.*
WITSKI,	*Mr Fawcett.*
NACLO,	*Mr Caulfield.*
ROSOLIA,	*Mrs Kemble.*
RACHEL,	*Miss Leak.*
WINIFRED,	*Mrs Bland.*

Peasants, Soldiers, Assassins, &c.

ZORINSKI.

ACT THE FIRST.

SCENE I.

Cracow—A View of the Diet—Bells ringing—A number of People discovered ; among them RADZANO, *disguised.*

Enter WITSKI.

Wit. Make way there for the king !—Here he comes !—here comes great Casimir !

Rad. That slave I do remember.—Save thee, fellow—whose vassal art thou?

Wit. Marry, courteous stranger ! I tend the mill of the lord Rodomsko, castellan of Wounitz, here in Cracovia.

Rad. Rememberest thou the lord Radzano ?

Wit. Remember him !—Alack ! the day—the last time I beheld his gallant form was on the battlements of his castle—then a very stripling—when my present lord besieged it.

Rad. So then Radzano was by force expelled—Pr'ythee the story.

Wit. If this addle pate of mine play me no trick,
marry, thus it was:—During the troubles of the late
reign, peaceful right was elbowed out by warlike
might: Then Rodomsko, our present lord, taking
'vantage of the time when our troops were on the
frontier, tugging with the common enemy, made inroad on us: On this Radzano hied him back to the
castle; but, alack! might cuffed down right; and, in
the encounter, our good brave lord was slain.—Ah,
stranger! that was a grievous day!

Rad. So—I still am lord then of my vassals' hearts.
——Fellow, I thank thee for thy story: A day may
come when I'll requite thy love for thy lost lord.—
But soft, the king!

Wit. Ay, here he comes—so majestic, and yet so
humble; so just, and yet so merciful.—The benizon
of Heaven light on him! He's the poor man's friend.

Rad. (*Shewing a paper.*) If thy report be true,
the wrongs here written may meet atonement.—
Stand back; he approaches.

Chorus of Peasants.

Hail! mighty king!
'Tis love that elevates our strains,
'Tis joy the swelling note sustains,
To thee we call!
Welcome as the God of day,
Who pours his animating ray
Alike on all.
Hail! mighty king!

*During the chorus, Guards, Officers, and Nobles enter
in procession:—At the conclusion, the King, Cardinal, and Nobles.*

Cas. (*To the Cardinal.*) By my faith, well urged!
—Lord Cardinal, your words befit as well the objects
of true policy as they attune with the holy mandate

of your calling.—Yes! our country shall have peace!
—True, these Teutonic knights have disgraced their
order, turning from Christian service and true chivalry, to deeds of usurpation and dominion: Yet,
nerved though we are to check these ravagers, it
befits us rather with firm expostulation to meet our
enemy than risk our subjects' blood in keen encounter. Let conquerors astound the ear with the din of
war, the trumpet's clangour, and the groans of cap-
tives—be mine the clamours of my people's love.

As the King passes on RADZANO *kneels*—CASIMIR
*takes the petition—looks at it—stops suddenly, and
with scrutinizing eye examines* RADZANO — *approaches him.*

Cas. (*In a low tone.*) Radzano!
Rad. He.
Cas. Amazement!—My good lords, proceed you
to the diet.   [*Exeunt Lords.—He waves his hand
to the People, who exeunt.*
Rad. My gracious king! (*Kneels.*)
Cas. Rise to my heart—Say what fair fortune has
preserved thee to me?
Rad. A woman, good my liege, and fair as fortune
e'er was pictured; yet, in sooth, without her fickle-
ness, and only blind in her fond love of me.—My
king may well remember when I left the embattled
frontier.
Cas. Remember it! By my sword I had reason;
for with thee went this body's buckler.—O, my best
soldier! 'twas this arm first taught thee the rudiments of war, when scarcely truncheon high.—But
my love breaks in upon thy story—On.
Rad. I reached my castle time enough to see its
ruin—Rodomsko triumphed. In a remote apartment,
constructed for concealment, I lay hid, hoping for
life and better days: that apartment was selected
for Rodomsko's daughter, the beauteous Rosolia:

To her pitying ear I told my story; and her soft bosom, rich in nature's best endowments, soon matured compassion into love.—At a fit time I fled.

Cas. Whither, good Radzano?

Rad. To England, my loved lord! There I sojourned till Fame proudly proclaimed that Justice was again enthroned in Poland; for there reigned great Casimir. For that justice thus I bend my knee; and my boon is, that my tongue may denounce Rodomsko villain, and my good sword avenge my wrongs!

Cas. Then I refuse thy boon.

Rad. Dread liege! Heaven will make the good cause prosperous!

Cas. Radzano, link not Heaven with murder!—If Heaven recognized the sword's arbitrement, Rodomsko ne'er had triumphed.—Droop not, my friend—by my crown, thou shalt have justice!—Even now in angry parley I meet Rodomsko!—These hot lords, who live but in a storm, urge me to renew the war—But of that hereafter.—Uncloud thee—be thyself—attend me at the diet.—Once more, Radzano, welcome! [*Exeunt.*

SCENE II.

Draws, and discovers the Country near Cracow.—
RACHEL *and Slaves at work.*

Enter AMALEKITE—(*the Slaves bow.*)

Ama. Again, again; dat ish goot.—Now vork, you damned Polish dogs! or bastinado's the vord.—Rachel, come here, you slut—you audacious—Delicious little tit! (*Aside.*) Come here, I say. (*Angrily.*)—

Must speak cross before dem—but, my little plump
cherry, I be's not angry.

Rac. Dear sir! then what makes you look so terrible?

Ama. It's the mild tender passion of love.—(*With
amorous fervour.*)—You know, Rachel, 'twas for your
sake I did not turn your fader Witski out of his mill
to starve, though he dare laugh at me—me, Amalekite
Grabouski, chief agent to Lord Rodomsko, castellan of Wounitz in Cracovia; so you sees how I loves
you.

Rac. Oh! I'm sure you don't; for lovers sigh, and
kneel, and——

Ama. Kneel! Oh dear! I cannot does dat—What
a pity's love is such a foe to dignity!—I say, Rachel
—(*Looks to see whether the peasants observe him*)—
I say—how do you contrive to have so soft a hand?
(*Enter* WITSKI.) I should suppose labours would
make it hard—(*Fumbling and kissing it*)—but I declare it's as smooth and as soft—Bless my soul——
(*During this,* WITSKI *advances, bows low, and close
to* AMALEKITE, *who, by accident, lays his hand on his
head.*) Oh, Lud! vat ish dat—Stand off.

Wit. You know, sir, you always told me to shew
you homage.

Ama. Yes! but at an awful distance.

Wit. True; but seeing your honour so close to
my daughter, I thought I might be treated in the
family way. (*Laughs aside.*)

Ama. Now he's grinning again!—Rachel had behaved ill, so I was punishing her—vas not I punishing you, young vomans?

Rac. Yes, indeed you were, sir.

Ama. Go to work, hussy!—So, Witski, you've
been at Cracow?

Wit. Yes, your honour! and here is the produce
of the flour for our lord—(*Gives a purse*)—and here,

you know, sir, is the——for the steward. (*Gives
another.*)

Ama. (*Putting one in each pocket.*) Yes, yes! Dat
ish vary goot—Vare you going?

Wit. Home to my wife.

Ama. (*Turning quick round.*) Ah! how does she
do? She's a very pretty little vomans!

Wit. My wife too! Was there ever such an old—

O'Curragh. (*Without.*) Hollo!

Enter O'CURRAGH.

O'Cur. Pray, is there ever a Jew-faced creature?
(WITSKI *points to* AMALEKITE, *and exit.*) Pray, Mr
Jew, is your Christian name Amalekite?

Ama. Amalekite ish my name.

O'Cur. Then how are you? how are you? (AMA-
LEKITE, *in action, demands obeisance.*) Well, I'll indulge you—There—(*Bows*)—but you might have
the civility to return it.

Ama. I'm in office!

O'Cur. And, I suppose, like other great men, you
have stooped so low to get there, that your back has
been cramped ever since. But come, to business—
look there—(*Shews a letter*)—and be secret, snug—
dumb as a potatoe.

Ama. (*Reads.*) " Your Lord Radzano greets you."
—Holy Abraham! is he alive?

O'Cur. Hush!

Ama. " Your Lord Radzano greets you : e'en now
he is arrived in Cracow, to claim his rights, and crush
that usurper Rodomsko"—Bless my soul!—" Do you
win the vassals to his interest.—He who brings this
will instruct you farther.—Be faithful, and you will
be rewarded. RADZANO."
Bless my soul, what shall I do? Radzano has the
right, but then Rodomsko has the possession.—Bless
my conscience, what shall I do? Then Radzano is in
great favour with the king.—Bless my conscience,

what shall I do? But then Rodomsko is in great favour with the nobility.——Bless my conscience, what
shall I do?

O'Cur. Who comes here?

Ama. Stand aside—it is the lord Rodomsko, who
passes here in his way to the diet—Stand aside. (*Puts
up the letter, and* O'CURRAGH *retires.*)

Enter RODOMSKO *and Train*—AMALEKITE *bows very
low—the Slaves prostrate themselves.*

Ama. Heaven save our gracious lord!

Rod. Hast thou aught to impart?

Ama. Nothing, dread lord.

Rod. Are the slaves obedient.

Ama. Yes, dread lord.

Rod. On to Cracow. [*Exeunt* RODOMSKO *and train.*

O'Cur. (*Comes forward.*) I say, this lord Rodomsko is a stiff, crabbed kind of a——

Ama. Oh! he keeps the slaves in proper subjection.

O'Cur. Proper subjection! I'll tell you what; he
appears to me like the great tall thistle in the potatoe
garden, which bothers every one who touches it, and
prevents the humble fruit from arriving at the whole-
some maturity Nature intended. Oh! I wish I had
the docking of him.——Now my lord Radzano is so
humane, so polished, so—gallant—so—

Ama. Hah! hah! I suppose he has brought over
with him what will please the ladies.

O'Cur. Faith, you may say that, for he has brought
me over with him.

Ama. And I hope he is hospitable and charitable,
and all——that damned stuff! (*Aside.*)

O'Cur. Oh! he has been sucking in the breath of
it in little England, Mr Amalekite. Oh! confound
your name: Could they not have called you Ne-
buchadnezzar, or MacLaughlin, or O'Shaughnessy,
or any easy agreeable name of that sort.——Oh! we

shall have such jolly doings: every heart will wear the face of joy, and all countenances, men, women, cows, Jews, and sheep, must all be on the broad grin.

Ama. I must consider—which of my lords shall I betray?—Bless my conscience!—Slaves, treat this stranger with all respect, and give him the song of welcome.—You will follow me.—It's a very puzzling case:—Radzano has the right—Rodomsko has——Bless my conscience!　　　　　　　　　　[*Exit.*

Slaves approach, and prostrate themselves to O'Cur-RAGH.

O'Cur. Thank you, thank you! Oh! low enough in conscience.—What are you at? what are you at, jewels?—Keep your fore-paws off the ground, and don't make bulls of yourselves--Stand up, I say—Heaven never meant its own image should be so degraded!

SONG.—RACHEL.

I.

Courteous stranger,
Now free from danger,
And laughing at departed care and labour;
Thy cares unbending,
Thy journey ending,
Now frisk it to the merry pipe and tabor.

II.

Welcome stranger, welcome here,
An humble welcome, but sincere;
From the lowly slaves receive,
All, alas! they have to give.
　　　　　　　　Courteous stranger, &c.

III.

May the savage beast of prey
Ne'er cross thee on thy lonely way!

And, returning, may'st thou find
Thy friend sincere, thy mistress kind!
     Courteous stranger, &c.
       [Exeunt, different sides.

SCENE III.

The Diet.

The King (seated), Cardinal, RODOMSKO, *Nobles,&c.*

Cas. In pursuance of our purpose, we have appointed my Lord Cardinal our ambassador, to conclude a peace with the Teutonic knights.

Rod. Peace! Is then a soldier, the world's right arm, to wither and decay, that hordes of priests, with their beads and crosiers, may preach us into cowards? But I wonder not; for since the great Zorinski was disgraced——

Cas. What of him?

Rod. He was honest.

Cas. He was proud and inflexible! But forbear to name him.

Rod. Since, sire, you have banished from your councils those hardy spirits who alone were fit to aid the public weal, naught now will down but peace—the general good—these are the entrapping blandishments held out for emancipating slaves, privileging towns, and using every circumventive art to crush the power of the nobility!—Peace! Let my Lord Cardinal preach its blessings—I hate it! What! gentlemen of Poland! shall your goodly scymitars canker in their sheaths, while those usurping knights despoil your borders?

Cas. (*Coming forward.*) Fiery lord! hear me.   If
it be my duty to root out usurpation and foul conspiracy, why need I wage the war on Pomerania's borders, when my eye's scope comprehends an object
that would give vengeance full employment?

Rod. Sire! Rodomsko scorns base fear, nor will
he shun inquiry.—Thou would demand, how came I
by my power? My answer is, by valorous achieve-
ment—by conquest—the soldier's tenure! But why
waste we words? Radzano being dead—who is there—

Cas. (*Holds up his finger.*) Indeed!

Enter RADZANO.

Rod. Lightnings blast him!

Cas. Behold the wronged Radzano :—What canst
thou urge?

Rod. I cannot battle it with words.—'Twas this good
arm that gave me power, 'tis this good arm that will
maintain it!—Follow me.—Thou wilt not find it palsied, boy. (*Both going.*)

Cas. On your allegiance, hold!—Still the friend to
gentle peace—still anxious to preserve the most re-
bellious drop of subjects' blood—let me propose between you terms where love may grow, and honour
ratify them.   Rodomsko, Radzano loves thy daughter

Rod. Indeed!

Cas. Let her be mediatrix between you: let holy
marriage with their hands unite your hearts ; so live
in equal power and love—What says Radzano?

Rad. My king has spoken my soul's fondest hope!

Rod. (*Aside.*) Hold—hold—this marriage has some
promise in't—it gives Radzano to my power—and
should the confederate lords—It shall be so.

Cas. That scowling brow looks not consent.

Rod. Then, my liege, it wrongs my heart.   'Tis
true, I have not that April face that clouds and shines
at every gust of grief or joy ; but 'tis my rugged na-

ture—I pray you bear with it.—Radzano! here's my hand.

Rad. (*Pressing it to his bosom.*) Thus let it stamp upon my heart a son's obedience, and to oblivion give each hostile thought.

Cas. Rodomsko, hie you to your castle; for e'en this night in person we will progress thither, and consummate this happy union. (ROD. *bows.*)

Rod. (*Aside.*) So then a lord of Poland, great in birth and arms, preserves his dignities by the arch dimples of a puling girl.—Oh, Cupid! how I honour thee!   [*Exit.*

Cas. Oh, Radzano! let me pour into thy breast my griefs—The wrongs I bear from these injurious lords press hard upon me; but I am rich in poor men's prayers, and that's a kingly solace. Oh! I would rise unto my people like the god of day to Lapland's icy sons after his wintry absence!—What! not a word, Radzano? I see the lover dulls the patriot—but I forgive it.—Away to thy Rosolia—Yet mark her father —watch well Rodomsko—E'en now conspiracy's at work against my throne and person, yet, 'spite of impending death, I'll on!—Farewell, my friend! (RAD-ZANO *bows, and exit.*) My good lords, attend me!— Oh, my country! let me but save thee.   [*Exeunt.*

SCENE IV.

RODOMSKO'S *Castle.*

Enter RODOMSKO, *reading a letter.*

Rod. " The confederates greet thee, brave Ro-domsko! If they have appeared inactive, 'twas as na-ture stilly pausing, before the coming storm; for 'tis

resolved that Casimir shall fall." Vengeance, I thank
thee! " Forty chosen men are ready for the achieve-
ment, waiting but a leader.—Know, Rodomsko, in thy
mines dwells a man fashioned to conduct the daring
enterprise—seek him instantly.—The brave fellow who
brings this, by whose dejected brow thou'lt see he's
ripe for murder, will conduct thee to the man we
seek.—Farewell! and triumph."—Now tremble, Casimir.—But soft :——the messenger from the lords ap
proaches.—What says my letter? (*Enter* O'CURRAGH,
smiling.)—Dejected brow! If the mind's construction
be indexed in the face, this man bears sweet content
about him.—Health to thee, friend!

O'Cur. (*Aside.*) Mighty civil, however.

Rod. Instruct me in your fortunes.

O'Cur. What, my history?—Oh! I'll tell your
lordship; and a sweet piece of geography it is.——
The first thing I know is, that I don't know where I
was born, for nobody could tell me, and being young
myself at the time, it has slipped my memory.

Rod. Shallow babbler—thy name?

O'Cur. O'Curragh, the faithful servant of Lord
Radzano.

Rod. (*With irritation.*) Com'st thou from him?
Well—well—what of him?—Dispatch.

O'Cur. He sent me, his humble servant, to express
his sorrow that he can't, where he is, throw himself
at the feet of the fair Rosolia. I make his excuses
clumsily ; but, were he here himself, he'd make a
much better apology for his absence.

Rod. Be gone, fellow!

O'Cur. I have the pleasure to take my leave. Oh!
how my master sighs—and then he closes his eyes,
and looks so tenderly.

Rod. Away! I say—that gallery leads to my
daughter's apartment—prattle these gewgaws there
—each mawkish nothing will, on her love-sick taste,
drop sweet as Hybla's honey.—Away!—(*Exit* O'-

CURRAGH;) for here comes one who embodies well
the picture given.

Enter NACLO.

Nac. The confederated lords greet thee!

Rod. Thou art welcome!—Approach—nearer—
nearer—Know'st thou the drift of this?

Nac. Ay, dread lord!

Rod. Then bring me to him we seek.—Yet hold:
—Tell me the manner of the man, that I may better
wind about his heart, and trap him to my purpose.
—Is he——

Nac. By turns, my lord, every thing.—Sometimes,
mocking the horror of his fate, he out-toils the slave;
anon he starts from his labour, and with indignation
grasps his spade, as 'twere the sceptre that swayed
the world. The foolish knaves in the mine say that
love hath crazed him; but, to my thinking, he resembles more the hungry vulture than the sorrowing
dove.

Rod. The picture's big with promise.—Conduct
me to him—How shall I best approach him? Nay,
pr'ythee lead.—'Tis strange!

[*Exeunt, ruminating;* NACLO *leads.*

SCENE V.

The Country.

Enter O'CURRAGH.

O'Cur. Upon my honour, this Lady Rosolia is a
bewitching creature; and now that she has passed
the ordeal of constancy, which is by looking me over
without so much as an ogle at me—why, my master

may call himself a happy man. I don't know how it is, but I think this snug agreeable person of mine is a sort of a female test; just like a bit of rough glass that they try money on—and have you found any bad ones, O'Curragh? Oh! sweet Mrs Flannigan for that—never shall I forget!

SONG.—O'CURRAGH.

(*At the Dead of the Night.*)

I.

At the dead of the night, when by whisky inspired,
And pretty Katty Flannigan my senses had fired,
I tapped at her window, when thus she began,—
Oh! what the devil are you at ?—get out you naughty man

II.

I gave her a look, oh! as sly as a thief,
Or, when hungry, I'd view a fine sirloin of beef:
My heart is red hot, says I, but cold is my skin,
So pretty Mrs Flannigan—oh! won't you let me in ?

III.

She opening the door, I sat down by the fire,
And soon was reliev'd from the wet, cold, and mire;
And I pleased her so mightily, that ere it was day,
I stole poor Katty's tender heart, and so tripped away.

Thinking of old times has given me such a comical feel, that if any pretty creature was to come across me, I fancy I should be rather agreeable company. In faith you are in luck, O'Curragh, for here comes that delicious morsel that sung her Polish planxty so sweetly.

Enter RACHEL.

Rac. Heigh ho! where can my dear Zarno tarry

so long? He knows I have but an hour from work, and yet he is not come. (*Seeing* O'CURRAGH, *bows.*)

O'Cur. Bend not to me, sweet one; rather let me kneel to you: You ladies are the lords of the creation. (*Kneels.*)

Enter ZARNO—*starts.*

Zar. Rachel! (RACHEL *runs to* ZARNO, *and embraces him.*) How dare you insult *my* Rachel? She's mine, alone mine—I love her.

O'Cur. Then she's alone mine too, for I love her; and if I've insulted her, I flatter myself I can give her satisfaction.—Insult! I don't like that.—Pray, sir, would you just step aside, and condescend to explain that word insult? Here's the prettiest chopper of logic. (*Pointing to his sword.*)

Zar. I understand you, but I dare not.

O'Cur. Dare not! You paltry——

Zar. Hear me.—Not for myself I fear, but for her. Should a freeman be killed in a slave's quarrel, she would suffer—she would be punished.

O'Cur. In love with the girl, and yet for her sake dares not defend her! That's hard, that's hard: but can't we manage it any how?

Zar. Yes; if you're a man, conceal our cause of quarrel, and I'll shew you what I dare.—I can find a sword.

O'Cur. Poor fellow! Oh, what a pleasure it will be to fight him!—Upon my honour, our cause of dispute shall be a secret.

Zar. Thank you, thank you.—Come along.

Rac. Oh, pray don't quarrel, sir!

O'Cur. Quarrel! Not at all, not the least animosity. If I should kill him, I'll give you leave to ax him whether I did it in passion.

Rac. But why fight at all?

O'Cur. Upon my conscience, I can't immediately tell why we fight.—Oh! it's for your sake.

Rac. I shall hate you.

O'Cur. Hate me ! Upon my honour, I'm so unused to hear a woman say that, that it confuses—Oh, this head ! this head ! What am I at ? going to kill a man about a woman that don't care for me !—Come here, come here.—There, my dear boy, there's satisfaction. (*Joins their hands.*)

Zar. You're a generous fellow !

O'Cur. But why don't you marry ?

Rac. Because I am a slave, and Zarno can't afford to buy me.

O'Cur. Buy you! Upon my conscience, I should like to buy a flock of such pet lambs !—But as you both seem tolerably built for running, why don't you trot off in a canter ?

Zar. Because, if Rachel were taken, her lord would kill her.

O'Cur. Then he'd be hanged for it.

Zar. Ah ! no. I have heard there was a good law once, that made a lord pay a fine for killing a man ; but it's never put in force now.

O'Cur. A fine for killing a man ! A good old law do you call that ?—What a devil of a spot have I got into here! Oh ! what a picked place is little Ireland to this ! We're poor enough to be sure, but what of that ? We can fight when we please, can work when we please, ay, and starve when we please ; and we can flourish our shilalahs, and strut about our potatoe-garden like a collection of emperors !   [*Exit.*

Zar. Adieu, dear Rachel ! I must go back to the salt-mine.

Rac. Ah, Zarno ! why do you remain in that mine ? —Nay, don't bè angry.—You, who lived in Cracow with the great Zorinski, were dressed in furs and silk, and now you wear the basest garments.

Zar. My dear Rachel ! I have reasons I cannot explain.

Rac. What ! not to me, Zarno ?

Zar. Should Zorinski know I have divulged—

Rac. Zorinski!

Zar. Ugh! (*Putting his hand to his mouth.*) Eh!
—why should not I—Bless her! Does not she deserve to be trusted?—Rachel, I'll tell thee a secret,
which, if known, would cost Zarno his life.

Rac. Would Zorinski kill thee?

Zar. No; but I would kill myself for having betrayed him. Know then, in that dreary mine dwells
the great Zorinski! Mark, when Casimir was crowned, Zorinski, who was all in all with the late king,
could not bear the thwarts Casimir put on him; a
quarrel ensued, and my master, though I love him,
was much to blame—disgrace followed. His house,
which had been the hive of courtiers, became deserted; away they flew: his great soul could not brook
it: with despairing brow and knotted arms I saw him
leave the city; and sadly he walked along till he
reached the opening of the mine.

Rac. What! to throw himself down headlong, and
end his life?

Zar. I dreaded it, so fell at his feet. He took
me by the hand, a big tear fell on it, he blushed,
called me his faithful Zarno, bade me farewell, and
gave me liberty: From that moment I became his
slave. We descended into the mine, and I have attended him, and carried him his food—ay, and ever
will. Ah, my dear master, never will Zarno leave
thee! I shared his prosperity, and shall I desert him
now? No, no. Now, Rachel, thou hast the secret,
and thus I seal it up. Farewell.

Rac. But may not we hope for happier days, Zarno?

DUET.—ZARNO *and* RACHEL.

Rachel. When first this little heart began
　　　　To feel an impulse tender,
　　　You slily came, too faithless man,
　　　　And taught it to surrender.

Zarno. That dear reproach, which seems to chide
The conquest it confesses,
By words alone affects to hide
What every look expresses.

Both. Then let us hope for the wedding-day,
When we may merry make O.

Rachel. Care away, Zarno near.

Zarno. Lip to lip, Rachel dear.

Both. And when to church we hie away,
Ding dong, ding dong, ding dong will go
The merry bells at Cracow.

Rachel. Sweet hours of love ! but short as sweet,
For Rachel's bloom must alter,
And Zarno other girls may meet,
And then his love may faulter.

Zarno. My love will last while life endures,
Though Rachel look not younger ;
For time, that lighter passions cures,
Will rivet mine the stronger.

Both. Then let us hope, &c.

ACT THE SECOND.

SCENE I.

A Salt Mine.

Enter, down a stair-case, RODOMSKO *and* NACLO.

Rod. Begin your search. (*Exit* NACLO.) The place is awful—sighs and groans, mixed with the maddening laugh of drunkards, pour along these aisles a discord that chills the very heart.—How heavily must woe have weighed him down, that makes this den his dwelling.

Enter NACLO.

Nac. Look there, my lord! Behold him wiping from his brow the painful drop of toil.

Rod. He comes this way.—What gloomy dignity!—Back—back. (*They retire.*)

Enter ZORINSKI, *with a spade.*

Zo. Well toiled to day.—I often hope that when these over-laboured limbs do press their straw, sweet sleep will give a short oblivion to my cares. But oh! then this big heart, forgetful of its fall, beats high, and wakes my brain to recollections that go nigh to mad me.—Oh, Zorinski!—how, how long will this, thy body's hardihood, shake off the gripe of death!—Shut from the sun, without a hope, without a friend

—nay, that's not so neither. Zarno, let me not wrong
thee, varlet.—Zarno!

Enter ZARNO.

Come hither, fellow.—Hast been on earth to-day?

Zar. Yes, my lord; and there's great news above.

Zo. Indeed!

Zar. Going, my lord, to Cracow, to buy provision,
I passed the diet, just as the king—(ZORINSKI *starts.*)
My lord?

Zo. Go on.

Zar. Just as the king came forth; and he looked
so kindly on us all—ay, as if he'd been our father.

Zo. (*Much agitated.*) Father of all—and I alone
rejected!

Zar And with him came the lord Radzano, whom
every body supposed dead—he's to be the favourite
now—and the palace your honour possessed is to be—

Zo. (*Much agitated.*) Be dumb! Have I not often
told thee, villain, not to name—Be gone! (*Apart.*)
What! proud heart, must thou still play the tyrant
—will not this dungeon humble thee!—Oh, shame.—
Come near me, knave—I was to blame, Zarno.

Zar. To blame, my lord! That you were not:
You had a right to be angry, and if you had trod on
me, you would have treated me as I deserved. But
will you, dear lord, forgive poor Zarno?

Zo. Forgive thee! (*Wiping his eyes.*) Fond fool,
'tis ever thus he makes a woman of me.—On with thy
tale, Zarno.

Zar. Oh! that, that, that was all.

Zo. What was all?

Zar. That was all—about—about the—(*Hesitating*)
—that is, my lord—it's dinner time.—I've had such
an adventure.

Zo. As how?

Zar. Why, trotting past a kitchen hard by—I had
just been to see the king go—(*Stops suddenly.*) Trot-

ting past a kitchen hard by, as hungry as a hunter, a curious stew presented itself—my nose stumbled at it, and I made as dead a set as a dog at a partridge, and was just going to seize, when the chesnut-faced cook threw it all over me, and made that an outside covering that I intended for an inside lining.

Zo. Ha! ha! Come, we'll in, and laugh.

Zar. It smelt so savoury—'egad, it was fit for a king: (*Stops, hits his head :*) However, I have a most delicious platter of peas and garlic.

Zo. I cannot feed. (*Sighs.*)

Zar. Not feed, my lord?

Zo. No: In thou, and eat.

Zar. Yes, my lord—but you have taken away my appetite.

Zo. Ha! strangers.—Go in, good fellow.

Zar. I will, my lord—but could not you just pick a bit? (ZORINSKI *holds up his finger,* ZARNO *exit, bowing.*)

Zo. If my eye err not—the lord Rodomsko.— Should he know me! That's an idle fear: prosperity hath but a shallow memory—clothe its dearest friend in rags, and, on my life, it puts him clean beyond his knowledge.

Rod. (*To* NACLO.) Stand aloof! (*Approaches* ZORINSKI.) Your pardon; but when I behold shut out from man, man's paragon—when in this loathsome mine I find a gem fit to illumine Poland, wonder not that I should wish to take it to my bosom's interest; nor deem me, sir, impelled by womanish inquisitiveness, when I seek to know the fortunes of a man by fortune hardly dealt with.

Zo. My story is but a dull monotony of sorrow.— To repeat it were but to strike again the chord of dire calamity, and give a lengthened tone to melancholy.

Rod. Are you of Poland?

Zo. Ay, of the equestrian order.

Rod. Gentleman of Poland !—That envied dignity's
a blessing.

Zo. It has been my curse.—Born to command—
my stubborn nature will not bow to my condition.

Rod. Sure no crime has stained——

Zo. Oh! the most monstrous—poverty—that fiend
accursed—The slave whom he encounters prostrates
in the dust, and by humility escapes his fangs—but
meeting with a rough, imperious spirit, pride and he
around him twine their venomed knots, and hold the
victim sure—for know, lord, though penury and sorrow be the sad inmates of this bosom, my soul dis-
dains the curse of benefits—Rather than so, I dungeon here, litter with devils, and out-toil the hind.

Rod. Brother! Are our rights dear to thee?

Zo. By the sacred plain of Vola—dearer than sight,
for that shews me but a hated world—dear as to the
damned the joys of heaven—for I, like them, languish for blessings which I ne'er must taste.

Rod. Not so—for I will put thee on a purpose that
shall mount thy fortunes till they reach the noble
elevation of thy soul—make thee——

Zo. Pray be careful.—So long I've banished hope
from this sad breast, that its incursion now is aching
to the sense.—Drag not at once the dungeon'd
wretch before the orb of day, and blind him with his
blessings.   Oh, sir! so long misfortune's blasts have
driven this rugged trunk—so long has misery sapped
my roots, and torn away each fibre that sustained me,
that the sun of hope (that greatest good) warms but
to wither—shines but to destroy me.

Rod. Come, cheerly, cheerly.—In the chequered
play of fortune, the best regarded must expect mis-
chance.—See'st thou the sleeky knaves of the court?
—Be wise—mask thy heart, and learn to flatter.

Zo. Flatter! I tell thee, lord, as easy were it for
our stern Carpathian mountains to shake from their
rugged brows their everlasting snows, as for this

tongue to bring forth what this heart doth not beget
—flatter !—'Sdeath—join gripe with what I hate !—
strain to my heart its fixed antipathy !—by Almighty
truth, I swear, the poisoned twine of adders round
this breast were grateful to't —thou know'st me not.

Rod. Nor can scarce believe——

Zo. Yet, Rodomsko——

Rod. Ha ! my name !

Zo. Ay, lord ! Yet, I say, thou wilt believe, when
I tell thee that this abject, rugged, heart-broken
wretch was once Zorinski——

Rod. Zorinski here !

Zo. What could I do ? Live with men to blast me
with their pity ? No ! when disgrace pursued, I earth-
ed me here, lest, Acteon like, I should be hunted by
that yelping pack of courtly knaves my bounty had
given breath to.

Rod. Oh, Zorinski ! again to fold thee, and at an
hour of such dread moment.—Oft have I in the senate mourned thy loss—but instant leave this den.

Zo. To the world again ?—What should I there—
but cast a mournful look around, and, on the wide
surface of nature, see nothing I could claim, except
a grave.

Rod. Away with this—by manhood, 'tis baby weakness '—Oh, Zorinski ! there are purposes—(*The
noise of a bugle-horn is heard above*)—Casimir hawks
to-day.

Zo. Ay—again he treads upon me. (*Looking up.*)

Rod. He does—thy fall, Zorinski—nay, droop not,
man, at what should fire thee—thy fall shall be revenged——

Zo. Ha !

Rod Yes ! rouze thee, for vengeance is at hand !
The confederated lords, allied in wrongs, are ripe for
action ; and, let but thy aspiring soul resume its
energy——

Zo. Oh ! thou hast poured again into this breast

ambition's godlike impulse! Tell me, Rodomsko, can
the devotion of this life, this soul, forward the illustrious cause?

Rod. Most mightily; for the fate of Poland hangs
upon thy breath.

Zo. Shall I to the senate there?

Rod. 'Twere useless all.—Did reason use Jove's
hunder, 'twould be outroared by the clamorous
people who pay this Casimir a worship, e'en to the
wronging of high Heaven! Oh, my friend, action is
vengeance's language—thy arm, Zorinski!——

Zo. Ah!

Rod. I have for thy ear words of deep persuasion
nd mightiest import—but the time's unfitting—instant leave this hated place.

Zo. Foul den, I quit thee, and with thee impotent
despondency!—Lead—yet hold—I've here a faithful slave that must not be forgotten.—Zarno—

Enter ZARNO.

Prepare to leave this place.

Zar. My lord—eh—what—leave this place!—O
dear—ha, ha—I'm so glad of it—an't you, sir? (*To*
RODOMSKO, *who frowns.*)

Zo. Peace, familiar fool.

Rod. There. (*Throws him a purse.*)

Zar. There! (*Aside.*) Curse his money—a churl-
ish——

Zo. Thou'lt follow, Zarno.

Zar. Oh, to be sure I will. I'll only take leave of
my fellow devils, and mount in a twinkling. Oh,
I'm so happy! Hollo! hollo!

[RODOMSKO *and* ZORINSKI *exeunt up the stair-case.*

Enter Miners.

Ah! you miserable, jolly dogs, how are you?—In
sooth this digging in a salt-mine is very productive;
for, while many an honest gentleman above can't get

salt to his porridge, you may swallow it by shove full—farewell to you all.

Miner. Are you going to leave us, Zarno?

Zar. Yes; for though this is certainly a very delectable situation, yet I find, by consulting my glass, it rather annoys the complexion; and my physician say, that this air induces spleen and melancholy.

Miner. He's mad!

Zar. Mad, am I? Then there—(*Gives money*)—there's what will make you all drunk, and then you will be as mad as I am. There goes the old carle's money. Drink, devils, drink!

SONG.—ZARNO.

I.

Good bye, my fellow devils dear,
    Fal, lal, lal, &c.
Long time I have been pickling here,
    Adieu, adieu, adieu!
O weep not, friends, because I go,
Restrain your briny drops of woe;
Unmanly weeping is a fault;
And tears like yours are wondrous salt.
    Fal, lal, lal, &c.

II.

The mine has made me pale and wan,
    Fal, lal, lal, &c.
Salt cures a hog, but kills a man,
    Adieu, adieu, adieu!
I hope your liquor may be found
Not very dead, though under ground;
So rest ye merry while I go,
And thus I quit the shades below.
    Fal, lal, lal, &c.   [*Exeunt.*

SCENE II.

A View on RADZANO'S *Estate.*

Enter WITSKI, *followed by* WINIFRED.

Wit. But, my dear wife, my dear Winifred, now do stop that tongue of thine.

Win. I won't hold my tongue; and what's more, I'll tell Mr Amalekite how you use me.

Wit. Ay, there it is!—Oh, what a hard lot is mine! If I don't submit to her in every thing, then she threatens to encourage that old amorous Jew!—Now pray be quiet

Win. I won't be quiet—I will have my own way; and I won't be snubbed—and I will be heard!

Enter O'CURRAGH.

O'Cur. What's all this chatter about?

Wit. Winny, Winny, Winny, don't provoke me: you ought to know by this time I am a man.

Win. And you ought to know by this time I am a woman.

Wit. But zounds! why so loud? Do you want all the world to know you are a woman?

O'Cur. No quarrelling to-day! Come, you cooing turtle—did ever magpie keep up so damned a chatter?

Win. I won't hold my tongue.—Oh, here comes Mr Amalekite—obey me, or you know what!

Wit. Yes, I do know what—(*Rubbing his forehead*) and yet I won't submit.—If Heaven has willed it—why——

Win. Heaven's will be done, I say.

Wit. An't you surpriz'd, friend?

O'Cur. Faith! not much at the thing, but a good deal at her choice; for if horns be the word, 'tis allowed, I believe, that no one makes a bull more neatly than an Irishman.

DUET.—WINIFRED *and* WITSKI.

WINIFRED.

A piper o'er the meadows straying,
Met a simple maid a maying,
Straight he won her heart by playing,
　　Fal de ral, &c.
Wedded, soon each tone grew teazing,
　　Fal de ral, &c.
His pipe had lost the power of pleasing,
　　Fal de ral, &c.

WITSKI.

Wedlock's laws are hard and griping;
Women fretful—arts are ripe in;
'Twas his wife that spoil'd his piping,
　　Fal de ral, &c.
Her shrill note marr'd every sonnet,
　　Fal de ral, &c.
And crack'd his pipe, depend upon it,
　　Fal de ral, &c.

WINIFRED.

Silly wives too late discover
When the honey-moon is over,
Harsh grows every piping lover,
　　Fal de ral, &c.

WITSKI.

Zounds! why teaze morn, night, and noon now,
　　With fal de ral, &c.

9

WINIFRED.

Your pipe, my dear, is out of tune now,
　　Fal de ral, &c.

BOTH.

Why then teaze morn, night, and noon now?
　　Fal de ral, &c.

Enter AMALEKITE *and Slaves.*

Ama. Fall back there—fall back!—Ah, gossip
Winifred? (*Takes her hand.*)

Wit. O dear! O Lord! what shall I do?—I can't
bear it!—I say Winny, Winny, I yield—I submit—
any thing——(*Pulling her away by the gown.*)

O'Cur. Was there ever such a hen-pecked fool?
—But I say, (*To* AMALEKITE,) have you told the
peasants that they are now become the slaves of my
lord Radzano?

Ama. I have; but pray why be they assembled
now?

O'Cur. Because my master is coming hither with
his sweet bride that is to be, to receive their homage.

Enter RACHEL.

Rac. Oh, dear father, Zarno has left the salt-mine,
and he says he'll soon be rich; and then he'll buy me
of that old rogue Amalekite!

Ama. Vill he so, slut! The old rogue will prevent
him though. Old rogue! you and your fader shall
smart for dat.

O'Cur. Stand back!—here comes my lord and his
sweet, sweet bride! Now mind your hits all of you.
I say, have you the roll with the slaves names?

Ama. Yes; here it is.

Enter RADZANO *and* ROSOLIA, *attended.*

Rad. Surely, sweet! those whose loves run in un-
ruffled smoothness, and never feel Calamity's chill

blast cannot taste my joy. Oh, lovely, constant maiden, ne'er was Radzano proud till now.

Roso. Constant! bestow not praise on that which not to be, were to be nought. If constancy be worthy praise, be it thine, Radzano, for thou hast sojourned e'en in beauty's court, and yet forgot not thy Rosolia. Look, dear lord, your vassals are assembled: Ah! they little know the blessings that await them.

Rad. Amalekite, give me the roll, and bid the slaves approach.

Ama. (*Presenting the roll.*) I am much afraid he mean to favor dem!—I no like his looks—Oh, he has a damned benevolent countenance. (*Aside.*)

Roso. Poor wretches, how they tremble!

Rad. Approach, and fear not; in this you and your children are registered my slaves, and live but in my will; acknowledge ye your vassalage? (*The slaves prostrate themselves.*)—Rise then, and mark. By this you are recorded slaves; but by this (*Tearing the roll*) you are no longer slaves, but men. (*The most extravagant signs of joy are displayed.*) The world's before you:—who will remain with me?

Peasants. All, all.

Rad. The brightest page of nature's bounteous charter is freedom to her children; that I possess you of: but, oh! contemn not just restraint, else 'twill prove a curse more galling than the most abject slavery tyranny e'er compassed; see, therefore, you abuse it not.

Roso. Oh, impossible: while e'en the spade they toil'd with was their lord's, vice and sloth possessed them; for what incitement had they to industry? but when they find their labour will cheer their children, and throw content around their humble cots—ah, dear lord, these blessings strike too sweetly on the heart to fear abuse.

Rad. Fair advocate, see their hearts thank thee. Come hither, fellow (*To* WITSKI); fear not, man;

give me thy hand ; for the love I know thou bear'st
me, remember this—the mill thou long has toiled in
is thine own.

Wit. Oh dear! Oh dear! I shall run mad with joy
—I know I shall—*my* mill!

Ama. (*Aside.*) Oh, de devil! it is all over vid me.

Enter Messenger, who gives a paper to RADZANO.

Mess. From the king.

Rad. The royal mandate calls me to council; the
king doth here entreat thy pardon for thus antici-
pating widowhood, and bids thee, sweet! prepare thy
lute, that jocundly this night may pass in mirth and
minstrelsy : till night, then, farewell, dear mistress.

Roso. Heaven speed your councils : my lowly duty
to the king.

Rad. Guards, attend. [*Exit* ROSOLIA *attended.*]
O'Curragh, my faithful fellow, observe Rodomsko : if
you should suspect him—

O'Cur. Oh, I don't suspect him at all; I know
he's a rogue.

Rad. Should his conduct threaten danger, on the
instant hie thee to Cracow; remember. Freemen,
farewell.   [*Exit.*

Wit. Yonder he goes;—now he's at the top of
the hill; see, he waves his hand to us;—heaven bless
him! heaven bless him !——" Freemen, farewell."
—Oh! my head, my head.—I'm sure I shall go mad ;
I feel I shall.   I'll run home and tell the cow and
the mill :—*my* mill, only think of that!—(*Walks
backwards and forwards, and each time jostles* AMA-
LEKITE, *without noticing him.*)—Damme ! I'm a man,
a freeman, and a gentleman.   (*To* O'CUR.) Sir, I
shall be proud to see you at my mansion—*my* mansion—that's right, is not it ?

O'Cur. To be sure; you are lord of it, and may
knock any man's brains out that comes in without
your leave.

Wit. May I though ?—ecod, that's jolly—he ! he ! he !—Then, I'll tell you what, (*To* AMALEK.) if ever I catch that black muzzle within the portico of my mill, I'll grind you into sausages ; I will, you ugly dog ! Wife, now, we'll see who's man of the house.—Wife.

Win. Oh ! my dear Witski !

Wit. Silence, silence ; there. (*Gives her his hand to kiss.*) That's right, is not it ?—he ! he ! he !

Win. I'm dumb, but don't be angry.

Wit. Angry ! I could not be angry if I would—he ! he !—come buss me.

Ama. Gossip Winifred.

Win. Keep off, man ! I only encouraged you as a scarecrow to frighten my husband :—but now—faugh !

Wit. Well said, Winny.—Ah, Rachel, my girl, kiss thy honoured parent.

Rac. Oh, father, won't you let me marry Zarno ?

Wit. Ay, to-morrow morning, with all my heart and soul.

Rac. And here he comes.

Enter ZARNO.

Zar. Joy, joy, joy to ye all !—I've heard the news. Ah, dear Rachel, (*Pushing aside* AMALEK.) I'm so happy.

Rac. And so fine !

Wit. Ecod, that he is.

Zar. Am I, think you ?—yes, pretty well :—sword, and cap, and altogether, eh !—yes, it's not shewy, but neat : it's becoming. Now, my jolly dad that is to be—(*Walks about, jostling* AMALEK.)

O'Cur. How do you do, Mr Amalekite ; you don't seem to comprehend what's going forward here : will you try your hand at that, (*Gives a paper,*) there's your quietus for you.

Ama. (*Drops the paper.*) My discharge! bless my conscience.—(*Is going out despondingly.*)

Zar. You move rather slow; come, for old acquaintance sake, I'll give you a lift (*Pushes him off.*) —Just set him a-going.

O'Cur. Oh, it was time to put a stop to such a rogue. Now I'm to be steward; which is an office —an office—oh! first I am to take particular care to receive the rents of such tenants as won't pay; and, secondly, to see that no one behaves improperly, without my overlooking him: yes, that's it.—Now I must away to the castle.

Zar. O, there are to be great doings there; the king is to be there; and, Rachel, you shall be there: I'll meet thee to-night in the wood, the old place; and then, to-morrow, when the friar comes—oh, you blushing, tempting rogue!

Wit. Now, brother freemen, to our homes—drink prosperity to our deliverer, and be merry and happy all the rest of our lives.

SONG *and* CHORUS.

WITSKI, WINIFRED, ZARNO, RACHEL, *and* O'CURRAGH.

WITSKI.

No longer a ninny,
  But lord of my mill,
With my jug and my Winny,
  Full jorums I'll swill.

WINIFRED.

Ever constant and humble,
  Your Winifred shall prove,
And, without e'en a grumble,
  Obediently love.

CHORUS.

La, la, la, &c.

RACHEL.

In a salt mine so drearily,
   Of the dumps you'd your swing,
But now brisk and cheerily,
   With Rachel you sing.

ZARNO.

Let the tabor go bing bang,
   The pipe shrilly play,
The sweet guitar go ting tang,
   On Zarno's wedding day.

CHORUS.
La, la, la, &c.

O'CURRAGH.

Then dance, sing, and caper,
   Ye merry men so gay,
And while briskly plays the scraper,
   For liberty huzza!

CHORUS.

Then dance, sing, and caper,
   Ye merry men so gay, &c.   [*Exeunt.*

SCENE III.

An Apartment in RODOMSKO'S *Castle.*

Enter RODOMSKO *and* NACLO.

Rod. I tell thee, fellow, Zorinski will be won.—
Where are thy comrades?
   Nac. Shrouded in the neighbouring forest.
   Rod. Bring them hither; but see they hold no

converse with my people. Be firm, good Naclo; for my
confidence rests weightily upon thee. [*Exit* NACLO.
Within there!

Enter Servant.

Bid anon my daughter touch her lute.—[*Exit Servant.*]—For now the bloody purpose being unfolded,
all traps must be set for him.—Ha! he approaches,
and in heavy rumination.

Enter ZORINSKI.

Zo. Though Casimir has sorely urged me to revenge, by the most galling wrongs, yet to murder—

Rod. (*Taking his hand.*) Was Brutus then a murderer? Genius of Poland, where sleepest thou, when
thy patricians shrink from achieving what those of
Rome contended for?

Zo. Grant he ought to die, yet—soft—(*A lute is
heard behind, which plays some time*)—what heavenly
sounds!—much I thank thee, unknown minstrel, for
thy enchantment has prisoned down the hell-born passions that possessed me, and soothed my soul to tranquil melancholy.

Rod. 'Twas my daughter's lute.—Within there—
Rosolia!—see, she approaches.

Zo. (*Starts.*) What magic sweetness!—do not
wonder at me; for so long these eyes have been unused to look on beauty, that its inroad now riots my
pulse, e'en, perhaps, to boyish folly—let me avoid
its witchery. (*Going.*)

Rod. Hold!

Enter ROSOLIA.

Ros. What wills my father?

Rod. Where hast been, my girl?

Ros. Enjoying the richest luxury of greatness—
seeing the poor made happy.

Rod. Ay, by whom?

Ros. E'en my intended lord—(ZORINSKI *starts*)—
this day he hath given freedom to his vassals, and
much I joyed to behold wretched man rescued from
abject slavery.

Zo. Loveliest maiden, thy tender nature ne'er can
impose chains, save those of love's soft thraldom.

Rod. By heaven he's caught—Rosolia, I here present thy father's dearest friend.

Ros. Deign, sir, to receive my hearty greeting.

Zo. (*Salutes her.*) The fascinating poison thrills
my every nerve—all powerful love—love—art mad,
Zorinski—thou who scorn'st to flatter others—be to
thyself consistent—Is this rugged frame shaped for
love's soft dalliance—do amorous whispers, soft as
the zephyr, come from a voice chill and surly as the
northern blast?—is this scowling eye, now rife with
murder, a place for Cupids to ambush in?—mockery
all—yet, on my soul, I dare not trust my eyes to
look upon her.

Roso. He seems much moved.

Rod. Thou hast done well, my girl—bid him farewell, and get thee in.

Roso. Tho' ignorant in what, I am right glad I've
pleased you, father—Courteous sir! sweet peace be
with you.   [*Exit.*

Zo. That will never be again—(*Aside*)—talked she
not of marriage?

Rod. Ay, with the young lord Radzano—'tis a
match of the king's making.

Zo. (*With surly irritation.*) Casimir, dost thou
again thwart me?

Rod. E'en now the king is journeying hither with
his young friend, to consummate the union.

Zo. Happy Radzano—wedded, and to-morrow?

Rod. Ay, but should a real friend to Poland think
her worthy——never.

Zo. Ha!

Rod. Oh, Zorinski! act but to-night as doth be-

come thee—vindicate thy own wrongs, avenge the
lords of Poland, and receive my daughter to thy arms;
for by her blushing beauties I swear she's thine.

Zo. Oh, Rodomsko! tempt me not beyond man's
bearing.

Rod. Dull man, I tempt thee to a throne—Casimir
being disposed of—his place must be supplied; and
whom will thy peers deem so fit to guard their rights,
as he who crushed their fell destroyer!

Zo. If thou wilt place before me temptations more
than mortal, he must be more than mortal that re-
sists—by hell I'm thine—Casimir or Zorinski falls—
so may my soul find life or death eternal.

Rod. But this night.

Zo. The better.

Rod. And mark; should chance so order it, bring
Casimir alive—the confederate lords demand him for
their vengeance—a band, whose steely hearts are
rivetted with oaths, will aid thee.

Zo. I need them not—let daws cling together—
the eagle flies alone.

Rod. Away with this romantic folly—within there
is prepared a solemn sacrament, think on't.

Zo. If thou wouldst have me act this deed, oh
let me *not* think, Rodomsko—but on the instant give
me the deadly oath—ay, 'tis well conceived—'twill
save revolt and cowardly compunction—for oh, the
dread interval will be a hellish purgatory, but it leads
to a heaven of bliss—so love and proud ambition receive your votary! [*Exit.*

Rod. My soul is satisfied.

O'CURRAGH *enters behind, seeing* RODOMSKO *retire.*

Now bustle all—Rosolia—my daughter—stir, wench.

Enter ROSOLIA.

Prepare to leave the castle instantly.

Roso. My father!

Rod. Question not why nor where.
Roso. O! sir.
Rod. Be dumb—within there.

Enter Servant.

Arm fifty chosen vassals—and to the southern inlet
of the forest speed with my horses—away.
                                        [*Exit Servant.*
  Roso. (*Kneels*) Oh, my father! if humanity dwell
in you, ease this heart—kill not your daughter's happiness.
  Rod. Thy happiness, weak girl! Zorinski will take
good care of that.
  Roso. Zorinski!
  Rod. I tell thee, the fate of Poland is in suspense
—along I say.
  Roso. Rather take my life.
  Rod. It will not serve my turn—No struggling—
your chamber—your chamber.   [*Exeunt.*

O'CURRAGH *comes forward.*

  Oh, oh! there bids fair to be foul play here. Oh,
the confusion of all Ireland upon that Rodomsko,
I say! What the devil shall I do? If I go to my lord
at Cracow, I can't very conveniently stay here to
see what will become of his lady—Oh! if this head
would but prevent a mistake by blundering on what's
right—I have it—I'll follow her, and if losing my
life will enable me to take her away with me, I'll
do it with all the pleasure in nature. Oh! to die for
such a lady, and such a master, is what no faithful
servant would ever repent of.   [*Exit.*

Enter RODOMSKO *and* NACLO.

  Rod. Now, good Naclo, spirit up thy comrades.
Are they at hand? (NACLO *beckons.*)

Enter Assassins.

Ye spirits of noble daring! this night acquit yourselves, and you are made for ever; there's to cheer
you. (*Throws money.*) Naclo, your leader will anon
meet you—be firm, good Naclo.   [*Exit.*

Naclo. Now, gentlemen, set hands and hearts to
the business—night is coming on apace, and then
——(*Laying his hand on his sword.*)

1st Assassin. Fear us not, comrade.

CHORUS OF ASSASSINS.

While the hideous night is scowling,
While the savage bear is growling,
Thro' the dismal forests prowling,
First with stealing step, and hush,
Then, like a torrent, on we rush,
And immolate our foe.   [*Exeunt.*

ACT THE THIRD.

SCENE I.

A Wood.—Night.

Enter O'CURRAGH.

O'Cur. Oh! I'm sure mischief is going forward,

every thing is so peaceable, and torches keep flash-
ing about like a battalion of jack-lanterns—one good
thing is, that the old rogue Rodomsko has lost his
way and his attendants; there was such a train of
them, that I found the best mode of pursuing was
getting before them. Oh! he hauls my sweet lady
along there, as if she were his wife instead of his
daughter——now's your time, O'Curragh! Oh, St
Patrick! I'll just beg leave to trouble you for five
minutes. (*Retires.*)

Enter ROSOLIA, *leaning on* RODOMSKO.

Ros. Indeed, I can no further.

Rod. Nay, good Rosolia! come—wayward and
stubborn! on, I say—those vile erring slaves, not to
return—my curses on them! entangled in this labyrinth, each step bewilders more—ha! their torches
gleam thro' yonder valley—(*During this*, O'CUR-
RAGH *attracts the attention of* ROSOLIA.) Who's there?

Ros. (*With apprehension.*) 'Tis your faithful slave,
Kalish.

Rod. Right glad am I of that—(*Still looking after
his vassals*)—death and hell! they take their course
athwart! good Kalish! tarry with Rosolia—stir not,
be sure—but I know thy honesty.   [*Exit.*

O'Cur. For once, old gentleman, you have spoken
truth by mistake.

Ros. Oh! save me, good fellow.

O'Cur. This way, sweetest lady!

Ros. Oh! Radzano, where art thou? perhaps e'en
now the victim of foul conspiracy; where will my
sorrows end!

O'Cur. Oh! put your trust in St Patrick, out and
out the genteelest saint in the calendar.   [*Exeunt.*

SCENE II.

Another Part of the Forest.

Scene draws and discovers ZORINSKI *with a Sabre in his hand, leaning despondingly against the Arm of a Tree.*

Enter ZARNO.

Zar. What can make Rachel tarry so? it's an infernal night! it rains, blows, thunders, and whew!—this is weather to try a lover in—Where can Rachel be—(*Sees* ZORINSKI.) What—eh! my master here, and his sabre in his hand—my mind misgives me! Oh! some villainy of that rogue Rodomsko. (*Seeing* ZORINSKI *coming forward, retires.*)

Zo. Oh! Zorinski, how art thou fallen?—confederate with hired assassins—fettered by deadly oaths ——how changed the face of all things?—the heav'ns seem grim'd with pitch as black as Acheron, and the rustling wind strikes on my ear e'en as the hissing of hell's serpents. (ZARNO *approaches,* ZORINSKI *starts.*) Oh, all the devils, do I tremble?

Zar. My lord!

Zo. Zarno, thou did'st not say I trembled!

Zar. Dear lord! you are pale, and your voice faulters—I fear you are very ill.

Zo. Yes, that's it, that's it, good Zarno—my pulse is fevered, and that affects the brain—(*With solemnity*)—a little blood spilt, and all will be well—leave me, Zarno.

Zar. What! Zarno leave you when you are ill? oh, no! Ah, master! don't you remember in the

mine when an ague shook you, how Zarno watched
you, and when I blubbered over you—you wept too.

Zo. Yes, there was a time when I could weep.
Zarno, I charge thee leave this place!

Zar. Oh! dear lord—

Zo. (*Hearing a noise.*) Hush! not a breath. [*Exit.*

Zar. Some horrid purpose possesses him—now he
stops.

Enter ROSOLIA *and* O'CURRAGH.

Zar. Who's there?

Ros. Oh, stranger! aid an unhappy maiden, who,
torn from her soul's only hope, and well nigh dead
with weariness, humbly implores thy succour, to un-
wind the mazes of this wood, and lead her on her
way to Cracow. (ZARNO *still looks after his master.*)
Radzano will reward thee.

Zar. (*Turns round.*) Good heavens! the lady Rosolia, and here—dear lady, I'll go with you to the
world's end—only I've a little business here, that—
(*Returns to his observation.*)

Ros. Come then, good fellow!

Zar. Yes; I'm coming. (*Moving from her.*)

O'Cur. Hark you; that may be coming; but it
looks so like going, that you will please to move this
way.

Zar. Unhand me, or—lady, pardon me—but you
—I—my master—I won't leave him—I have it—hard
by there's a mill, mention the name of Zarno, and
you'll find protection. (*Again looking out.*)

Ros. Oh! guide us to it.

Zar. Well, I'll walk a little way with you : there,
(*Walks a few yards and then stops,*) there now, that's
the road, right along there, (*Pointing one way, and
looking another ;*) good fortune attend you, lady! Oh,
my unhappy master!

O'Cur. Is it kept by one Witski?

Zar. It i

O'Cur. How lucky! an old friend of mine, that I made acquaintance with this morning.

Zar. Oh, Zorinski! oh, my master!

Ros. Zorinski! away—away—

O'Cur. Don't droop, dear mistress; for tho' you have but one man to protect you, yet consider, that one is an Irishman.

                 [*Exeunt* ROSOLIA *and* O'CURRAGH.

Zar. What can this mean? she afraid of him— Eh! here he comes again.

Enter ZORINSKI.

Zo. Will the hour never cone? I'm glad my faithful Zarno left me—his fondness tore my heart-strings! —not gone!—avaunt! I say.

Zar. Don't look so terrible—oa! don't—you frighten me so, I can't go—oh! master, there is murder in your eye! if it were day-light, I would not mind it—I should like to see you fight in day-light; but none but assassins stab in the dark.

Zo. Horrid truth!

Zar. Oh! master, quit this place; let us return to the dear dreary mine again!—Did not I hear the tread of horses? (*Agitated.*)

Zo. Look out!

Zar. Yes, I will—but pray don't leave me. (*More alarmed.*)

Zo Look out, I say!

Zar. Yes; oh lord!   [*Exit.*

Zo. My senses are benumbed—I'm very faint— but thy oath, thy oath, Zorinski! there I'm firm again.

Enter ZARNO.

Zar. Oh! dear master, all my fears are over.

Zo. Who is it?

Zar. Pardon, dear lord, what a rogue was I to think the great Zorinski could swerve from honour—I feared it was some rival, or——

Zo. Who is't, I say?

Zar. Thank heaven, none that you can harm! It's the king. (*With a smile.*)

Zo. Ha! (*Grasps his sword.*)

Zar. O God! O master!—What?—Impossible!

Zo. Discord is at large!—Oh, for a tyger's fury!—

Zar. (*Lays hold of his cloak.*) Oh, think a moment——

Zo. Cling not to me thus—away, I say! (ZARNO *runs round, and falls on his knees before him.*) Villain!

Zar. Yes, I am—any thing; reproach me; spurn me; kill me——Zorinski an assassin! *my* lord a traitor!—I can't bear it. Oh, think of dishonour! think of your soul! think of Zarno!

Zo. In vain, in vain: were he guarded by the furies I would seize him! (*As he is rushing forward,* ZARNO *jumps back, draws his sword, and opposes him.*) Ha! raise thy arm against thy master's life!

Zar. Do not you raise your arm against your master's life.

Zo. O hell! he's right!—Zarno, thou art sadly changed; I've seen thee draw to *save* my life.

Zar. And now I draw to save what's dearer, your honour, your soul. You pass not—no! I would rather see you dead at my feet, and I the man that laid you there, than suffer you to pass.

Zo. Baffled by a slave! (*Clashing of swords without.*) Ha! the work of death's begun! see how their sabres gleam!—Brave not my fury—give way——

Zar. No, by heaven! (*With firmness.*)

Zo. Hark! 'tis Vengeance calls—then take thy death, vile slave! (*Fight, he wounds* ZARNO, *and exit.*)

Zar. Heaven forgive him! Let me but live to see —(*Staggers to the side of the stage, supporting himself on his sword.*) How dim my eyes are—ah! see he rushes among them; he bears down all before him—ah! now he seizes the king—and now he——Oh! (*Falls.*)

Enter RACHEL.

Rac. What clashing of swords!—oh! I shall sink with fear! Zarno! Zarno!

Zar. (*Faintly.*) Here.

Rac. O Zarno! bleeding!

Zar. O cruel master! cruel master!

Rac. Was it he that did it? Monster! is this a return for a fond servant's love?

Zar. Did I say it was my master? did I?—no, Rachel, no.

Rac. Come, try to reach the mill; for poor Rachel's sake try.

Zar. Well, I'll try. (*Rises.*) Only this—you know, Rachel, the words of a dying man are awful: then hear mine—it was not my master that did this—remember, Rachel, it was not my master.

[*Exeunt,* RACHEL *supporting him.*

SCENE III.

Another Part of the Wood—Thunder and Lightning.

Enter ZORINSKI, *pulling in* CASIMIR.

Zo. On, I charge thee!

Cas. This wounded frame can go no farther.

Zo. Now, ye fiends! ye who first instilled into my soul your damning purpose, nerve but my arm to strike the blow! (*Thunder.*) O God of Justice! why hurl thy bolts of fate to scare the peaceful grove, when I stand here a wretch, and court the vengeful shaft? Hark! a noise again!—delay were fatal—on, on, or here thou diest!

Cas. Here be it then—I tell thee, base assassin!—

Zo. Thou wrong'st me, king! I am no common stabber—view me well—have the wrongs thou hast inflicted on me so furrowed o'er my visage—has despair so grimly marked me for her own, that thou rememb'rest not?——Know then 'tis Zorinski strikes.

Cas. Zorinski!—But oh! is't possible—can thy soul be reconciled to treason?

Zo. (*Aside.*) How that shot through me!

Cas. Art thou content that future ages shall use thy great name to curse with?

Zo. My hair bristles, and my teeth chatter!—— Peace, I charge thee!

Cas. Those convulsive throbs speak virtue in thee. Oh, obey its sacred impulse! behold thyself thy king's deliverer! see hands and hearts hail thee thy country's saviour! think how the good will pray for thee, and ages bless thy name!

Zo. O let me with repentant—ah! is not the deadly oath sworn?—Hell, I'm faithful to thee!—Who is't that holds my arm?—(*A bugle is heard at a distance.*) Ha! again——now——(*Raising his arm.*)

Cas. A moment's pause.——O God, shield with thy arm omnipotent my dear, ill-fated Poland! receive my parting spirit! and oh, forgive this man!—Now, traitor, strike.

Zo. (*After a struggle.*) Oh, impossible! (*Falls at the King's feet, then recovers himself on his knee.*) Oh, Casimir! oh, my king! how shall I look upon that injured face!

Cas. Zorinski! the fiery trial past, gives thee to my heart more pure—(*A whistle.*)—Hark! thy comrades!

Zo. (*Starts up and recovers his sword.*) Let them come on; this weight of guilt taken from this arm, I will protect thee, king. Virtue's electric fire so springs each nerve, that, did Nature loose her ravenous kind—did hell oppose its ministers of blood, I seem as with one blow I could sweep them to destruction.

Cas. I'm faint—my wound begins to torture.

Zo. Horror! 'twas not my sword—'twas not my
sword, my king, that wounded thee; for e'en in that
guilty moment, I struck the villain dead that did inflict it.

Cas. Give me thy arm.

Zo. See, the moon dares shine again!—Canst thou
forgive me?—Thou may'st; but can heaven!

Cas. No more: thou hast unclogg'd thy soul of treason—Treason, that most hideous monster, which with
one blow severs a nation's peace, tramples down law,
that barrier of existence, and gives to him most triumph, who most shall murder and destroy.

[*Exeunt,* *King leaning on* ZORINSKI*.*

SCENE IV.

A Mill.

Enter WITSKI *from the Mill.*

Wit. O dear, O dear, I do so overflow with joy,
that I'm quite miserable! I can't eat, and I can't
sleep—thank heaven, I can just contrive to drink a
little, else—what a rate my mill went all day!—clack,
clack, clack! Winny's tongue had no chance with
it.—And then to think of the sweet lady Rosolia
seeking protection in my mansion—there's an honour!

Zo. (*Behind.*) Hollo!

Wit. What! an enemy may be. Then I'll retire
into my castle, and parley from the battlements.

(*Goes in.*)

Enter CASIMIR *and* ZORINSKI.

Zo. Within there. (*Strikes his sword against a window.*)

Wit. (*Above.*) Stand off, or I've a cross-bow here will send a choice collection of bullets into your pate. Break one of my windows, you robbers!

Zo. Give instant entrance, or I'll force my way.

Wit. Know all men, I am lord of my castle; have been so—ay, thirteen hours; and will knock any man's brains out that enters without my leave.

Cas. Are you lord of it?—Prove then you deserve the title, by giving succour to the unfortunate.

Wit. Oh, there's no standing that. (*Comes down.*) You must know I am lord of this—

Zo. Leave prating, and instant lend thy aid.

Cas. Your king demands it—(WITSKI *drops on his knees*)—give me your assistance.

Wit. Oh no, heaven forbid that I should dare to think of such a thing.—Oh no.

Cas. I want not thy obedience, but thy service; I faint for very weariness.

Enter ROSOLIA, O'CURRAGH, *and* WINIFRED, *from the Mill.*

Ros. Sure that voice—heavenly powers! the king!

Cas. With equal wonder I behold thee, fair maiden.

Ros. Oh, sire, forgive me, if thus untimely I press my private griefs:—Where is my lord?—Oh! does Radzano live?

Cas. E'en now we parted near your father's castle.

Ros. O'Curragh, fly!   [*Exit* O'CUR.

Cas. But whether he live or no—(*Looks at* ZO-RINSKI, *who is agitated with shame and remorse.*)

Ros. Oh, horror! he here!

Zo. Fear not, wronged lady, the basilisk has lost its power to harm.

Cas. Lead me in.   [*Exit with* ROSOLIA.

Zo. Fairest innocent! and has this withering arm blasted thy joys?—Oh, was not my agony enough be: !—How came she here?

Wit. Zarno sent her.　Would you choose to walk
in ? (*Goes towards the door.*)

Zo. Zarno! Zarno!—(*With vacant wildness.*)　Soft
—good brain, collect thyself.—Sure I saw him in
the forest—and he went—no—ah! now hellish recollection darts upon me—he wept—he begged me—
he clung to me, and I—(*As if choaked with grief,
makes the motion of stabbing.*)—Oh! I am deeply
damned for that—the only soul on earth that loved
me; never servant so loved a master—(*Weeps*)—and
I to stab, oh!—eh! perhaps he yet lives—perhaps
—here, slave.

Wit. I beg your pardon, sir, but I am not a slave.

Zo. I care not what thou art.

Wit. I am—

Zo. Be dumb.—Mark; take this sword; guard
well the door; I'll return anon.—Oh, Zarno! Zarno!
[*Exit.*

Wit. He's mad—the poor devil's mad!

Win. Now, my dear Witski, I'll tell you what—

Wit. What, you are beginning your chatter?

Win. Nay now, only hear me, that's a dear man.
You know, husband, his majesty has favoured us with
his company at our house; very well! then, you
know, it will be but civil to return the visit.

Wit. Certainly; he'll naturally expect it.

Win. Well; and so I was a thinking that some
new fur put upon my Sunday's cap, with rose-colour-
ed ribbons, and my new russet gown will do to—

Ros. (*Within.*) What, miller, ho!

Wit. (*Stopping* WINIFRED's *mouth.*) You will keep
gabble, gabble.　Confound you, is not his majesty
within hearing? and an't I his sword bearer?—Hush,
I must guard the door; and, do you hear? keep the
cats and the dogs quiet—hush, softly.
[*Exeunt into the mill.*

SCENE V.

Wood.

Enter RACHEL, *leading in* ZARNO.

Rac. Come, dear Zarno, see, yonder's the mill;
—you look better.

Zar. Do I, Rachel?

Rac. Far better, since with my hair I stopt the
bleeding of your wound.

Zar. 'Tis not my wound, Rachel; it's here; it's here;
my heart's broken, Rachel.—Oh, my master——Let
me rest here a while, it will give me strength. (*Lies
down.*)

Enter ZORINSKI.

Zo. Zarno—alive——(*Runs to him, and kneels.*)

Zar. Ah, Rachel, hide me—don't touch me—don't
touch me——

Zo. How art thou, Zarno? Shrink not from me—
I come to comfort thee.

Zar. Comfort—say, then, (*In a low tone, and getting near him,*) lives the king?

Zo. What is that to thee? (ZARNO *shrinks from
him.*) He does! he does!

Zar. What, lives!—lives!—ha! ha! ha! (*Faints.*)

Zo. Soft, he recovers—how art thou, Zarno?

Zar. Better—well—very well—but are you not
deceiving me?

Zo. No, on my soul——Zarno, I am not so damned
a villain as thou think'st me. (*With an agony of grief,
hiding his face.*)

Zar. I think you a villain! dear honoured master,
where is your hand? (*Kisses it.*)

Zo. Let me convey thee to a place of safety.

Zar. I can walk—can walk very well.

Zo. Art thou—art thou—much wounded, Zarno? (*With shame.*)

Rac. Oh yes——

Zar. (*Stopping her.*) A scratch—a scratch—it's joy makes me so weak—I'm very troublesome—I can walk alone.

Zo. Psha! rest on me, good fellow.

Zar. I'm afraid I lean very heavily.

Zo. Pr'ythee be quiet—see'st thou that mill—the king is there—we shall easily reach it.

Zar. O yes, dear master, unless I die with joy by the way—I'm quite asham'd.

Zor. Come, rest firmly on me—there—there

[*Exeunt.*

SCENE VI.

Inside of the Mill.

CASIMIR *discovered asleep on a Pallet,* ROSOLIA *watching him,* WITSKI *guarding the door.*

SONG.—WINIFRED.

I.

Than envied monarchs happier still,
  O! happier far, the peasant;
No treason lurks around his mill,
  No terror breaks his slumbers pleasant.
Yet one must fill the regal seat,
  With care incessant pressing;
E'en to preserve those slumbers sweet,
  His lowly, happy cottage, blessing.

II.

Then fly not now, O gentle sleep,
    Fly not our humble dwelling,
His anguish in oblivion steep,
    The image of the past repelling.
And such soft visions of delight,
    From airy fancy borrow,
As he deserves whose watchful night
    From us poor peasants drives forth sorrow.

(*A knocking at the door.*)

Cas. (*Awakes.*) What refreshing sleep—heaven,
accept my thanks—Rosolia! droop'st thou for thy
love—fear not his safety—have I not seen him in the
field—believe me, he must be champion, indeed, who
spoils Radzano—hostess, I thirst.

Win. Here, your majesty, 's a cup of wine; all our
poor house affords.

CASIMIR *is about to drink, when the knocking at the
door is repeated.*

Cas. Open, good fellow—and fear nothing.

Enter ZORINSKI *and* RACHEL, *leading* ZARNO.

Poor wretch—he faints—lead me to him: (*Approaches*
ZARNO, *who looks faintly on him :*) here, poor knave,
drink this ; thy wants far exceed mine—drink, 'twill
refresh thee.

Zar. Oh no.

Cas. Do as I bid thee.—(ZARNO *drinks.*)—has't
done thee good, knave ?

Zar. Oh yes.

Cas. And me abundant. Come, thou look'st more
cheerly ; thou art better.

Zar. Better! I never was so well in my life.

Ros. It grieves me in such base sort to see your
highness.

Cas. Not so, fair one! am I not with my people,
with those who love me?—Come, mine host, thy fire.
(*To* WITSKI.)—Wilt thou to court, and grow great?
(*Sighs, and shakes his head.*)

Wit. Please your majesty, I can't leave my trade.

Cas. Why, knave?

Wit. Because I have a wife; and, to confess the
truth to your majesty, Winny has certainly a happy
knack at sprightly conversation.

Cas. (*To* ROSOLIA, *smiling.*) Hear'st thou the
slanderer?

Wit. So when she lets her tongue go, I let my
mill go, clack for clack: I could not manage without my mill.

Cas. Ha! ha! I'll build thee one upon the Vistula; thou shalt be the greatest miller in Poland.
(*Trumpet without.*)

Enter RADZANO.

Rad. My gracious king! (*Kneels.*)

Cas. Radzano, thrice welcome—said I not, Rosolia, this arm would prove victorious?

Ros. My dearest lord!

Rad. Pardon, dear mistress, what stern duty compels—Rodomsko was found wandering in the forest,
deserted by his people.

Ros. (*Kneeling to* CASIMIR.) Oh, merciful Casimir!

Cas. (*Raising her.*) Fear nothing—let him live—
but not in Poland.

Rad. See, how your loving subjects, bearing their
rustic arms, press on to guard you.

Enter Soldiers and Peasants armed.

Cas. What a proud moment!—heaven give me
strength to bear this rushing joy—trust me, my people, the dangers I have passed will but give energy
to fresh exertion—yes, like the fertilizing Vistula,

mild, yet irresistible, I'll open wide the current of my justice, until the humblest peasant of my state shall taste its blessings.

FINALE.

CHORUS OF SOLDIERS.

Let the loud rattling drum and the trumpet's shrill clang,
    That in battle our heroes have nerved;
Now aid the rough soldier in rapturous song,
    For his king and his country preserved.

PEASANTS.

Let the happy peasant join,
And his humble lay combine,
While joy in every face shall shine,
Throughout the realm of Poland.

Every honest tongue shall sing,
Every happy valley ring,
For Heaven has restor'd our king,
And happiness to Poland.

ZARNO.

Blessed with peace and liberty,
My life shall pass in merry glee,
With little Zarnos on my knee,
And Rachel dear so clever.

WINIFRED *and* RACHEL.

Should our artless story move,
And you, our valued friends, approve,
With warmest gratitude and love,
We are your slaves for ever.

CHORUS.

Let the happy peasant, &c.

SECRETS WORTH KNOWING;

A

COMEDY,

IN FIVE ACTS.

AS PERFORMED AT THE

THEATRE-ROYAL, COVENT-GARDEN.

BY

THOMAS MORTON, Esq.

DRAMATIS PERSONÆ.

GREVILLE,	*Mr Pope.*
EGERTON,	*Mr Holman.*
ROSTRUM,	*Mr Lewis.*
UNDERMINE,	*Mr Munden.*
APRIL,	*Mr Fawcett.*
PLETHORA,	*Mr Knight.*
NICHOLAS,	*Mr Quick.*
VALET,	*Mr Klanert.*
BUTLER,	*Mr Abbot.*
COOK,	*Mr Thompson.*
COACHMAN,	*Mr Rees.*
MRS GREVILLE,	*Mrs Pope.*
ROSE SYDNEY,	*Mrs Mountain.*
SALLY,	*Mrs Mattocks.*

SECRETS WORTH KNOWING.

ACT THE FIRST.

SCENE I.

An Apartment in Greville-House.

Servants talking without.

Enter Valet, Butler, Coachman, Cook, and Footmen.

Val. Silence, I say! Why, you keep as loud a gabbling as if you were settling the balance of Europe in the lobby of the house of commons. Order, I say—the question is this. Our old master being dead, and our young one expected every moment from abroad, ought we, when he arrives, to laugh or cry? Hear the cook!

Cook. Why, I thinks, that, for the death of an old master, a little dripping from the eyes would be quite natural.

Val. It may be natural, Master Cook; but, Lord bless you, the genteel feel of your tip-top folks is no more like nature, than one of your fine kabobbed fricassees is to plain roast and *taties*. Besides, when a man leaves behind him a good ten thousand a-year, I think it quite natural for the heir to laugh. What say you, Coachy?

Coach. I pulls with you, Mr Valet—young master must in the main be glad, for we all know that the old gemman, seeing that he run skittish, kept him upon low provender beyond sea. So my verdict is, Mr Butler, that we all smiles agreeably.

But. So say I. Dam'me, I'll look as pleased as punch, ha! ha!

Val. Softly. And will you, sir, who have but thirty pounds a-year, dare to be as pleased at seeing your master, as I, who have fifty? No, no—subordination is every thing.

Coach. Ecod, the best reason we should not be sorry, is, that the old buck left us no legacies.

Val That settles it. (*All laugh.*) (*A knocking at the door.*) Here he comes—I am to look most pleased, and stand in the front. Back a little, Coachy, and remember I am to speak.

Enter Mr *and* Mrs Greville.

Grev. Why this boisterous mirth?

Coach. You are to speak, you know.

(*To the Valet.*)

Grev. Is it thus you honour the memory of your departed master? My love, welcome to England, and to my father's house. If I can trust my heart, the greatest happiness I shall feel from prosperity, (should it await us,) will be in placing my Maria in the elevated station her virtues will illumine.

Sally, *in a travelling dress, speaks as she enters.*

Sally. Travelling indeed! nothing but extortion

1

I declare—Such a gang of them! First, in comes
the bill; then, remember the waiter—John Osuer,
sir—the chamber-maid, ma'am—don't forget your
Boots—I am the porter—the post-boy, your honour
—so that your hand keeps constantly moving up and
down, like the great lump of wood at Chelsea water-
works—(*The Servants nod and wink to her.*)—What
are you all nodding and winking at? why don't you
set chairs? (*Servants set chairs.*) Now, go along all
of you, and see the luggage unpacked—(*Servants surprised*)—why don't you go?

(GREVILLE *waves his hand.*)

Val. To be ordered about by such a dowdy! My
dear Coachy, this will never do for us.

[*Exeunt Servants.*

Sal. A parcel of lazy chaps, I dare say—but I'll
make them stir their stumps. Well, here we are at
last. Oh, gemini gig! how my poor bones do ache!

Mrs Grev. My Greville, excuse her familiarity—
she has lived with me from my infancy, and is, indeed, a faithful, affectionate creature.

Sal. Ay, that I am. Oh, bless its pretty face!

(*Patting her mistress's cheek.*

Mrs Grev. Leave us, good Sally.

Sal. Leave you?

Mrs Grev. Yes.

Sal. Well, I will. I am a foolish, good natured—
I'll go and scold the servants.   [*Exit* SALLY.

Mrs Grev. You look uneasy, Charles.

Grev. 'Tis for thy sake, Maria. Between hope and
fear, my mind is tortured: when I reflect on my father's determined, but just resentment, at my dissipated conduct while in England—so determined, that
I dared not acquaint him of my union with my adored
Maria—then, I fear that he died without blessing me,
and has estranged me from his house and fortune.
When I reflect that I am, perhaps, destitute of the
means of supporting thee—surrounded by creditors
—(*A knocking at the door*)

Enter SALLY.

Sal. Oh! master, here is such a frightful old fellow
wants to speak with you!—Such a—O Lord! here
he is.

Enter NICHOLAS, *his face wrinkled, hollow cheeks, and
every exhibition of dolefulness, age, and decrepitude.*

Grev. Your name, friend, and business?

Nich. Sir, my name is—so there *is* a lady in the
case—my name, sir, is Nicholas Rue, and my business will be explained by this letter. (GREVILLE
reads the letter, and seems elated with pleasure.) Now
to have a peep. (*Puts on his spectacles.*) Eh! as I
hope to live these fifty years—Miss Egerton. How
my master will be surprised!

Grev. What happy tidings! present my best respects to your master—I will wait on him immediately.

Nich. Very well, sir. How my master will be surprised!   [*Exit.*

Grev. This letter, Maria, is from my father's executor. (*Reads.*)

" SIR,—As executor to my dear departed friend,
Mr Greville, I have to inform you, his will leaves
you, conditionally, his sole heir."

Sal He! he! how happy I am!

Grev. The familiarity of this girl is intolerable.

Sal (*Pouting.*) Tolerable, indeed! Oh, Mr Egerton, her noble brother, behaved different: He never
thought me tolerable.

Mrs Grev. For shame, Sally!

Sal. And so it is a shame that a poor servant
should be out of her wits for joy at hearing her dear
lady's good fortune? Sir, I has as much right to be
happy as you *has*, and I will be happy, tho' you make
me cry all day for it.

9

Grev. Well, well—loving Maria atones for a thousand faults.

Sal. (*Significantly.*) Ha! ha! perhaps this is as lucky for Mister Somebody, as for Sally Downright.

Mrs Grev. Dear Sally—

Sal. Do you say dear?

Mrs Grev. Pray be silent.

(SALLY *puts her hand to her mouth, and retires.*)

Grev. My love, I must hasten to Mr Undermine.

Mrs Grev. Who?

Grev. Mr Undermine, my father's executor.

Mrs Grev. Heavens!

Grev Do you know him, Maria!

Mrs Grev. Alas! too well.

Sal (*Advancing.*) Know him! he is the blackest villain, sir—it was he who ruined her dear brother, and drove him from England, to wander, nobody knows where.

Mrs Grev. O Greville! I doubt the goodness of that fortune to which he is harbinger.

Grev. You alarm me, but I will hasten to him.

Sal. And I'll go with you, and, by gemini gig, I'll give it him——

Grev. For heaven's sake, be quiet! Droop not, my dearest love! 'tis prosperity awaits us. I go to seize the prize, and lay it at thy feet, a fit oblation to thy surpassing virtues.   [*Exit.*

Mrs Grev. Heigho!

Sal. Don't sigh, dear lady! I know from experience, riches don't give happiness. When poor, I was happy, and now that I am independent. having 3*l*. 10*s*. a-year in the consolidated real grand Bank of England, yet I'm not happy; but I shall be so, when my darling mistress is a great lady, and her dear brother comes home a general.

Mrs Grev. Poor Egerton! What perils has he not encountered for my sake——perhaps his precious life——

Sal. Oh, no, no—take comfort, for sure nobody

wou'd go to kill so handsome and good a creature as he is—besides, ma'am, has not he a mole on his right arm? Was he not born with a cawl? and has he not a pocket-piece that I got conjured?

Mrs Grev. Peace, foolish girl! Yet I will take comfort, for he has the protecting arm of heaven.

[Exeunt.

SCENE II.

A Room in UNDERMINE's *House.*

Enter NICHOLAS.

Nich. (*Crossing the stage.*) That the sister of Egerton shou'd be the lady—this is news, indeed. They must be married, and then my old rogue of a master gets the estate, and poor I only a thousand pounds for assisting in the roguery; but 'tis a snug sum.

Enter UNDERMINE, (*yawning.*)

Und. Good morning. You look ill, Nicholas.

Nich. Oh dear! don't say so—I feel pretty much in the old way—eat little, to be sure—sleep less.

Und. Ah! but you have been a sad old rogue, Nicholas.

Nich. I have always executed your honour's commands faithfully. Sir, I don't like twelve o'clock at night. All dark as pitch! The church-bell tolling, and nothing else to be heard but the rats in the wainscot.

Und. Don't talk of it.

Nich. Then, somehow a trembling seizes me—

Und. And you feel a kind of shivering damp, don't you?

Nich. Yes.

Und. I know—I know   Then the dreams. I dreamt that old Greville came to my bed, and demanded justice to his son, with horrible ghastly eyes like—just like yours, Nicholas;—and——pshaw! I'm becoming a superstitious fool. Away to Greville with my letter.

Nich. I have already been there. You see how anxious I am to put you in possession.

Und. How anxious you are to touch the thousand pounds, Nicholas!

Nich. Well, sir! he is arrived, and with him——

Und. Ay!

Nich. A lady.

Und. His wife, think you?

Nich. I'll tell you who she is, and leave you to judge—the sister of Egerton.

Und. Indeed!

Nich. Whom you ruined.

Und. And he deserved it for his folly. What chance had he, with only old blind justice on his side, while I had possession, a long purse, and a Chancery suit, ha! ha! you don't laugh, Nicholas?

Nich. Lord, sir, I have not laughed these thirty years.

Und. Ah! you have been a sad rogue. But when am I to expect Greville?

Nich. Directly, sir.

Und. Then give me his father's will out of that drawer.

Nich. (*Significantly.*) Which will, sir?

Und. Which will? why, you are a wag, Nicholas. Not his *second* will, which you burnt. Ha! ha! you are a wag. No, no—this is the will for us, Nicholas; the second did not suit quite so well—it did not contain this beautiful proviso—" But in case my said son shall have acted, or shall act, contrary to this my will, I then bequeath all my estates, whatsoever and wheresoever, to my herein named executor, adviser, and valued friend, Urban Undermine, esquire."—And

was not I a good adviser, eh? But then, Nicholas,
what trouble I had, to make the old superannuated
fool sign it. How I had, to enforce the sin of disobedience, read to him all the tragical stories of impro-
vident marriages—yet, Nicholas, we are not quite
safe, while my late servants, the witnesses to the burnt
will, are forthcoming. Have you been to Newgate
to see them?

Nich. Yes, sir; and says I to them—you know my
master's plate was found at the bottom of your trunks,
(which, you know, sir, I put there myself,) and the
law has condemn'd you to be hang'd—now, your kind
master has got your sentence softened to a *mere* trip
to Botany Bay.

Und. And they were quite happy, I suppose?

Nich. No, sir—they grumbled.

Und. Ah! man—man—never contented. This is
my reward for sending them to a charming flourishing colony, where there is every luxury—even a play-
house, Nicholas.

Nich. And I am told, sir, there are very good
actors there.

Und. I dare say there are. (*A knocking at the door.*)
Run to the window, and see if it be Greville.

Nich. Lord, sir, I can't run—nor I can't see.

Und. (*Aside.*) Pshaw! old withered dolt!—can't
see—one comfort is, you will soon be dead.   [*Exit.*

Nich. But I can hear—Soon be dead, eh? Oh,
dear me, no—equally obliged to you, notwithstanding—I am pretty well—indeed—excepting a slight
liver complaint, a flying gout, and a touch of the drop-
sy, I am quite well—Ah! the one thousand pounds
must be first duly and truly paid, or I'll shew you a
trick you little expect, old master of mine.

Enter UNDERMINE.

Und. 'Tis he—'tis Greville—run to the door.

Nich. I can't run, I tell you.   [*Exit.*

Und. If he be but married ! Now for management
—If he be but married——

Enter GREVILLE.

Mr Greville, I presume—allow me to congratulate
you on your arrival in England. I hope you enjoyed
your health abroad?

Grev. Perfectly so.   Excuse me, Mr Undermine;
but my anxiety——

Und. I understand—There, sir, is your good father's will.

Grev. (*Reads.*) " I, Robert Greville, do make and
declare this my will. To my only son, Charles Greville, I bequeath my forgiveness and blessing, (*Bows
in thankfulness,*) together with all my estates, real and
personal, provided my said son has not, during my
life, contracted, nor does not, till he has fulfilled his
twenty-fifth year, contract—matrimony."

(Greatly agitated.)

Und. He is miserable—I am a happy man !

Grev. (*Reading.*) " And in case my said son shall
have acted, or shall act, contrary to this my will, I
then bequeath all my estates, whatsoever and wheresoever, to my herein-named executor, adviser, and
valued friend, Urban Undermine, esquire." (*Aside.*)
Most accomplished ruin ! O, Maria.

Und. You seem indisposed.

Grev. How shall I act? Sir, the dying blessing of
a justly-offended father has agitated my spirits. (*Aside.*)
And shall this wretch, the enemy of Maria, riot in
the blessings she should enjoy ?

Und. Mr Greville !

Grev. (*Aside.*) Suppose I conceal my marriage—
The clergyman, who officiated abroad, being dead,
and the certificate safe in my possession, detection
is impossible.

Und. Sir, the pleasure I might otherwise feel at so
large an acquisition of property as your *marriage*

gives me, is really, sir, changed into anguish on your
account.

Grev. (*Aside.*) I'll conceal my marriage—I'll torture him. Mr Undermine, how happy am I to relieve
your benevolent heart from the anguish which op-
presses it, and make you happy by declaring, I am
not married; but you don't seem happy.

Und. N—no—not married!—Is *it* possible that—

Grev. It is quite possible.

Und. That is—I mean—I—I—have the pleasure
of knowing Miss Egerton.

Grev. True, and she says she knows you *well*.

Und. Yet, on reflection, who can wonder——

Grev. What do you say?

Und. Who can wonder, I say, that the sister of a
proud beggar should be lost to those celestial virtues——

Grev. 'Tis false! virtues! she is their representa-
tive on earth.

Und. Except chastity.

Grev. (*Aside.*) Distraction! Oh, my wrong'd wife!
am I the assassin of thy fame?—If I remain here, I
shall betray myself.

Und. Yet, I say——

Grev. Say no more, sir.

Und. Allow me to advise——

Grev. Pardon me, *good* sir—the advice you have
here given is so excellent, (*Returning the will*,) that
I should be deemed a monopolist, did I engross more.
Let the world benefit—my family have had quite
enough of it.

Und. In short, then, Mr Greville——

Grev. In short, then, Mr Undermine, I am equal
to the attendance on my own affairs. Do you prove
your attention to yours, by promptly attending me in
the capacity of executor, and not as heir, to my father.   [*Exit.*

Und. So, so, so—Yet he must be married : but then how to prove it—how to manage—

Enter NICHOLAS, *running and capering.*

Nich. Well, sir, here I am—ready to touch.

Und. You *can* run, I see.

Nich. Why, after a thousand pounds, I can hobble a bit.

Und. Can you ? then hobble to Lucern, in Switzerland, and obtain proof of their union—he denies being married.

Nich. Deny being married ! but I'll take my oath he is.

Und. I dare say you will—But who will believe you, Nicholas ? I'll probe him to the quick—a licentious profligate ! Ah, Nicholas ! let this be a lesson to you. Avoid the sin of seduction.

Nich. I will, sir.

Und. To rob innocence of its thousand charms !

Nich. To rob me of my thousand pounds !

Und. But he is married. I'll after him directly.

Nich. Sir, you forget the steward is coming.

Und. True, true, old April—a full twenty years since we met.

Nich. He must be tottering on the grave, poor old fellow.

Und. He tells me he has brought Rose Sydney to town with him, our joint ward. I have left the care of her entirely to him, because it never struck me how I could get any thing by her.

Ap. (*Without.*) Up stairs, do you say ? Come along, Rose.

Und. The old fellow is fumbling his way up. Don't hurry yourself, friend April, I'll help you.

Enter APRIL *and* ROSE SYDNEY—APRIL'S *figure representing the* " *lusty winter*" *of life, strong, corpulent, a ruddy complexion, and long, flowing, silver hair.*

Ap. Who the devil wants your help!—Friend Undermine, how are you?—heartily glad to see you. (*Shaking him violently by the hand.*)

Nich. Ah, Mr April!

Ap. What, old Nick! alive! You grow devilish like your name-sake! Ha, ha! (*Stops laughing suddenly.*) My dear Rose, ask pardon—forgot to introduce, and all that—Undermine, this is our ward, our pretty Rose—brought her up to town t see all the devilments and things, and marry her to my grandson Plethora, who is by this time, I warrant, a celebrated physician.

R. Syd. That is, Guardy, if I like him.

Ap. To be sure—no compulsion—w—n—You see mine has been a difficult task, friend Undermine —not only to take care of a large lump of land, but also this pretty little morsel of live stock.

R. Syd. Which is certainly the harder task of the two: for where you leave a pasture at night, there you are sure to find the pasture in the morning; but you may leave me peaceably browzing in that pasture in the evening, and, the next day, hear of my curvetting and frisking it on a certain green, called Gretna.

Und. Ha, ha! madam, you will be esteemed a wit.

Ap. She will—for she has three thousand a-year, ha, ha! But, old Nick, have not you a bit of dried wainscot in the house, commonly called a housekeeper? Rose will want an army of milliners, haberdashers, and odds and ends.

Nich. Do you imagine, sir, we exist without the blandishments of the softer sex? Allow me to conduct you—don't be alarm'd, miss, you may rely on my prudence and delicacy.

[*Exeunt* NICHOLAS *and* ROSE.

Ap. Come, let me look at you, old boy. You are grown devilish rusty.

Und. Impudent blockhead!

Ap. My countenance is the same.

Und. Yes, brass never rusts; but you must want repose.

Ap. Repose, ha, ha! Why I walked good twenty miles yesterday, over hedge and stubble, to shoot you a bag of birds, old boy. How you stare!

Und. How the devil have you contrived to keep so ruddy a face?

Ap. By keeping clean hands, friend Undermine.

Und. And how do you manage to keep your body upright?

Ap. By keeping my heart in the same attitude; for I soon found out that the weight of every ill-gotten guinea is laid on a man's shoulders for life—bends him down—there is no getting rid of the load. (UNDERMINE *tries to hold up his head, but fails.*) So I preferr'd a long life to a long annuity, and a light heart to a heavy purse, eh, Mr Undermine?

Und. A most excellent plan indeed—for the country.

Ap. Well, but the news—is Greville arrived? The young heir—the dear boy, Charles—is he well?

Und. Yes, a pretty chick he is—a profligate! a seducer.

Ap. What! Oh, I see—a joke of yours, to try to prevent my laughing, ha, ha! Eh, you shake your head though.

Und. What would you say, if I told you he had basely seduced a virtuous and superior woman?

Ap. I would say it was a lie.

Und. Go then, and convince yourself.

Ap. What! Charles Greville guilty of dishonour, merely to get a fashionable name?

Und. And even there he will be disappointed. Formerly, indeed, the ruin of an innocent woman was thought wickedness enough to entitle you to a seat in the coterie of fashion; but now, unless that woman be the wife of your friend, or the daughter of your benefactor, your gusto is scouted, and you are blackballed, for want of a due qualification.

Ap. Oh, rare London, ha, ha! Should not laugh though.—Sad doings. I'll go to him; if what you say be true, he won't dare to look even me in the face—but it can't be.—Oh! he was the bravest, noblest lad! I'll tell you stories of him, will make you so laugh, ha, ha! And I'll tell you stories will make you so cry!   [*Exeunt.*

ACT THE SECOND.

SCENE I.

An Apartment in UNDERMINE'S *House.*

Enter APRIL *and* UNDERMINE.

Ap. But tell me, tell me—have you seen my grandson Plethora lately?

Und. No, not lately.

Ap. Is he one of your *first* rate doctors, eh?

Und. (*Concealing a laugh.*) Not quite, I believe.

Ap. He must be grown a tremendous fellow. Sent him to town in high condition—full of health—all sinew—strong as a castle.

Und. You'll find your castle reduced to mere lath and plaster. (*Aside.*)

Ap. And a power of money in his pocket.

Und. Ay, how much?

Ap. All I was worth.

Und. The devil you did?

Ap. To be sure The road of life is confoundedly up hill, so I determined the boy should not want provender. Besides, they say money gets money—and by this time I dare say he has doubled, ay, trebled it.

Und. (*Aside.*) Ha! ha! Give all she has to a young spendthrift. Well, you'll follow me to Greville's?

Ap. Never to do things by halves, is a maxim in the family of the Aprils.

Und. (*Aside.*) And you have certainly proved yourself the first of the Aprils, ha, ha! [*Exit.*

Enter ROSE SYDNEY.

Ap. Ah, Rose, my girl, I expect your lover every moment. (ROSE *shakes her head.*) Nay, fair play—see him, and hear him—let us have no sending adrift without a fair trial. Egad, you'll see a man fit for a hasband; like—like what I was fifty years ago.

R. Syd. Of this I am sure: I never can hate any thing that resembles my dear Guardy.

Ap. Bless thee!—(*Knocking.*)——Eh—here he comes—the head of Apollo, the strength of Hercules, the voice of a Stentor, the——

Enter PLETHORA, *his visage thin and emaciated, his figure lean, his voice tremulous. A man of twenty, with a constitution of eighty.* APRIL *jumps with surprise.*

Ap. Eh! what! no!

Ple. How are you, Grandad?

Ap. Rose, my love, speak to it.

R. Syd. Alas! poor ghost!

Ple. How goes it, I say?—Grown quite slim and genteel since you saw me last, an't I?

Ap. Quite.

Ple. This is shape and make, is not it?

Ap. Why, Bob—ha, ha! should not laugh—Poor fellow! perhaps 'tis intense study.—But, he, he! zounds, doctor, instead of giving it to others, you seem to have taken all the physic yourself.

Ple. Yes, of cherry-bounce quantum-suff,—and old Oporto,—a couple of magnums—that's my physic—a short life and a merry one, ha, ha!—Ugh, ugh! But you sent word you wanted me on business. What is it, eh?

Ap. Why, I had an intention of proposing a marriage between you and that sweet girl. But I don't know what to say—you don't seem exactly calculated. What do you think, Rose? (*She shakes her head and laughs.*) Nay, don't laugh at my grandson. Age is respectable. I say, old one, what do you think of marriage?

Ple. With that fine girl?—with all my heart. A short life, and a merry one.

R. Syd. Don't be rash, sir. And will you venture to run away with me?

Ple. That I will. Easy stages though.

R. Syd. Easy stages!—It won't do, Guardy.

Ap. No; we must give it up. But what have you done with all the money I gave you?

Ple. Why, I duly considered the hardness of the times, and so threw it into circulation.

Ap. Indeed! And pray how do you intend to live?

Ple. I am one of the host of Pharoah.

Ap. Dam'me, you are one of the lean kine, ha, ha! But zounds and fury!——(*Going up to him.*)

R. Syd. Oh, don't!—If you touch him you'll kill him.

Ple. You have arrived in time; for I have just de-canted the last hundred. Come, tip a rouleau.

Ap. I heard you kept a carriage.

Ple. Two—a gig, and a tandem.

Ap. You a physician! Why, you ignorant—

Ple. Come, tip. (*Holding out his hand à la medi-cin.*)

Ap. Eh! ignorant—I beg your pardon—No, I see you understand at least the grand principle of the profession, (*Imitating,*) ha, ha! But, 'sdeath! what have you to shew for all the money?

Ple. Shew! Ask at the College.

Ap. Oh! in Warwick Lane.

Ple. Warwick Lane! Curse the old quizzes! ha, ha!—ugh, ugh!—No, I mean the Horse College.

Ap. The Horse College!

Ple. To be sure. Farriery is now the only learn-ing fit for a man of fashion. Why, have not you read the Rights of Cattle?

Ap. No.

Ple. No! Then you **are a** Yahoo.—Nor Loose Thoughts on a Horse-shoe, six volumes folio, price twenty guineas?

Ap. No.

Ple. Nor you, ma'am?

R Syd. No, sir.

Ple. What! both ignorant of horse-shoeing! Why, you an't fit to shew your heads in polished society. I tell you, 'tis the only thing going.

Ap. Indeed! Well, as it is a thing going, there can be no harm in wishing it gone.

Ple. Gone! Why, bless you, so far from that, there's Lord Snaffle learning to read on purpose. But I must be off.

Ap. Where?

Ple. To the College to be sure—never miss—fa-mous day. Two lectures—one, a grand dissertation on the use and abuse of cruppers.

Ap. Amazing!

Ple. The other, on the proper application of the horse-whip.

Ap. You need not go on that account. I'll shew you that in two minutes. (*Is restrained by* ROSE.)

Ple. But, I say—if I am to match with that nice girl, say the word, that I may go into training accordingly.

R. Syd. Certainly not, sir.

Ple. Then good bye.—I say, a short life and a merry one, he, he! ugh, ugh!   [*Exit.*

Ap. So, all my property gone to make a farrier. I say, did you ever see such a bit of blood, ha, ha! But I must away to Greville's. Good bye, my girl! Horse-shoeing!—Egad, doctor, you shall have a bellyful of it; for into the country you go, and farrier you are for life.   [*Exeunt.*

SCENE II.

A Library at GREVILLE'S.

MRS GREVILLE *discovered, dejectedly leaning her cheek on her hand*—SALLY *looking out of the window.*

Mrs Grev. Greville not yet returned?

Sal. There he is, ma'am, pacing up and down the Square, with his arms crossed—now he stops—now he walks quick.

Mrs Grev. Oh! call him to me.

Sal. He is coming, ma'am. Don't agitate your dear spirits.——

Enter GREVILLE, *under great agitation ; not observing his wife, he draws a chair, and sits down.*

Grev. To conceal my marriage—How can I ask it of my wife? To confess it, then! (*Rising.*) Ruin without hope. I cannot bear the thought. Unfortunate Mária!

Mrs Grev. (*Leaning on his shoulder.*) Not so—while I possess your love—Oh, tell me, Charles! the wild disorder of your eye terrifies me. (GREVILLE *points to* SALLY.)—Leave us, good Sally. (*Exit* SAL.)—Tell me, oh! tell me the worst.

Grev. I will—it is—for us, a prison during life. Beggary for our child. (MRS GREVILLE *weeps.*) This horrid fate you can alone avert.

Mrs Grev. (*Smiling through her tears.*) O Charles! how unkind to think that misfortune shall for a moment oppress your heart, which I can avert. 'Twill be a happiness——

Grev. (*Mournfully.*) Happiness, Maria! mark me. To prevent the heavy hand of poverty from crushing us, you must declare—how shall I utter it?—that we are not married. Should that be known, I am disinherited.

Mrs Grev. Oh! must we part?

Grev. I mean not that. Consent to live with me, yet——

Mrs Grev. Say on.

Grev. Declare yourself—think the rest.

Mrs Grev. Your mistress. (*Faintly.*) I will. Pardon me a moment's agitation. (*Recovering.*) Yes, cheerfully.

Grev. Think, my love, 'twill be but a transient sorrow.

Mrs Grev. Alas! I think but this—it was my Greville asked it ; and I solemnly swear by the holy marriage vow, never to claim the honour'd name of wife, but at your command.

Grev. Let me adore thee!

Mrs Grev. Yet, oh! (*Bursting into an agony of tears.*)

Grev. Is this cheerfulness, Maria?

Mrs Grev. 'Tis not for myself—the title of mistress gives not this pang. But O, Charles, what name will attach to our pretty innocent?

Grev. I cannot bear the conflict. Let ruin come.

Mrs Grev. Oh no! forgive me—but at that moment the mother felt strong within me. Indeed, I will be all you wish. Pray look happy. Come, you shall see I'll act my part to admiration! Be gay. (*Faints.*)

Grev. Maria—my love!—

Mrs Grev. (*Recovering.*) I am better. It was my last struggle. Indeed, I am better.

Grev. Within there! (SALLY *makes one step on the stage.*) You were very near at hand. Her secrecy will be necessary. By your alacrity, I judge it would be needless to repeat what has now passed?

Sal. Why, sir, to speak the truth, I overheard every word you said.

Grev. This, then, is your duty.

Sal. Ah, sir!—if my love for my dear mistress had not been stronger than my duty, you would not have been so long troubled with Sally Downright.

Grev. Well, well—have the servants asked you any questions about your mistress?

Sal. A thousand.

Grev. What answer did you give them?

Sal. None.

Grev. That was right. Now attend to my orders. You must deny my marriage with your mistress.

Sal. I won't.

Grev. What!

Sal. I will not. (*With firmness.*)

Grev. I am not to be trifled with. Will you obey

my orders? (*She shakes her head.*) Then leave this
house instantly.

Sal. I won't go. (*Takes a chair and sits down between them.*) Her dear noble brother left her to my
care——

Grev. But your charge is superseded by a husband's protection.

Sal. Act like a husband, and I'll go, bag and baggage.—'Till then, here I sits.

Mrs Grev. Would you see us reduced to want?

Sal. Want!—Nonsense! Have not I a pair of hands
strong enough to work for you? And I suppose his
are strong enough to work for himself. Want, indeed!

Mrs Grev. Leave her with me. I know I can prevail. Retire, my love.

Grev. My mind is too oppressed to meet Undermine. Tell him to return in two hours.

Mrs Grev. Compose your spirits.

Grev. Thanks, my kind Maria. [*Exit.*

Sal. What! deny his own honourable, real, lawful spouse, and such a lady! And then expect me
to encourage——

Mrs Grev. Come, come—you can refuse me nothing.

Sal. I cannot say it.

Mrs Grev. But you can be silent.

Sal. That I can.

Mrs Grev. Then promise me to remain so, should
the subject be mentioned to you.

Sal. I do.

Mrs Grev. Ay, but seriously?

Sal. Or may I never see your dear brother again.
'Tis lucky he does not know of these doings.

Enter Servant.

Serv. Mr Undermine. [*Exit.*
Mrs Grev. Be prudent, Sally—remember.

Enter Undermine.—Mrs Greville *bows coldly,*
and retires up the Stage.

Und. This is the confident, I suppose. (*Beckons
her towards him.*) I'll try a dose of flattery: that
costs nothing. You are as handsome as an angel.

Sal. So are you, sir.

Und. Me! no, that won't do. Ah! then I must
apply to the grand specific; (*Takes out a purse;*) put
that in your pocket for my sake, but don't talk about it.

Sal. You shall never hear of it again, depend on't.

Und. I say—a handsome couple.

Sal. Very.

Und. I suppose you had a very jolly wedding.—
(*She remains silent.*) Come, come, you may trust me.
Why should you suppose me a babbling idiot, that
cannot keep a secret?

Sal. Why should you suppose me one?

Und. (*After looking at her with suspicion.*) I'll
thank you just to look at that purse again.

Sal. Certainly, sir. (*Feeling for it.*) But can you
really be snug?

Und. I can—keep the purse—I insist on it—I have
her!—I have her.

Sal. Can you be secret?

Und. Yes.

Sal. So can I.   [*Exit.*

Und. God bless my soul!—She is gone—and the
purse is gone.—Somehow, I didn't manage quite so
cleverly. Eh! but now for the mistress. I'll humble
her, however—yes—with the earth——Madam, I am
under the necessity of asking by what name I am to
have the honour of addressing you?

Mrs Grev. (*Coming forward.*) By a name most
unhappy, most wronged—yet, by the still proud name
of Egerton. Mr Greville cannot see you at present.
In two hours he will be at leisure. That is the door.

Und. Alas! madam, I pity you.

Mrs Grev. (*Stifling her indignation.*) I thank you
for thinking I deserve it. How superior, then, am I,
to that wretch who basely defrauds worth, and drives
from his friends and country a noble youth, to encounter calamity, perhaps death ;—for, in the awful hour
of retribution, who will pity him ? That, sir, is the
door. [*Exit.*

Und. God bless my soul! I have not triumphed
quite so much as I expected. I don't exactly know
what to do. I see no particular use in staying here,
and, as she observed, that certainly is the door. God
bless my soul ! [*Exit.*

Enter SALLY *and* APRIL.

Sal. (*Bobbing a curtsey.*) My master is not at home,
sir.

Ap. Puph—pugh—tell him 'tis April come to see
him. I am his steward.

Sal. Indeed, sir——

Ap. And who are you ?

Sal. I am Sally, sir—I came with them from foreign parts.

Ap. Then I suppose you can prattle German, Sally ?——

Sal. Me jabber their outlandish stuff! Sir, I'll give
you my opinion on that subject. I thinks, that, for
a true-born Briton to speak one word of foreign lingo,
is a mortal sin.

Ap. Bravo, English Sally! and how did you like
the people ?

Sal. Not at all—a parcel of conceited chaps—pretended not to understand me, though I spoke as le-
gibly to them in the real vulgar tongue as I does to
you.

Ap. Ha, ha! and how did you like the country?

Sal. Not a bit—high frightful mountains all covered with ice. Ugh! (*Shivering.*) And horrible roaring
cascades, making such terrible noises. No—Taun-

ton Dean for my money.   Regular hay-fields, and
corn-fields, and a good turnpike-road.

Ap. Egad, you are a girl to my mind.

Sal. And I am sure you are a nice old man.

Ap. Do you think so, ha! ha! Now to sound her.
Pray, Sally, how long has our young master been married? (*She is moving off silently, he gets between her
and the door.*)   And so you think me a nice old
man, eh?

Sal. Yes, that I do—ha! ha!

Ap. And so they were married abroad, eh? (SAL-
LY *looks grave again, and exit.*)   Then it is so.   Ah,
here he comes—he is grown a noble fellow.   Pity
that so fine a tree should be rotten at the core.   Ah!
I see he is a man of pleasure, he looks so miserable.

Enter MR *and* MRS GREVILLE.

Grev. Ah! April, the same man I left.

Ap. Yes, the same—body and heart.—Can you
say so to me, Charles?

Grev. So, so—more torture.

Ap. What a charming creature! (*Addressing* MRS
GREVILLE.) Don't be offended, madam—you look like
an angel—nay, don't droop—I dare say you will be
one.   Heaven is merciful! give me your fair hand.
An old man's blessing will not harm you, lady. (*Wiping his eyes.*)

Mrs Grev. He weeps.   O, Greville! let us retire!
Even the pity of a villain did not move me; but the
virtuous tears of that old man press on my heart with
agony insupportable.

Ap. O, Charles! Charles!

Enter SALLY.

Grev. Mr April, are you content to be a silent ob-
server of my conduct?

Ap. I cannot—I cannot.

Grev. Then, sir, you must estrange yourself from this house.   [*Exeunt* MR *and* MRS GREVILLE.

Ap. I'll go—I'll go—Is this my once noble boy— my pride?—forbid me his house!

Sal. Never mind his forbidding. I shall always be proud to see you, sir.

Ap. Thank you, Sally. I, that taught him to shoot flying, and now have his dogs so trained—coveys waiting for him to come and shoot them—'tis all over. Pray, (but tell me if I am impertinent,) who is that lovely creature?

Sal. The sister of Mr Egerton. Ah! there *is* a man. How I loved him! Platonic, I assure you. And the regard was mutual; for, excepting the old greyhound, I was first favourite.

Ap. What, he likes greyhounds—then I dare say he is a fine fellow. I'll think no more of Greville— And so your love was Platonic, eh?—Ha! ha!—nay, if I can't laugh, 'tis all over with me. Yes, I will leave your house. Lend me your arm, my good girl; for, to say the truth, Sally, this quarter of an hour has shook me worse than the last twenty years wear.
                                        [*Exeunt.*

ACT THE THIRD.

SCENE I.

An Apartment in UNDERMINE'S *House.*

Enter UNDERMINE *and* NICHOLAS.

Nich. Well, sir, what news of Greville? Does he confess?

Und. No.

Nich. Dear me, I should like to touch. I am an old man, and I can't, I suppose, hope to live always. Do you think I can, sir?

Und. Not always, I shou'd think.

Nich. Ah! (*Sighs.*) Then, sir, if—ever—I should, by any accident, happen to die—it would be consoling to clutch the thousand pounds first. Oh dear—I forgot.—Your nephew Rostrum, the young auctioneer, is below.

Und. What does he want?

Nich. Every thing—riches, title, sense, elegance; because, (to express myself in one grand energetic word,) he wants the *cash.*

Und. Well, well, give him a guinea—stay, I have a thought. Suppose I make him an engine to torment Greville—but he is such a sneakup! Were he a boy of metal, I would adopt him—but he is so honest, Nicholas.

Nich. 'Tis excusable in youth, sir.—Time and your instructions——

Und. Then he is deficient in spirit.

Nich. Lord, sir, you have never allowed him fair play: give him a purse full of gold—try that—adod! it would make a buck of me.

Und. I will try it.

Nich. And, sir,—a thought has struck me too.

Und. Out with it.

Nich. I don't think, sir, we lead very happy lives.

Und. No—not remarkably so.

Nich. Suppose then, sir, when you get the Greville estate, and I get the thousand pounds, that we get rid of the cold damps and shiverings.

Und. Ay, but how !—how !

Nich. Lord, sir, don't you see how the great contrive it ? Instead of passing twelve o'clock at night in darkness, and the blue devils—their houses are illuminated, full of company and jollity.

Und. And a most excellent plan it is—I'll do it. —Yes, I'll pass the next fifty years of my life in luxury and honourable uprightness.

Nich. Except, I suppose, any snug bit of roguery shou'd occur in our way.

Und. Certainly, and I'll become a man of taste and virtù.

Nich. What, become a man of virtue, sir ?

Und. No—no—you blockhead—I'll explain to you, Nicholas—Virtù is an admiration of every thing useless, or monstrous; as old books full of lies—teacups—bad sixpences—butterflies—kittens with two heads, and so forth ; while Virtue is, that—I say Virtue is a—every body knows what Virtue is.

Nich. And, edod, I'll have my jollifications, and who knows but in time I may learn to laugh again ?
                                                    [*Exit.*

Und. Now, how to provide handsomely for my nephew, without its costing me a farthing—I have it

—marry him to Rose Sydney—ah! let me alone for management. Ah, here is my young auctioneer.

Enter ROSTRUM.

Ros. How do you do, sir? (*Bowing low.*)

Und. Curse your bowing—come here, sir—hold up your head.

Ros. Civility, sir, in my line, is every thing.

Und. Yes, but I am going to make a dashing buck of you, and in that line—civility will be all against you.

Ros. What, sir, am I to leave my pulpit—and part with my little hammer?

Und. (*Throws him a purse.*) There is something better than your little hammer.

Ros. Oh dear, and what am I to do with all this?

Und. What you please.

Ros. I'll go to a sale.

Und. Go to a sale—I gave it you to throw to the devil.

Ros. I'll take it to my attorney's.

Und. Take it to Bond Street—purchase expensive clothes, horses, carriages—I'll make a man of you.

Ros. Well, I should not have thought that becoming a sprig of fashion was the way to make a man of me.

Und. I say, how do you feel with a heavy purse?

Ros. Quite light, sir—the cash certainly loosens a man's joints, and gives a sort of a—I—don't—care—a—damn—for—any—body, kind of a feel—

(*Strutting about.*)

Und. Obey me, and my fortune's yours—disobey me, and you are a beggar. In the first place, forget your absurd auctioneer jargon—you understand.—

Ros. Sir, I take your bidding—I mean, I take your hint.

Und. And get rid of that respectful manner: the age of supple adulation is passed; bend now to the great, and they will sink you lower.—No, you must assume a superiority—you must hold up your head.—Do you think, for instance, you can get rid of your respect for me?

Ros. With the greatest ease possible.

Und. Very well. Observe, every thing may be done by management. *I,* who am now look'd up to—ay, sir, look'd up to; once kept, you know—a paltry grocer's shop.

Ros. It was a chandler's shop.

Und. Was it?—well—well—how have, I become what I am?—by management—for instance—I am thought to possess a strong understanding—is it so?

Ros. It never struck me that you did.

Und. Very well——again—the world calls me a man of scrupulous integrity—am I so?

Ros. Certainly not, sir.

Und. Very well, then—all the effect of management. Say little—yet never seem ignorant; but, by significant nods and smiles, seem to say, I know all—but won't tell.

Ros. Oh! whenever I don't understand a subject, I must nod.

Und. Yes.

Ros. Then, my dear uncle, I shall nod my head off to a certainty.

Und. No, no, you may manage—get a smattering of politics at a party bookseller's—morality you may learn at the play-houses—mechanism at Merlin's—and the fine arts——

Ros. At my own auction room.

Und. Confound your auction room—away and begin your career.—Stay; a little trifle I had forgot—I am going to marry you to a——

Ros. Marry me!—Oh lock, sir! (*With bashfulness.*)

Und. Oh lock, sir!—You sneaking——

Ros. Upon my soul, I meant, sink me—I meant to say—so you are going to marry me. Sink me.

Und. Yes; and to a lady who has all the requisites

for an excellent wife. In the first place, she is esteemed beautiful by all who have seen her—fine estate in
Worcestershire.

Ros. Fine estate! I shou'd like to sell it—freehold or copyhold.

Und. Freehold, I believe.

Ros. Within a ring fence.

Und. How the devil should I know? In the next
place, she is remarkably sensible and witty—that I
had from a gentleman, who says her estate is the
prettiest in the county.

Ros. A most excellent authority.

Und. And thirdly, she has a crowd of lovers, which
certainly proves——

Ros. That her estate is the prettiest in the county.
Quite natural, for, now a-days, no gentleman comes
more frequently to the hammer than little Cupid—
but I must away; this purse makes me very fidgetty.

Und Success attend you—don't forget my lessons
—(*They nod to each other.*)—Management is every
thing—remember—hypocrisy.   [*Exit.*

Ros. Hypocrisy! I am sure I ought to nod now,
for, thank heaven, that is a subject I am completely
ignorant of.   [*Exit.*

SCENE II.

Bond Street.

Enter EGERTON *in a military great-coat and cross-belt,
with every appearance of distress, and dejection of
mind and body.*

Eg. 'Tis strange, that I should pass unheeded
amidst a crowd of friends, that none should know me;

surely, the necromancers of old were fools to study
life away in vain attempts to become impervious to
human sight, when, to render themselves invisible to
their nearest friends, 'twas only to put on the garb of
wretchedness. (*Takes out a miniature.*) This is the
only treasure I have left—my sweetest Rose. (*Kisses
the picture.*) But what have I to do with love or
happiness? Yet I will not part with thee, sweet re-
membrancer, though nature's calls are most imperious, and I sicken with hunger.

Enter ROSTRUM.

Ros. Plague take this purse; I don't know what to
do with it. I don't care twopence for horses—I hate
gaming. I can't drive curricles. And as for the once
concealed charms of the fair—no need of a purse for
that—now-a-days, they are all to be seen gratis.—
Heigho! I am no more fit to be a blood, than my
uncle is to be a bishop—I have nothing to do—no
where to go—Oh! what a cursed bore it is to be a
gentleman.—Eh! what have we here—Oh! I see, a
soldier returned from the wars in the full dress of vic-
tory.—As we *conoscienti* say, 'tis a grand head, and in
nature's best manner. On canvass, it would fetch
twenty guineas; but on the shoulders of a poor soldier, nobody will give sixpence for it—throw this to
the devil!—No—suppose, instead, I try to get my
name inserted in a better catalogue.—Sir, your most
obedient—this fine sharp air gives a keen appetite.

Eg. It does, indeed.

Ros. Comical place this Bond Street—brilliant equi-
pages dashing along—most of the owners though are
in the predicament of your coat—rather out at the
elbows.

Eg. Sir!

Ros. I don't mean to offend.—You seem a stranger;
give me leave, sir, to shew you the lions—that small
gentleman, with a large coronet, is a new peer of

ninety-seven—that lady all the bucks are ogling, is an old woman of ninety-seven—that seven-feet giant is a milliner—that gentleman running across the way to shake hands with a bailiff, is over head and ears in debt: don't be surprised, he is in parliament—in the phaeton, with little ponies, sits a female gambler, and a great orator : The female gambler, the great orator, and the little ponies are all upon sale, and may be knocked down to the best bidder. I was once a delightful auctioneer—my present trade is buckism —pray, sir, what may your trade be?

Eg. Alexander's.

Ros. By my soul, 'tis an interesting picture, and it sha'n't be my fault, if it has not a gilt frame. Sir, will you have the goodness to lend me twenty pounds?

Eg. Do you mean to insult me?

Ros. I do not, indeed—will you, then, have the goodness to let me lend *you* twenty pounds?

Eg. No, sir.

Ros. Proud as Lucifer—I'll lose some money to him —A remarkable clear bright sun-shiny day.

Eg. Yes.

Ros. I'll bet you ten pounds, it rains—

Eg. Madman—leave me.

Ros. Leave you! oh, very well—if you insist— good bye to you. (*Drops his purse, which* EGERTON *picks up.*)

Eg. Sir, here is a purse which you dropt.

Ros. I dropt—oh! you sly dog—is that your trick —ring dropping—a brilliant, and a draft—I understand it all—my dear fellow, it won't do—Oh, for shame of yourself!   [*Exit.*

Eg. A most extraordinary character, but benevolence fills his heart, and I will not insult it, by refusing to take from his purse such benefits as nature so strongly craves.——(SALLY *crosses the stage singing a ballad.*

'Tis of a sailor that I write,
Who on the seas took great delight.)

Do my eyes deceive me—my sister's servant in England! Sally!

Sal. (*Turning round and running into his arms.*) Oh! my dear master; alive!—he! he! he! ah! but you are not well.

Eg. Not quite well.

Sal. And in poverty.

Eg. Oh! 'tis the soldier's lean inheritance. He must feel nothing a misfortune—but disgrace. But tell me—why do I meet you in England—surely, Sally, you have not deserted Maria?

Sal. I desert her!—have you received no letter?

Eg. None. You seem agitated—is my sister well?

Sal. Yes—Heaven bless her——

Eg. Then I guess the cause—she is married?—(*She looks perplexed.*)—Ah! did'st thou not hear me—she is then married?—(*A pause.*)—No answer—damnation—the thought is madness.—On thy soul, I charge thee speak. Is she a wife?—yet silent—oh! while strength and reason hold—lead me to her.
[*Exeunt.*

SCENE III.

An Apartment in GREVILLE'S *House.*

Enter MRS GREVILLE.

Eg. (*Without.*) Where is she?
Mrs Grev. Ah! that voice.—It is my brother!

Enter EGERTON—*he sinks into a chair.*

Eg. Stand off.

Mrs Grev. What means my brother?

Eg. Come not near me, but answer.—Art thou a wife?

Mrs Grev. Ah! have I not sworn to conceal my marriage!—Oh! William!—pardon my silence—I am most unhappy, yet most innocent.

Eg. The laws of honour are simple unsophisticated —thou art an angel, or—'tis plain—I see the burning blush of guilt—and are my sufferings for thee thus repaid?

Mrs Grev. Sufferings! oh tell me——

Eg. I will tell thee, for thou hast deserved to know them—When I had given thee all, I sought my fortunes in a German regiment in the pay of England; we were ordered to the West Indies—there, slowly recovering from the pestilential fever of the island, my emaciated state would not allow me to dress in the ranks with my usual alacrity; the consequence was, that, from the cane of a young ensign, I received on my shoulders a blow. (*Rising.*) Yes, a blow— in the paroxysm of madness I felled him with the earth. (*Sinks again into the chair.*) Yet, it was cowardly in me, for it was a boy that struck me.

Mrs Grev. Oh! (*Weeps.*)

Eg. The punishment of death I was prepared to meet—but, Maria! picture the agony of this proud heart, when I was ordered to the halberts—yes, to be punished with ignominy.

Mrs Grev. Oh! my brother.

Eg. I shall soon conclude—I flew with desperation on my guard, hoping from them to meet the death I longed for—I was deceived, they favoured my escape—at that moment thy image rushed upon my heart, and nature bade me struggle with my fate, and find a sister—I have found her, and may the heavy curse——

Mrs Grev. (*Catching his arm.*) Oh! do not curse me—suspend it but a day—an hour—grant me this, William, or you do not love me.

Eg. Not love thee!—unhappy girl—even now, spite of its wrongs, my heart throbs as it would burst to meet thee.—Yes—one embrace, for her honoured sake who bore thee—no more——curse on my feeble nature. (*Sinks into the chair.*)

Mrs Grev. Ah! you look faint.

Eg. It is not strange—I have not lately tasted food.

Mrs Grev. Oh! William, protect your valued life —take this—on my knees let me intreat it——

Eg. (*Rising with a smile of dignified disdain, and dropping the purse.*) Do not insult me, girl!

Mrs Grev. Indeed I meant it not.—Oh! Greville, come and save my heart from breaking.

Eg. Greville! ah! that, then, is the villain's name.

[*Exit hastily.*

Mrs Grev. Oh stay!—my brother—hear me!

[*Exit, following.*

SCENE IV.

An Apartment at UNDERMINE'S.

Enter ROSE SYDNEY.

R. Syd. Heigh ho! no information yet of my dear Egerton; I fear to enquire for him, for should my guardian, Undermine, know of my attachment, I should become the object of his fixed malevolence. —Pshaw—here comes his nephew to make love to me.

Enter ROSTRUM.

Ros. There she stands.

R. Syd. (*Sings.*)

" Dee'l take the wars that hurried Willie from me."

Ros. Who the devil is Willie?—I feel very awkward. (*Aside.*) How do you do, ma'am?

R. Syd. Now for a specimen of a modern lover.

Ros. I hear, ma'am, you have a charming estate.

R. Syd. A modern lover indeed—Which estate, in my opinion, sir, you value above its merits.

Ros. I beg your pardon, ma'am—no—when I am call'd in to value an estate, I——

R. Syd. Sir!

Ros. Zounds! no, ma'am; what I wish to speak of is quite another article, I mean quite another lot —I mean quite another affair—'tis not the fine estate in Worcestershire; but, (*Blushing,*) but the holy estate of matrimony, ma'am.

R. Syd. Well, sir, what of it?—pray speak.

Ros. (*Aside.*) I am tongue-tied—'tis damn'd hard, I can only preach in my own pulpit.

R. Syd. What did you say, sir?

Ros. I said, ma'am, that—I'll try my uncle's way. (*Nods to her.*) You understand?

R. Syd. Indeed I do not.

Ros. Nor I neither. (*Aside.*)—Ma'am!

R. Syd. Sir!

Ros. I say—(*Aside.*) I have it—I'll pour forth a torrent of eloquence.—Oh! miss, believe me, I despise riches—ah! how blessed should I be to live with you in a retired and peaceful cottage, situate in a delightful sporting country, with attached and detached offices, roomy cellaring, and commodious attics!

R. Syd. Sir!

Ros. Together would we inhale the vernal breeze in an acre and a half of garden ground, crammed with esculents and choice fruit-trees—well stocked and cropped.

R. Syd. The poor man is mad.

Ros. With content smiling round us. I would not languish for town enjoyments—no—though situated only an agreeable distance from the turnpike road, with the accommodation of a stage coach passing daily to London.

R. Syd. But, sir, I hate a cottage—and when I marry——

Ros. The premises may be viewed with tickets, and immediate possession had.

R. Syd. Quite—quite mad.—

Ros. Well, miss—after all that, don't you love me?

R. Syd. No—(*Sings.*)

" The pride of all nature was sweet Willie O!"

Ros. Damn Willie—my name is Tom.

R. Syd. Tom, is it? ha! ha!

Ros. She is a sweet creature—perhaps, ma'am, your heart has been previously disposed of by private contract?

R. Syd. It has—(*Sings.*)

" He wou'd be a soldier, wou'd sweet Willie O."

Ros. Oh! Willie is a soldier, is he? then what chance has a simple auctioneer, with his little hammer, against a soldier with his long sword—so, ma'am, you can't bid for me—I mean, you can't love me?

R. Syd. No, sir!

Ros. What a pity—is there no agreeable attitude I could put myself into—no way—what would I give for one kiss?

R. Syd. I'll tell you how you may obtain twenty.

Ros. How?

R. Syd. By giving up the lover, and assuming a character I am sure you will succeed in—a sincere friend.

Ros. Indeed! thank you—quite happiness enough for me—only place me next to sweet Willie O in your heart, and I am satisfied—What shall I say—I'll serve

you with fidelity—pugh!—that I would do for any
body else—I'll—I'll fight for you; and that I would
not do for any body else.

R. Syd. Oh! sir, could I but learn where my soldier is——

Ros. I'll run and inquire at the War Office.

R. Syd. (*Embracing him.*) Thank you, dear sir.

Ros. Oh, charming—farewell. Would it not be as
well though if I knew his name, because, if I ask the
clerks for Sweet Willie O! they may not comprehend——

R. Syd. True! true!—his name is William Egerton.

Ros. Happy fellow—one more friendly hug.

Enter at opposite doors UNDERMINE *and* APRIL.

Ap. Hey-day!

Und. (*Aside.*) There's management—he'll do—
he'll do.

Ap. More vexation!—Shame, girl—in the arms of
a stranger!

Und. He is my nephew—will be my heir—and he
is a very clever fellow. (ROSTRUM *nods.*)

Ap. He has a queer way of shewing it.

Und. A tolerable well-looking man, is he not?

Ap. I can't tell.

Und. He has an excellent heart.

Ap. I don't know.

Und. Do you think I would deceive you?

Ap. I can't say—you may be all alike—my grandson has ruined my fortune—Greville has ruined my
happiness, and, perhaps, I may find him a coxcomb—
my Rose ungrateful—and you a scoundrel—so I'll
to the country again, and in the mean time, my dear,
you shall see as much of this virtuous town as you
possibly can, out of a two pair of stairs window. (ROSE
and ROSTRUM *kiss their hands to each other.*)

[*Exeunt* APRIL *and* ROSE.

Und. You are a clever fellow—an exceeding clever

fellow. I say, how did you manage to win her so soon?

Ros. I don't know—I believe I have an odd agreeable tickling way with me. Did you never see me coax the ladies to bid at my auctions?——adieu, uncle——

Und. Come back, sir—I can't part with you—this match with management, I conclude, is as good as settled.

Ros. Exactly.

Und. Very well—now you must get a mistress—

Ros. A what?

Und. A mistress—you rascal—do you blush?

Ros. I blush!—sir, I blush to think, that you should' think, that I should think of blushing—(*Fanning himself with his hat*)—only getting a mistress, when a man is going to be married——

Und. Well, sir.

Ros. I can only say the necessity of it does not strike me.

Und. Necessity!—I tell you 'tis the etiquette

Ros. Oh! the etiquette is it?

Und. Now for my grand attack on Greville—follow me, sir. [*Exit.*

Ros. This will never do for me. Oh! I foresee a dissolution of partnership here—but he is a relation —what then—am I therefore to sacrifice principle to duty—no—I remember our school adage was " *Amicus Plato sed magis amica veritas;*" which I thus interpret—Undermine is my uncle, but integrity is my father. [*Exit.*

ACT THE FOURTH.

SCENE I.

A Library in GREVILLE'S *House.*

Servant introduces UNDERMINE *and* ROSTRUM.

Und. Tell your master I wait for him——

Serv. My master is from home—I will acquaint my mistress with your arrival——   [*Exit.*

Und. A noble mansion, is not it?

Ros. A charming tenement, indeed.   What is the ground rent?

Und. How should I know?—Here she comes. What think you of this encumbrance with it, eh? Is not she beautiful?

Ros. Very; but she seems unhappy.

Und. 'Tis the more incumbent in you then to endeavour to make her otherwise——

Enter Servant.

Serv. My mistress.   [*Exit.*

Enter MRS GREVILLE.

Mrs Grev. Gentlemen, I expect Mr Greville home every moment. Oh, would he were come! (*Aside.*)

Und. Madam, Mr Rostrum, my nephew—now address her.

Ros. But she is in tears, sir.

Und. What's that to you, sir? tears! nonsense! is she not a mistress?

Ros. Is she not a woman?

Und. Come, let us have a specimen of the agreeable tickling way you were talking of.

Ros. (*Approaching her.*) What shall I say? Ma'am, what a capital room, ma'am, this would be for a sale.

Mrs Grev. (*With surprise.*) Very probably, sir.

Ros. That is all, ma'am.

Und. S'death, is that your tickling way? Make love to her, you rascal.

Ros. Yes, sir.

Und. Be sprightly.

Ros. Yes, sir.

Und. Dance up to her, you dog.

Ros. Yes, sir. (*Addressing* Mrs Greville *in a melancholy tone.*) You are the most charming creature.

Mrs Grev. Sir! (*Shrinking in alarm.*)—(*Enter* Greville.) Oh, I am glad you are returned.

Grev. What is the matter?

Mrs Grev. Nothing.

Grev. No insult has been offered?

Mrs Grev. No—I am so timid—Indeed, quite childish; but oh! I have a tale to tell you, Charles. Yet that wretch shall not triumph in our agitation. No—until he is gone I am calm.

Grev. Matchless girl! Come, sir, dispatch.

Und. My nephew, sir. (Greville *bows.*) If I can but put him off his guard.—Now is your time.

(*To* Rostrum.)

Greville *and* Undermine *sit at a table with their eyes fixed on* Rostrum, *who addresses* Mrs Greville *in dumb shew.—She appears distressed at his attentions.*

Und. These, sir, are the ready money securities.

Bonds to the amount of five thousand pounds. (GRE-
VILLE *snatching the papers, and eagerly returning to
his observation.*) Bravo! (*Eying* ROSTRUM *and* MRS
GREVILLE.)   These are exchequer bills—that is an
India bond.

Grev. (*Quitting his chair and running to his wife.*)
I cannot bear it; 'tis torture insupportable! I will declare thy innocence.—Poverty, death, I can endure,
but not thy tears, Maria.   Mr Undermine——

Mrs Grev. Hold—Greville—

Enter SALLY.

Sal. Stand aside ; here comes somebody will soon
tell who is who.   I'll get out of the way.   [*Exit.*

Enter EGERTON.

Eg. Who answers to the name of Greville ?
Grev. I do.
Eg. Give me your hand.
Grev. What do you mean ?
Eg. (*Seizing his hand.*) The gripe of everlasting
friendship—for 'tis death must part us.   You are a
villain. (*Presents pistols;* GREVILLE *snatches one;*
MRS GREVILLE *rushes between them.*)

Mrs Grev. Oh, my brother !
Grev. Brother ! (*Throws away his pistol.*)
Mrs Grev. Oh, raise not your arm against——
                                              (*Pauses.*)

Eg. Who? (MRS GREVILLE *pauses.*)
Grev. Her husband.
Eg. and *Und.* Her husband !
Grev. Yes; spite of the poverty that name entails
on me, spite of impending ruin, my heart triumphant-
ly exults in proclaiming her my loved, my honoured
wife! (*Kneeling to her.*) By my soul, Maria, I would
not raise another blush upon that angel cheek to purchase the world's dominion.

Und. Then the estate is mine. Strut, you dog.
(*To* ROSTRUM.

Ros. I do, sir. (*Reluctantly.*)

Eg. My darling sister! my pride! let me now hold
thee to my heart with rapture. (*Puts his handkerchief
to his eyes.*)

Und. Tears from a soldier! (*Sneeringly.*)

Eg. Unfeeling man! did not tears of joy start from
me at beholding beauty and innocence restored to
their native lustre, I were unworthy of the name of
soldier.   And, sir, it may be prudent for you to remember, that a soldier's heart is like his sword, formed
of tempered steel: for, while it bends with sympathizing pity to the touch of woe, it can resume its
springing energy to punish arrogance or crush oppression.

Ros. Strut, uncle!

Und. No, no, a little is very well.   It would not
be feeling.   When will it be convenient, Mr Greville,
to give possession?

Grev. Immediately. (*With spirit.*)

Und. I say—I'll triumph by and by—at present
we'll go home, snug and quiet.   Ten thousand a-year,
here is management, you dog. [*Exit.*

Eg. (*To* ROSTRUM, *who is following.*) Sir, allow
me with gratitude to return this purse.   You will find
that I have been greatly benefited by your generosity.

Ros. Nay, don't.

Eg. I insist, sir.

Ros. Conceited fellow! but I must away to enquire
for Sweet Willie O.

Grev. Come, Mr Egerton.

Ros. (*Turning round.*) Egerton? did I hear rightly? Sir, one word, if you please.   Will you take this
purse again?

Eg. No, sir.

Ros. You won't! We'll see that.   Have you forgot a lady called Rose Sydney?

2

Eg. Have I forgot her! (*Sighing.*)

Ros. I have just parted from her, and she said—will you take this purse?

Eg. Excuse me—but tell me—

Ros. She said—you had better take it, or the devil a word will you get out of me.

Eg. Well, well. (*Takes it.*)

Ros. Now you are an honest fellow again—she loves you sincerely—and, if you will meet me in an hour in Berkley Square, she shall tell you so.

Eg. Don't trifle with my feelings.

Ros. By Heaven, I am serious. You shall have a kiss, and I'll have another. And I say—bring a parson with you.

Eg. I don't know any. Who will introduce me?

Ros. Who will introduce you to a parson! look at your friend on your right hand, my dear fellow—he is gentleman-usher to all mankind, in court or in city.—In public he will escort you to a great man in his state-chamber, or in private to a pretty woman in her bed-chamber.   [*Exit.*

Mrs Grev. You are not happy, Greville.

Grev. Yes, Maria——though bereft of fortune; though a prison opens its gates to receive us, yet, blessed with thy love, and my heart's approbation, I feel that I am happy. Accept my homage, oh, celestial virtue! Nature's sweet nurse—'tis thou alone can pour a healing balm upon the wounded spirit, and lull the throbbing heart to rest.

Enter SALLY.

Sal. (*Speaking as she enters.*) Oh, now 'tis Mrs Greville, is it? Did not I say it would be so? Now every thing is as it should be, and my tongue can wag again. (*To* EGERTON.) Oh, my dear master—Well, you must tell me how you have been, and where you have been; and—sir, (*To* GREVILLE,) I am entirely satisfied with your conduct, and, to shew I am perfectly reconciled, you may, if you please—(*She wipes her mouth,* GREVILLE *smiles, and salutes her.*) But here am I talking a heap of nonsense, while he wants rest and refreshment.

Mrs Grev. Oh, true.

Eg. Maria! how could I mistake the glow of virtue for the blush of guilt! This lovely cheek resembles that of the chaste queen of night, which can only be illumined by a ray from Heaven. Come, my sister. (*Takes her hand;* SALLY, *on the other side, presents hers; he smiles, takes it, and exeunt.*)

Grev. Ah! here comes my early, my excellent old friend. Circumstances obliged me to behave harshly to him; but I know the way to his honest heart.

Enter APRIL.

Ap. (*Softly.*) Huzza! he is my own boy again. Ecod, I could jump over the moon. But he sha'n't see my joy, that is—if I can help it. Ha, ha! No, he has insulted my regard for him, and it demands satisfaction.

Grev. Well, good April—

Ap. (*Assuming sulkiness.*) Called for orders, sir.

Grev. Sir! Is that language to a friend, to your own boy? Come, if I have been a little frolicsome, pray, who was my instructor?

Ap. (*Stifling a laugh, and appearing sulky.*) I don't know.

Grev. No—don't you remember the mischievous pranks you taught me?

Ap. Yes—ha, ha!—No, I don't.

Grev. What! not making me fill the apothecary's boots with cold water?

Ap. (*Aside.*) He, he, he! (*Sulkily.*) It was not cold water, it was hot hasty-pudding.

Grev. True; and then, April, in our shooting excursions, how you assisted me in climbing the hills. I think I feel at this moment the pressure of your

friendly hand upon my infant fingers. I wonder how
it would feel now. *(Presents his hand.)*

*Ap. (No longer able to resist his joy, turns round
and embraces him.)* Oh! my dear Charley, boy! *(Sobbing.*) Now you shall see how merry an old man can
be, ha, ha!—The old pye-bald poney is dead tho'.
Ecod, I'll tell you a good joke. My dog of a grandson has spent every shilling I am worth, ha, ha!—
But you look grave.

Grev. Have I not reason?

Ap. What reason?

Grev. Are you, then, ignorant, that, by my marriage, I forfeit my father's estate to Mr Undermine?

Ap. Eh! what! forfeit! 'Tis impossible.

Grev. Such is my father's will.

Ap. That your father's will? Then my old master, Heaven rest his soul! is gone to the devil to a
certainty. But Undermine can't think of keeping it.

Grev. Ah, you then know little of Mr Undermine.

Ap. But I will know him, ay, thoroughly. There
must be villainy. I'll to him directly. He possess
the Greville estate—no, no, no! Though his majesty
has not a more peaceable subject in his dominions
than myself, yet, rather than that, I would throttle
him to a certainty. Come, come, cheer up. That's
right—don't droop; for, while the left side is the
stoutest, I warrant it will some how contrive to prop
up the other.   [*Exeunt severally.*

SCENE II.

An Apartment in UNDERMINE's *House.*

Enter UNDERMINE *meeting* ROSTRUM.

Und. Well, nephew, I am a made man; and if I
could but see you married to Miss Sydney !

Ros. (*Aside.*) Now for a little swaggering!—Make yourself easy. I mean to marry her in an hour.

Und. The devil you do! But how will you get April's consent?

Ros. (Snapping his fingers.) That for his consent. I'll carry her off.

Und. You don't say so!

Ros. I will—sink me!

Und. But are you sure of her consent?

Ros. I don't care that for her consent neither. I'll carry her off, whether she will or no.

Und. Amazing! I didn't think it was in you. But I say—you must have somebody to assist in carrying her off.

Ros. I will—I'll get two of our auction-porters—careful fellows—carried home a Venus the other day without the smallest fracture.

Und. Nonsense!—They won't do.

Ros. No! Then I'll get an officer in the army to assist me in the elopement.

Und. That's right—they are used to it. Now for management! Take that. Observe—that key——

Ros. Is a patent one.

Und. Psha! It opens the escrutoire up stairs.—In the right-hand drawer you will find the title-deeds of her estate, which April put into my care; and possession——

Ros. Is every thing.—Bravo! This is luck indeed. *(Aside.)*

Und. But stay—I must not seem to consent to your carrying her off.

Ros. Certainly not.

Und. I must resist you, and you must push me about.

Ros. I will.

Und. Ah! but may I depend on you?

Ros. You may, upon my soul. Good b'ye, ha! ha!

Und. I say—this is management.

Ros. It is.

Und. You'll trick the old one.

Ros. I mean it, I assure you, ha, ha!   [*Exit.*

Und. I did not think it was in him.

Enter NICHOLAS.

Nich. I give you joy, sir, with all my heart and soul.

Und. Ay, Nicholas, 'tis all settled, so say no more about it. All quite settled.

Nich. Except the one thousand pounds, sir.

Und. What? Oh, true. But at present I have not any cash in the house.

Nich. A check on your banker, sir.

Und. Eh! but without pen and ink——

Nich. Here they are, sir.

Und. Well, well—a thousand pounds, isn't it?

Nich. And interest.

Und. Interest!—It has not been due an hour.

Nich. A little interest, sir.

Und. How much?

Nich. Five hundred pounds, sir.

Und. (*Aside.*) Here's a damn'd villain.—There's no need for hurry.

Nich. I am an old man, and have no time to lose. (*Presenting the pen.*)

Und. (*Avoiding him.*) You must hire servants.

Nich. I will, sir. (*Pursuing with pen.*)

Und. I mean to sup in my new mansion.

Nich. You shall, sir.

Und. And let me have a band of music——

Nich. I'll go directly. I can hire them in St James's Street.

Und. Ay, go directly, Nicholas.

Nich. And as your banker lives in Pall Mall, it will be quite handy.

Und. By and by.

Nich. It must be paid directly; for being due for a little roguery, it of course becomes a debt of honour.

Enter APRIL *(unobserved.)*

Und. Zounds! don't teaze so. Interest, forsooth! Consider what an enormous sum a thousand pounds is, for only just popping a will into the fire. I won't be hurried I tell you. [*Exit.*

Nich. And if I had popped it into the fire, what a pretty way I should be in! Ah! you had no such fool to deal with. No, it is sewed up safe here in my coat—by day the comforter of my heart, by night the companion of my pillow; and it shall not be burnt till the thousand pounds are paid. Ay, and with swinging interest too. *(Alarmed.)* Ah! Mr April, I did not see you.

Ap. What do you say?—I am very deaf.

Nich. I am devilish glad of it. Then all is snug.

Ap. Burnt will! *(Aside).*

Nich. Mr April.

Ap. How to fathom it——*(Aside.)*

Nich. I say, I shall be steward now—'tis a great undertaking; but I suppose I shall contrive not to lose much by it.

Ap. I dare say you will.—A thousand pounds?

Nich. Prepare the tenants for my arrival.

Ap. Yes; I'll tell them old Nick is coming among them.—What the devil did he say about sewing up?

Nich. The country air may be of service.

Ap. Yes, with the help of that you may live some weeks.

Nich. Oh dear! some weeks—A large quantity of years you mean? Well, good b'ye, April. *(They embrace, and* APRIL *lays his hand on the left side, where the will is deposited.)*

Ap. Eh—What—By Heaven, I felt something like parchment—If it should be—I'll be convinced—Good b'ye, Nick—a last embrace. *(Embraces him closely, and feels for the parchment.)*

Nich. 'Tis suffocation!

Ap. 'Tis parchment.

Nich. Zounds! it had like to have been a last embrace, indeed.

Ap. How shall I get at that parchment? I can easily persuade him he is ill—perhaps, by that means—I'll try—once more.

Nich. No, no—there is my hand.

Ap. *(Taking it.)* Eh!—what! good God!

Nich. What is the matter?

Ap. Let me look at you—good God!—don't be alarmed.

Nich. But I am very much alarmed. Am I ill?

Ap. *(Shakes his head.)* I dare say you feel—flurried.

Nich. Exceedingly.

Ap. Palpitation at the heart?—'Tis parchment!

Nich. Oh yes—very sudden this. I felt quite well just now.

Ap. Did you? That's an alarming symptom; for I have always observed, that nothing makes the physician look so grave, as the patient's saying he feels quite well. My dear friend, send for one directly.

Nich. I don't know what to say. They sometimes save your life, but then it is sure to cost you a guinea.

Ap. *(Aside.)* And saving yours is certainly not worth it. But I see you are a philosopher—You are prepared for death.

Nich. Oh dear! not at all—I am quite terrified. If perspiration is good for me, I feel that copiously. —What shall I do?

Ap. Come, for old acquaintance sake, my grandson shall attend you gratis.

Nich. Oh, thank you.

Ap. Wonderful physician! Never lost a patient!— *(Aside.)*—because he never had a patient to lose. I expect him here in five minutes. You had better go to your room.

Nich. Ay.

Ap. Keep yourself warm.

Nich. I will.

Ap. Above all things, don't change your clothes.

Nich. I won't.

Ap. Shall I button your coat?

Nich. No, no—I'll do that myself.

Ap. Go, I'll follow, and talk to you of your latter end, and keep up your spirits.

Nich. I believe I am dying. 'Tis very good of you to get me a doctor gratis. *(Exit, and re-enters.)* But I say—who is to pay the apothecary?

Ap. I'll settle that too.—*(Exit* NICHOLAS.*)*—Now for Undermine—If he have one spark of humanity in his composition, I'll call it forth; if not, and I can get that coat——

Enter UNDERMINE.

Und. Nicholas! What, April here—I guess your errand, and am sorry, sir, I cannot continue you as steward.

Ap. (Aside.) I your steward! No, that is not my errand. I am a feeble fellow, sliding out of the world; but Greville is a noble fellow rising into it. 'Tis respecting him I come. You must assist him. How is he to live?

Und. (Sneeringly.) Oh! his integrity will support him.

Ap. True; but consider what a way you would be in, if you had nothing but your integrity to support you.

Und. Sir, I see you only want to trifle with me.

Ap. True; I only want a trifle of you.

Und. I am flint.

Ap. Well; but even flint, when properly hit, will send forth warm, vivid sparks.

Und. I must leave you. Time presses.

Ap. So do his wants.

Und. A nobleman is waiting for me.

Ap. A bailiff is waiting for him.

Und. If you proceed, expect some personal insult.

Ap. Throw your purse at me.   Come—

(*Takes hold of his coat.*)

Und. I shall burst with rage.

Ap. They will famish with hunger.

Und. Unhand me, I say. (*Strikes* APRIL *from him.*)

Ap. What, a blow! *(With subdued irritation.)*

Und. Yes; take him that.

Ap. No, no, that you meant for myself, and I'll take it, so you will give something better to poor Greville.

Und. I will not.

Ap. (*Shaking him.*) You scoundrel! And do you suppose, that, because I would submit to a blow to endeavour to save a friend from ruin, that I want the spirit of a man to resent an indignity! Ask my pardon.

Und. Pardon!

Ap. Ay.

Und. I do—help! help!

Ap. On your knees, or your last hour is come.

Und. Well.   I do—I do. Help! help!

Enter two Servants.—APRIL *throws* UNDERMINE *from him, who retreats behind the Servants.*

Und. Leave my house, sir, leave my house. By Heaven, I'll be revenged.

Ap. By hell, you are a villain. [*Exeunt severally.*

ACT THE FIFTH.

SCENE I.

Outside of UNDERMINE'S *House.*

Enter ROSTRUM *and* EGERTON *with caution.*

Ros. That is the house.

Eg. Does that contain——

Ros. Softly—recollect, sir, you are only a subaltern in this affair, and that I am your commanding-officer; so, obey orders.

Eg. How do you intend to proceed?

Ros. I am too great a general to communicate my plan of operations; I shall do my duty in giving you possession of the lovely citadel, and then take care and do your duty. (*Going.*) I say, when the alarm is given, do you retreat—you know how to do that, I dare say.   [*Exit into the house.*

Eg. I fear to trust my happiness. Can it be possible that my adored girl still thinks with kindness on her poor Egerton? Ah! a noise—what an anxious moment! (*Retires.*)

Enter ROSTRUM *from the house, with* MISS SYDNEY *in one hand, and repelling* UNDERMINE *with the other.*

Ros. I will carry her off.

Und. You shall not, sir: I am her guardian.

Ros. Do you think I care for guardians? dare to

stir hand or foot, and I'll crush you into atoms, you
old scoundrel. (*During this* EGERTON *discovers himself to* MISS SYDNEY, *who runs into his arms.*)

[*They exeunt.*

Und. That will do—zounds! be quiet—they are
gone, I tell you.

Ros. Eh! so they are, ha, ha!—well, how did I
do it?

Und. Oh, capitally—(*Rubbing his arm.*) Has the
soldier got her?

Ros. Yes.

Und. That's as it should be.

Ros. Exactly.

Und. Well!

Ros. Well!

Und. Are you mad?

Ros. What's the matter?

Und. The matter! why don't you go?

Ros. Where?

Und. Why, zounds! how can you marry the girl
if you stand here.

Ros. I marry! oh, very true. I declare it quite
escaped me.

Und. 'Sdeath! run.

Ros. I am a-going, a-going, a-going—(*Returning.*)
Sir! where shall I bring the bride?

Und. To Greville's. Go along.

Ros. (*Returning.*) I say—this is management.

Und. Yes, yes—but go along.

Ros. (*Returning.*) Sir, you would make a capital
puff at an auction.

Und. Zounds! go. (*Exit* ROSTRUM.) So that's
settled—and now to Greville's in triumph. I'll walk
in with erected crest, and—ugh! confound the fellow,
how he has bruised me! [*Exit.*

SCENE II.

An Apartment at MR UNDERMINE'S.

NICHOLAS *discovered on a couch.* APRIL *sitting by him with a book.*

Nich. I wish the doctor were come.—Bless me, I hope I sha'n't die—I don't care what pain I suffer, so I don't die. Oh! for a swinging rheumatism that would last me twenty years—do read a little to me.

Ap. (*Reading.*) " Crumbs of Comfort for an Aged Sinner."

Nich. These books are quite new to me.

Enter PLETHORA.

Ap. (*Apart to* PLETHORA.) Have you had my letter?

Ple. Yes.

Ap. Don't forget—'tis the coat I want—and remember you are a physician, not a farrier.

Ple. I will—and if I succeed, remember you tip. How do you do?

Nich. That's what I want to know of you.

Ple. True—Oh, I see——-

Nich. Shall I detail my symptoms?

Ple. No—'tis a clear case—if you were to talk for an hour, I should not know more of your complaint than I do at present.

Ap. (*Apart.*) Bleed him—

Ple. (*Feels his pulse.*) I will. You have no objection to part with a little blood?

Nich. I have no objection to part with any thing.

Ple. Except to advantage. Now, if by sinking an ounce or two of blood, you can produce an income of sixteen pounds of flesh, the advantage is immense.

Nich. How sensibly he talks! Why, 'tis five thousand per cent. profit. I'll be bled directly. (*Taking off his coat.*)

Ple. Help him.

Nich. No, no, I can do that myself. (*Places the coat carefully under the cushion of the sofa.—As he sits down,* APRIL *slips the coat from under the cushion, winks to* PLETHORA, *and exit on tiptoe.*) 'Tis very terrifying—I'll read a little more. But, doctor, are you sure now I shall not be suddenly called to Heaven?

Ple. I am very sure of that.

Nich. Oh, you are. (*Throwing away the book.*)— Then, pray, sir, what is my complaint?

Ple. Complaint? what shall I say? I wish he would return—oh, 'tis the—the glanders.

Nich. The glanders! zounds! do you make a horse of me?

Ple. No—we will be content with making an ass of you. (*Aside.*)—(*Enter* APRIL *with the coat and will, which he exhibits to* PLETHORA *in triumph.*) Or perhaps the disorder may be seated in the coats belonging to the stomach.

Ap. (*Coming forward.*) No, no—the disorder was seated in the coat belonging to the back, ha, ha! but now 'tis removed. (*Throwing him his coat.*) Do you see this? (*Shewing the will.*)

Nich. I am undone.

Ap. And how the devil could you expect a moment's ease with such a thing as this lying next your heart—you may go—you are quite cured.

Nich. Cured! I am ruined. Oh! If I had but touched the thousand pounds, I would not mind the interest—perhaps 'tis not too late.

Ap. (*Examining the will.*) Sole heir, without reservation or restriction; huzza!

Nich. Sir, honourable sir, will you allow me to ask you one small favour?

Ap. What is it?

Nich. Only to delay mentioning this (*Sighing*) joyful discovery for a few moments. My master and I have a little account to settle, and I should like just to strike a balance before he knows what has happened.

Ap. Oh, I understand—we have bled you, and now you want to go and bleed him?

Nich. Just a little, sir.

Ap. With all my heart, old Nick. Devil claw devil.

Nich. O, thank you, sir.

Ap. But dispatch——

Nich. I fly, sir. [*Exit, hobbling.*

Ap. Now, with heels as light as our hearts, we'll away to Greville's.

Ple. Stop—stop for me, grandfather.

Ap. I beg your pardon, old one. Here take my arm—let your grandfather assist you. Upon my soul, I quite forgot you. [*Exeunt.*

SCENE III.

An elegant Drawing-Room in GREVILLE'S *House, illu-minated.—A Band of Music playing.—A number of Servants dressed in splendid liveries.*

Enter UNDERMINE *in great elation, joining the music in,* " See the conquering hero," *&c.*

Und. Approach! Is Greville gone?

Serv. Not yet, sir.

Und. Any of my guests arrived?

Serv. No, sir.

Und. Has the traiteur furnished a splendid entertainment?

Serv. Yes, sir.

Und. Let music usher in the guests. (*Music plays.*)

Enter APRIL, *singing* " See the conquering hero,"
&c. *flourishing the will in his hand; seeing* UNDER-
MINE, *he conceals it.*

Und. Zounds! he here.—(*To the Servant.*)—Don't
go away, sir.

(*Places the Servant between him and* APRIL.)

Ap. How do you do?

Und. How do you do? (*With alarm.*)

Ap. I have overcome my passion, and thought
better.

Und. Oh, very well—then 'tis all over?

Ap. Yes.

Und. (*To the Servant.*) You impudent rascal, how
dare you stand between me and my friend?—Be
gone, you scoundrel!—I thought you would see the
absurdity of my supporting Greville.

Ap. Oh yes; it would have been quite out of character.

Music plays. ROSTRUM, *singing* " See the conquer
ing hero," &c. *enters, leading in* EGERTON *and* ROSE
SYDNEY.

Ap. Hey-day! my ward here! why, girl—

(*Goes up to her, and they converse in dumb shew.*)

Und. (*To* ROSTRUM.) Come here—come here—
give me your hand, you dog—I suppose 'tis all settled.

Ros. It is—the wedding's over.

Und. I say, what will that old fool April say, I
wonder?

Ros. We shall hear.

Ap. (*To* MISS SYDNEY.) I understand. Mr Undermine, have you given our ward permission to
marry?

Und. To be sure I have.

Ap. If that be the case, my dear, you have mine.

Eg. Gentlemen, I thank you.

Und. He thank me! what has he to do with it? Oh! I forgot he helped you to this delicious morsel.

Ros. No, he did not; he helped himself—and what is more, persuaded a parson to say grace.

Und. Egerton her husband! did not I order you to marry her? Did not I bid——

Ros. You did bid, sir; but honour bid more.

Ap. I give you joy, my girl. You have chosen a noble fellow.

Und. Well, and I give her joy, for she has chosen a beggar.

Ros. On that point I beg to be heard. You remember you gave me a key—here it is.

Und. Well, sir?

Ros. It belonged, ladies and gentlemen, to an escrutoire, with a secretary drawer—pannels richly fineered—scrole pediment head—bracket feet—the whole finished in a workman-like manner, and well worth the attention——

Und. At the auctioneer again—Zounds! you are so fond of it, I dare say you would sell me.

Ros. Sir, I would knock you down with all the pleasure in life.

Und. But what of the key?—the key——

Ros. The key certainly opened the drawer you mentioned; and it as certainly opened a drawer you did not mention.

Und. What?

Ros. Be quiet. There I found a parcel of papers and title-deeds, which you must have put there entirely by mistake, my dear sir, because I perceived they belonged to Mr Egerton.

Und. Give them to me directly—I say, sir, restore——

Ros. Every thing to its right owner. Certainly—I don't wish to keep your, or any man's property—so, Egerton, there are your papers again—and, uncle, there is your key again—

Ap. Ha! ha!

Eg. What disinterested integrity!

Und. What damned rascality!

Ros. Oh fie! no, no.

Und. What is it then?

Ros. Management.

Und. Well, you have managed finely for yourself
however—I discard you. Had you followed my instructions, you would have been exalted—

Ros. To the pillory, I suppose.—No, sir, though
you don't scruple it to others, far be it from me to
rob *you* of your natural inheritance.

Und. I would have left you all I am worth.

Ros. What then? you forget all you are worth belongs to other people. When you were gone, they
would naturally ask me for their own, and how could
I have the face to refuse them?

Ap. Give me your hand. You have acted your
part nobly, and now 'tis my turn.

Und. All this I laugh at. Am I not possessed of
the Greville estate? Who has any thing to say on
that subject?

Ap. I believe I shall trouble you with a word or
two.

Und. I see Greville is about to depart, and I must
beg you will all follow his example.

Enter MR *and* MRS GREVILLE, SALLY *following with
a small bundle, and weeping.*

Eg. My best friends, allow me to present to you a
sister. By this gentleman's kindness, Maria, happiness
again dawns upon us.

Ap. (Aside.) And I will make it blaze with meri-
dian splendour.

Grev. Let us then leave this man to the full enjoyment of such reflections as his conscience may administer.

Ap. I beg your pardon a moment. Umph! Mr

Undermine, I hear doubts have arisen respecting the authenticity of the late Mr Greville's signature.

Und. (*With a confident smile.*) Indeed!—Sir, to shew my fairness, I'll leave this point to your decision. (*Shewing the will.*)

Ap. 'Tis genuine, it must be confessed.

Und. Must it so?

Ap. Any objection to my reading it?

Und. None.

Ap. Perhaps it may tire you.

Und. By no means. I think it remarkably entertaining.

Ap. (*Substituting the second will, reads.*) " I, Robert Greville, do declare this my last will.—To my only son, Charles Greville, I give and bequeath my forgiveness and my blessing, together with all my estates, real and personal."—Umph! that is very entertaining.

Und. Very—but I prefer the remainder—" Provided my said son"—go on—go on.

Ap. What do you say?

Und. 'Psha!—" Provided my said son has not contracted"—why don't you go on?

Ap. I don't see any thing like it.

Und. You don't, ha, ha! give me leave to direct your attention. (*Looks at the will, drops his hat and cane, and groans deeply.*)

Grev. What does this mean?

Ap. Mean!—That my young master, my friend, my dear Charles, is happy—that my old master is in Heaven, and that I am in Heaven. Two wills were made; by the last, which he endeavoured to suppress, you are sole heir, without reservation.

Mrs Grev. Is it possible?

Grev. How shall I express my gratitude for this discovery?—for giving happiness to my Maria?

Sal. And to me too. Oh, you are a nice old man!

Und. He must have dealt with——

Ap. Old Nick—You are right—I did—and here he comes.

Enter NICHOLAS.

Und. Ah, Nicholas, Nicholas!

Nich. Ah, master, master!

Und. A dreadful affair this!

Nich. Very shocking indeed, sir.

Und. Eh—zounds! I have given him a draft for a thousand pounds. *(Coaxingly.)* Nicholas—Come here, Nicholas. I am not angry. My consolation is, what's done can't be undone. I gave you a draft—

Nich. You did, sir. And my consolation is, what's done can't be undone.

Und. Indeed! but it will be of no use. I have no cash at my banker's.

Nich. Dear sir, what credit you have! They paid it without a word.

Und. *(Eagerly.)* You have not been—

Nich. Yes, sir—I just contrived to hobble there.

Und. You infernal! *(Gulping down his passion.)* Old friends should not quarrel, Nicholas:—Suppose we go home, and talk it over agreeably. I'll propose something reasonable.

Nich. It must be very reasonable.

Und. It shall. Gentlemen———*(Bowing.)*

Ros. What, bowing! You forget, sir, your own lessons.—Be erect, and I'll tell you how you may be so;—become an honest man, and on my life, that will make you hold up your head more gallantly than the first dancing-master in Europe can—depend on't, sir. Roguery is the worst trade a man can follow; for (to the credit of human nature) I sincerely believe, that where one fortune is raised by pursuing the devious mazes of chicanery, a hundred are acquired by walking in the simple path of industrious integrity.

Und. Indeed!

Nich. You had better stick to management!

Und. Management!—Oh, I have had enough of that.   [*Exeunt* UNDERMINE *and* NICHOLAS.

Ap. Now, being all as happy as heart can wish, come along with me, Sally. Good b'ye to you——

Grev. Where are you going, April?

Ap. To the kitchen. I have no notion of your houses, not I, where all the joy is confined to the drawing-room. Let there be degrees in every thing but happiness; and 'fore George, if any servant in this house be sober enough to wait on you at supper, I'll discharge him to-morrow morning.—Poor fellows! must not make them ill though. Never mind—Come along, Sally.

Sal. Oh, you are a nice old man!

                        [*Exeunt* APRIL *and* SALLY.

Ros. (To EGERTON *and* GREVILLE.*)* If I must have thanks, gentlemen, let me receive them here!— (*Kissing the ladies' hands.*) Happy fellows! you are to be envied.

Mrs Grev. So are you. We have *received* happiness, you have *given* it.

R. Syd. Your fortunes, sir, will be our peculiar care.

Ros. Thank you, dear ladies; but, with your permission, I'll stick to my trade.

And oh! could all my pray'rs but gain this lot.
To raise my pulpit nightly on this spot;
Then your poor auctioneer would prize his station,
While you vouchsafed one nod of approbation.
                              [*Exeunt.*

WHO WANTS A GUINEA?

A

COMEDY,

IN FIVE ACTS.

AS PERFORMED AT THE

THEATRE-ROYAL, COVENT-GARDEN;

BY

GEORGE COLMAN, THE YOUNGER.

DRAMATIS PERSONÆ.

Torrent,	Mr Munden.
Heartly,	Mr Chapman.
Hogmore,	Mr Waddy.
Solomon Gundy,	Mr Fawcett.
Barford (or Delamere),	Mr Kemble.
Jonathan Oldskirt,	Mr Simmons.
Sir Larry MacMurragh,	Mr Lewis.
Andrew Bang,	Mr Emery.
Carrydot,	Mr Davenport.
Henry,	Mr C. Kemble.
A Boy,	Master Horrebow.
Fanny,	Mrs Gibbs.
Mrs Glastonbury,	Mrs Mattocks.
Amy,	Miss Waddy.

SCENE—*Yorkshire, near the Coast.*

WHO WANTS A GUINEA?

ACT THE FIRST.

SCENE I.

An Apartment in HEARTLY'S *House.* HEARTLY *and*
HOGMORE *seated at a Table*—HOGMORE *smoking*
—*A jug of Ale at his elbow.*

Heart. Yes; an hour after midnight, the flames
had consumed two-thirds of our adjoining village.

Hog. Very bad fire last night, to be sure, Mr
Heartly.

Heart. Think, then, on the destitute situation of
its inhabitants.

Hog. They're in a pretty pickle, I warrant 'em.
My service to you. (*Drinks.*)

Heart. Come, come, Mr Hogmore, Providence
has bless'd you with abundance; and you must assist
me in my poor endeavours to succour our rustic
neighbours. The wealthy of this land forbid the
drops of disappointment to fall from labour's eye, and

rust the ploughshare.   Industry is the source of our
country's riches ; and English policy would teach
opulence to dry the peasant's tear, if English justice
and generosity did not continually prevent its flowing.

Hog. (*Smoking.*) Plaguy good tobacco this of
yours, Mr Heartly.

Heart. I am glad you like it.   But the poor cottagers' calamity—I am sure, Mr Hogmore, you feel
for them deeply.

Hog. Monstrous deep, for certain.   How much a
pound for this tobacco, Mr Heartly ?

Heart. 'Tis a present from a friend in London.
Now, as you are wealthy, Mr Hogmore, I trust you
will co-operate with me (whose means are circum-
scribed) to alleviate their miseries.

Hog. (*Taking the pipe from his mouth, and looking
at it.*) These are nice pipes, rabbit me if they ar'n't !
You have every thing mighty snug about you here,
neighbour Heartly.

Heart. But to the point in question.

Hog. Well, well—I pity the poor devils—I do indeed.   I looked out of my window last night, just at
eleven o'clock—Here's to you. (*Takes the jug.*)—I
was going to bed—Rabbit me, Suke, says I, to my
wife, what a blaze ! (*Drinks.*) Now, I say that ale
sha'n't be bad—So I shut the window, and Suke and
I bundled in.

Heart. You did ?

Hog. Ay ; for as I live a quarter of a mile off,
you know, we were all safe, and had nothing to hinder us from going to sleep as usual.   But you are
nearer to 'em : I warrant me you was in a fine pheese
about your moveables ! What was you doing about
that time, neighbour Heartly ?

Heart. At the time you were shutting your window ?

Hog. Ay.

Heart. I was then, neighbour, opening my door,

to give every relief in my power to the sufferers; and just as you were " bundling in," as you call it, at your home, I was inviting them to bundle in at mine.

Hog. (*Sulkily.*) Perhaps, Mr Heartly, I may be as charitable as you, though I can't speechify.—I I don't want eeling. I pay the poor's-rates punctually.

Heart. That, Mr Hogmore, is rather a feeling of the legislature, which enacts, in some cases, lest feeling should not prompt.

Hog. Englishmen don't want to be rous'd to feeling, Mr Heartly.

Heart. I never knew a nation more sensibly alive to it; but here and there, neighbour, an individual may nod; and our laws, vigilant in the cause of general good, search every corner where charity happens to slumber; then, giving her a jog, whisper to her to get up for the welfare of the community.— But, surely, Mr Hogmore, you will contribute to the relief of these sufferers ?

Hog. Not a souse—I've a wife and family.

Heart. That is the very reason why you should not refuse.

Hog. How do you make out that ?

Heart. Because a husband and father can best judge of *their* anguish, whose wives and children are starving around them.

Hog. So, then, I must strip my fire-side, to warm theirs ?

Heart. By no means. Our fire-sides are naturally our first care, but you are affluent—a rich man's superfluities are often a poor man's redemption; and you cannot conceive, neighbour, how much more cheerfully the faggot would crackle on your hearth, if you sent its fellow to save a family from perishing.

Hog. 'Tis my opinion there has been fire enough in the village already. However, there is a great man coming down among us, who is to smother us

5

all with guineas. He has bought the manor, they say,
and the old mansion, and the park—all the estate;
but, for all that, he may turn out at last as arrant a—

Heart. Softly—Mr Torrent is my friend.

Hog. Then let Mr Torrent, if that's his name, take
care of his tenants. For my part, I know the duties
of humanity, without a lesson. As to the tender feelings of a father and a husband, my family shall never
want good clothes, food, or physic ; and I say it without boasting. As to good will to my neighbours, I
never wronged a man of a brass farthing.—In short,
I pay my bills punctual—I do the upright thing—
I've finished your ale, and I wish you a good morning.   [*Exit.*

Heart. This fellow now has obtained respect in
his neighbourhood, by a dry performance of duty to
every body, without a grain of feeling for any body.
How I detest your worldly moral man, who is just as
honest as the law directs, and just as kind to his family as decency requires. He paces through the
proprieties of life as a bear moves a minuet ; and is
an upright brute of good carriage and decorum : But
surely, ere Society established rules, Nature traced
her precepts upon the yielding tablet of the human
heart, and, with a glowing hand, she wrote on it—
" Compassion."

Enter SOLOMON GUNDY.

Now, Solomon Gundy, how are they going on in the
village ?

Sol. The conflagellation has been dreadful—all
smother and rubbish. 'Tis the greatest calamity to
our hamlet since my father was schoolmaster.

Heart Don't get on the old subject now. We'll
wave the schoolmaster, till we have more leisure.

Sol. De toot mong cure :—though 'twas under him
I made all my deficiency in the English tongue before I went to France, and learnt to *parly voo.*

Heart. Well, well, your father has been dead these eleven years.

Sol. Dead as Malbrook. He's *more,* as the French say; which, in English, means he is *no* more. So, peace to his remainders!

Heart. Now, tell me of the cottagers.

Sol. Most of 'em ruined, and nothing to turn their hands to.

Heart. Poor fellows!

Sol. Ay; all poor indigenous pheasants. Thanks to industry, I've better luck. I snatched the board from over my door when I was burnt out, and ran off with it under my arm. Here it is. (*Reads it.*) "Rats and gentlemen catched and waited on, and all other jobs performed by Solomon Gundy."

Heart. You have still a livelihood, Solomon.

Sol. Edication and travel fit a man for any thing, and make him a *jolly garsoon.* You'd hardly think it, but at fourteen years old I could read.

Heart. You don't say so?

Sol. Fact, upon my *patrole ;* and any sum in arithmetic, that didn't demand addition, substraction, or multiplication, I looked upon as a *petty kick shose.*

Heart. Why, you are a perfect prodigy of genius.

Sol. I believe I have picked up a little; and the captain of the cutter on our coast, that traded in brandy, taking me to Dunkirk for six months, perhaps has given me a *jenny see quaw,* to which the commonality seldom perspire.

Heart. Who was that captain, Solomon?

Sol. Quite the gentleman—an *Ellygong,* as the French say; and felt such a sympathy against vulgar custom-house officers, he'd have no dealings with 'em; so he always smuggled.

Heart. But I hope no lives are lost among our neighbours?

Sol. Not a Christian soul, except the old village bull, and a porker. Their loss is to be implored, though they are but quadlipeds. But a number of accidents.—Jacob Grull, the hump-backed taxman, jumped out of his cock-loft into the water-tub, poor reformed creature! If we hadn't heard him bawling " Fire !" he'd have been drowned. And fat Mrs Doubletun, scrambling down a ladder in her husband's short frock to the farm-yard, was so peck'd at by the cock-turkey, she won't be able to *assayez voo* for a fortnight.

Heart. These calamities are not very serious ; but a number of buildings are, doubtless, destroyed.

Sol. All down but the house of deception for travellers, and the contagious brick messages beyond it. We worked hard to save 'em, laboured like gallypot slaves.

Heart. I will do all in my power to be of service, in the general calamity.

Sol. We know that. You are full of *amour proper* for your neighbours, as we say at Dunkirk. Nobody doubts the malevolence of your heart.

Heart. An hour hence I shall be among you in the village.

Sol. An hour! Then your *amee*, who has been overturned, will be put out of patience.

Heart. A friend of mine overturned in the village !

Sol. Plump into the horse-pond—shot from a chaise out at elbows, with four posters. Don't be frightened, he fell too much in the mud to be hurt.

Heart. You're sure he's safe ?

Sol. As his most sanguinary friend could wish.

Heart. What's his name ?

Sol. Can't tell. He's at the Spread Eagle. The carriage broke into twenty *morso's*. I helped to drag it. No coach-maker by, I offered to impair it. The great man was daub'd, and looked like a hog. No servant with him, I scraped him. He read my board as I was rubbing him down. Wanted to send you a *billy*—no messenger at hand—I've brought it. He

gave me a guinea ; I called him an angel ; he bid me
run like a devil; I told him I would ; so I have, and
there's the contentions. (*Gives a letter.*)

Heart. (*Reading the letter.*) " Dear Heartly, I
have just *tumbled* into my estate.   Let none of the
villagers know who I am till I get to my house.   I
hate fuss—Don't say I am a rich man.   Come to me
at the alehouse.   JOHN TORRENT."
He arrives just in time to assist his tenants in distress ;
but I dread his impetuosity, and carelessness of dis-
crimination.   Ever in haste to make people happy,
he defeats his own purpose.   His heart runs away
with his head, and he often produces most harm when
he shews most benevolence.   I'll wait on the gentleman, Solomon, directly.

Sol. That's just what I should like to do myself.
Speak a good word for me to him, your honour.
Pauvre Solomon Gundy, just burnt out—kills vermin,
and dresses gentlemen.   I know he'll attend to your
imprecations.

Heart. There's no hurry—he'll stay in the neighbourhood some time.

Sol. Will he ? Take a *chateau*, perhaps.   I'm up
to every thing about a house.

Heart. Well, well, follow me, and we'll see what
can be done for you.

Sol. Thank your honour. I'm very graceful.   If I
am but burnt into a good place, after all, this fire
will turn out as fine a *few de joy* of misfortune to me,
as could possibly happen.   I follow your honour.
                                        [*Exeunt.*

SCENE II.

A Room in the Village Inn. TORRENT *discovered ;*
AMY *is attending him.*

Tor. And so your name is Amy, and you are
daughter to the Spread Eagle ?

Amy. Yes, your honour. We are in a sad pickle,
to be sure.

Tor. Ay, ay; all owing to the fire, as you say.

Amy. Yes, your honour. It broke out unawares ;
but we hope you'll excuse it. (*Curtseying.*)

Tor. It carries its own apology. Whereabouts did
it begin ?

Amy. It began about ten o'clock, your honour.

Tor. Umph ! In what part of the village, my dear ?

Amy. Oh !—At the corner of the—but you're a
stranger—it was as you go by the—but perhaps your
honour knows the horse-pond.

Tor. Very well :—I've just come out of it.

Amy. There's a power of mischief done ; and all
in a moment, as one may say. Lord knows, when I
was stepping into bed last night, I little thought that
ruination was just a-coming !

Tor. Like enough. Ruination, my dear, often
comes, when giddy girls like you least think about it.

Amy. But what a thing if it had happened to our
house, now my poor father's bed-ridden !

Tor. What ! bed-ridden !—Poor fellow ! Is he a
good father to you ?

Amy. The best in Christendom. He's the kindest
neighbour, and the kindest parent—But we have
had a power of misfortune, and he's nigh broken down
in the world,

Tor. I'm glad of that.

Amy. Glad ?—Dear !

Tor. Here's an honest man, up to his ears in misfortune, and I'm his landlord ! Come, that's charming ! I have something to begin with. You take in the weekly paper, you said ?

Amy. Yes, your honour.

Tor. Fetch it me. (AMY *is going.*) And, hark ye —your father is *very* poor and *very* sick, you say ?

Amy. Very, indeed.

Tor. Then mind, if he recovers this bout,—I'll do for him.

Amy. Do for my father ! Bless us !

Tor. If I don't, hang me.

Amy. Why, sure, you—

Tor. Go, and get me the paper.

Amy. Dear ! what a strange old gentleman !

[*Exit.*

Tor. This fire is delightful ! It has destroyed two thirds of my poor tenants' houses. Huzza ! I shall have the pleasure of building them up again. They shall be as merry as the day is long. Their dirty village shall rise in splendour, like a phœnix out of a crow's nest ; the hod and trowel shall catch their tears ; and I'll block up all their grief with brick and mortar.

Re-enter AMY (*with the paper.*)

Oh ! the newspaper. Is the messenger come back from Mr Heartly ?

Amy. Not yet, your honour.

Tor. Damn it ! how slow he is !

Amy. Slow ! There's not a cuterer young man in the village than Solomon Gundy.

Tor. How the devil do you—O ho ! I smoke—a sweetheart of yours, I perceive.

Amy. He, he ! Yes, your honour ;—but don't you tell ; for, till he gets twenty pounds to set us a-going, 'tis a secret to every body but father, and the rest of our village.   [*Exit.*

Tor. Twenty pounds!—He shall have—No, damn it, I won't marry people rashly neither; for they may hate me for it afterwards, as long as they live. I was apprehensive, when I left London, that I had acquir'd an overgrown fortune there to little purpose; for I see no good in getting an overgrown one, but to make those around us happy. It would have been an irksome thing to me, now I have left the bustle of business, to have found every body's happiness ready made to my hands;—but, thank Heaven, my tenants are as miserable as their best well-wisher can desire!

(*He sits down to read the newspaper, with his back turn'd to the door, through which enters* BARFORD, *without observing* TORRENT, *and throws a small bundle on the table.*)

Bar. Rest there, my whole property!—the remains of many a wreck, rest there!

Tor. (*Starting up.*) Eh! Zounds! Wreck! He looks like a gentleman. Pray, sir, how came the wreck of all your property to be tied up in such a cursed small pocket-handkerchief?

Bar. By what right, sir, do you inquire?

Tor. By the right that lugg'd me out of the horse-pond—the right of running to any man's assistance who seems to be stuck in the mud.

Bar. (*Turning from him.*) Pshaw! Sir, you are obtrusive.

Tor. Why, it was rather rude to be reading the newspaper in my own room, when you chose to walk in, and interrupt me.

Bar. This is the parlour of a village inn, sir, where 'tis the custom to huddle people together indiscriminately. 'Tis an emblem of the world: men mingle in it from necessity, as we do now, till they part in dislike, as we may do presently.

7

Tor. We seem to bid fair for it; for I detest misanthropy.

Bar. 'Tis the opium to our affections; an antidote
to the drivelling unwillingness dotards feel to be swept
from hypocrites who have profess'd to regard them.

Tor. Opium—and antidote!—You've dealt with a
damn'd bad apothecary. Hatred to mankind is Lucifer's own laudanum; and whenever he coaxes a
Christian to swallow it, he sends one of his imps to
shake the bottle. All men hypocrites! Zounds! here's
a doctrine! So, then, love, and friendship, and—

Bar. Love and friendship are, at best, Life's fading roses; but reject the roses, and you escape many
a thorn.

Tor. How should you like to lose your legs?

Bar. Why my legs, sir?

Tor. They are part of the fading blessings of life,
like love and friendship; but you may have the gout.
Reject your legs, and you escape many a twinge in
your great toe.

Bar. I have suffer'd deprivations enough already,
sir.

Tor. I give you joy of them; for, according to your
own account, they must make you very comfortable.
But you have deprived yourself of that, which your
worst enemy's malice should never have taken from
you.

Bar. What is it?

Tor. Universal benevolence: the chain of reason
in which we all, willingly, bind ourselves. Nature gave
us the links, and civiliz'd humanity has polish'd them.

Bar. And how often are the links of Reason and
Nature broken by sophistry and art!

Tor. I'm sorry for it. I know there are rascals;
but the world is good in the lump; and I love all human kind; kings, lords, commons, duchesses, tallow-
chandlers, dairy-maids, Indian chiefs, ambassadors,
washer-women, and tinkers. They have all their claims

upon my regard, in their different stations; and, whatever you may think, hang me if I don't believe there are honest attorneys!

Bar. You *have* been fortunate in the world, I perceive.

Tor. I have been fortunate enough in my temper to keep the milk of human kindness from curdling.

Bar. By having no acids squeezed into it.

Tor. Plenty: Who hasn't? But, when you were put out to nurse, curse me if I don't think you sucked a lemon! You have a fine field to fatten in, upon others calamities here. Only look out. (*Pointing to the window.*) Pretty havoc from the fire! There's a house, now, that would just suit you. It sticks up by itself, gloomy and gutted, in the midst of the rubbish.

Bar. That *was* my residence, sir; my refuge, as I hoped, during the remainder of my life, from ingratitude and treachery.

Tor. Did—did—did you live in that house?

Bar. Eight months ago, I enter'd its door, to take possession of an humble lodging; and last night, I leap'd with difficulty, amidst the flames, through its window.

Tor. Out at—that window?

Bar. Yes; with that wreck of property, on which you have been pleas'd so much to question me.

Tor. My dear sir, you are an unfortunate man: I have behav'd like a brute, and I beg your pardon.— (*Seizing his hand.*)

Bar. I feel no anger, sir. (*Coldly.*)

Tor. Damn it, then, you despise me. I know you must, for I have treated you cruelly; but, as you have taken offence at all the world, don't think me too contemptible to be left out of the number. Pray, be angry with me, then shew me you forgive me by telling me how to serve you—I happen to be rich.

Bar. And I happen to be poor; but I will always be independent, and will accept no favours.

Tor. That's right : but I have taken a house in the neighbourhood—Dine with me every day. That will only be doing me a favour, you know.

Enter AMY.

Amy. Here's a letter for you, sir. (*To* BARFORD.)
Bar. To me ! Who should write to *me ?*
Amy. 'Tis from the parson of next parish.

[*Gives the letter, and exit.*

(BARFORD *opens the letter, and reads to himself.*)
Tor. (*While* BARFORD *is reading.*) Independent! That's the proud lie of a decay'd gentleman—It sometimes gives truth the ear-ache ;—but it always gives pity the heart-ache,—and, to prove that I don't believe you, (*Going to the table,*) here goes my pocket-book into your bundle ! There ! (*Stuffs it in.*) You are, now, a hundred and fifty pounds nearer to independence than you imagine.

Bar. (*Folding up the letter.*) This bears the semblance of kindness, and 'tis from a clergyman. His profession commands respect. I will wait upon him, and decline his offer.

Tor. (*Hastily.*) What is it? (*Checks himself.*) I beg pardon ; but I——

Bar. His house, sir, if you must know, in my calamity.

Tor. That's right—don't take it—cut the parson, and come to me.

Bar. I fix in no residence, sir, which I cannot call my own.

Tor. Well, you may call mine your own ;—and bring the parson with you :—I like that parson.

Bar. Excuse me; (*Takes his bundle from the table ;*) but, before I leave you, sir, one word, which, I think, I owe you.

Tor. I won't take back a shil—I mean, you don't owe me a syllable.

Bar. Pardon me, and I must pay it.   Your impulses, apparently, proceed from benevolence ; but your impetuosity may render you an offence to the sensitive, and a dupe to the designing.   Farewell, sir.   [*Exit.*

Tor. That advice is a little too late to a man at fifty. My impulses are like old radishes ; they have stuck so long in the soil, that, whenever they are drawn out, they are sure to be hot.

Enter HEARTLY.

Ah! Heartly! my dear old friend! give me your hand! I hav'n't shaken it these ten years. I'm so glad to see you, that I—Well, and—Zounds! my heart's so full, that I had better hold my tongue.

Heart. Moderate yourself! I need not tell you how happy I am to see you.

Tor. Well, old school-fellow! I've closed all accounts of business at last : but we have a deal to think about :—The estate, and the tenants, and the fire, and all that. We must go to work directly, old Franky!

Heart. (*Smiling.*) I thought you had done with business.

Tor. Pshaw! this isn't London business. That is a constant fatigue. This is country bustle, that keeps the mind from stagnation.—But, damn it, how well you look!

Heart. And you wear well, my friend.

Tor. No, no ; city smoke and a counting-house ; —but, with your air, in a fortnight, I shall get as fat, and as red about the gills, as a cramm'd turkey. By the by, did you meet any body, as you were coming in, with a bundle under his arm?

Heart. You mean Mr Barford.

Tor. That's his name, is it? What is he?

Heart. Nobody can tell. I fancy he has serv'd in the army. He avoids the gentlemen in the neighbourhood, and is a mystery to the villagers.

Tor. He seems a strange fellow.

Heart. You have conversed with him, then?

Tor. Yes—He appears to be a gentleman; but I'm afraid he's poor.

Heart. I hope you gave him no hint of such a fear.

Tor. Why, yes, I did—One or two, plump to his face.

Heart. Which, no doubt, offended him.

Tor. Yes; and so I dropp'd the rest behind his back.

Heart. Oh! I begin to perceive.—And how were they dropp'd?

Tor. Pshaw!—Why—into his bundle, if you must know.

Heart. To no small amount, probably; and without investigating his character.

Tor. I hadn't time.—He was in want—I may never see him again; and, in such a case, 'tis better to take our chance for a knave, lest caution should let honesty go away unsuccour'd.

Heart. Here you may have chanced right; for I fancy he only affects misanthropy.

Tor. I fancy so, too.

Heart. I have many reasons to think so; and one of the strongest is, his only having that small bundle with him.

Tor. How so?

Heart. He relinquished the material part of his property, to save his landlord's infant son.

Tor. Zounds! Then his landlord is a rascal. Not run the first to his own child, when the house was on fire!

Heart. My dear, impetuous friend! a father, who was, three days ago, struck with a palsy, occasioned, perhaps, from grief for his wife's recent death, finds some difficulty in running, even to his child. This was the landlord's case, Barford knew it, when the house was burning beneath him.—He rushed to the poor cottage-garret, clasp'd the sleeping baby under one arm, and, with the poor bundle (which you saw) under the other, leap'd to the ground.

Tor. And where's his landlord?

Heart. Barford recollected him, as soon as he had placed the child in safety. A ladder was at hand; he ascended it to a room, from which the smoke was rolling in columns; he dragged the father through the flames, and seated him by his boy! But this man professes misanthropy.

Tor. He lies! he lies! God bless him! he lies! I'll run after him, and stop him from going to the parson. (*Running out.*)

Heart. (*Detaining him.*) Stay, stay; he is not leaving the neighbourhood. He has a bed here, I find—and you have enough to do besides.

Tor. Why, that's true: the man of the house is sick—a good fellow;—and I must think of Amy, who is in love with Sólomon Gundy.

Heart. (*Laughing.*) Ha! ha! ha! These are minor considerations, when you have the distress of a whole village to remedy: but for Solomon Gundy I must be an advocate.

Tor. Do *you* recommend him?

Heart. He is an industrious fellow, and a proper object.

Tor. I know him; he's burnt out—I read his board. —He's a rat-catcher—I'll make him my valet de chambre directly.

Heart. Softly:—What may your present household consist of?

Tor. Why, some I shall find, as you wrote me word, on the spot. Two footmen I sent on before me to the house, to avoid fuss. A cook was pack'd off a week ago. A housekeeper I expect every hour. That's all for the present.

Heart. Who recommended the housekeeper to you?

Tor. Her distresses.

Heart. So! I hope she is a steady, methodical woman. I think, my good friend, you will want one of that description.

Tor. Why, distress generally makes people think; and when 'tis accompanied by virtue, it should never want a place in a rich English family.

Heart. What is her age?

Tor. Nineteen.

Heart. Rather young for a steady housekeeper What threw her in your way?

Tor. An advertisement in the newspaper.

Heart. I see—" To the affluent who can feel."

Tor. Psha! damn it, now you are sneering at me. If you had read it, it would have broken your heart! I've never seen her, but my agent in town tells me she's a good girl, and as handsome as an angel.

Heart. I wish you joy. A handsome housekeeper of eighteen will give you *eclat* in the county.

Tor. Pooh! nonsense! How can you be such a blockhead! You know I'm too old for—Psha! and as to my character, I don't care a button for the rural backbiters.—Come, let's go up to the house to dinner.

Heart. Why didn't you go there first?

Tor. To avoid the cursed parade of an entrance upon an estate. I hate to be huzza'd like a return'd member, or the man in armour, at lord-mayor's show. Walk with me up the hill, and let me slink into my splendour. But first we'll call Solomon Gundy. Solomon.

Enter SOLOMON GUNDY.

Solomon Gundy, can you keep a secret till you get to the top of a hill?

Sol. A secret is a sacred deposition, and I never revulge.

Tor. Then I'm going to live on the hill, that overlooks the village.

Sol. The manor-house !

Tor. Yes ; 'tis mine, and you shall be my servant.

Sol. Shall I ? Then, damn my board, when I've got such a lodging !—(*Throws the board away.*)

Tor. Go out, just three paces before me. You sha'n't talk to Amy. I know you love her ; and I'll never trust a man with a secret, out of my sight, when there's a woman in the case. The moment you get to the house, you shall have a horse, to ride for a doctor, to visit the sick Spread Eagle ; then, if your cursed jabber should raise a clamour, by calling the neighbourhood about my ears, dam'me if I won't order my cook to baste you. Come along, Heartly.

[*Exeunt.*

ACT THE SECOND.

SCENE I.

A cross Road.

Enter OLDSKIRT *and* FANNY.

Old. Well, I hadn't been out of the bills of mortality since I set up shop ; and now we're in Yorkshire, a hundred and seventy miles from Whitechapel. This cross lane is as boggy as Tothill Fields, and as rough as Cranbourne Alley pull'd up for new paving.

Fan. We cannot be far from Mr Torrent's now.

Old. Far ! We've waddled a good three miles of bad way, since we left the stage at the corner of the high road. Miss Fanny, ar'n't you monstratiously tired ?

Fan. Not in the least.

Old. I'd carry the bundle for you myself; only, ten to one, I shall tumble and daub it.

Fan. Indeed, I want no assistance, and the plough-man, we just met, says it is but half a mile further to the manor-house.

Old. At any rate, I'm glad we're out of the coach. Six inside—two squalling children in lap, and a point-er as big as a hog. At every jolt, the sleepy quack doctor plump'd his fat head smack in the pit of my stomach; and, when I popp'd my mouth out o' window to fetch breath, the long-legg'd Scotchman on the roof gave me a kick in the jaws with his heels.

Fan. But, my dear sir, I—I have a favour to ask.

Old. A favour ?

Fan. Consider, I am going to Mr Torrent's in a humble situation.

Old. Ay—as housekeeper. You ought to have a palace of your own. If fortune isn't quite blind, I wish, for your sake, she'd send for some eye-water.

Fan. As it is, let me persuade you not to appear with me at the house.

Old. What ?

Fan. I only mean, not immediately.

Old. Oh ho ! I smell a rat ! What, then, Miss Fanny, you're beginning to feel asham'd of Jonathan Oldskirt, the little remnant-seller from the back of St Clement's ?

Fan. How can you fancy so ?

Old. Why, you are a gentlewoman born ; and I

suppose I am but a stiff-rump'd jockey, to go to a grand house : the members of our club call'd me old Deadwig ; and last week, when business took me a trot up Bond Street, a pert puppy, in pantaloons, ask'd me after my uncle Noah, and hop'd all my relations were well in the ark. But I didn't think Miss Fanny would have turn'd up her nose at me, neither.

Fan. Can you think me capable of—Sir, you have been my preserver.

Old. I can see—'tis the way of the world—shake hands with a shoe-black, when your boots are dirty, and kick him as soon as they're shin'd.

Fan. How can you wrong me so?

Old. Póoh! What could have made me leave shop at sixes and sevens, but to see you well plac'd? I've been bump'd and bruis'd in the stage, into as many colours as a tailor's book of patterns.—And, now we're within half a mile of the house, you are for shuffling me off in the middle of the mud.

Fan. Hear me, sir—recollect what I have already suffered, and do not add to my sorrows. In an obscure corner of Jamaica, after fifteen years of penury and affliction, it was my lot to receive the last breath of a wretched mother, who expired, heart-broken, in my arms.

Old. I wish you'd hold your tongue, Miss Fanny. I'm a soft old fool, and that plaguy Jamaica story is, somehow, as bad for my eyes as all the pepper and spice of the island.

Fan. You have rous'd me, sir, to recapitulate, and I will proceed. Her dying hand plac'd mine in Henry's. Plung'd in poverty, like myself, he promis'd to be my protector and future husband. He sail'd with me for England, where he had friends to solicit, and we cherish'd expectation. On the day of our arrival in London, he was snatch'd from me, (Heaven knows how!) and left me destitute, even of hope.

Old. He was crimp'd, I'll lay a penny—I always said so. Poor, dear soul! you've gone through a great deal.

Fan. I have, now, endured the worst, sir; for you—you have upbraided me——Sir, without your humanity, I must have perish'd.   An ingenuous bosom can feel no keener wound than the charge of ingratitude from such a benefactor.

Old. Then, why won't you let me go with you to the place? You know, I've set my heart upon seeing you done justice by.   Don't be cast down.—I look on you, Miss Fanny, as my own child.   I shall never forget how you came to me first, as my lodger.

Fan. Pennyless.

Old. Why, at the end of a week, when I ask'd you for rent, you told me so, and fell a-crying.   Now that, Miss Fanny, was the first thing that made me take a liking to you.   When a tradesman is never to be paid, you can't think how much more satisfactory your way is to him, than being told, month after month, by a great man's porter, that the fellow must call again.   Come, let us go on to the house.

Fan. Pray, oblige me! pray, be patient with me! To present myself, in my new office, with a person, determin'd, as you are, to fix there for some days, would be thought presuming.

Old. But what the plague am I to do?   Stick here, in the dirt, like a skewer in a marrow-bone?

Fan. There appears to be a village to the left yonder, scarcely a quarter of a mile distant.

Old. I see a few chimneys, and a deuced deal of smoke.

Fan. No doubt you will find an inn in the place. Wait there till evening, then come to me.   I shall then have spoken to Mr Torrent, concerning your care and kindness for me.—'Twill be better so on both our accounts—indeed it will.

Old. Ah! bless you, Miss Fanny! you can per-

suade me to any thing.   But how will you get safe?
We're so far from town, it must be monstrous dangerous.

Fan. Oh! I have no apprehensions.

Old. Well, I see you are resolv'd and desperate.
Heaven bless you! This is a wild country for a Lon-
doner! and, somehow my mind misgives me, I shall
never see you again.

Fan. (*Smiling.*) There is no danger, believe me.

Old. Farewell!——(*Going, returns.*) Miss Fanny,
my will's in the left hand pigeon-hole of my bureau,
in the back room, up two pair of stairs. I've neither
chick nor child;—so I've made you sole executrix
and legatee.—Jonathan Oldskirt may cut up richer
than some people think.   Heaven knows the depth
of these mud lanes!   I measure but five foot three;
—and if I happen to be missing, it will be but
respectful to send somebody to dig for me.

[*Exeunt severally.*

SCENE II.

A spacious Hall in a Country House.   ANDREW
BANG *discovered asleep in a Chair.—A violent
ringing of Gate Bell is heard.*

Enter SIR LARRY MACMURRAGH.

Sir Lar. (*Without.*)   Hollo!—If there's nobody
within hearing, cannot you say so?—(*Enters.*)   As
I am an Irishman, I believe every living creature in
this house is dead; for I've pull'd the bell for them
this half-hour, like a sexton. (*Sees* ANDREW.)   By
my finger and thumb, I see a nose!   I'll pull that,
and, perhaps, I'll get an answer.—(*Pulls his nose.*)

And. (*Bawling and starting up.*) Awgh! awgh!

Sir Lar. (*Bowing.*) Sir, my compliments of the sleeping season. There's the handle of the gate-bell. (*Throws it to him.*) Hang up the handle of your own ugly mug in the room of it, and plenty of visitors and runaway rings to you!

And. Bless us, zur!—Seeing you be a stranger, how did you get in?

Sir Lar. Like a tom cat.—I walk'd in at the outside gate, over the wall. Where's my lord's steward?

And. Mr Carrydot be taking a morning's ride, zur.

Sir Lar. Upon business?

And. Na; upon Dobbin.—Can't ye wait a bit, zur?

Sir Lar. I'll wait a little; but if he hasn't done airing in six weeks or two months, the chance is, I'll be gone from the premises.

And. Two months!

Sir Lar. I will;—my estate to nothing.—So, 'tis an even bet, you see.

And. Be you come to stay at my lord's so long, zur?

Sir Lar. Don't be asking questions—I'm our master's—Lord Alamode's friend;—I'm here, *incog.*; —and if you are after blabbing it to a soul here, in Yorkshire, that I'm Sir Larry MacMurragh of Ballygrennanclonfergus, by the honour of an Irish baronet, I'll crop your ears as short as St Thomas's day. Never you tell secrets.

And. I never do, zur, but when I'm fuddled.

Sir Lar. I must bribe this sot. Don't you go to the alehouse, and there's something for you to drink. —(*Gives money.*)

And. Thank ye, zur.

Sir Lar. Mind—let nobody learn my name of you.

And. I defy 'em—It's so plaguy long, I shall never learn it mysen.

Sir Lar. Here, now—(*Putting his hand in his purse.*) Go you, and give this to my two post-boys at the gate.—I paid for the chaise beforehand.

And. Ees, zur.

Sir Lar. Tell the rascals they crawl'd like a couple of flies in treacle. They would have had half-a-crown each for driving fast; but now there's only a seven-shilling piece between 'em; and damn the rap more do they get.

And. (*Aside, and going.*) He, he! if they'd ha' stood still, dang me if he wou'dn't ha' given 'em half a guinea.

Sir Lar. And, hark ye, what family has my lord left in the house?

And. There's na' but ould steward, Mrs Glastonbury the housekeeper,—and I, zur.

Sir Lar. And who are you, you Judy?

And. Andrew Bang, my lord's game-keeper.

Sir Lar. You and I'll have a slap at my lord's partridges, Mr Bang.

And. Be you a good shot, zur?

Sir Lar. A good shot! I'm an Irishman, you devil.

And. Have they much practice that way, zur?

Sir Lar. A pretty deal with a single ball, Mr Bang.

And. (*Going.*) Shoot partridges wi' a single ball! You ha' been used to shoot wi' a long bow, or I be plaguily mistaken.   [*Exit.*

Sir Lar. I wonder is Mrs Glastonbury pretty. A smart housekeeper is a mighty convenient article for an Irish gentleman, in an empty house, all alone, by himself. Oh! this old-fashion'd man must be the steward.

Enter CARRYDOT.

Is it Mr Carrydot I'm talking to?

Car. I am very sorry, sir, I wasn't at home to receive you.

Sir Lar. Short speeches, my dear creature, for we're upon business. Just run your spectacles over this small bit of a letter.—(*Gives it.*)

Car. 'Tis my lord's hand, I see.

Sir Lar. You may say that.

Car. (*Opens the letter, and reads.*) " Mr Carrydot, the bearer of this is my dear and intimate friend, Sir Lawrence MacMurragh of—of Ballygrennanclonfergus."

Sir Lar. That's my estate in Ireland.

Car. You'll excuse me, Sir Lawrence, but I find it rather difficult to get through that name.

Sir Lar. Never you mind the name ;—I've found it mighty easy to get through the estate.

Car. (*Reading on.*) " You will shew the baronet every attention, while he does me the honour to remain in my house. His situation requires secrecy, which you will scrupulously observe, if he condescends to place you in his confidence—Yours,

ALAMODE."

Sir Lar. Now I'll place you in my confidence, ould gentleman, before you can throw sixes. The short and the long of the story is, I'm dish'd.

Car. Dish'd, Sir Larry ! Pray what is that ?

Sir Lar. 'Faith, I'm always bother'd at derivations ; but, according to the most learned Greeks on the subject, 'tis agreed that dishing comes from dashing.

Car. I don't comprehend.

Sir Lar. Sure, 'tis as easy as nothing at all.— Only, when it happens in the city, you're a duck ; but at the west end of the town, you're a pigeon.

Car. I protest, I am still in the dark.

Sir Lar. This is it in the west, do you see—Run to London, give grand dinners, and set your champagne going like whisky—Sport your carriages, belong to the clubs, lose to gamesters, borrow of Jews, bet upon boxers, keep a stud, keep a Dolly.

Car. A Dolly! Bless us, what is that?

Sir Lar. A sort of moveable in a house, sometimes of mighty little use to the owner.—And so, you see, when you have completely over-run the constable, you must try to out-run the bailiff; and then you're dish'd, after the newest receipt of the present season.

Car. I fear, Sir Lawrence, you may have been duped at play.

Sir Lar. Duped! What, Sir Larry MacMurragh! Sure, and wasn't I ruin'd, at last, in the most honourable manner, by an intimate friend?

Car. Ruin'd in an honourable manner, by an intimate friend? I can't conceive how that can be.

Sir Lar. That all comes of your ignorance of fashionable life, Mr Carrydot. 'Twas my friend, your own natural lord and master, that finish'd the job.

Car. Lord Alamode?

Sir Lar. His own dear self;—fair and easy, about six in the morning. The run had been against me pretty smart, and I grew desperate like. Will you set ten thousand, says I, against the remaining third of all the estate I have in the world at Ballygrennanclonfergus? With all my heart, Sir Larry, says my lord. Seven's the main, says I. Throw, says he. Crabs, says I. 'Tis mine, says he. Then damn the luck on't! says I; for, Heaven bless you, my bosom friend, you have made me a beggar, like a man of honour as you are, all at a stroke.

Car. A stroke of thunder, I should think!

Sir Lar. Upon my soul, it was much more like an earthquake; for it swallow'd up three thousand acres, and a great big family-house, before you could say shamrock.

Car. I am sorry my lord should have done this.

Sir Lar. Indeed, and I sympathise with yourself: but rather he than another; for mind how friendly.

Now I have won the last stick and guinea you have, my dear friend, says he, you'll want a house to be out of the way of your creditors. You are welcome to hide yourself at mine, in Yorkshire, till you can turn yourself about.

Car. Did my lord, then, advise you to fly from them, Sir Larry?

Sir Lar. Sure, and he did; for you can't beat it into their brains, that a man of honour must ruin twenty tradesmen sooner than not pay one man of honour who has ruin'd *him.*

Car. But I should hope, Sir Lawrence, that with the assistance of friends, and the exercise of economy—

Sir Lar. Economy! Only look at that book. (*Gives him a pocket-book.*) See how methodical I was when I first went to London. All my expences set down:—only you'll see, at the bottom of a leaf, I cou'dn't cast up the sum total.

Car. (*Reading.*) " To the sweeper of the crossing in Bond Street, one shilling." This is methodical indeed, Sir Lawrence.

Sir Lar. Oh! I was resolute to be mighty particular.

Car. " To sundries,—seven thousand pounds." That is not so mighty particular, Sir Larry.

Sir Lar. I was busy that day. I lump my expences, now and then, when I'm bother'd.

Car. " To a collar for Lady—half-a-guinea."

Sir Lar. A female of Dutch extraction—a pug, that belonged to me once, Mr Carrydot. That's a cheap article.

Car. " To a diamond necklace for Eliza,—nine hundred pounds."

Sir Lar. A female, whose extraction I could never make out; but she belong'd to me once, Mr Carrydot. That article's a trifle dearer.

Car. A great deal indeed!

5

Sir Lar. No matter for that. They both ran away from me one day, and I advertis'd them the next. " Whoever will bring Lady without a collar, or the necklace without the lady, shall be handsomely rewarded."

Car. " Promised my tailor four hundred pounds." Is that to be put down as an actual expenditure, Sir Lawrence?

Sir Lar. Sure and it is. Isn't a promise to a tailor fashionable payment all the world over?

Car. " Lost to my best and dearest friend, all I have in the world."

Sir Lar. That's the end of my fashionable atlas for the year eighteen hundred and five; and it saves a great deal of trouble in casting up the articles.

Enter ANDREW.

And. I ha' pitch'd all your bundles out o' the chaise, zur, into our court-yard.

Car. The court-yard! Why, there's a soaking shower.

And. That's why I left 'em there, zur. I'll take 'em in the moment it's over, you may depend on it.

Sir Lar. Let him manage it. He's a careful person, I see.

And. Ees, I be, zur. If I hadn't rummaged chaise, they'd ha' drove off wi' summut.

Sir Lar. Was it my little shaving-case?

And. Na;—'tware a little boy.

Car. Drove off with a little boy!

Sir Lar. By the powers! that's my man-servant. I'd forgot him—clean and clever.

And. He was fast asleep, in a laced jacket, up in the corner.

Sir Lar. And how did you wake him?

And. Why, zur, first I pull'd his nose; and then, says I, " Zur, my compliments o' the sleeping season."

Sir Lar. But has he taken out the sparring-gloves, and the pistols, and the German flute, and Hoyle's Games, and the usquebaugh, and the rest of my creditors?

And. Here they all be, zur.

Sir Lar. By my soul, I levanted from London in such a hurry, I can't tell if one parcel is itself or another! What did he say is that thing like a wafer-box in your hand?

And. It's all your ready cash, Sir Larry.

Sir Lar. And what's that big bag at your back, you devil?

And. Boy says it be all your unpaid tradesmen's bills, Sir Larry. Which room be the bag and the baronet to be put into, Mr. Carrydot?

Car. The blue chamber. Get a fire,—see every thing arranged.   [*Exit* ANDREW.
Well, Sir Lawrence, every thing in my power, to render my lord's house comfortable to you, it will be my duty to perform. I will go and give the house-keeper directions for your accommodation. (*Going.*)

Sir Lar. You'll mind to sink my name in the neighbourhood, you know.

Car. Rely on my discretion, Sir Larry. I am as faithful to my lord's friends as to my lord himself.
                                         [*Exit.*

Sir Lar. That you may be, and cheat 'em most confoundedly, steward-like. I'll be mighty dull in this house. The worst of us fine fellows of high style is, when we are left by ourselves, we have hardly any resource, but Hoyle's Games and a German flute.

Re-enter ANDREW BANG.

Have you a fire in my room yet, Mr Bang?

And. I think so, zur; for it be plaguy full of smoke.

Sir Lar. Hark ye, is that Mrs Glastonbury, your housekeeper, a smart sort of good-looking creature?

And. He, he!—She be round and plump-like.

Sir Lar. Plump! Well, well,—sure a person may be pretty for all that.

And. I know that, zur;—I'se plump mysen.

Sir Lar. I think she may help me out in passing the time. I think I fancy her a neat, round, inviting Yorkshire Hebe, that—

Enter MRS GLASTONBURY.

Mrs Glas. Your room is ready, sir; and I hope I shall make all things agreeable.

Sir Lar. And are you Mrs Glastonbury, the housekeeper?

Mrs Glas. At your honour's service. I'll shew you all the pictures to-morrow, sir. This house was erected in King William's time. I was born in it, sir.

Sir Lar. That you were, the day before it was built, I'll be bound for you. (*Aside.*)

Mrs Glas. This way, if you please, sir.   [*Exit.*

And. Don't you go to be roguish wi' our house-keeper, zur. Her reputation be tender, you do know.

Sir Lar. Then, upon my soul, it isn't at all like her person:—for, any how, that's tough.

And. You'll always find her mighty civil to ye, zur.

Sir Lar. 'Faith, and I'll return the compliment; for damn the bit shall she complain of my being rude.

And. He! he! he!

Sir Lar. Oh, curse you—and are you laughing? Shew me the way, you sneering spalpeen!   [*Exeunt.*

ACT THE THIRD.

A Still-Room in LORD ALAMODE'S *House.   Bottles on Table, &c. &c.*

Enter MRS GLASTONBURY *and* ANDREW BANG.

Mrs Glas. Bless my stars!—He's up the house and down the house! skipping, jumping, boxing, swinging the dumb-bells, blowing the flute—all within this half-hour.   For my part, I think he's a madman.

And. So do I.—But he do say he's na' but a baronet.

Mrs Glas. And who is he? Where does he come from?

And. That's tellings.—He ha' put I upon honour.

Mrs Glas. Put you upon a pin's head! I wouldn't give a farthing for your honour.

And. He gi'd I nine and sixpence.   I said nought but liquor should make I betray un.   Be that cherry-bounce you ha' got on table, Mrs Glastonbury?

Mrs Glas. Tell me all, and you shall have two glasses.

And. Fill away then.   (*She fills a glass, and gives it to him.*) Why, then you must know his name be— Here's wishing you well through this world's trouble, and very soon out on't. (*Drinks.*) Fill up t'other glass. (*She fills and holds it.*) His name be Sir Some-

body Summut, as long as your bills ; and—gi's t'other
glass—he do come from a place fit to break more
teeth than you ha' left in your head.

Mrs Glas. And that's all you have to discover ?

And. Ees—don't you tell. (*A horn is blown without.*)

Mrs Glas. What's that ?

And. He be gi'ing a tantivy upon your old rusty
French horn, that do hang up in the hall.

Mrs Glas. My legacy !—I wouldn't have it hurt for
fifty pounds. He'll turn the whole house topsy-turvy.

And. Wool he ? It will be a comical sight then to
walk into your room.

Enter SIR LARRY MACMURRAGH.

Sir Lar. The rain's done, all but drizzling, Mr
Bang, and we'll pop at the partridges. Oh ! and is
it there you are again, Mother Glastonbury ?

Mrs Glas. Marry come up !—Mother !—I never
was called so before, sir.

Sir Lar. Then it's too late in the day with you
now to hope for a true title to that appellation. And
whose is that horn hanging up in the hall, old gentlewoman ?

Mrs Glas. Old gentlewoman ! Why, sir, that horn
belonged to my dear deceased husband, who was
huntsman here ; and, if you must know every thing,
my late lord gave him a pair of them.

Sir Lar. And did your late lord do that ?

Mrs Glas. That he did—bless his memory for it.

Sir Lar. That's right : you mayn't meet such another good-natured person again in a hurry.—Mr Bang,
isn't that sweet lady a most infernal sour old woman ?

And. Nation ! Plague her a bit, do, zur. Say my
lord ha' hired another housekeeper.

Sir Lar. Be asy, Bang. Mrs Glastonbury, I—
you're a fine bustling body—But now I'm come here,
mayn't I chance to fatigue you a small matter ?

Mrs Glas. Perhaps you may, sir. (*Sulkily.*)

Sir Lar. That's what I'm thinking—And you might be even with me, you know—So I told my friend, Lord Alamode, I had just made bold to order a new housekeeper in the room of you.

Mrs Glas. What !—I've been here these five-and-forty years, and if my lord himself offered to discharge me, I wouldn't turn out, and that's flat.

And. Dang me, but he ha' set the old one's back up now !

Enter CARRYDOT.

Car. Sir Lawrence, a young person at the gate inquires for you.

Sir Lar. A young person? By the powers, a sucking bailiff !

Car. 'Tis a woman, Sir Lawrence.

Sir Lar. A woman! And is she handsome, Mr Carrydot?

Car. That, sir, it is not in my department to determine.

And. Let I go, and look at her, zur. I be reckon'd a tightish judge.

Sir Lar. Bang, don't you bellow. (*Stopping his mouth.*)

Mrs Glas. I see what's going on. The family mansion will be made quite scandalous.

Sir Lar. (*Putting her aside.*) Hold your tongue, you punchy lady ! Mr Carrydot, I respect the roof of my bosom friend; and, if the young person isn't fitting to come under it, by St Patrick ! rather than let her in, I'll marry Mother Glastonbury.

Car. Her appearance is most respectable, sir ; but I think there must be some mistake.

Sir Lar. Explain me the rights of it, Mr Carrydot. Don't bother, now, you two keepers, game and house.

Car. She has inquired for the gentleman who is
just arrived on the estate.

Sir Lar. That's myself, you know.

Car. Doubtless, sir; but she says that she is come
here, engaged by you, as housekeeper.

Mrs Glas. I won't budge an inch. I'll stay here,
and tear her eyes out.

Sir Lar. (*Apart.*) Mr Bang, how will I get rid of
that tremendous old tabby?

And. Bide where you be, zur; I'll ha' her out
in no time.   [*Exit.*

Mrs Glas. Service is no inheritance, that's a sure
thing; but if my deceas'd husband was alive, he'd—
(BANG *plays upon the French horn without.*) Bless
me! what's the matter now?

Sir Lar. It's Mr Bang playing " Variety is charming," on the horn of your deceas'd husband. (*The horn
falls with a crash.*)

Mrs Glas. (*Screaming.*) Augh! he has broke it all
to pieces. (*Runs out.*)

Sir Lar. I'll thank you now, Mr Carrydot, just to
send in the young woman, and keep out the old one.

Car. I shall, Sir Lawrence. But I had almost forgot—The young woman desir'd me to give you this
card, which will instruct you whence she came; and
then, she says, you will recollect who she is. [*Exit.*

Sir Lar. (*Reading the card.*) " Jonathan Oldskirt,
remnant-seller, back of St Clement's."—What will I
make out of this? Sure a young woman, come here
for housekeeper, can't be Jonathan Oldskirt, from
the back of St Clement's.—" Deals for ready money
only."—By St Patrick, you are little likely to get me
for a customer!

Enter ANDREW BANG.

And. I think, zur, I ha' blow'd out Mother Glastonbury.

Sir Lar. And who is it you have bid to be asking after me, to bother her?

And. Come, that be a good un! You do know who it be better nor I, zur.

Sir Lar. Look at this card. Mr Bang, can you read?

And. I left off schooling, zur, afore I got to that part o' my edication.

Sir Lar. And you don't know the back of St Clement's?

And. Na, zur; nor his face neither.

Sir Lar. Look ye, Mr Bang, you rapscallion! if you have been sending any female here according to my order, which I never gave, you have taken an unpardonable liberty with my name,—provided she's ugly.

And. Why, how could that possibly be, zur? Putting the case, I had got your order in earnest, who could I gi' it to as would mind it?

Sir Lar. Not mind my order! Would you make me believe every body here is like my banker?

Enter FANNY.

Oh, Venus! here's a creature! Are you the person that came from the person, that—

Fan. Sir!

Sir Lar. By the powers! the dazzle of her eyes has blinded my utterance! Are you the person, my dear, come here as housekeeper?

Fan. Yes, sir; I am come from London in obedience to your commands.

Sir Lar. My comma—Seat yourself, my jewel. Mr Bang, get some refreshments. Fly, you devil!

Fan. Indeed, sir, you distress me.

And. (Going to the table.) Mother Glastonbury ha' left out her brandy bottle. I'll fill the young woman a bumper

Fan. *(Doubtfully.)* I hope I have not mistaken the house, sir.

Sir Lar. Oh,'faith, you are under no mistake. This, my dear, is the house that—the house that Jack built, for all I know to the contrary. *(Aside.)*

And. *(Presenting a bumper.)* Take a drop o' this, miss; it will comfort you up, like.

Fan. Not any, I thank you.

And. Then here's wishing you joy o' your safe arrival. *(Drinks it.)*

Fan. Then this, sir, is the manor-house?

Sir Lar. Is this the manor-house?—Isn't there the game-keeper?—Only ask him—Sure he shou'd know.

And. *(Aside to* SIR LARRY.*)* It be half a mile up the hill, on the hill, zur.

Sir Lar. Lie through half a mile up hill—it won't tire you.

And. I wool.—Ees, miss, this be the manor-house.

Fan. *(To* SIR LARRY.*)* And are you the master of the house, sir?

Sir Lar. Ask the game-keeper again, my little one.

And. What be I to say, zur? *(Aside to* SIR LARRY, *who holds up half-a-crown.*) Hem!—Oh! half-a-crown—Yes, miss, this be master.—He be landlord in fee. *(Takes the money.)*

Fan. I had been taught to expect a gentleman of a more elderly appearance, sir.

Sir Lar. Would you be after my parish-register, my darling?—But, *je me porte bien*, as the French say;—and, standing by the side of this ordinary man is a mighty advantage, you know.

Fan. You will think me very presuming, sir; but I imagined also that my employer was a native of England.

Sir Lar. Is it just a little twist of the tongue you are noticing?

Fan. I confess it is, sir.

Sir Lar. Oh—pooh—that's Yorkshire, my darling.

Fan. Yorkshire, sir!

Sir Lar. That's why I took this estate. I'm partial, you see, to the county I was born in.

Fan. To say truth, I am ignorant of dialects here, sir. Except the last six months at London, my whole life has pass'd in Jamaica.

And. That's where the rum do come from.

Sir Lar. Hold your tongue, you—

Fan. But, if your accent be of this country, sir, your game-keeper, or my ear deceives me, cannot be Yorkshire also.

And. Na, miss—I'm Irish.

Fan. Forgive the questions I ask, sir.—A heart, like yours, that can compassionate female distress, slightly sketch'd as mine was, in a newspaper, will account for my apprehensions.

Sir Lar. (*Aside.*) A newspaper! You'll find many an honest man, every day, mighty tender-hearted, in a case like yours.

Fan. I have found only one, except yourself, sir.

Sir Lar. Only one! and who is he?

Fan. The person who had the interview with your agent in town, sir, and engag'd me in your service.

Sir Lar. And what's his name, my little one?

Fan. I sent you in his card just now, sir.

Sir Lar. (*Looking at the card.*) Oh, I remember—Jonathan Oldskirt.

Fan. Your first notice of my advertisement was address'd to me, under cover, to his initials, sir.

Sir Lar. His initials.—Yes—that's—(*Referring to the card*)—that's *I, O,* my dear.

Fan. Yes, sir, you writ me word you had enter'd them in your pocket-book.

Sir Lar. Yes, you may say that—There's *I, O,* in my pocket-book;—with a damn'd sight of thousands at the tail of it. (*Aside.*)

Fan. His house has been my asylum, sir.

Sir Lar. And didn't you find the asylum rather dark and dingy, my dear, at the back of St Clement's?

Fan. Oh, sir, gilded roofs escape the eye of affliction; but the smile of welcome, the tear of pity, strike forcibly upon the heart, when benevolence shelters misery;—and the meanest cabin true charity inhabits affords gratitude a palace.

Sir Lar. It's my notion you love this same Jonathan Oldskirt, my darling.

Fan. Dearly, sir;—I love him as a father: Anxious for my welfare, he hopes you will not think him intrusive, by requesting to be admitted here a few days, till he sees me properly settled.

Sir Lar. And is he come with yourself?

Fan. He would not presume so much, sir, without your permission; for which he waits in the neighbouring village.

Sir Lar. (*Aside.*) I wish, with all my soul, he was waiting in Constantinople.

Fan. He will be here in the evening, to know if he have your leave to remain, sir.

Sir Lar. Oh, 'faith, let him take leave, and welcome. Mr Bang, you'll do the honours to Mr Jonathan Oldskirt.

And. Ees, zur.—*(Apart.)* I ha' lock'd Mother Glastonbury up in china-closet, putting by her husband's horn; when Mr Oldskirt do come, I'll lock he up wi' her, for company.

Sir Lar. Do that thing—My dear, I—I—the family is a little unsettled just now, you see; so you'll take a mutton-chop to-day with me, you know.

Fan. With—with you, sir!—I heard, indeed, you were but just arrived on the estate—the family unform'd, and—but still, I—

Sir Lar. Damn the soul's in the house but ourselves, good or bad, except the old steward, and that ill-looking game-keeper.

Fan. Indeed!—this is very strange! (*Aside.*) Sir, I—

Mrs Glas. (*Without.*) Let me out—I insist upon it.

Fan. Bless me! what's that?

Sir Lar. That? Oh! that's a rumpus.—You must know, among other live lumber, I found an old house-keeper on the estate, and—and she's lock'd up.

Fan. Good Heavens! this is very alarming.—Lock'd up, sir?

Sir Lar. Yes; she's crazy, poor soul!

And. Don't ye be frightful, miss.—It ben't often here we do lock up the housekeeper.

Sir Lar. Make yourself easy, my darling. The game-keeper shall take you to t'other side of this great big house, and the devil the bit will you be plagued with that woman's bawling. I'll come to you, and we'll go over the apartments, and we'll—Shew the way, Mr Bang.

And. This way, miss.

Fan. Go on—I know not what to think: but if I betray my suspicions, I—(*Aside.*)—Go on.

[*Exit* ANDREW, *conducting her.*

Sir Lar. Whether, now, is this one of the deserted ladies, who are unhappy in the Morning Post every day, thirteen to the dozen, or real virtue in misfortune? Any way, she'll procure me an agreeable companion, in the long afternoons. If she's kind, we'll make a merry duet; if she's immaculate, I'll have no bad *tête-à-tête* with my own conscience,—for dismissing innocence, with its due honours, when I had it so much in my power.   [*Exit.*

SCENE II.

A Room in the Manor-House.

Enter TORRENT *and* HEARTLY.

Tor. It shall all be done, slap dash—on the spur
of the moment. By this day se'ennight, every tenant,
man, woman, and child, shall meet me with a grin of
joy, and a face as round as a dumpling. They shall
all buz in sunshine, like a hive of bees.

Heart. Are the drones on your estate to profit
equally by the heat of your munificence?

Tor. Pshaw! Why won't you let the poor devils
be happy, if they can?

Heart. Certainly you have a right to command here;
but I think you are too hasty in such indiscriminate
kindness.

Tor. Too hasty in doing good to the poor!—No,—
no;—come;—there is a warm adviser, old boy, in that
case, that tells me I am right.

Heart. Who is that adviser?

Tor. My heart.

Heart. 'Tis too warm for an adviser—'Twere better to consult a cooler.

Tor. Yourself, I suppose?

Heart. No; you can spare *me*, at times. 'Tis one
you cannot live without for a moment.

Tor. Who is that?

Heart. Your head.

Tor. I should make an awkward figure without it,

that's certain.—But what's the use of a consultation about relieving want, if I can afford it ?

Heart. To distinguish between an ardour and a rage for charity ; to regulate patronage, that we may not injure society at large, by squandering relief upon distress'd knaves ; and to prevent one of the worst national principles affluence can inculcate, that want is to place Virtue and Vice upon a level.

Tor. Well, but there are some points that speak for themselves. The poor widow, for instance, who left her petition at the house against my arrival. Her case is notorious to all the parish.

Heart. Yes—and to half the next, they tell me.

Tor. Why, you hard-hearted Turk ! She has five little children,—and without her husband.

Heart. That was well known before she was a widow.

Tor. What ?

Heart. That she had five children without her husband.—She's a scandal to the place.

Tor. Indeed !—At all events, the children must be brought up to some honest employment.

Heart. There I agree with you. To train an infant of the abandon'd to industry is a noble mode of serving the public, by saving the individual.

Tor. I am glad I have got you to agree to something at last. You'll allow, too, I was right to make a present just now to the thatcher ?

Heart. Clearly ;—if you were certain he is a worthy object.

Tor. Where's the doubt ?—Isn't he disabled from work ?—Wasn't his hand scorch'd last night at the fire ?

Heart. He is used to that.

Tor. Used !—how ?

Heart. He was burnt in it at the last assizes.

Tor. Curse me, if I think you have any thing decent in the parish ! You have decoyed me into a neigh-

bourhood of ill fame ; and I must go about at noon-
day, like Diogenes, with a lantern, looking for an honest man.

Heart. Oh ! he was a cynic, or he might have
found plenty, without the help of a candle.

Tor. Hang it ! after all, it matters little how my
money goes. My young brother, mad Tom, as I
used to call him—was the last relation I had in the
world, and he has been gone many years. If he
hadn't been a bad subject, rambled away from all his
friends, turn'd soldier, and died abroad, nobody
could hear exactly where or how, he should have in-
herited my fortune. Well, it can't be help'd, and—

Sol. (*Without.*) I'll denounce you to my master
in a *petty momong.*

Tor. There's that infernal Solomon Gundy!—the
rat-catcher, whom you have made my valet-de-cham-
bre.

Heart. *He's* honest, I'll be sworn.

Tor. Confound him!—he does nothing but run
about and talk. He's all legs and mouth, like a
Dutch oven upon a trivet. He knocks the furniture
about as he does French and English, and makes as
much havoc in a house as in a language.

Enter SOLOMON GUNDY.

Well, what have you been doing this last half hour ?

Sol. A multiplication of affairs !—I've laid the cloth,
fed the mastiff, comb'd your best wig, tapp'd the ale,
hunted the pigs from the pleasure-ground, and clean'd
the parlour windows.

Heart. A pretty good half-hour's employment.

Tor. But why will you be in such a devil of a
bustle ?

Sol. Bless your honour ! I'm very jealous to learn,
till when you'll pardon my defection. Mr Thomas
is so condescending as to say he'll do nothing at all,
that I may get versified in all the work of the house.

Tor. Is he?—Then I'll tell you how you are to dust my coat.

Sol. Commong? as they say at Dunkirk.

Tor. Put it on Mr Thomas's back, and beat it as hard as you can with a horse-whip. Tell him 'tis my order. What was that smash I heard just now in the hall?

Sol. A fraction.

Tor. A vulgar one, I'm sure, if you were concern'd in it. I heard you letting down the great lamp by the pulley—so, I suppose, you have broke it?

Sol. Into a thousand anatomies. It came down with so much voracity, that it forced my head through the glass bottom, and wedged me in down to my shoulders.

Tor. Fine mischief you have been doing already.

Sol. Don't be concern'd: I'm very little hurt. A slight confusion in my head, but soon heal'd, your honour.

Tor. Curse me if the confusion in your head isn't incurable! And where is Thomas?

Sol. Tasting the ale.

Tor. Then I hope 'tis sour.

Sol. He thought so the third jug—so he's drawing a fourth, to be certain.

Tor. I've a great mind to be plagued with that drunken rascal no longer.

Heart. Why have you been plagued with a drunken rascal at all?—Nobody but yourself would keep him a week.

Tor. That's the reason I have kept him these seven years. He'd starve if I turn'd him away.

Heart. That's *his* affair.

Tor. No, it isn't: 'tis the affair of a sober woman and two squalling brats, who must starve along with him.

Sol. Ah! you've got a *cure,* as the French say.

Tor. Curse the French!—What brought you in here ?

Sol. I came to say that——

Tor. But stop—First remember to keep that sot out of my sight during the rest of the day. Let him come to my chamber as soon as I rise to-morrow, and I'll lecture him when his head aches.

Sol. What time do you get up ?

Tor. Nine.

Sol. Not till nine ?—Then, before I shave you I'll catch a few rats.

Tor. This fellow will lather me with arsenic ! Now why did you come in?

Sol. With a message.

Tor Deliver it.

Sol. I came to denounce that a gentleman in the hall is——

Voice (Without.) Solomon Gundy !

Sol. That's Mrs Cook's voice.—The jack's down. —I'll be back *dong le momong*, as they say.   [*Exit.*

Tor. An active booby !—He is as provoking as a bad barometer; his quicksilver only causes confusion.

Heart. Nay, give him a fair trial.

Tor. I intend it:—But where is your grand recommendation ? the person you writ to at London, to come down and lay out my grounds ?

Heart. He was to have been here yesterday.

Tor. Is he clever ?

Heart. Very; and as cheap as any dirt he has beautified.

Tor. I don't mind expence, if he has taste ; but if he throws Chinese bridges over a dry English ditch, Solomon Gundy shall kick him into it. I never heard of him.

Heart. Few have.—He is a man of talent and acquirement, but modest, even to shyness; and of too simple manners to make a fortune, as many bustlers do without one tythe of his ability.   His mind is like the landscape he adorns; the height of its polish has not disturb'd the quietness of nature.

Tor. He is just what I want. I hate to hear fashion cry up an architect, or a painter, or a playwright, as the only man, to the degradation of all others. A fury for individual artists pinches the arts; and when people have patronage they should always draw modest genius from obscurity.—But why isn't he here?

Heart. I think there must be some mistake—You dine late—I must leave you for half an hour to go into the village; and I will make inquiries about him at the inn.—(*Going.*)

Tor. Heartly——

Heart. Eh?

Tor. The Spread Eagle has got the gout in his stomach.

Heart. I intend calling there.

Tor. Aren't his liquors very bad?

Heart. Execrable.

Tor. I've laid in some famous old Madeira.

Heart. I shall taste it at dinner.

Tor. If you don't mind a little bumping behind you, perhaps a bottle in each of your coat-pockets may do the poor fellow a service.

Heart. I'll take care of him, depend upon it.

[*Exit.*

Enter SOLOMON GUNDY.

Sol. A man in the hall wants your ear.

Tor. My ear?

Sol. Yes—your *orell.*

Tor. What's his name?

Sol. I forgot to ask:—that was a little *forepaw,* as the French say.—I'll run and——(*Going.*)

Tor. Zounds! come back; and stand still, if you can!—Did you ask his business?

Sol. As I am but a menial, I thought it might flavour of curiosity.—But he comes from London.

Tor. From London?—Oh! Heartly's friend that's to lay out the ground.—I'm glad he's arrived.——Doesn't he say he comes recommended to me?

Sol. He says a person, now in the house, was to give you some intimidation.

Tor. Ay, ay, 'tis he: desire him to walk in.

Sol. Shall you want me again till I wait at dinner?

Tor. No, I hope not.

Sol. Then I'll bait my traps, just to *passy le tongs,* as they say. [*Exit.*

Tor. I'm glad the surveyor is come. We'll go at it ding dong!

Enter JONATHAN OLDSKIRT.

Oh, pray come in! I have been expecting you, and am very happy to see you.

Old. Then Miss Fanny has mention'd me. (*Aside.*) I should be sorry to intrude, but——

Tor. Intrude!—Nonsense. Merit never intrudes; and you have just been mention'd to me by a person I sincerely regard and respect.—Sit down.

Old. Regard and respect! How pretty he talks of Miss Fanny already! (*Aside.*) Why, sir,—(*Both of them sitting*)—the long and the short on't is, I had set my heart upon coming.

Tor. Had you heard a good account of the situation?

Old. A friend or two told me it was a situation for any body that wanted one, to jump at.—" But," says I, " though prospects are good, my advice is wanted, and I had better be on the spot, to see how I may mend them."

Tor. Certainly. The only way, I suppose, to mend the prospects, is to be on the spot.

Old. Well, I hope you don't think I have come up, on bad grounds.

Tor. In that I must bow to your opinion. You must be a much better judge of any grounds you come upon than I am.

Old. (*Aside.*) The sweetest temper'd man I ever met with!—Ah, sir, we might be of much service between us :—and I have great hopes; for, to say truth, I am prodigiously pleased with what little I have seen of your manner.

Tor. Why, the manor, they tell me, isn't a bad one; but there's room for improvement.

Old. Indeed I think it vastly agreeable.

Tor. Then, on the whole, you don't dislike the place?

Old. In my opinion, the place bids fair to turn out all I could wish.

Tor. Well, well, we must lay our heads together, how to make it better.

Old. Begging your pardon, that will depend upon the master.

Tor. Pooh! if you mean money, I don't mind that.

Old. Why, money is an object in a place to be sure; but good treatment is a prime matter with me.

Tor. Treatment? Ay, true;—as the poet says—
" In all, let nature never be forgot :"—We mustn't have too much labour.

Old. That's a good hearing : for she's very delicate.

Tor. " But treat the goddess like a modest fair !"

Old. The goddess !

Tor. " Nor over-dress"——

Old. That would be ridiculous.

Tor. " Nor leave her wholly bare."

Old. (*Starting up.*) Dam'me if I'd stand by and suffer such a thing for the universe !

Tor. (*Rising.*) This man's an enthusiast in his business. He'll do! We'll begin our operations betimes to-morrow morning. Are you an early riser ?

Old. First up in the house, this thirty years.

Tor. Indefatigable in your profession, I dare say.

Old. I was always fond of my business. When I was a boy, I had the watering-pot in my hand by day-break, and had generally done sprinkling before a soul was stirring.

Tor. The watering-pot!—So—began with the lowest rudiments of his art, I suppose, and was a common gardener—(*Aside.*) Well, application added to genius is always sure to rise—And 'tis amazing how much we have mended in your line, within the last century. Quite another taste. Hardly a remnant of the old style to be seen.

Old. Now and then a remnant of that kind comes in my way, but very scarce.

Tor. So much the better—Our forefathers were too formal;—too stiff by half;—no grace, no ease, no sweep;—they could never boast any thing like the lawns of the present day.

Old. Lawns are a nice article, and brought to amazing perfection, that's certain.

Tor. I see we shall agree in our notions on all points. We'll talk more about it, when the cloth is removed. You'll dine with me of course. I have only Heartly.

Old. Dine with you? Bless me! that honour is too great.

Tor. Why, where the deuce wou'd you dine?

Old. With your leave, as long as I stay, I'll take my victuals in the housekeeper's room.

Tor. (*Aside.*) Zounds! he is modest even to shyness, indeed, as Heartly says. You are to do as you like, but——

Enter SOLOMON GUNDY.

Sol. There's a man in the hall——

Tor. Wants my *other* ear, I suppose. What's his name?

Sol. Mr Barford, of our village.

Tor. The gentleman I met at the Spread Eagle, who was burnt out?

Sol. Yes;—one of the unhappy incendiaries.

Tor. Shew him into the breakfast-parlour.—And conduct this gentleman to the housekeeper's room— (*To* OLDSKIRT.) But suppose you let him take you into the park first—Do—perhaps you'll catch a hint.

Old. (*Aside.*) Catch a hint!—Bless me! I'm more likely to catch a cold, this rainy day.—By all means, whatever you please.

Tor. Attend the gentleman, then, Solomon. We shall meet by and by, you know.   [*Exit.*

Old. I'm always at your commands—(*To* SOLO-MON.) Shew me to the housekeeper's room at once.

Sol. That's *tooty fay imposseeble.* My master has laid his conjunctions upon me to take you a *prome-nade.*

Old. (*Bowing.*) Thank you, sir. Now, whether this foreigner is going to take me out of doors, or into the housekeeper's room, I wish I may be burnt if I can understand.   [*Exeunt.*

ACT THE FOURTH.

*An Apartment in the Manor-House—*BARFORD *discover'd.*

Bar. The wealthy man takes his time:—but poverty, it seems, must always wait the leisure of the rich. Oh! I hear him coming.

Enter TORRENT.

Tor. Ah! Mr Barford! this is kind! you are come to dinner, as I requested.

Bar. I am here, sir, upon business.

Tor. Well, we'll settle it after our bottle, and——

Bar. Pardon me; I——

Tor. But why didn't you bring your friend the parson? I respect the cloth, and there's a plum-pudding.

Bar. Look at this pocket-book, sir. (*Putting it into his hands.*)

Tor. 'Tis a—hem!—'tis a mighty neat one, indeed.

Bar. You certainly recollect it.

Tor. I—I think I have seen a clasp of this pattern before.

Bar. Nay, sir, I know it is yours, and I must insist upon restoring it to you. There are bank-notes to the amount of a hundred and fifty pounds. See if they be right.

Tor. Pshaw! I'll tell you what—If you come to cut
my throat, for trying to do you a favour, you are too
late. I could have quarrell'd with you to your heart's
content, at first, for your doctrines, till I saw they
arose from disappointments. I am always inclin'd to
affront a surly hater of man; but never able to offend,
nor be offended, by a man in misfortune.

Bar. You mistake the motive of my visit, sir. I
came to thank you; but there is something, beyond
a poor man's pride, which forbids me to accept of
your assistance.

Tor. 'Tisn't misanthropy, though you make such
a boast of it.

Bar. You cannot penetrate my sentiments.

Tor. Better than you yourself, perhaps;—and,
with all your pride and hatred, I have a great mind
to send you on a message, and you will skip for joy
at the office.

Bar. Sir!

Tor. Carry this pocket-book to your palsied landlord, with his little boy, whom you rescued from the
fire, at the risk of your life; and ask your feelings,
by the way, whether you hate your fellow-creatures.

Bar. (*Eagerly.*) Give it me. I—No—(*Checks
himself.*) He is an humble son of labour. Whenever
you can remove distress, without wounding sensibility, you must not lose the pleasure of drying a tear
with your own hand. But how should you know
that transaction?

Tor. Because the world isn't so bad as you pretend
to think. If there are too many to chatter tales to
a man's disadvantage, there are enough to proclaim
a fact to his credit; and one steady sound of Candour's clarion is heard through a thousand squeaks
of Scandal's penny trumpets. But how came you to
know, to a certainty, that this book is mine?

Bar. You forgot that the inclos'd memorandums,
and your own written name, (which had I perceiv'd

11

first, I should have search'd no further,) must lead
to a discovery.

Tor. Confound my stupidity!—The next pocket-
book I buy, I'll make a *nota bene* in it, never to forget remembering my memorandums.   However, it
has brought you here, and bids fair to make us better
acquainted.—And there's my friend Heartly, and
myself, and—come, come—we'll try to make this
country pleasant to you.

Bar. Perhaps, Mr Torrent, when you know my
history, you are the last man who would endeavour
to make any country pleasant to me.

Tor. Hey! the devil! I wish to make any body
comfortable but a downright rogue; I—I am sure
you can't be that character.

Bar. I have punctually discharged all moral obligations, sir.   I have serv'd, too, in his majesty's
army; I have retired from it with unblemish'd honour, and so I mean to retire to my grave.

Tor. Then you'll want no flourishes on your tomb-
stone.   A homely chisel chipping out plain duties,
faithfully performed to king, country, and relatives,
beats the best poetical epitaph I can remember. 'Tis
a blunt question to ask,—but you see that's my way
—Who are you?

Bar. One who, by the intelligence you have given
him this morning, is willing to disclose himself.

Tor. I have given!

Bar. I once possess'd a moderate independence:
youthful ardour threw me into the army, and I was
order'd abroad.   At the time of my departure, the
hand of the woman I almost ador'd was given to me
in marriage by the friend I most lov'd.   That friend
was an officer in our regiment, who, having no resource but his profession, shar'd my purse, as he
shar'd my confidence.

Tor. I like that sharing.   When an officer is independent, every little bandy-legg'd drummer in his

regiment should at least be, once in a winter, a pair of stockings the better for him.

Bar. My wife resolv'd to be the partner of my voyage. Flush'd with the hope of fame, and ardent in my country's cause, I gaz'd from the deck upon my native cliffs, without one sigh as I receded from them; for I had the wife of my bosom on one side, and the friend of my bosom on the other.

Tor. I wish I were young—I'd marry, and go into the army, to-morrow morning.

Bar. Mark the reverse.—After five years residence in the West Indies, the friend, whose need had been supplied by my unsuspecting love, seduc'd the innocent he had given to me at the altar; and, at one blow, struck two of the keenest wounds upon his benefactor's heart, the heart of man can suffer.

Tor. Damn him for a scoundrel!

Bar. The guilty fled together. I pursu'd, and overtook their carriage. The bosom traitor threw out his sword, unsheath'd, and exclaim'd he was ready, on the instant, to give me satisfaction.

Tor. What? By—Oh, true—I had forgot:— The modern notion of satisfaction is, that the injur'd is to enjoy a chance of being murder'd by his injurer.

Bar. The hilt of his sword stuck deep in the soil of the road, while the blade pointed upwards to that heaven which had witnessed his villainy. In leaping out, he fell upon it; it pierc'd his body, and he expired at my feet.

Tor. And by almost the only sword that would not have been disgrac'd by ridding the world of such a monster. Who was he?

Bar. Your brother.

Tor. My bro—I—You—So, then, it seems he died at last, by—I don't mean to insult you by being shock'd at his death; but he was my brother, and I can't help it. What became of your wife?

Bar. We had a daughter, four years old. The wretched woman hurried from the scene of death, to give a last kiss to her little one, before she shrunk from the eye of an outrag'd husband ; but, while the smiling baby twin'd its arms about her neck, a mother's tenderness urg'd her to add to a wife's cruelty; and, as she rush'd from my roof for ever, she bore away my infant.

Tor. Pray, say no more :—he was my brother, but i'm afraid he deserv'd to——

Bar. Deserv'd! Oh! Probity, Honour, Domestic Peace! how often are your sacred bonds rent asunder, and how lenient is law to the offender !—If the famish'd criminal be executed, who purloins a little food to preserve life, what sentence can be too severe for the libertine wretch, who has plunged his friend's family in anguish, to gratify his passions!

Tor. You have too much reason, I believe, to abhor my brother's memory.

Bar. He has disgusted me with the living, but I wage no war with the dead ; although his death ruin'd my fortunes, as his life destroy'd my happiness.

Tor. Your fortunes !

Bar. At the moment he was planning my misery, and my wife's shame, I had become his security to so large an amount, that my paternal income was annihilated in discharging his creditors.

Tor. Bring your claim against his relations. I am the only one surviving, and will discharge the bonds directly. Where are they ?

Bar. Here is your brother's note, bearing a reference to those bonds, for seven thousand pounds. —(*Shewing it to* TORRENT.)

Tor. I'll swear to the hand. Let me cancel the debt, though I blush at the relationship.

Bar. I cancel it now, sir. (*Tears it.*) That pocketbook, which I have just return'd, has given me a far,

far more valuable claim; my title is indisputably legal, and I am here to assert it.

Tor. Pocket-book! There's nothing that I recollect, but—but the paltry notes and—(*Searching it*) —and some memorandums—and a long letter here, without an *envelope*, from a poor girl in distress, who is coming to be my housekeeper.

Bar. I must see her.

Tor. See her!—Why?

Bar. That this heart, so long cold and desolate, may feel the aching transport of a father, when it beats against the bosom of my child.

Tor. Child! What, is she the infant daughter that —Hollo! (*Calling.*) You shall be—Solomon!—I'm as much pleas'd as if—Thomas! Pooh!—he's drunk —My dear sir, if she's not arriv'd yet, you'll see her to-night to a certainty.

Bar. Not arriv'd! The letter says she would be here this morning.

Tor. Yes; but she's not come.—The moment I— that is, she—I mean that—Zounds! I'm too much flurried to speak plain. But don't distrust me:—If my brother has sullied his memory, by making a husband wretched, don't suppose I can't jump for joy in making a father happy.

Enter SOLOMON GUNDY.

Tor. Is Miss Fanny—is—the housekeeper arriv'd?

Sol. No.

Bar. No!

Tor. No!

Sol. *Nong paw*, as the French say; but the little man in the bob wig is run out of his senses.

Tor. Then I wish you had run into them.—What's the matter with him?

Sol. A total arrangement of his ineffectuals.—He's what we call *foo* at Dunkirk. He says you sent him into the park to take him in; calls all the prospects

a blind; and when I shewed him the stags, he ran
into the *chateau*, and said he wouldn't be kept from
his own little dear.

Tor. Why, what is all this?—Don't be impatient.
(*To* BARFORD.) This is only a strange surveyor
that—You shall soon be made easy.

Bar. I shall expect it, sir.

Enter JONATHAN OLDSKIRT.

Old. I've been from the top of the house to the
bottom; but I sha'n't be bamboozled.

Tor. Hey-day!

Old. Mr Torrent, you know what business brought
me here.

Tor. To be sure I do.

Old. Then I'm a reputable man, and insist upon
joining the party.

Tor. Joining the party!—When I ask'd you to
dine at my table, didn't you tell me you would take
your victuals in the housekeeper's room?

Old. That's what I wanted; but, instead of that,
this outlandish fellow has kept me capering about
the park, after a parcel of live venison.

Sol. 'Twas my master's *ordonnance*, and I acted
according to *riggles.*

Tor. Hold your tongue!—If you wish to go to
dinner, go to dinner; and when you like; nobody
hinders you.

Old. Damn the dinner!—that isn't my object.

Sol. *Tezzy voo*, according to the French; for if
you are saucy to my master, I shall kick you out,
agreeable to the English.

Tor. Leave the room.   [*Exit* SOLOMON GUNDY.

Old. Don't tell me; I'll raise the whole county,
but I'll know the rights on't.

Tor. Heartly has sent me a maniac. Aren't you
welcome to all the house affords?—What more do
you want?

Old. Want?—I'll have a beautiful young woman.

Tor. The devil you will!

Old. Yes; and I won't rest till I'm satisfied.

Tor. I'll tell you what, my friend; for a man, modest even to shyness, you are as brazen a dog as ever threw up a clump.

Old. I've clump'd here up to my neck in clay; and it's well I did, or I might have been cheated out of my charge.

Tor. I never knew such assurance!—How dare you talk to me of being cheated of a charge, when you have no title yet to demand one?

Old. We shall see that.—I'll swear to our parting this morning in the lane, in the direct road to your house.

Tor. 'Tis my opinion that you'll swear to any thing; but, so far from parting with you in a lane, curse me if I ever saw your extraordinary face any where but in this parlour!

Old. Who says you did?

Tor. You, this minute—But here comes a gentleman who will settle matters, and rid my house of you directly.

Old. With all my heart. Let him clear up all. I've no objection to meeting a gentleman, for my part, when he behaves as such.

Enter HEARTLY.

Tor. So, Mr Heartly, here's a mighty modest person, according to your notion of things, to whom I must beg you to talk a little, if you please.

Heart. (*Bowing to* OLDSKIRT.) Sir, your most obedient.

Old. (*Returning the bow vulgarly.*) Sir, yours.

Tor. And now, let me tell you, (*To* HEARTLY,) if you had search'd all England for a shy and a cheap man, you couldn't have pick'd out a more impudent or extortionate fellow.

Old. I don't value what you say of me a button.
Come to the point.

Heart. I'm thunderstruck!—Who can this be?

Tor. Who should it be—but your precious recommendation, the surveyor.

Old. Surveyor!

Heart. You are mistaken—I never saw this person
before.

Tor. No!

Old. You know that as well as he. But that fetch
won't pass.—I'll have what I came for.

Tor. And what the devil did you come for?

Old. For one who is as dear to me as the eyes in
my head. Didn't I tell you I came to better her
prospects, now she had got a place?—And didn't
you cajole me by saying you'd help me to mend 'em?
But old Jonathan Oldskirt had rather see all his
remnants on fire, than return to the back of St Clement's before he knows Miss Fanny Delamere is
safe.

Bar. How!—Are you the person she mentions in
her letter, who has shewn her so much care and
kindness?

Old. What's that to you?—I know none of you;
but let her be forth-coming.

Bar. (*Warmly*). She shall be forth-coming.

Tor. Oldskirt!—Zounds! then you are the remnant-seller who settled every thing for the place with
my agent in London.

Old. Pooh! pooh!—You knew that all along.

Bar. 'Tis fit that I, as her father, Mr Torrent,
should know every thing.

Old. Her father!—What!—Will she find a father
after all?—Lord, Lord! I—But first, let her father
find *her.* Have the house search'd directly.

Tor. Why, what is it you mean to insinuate?

Old. I'll take my oath to leaving her a few hours
ago, not half a mile off, in her way to the house;

and, when I got here myself, you said you expected
me, because she had just mention'd to you I was
coming.

Bar. You hear that, sir.

Tor. Yes; but I said no such thing.

Old. Don't believe him—Fie upon you! You are
no better than a kidnapper.

Tor. Dam'me, if I—

Heart. (*Interposing.*) Softly— Here must be some
mistake. Mr Barford, if you have that claim to inquiry to which the tender name you have just mention'd gives you a title, we had better leave you to
investigate the matter coolly with my friend. Come,
Mr Oldskirt, to avoid clamour, suppose you and I
withdraw to another apartment.

Old. (*To* BARFORD.) Do you say I should?

Bar. I think it would be better.

Old. Well, I—But don't be bamboozl'd—We're
in bad hands.

Heart. Come, come.

Old. (*Going.*) Curse me, though, if I quit the premises till I see her!

　　　[*Exeunt* HEARTLY *and* OLDSKIRT *on one side,*
　　　　TORRENT *and* BARFORD *on the other.*

SCENE II.

*A substantial House on a Heath.   Barns and Out-
Houses adjoining.—A slight Railing in Front of
the House, and a Wicket, to which a Bell is attach'd.
—A Cart under a Shed, and at the end of it is in-
scrib'd " Barabbas Hogmore—Tax'd Cart."—The
Sea at a distance.—Bright Moon-light.*

Enter HENRY.

Hen. After a painful walk from the beach, here
is a house at last. I need not doubt a reception,

for I am on British ground.   The mastiff barking,
as a nocturnal terror at an Englishman's gate, gives
sure token of comfort to the wanderer in search of
a habitation. (*Rings at the wicket.*)

Hog. (*Looks out at one pair of stairs window.*)
Who's that?

Hen. A stranger in quest of a night's lodging.

Hog. We don't let any here.   (*Going to shut the
window.*)

Hen. Stay a moment.   I do not want to *hire* a
night's lodging—I *entreat* one.

Hog. That's a genteel way of begging, I suppose.
Where do you come from?

Hen. The coast of France.

Hog. O ho! I understand.   If you have any run
brandy, I should like a keg, snug and reasonable.
I'll come down to you.

Hen. You mistake me.   I was, six months ago,
impress'd into the king's service;—I was captur'd
by the enemy;—have escap'd from a French prison;
—and, after many hardships at sea, was put on
shore, in an open boat, an hour since, on this coast.

Hog. That may be all gammon. Coast of France,
indeed!   'Tis a mighty extraordinary story.   Are
you an Englishman?

Hen. I am a British subject, and want shelter.

Hog. You don't get any here.

Hen. Then your want is more extraordinary, for
an Englishman, than mine.

Hog. What's that?

Hen. The want of hospitality.

Hog. Look ye, my man; I'm a Yorkshire free-
holder : my young ones are just going to bed, and
I am obligated to keep 'em safe : if you hover outside of my warm dwelling, because you are in want
of house and home, I'll fire at you, as every tender
master of a family is in duty bound.   (*Shuts the
window.*)

Hen. Brute! You form, I hope, a strong exception to the rule of that country's generosity in which you are born. His young ones!—What a litter of cubs must spring from such a bruin! I am very faint, but I will stagger on. (*Going.*)

(*A Boy, apparently seven years of age, puts his head from a window of the ground-floor, and calls to* HENRY.)

Boy. Hollo! Master!

Hen. (*Turning back.*) A child's voice!

Boy. Don't you go.

Hen. Why not, my little fellow?

Boy. Because I'm locked in to go to bed. I've all this closet to myself; so, if you creep in at window, you shall sleep in my room if you like.

Hen. Can so sweet a baby belong to that savage?

Boy. But stay, I had better come out, for Tiger's unchain'd—He'll bite you if he don't see me with you; he won't bite you when he does, for I ride upon him. I'm coming.

Hen. No, no; you'll fall and hurt yourself.

Boy. No, I sha'n't. I clamber out of this window very often, and in again too, when brother John plays with me at hide-and-seek.

Hen. Take care.

Boy. Stop, though—Mother puts her cold ham and cordial bottle in my cupboard; and I dare say you are very dry and hungry. (*Goes back.*)

Hen. Infantine simplicity, how powerful is thy appeal to Nature! How do thy tones and gestures awaken in us that softness which age, with all its acquired austerity (sour vintage of life!) cannot resist.

(*Boy having come from the window to* HENRY, *with bottle and meat in a basket.*)

Boy. Have you got a knife in your pocket?

Hen. Yes, my sweet fellow.

Boy. Then cut the ham very smooth, and father

12

won't miss it ; else, if he finds me out to-morrow morning, he'll larrup me.

Hen. Can he ever have the heart to beat you ?

Boy. Never very hard when mother's by, for then he'd get it himself. Come, why don't you eat ? And then we'll go to bed.

Hen. I am too ill to eat, my dear boy ; but the contents of your bottle will cheer me.

Boy. Oh! nobody will miss that. When mother gets up, she never remembers if she left any in it over night.

Hen. (*Drinks.*) What is your name, my dear ?

Boy. I'm Bill.

Hen. Won't you lose a keep-sake, if I give you one ?

Boy. No, that I won't.

Hen. See—here is a silver whistle for you. I tore it by accident from a poor boatswain, as I was endeavouring to pluck him from the waves, when he was drowning.

Boy. What!—and was he drowned for good and all ?

Hen. Yes. Be sure to keep this till you are a man, and it will put you in mind to do then what you are doing now.

Boy. What's that ?

Hen. (*Lifting him up in his arms.*) To struggle all in your little power to save a fellow-creature from sinking. (*Kisses him, and puts him to the ground. As going.*) Farewell.

Boy. Oh, but you won't go ?

Hen. Yes, my love. But I must see you get into your room first.

Boy. Oh, but stay, and see how nice I'll blow this whistle. (*Blows it.*)

Hen. Hush! you'll alarm the house.

Boy. Oh dear! I forgot that.—There's father at

the window—Let us get under the great elm. (*They retire.*)

Hog. (*Looking out.*) Who's that ?

Enter SOLOMON GUNDY.

Sol. Mr Hogmore, I wish you a very *bong soir.*

Hog. What do you want here, after sun-set, you rat-killing vagabond ! No good, I'll answer for you.

Sol. Whoever answered for you, at your christening, to teach you the vulgar tongue, kept his word with the strictest voracity. And as to killing rats, you have always been my victorious competitioner.

Hog. How do you make out that ?

Sol. While I have poisoned one, you have starved twenty. But suppose now, our new lord of the manor had placed me at the top of his house ?

Hog. Then I shouldn't be plagued with you under my wall.

Sol. He has sent me here, officiously, to implore the country in search of a wanderer. Have you seen one ?

Hog. There was one wanting to get in just now.

Sol. Huzza ! What did you do ?

Hog. I'll shew you. (*Slaps down the window.*)

Sol. That man is what I call a *Poissarde.* I could hear no news of this housekeeper at the Spread Eagle. I'm afraid we must look upon her as lost, like an *ong-fong trouvay.* But I suffused a sigh into the ambrosial ear of my Amy, and murmured my youthful vow of everlasting detachment.

(HENRY *and the Boy come forward.*)

Who's that ?

Hen. The wanderer, you have just been told, was refused admittance to that dwelling.

Sol. This can't be the housekeeper, for she's a *song culotte,* as the French say. Where do you come from ?

Boy. He came out of a boat ;—all the way from France.

Sol. From France ! Hem ! *Parly Fransay un pew,* I suppose, *Musseer?* (*To* HENRY.)

Hen. I understand French better than I speak it.

Sol. That's not my case : I speak it, *toote le maim,* as well as I do English. What part did you *voyagy* from last ?

Hen. From Dunkirk.

Sol. Dunkirk ! that's astonishing ! The place where I received my foreign polish. Perhaps you lodged at the *Tetty de Buff?*

Hen. I lodged in a prison.

Sol. A prison !

Hen. And the most wretched of its kind.

Sol. Now, that's what I call *le diable momporte.*

Hen. My story is brief. I was taken in the English service by the French, and have escaped, first from their prisons, then from the storms that have driven me so far northward on the English coast. Be my guide to any place where I may rest for the night, and I will reward you for your labour.

Sol. I'll tell you what you shall give me.

Hen. Make your terms.

Sol. A cursed thump on the head, if I take a farthing for helping a distressed English seaman, thrown on his own shore, from the clutches of the enemy.

Hen. My good friend, whatever your proficiency may be in French, such language is pure English, and that of the best subjects in the British dominions.

Sol. Don't be surprised at my orthography of utterance, for my father was schoolmaster at the contagious village ; so learning to me is hereditary.

Hen. Well, shew me the nearest habitation, for I am almost dropping with fatigue.

Boy. My lord's house is just a' top of our hill.

Sol. I must go to Lord Alamode's to make inquisitions about our housekeeper ; but they have no family

there now.   I'll take you afterwards to my master's,
where you will be treated *cummy fo*, as we say.

Hen. Oh ! the very first place of rest.

Sol. 'Tis but a few hundred yards, and the night
is quite lunatic.

Hen. First let me take care of my little friend.
Come, William, I must see you safe into your room.

Boy. Oh ! I can get in easy enough.

Hen. Won't you let me help you ? You have been
ready enough to help me.

Boy. Yes, that you shall, if you like.   Softly,
though, for fear father should hear us again.   Come
along. (*Goes to the window.*)   Now for it. (*Gets in,
and remains in sight.*)

Hen. (*To* SOL.) My good friend, give me that
basket.   God bless you ! (*To the child.*)

Boy. Good b'ye !

Sol. (*Giving the basket.*) Here's a ham ! A *jam-
bong*, as we call it at Dunkirk.

Boy. (*To* HENRY.) If you come this way again,
I shall be very glad to see you.

Hen. And if I do come this way again, it shall go
hard but I *will* see you.   Good night, my sweet little
fellow ! (*Kisses him.*)

Boy. Good night : I'll take care of the whistle.
(*Goes in.*)

Hen. Come, friend, come.   [*Exeunt.*

ACT THE FIFTH.

SCENE I.

A Room in LORD ALAMODE'S *House.*

Enter MRS GLASTONBURY *and* FANNY.

Fan. My presence here arises entirely from mistake, believe me.

Mrs Glas. Well, well; I take your word for it.—— But that brute Bang did not lock me up by mistake, that's certain. You are the new housekeeper, you say, at the manor-house.——You are prodigiously young, child, for the mysteries of so important an office.

Fan. There is no mystery, I imagine, in being strictly honest to my employer.

Mrs Glas. Honest! Fiddle faddle! Can you raise paste, and make lemon-cheesecakes? Do you know what is good for an inward bruise? Have you studied the whole art of preserves, pickles, jellies, cakes, candies, dried fruits, made wines, cordials, and distillery?

Fan. No, indeed.

Mrs Glas. I thought so; but, as you let me out of the closet, I owe you a return of favours.

Fan. And I entreat your assistance, madam, immediately.——Enable me at present to fly from this house.

Mrs Glas. Don't be alarmed, young woman. Has that madman, my lord has sent here, been rude to you?

Fan. Indeed he has! By proposals which, how-ever speciously worded, a virtuous woman bears with indignation.

Mrs Glas. Oh! I wish he had been rude to me! I would have given him such a look! my looks freeze a libertine, they are reckon'd so very repell-ing.

Fan. In this lone house, and in his power, I have nearly sunk with terror; but the wine he has drank, which at first increased my fears, gave me an oppor-tunity of escaping from his apartment.

Mrs Glas. And, in running along the gallery, you heard me calling help through the key-hole.

Enter CARRYDOT.

So, Mr Carrydot! fine doings, truly!

Car. What is the matter, madam?

Mrs Glas. Matter! I have been made prisoner in my own china-closet, by that beast of a game-keeper.

Car. Bless me!

Mrs Glas. Bless you? Bless me, if you go to that! and while one ruffian has lock'd me up, t'other has made advances to her, which make every virtuous housekeeper tremble!

Enter ANDREW BANG, *drunk.*

And. I say, old Carrydot, do you go and fetch coffee for the baronet.

Car. Drunk as an owl! how did you get in this sad condition?

And. Sad? That be your mistake. I've been get-ting merry.

Mrs Glas. So, sir, I am obliged to you for locking me up.

And. Don't ye mention it.—You be kindly wel-come,·I do assure ye.

Car. Answer me, you abominable!—How came you in this pickle?

And. Mother Glastonbury forgot to lock up her cherry-bounce before I lock'd up she.

Mrs Glas. And you have drank it all?

And. Damn the drop's left, as the baronet said, e'en now, a'ter his third bottle o' claret.

Car. His third! Why, I only sent up the third, because you told me the second was cork'd.

And. So it ware then; but when I uncork'd it, he drank it. Miss, the baronet do want you to pour out his coffee.

Fan. I shall never—but I cannot give you an answer.

And. Nor I you, hardly; so we be much of a muchness. (*A ring at the gate.*)

Car. There's a ring at the court-gate.—Inquire who it is, if you can.

And. Pooh! I'm sober enow, you'll see, and——
(*Ring again.*)

Car. Go to the gate.—Let me see that, you hog.

And. I wool; but if you want to see a hog in a gate, you had best go to't yoursen wi' a looking-glass.   [*Exit.*

Fan. And now, sir, set me free, I beseech you.

Car. Nay, nay, be advised.—I am unable, while matters are in this state, to leave the house myself to-night; and your venturing alone would be dangerous.—To-morrow, early, I will see you safe.—Rest easy, child, till then, under my care.

Fan. Till to-morrow, then, to your care, though with a trembling heart, I confide myself.

Mrs Glas. Ay, ay, you needn't fear trusting yourself to him.—We have pass'd many a winter's evening together; and he's as harmless a man as any in Christendom, I'll answer for him.   [*Exeunt.*

SCENE II.

The Hall at LORD ALAMODE'S.

ANDREW BANG *admitting* SOLOMON GUNDY *and*
HENRY.

Sol. Thank you, Mr Bang, for letting us in.—*Mill grass*, as we say at Dunkirk.

And. You be kindly welcome, as we do say in Yorkshire.

Sol. My business here———But, first, for this gentleman—he has just deliberated himself from the clutches of our incapable enemy, the French.

And. The French!—How the dickens did he get here?

Hen. The usual mode of crossing from the Continent to an island is by sea, friend.

Sol. Yes; he's just come off the *mer*.

And. Cross the sea upon a *mare*!—Dang me! but that be a rum way of coming over!

Hen. Permit a fatigued stranger to remain here till day-break, friend, and I shall be thankful.

And. You be welcome to our arm-chair, zur. (*Pointing to one.*)

Sol. Hav'n't you, *par accidong*, such a thing in the house as a bed?

And. Plenty i' the wash.—All ours, bating they in use, be pull'd down for cleaning.

Sol. Nothing to eat?—A few eggs, perhaps, for a *hamlet*.

And. I emptied my lord's hen-roost at my dinner-time; for he do keep I upon board wages.

VOL. III.   2 A

Sol. And—hem—I see you never have any thing to drink.

And. Bless ye, ours be an unaccountable sober family.

Hen. A roof over my head is all I desire. (*Throws himself in the chair.*)

Sol. Now for my own business.—Come here, Mr Bang—have you *wrong-countered* a refugee ?

And. Anan ?

Sol. I am looking for one that is not to be found.

And. Who be it ?

Sol. A hapless female ! wandering, benighted, through the *beau monde*, exposed to insults from the licentiate !

And. Now just put that into English, will you ?

Sol. The housekeeper's lost out of the stage-coach, who was to come to-day to the manor-house.

And. Is she, by golls !

Sol. She is, *parblew !*—Have you seen any thing of her ?

And. I'll step and ax the baronet.

Sol. Ask a baronet ?

And. Ees ; we ha' gotten one come down to our house.

Sol. Have you ?—A *shevalleer*, as we call 'em at Dunkirk. But can't you tell whether you've seen a young woman, without asking a baronet ?

And. Na, sure.—Why, I shouldn't know when I'd seen a baronet, himsen, if somebody didn't tell I what he ware.

Sol. This man's almost a naturalist.

And. Bide where you be—I'll be wi' ye in no time. So there be a hue and cry a'ter miss ! I wonder where be the baronet's conscience.—Dang me, if I tell a lie for him, about her, under five shillings !

[*Exit.*

Sol. (*Turning towards* HENRY.) The stranger is fast asleep.—Ah ! how little the terraqueous lands-

man thinks on the hardships of the poor fatigued ma-
rine! (*A ring at the gate bell.*)—Somebody *sonnys*
the *closh*—Mr Bang's busy, and I'll open the gate.
Sir! (*Jogging* HENRY.)

Hen. Well, friend, why have you waked me?

Sol. Only to tell you not to be disturb'd, if any
body comes in.   [*Exit.*

Hen. Why should I endeavour to repose, when I
am tortured with such anxieties? Sleep descends upon the eye-lids of the happy, like Heaven's dew-drops
on the earth, cool and refreshing; but the dosings of
a disturb'd mind add listlessness to the fever'd limbs
of the slumberer.

Re-enter SOLOMON GUNDY, *escorting* TORRENT *and*
BARFORD.

Tor. But is she to be found?

Sol. All my derogatories have been crown'd with
disappointment.

Bar. No tidings!

Sol. Poing de too.

Bar. 'Tis very unaccountable.

Tor. So it is:—but what would you have me do
more? Isn't this almost the only house that we
haven't searched? What would you infer?

Bar. The inference, under all the circumstances,
is, that as she is to be found in no other house, she
may still be conceal'd in yours.

Tor. Zounds! Then, to convince yourself, spring
a mine upon it with gunpowder; that will search
every cranny. You'll blow up a hump-back'd cook
and a pimple-faced footman; but if you throw out a
handsome housekeeper, I'll suffer the fate of Guy
Fawkes

Bar. One way or other my doubts must be satisfied.   [*Goes up the stage.*

Tor. This comes of doing kindnesses; but if ever
I am caught at another—I'll harden myself against

all manner of pity ; I'll——Who's that asleep in the chair ? *(Seeing* HENRY.)

Sol. A *maleroo.*

Tor. What the devil's that?

Sol. An English seaman, lately inkarkerated in France, that wants a bed to lie down on.

Tor. Wants a bed! And who are the unfeeling scoundrels that let him lie there ? Stay—He's waking. (HENRY *rises.*) Young man, you are in need of help, they tell me—my house is close by, and I have bed, board, and lodging at your service.

Hen. To whom am I indebted for this kindness?

Tor. To one who has just resolv'd to feel for nobody; but, curse me, if any thing could be more illtimed to a man, beginning to be hard-hearted, than the sight of an English seaman in want of assistance.

Enter ANDREW BANG.

Tor. Who's this ?

Sol. My lord's game-keeper—his *gardy sash,* as the French say. Any news of the young woman, Mr Bang?

Bar. (*Starting up.*) What? we have still a chance here then ?

And. The baronet do say he'll answer all questions himsen.

Bar. The baronet ?

And. Ees, he be an old friend o' my lord's ; though he and I haven't been long intimate.

Bar. Let us see him immediately.

Tor. Let me see him first by myself.

Bar. Why so ?

Tor. I suppose you don't want to make a hubbub of inquiry; and as I am a neighbour, fixing in this country, the thing will be done more quiet and more proper.

Bar. Perhaps you may be right, sir. I will wait for you here.

Tor. Conduct me to this baronet directly.

And. Mind how you do come through our gallery, zur. It be nation dark, and a'ter dinner, you mayn't be quite steady.

Tor. Solomon Gundy, come with me, or this drunken rascal will lead me into the cellar.

Sol. Voos avy rasong. Besides, this building's very antic, and, I dare say, full of rats. Mr Bang, pray go first.

And. A'ter you, if you please, Mr Gundy.

Tor. Oh! confound you both! Get on, and shew me the way.   [*Drives them before him, and exit.*

Hen. Who is that gentleman, sir, who has made me so hospitable an offer?

Bar. His name is Torrent.

Hen. Torrent! Had he a relation who served several years ago in an English regiment, in Jamaica?

Bar. (*With a movement of surprise.*) Did you know any thing of such a relation?

Hen. I know he was a villain. He was guilty of the deepest treachery to a generous friend, and entail'd many a year of misery on that friend's penitent wife, whom he had seduced from her duties.

Bar. Was she penitent? Are you certain, sir, of that circumstance?

Hen. Remorse preyed upon her lovely frame, and sunk her to the grave: and, as the head of the poor dying soul reclined on the bosom of her daughter, she fervently bless'd her husband, and implored Heaven's and his forgiveness.

Bar. Did—did you witness this distressing scene, sir?

Hen. Yes; had the husband been present, I think the sense of his wrongs would have yielded to his pity, and he would have pardon'd her.

Bar. The sight would have wrung his heart. The thoughts of former mutual affection, in her bloom of innocence, might have rush'd upon his mind, while

he beheld her agony, and forced him to obey the
mild precept of divine mercy, when crime is expiated
by repentance.

Hen. Did you know her husband, Captain Delamere ?

Bar. I—I was acquainted with him, sir.

Hen. Can you inform me if he be still alive ?

Bar. Why do you inquire ?

Hen. To little purpose, perhaps, at this moment.
Six months ago I had a treasure of his in my care to
restore to him.

Bar. What was it, sir ?

Hen. His daughter.

Bar. His daughter ! Then 'twas to you she was
consign'd, by her dying mother, as your intended
wife ?

Hen. How came that to your knowledge ?

Bar. You may be inform'd hereafter. But the
instant you arrived with her in London, you abandon'd her.

Hen. I would sooner have abandon'd life.

Bar. If you betray'd her innocence ; if, with the
smile of protection, you lured her to infamy, and
then left her to famine, your life, sir, must be answerable to her father, on your first encounter with
him. Suppose I were intimate with Delamere ? Suppose I felt as warmly for his interest as my own ?

Hen. You might then inform him (it would be
my duty, could I discover him) that on our arrival
in London, as I left her at our inn, to seek for her
an humble, but proper habitation, I was hurried on
board a vessel, sent into action, immured afterwards
in French prisons, whence I have escaped to England, in the anxious hope that I may recover and
again protect her.

Bar. But was not a father's consent necessary to
your union ?

Hen. 'Twas my ardent wish to obtain it; but where

was I to find him? In such a case, had he re-appear'd, a father's anger would not have fallen upon us, when I had married his friendless daughter, that I might afford her an honourable claim to share the humble income my professional pursuits might obtain for me in England.

Bar. Take his consent, young man; take the gratitude of an unhappy husband, for soothing the last moments of a deluded, heart-broken wife. Accept the tears of a father, for the protection you have given to his child.

Hen. Her father! Are you, then, sir——

Bar. Yes, yes; say no more now. Spare me.—— The heart that has been so long torpid in the sullenness of misfortune, can scarcely bear this aching surprise of the affections.

Hen. But have you intelligence, sir, concerning her?

Bar. I have. A letter, which she writ to Mr Torrent, who has just left us, gave me this morning much of her history.

Hen. Can we trace her?

Bar. Perhaps we may; but I fear some treachery, even from the person who ostensibly protects her—— this Torrent—'tis a hateful name! Come with me further into this house—we must search every angle of it.

Hen. Rely on my activity.

Bar. Oh, young man! You are beginning to wake me from dreams of gloom, which I fear I have too much encouraged. Misfortunes have made me hate the world; but afflictions are the test of religious patience, and repining is impious, when Providence has ever so many unforeseen blessings in store for us.

[*Exeunt.*

SCENE III.

An Apartment in LORD ALAMODE'S *House.*

Enter SIR LARRY MACMURRAGH *and* TORRENT.

Tor. But, sir, you won't tell me whether you do or don't know any thing of her.

Sir Lar. That all comes of my having had my claret.

Tor. Had your claret!

Sir Lar. A man of fashion, you know, never bothers his head after dinner about business, without 'tis gaming.

Tor. But zounds, sir, here's a beautiful girl lost; the whole country is running after her.

Sir Lar. Then, upon my conscience, the whole country has a deal of taste.

Tor. I cann't tell what to make of this buck! He seems half tipsy, and he either knows nothing about her, or too much. I'll at him again. Sir, my housekeeper, I tell you, was lost almost close to my park pales this morning.

Sir Lar. You'd have hinder'd that, if you'd just done as I did, a week ago.

Tor. What was that, sir ?

Sir Lar. I lost my park itself, and every pale and stick about the good-looking premises.

Tor. Nay, sir, trace with trifling. She is a poor young handsome creature, who—

Sir Lar. Yes, I understand—She advertised, you told me.

Tor. Yes; she was among the numerous children of misfortune who wanted comfort.

Sir Lar. Och! faith, there's no small lot of handsome ladies to be comforted, if a man gives his mind to pity. Quite a beauty, you say!

Tor. So they tell me ; and her distresses, of course, must interest me.

Sir Lar. Ay, humanity, and charity, and all that. A retired citizen, you know, must be decorous.

Tor. A retired citizen!

Sir Lar. Snug, you know.

Tor. Damn snug ! I can't tell what you mean. If humanity and charity be decorous in a retired citizen, his *decorum* is only what it was before he *did* retire.   Look at the commercial names that swell every list of national subscriptions, and then tell me whether men of the highest rank do not acknowledge, with pleasure, the merchant's kindred ardour in the country's welfare.

Sir Lar. Long life and prosperity to the city, sir, say I.   But take my advice, as a friend,—don't be coming out, at moon-shine, after distress'd young creatures, or, upon my soul, you'll bring a scandal upon the corporation,

Tor. I come out after——Sir, my character has bid defiance to scandal these forty years.

Sir Lar. That's a mighty long provocation.

Tor. Zounds! Sir, you'd provoke a parson.

Sir Lar. Then you may keep cool till you take orders, you know.

Enter HENRY.

Hen. You must pardon my abrupt entrance, sir, for I have pressing business.

Sir Lar. Oh, murder! I see how it is.

Hen. In which business I have a friend in the house who is jointly concern'd.

Sir Lar. The game's up : tell me at whose suit, you divel, at once.

Hen. Suit !

Tor. Eh ! the young seaman I left just now in the hall.

Hen There is a servant in this house, sir, from whom I have gathered (thanks to his intoxication) that a female arriv'd here this morning, on whom you have basely impos'd, and who—

Sir Lar. Asy one moment, if you please, sir. We always take matters cool in Ireland, when it looks like a bit of a quarrel. May you chance to know who I am, sir ?

Hen. A baronet, whose appellation, the servant tells me, 'tis very hard to remember. I congratulate you on this difficulty, which, should your exploits be publish'd, may prevent your name from being coupled with your transactions.

Sir Lar. It's my notion, one day, I'll print my memoirs myself, sir, and set my hand and seal to the back of 'em. Such a work, you know, must be address'd to the most impudent person born ; and I hope you'll allow me the pleasure to write you a dedication.

Hen. In the mean time, sir, I have every reason to suppose that the female I have mention'd is still in this house : but the building is intricate. My friend is searching it on one side ; I on the other. I have luckily stumbled on your apartments, and insist upon your immediately producing the person we seek, or giving me a strict account of your conduct.

Sir Lar. That same *insist* is rather an awkward bit of an expression. Indulge me, sir, in a trifling question :—May you, by any chance, just happen to be a gentleman ?

Hen. Birth and education give me a claim to that character. And I have never forfeited my title by practising fraud on an unprotected woman.

Sir Lar. That's quite enough.——Mr Bang !—— (*Calling.*)

Bang. (*Without.*) Zur.

Sir Lar. Bring in my pistols, and make haste with the coffee.

Enter ANDREW BANG *with coffee and pistols.*

Tor. I won't have any fighting.

Sir Lar. Don't you meddle, you old Cheapside—sure we must have all in readiness, providing that gentleman don't think proper to make me a small matter of apology.

And. There be the coffee, Sir Larry, smoking hot.

Sir Lar. Set it down on the table, and take out, in your arms, that little old gentleman.

And. Where be I to carry un to, zur?

Tor. If any body dare to—

Sir Lar. Fie upon you! Keep the peace! I am wishing to shew you all manner of respect; so, till this business is over, (which it is not decent for you to see,) what part of the house will we bind you over to?

And. There be plenty o' room for him in our hen-house.

Sir Lar. Then, by the powers, I'll send him to the Poultry.

Tor. Gentlemen, you think the game is in your own hands!—But I shall not suffer you to commit murder.

Sol. (*Without.*) Murder!

Sir Lar. Sure that's an echo!

Tor. Then you've brought it with you from Ireland; for 'tis as different from the reverbation of sound, as a cart-load of iron bars and an opera-singer.

Enter SOLOMON GUNDY.

Solomon Gundy! What the devil's the matter with you now?

Sol. There's a tame goat in the gallery.

Tor. Well?

Sol. As I was imploring, in the dark, through the intrikasies of this *chateau*, he butted me down as flat as a *six livre piece.*

Enter BARFORD.

Bar. This way the light directs me; and I——

Sir Lar. 'Faith, now, and here's another.—Is it a lady you are asking after, or are you running away from a goat in the gallery?

Bar. It is a lady, sir, I am seeking.

Sir Lar. I'm just going to give this gentleman an explanation of the whole affair in one word.

Bar. What is that one word, sir?

Sir Lar. Pop—A long Irish phrase, that stands for the English monosyllable, satisfaction.

Tor. No, you don't.—Come here, you drunken game-keeping rascal!—There are two pistols—take them away;—there's a guinea—and now go to the devil.

And. A guinea! I'd better go to the ale-house.
                                                    [*Exit.*

Bar. (*To* SIR LAR.) I conceive, sir, you are possessed of some intelligence of the person whom we are anxious to discover.

Hen. I am convinced he is.

Tor. So am I.

Bar. Are you a father, sir?

Sir Lar. Upon my soul, sir, that's a mighty difficult question to answer.

Bar. Levity apart, sir, I am the father of the young person for whom we anxiously inquire. If you have any thing to disclose relative to my daughter, let me invoke your humanity rather than suspect your subterfuge.

Sir Lar. This is the case, sir, you see. Does an Irishman like a pretty woman? Sure, sir, he does; but when he's bullied by a wicked advertising alderman on one side of him, and a man in trowsers on the other, damn the bit of answer will he give.—I—Give me your hand, sir—there's no standing a father's asking for his child. Sir, I'm a gentleman, a little wild, perhaps. But upon my honour and conscience, she's safe ; and damme if an Irish gentleman will ever do a dirty action.

Bar. But is my daughter in this house ?

Sir Lar. Hollo there, ask old Carrydot where's the young lady ?

Enter JONATHAN OLDSKIRT *conducting* FANNY.

Old. I've got her ! I've got her ! I've got her !— I've hunted all the neighbourhood, and burn all my remnants, rather than not find her.

Fan. (*To* OLDSKIRT.) Under your protection, sir, I venture again into this gentleman's apartment ; but whom else I am to meet, I—Henry ! Ah !—

Hen. (*Runs to her.*) You encounter none but friends.

Fan. Whither have you—

Hen. Cease—cease to inquire now—my heart is too full ; but here is one who claims every immediate attention.

Bar. (*Singles her out, and brings her forward.*) You—'tis fifteen years since you were torn from me, in—I mean, young lady, that I—Oh God ! my child ! my child ! (*Falls on her neck.*)

Fan. My father !

Tor. Tol de riddle lol, lol, &c. Whoever says I am hasty in charity, I'll kick him.—Heartly may lecture as much as he pleases, but I'd rather hire twenty housekeepers, who would let my jellies turn mouldy, than lose the chance of this meeting. I'll make you all happy—I perceive you two are inclined to be *very* happy together, (*Pointing to* HENRY *and* FANNY,) and I owe it in justice, sir, to you, (*To* BARFORD,) to take care of their fortunes, if you'll permit me.

Bar. I begin not to be quite so fastidious relative

to obligations as I have been, sir ; but still I dislike
favours.

Tor. Well, well, we'll talk over all that. Master
Oldskirt, you are a worthy fellow for taking care of
this poor girl, and I must take care of you. As for
you, Solomon Gundy, I suppose I must portion you
off with the daughter of the Spread Eagle, and be
pestered with your brats and jabber in my house, to
the last hour of my life.

Sol. *See voo play,* as we say at Dunkirk—But I'm
full of thankfulness and remorse.

Tor. (*To* Sir Lar.) As for you, sir—

Sir Lar. Make yourself easy on my account, old
gentleman. You seem a worthy person, and I'm
sorry I've afforded you any kind of offence. But as
I didn't know the case of this mighty pretty couple,
the lady will forgive all errors, and I'll look over the
small words that happened to slide out of a wrong
corner of that young gentleman's mouth.

Tor. All must be forgotten that requires to be forgiven ; and I will (if I can) try to convert my haste
of charity into (what Heartly calls) thinking benevolence.

Bar. And I, Mr Torrent, must endeavour to convert my mistaken tendency to misanthropy into a
fair appreciation of mankind. To be soured with the
world by the treachery of a few is judging millions
by individuals. Men were born to endure ; but half
the measure of our grief depends upon our own sentiments.—And, gloomy as my thoughts have been,
my anxious wish now is, to observe all around me in-
dicating a light heart, and a good-humoured countenance.   [*Exeunt.*

WERTER;

A

TRAGEDY,

IN THREE ACTS.

AS PERFORMED AT THE

THEATRE-ROYAL, COVENT-GARDEN.

BY

F. REYNOLDS, Esq.

DRAMATIS PERSONÆ.

ALBERT (*betrothed to Charlotte*),	*Mr Harley.*
SEBASTIAN (*Friend to Werter*),	*Mr Williamson.*
LEUTHROP { (*Werter's confidential Servant*),	*Mr Claremont.*
WERTER (*in love with Charlotte*),	*Mr Holman.*
CHARLOTTE,	*Miss Wallis.*
LAURA (*her Confidante*),	*Miss Logan.*

Servants, Friends, &c.

Scene—Walheim, throughout.
Time—A Night and Day.

WERTER.

ACT THE FIRST.

SCENE I.

CHARLOTTE'S *Apartment.*

Enter CHARLOTTE *and* LAURA.

Char. (*Reading a letter.*) Albert returns to-night
—he little thinks
What ravages a few short hours have made
In this distracted breast: Laura, he comes
To take possession of my promis'd hand,
And claim that love his virtue well deserves!
How will his hopes be dash'd, then, when he finds
That all the labours of three tedious years,
One night, one fatal night, has quite eras'd?
    Lau. Banish these thoughts—they serve but to en-
    hance
The sad remembrance of an hopeless love.
    Char. Talk not of love, it has destroy'd my peace:
Oh! had not Werter's lovely form appear'd,

I still had liv'd unconscious of these pangs!
And Albert's friendship Werter's love supply'd;
But he has shewn the god in all his charms,
With each allurement to seduce the soul,
And then has left me to deplore and die!

Lau. Think not of Werter—'Twas thy solemn vow
To wed with Albert.

Char. And I'll maintain that vow;
Think'st thou that honour will descend to kneel
At love's fantastic throne? No, Laura! no;
Albert deservedly has gain'd my heart;
Some sighs may heave, some tears in pity fall,
When memory muses on another's fate;
But truth and constancy shall never cease
To pay that debt the generous Albert claims.

Enter WERTER.

Wer. My better angel!—Oh! at sight of thee
The gloomy winter in my bosom thaws,
And sunshine smiles again.

Char. O, Werter!

Wer. What means my Charlotte?

Char. Alas! my Werter,
There, in that letter, read thy hopeless fate.

Wer. (*Having read the letter.*) Albert return to-
night!—Then am I curs'd indeed.

Char. Wou'd I could sooth the anguish of thy soul;
But well thou knowest honour denies thee that
Which best might give relief—yet, if the balm
Of healing pity will assuage thy pain,
Still thou art somewhat blest! for even now—
My heart is bleeding for the wounds of thine.

Wer. Generous Charlotte!—But oh! what needed
this?
If sympathy could heal my rankled wounds,
I knew that thou wouldst pour the balsam on;
'Twas madness only that has made me thus,
And only that can save me!

11

Char. No, Werter;
'Tis Charlotte only that has made thee thus—
She is the origin of all thy woes!

Wer. Perish the thought!—I am myself the cause;
Thou art the lovely soother of my cares;
My guardian angel! sent by pitying Heav'n
To compensate my every other ill;—
And yet there is another that should claim
My warmest gratitude.

Char. O shun me! fly me!
I am a syren fatal to behold,
And ruin those I ever should protect.

Wer. Tell me delusion lurks beneath thy smiles;
Tell me destruction dwells within thine eye;
Tell me contagion hangs upon thy tongue;
And I will still love on, and still be happy;
But when thou tell'st me to avoid that form,
Death has no terrors! hell no pangs like mine!
Ah, whence those cruel tears!

Char. Thou best of men,
For thee they fall—anguish must have its vent,
Or the heart's blood would gush.

Wer. If I have liv'd
To give one moment's misery to thee,
That moment I have liv'd too long—by Heaven!
The frantic thought of adding woe to her,
Drives each ungenerous selfish sorrow hence,
And shews me what a shallow soul I have:
Oh! cease to weep; in a far worthier cause
Thy sorrows might be shed.

Char. Never, Werter.
When virtue such as thine is tortur'd thus;
When love, the purest, is so ill bestow'd,
And noblest talents are in love so lost,
The sympathizing heart may surely melt,
And melting, thus may pour its wishes forth:
Fly then far hence—seek some more generous fair;
And should she ask the story of thy life,,

Tell her that Charlotte did abuse thy love:
Tell her, the only recompence she shew'd
For all thy sufferings was—to leave thee thus—
My heart no longer can support its pangs!   [*Exit.*
   Wer. (*Solus.*) If you have mercy, Heaven, O shew
    it now!
For never wretch did need your mercy more.
But hold—How shall my troubled mind resolve?
If I remain—'tis but to mar her peace—
'Tis but to check the generous Albert's bliss:
If I depart, the pain is all my own!
Where is that virtue then, that boasted honour,
That ever was my pride? O shame! 'tis fled,
And Werter's but the shadow of himself!
Yet will I shew some firmness still remains,
And shake these demons from the dens they haunt!
Yes, I will leave her—e'en now I'll seek my friend,
Take one short farewell, and depart to-night!
So may I live to bless that happy hour,
When honour nobly triumph'd over love!   [*Exit.*

SCENE II.

Garden, by Moonlight.

Enter ALBERT.

Enough is known; and I with pity see
A youth the noblest struggling to subdue
A generous passion; whilst I in peace possess
The valued treasure he so much admires—
As the disturber of another's peace,
Honour compels me to attempt relief.

Enter CHARLOTTE.

Alb. At length the wish'd-for moment is arrived!
At length I clasp thee in a fond embrace!

Char. Oh, 'tis an age since last we met!

Alb. The pangs of absence have indeed been great;
Yes, most severe—But I'll no more complain;
Propitious Heaven has granted all I ask'd;
Has yielded thee, the summit of my hopes!
And we shall part no more.

Char. May Heaven so grant!

Alb. Why those doubtful words?—and why that
　　　　pensive look?
Oh! had I thought of meeting thee in grief,
The pangs of absence never had been borne—
'Twas the fond prospect of our future bliss,
That only cheer'd my pains!

Char. Alas! my lord,
When the great secret in my breast is known,
You will not wonder at my present grief—
Perhaps you'll think I merit all I feel,
And wound me with reproach!

Alb. Banish thy fears—
I know that secret—I approve its cause:
It adds new honour to the best of hearts,
And makes me worship, where before I lov'd—
Oh, if that only interrupts thy peace,
Thank Heaven, for Albert can dispel thy grief!

Char. Heavens! is it possible?—Yes, 'tis Albert;
The same unalter'd Albert I esteem!

Alb. And couldst thou think that Albert was so
　　　　base,
As not to sympathise in Charlotte's woes?—
I scorn suspicion and its jealous train;
'Tis only nourish'd where pollution lives.
For ever, in the pure unspotted breast,
The poisoning canker starves.—But, O my Charlotte!
Long have I known thy honour, love, and truth;
Have seen these jewels stand such trying tests,

That when I doubt them—may I cease to live!

   Char. Who could be false when truth is thus
      esteem'd?
Albert, there needed not my truth alone,
To make thy peace secure—for had I wish'd
To prove unfaithful—I had wish'd in vain.
Werter had scorn'd me for a thought so mean;
For, oh! his honour only stoops to thine.

   Alb. Then as his honour has preserv'd my peace,
Mine shall instruct me to restore him his—
Yes; I will shew this all-excelling youth,
That Albert never was out-done by him.
I'll seek his friendship and his sorrows share;
And, if my Charlotte shall approve the thought,
Entreat him to remain and share our bliss.

Enter WERTER.

   Wer. Ha! Albert here—'twas him I would have
      shunn'd—

   Alb. Come to my arms, thou honest noble youth!

   Wer My heart o'erflows—I know not how to thank
This generous kindness!

   Alb. Come, Werter, let us contemplate
The beauties that surround us.
How sweet the solitude of this retreat;
'Tis solemn silence all—and yon pale moon,
That dully glimmers on the passing stream,
Completes the awful scene.

   Char. Yes, 'tis most awful;
And ever when I walk by Dian's light,
A musing melancholy wraps my soul,
And memory ponders on departed friends;
On friends I never shall again behold!
O Werter, shall we converse after death?
Shall we in unknown climes again exist,
And once again be known?

   Wer. (*In agitation.*) Charlotte, Charlotte!
Here and HEREAFTER we shall meet again.

Char. And do the buried know the living's thoughts?
Are they partakers of our various scenes?
Oh, if my long-lost parent could be told,
That I my proffer'd promise had fulfill'd—
To be protectress of her children's youth;
Could she be witness of the social love,
The mutual harmony that now subsists,
How would she worship that great power above,
Whom in her dying prayers she so implor'd
For our protection!

Alb. These thoughts, my Charlotte,
May please remembrance, yet—

Char. O Albert!
You well remember her exalted soul,
And oft have wonder'd at its various charms!
Oft call'd her generous, cheerful, mild, and fair:
And Heaven can witness she deserv'd thy praise.—
Ah me!—how often have I vainly pray'd
To be the image of such great perfection.

Wer. (*Throwing himself at her feet.*) Thou art that
image, 'tis by Heaven proclaim'd!
The gods' own blessing, all thy mother's charms,
With double splendour grace an angel now!

Char. (*Laying hold of his hand.*) You should have
known her, Werter:
Yes, she was worthy to be known to thee!
A heart so good deserv'd a friend so great:—
Yet, in the midst of happiness and life,
She was to perish, she was to be lost.
Alas! how hard to part with those we love!
Werter—'tis sharper than the stings of death.

Wer. Charlotte, 'tis more than nature can support!
'Tis agony extreme! 'tis horrible to think on!—
Gracious powers above!
Why am I tortur'd with these questions now?

Alb. Be patient, Werter; let not reason yield
To these tumultuous transports of the soul!

Wer. Fools may be patient—my controuling woes

Shall ne'er be silent; they must roar aloud,
Else my expanding heart would burst.—Albert,
Thou hast not drunk of sorrow's bitter cup,
Thou hast not borne the miseries of love,
Nor felt one agony that Werter feels!
Oh! if thou hadst—thou wouldst invoke the gods,
Thy ceaseless groans would be as loud as mine,
Thy madness—raging madness!—wild as mine!

    Alb. Werter, farewell—'tis time we should be gone.
    Wer. And canst thou leave me on the brink of
        fate?
Can Charlotte leave me like a wretch cast off?
Stay but a moment—oh, one parting look!
Am I so lost she will not grant me that?
I am content—now leave me to my fate.
Farewell to both!—and may you never bear
What I have borne!—but we shall meet again—
'Tis not for ever that we now divide.

    Char. No, for to-morrow we will meet again.
    Wer. To-morrow, Charlotte—oh! oh! oh!
    Alb. Werter, farewell!
Some pitying angel guide thy steps,
And sooth thy soul to peace!

                [*Exeunt* ALBERT *and* CHARLOTTE.
    Wer. (*Solus.*) She's fled! the image of my soul
        is fled!
My other self, my only refuge gone!
Then what remains for Werter but—despair?
Now, Grief! now, Sorrow! I am all thine own.
Ye shades of night expand your sable wings,
Cover in darkness a deserted wretch!
Hide him from Heaven, the world, and from himself!
Here let him fall forsaken and forgot,
And sigh in solitude his life away!

              (*Throws himself on the ground.*)

Enter SEBASTIAN *and* LEUTHROP.

Seb. I fear the generous Albert has prevail'd,
For I have waited at the gate in vain!
This way I know they met—Alas! how's this?
O, Werter, speak!
   Wer. Away! I'll perish here.
   Seb. Look up, my friend!——thy lov'd Sebastian
      calls;
Perhaps he brings thee peace!
   Wer. (*Starting up.*) Who talks of peace!
'Tis not to be found!—the cherub sits on high,
And, smiling, mocks mankind—pursue it not,
For it will lead thee to a dangerous sea,
And there will vanish! rather thou, like me,
Plunge deep in sorrow; millions of fathoms deep;
And gorge upon despair! 'twill satisfy
The hungry soul, and leave it nothing wanting!
   Seb. Oh Heaven! the thought of leaving all his
      soul holds dear
Has, for a while, depriv'd him of his senses:
We must delude him hence.
   Wer. Look, look, and read;
'Tis fate's dire volume! and on the bloody page,
Self-murder's doom'd damnation!—and see! around
Avenging demons wait to lash their prey——
Hark how they yell! and now they pull—they tear—
O torture, torture!
      (*Falls on* LEUTHROP, *and is supported off.*)
                     [*Exeunt.*

ACT THE SECOND.

SCENE I.

ALBERT'S *Apartment.*

Enter CHARLOTTE *and* LAURA.

Char. If dreams are ominous, some dreadful woe
Is not far distant, Laura, from thy friend—
For even now, oppress'd with heaviest care,
I sought for comfort in a short repose ;
And my wild brain was harassed with a dream
So terrible ! that it will banish sleep
For ages from my soul.
    Lau. Oh, heed it not!
It can portend no harm.
    Char Hear then, and judge—
Methought, alone, and in the dead of night,
Whilst lightning fill'd each pause the thunder made,
And the pale moon in blackest clouds was lost,
I wildly wander'd to that dreary vale—
That vale ! where Werter first confess'd his love,
And oft in secret sigh'd !—But to my tale—
The lightning's fire, and moon's few scatter'd rays,
Just shew'd the awful horror of the scene ;
Loud roaring waves rush'd o'er the fertile fields,
And the whole valley seem'd a tossing sea ;

Sad echo doubled every hollow sound,
And nature with complete disorder groan'd!
   Lau. How could your fancy form so wild a scene?
Indeed, 'twas terrible!
   Char. But mark the end.
The forked lightning flashed a sudden glare,
And far, far off, a towering cliff appear'd!
Urg'd, at the moment, by a secret wish
To gain its summit—in the flood I plung'd!
And driven by the torrent, reach'd its foot—
Loud howl'd the wind, the tempest still increas'd—
Trembling—sad omen! I began to climb—
And midway saw—oh, horrible to tell!
An human being on the highest verge,
With arms outstretch'd, propending o'er the deep—
I scream'd aloud—struck with the sudden noise,
He started—madd'ning I flew to his relief,
And saw with eyes as frantic as his own—
The lost, deserted Werter—O Laura!
I wak'd in terrors; and countless centuries
Can never wear the image from my mind.

Enter ALBERT.

   Alb. And still will Charlotte fly her Albert's arms!
Still will she leave him to lament alone!
Oh! if my soul could find a secret charm,
That gently could attract thy heart to mine,
Or gain me but a share of that dear treasure!
High Heaven itself would be a poor conceit
Of Albert's happiness!
   Char. Nay, talk not thus—
It stings me to the soul to hear thee chide.
Love's deepest wounds, affliction's sharpest pangs,
Would be indulgence to reproof from thee!
   Alb. Thou little know'st
How thou art rooted here!—In early youth
Thy lovely form first planted in my soul;
There long it liv'd, and charm'd my wandering senses;

But, nurs'd by time, it grew into esteem——
And friendship budding blossom'd soon to love:
The fruit, alas ! has not fulfill'd my hopes;
But, oh ! the plant is firmly rooted here,
And here shall flourish till the stock decays!
How canst thou wonder then that thy sad eye
Attracts unwilling frowns from mine !

    Char. Oh, Albert!

Ere this thou shouldst have known, 'tis Charlotte's
    fate
To torture most where most she means to please.

    Alb. Be what thou wilt,
Be pleas'd, be silent, be content or sad,
I will still love thee, and be blest to share
Thy pleasures or afflictions—but come, my life !
I came to tell thee that some sudden news
Compels me hence until to-morrow noon—
'Tis hard to part so long !

    Char. Alas ! my lord,
What news so suddenly can force thee hence ?

    Alb. I am compell'd to hasten to the court—
No common mandate forces me away:
But I have done—in this one fond embrace,
Let my farewell be known ! Ere noon to-morrow
I shall again my only joy behold !   [*Exit.*

    Char. (*Solus.*) Farewell ! and may the unrelenting
    heavens,
That shower down curses on this wretched head,
Lavish their blessings on the generous Albert.
Oh ! how my soul still struggles to forget
What most it meditates, what most it loves !
But ah ! how vain !—O Werter, Werter !
Yes, I may blame, but never can forget thee;
A secret sympathy attach'd me first;
Time since has stamp'd thine image on my heart
And the impression is engrav'd for ever !
Should we e'er meet again ;—deluding thought !

It thrills like lightning through my trembling frame,
And penetrates my soul.—Ha!—Werter!

Enter WERTER.

Wer. That very wretch!
Char. (*Turning away.*) Some kind protecting an-
  gel guard me now!
Oh, watch me at this awful moment!
 Wer. Heavens!
Is it possible?—can she abandon me?
She—who would smile if Werter was but pleas'd!
She—who would weep if Werter did but sigh!
 Char. We must not be alone——
The scene is alter'd since we parted last—
Laura, I say—yet hold—a moment hold—
Am I so lost that I distrust myself?
So mean, so cowardly! must I be watch'd,
Lest I prove false?—Hence, idle visions, hence!
I am alone protectress of myself,
And dare defy all love's seducing arts,
To shake one atom of my virtue!
 Wer. Oh!
It was not always thus!—the time has been
When Charlotte would have flown to soothe her Wer-
  ter.
But now 'tis well! he'll trouble her no more—
He came oppress'd with sorrow and despair—
Yes, almost broken with a weight of woes,
To seek for succour in his only hope.
Like one that's shipwreck'd in a dreadful storm,
Struggling he sought the last remaining plank
To save his sinking soul!—but that avoids him—
Even there his hopes are lost—then let the storm
Come on! it cannot injure now!
      (*Throws himself on the couch.*)
 Char. (*Looking sometime at him and flying to him.*)
  O Werter!
Why will you plunge in misery again?

Why will you leave the shelter of your friends,
For this distracted scene?

   Wer. Charlotte, I came
To you alone! One gentle hour of love,
Snatch'd at a time so circumstanc'd as this,
Is better than an age of other life!

   Char. Werter, no more—this is no time for love—
Oh! let the torturer for ever sleep
In silent peace! for shou'd he wake again,
'Tis but to lead us to the brink of horror!
Once more I charge thee to subdue a passion
So vainly, madly form'd! a passion join'd
To sure destruction!—why is it only me?
Me, that's another's—Alas! I much, much fear
The conscious thought—I can be never thine,
Only encreases the enraged desire!

   Wer. Did Albert furnish thee with this reflection?
'Tis a profound one.

   Char. Nay, think me not severe!
By Heaven, e'en now my struggling heart recoils
While thus it chides! and could the trembler speak,
'Twould tell thee that it pants to sooth and share
Each pang that tortures thine—but as the cause
Of all thy sorrows, it should seem not harsh
That pity prompts me to invent a cure!

   Wer. And know'st thou of a cure?

   Char. Return to Manheim—
Time may do much—absence, perhaps, much more;
Another object too may change the scene—
One who deserves thy love, who'll hear thy tale,
And by dividing dissipate thy woes;
And when past sorrows shall be quite forgot,
Bring her to Walheim, and with us enjoy
The purest pleasures perfect friendship yields.

   Wer. All will be well ere long—all will be well.

   Char. Do not oppose my wish—for you well know
Albert has been most kind—his generous love
Merits return—and I could rather die

Than willingly torment him with a care!
Therefore, alas! I tremble as I speak!
We meet with prudence, or we meet no more.
　　　　　　　　　　　　(*Here they both rise.*)
　Wer. 'Tis well—'tis very well!
　Char. Honour incites
The fixed resolve!—Heavens relieve me now!
I scarce have power to speak.—Ha, thou art pale!
　Wer. Or meet no more!
　Char. What passion shakes thee?
　Wer. Or meet no more!
　Char. What wild mysterious words!
Some smothered passion struggles in thy breast:
Speak——
　Wer. I dare not.
　Char. Oh speak, in mercy speak.　　(*Bell tolls.*)
'Tis Walheim abbey bell
That tolls for some poor wandering pilgrim's death!
　Wer. Death—ha! didst thou say death!——Lo!
　　　where he stalks!
Hence, thou pale warrior, hence,
　　　　　　　(*Takes* CHARLOTTE *by the hand.*)
You shall not, cannot part us!
Alas! where am I?—Ah, my brain is turn'd!
Pity me, Charlotte, pity me! I am
The veriest wretch alive.
　Char. Alas! my Werter!
　Wer. Oh! forgive me; the raging tumult's o'er,
And I'm again myself—'twas but a fancy
Of my too troubled mind—think on't no more;
Some better subject may employ our thoughts.
Oft have we chaced the heavy hour away
In reading Ossian—may we not read again?
　Char. Here is your own translation of his songs.
　　　　　　　　　　(*Here they seat themselves.*)
　Wer. O Charlotte, what ravages hard time has
　　　made
Since last I read them!—Of that no more——

Alas! the leaf's turned down
Where hopeless Armin mourns his murdered child.
(*Reads.*) " Alone on the sea-beat rock my daughter
was heard to complain—frequent and loud were her
cries, nor could her father relieve her. All night I
stood on the shore—I saw her by the faint beam of
the moon, and before morning appeared, her voice
was weak—it died away, like the evening breeze
amongst the grass of the rocks—Spent with grief, she
expired, and left thee, Armin—alone!"

> (*Here* WERTER *throws down the book, seizes* CHAR-
> LOTTE'S *hand, and weeps over it—she leans on
> her other arm, holding her handkerchief to her
> eyes—They are both in the utmost agitation.—In
> this unhappy story they feel their own misfortunes.
> —At length* CHARLOTTE *says,* Go on.)

Wer. (*Reads.*) " Why dost thou awake me, O
gale!—It seems to say I am covered with the drops
of Heaven—The time of my fading—is near, and the
blast—that shall scatter my leaves—to-morrow—shall
the traveller come—He that saw me in my beauty
—shall come—His eyes shall search the field—But
—they will not—find me!"

> (*These words fall like a stroke of thunder on the heart
> of the unfortunate* WERTER—*in despair he throws
> himself at her feet, seizes her hand, and puts it to
> his forehead. An apprehension of his fatal pro-
> ject, for the first time, strikes* CHARLOTTE—*she
> is distracted.*)

Char. (*Starting from the couch.*) Heavens! Sui-
cide-- am I to be so curs'd?
Is there no mercy to be found in Heaven?
O Werter! O Werter! (*Falling on him.*)

Wer. I will not lose thee——
Thus let me ever clasp thee to my heart.

> (*Here they lose sight of every thing, and the whole
> world disappears before them.— He clasps her in
> his arms, and strains her to his bosom.*)

12

Char. Werter! (*With a faint voice.*) Werter!
(*Gently pushing him away.*) Werter! (*With a firm
voice of virtue.*) This is the last time——we never——
never—meet again.   [*Exit.*

Wer. (*Solus.*) Now art thou satisfied, indignant fate!
Is not thy vengeance glutted now ?—Then look,
And sate thy soul with triumph and revenge,
For I am curs'd beyond the reach of hope !
Heavens ! how the tempest rages in my brain !
'Tis all on fire !—O Charlotte, Charlotte,
Once more come forth and soften me to calmness !
                    [*Throws himself on a couch.*

Enter ALBERT.

Alb. The night and ceaseless fury of the storm
Compell'd me to return—strange fancies too
Perplex'd my mind, and agitate me much.
I know not what to think—How ! Werter here !
This is most strange !—But, Albert, have a care,
Suspect not without cause, for when thou dost,
Then thou art damn'd indeed !—Of all calamities,
Suspicion I have yet avoided most—
And ever will!—Welcome again to Walheim.

Wer. (*Not looking up.*) Away—away—and leave
            me to my sorrows.

Alb. Still on affliction, Werter—I hoped ere this
Thy friends had chac'd each dismal care away,
And quite restored thee to thy former peace.
Oh ! 'tis a weakness to be ever thus !
Look up, my friend—'tis Albert speaks.

Wer. Albert!
The last on earth I would intrude on thus :
O Albert, do I merit this from thee ?
Am I not most unworthy of thy friendship.

Alb. Unworthy !—Now by yon heaven I swear,
There's not an action, (unallied to sin,)
However dangerous, however painful,
But I would willingly attempt for Werter !

Wer. (*Taking* ALBERT *by the hand.*) Then, Al-
    bert, hear!—and O ye powers above!
That ever blast the wishes of my soul,
For once be merciful, and grant my prayer!
Let anguish, sorrow, and despair combine,
To form in unison one perfect wretch!
And let that wretch be Werter!—but, gracious
    Heaven,
Let all the curses that are lavish'd here
Be doubled in thy mercies—blessings there.
Let purest pleasure, let perpetual peace,
Eternal happiness, and constant love,
Attend him even to the hour of fate!
But long avert that hour!—he deserves it all—
I can no more—my spirits weaken fast—
I pr'ythee bear me hence.
   Alb. Bear on my arm.
A little quiet will restore thy strength——
Thou shall rest here to-night
   Wer. I thank thee much——
But I have business that compels me hence:
Yes, I have that which cannot be delayed.
   Alb. Nay, sigh not, Werter; you will be soon at
    peace.
   Wer. Yes, Albert; very soon.—I would be gone.
   Alb. Nay, say no more—bear up, my friend—bear
    up—
Time will restore you to your wonted peace.
                   [*Exeunt.*

ACT THE THIRD.

SCENE I.

WERTER'S *Apartment.*

Enter WERTER *and* LEUTHROP.

Wer. (*Giving* LEUTHROP *letters.*) These to my
    mother—for Sebastian these—
Get them convey'd, and meet me here again ;
And mark me—that I prevail'd upon my friend
Not to depart from Manheim till to-night,
Must be divulg'd to none.

    Leu. I shall obey, sir.

    Wer. How goes the night ?

    Leu. 'Tis near the second watch.

    Wer. Then, Time, I must no longer trifle with thee—
Something must be done—and that most quickly—
Oh ! 'tis an awful
Moment ! and I must use it like a man—
Away, and leave me.

    Leu. His disorder'd speech,
And the wild fury in his looks, foretel
Some new misfortune—I will not leave him.

                      [*Goes up the stage.*

    Wer. (*Pausing.*) Death is the common medicine
    for woe—

The peaceful haven, which the shatter'd bark
In tempest ever seeks.————
Then why delay?—Why yet these doubtful fears?
Oh! tis the mind that shudders at the thought
Of dark uncertainty!

   Leu. (*Coming forward.*) O sir, forgive the ardour
      of your slave,
Who rudely thus intrudes—but much I fear
Some new affliction wounds my master's peace,
Which I perhaps can lessen or avert.

   Wer. Away! Away!

   Leu. O, do but try me, sir!
I would walk barefoot o'er the boundless world,
And every step that wrung my aged feet
Should be a shoot of comfort to my soul,
Could I but mitigate my master's woes!

   Wer. If thou wouldst shew obedience to my will,
This instant leave me, nor increase my pain.

                 [*Exit* LEUTHROP.
(*Pausing again.*) Yet in this world can I e'er hope
    for peace?
Peace!—when my Charlotte is another's wife.
E'en now perhaps she languishes away,
And melts transported in her Albert's arms—
Ha! that dread thought works inward on my soul
Like darting poison—and my madd'ning brain
Is swell'd with desperation.—Oh, 'tis an hour
Of horrors! and it calls for horrid deeds————
One of the three must die—that Heaven decrees—
Shall it be Albert? shall these yet spotless hands
Shed virtue's blood? and shall the honest fall,
To let the guilty take their happier seats?
O damn'd thought!—I shudder at myself,
For bare imagination of the deed!
Shall Charlotte then? shall that sweet angel form
Be torn—be mangled—and in Werter's cause?
O cruel, cruel fate!—I'll pause no more————
One thought alone possesses all my soul,

And that shall be obey'd—Werter himself shall die !
This long has struggled in my wither'd brain,
And now it bursts, and my whole soul's at peace !
Now, Albert, live ! and bless that perfect fair,
For whom I liv'd, for whom—I soon shall die—
And, Charlotte, when the grave holds all that's left
Of that unhappy agitated being,
Who knew no pleasure but in sight of thee !
Oh, when you wander through your long-lov'd vale,
Then think of Werter !
Think how oft his sighs
Have fill'd the sounding woods ! how oft his tears
Have dew'd the weeping grass ! and if you wish
To feed on sorrows never tasted yet,
Look—towards the church-yard that contains his
          bones,
And see ! with pity how the evening breeze
Waves the high grass that grows upon his grave !
Alas !—these thoughts recal such tender scenes !
They quite unman me.

Re-enter LEUTHROP.

   Leu. In tears—O heavens !
Teach me some way to soothe my master's woes—
My gentle-master——
   Wer. Whence this intrusion ?
   Leu. I have obey'd your orders, sir.
   Wer. 'Tis well———   *(Pausing.)*
This night shall close the scene—the midnight watch
Shall be the hour—ere that—she may be seen—
Attend me to my chamber—and now, high Heaven !
Aid me with calmness till I meet my fate ! [*Exeunt.*

SCENE II.

An Apartment in ALBERT'S *House.*

Enter CHARLOTTE.

Char. O what a fate is mine! a generous lover
Ere now resolving on a sudden death,
And I his murderer! a faithful husband,
Who long has lov'd, long watch'd my cruel heart,
Offended and incens'd!—ah! there's the rock
On which my shatter'd vessel will be crush'd;
Reproof from Albert will afflict me more
Than all my sorrows past.

Enter ALBERT.

Alb. The more I think, the more I am perplex'd—
E'en now I met Sebastian at the portal,
And Werter left her not an hour ago:
Can she be false?—Can Heav'n's own image?
Can Charlotte? but, ah! I reason as I wish—
Wou'd she were true! and memory cou'd forget
The various follies that my fondness lavished—
Oh! I deserve the torments I endure.
        Char. Ha!—so disturb'd—then are my fears con-
                firm'd:
I hope, my lord, no sudden accident
Delay'd your journey.
        Alb. I crave your pardon, Charlotte:
It is impossible! that angel form
Would blush at frailty—
O my dear partner!

Char. In tears, my lord:
What can this mean?
  Alb. Have I no cause to weep?
  Char. I know of none.
  Alb. Of none! my Charlotte.
  Char. No: on my soul—if innocence——
  Alb. Innocence!
  Char. Oh! on my knees let me intreat thee, Albert,
Unfold this mystery!—let not my mind
Be tortur'd with suspense—speak! quickly speak,
Or sudden madness will distract my brain.
  Alb. Nay, do not kneel—I pr'ythee leave me now—
My mind is much disturb'd——
  Char. No! kill me quite.
Let me not linger in my pain—Oh, Albert!
Thus, thus I'll cling, thus grovel at thy feet,
Till thou hast freed my doubts! if I'm the cause,
Thy fears are false—oh, by mine honour, false!
  Alb. Honour!
  Char. Ha! you mock me still.
  Alb. Yet leave me:
A new unusual fury rages here,
And soon 'twill blaze abroad—away——
  Char. 'Tis well.
Albert mistrusts his Charlotte—yes, high Heaven!
He doubts her honour, he suspects her love:
O hear! and answer if she merits this!
  Alb. (*Laying hold of her.*) Werter!
  Char. (*Much confused.*) Ha! what of him?
  Alb. O! guilt! guilt!
  Char. Guilt?
  Alb. Yes, guilt!
Hast thou not art enough to hide thy shame?
But thou must boast it thus! to the very face
Of him thou hast abused
  Char. If it be guilt to suffer keen reproach,
Regret, affliction, error, and despair,
With every torture that can rack the soul!

Rather than wander from my truth to thee,
In action, word, or thought—if this be guilt!
I own, my lord, the justice of your charge,
And well deserve the phrase.

  Alb. This syren's song
No more shall captivate my pliant soul;
I've been too long amus'd, too long deceiv'd;
My love has been long abus'd, my liberal conduct
Scorn'd and derided—but thou shalt know
I'm not that dupe, that easy, placid fool
Thy falsehood wish'd! no, I'll exert my powers,
Enforce my rights, and be a tyrant too:
Yes; mark me, madam: I charge thee on thy truth,
Nay, on thy peril, never to be seen
Or found in converse with thy minion more.

  Char. Minion! must I bear this?

  Alb. Ay, and much more.

  Char. No, Albert; a little while ago
You found me fond, affectionate, and weak,
Made up of folly, levity, and fears;
But your own rashness has restor'd my sense,
And I despise your threats—Minion! O shame!
Use such another word, and here I vow,
If e'er I deign to listen to you more,
'Tis but with scorn—unalterable scorn.

  Alb. This poor pretended spirit is in vain;
Thy stubborn heart shall bleed.

  Char. You little know
The heart of Charlotte, if you think 'twill bleed
At folly's idle rage—no, my lord,
When you return to your accustom'd peace,
And converse like yourself, I am your own,
Proud to indulge, and happy to obey you;
But when you lose that calmness you profess,
And thus insult me, I am only taught
That Albert is no better than a tyrant,
Whose vain presumption merits my disdain.

  Alb. Away, away—I'll trifle time no more:

Now hear my last resolve :—By Heaven I love thee
More than romantic fancy can express,
And would not leave thee for eternal peace :
But if you still persist
To let another triumph in your heart,
Thou art no longer mine—we part for ever.

 Char. Ungenerous man !
Is it for this my soul resign'd its love,
And kept its vow to thee ! is it for this !
He you abuse in endless anguish lives,
Perhaps—I cannot speak—*(Weeps.)*

 Alb. Ha ! do'st thou weep ! perfidious woman, go,
Go to thy Werter, revel in his arms;
Albert will never interrupt you more.   [*Exit.*

 Char. When, angry Heaven, shall thy vengeance
   cease ?
When shall this little victim be allow'd
A momentary calm—never, never—
Yet something—myself shall save him from
The horrid deed.

  Enter WERTER *(supported by* LEUTHROP.)

 Wer. A little onward bear me, faithful Leuthrop,
To sigh my life out at my Charlotte's feet,
And I shall die content.

 Char. Oh Heavens ! was Sebastian——

 Wer. He was deceiv'd—I yielded to his wish,
And while he left me to prepare for Manheim,
Completed my design—It was my fate
To catch a sad distemper in the heart,
Which grew contagious, and while it canker'd here
Infected all who sooth'd—Could I then live
But to destroy the sharers of my pains ?

 Char. Haste to Sebastian, tell him all—away—
Some speedy antidote may yet be found :
He cannot, shall not die.

 Wer. Give me some comfort ;
For I am coward all—I fear'd to brave

Life's common chances, and I shudder now
To meet that death I sought—horror! horror!
I dare not think upon the deed I've done;
I have invaded nature's sacred law,
Repell'd against Heaven itself!—O my Charlotte!
Is there no hope of pardon?

Char. Cruel, cruel hour!
And must I lose thee, Werter!

Wer. Tell Albert to forgive me,
For I have injur'd and abus'd him much:
Forgive me too thyself!—Could I but live!
It will not be—Ha! that pang was Death's:—
It will not be—mercy, mercy, Heaven!   *(Dies.)*
          (CHARLOTTE *falls on the body.*)

Enter ALBERT, SEBASTIAN, *and* LEUTHROP.

Seb. The sharpest torments cruelty suggests
Wou'd be indulgence to the pangs I feel:
Who but Sebastian wou'd have left his friend?
Had I remain'd and sooth'd him as I ought,
This ne'er had happen'd—curst, curst reflection!
I am the fatal cause of all these sorrows.

Alb. (Weeping over CHARLOTTE.*)* No, 'tis from
          Albert ev'ry sorrow flows.
Had I not been the weakest, worst of men,
I had resign'd my Charlotte, and been happy
In seeing her so exquisitely blest.
What am I now? thou injur'd innocence!
Pronounce my doom!

Char. (Starting up.) Talk not to me—away!
Be swift as lightning, or you'll be too late:
He's in yon fatal vale!—I left him there;
His sword was drawn, and death sat brooding by;
Fly, or he's murder'd!—hark! a shriek—a shriek!—
Ah! now 'tis past, the sweet deluder's vanish'd,
And I must wander o'er the world alone

Seb. (To CHARLOTTE.*)* Let not excess of grief

O'ercome thy reason, but with pity look
On wretched Albert.

   Char. Albert! I know him well,
He is my husband, guardian of my honour!
Honour! no more of that—no more of that—
That kill'd the innocent!—oh! my poor heart!

   Alb. Hold, hold, my brain!—will none attempt to
      sooth her?
Will none assist? I can no longer bear
The maddening sight!   *(Falls on* LEUTHROP.*)*

   Char. There—there's his sepulchre—
Ha! see it shakes—the tomb is all convuls'd!
Soft—now it yawns, and gently steals apart—
'Tis burst asunder—here the body lies!
Alas! how changed!—these tears, neglected shade,
Shall wash thy rankling wounds—these hands—ah!
      look,
His eye-balls roll! he trembles in his shroud—
He is alive! and all will still be well.
See! see! to Heaven he mounts;
Legions of angels hover round his form;
He beckons me! Werter, I come! I come—
And now let honour part us if it can!
            (Falls on WERTER's *body.)*

Curtain drops, with slow Music.

END OF VOLUME THIRD.

THE MODERN THEATRE

THE

MODERN THEATRE;

THE MODERN THEATRE

A collection of plays

selected by

MRS. ELIZABETH INCHBALD

First published London, 1811

in ten volumes

Reissued in 1968
in five volumes
by Benjamin Blom, Inc.

Benjamin Blom, Inc.

New York

THE

MODERN THEATRE;

A COLLECTION OF

SUCCESSFUL MODERN PLAYS,

AS ACTED AT

THE THEATRES ROYAL, LONDON.

PRINTED FROM THE PROMPT BOOKS UNDER THE AU-
THORITY OF THE MANAGERS.

SELECTED BY

MRS INCHBALD.

———

IN TEN VOLUMES.

VOL. IV.

DUPLICITY.   HE IS MUCH TO BLAME.
SCHOOL FOR ARROGANCE: SEDUCTION.
            SCHOOL FOR PREJUDICE.

LONDON:

PRINTED FOR LONGMAN, HURST. REES, ORME, AND BROWN,
PATERNOSTER-ROW.

1811.

First published London, 1811
Reissued 1968,
by Benjamin Blom, Inc. Bx 10452

Library of Congress Catalog Card No. 67-13004

Manufactured in the United States of America

DUPLICITY;

A

COMEDY,

IN FIVE ACTS.

AS PERFORMED AT THE

THEATRE-ROYAL, COVENT-GARDEN.

BY

THOMAS HOLCROFT.

VOL. IV.

DRAMATIS PERSONÆ.

MR OSBORNE,	*Mr Henderson.*
SIR HARRY PORTLAND,	*Mr Lewis.*
SIR HORNET ARMSTRONG,	*Mr Wilson.*
SQUIRE TURNBULL,	*Mr Lee-Lewes.*
MR VANDERVELT,	*Mr Wewitzer.*
TIMID,	*Mr Edwin.*
SCRIP,	*Mr Stevens.*
SERVANTS,	{ *Mr J. Wilson.* *Mr Newton.* *Mr Joules.*
CLARA,	*Miss Younge.*
MISS TURNBULL,	*Mrs Wilson.*
MELISSA,	*Mrs Inchbald.*
MRS TRIP,	*Mrs Pitt.*

DUPLICITY.

ACT THE FIRST.

SCENE I.

SIR HARRY PORTLAND'S *House.*

Enter CLARA *and* MELISSA.

Cla. Well, my dear Melissa, you will be a happy woman!

Mel. I have no doubt of it. The attention which Mr Osborne has shewn me was not that of a man eager to gain the affection of his mistress by humouring her caprices, praising her beauty, and flattering her follies. He is obliging and well bred, but sincere ; yet his disapprobation is delivered with a delicacy that makes it more agreeable than some people's compliments.

Cla. If time, instead of mellowing the strokes, should wear away this smooth varnish, and discover

a harsh outline, should you not be offended at the
severity of his manner, think you ?

Mel. Believe me, dear Clara, there is no danger;
for if there be one man on earth more capable of making a woman happy than another, it is Mr Osborne.

Cla. It would be heresy in you, my dear, to hold
any other opinion ; and I have no doubt but you
will continue orthodox after marriage.

Mel. Yes—I shall certainly die in that faith.

Cla. Your brother, Sir Harry, I believe, is of your
religion too.

Mel. Entirely—The friendship of Mr Osborne and
my brother is as sincere as the commencement of it
was remarkable—Have you ever heard their story ?

Cla. Never. You know my acquaintance with your
family is but just begun ; but I hope you will not
think them words of course when I assure you that,
short as it is, I feel myself interested in its happiness.

Mel. Oh ! I am sure you are sincere—I know it
by sympathy—Well then, I'll tell you.—Harry and
Osborne happened to be both abroad at the same
time. As my brother was going to Italy, and passing
through the mountainous part of Savoy, he came to
a hollow way, among the rocks, surrounded by trees
and caverns. All on a sudden, at a turning in the
road, he beheld Osborne and his servants attacked
by six banditti, and ready to sink under their wounds.

Cla. Was Sir Harry alone ? (*Alarmed.*)

Mel. He had his governor, two servants, and the
postillion—My brother instantly leaped from his carriage, snatched up his sword and pistols, and flew to
the place of action.

Cla. I declare you terrify me !

Mel. He was not seen by the combatants, and
took care to advance so near before he fired, that he
could not fail to do execution—He laid two of the
banditti dead ; and their companions, who had discharged their fire-arms, and beheld Sir Harry's peo-

ple running to the attack, and levelling their pieces, fled.

Cla. Thank you for that, my dear—you have given me breath.

Mel. The intrepidity with which Sir Harry saw Osborne defend himself, and the fortitude he discovered when he was informed, as it was at first believed, that his wounds were mortal, attached my brother so powerfully to him, that he resolved not to leave him in the hands of strangers, but anxiously waited while he was under cure.

Cla. This was a noble generosity!

Mel. It was; and Osborne was so sensible of it, that, though he was going the other way, he would return with Sir Harry into Italy; and their friendship has continued ever since.

Cla. But is it not strange, my dear, that he cannot detach his friend Sir Harry from the *gaming-table?*

Mel. My brother is infatuated—It is his greatest, almost his only weakness.

Cla. But the report is, that Mr Osborne takes advantage of this weakness; that while he publicly satirizes the practice, he privately benefits by his superior address, and, in fact, has half ruined Sir Harry himself.

Mel. The report of malice, my dear.

Enter SIR HARRY PORTLAND *and* MR OSBORNE.

Sir Har. Ladies, your obedient—Pray, when did you arrive in town, madam? (*To* CLARA.)

Cla. Yesterday—But how came you to quit Bath so suddenly, gentlemen? I understood you intended to stay another week, and you were gone before me.

Sir Har. Mr Osborne, madam, was *horriblement ennuyé*—dull as an alderman at church, or a fat lapdog after dinner—thinking on marriage, Melissa, and other momentous matters; and so——

Osb. Come, come, Sir Harry, this is mighty ingenious; but you were at least as willing to be gone as myself—The truth, madam, is, my *modest* friend here heard *you* were to set off in a day or two, and from that moment was continually giving hints, and asking me how I, as a lover, could exist so long without a sight of my mistress; and, in short, began, all at once, to talk so sympathetically about absence and ages, that I, who had made the excursion purely to oblige him, was, I acknowledge, exceedingly happy to find I could oblige him by returning.

Cla. What say you to this, Sir Harry?—But I know your politeness—you will confess it all to be true, and begin to say civil things upon the subject, that will only put me to the trouble of blushing and curtseying; so we'll suppose them all, if you please— But come, tell me—what's the news of the day?

Mel. News! Oh, that's true—Look here, my dear! —I thought I had something to tell you—(*Reads a paragraph in a newspaper.*)—" We hear, from very good authority, that a hymeneal treaty is concluded between a certain beautiful ward, not a mile from St James's Square, and her old guardian; and that the lady is expected in town from Bath every hour, to sign and seal."

Sir Har. What say *you* to this, madam?

Cla. Say! I protest I don't know what to say!— except that these news-makers are a very pleasant, ingenious kind of people.

Mel. But a'n't you angry?

Cla. Angry! no, indeed. I am sure I am very much obliged to them for thinking of me—I shall be so stared at—I'll go into public continually, and my guardian shall go with me.

Mel. But is there any foundation for this report, my dear?

Cla. Nay, I am sure I can't tell: there may be, for aught I know—I have suspected the matter a great

while, you must know, by my guardian's simpering
and squeezing my hand so often—then he is continually talking about Methuselah and the Antediluvi-
ans, and making systems, to convince me how much
stronger and longer-lived some men are than others
—He read, the other day, in the Annual Register, of
a man, at Inverness, who lived to the age of one hundred and seventeen; and he has been talking ever
since of purchasing a country seat in the Highlands.

Sir Har. That would be pleasant.

Cla. Very—Then we should have a flock of goats,
I suppose!

Sir Har. Dorastus and Faunia.

Cla. Oh yes—quite in the Damon and Philida
way.

Osb. You are very happy in a lover, madam.

Cla. Exceedingly—quite proud of my conquest.—
There is no such great miracle in bringing a young
fellow, whose passions are all afloat, to die at one's
feet—The thing's so natural, that one does it every
day—But to thaw the icy blood of a grave old gentleman, to see him simper, sigh, dance minuets, and
look ridiculous for one—Oh! there is, positively, no
flattery equal to it.

Sir Har. He will make your winter evenings in
the Highlands quite entertaining, with relating the
wild pranks he committed, and the deeds of prowess
he was guilty of in his youth—then you will be so delighted with listening to his raptures, and tasting his
panada, and——

Cla. Oh yes—yes, yes—ha, ha—I—I think I see
him now, with his venerable bald head, his shrivelled
face, and his little pug nose, that looks as red and as
bright as the best Dutch sealing-wax, rising from
his chair, by the help of his crutch-headed stick, to
breathe forth vows of love and everlasting fidelity—
Ha, ha, ha!

Mel. It's whimsical enough.

Cla. Yes—Oh, now you talk of whimsical, I was
accosted by an old gentleman, the night before I left
Bath, in the rooms, who was the drollest being, and
had the most agreeable kind of whimsicallity about
him, I ever met with—I thought he would have made
love to me—swore I was an angel, and said a thousand civil things—quite gallant.

Osb. Oh, madam, the old men are the only polite
men of this age.

Cla. Upon my word, I begin to think so.

Osb. The young ones, taught in the modern school,
hold a rude familiarity to be the first principle of good
breeding.

Cla. Manners, like point ruffles, are now most fashionable when they are soiled.

Sir Har. No, no—they only hang the easier for
being deprived of starch—But who was this old gentleman, pray, madam?

Cla. A relation of yours, sir.

Sir Har. Of mine, madam?

Cla. I should suppose so, for he mentioned his nephew, Sir Harry Portland.

Mel. Our uncle, Sir Hornet Armstrong.

Sir Har. It is—I found a letter from him when I
came to town, in which he informed me he should
arrive in Bath the very day we left it.

Enter Servant.

Sir Har. Who brought this?

Serv. It came by the post, sir.   [*Exit Servant.*

(Sir Harry *reads the letter, and seems surprised.*)

Cla. I die to be better acquainted with him—I
must have him in my train of sighing swains.

Osb. You seem astonished, Sir Harry.

Cla. Some unkind billet from his mistress, I suppose.

Sir Har. No, indeed; it is the most unaccountable epistle I ever received, and from my unaccountable uncle too—There, read, read. (*To* OSBORNE.)

Osb. (*Reads.*)—" Dear Harry—You know, you dog, how your old uncle loves you—You will say so, when you are thoroughly acquainted with the occasion of this——In brief——I met with a young lady at Bath, the most extraordinary, take her all together, I ever beheld—She is a nonpareil! a phœnix!—But you will judge for yourself—She is coming up to town with her brother, who, by the by, is a country booby—but that's no matter—I saw her only once, and that was in the rooms; but once is sufficient——They intended coming up to London by way of seeing the town, for they are country people I find, though the sister has more accomplishments, ease, and good-breeding, than I ever yet saw in the drawing-room—I proposed a match to the brother, and he seemed happy at the offer—They will arrive nearly as soon as this, for they set out before it; and I shall follow, maugre the gout, as fast as I can.

HORNET ARMSTRONG.

" P. S. I forgot to mention their name is Turnbull."—*Turnbull!* Why, what, in the devil's name, is Sir Hornet mad!

Sir Har. In one of his right ancient whims, I suppose—Sir Hornet has had many such in his time.

Mel. But pray, who is this miraculous lady, Mr Osborne? for you seem to know something of her.

Osb. Do you remember, Sir Harry, a gawky girl, that stalked round the rooms, and stared prodigiously—she that was stuck to the side of a bob-wig'd country 'squire?

Cla. Oh!—what, the—the wench with her arms dangling, her chin projecting, and her mouth open —dressed in the—red ribband, tawdry style, and that looked as if she were afraid of being lost?

Sir Har. Yes—or as if she durst not trust herself

alone out of her own parish, lest somebody should catch her, put her in a sack, and send her for a present to the king of the cannibals.

Osb. The same; that is the accomplished Miss Turnbull.

Sir Har. How!

Osb. That is the easy, well-bred, drawing-room lady.

Sir Har. Is it possible?

Cla. Ha, ha, ha, ha, ha! well—(*With an affected gravity*)—and I don't doubt but she would make a sort of a—a—a very good wife—Understands the arts of brewing, baking, pickling of pork, curing of hung beef, darning of stockings, and other branches of housewifery in perfection.

Sir Har. Oh, no doubt.—Is perfectly skilled too in the science of feeding the pigs.

Cla. Yes; and will make her own and her husband's linen, and do all the needle-work and quilting at home—Believes in ghosts; and has got the wandering Prince of Troy, the Babes in the Wood, and the entertaining Dialogue of Death and the Lady by heart.

Osb. Such, and so numerous, are the wife-like properties of Miss Barbara Turnbull.

Cla. Turnbull, too!—Well, that is such a delightful name for a country lady—so pastoral!

Osb. The father was one of the greatest graziers in the west of England, and was so intent on getting money, that he bred his children in the most stupid ignorance. He is lately dead; and the son has commenced gentleman and 'squire, by virtue of the father's industry, and a pack of fox-hounds; and though he has scarce knowledge enough of articulate sounds to hold a dialogue with his own geese, yet does he esteem himself a devilish shrewd fellow, and a wit. His conversation is vociferous, and patched up of proverbs and out-of-the-way sayings, which he strings together without order or connection, and utters upon all occasions and in all companies, without respect to time, place, or person.

Cla. Well, well, Sir Harry, I shall have to wish you joy soon, I suppose. But I must be gone. Fifty visits to make this morning. Time flies; but agreeable company, and all that, you know. Oh, Sir Harry, you mean to attend the spring meetings this year, at Newmarket? I am told you understand the turf. I think of sending a venture of five hundred by somebody. But I shall see you often enough before then. Adieu. [*Exeunt* CLARA *and* MELISSA.

[*Manent* SIR HARRY *and* OSBORNE.

Sir Har. Well, what do you think of this lady, Osborne?

Osb. I think her a very amiable, accomplished lady, and one that, under an assumed levity, observes and understands every thing about her.

Sir Har. I am entirely of your opinion. If I may judge from an acquaintance of such short date, she is the first woman in the world.

Osb. Except one, Sir Harry.

Sir Har. You, Osborne, may make exceptions, if you please; I am not so captious. She has beauty without vanity, virtue without prudery, fashion without affectation, wit without malice, gaiety without coquetry, humour——

Osb. Hold, hold! stop to breathe. How was it? Vinegar without acid, fire without heat, light without shade, motion without matter, and a likeness without a feature.

Sir Har. Spite, by the gods! proud spite and burning envy.

Osb. But did you observe her Newmarket hint, Sir Harry, and the concealed significance with which it was delivered?

Sir Har. I did.

Osb. Which, being faithfully done into English, bears this interpretation :—" I, Clara Forrester, a beautiful, elegant, sensible girl, with a fine fortune, should like to take you, Harry Portland, with youth, spirit, and certain *et ceteras*, but"——

Sir Har. But that I am afraid of indulging a partiality for any man who is so intolerably addicted to gaming. Is not that the conclusion of your speech?

Osb. Oh fie! no, no : Gaming! That man has a body without a soul, that never felt an inclination to gaming.

Sir Har. Perhaps so; but that man has the greatest soul who can best resist that inclination.

Osb. Pshaw!—Gaming is the essence of fashion, and one of your strongest recommendations. Clara is a girl of spirit; and what girl, that comes under that description, would ever place her affections on a sneaking, sober, prudent fellow—a mechanical scoundrel, that knows the day of the month, sips tea, keeps a pew in the parish church, writes memorandums, and goes to bed at eleven o'clock? Poh! absurd!

Sir Har. Curse me, Osborne, if I know what to make of you: you are a riddle that I cannot expound. You have such an awkward way of praising gaming, that it always has the appearance of satire.

Osb. Satire! how so? Do you think I'd satirize myself? Who sports more freely than I do?

Sir Har. Why, there's the mystery. You are as eager, to the full, as I am. If I set an hundred on a back hand, you offer a thousand; nay, had I the fortune of a nabob, and were to stake it all, you would be the first man to cry covered, and be damned mad if any one wanted to go a guinea. Not because you have not generosity, but in the true and inveterate spirit of gaming.

Osb. Certainly. Gaming! why gaming is the best sal volatile for the spleen: it rouses the spirits, agitates the blood, quickens the pulse, and puts the whole nervous system in a continual vibration. No man ever yet died of an apoplexy that loved a box and dice.

Sir Har. But they have died as suddenly.

Osb. Oh! ay, ay; but that's a fashionable disease, an influenza; that's to make your exit with *eclat ;* that's to go out of the world with a good report.

Sir Har. True, true ; and indeed as to a few years more or less, that is, in reality, a mighty insignificant circumstance.

Osb. A bagatelle !—Let us live while we do live, and die when we cannot live any longer.

Sir Har. That's my comfort, that's my comfort.— Yes, yes, a pistol, a pistol is a very certain remedy for the cholic ! Nobody but a pitiful scoundrel would go sighing, and whining, and teazing other people with his griefs and complaints. When a man is weary, what should he do but go to sleep ?

Osb. To be sure. Life itself is but a dream.— 'Tis only sleeping a little sounder.

Sir Har. What, live to be pitied! Ha, ha! A decayed gentleman ! No, no, no. A withered branch ! —a firelock without a flint ! And yet—heigho !— this Clara—damn it, it's provoking.—Youth, beauty, affability ! She's a bewitching girl !

Osb. She is indeed.

Sir Har. A lovely girl !

Osb. Ay, enough so to make any man, that might hope to be in her favour, in love with life.

Sir Har. Any man, any man but me—no, no— undone, undone, undone !

Osb. Well, but, seriously, since you have such bad success, why don't you renounce play ?

Sir Har. 'Tis too late : I have sunk eighty thousand ; my resources almost all exhausted ; my estates all mortgaged to Jews and scoundrels.

Osb. All !

Sir Har. All, except the estate in Kent.

Osb. Well, then, if you cannot content yourself
with your present loss, your best way will be to make
another vigorous push.

Sir Har. That's exactly what I am determined to
do; and unless the devil possesses the dice, I think
I may expect, without a miracle, that fortune should
change hands.

Osb. One would think so, indeed. Will you dine
then at my house? There will be the chevalier, the
baron, and the usual set. They have engaged to
dine with me. They are spirited fellows, and will
play for any sum.

Sir Har. I don't know. Suspicion is a curs'd meanness; and yet I cannot help having my doubts of
some among that company. Nay, had you not so
often assured me you were perfectly acquainted with
them all——

Osb. Why, I tell you again and again, so I am.——
I will be answerable for their conduct; and that's
more than I would say for any other set of gamblers
upon earth.

Sir Har. Well, well, I'll meet you there.

Osb. We dine early—at five.

Sir Har. Agreed.

Osb. And then—hey for a light heart and a heavy
purse.   [*Exit* OSBORNE.

Sir Har. No, no—no light heart for me.—I am
sunk, degraded in my own opinion. Gaming alters
our very nature. Osborne used to hate it. He was
then an open-hearted, generous fellow. He now
appears to have contracted an insatiable love for
money, and a violent desire to win—he cares not of
whom; of me as soon as another. Were I in his
situation, and he in mine, I think I should find an
aversion to increase his distress.—He knows mine,
yet has no such aversion. Perhaps he thinks my ruin
certain, and that he may as well profit by it as ano-

ther. I know him to have the most refined and strictest sense of honour. I have lost most of my money to him, and in his company, and therefore have not been duped out of it.—That is some comfort, however.   [*Exit.*

SCENE II.

Enter MR OSBORNE *and* TIMID.

Osb. Well, Mr Timid, has Sir Harry sent to you for a further supply?

Tim. Lack-a-day, sir, yes; and a very large supply too.—He wants 5000*l.* immediately. Lack-a-day! I asked him how he thought it possible for me to raise such sums as he called upon me for every day; reminded him what a bad way his affairs were in; and what an usurious rate I was obliged to borrow all this money at.

Osb. What said he?

Tim. Lack-a-day! not much: seemed chagrined; said it must have an end, one way or another, soon; and demanded whether I could or could not raise the money. Lack-a-day! I told him I was no longer master of ways and means; and he said, then he must positively employ another prime minister, for supplies he must have.

Osb. Why did you tell him that? Go to him; inform him you have met with a tender-hearted Jew, who knows nothing of the situation of his affairs, that will lend him 10,000*l.* directly, if he wants it.

Tim. Ten thousand! On what terms?

Osb. Oh! the mortgage of the Kentish estate.

Tim. The Kentish estate! Lack-a-day! but suppose he should go to gaming, and lose it to somebody else instead of you?

Osb. Oh, I'll take care of that.

Tim. Lack-a-day! it must not be Benjamin Solomons who lends this?

Osb. True; no:—humph—Isaac Levi, agent to a private company at Amsterdam.

Tim. (*Writes in a pocket-book.*) " Isaac Levi, agent to a private company at Amsterdam." Lack-a-day!

Osb. Well, go you to him, and inform him that the money shall be ready in about half an hour.

Tim. Lack-a-day! good young gentleman! Heaven pardon me; I had like to have said, damn the dice. You'll be a true friend?

Osb. Be under no apprehensions.—This old fool is become suspicious : I must be sudden. (*Aside.*)

Tim. Had not we better inform him of all, before he goes any further?

Osb. By no means : leave that to me.

Tim. Lack-a-day! Well, the remembrance of a good deed is grateful on a death-bed.

Osb. Do you be expeditious. I'll instruct the Jew, and he shall meet you here.　　　[*Exit* OSBORNE.

Tim. Heaven pardon me! I had like to have said, damn the Jews.　　　　　　　　　　　[*Exit.*

ACT THE SECOND.

SCENE I.

Sir HARRY *and* MELISSA.

Sir Har. Heavens! what romance! I can scarce believe my eyes! Did you ever hear of so strange an affair?

Mel. Strange! it's miraculous!—Quixotism!—And our good uncle is the prince of madmen!

Sir Har. To send a foolish, illiterate, country dowdy and her block-headed brother a visiting on such an errand! What can I say to them? I declare I don't know how to behave; never was so embarrassed in my life. Where are they?

Mel. He has made an acquaintance with the groom, and is gone to the Mews, which seems to be his proper element, to examine the horses; and I left her with my woman, staring, like a Dutch doll, at every thing she fixed her eyes on. Here she comes.

Enter MISS TURNBULL.

Miss Turn. My gracious! Here be a power of vine—(*Staring about.*) I wonder if that be he that be to be my husband.—(*Aside.*)

Sir Har. I hope, madam, the fatigue of your journey has not injured your health.

Miss Turn. Zir!

Sir Har. I hope you are pretty well after your journey.

Miss Turn. Pretty well, thank you, zir.—Iveck, he's a handsome man. (*Aside.*)

Mel. This is the oddest affair.

Sir Har. I don't know what to say to her—I am afraid, Miss Turnbull, you wont find the town so agreeable as the Elysian fields of Somersetshire.

Miss Turn. Lisian vields!—There be no zuch vields in our parts—There be only corn vields and hay vields.

Mel. My brother, madam, means to say, you are not so well pleased with the town as with the country, perhaps.

Miss Turn. Oh!—Yes, but I be though, and ten times better—(*They stand silent some time.*) Pray, miss, when did you see Zekel Turnbull, my uncle?

Mel. I have not the honour to know him.

Miss Turn. My gracious!—What, don't you know Zekel?

Mel. No, indeed!

Miss Turn. Why, he do come to London zity vour times every year.

Sir Har. Is he in parliament?

Miss Turn. Parliament?

Sir Har. Yes.

Miss Turn. What, a parliament-man?

Sir Har. Yes.

Miss Turn. No; he be a grazier—(*Silent again.*) Pray, miss, have you been to zee the lions and the wax-work to-day?

Mel. To-day!

Miss Turn. Ees.

Mel. I never saw them in my life.

Miss Turn. My gracious!—What, never zaw the kings, and the queens, and the tom-stones?

Mel. No.

Miss Turn. Merciful vather !—Well, let's go and zee 'em now then.

Mel. People of fashion never go to those kind of places.

Miss Turn. Never !

Mel. Never.

Miss Turn. My gracious !—But I am zure I will go every day while I be in London zity, if I can vind the way.—Pray be this vair-time here—Where be all those volk gwain—and where do they all come fro' ?

(SQUIRE TURNBULL *without.*)

Barbara—Barbara—Where bist, Barbara ?

Miss Turn. I be here.

Enter Squire.

Sq. Well, Zir Harry, here we be—Madam, your zervant—I zupped wi' Zir Hornet three nights ago, an a zaid you be a vine lass—What though—I had never zeen you, but I gave yo', miss, in a bumper ; an Zir Hornet swore, that, except Barbara, a didn't knaw one to match you.

Mel. He did me great honour.

Sq. Why, to be zure a did—What though—a was wrong—I zee a was wrong—Barbara is well enough —But what though—the greatest calf isn't always the sweetest veal—Vor all the length of her spurs, she won't do pitted against this vine ginger pullet.

Mel. Your compliments quite over-power me, sir.

Sq. Compliments—No, no—What though—vather be dead, an' I ha' three thousand a-year, and the best pack of vox dogs in Zomerzetzhire—I a no need make compliments—I would as zoon over-ride the hounds, or vell oak zaplings vor vire wood— Barbara, mayhap, understands zic things ; her reads Kademy o' Compliments—vor my part, I a' no time vor zic trash.

Miss Turn. I'm zure it be a very pretty book.

Sq. Hold thy tongue, Barbara, an' then nobody will knaw thee bist a vool—Look ye me, miss—I do want a wife—an' I should like hugely vor you an I to zet our horses together, as the zaying is.

Mel. Sir—I don't understand—

Sq. Vor my part, I am none of your hawf-bred ones—What though—shilly shally and no thank you are always hungry—A lame tongue gets nothing, and the last wooer wins the maid—A bad hound may start a hare, but a good one will catch her.

Sir Har. I believe, sir, you never saw my sister before.

Sq. Why, no, to be zure—What though—Love and a red nose can't be hid—If you cut up the goose, I'll eat it—The hare starts when the hound least expects it.

Sir Har. Very true, sir—But here is a disagreeable misunderstanding—

Sq. Why, to be zure—I do knaw it—We misunderstand the thing parfitly well—it be very disagreeable, an' I be glad of it—I a brought Barbara to London to zee the lions, buy ribbands, an' be married—But what though—liking's liking, an' love's love—myzelf bevore my zister—If the mountain won't go to the man, the man mun go to the mountain—an vaint heart never won vair lady.

Sir Har. Don't you think, sir, that were my sister's affections totally disengaged, this abruptness were very unlikely to gain them? Is it not too violent, think you, for female delicacy?

Sq. Why, to be zure—vemale delicacy!—I hate it—and as vor your abruptness, why, gi' me the man that speaks bolt outright—I am vor none o' your abruptness—What though—he must a' leave to speak that can't hold his tongue.

Mel. Your proverb is quite à-propos, sir.

Sq. Why, to be zure—dogs bark as they are bred.

Sir Har. ⎱
Mel.   ⎰ Ha ! ha ! ha !

Sq. I am a staunch hound, miss, and seldom at vault; an' zo, wi your leave, I'll—

(*Offers to kiss* MELISSA.)

Mel. I beg, sir——

Sq. Nay, don't be bashful—I like fruit too well to play long at bobcherry—a's a vool indeed that can't carve a plumb-pudding—

(*Offers to kiss again, and is prevented by* SIR HARRY.)

Sir Har. I am sorry to be obliged to inform you that you are entirely mistaken, both with respect to the affections of my sister and myself. As a friend of my uncle's, sir, I shall be happy to shew you every respect, but nothing farther can possibly take place between the families.

Enter a Servant.   (*Delivers a card to* MELISSA.)
Exit MELISSA.

Serv. Mr Timid desired me to tell you, sir, that Mr Levi is quite tired of waiting, and says, if you can't come now, he will call again to-morrow.

Sir Har. Oh, tell him he must not go—I beg Mr Levi's pardon : I'll be with him in a minute. (*Exit Servant.*)—Sir Hornet has been exceedingly precipitate in this business, sir—He is coming to town, and must apologize for his error—As to my sister, I have no doubt but she has every respect for your merits they deserve ; but her affections are pre-engaged, the nuptials fixed, and are soon to be celebrated—While you remain in town, however, I beg you will command my house and services. (*Exit* SIR HARRY, *bowing.*)

Sq. Well, Barbara, what dost think on un ?

Miss Turn. Why, a be well enough—but I daunt rightly knaw what a means.

Sq. What a means—thee bist a vool—thee dust

na knaw the London tongue, thee means—A zaid, in
a kind of round-about way, that it's all right.

Miss Turn. Did a?

Sq. Did a—why, to be zure a did—didst na zee
how zivil a were, an what a low bow a made—But
thee has no contagion in thee—thee will never learn
what's what.

Miss Turn. Why, where be I to learn zic things
—I a never been no where.

Sq. Never been no where—well—what o' that?—
Where have I been? I a never been no where—
what though—I do knaw how to stir my broth without scalding my vinger—I can zee an owl in an oven
as soon as another.

Miss Turn. But when be us to go and zee the
zights?

Sq. Oh, we'll go all together on the wedding-day.

Miss Turn. My gracious!—I wish it were here.

Sq. Ay, ay—I daunt doubt thee—women, pigs, and
poultry be never zatisfied.

Miss Turn. An be you to be married as well?

Sq. Be I to be married as well? Why, to be zure
I be—thee bist a vool—Isn't vather dead? an hannot
I three thousand a-year, an the best pack o vox dogs
in Zomerzetzhire? An didst na hear me tell miss 'at
I would marry her?—What though—I do knaw how
to catch two pigeons wi' one pea—Shew a dog a bone,
and he'll wag his tail—He that is born a beauty is
half married, an like will to like.

Miss Turn. Well, then, take me to parliament-
house, an shew me the king, an the queen, an the
lord-mayor, an the elephant, an the rest o' the royal
vamily.

Sq. I tell thee thee shatn't.

Miss Turn. My gracious!—What zignifications
my coming to London zity, an' I must be moped up
a this'n : I will go, zo I will.

Sq. I tell thee thee shatn't.

Miss Turn. Why, then, an I munnut zee the king —I'll go into next room and zee his picter, that I will.   [*Exit* MISS TURNBULL.

Sq. A hoic !—Barbara—Barbara—The helve after the hatchet—He that holds a woman mun ha' a long rope an' a strong arm—Women an mules will go their own road in zpite of riders or stinging nettles.

[*Exit Squire.*

SCENE II.

The House of MR VANDERVELT.

Enter VANDERVELT, (*meditating.*)

Vand. Clara is very beautiful—but mankind is very censorious—They will tell me that sixty-seven is too late in life to undertake the begetting, bringing up, and providing for a family—What of that—Must I go out of the world as I came into it—nobody to remember me ?—Must the name of Vandervelt be forgotten ?—Must I leave no pretty picture of myself ? —Sixty-seven is but sixty-seven—Have not we a thousand examples of longevity upon record ?—— And then—as to cuckolds—I cannot be persuaded that they are as common now as they were when I was a youngster—Times, men, and manners alter— Children are born wittier, and the world gets more sedate—I myself am a living proof of it—I never go to bagnios now—I never break lamps, beat watchmen, and kick constables now—Once, indeed, I should have made very little ceremony about dignifying an elderly gentleman, that had a handsome wife ; whereas now I can lay my hand upon my heart, and with a safe conscience declare I have no such wicked inclinations.

Enter CLARA.

Cla. Ah! mon cher papa! What, ruminating!

Vand. Ah! Turtle! But why do you always call me papa? you know I don't like that word, turtle.

Cla. And why, papa, do you always call me turtle? —Have not I told you, fifty times, it puts me in mind of calipash—and aldermen—and other ugly animals.

Vand. Calipash! Thou art sweeter, tenderer, more delicate, delightful, and delicious, than all the calipash and calipee in the universe—A gem—a jewel—that all the sophies, sultans, grand signiors, and great moguls of the whole earth have not riches enough to purchase.

Cla. Ah! Mon cher papa!—You are so gallant— You do say the most obliging things!

Vand. *Say* the most obliging things!—Ay, and will —No matter—Deeds—Title-deeds—Rent-rolls—— India bonds—Well—Death and the day of judgment will make strange discoveries.

Cla. Oh yes:—I know you wise men often meditate on these serious subjects.

Vand. Ay—Life is treacherous ground—One foot firm, and the next in a pit.

Cla. But why so melancholy, papa?

Vand. I have no friends—that is, no relations—no children—have made a great fortune, by care, and labour, and anxiety, and debarring myself the pleasures and comforts of life in my youth—And why should not I sit down and enjoy it?

Cla. Very true, and why don't you?

Vand. Because men are fools, and laugh, they don't know why—I hate ridicule—Nobody loves to be thought ridiculous—The world has got false notions —A man of fifty is called old, and must not be in love, for fear of being pointed at—Whereas some men are older at thirty, than others at threescore.

Cla. Certainly.

Vand. What is threescore?

Cla. A handful of minutes!

Vand. That vanish like a summer shower.

Cla. Melt like a lump of sugar in a dish of tea.

Vand. That come you don't know how.

Cla. And go you don't know where.

Vand. Surely a man of sixty may walk through a church-yard without fear of tumbling into a grave?

Cla. If he can jump over it.

Vand. True—And I was once an excellent jumper—Sixty!—Why, Henry Jenkins, the Yorkshire fisherman, lived to a hundred and sixty-nine—So that a man of sixty, even in these degenerate days, has a chance to live at least an hundred years.

Cla. Well, I declare, papa, you are quite a blooming youth!—forty years younger, in my opinion, than you were a quarter of an hour ago!

Vand. Forty?

Cla. At least!

Vand. Why then, by dad, as thou sayest, I am a blooming youth—Ah, turtle!—I could tell you something—that would surprise you—I could tell you—Think what I could tell you.—(*Sings.*) " If 'tis joy to wound a lover"——hem——" how much more to give him ease."

Cla. " When his passion we discover." (*Sings.*)

Vand. (*Speaks.*) " Oh how pleasing 'tis to please."—Oh, I could tell—But no—no—no, no, no—You are sniggering—laughing in your sleeve—Ay, ay—I perceive it—You're a wit, and I am an old fool—Sneering—ridiculing me—I hate wit and ridicule.

Cla. Me a wit!—Lord, papa—I would not be such an animal for the world—A wit!——Why, a wit is a kind of urchin, that every man will set his dog at, but won't touch himself, for fear of pricking his fingers. A wit is a monster, with a hideous long tongue, and no brains—A dealer in paradoxes—One that is blind, through a profusion of light—A wit is a spectre, that makes a pair of stilts of his criss-cross-row, walks upon metaphor, is always seen in a simile, vanishes if you come too near him, and is only to be laid by a cudgel.

Vand. Frightful indeed!—Thank Heaven, nobody can say I am a wit.

Enter a Servant.

Serv. Mr Codicil the attorney desires to speak with you, sir.

Vand. Very well—I am coming.

Serv. Mrs Trip, madam, is in the house-keeper's room, and says she hopes your ladyship is well.

Cla. Desire her to walk up.   [*Exit Servant.*

Vand. Who is Mrs Trip, turtle?

Cla. A person that lived several years in our family. She is at present lady's maid to Melissa, Sir Harry Portland's sister—She will divert me with her fine language: besides that, I wish to ask her how she likes Sir Harry's family.

Vand. I know Sir Harry's uncle, Sir Hornet Armstrong, very well—an old friend.

Cla. Indeed!—I never saw him here.

Vand. Why, no—I don't know how it has happened, but I have not seen him above twice these two years myself—he's an odd mortal—a whimsical old gentleman—Well—by, by!

Cla. Adieu!

Vand. By, by!   [*Exit.*

CLARA *alone.*

This Sir Harry runs continually in my head—ay, and I am afraid has found a place in my heart—yes, yes—there's no denying that—but that *friend*—that Mr Osborne—whether it be my particular concern

5

for Sir Harry, or my superior penetration, I cannot discover, but that man wears to me a most suspicious, hypocritical face. (*Enter* Mrs Trip.) So, Mrs Trip, how have you done this long time?

Mrs Tr. Pretty well, thank you, madam, except that I am subject to the historicals, and troubled with the vapours; being, as I am, of a dilikut nirvus system, whereof I am so giddy, that my poor head is sometimes quite in a whirlpool; and if I did not bathe with my lady, the doctor tells me I should decline into a liturgy, and so fall down and die, perhaps, in a fit of apostacy.

Cla. And how long have you lived in Sir Harry's family, Mrs Trip?

Mrs Tr. I came soon after my poor dear lady, your mamma, died, and was interrogated; whereof I was at her funeral—My lady is a very good lady; that is, I mean, ma'am, my future lady, that I live with at present—she is to be married soon to Mr Osborne; and may Hydra, the god of marriage, tie the Gorgon knot—whereof I heard your ladyship is to be one of the ceremonials.

Cla. I am invited, and shall be there—But pray, Mrs Trip, what is your opinion of Mr Osborne?

Mrs Tr. Oh Lord, ma'am, consarning Mr Osborne—I heard a small bird sing.

Cla. A small bird sing!

Mrs Tr. Yes, ma'am.

Cla. Of what feather was this fowl?

Mrs Tr. Foul!—No, I assure you, your ladyship, as fair a speechified person as any in England—whereof he has a great valiation for me.

Cla. Well.

Mrs Tr. And so the secret is, that Mr Osborne has won almost all Sir Harry's estate.

Cla. Indeed!

Mrs Tr. And, moreover, has pretended to be a synagogue, and a Jew, and has lent money in other people's names, on mortgagees, and nuitants, where-of my friend has been a party consarned.

Cla. Good Heaven! what villainy! (*Aside.*) And pray who is your friend, Mrs Trip?

Mrs Tr. Oh, ma'am, I hope your ladyship won't intoxicate me on that head, for I know Mr Timid too well to—

Cla. Oh! it was Mr Timid.

Mrs Tr. Why—that is—ma'am—I didn't mean—Mercy!—What have I said?

Cla. You may assure yourself, Mrs Trip, I shall be careful not to do you any prejudice.

Mrs Tr. I am sure I am supinely obligationed to your ladyship. [*Exit* MRS TRIP.

CLARA *alone.*

Poor Sir Harry! He has a heart that does honour to mankind, that does not merit distress, yet, if I augur right, that must shortly feel the severest pangs a false friend can inflict—Ungrateful Osborne!—I must warn Melissa to beware of him, and, if possible, to detach Sir Harry from the gaming-table. [*Exit.*

ACT THE THIRD.

SCENE I.

SIR HARRY'S *House*.

Enter SIR HARRY, CLARA, MELISSA, VANDER-
VELT, *laughing*.

Cla. Ha! ha! ha! Sir Harry, you are a happy
man!

Vand. Ay, Sir Harry, you are a happy man!

Mel. Such an accomplished spouse!

Cla. And so kind an uncle!

Sir Har. Upon my soul, I can't help laughing;
and yet the more I reflect on the affair, the more I
am amazed—Sir Hornet is whimsical, 'tis true, but
no fool.

Vand. Fool! Sir Harry!—no, no, he is always the
readiest to spy the fooleries of other people—Many
a time have I laughed at his whims and jokes—an
odd mortal he is.

Cla. Nay, if he be so fond of a joke, who knows
but he may have sent them on this errand for the
joke's sake?

Vand. By dad, turtle, thou hast hit it.—As sure
as can be, that's it—it is for the joke's sake.

Sir Har. Impossible—The affair is too serious to
be intentional caprice.

Mel. But I thought, when I left you, you were
coming to an eclaircissement.

Sir Har. Coming to an eclaircissement!—Why, I told them, as plain as I could speak, that no alliance whatever could take place between the families.

Mel. 'Tis certain they have not understood you then.

Sir Har. Well, there the matter must rest, till I can find an interpreter, for I can't make myself more intelligible.

Cla. And you have not had one tender love scene yet?

Sir Har. Not one—I am amazed at the girl's simplicity—it equals her ignorance—she speaks and looks so totally unconscious of impropriety, so void of intentional error, that I don't know how to reply.

Cla. Suppose, then, you were to practise a little—Come, I'll stand up for the young lady.

Sir Har. I shall still find a difficulty to speak.

Cla. Surely!

Sir Har. In very truth, ma'am. But it will be from a quite different motive.

Cla. Oh, for the love of curiosity, Sir Harry, explain your motive.

Vand. Ay, Sir Harry, explain your motive.

Sir Har. I cannot, sir.

Vand. Cannot, Sir Harry! Why so?

Sir Har. For reasons, sir, which are far more easily imagined than described.

Vand. Nay, don't be afraid, Sir Harry.—My turtle knows how to answer interrogatories—you won't find her a simpleton, I'll warrant.

Sir Har. No, sir—the danger is, that she might find me one.

Vand. I fancy, Sir Harry, you are a little like me—cautious with the ladies, lest you should be made ridiculous—I am very circumspect in those matters.

Sir Har. You are very right, sir—It is not every one who has the gift of wearing a fool's cap with a grace.

9

Cla. Ay, but notwithstanding all this, Sir Harry, I should like to have a love scene with you.

Vand. How, turtle!

Cla. In the character of Miss Turnbull.

Vand. Oh!—Ay, do, Sir Harry, have a love scene with my turtle.

Sir Har. Any thing to oblige you, sir.

Vand. Come then—begin. (CLARA *sets herself in an awkward, silly attitude.*) Ah! ha, ha, ha!—look! look at my turtle lovidovey!

Sir Har. (*Addresses* CLARA.) My uncle, Sir Hornet Armstrong, madam, is desirous that I should gain the inestimable blessing of your hand.

Cla. Anan!

Vand. Ah! ha! ha! ha!

Sir Har. And give me leave to say, madam, however unworthy I may be of the happiness and honour intended me, no person can be more sensible of them.

Cla. What!——That be as much as to zay, you wun't ha' me, I zuppose. (*Whimpers.*)

Vand. Ah! ha! ha! ha!—Nay, but don't cry in earnest, lovidovey.

Sir Har. Oh dry those heavenly eyes, madam, and believe me, when I call every sacred power to witness my affection—I love, I adore, I die for you —Suffer me to wipe away those pearly tears, that hide the beauties of your cheek. (*Offering to salute her.*)

Cla. Hold, hold, Sir Harry!

Vand. Ay, hold, hold, Sir Harry!

Sir Har. Why so, sir?—'Tis quite in character.

Cla. Deuce take you, Sir Harry—You—you are too passionate in your feigned addresses—So warm and pressing——

Vand. Ay—so warm and pressing.

Cla. One was not aware.

Sir Har. I was taken by surprise myself, madam —The bounteous god of love kindly contrived an opportunity, which my profound adoration, and a conscious want of merit, had totally deprived me of—Pardon me, if, for a moment, I forgot that respect which every one who beholds you cannot help feeling.

Vand. Why, what's this, Sir Harry? You are not in downright earnest, are you?

Sir Har. Sincere, as dying sinners imploring mercy.

Vand. What, in love with my turtle!

Cla. Pooh—Why, no, to be sure—We were only acting a supposed scene.

Vand. Supposed!—Bedad, I think it was devilish like a real scene—You both did your parts very naturally.

Sir Har. Oh, sir! no actor who feels as forcibly as I do can ever mistake his character.

Vand. Feels forcibly!—Your feelings are forcible indeed.

Mel. Come, come, let us adjourn to the drawing-room : I want to have your opinions on a painting of Coreggio's, that my brother has made me a present of.

Vand. Favour me with your hand, young lady—And, Sir Harry, do you take my turtle's—but don't you let your feelings be too forcible.   [*Exeunt.*

SCENE II.

The Hall in SIR HARRY's *House.*

Enter SIR HORNET ARMSTRONG *and Servant, as just arrived.*

Sir Hor. Are the trunks safe, sirrah, George?

Serv. Yes, sir.

Sir Hor. And did you order that dog of a postillion to take care of the poor devils the horses?

Serv. I did, sir.

Sir Hor. And of himself?

Serv. I did, sir.

Sir Hor. You did, sir?—Why then, do you go, and take care of yourself, you rascal.

Serv. I will, sir.

Sir Hor. And do you hear, George!

Serv. Sir!

Sir Hor. If I find you disobey my orders, I'll break your bones.

Serv. I'll be very careful, sir, I assure you.

[*Exit Servant.*

Enter TIMID *and* SCRIP.

Tim. Brokerage comes rather heavy, Mr Scrip, when the sum is large.

Scr. Heavy! no, no—a damned paltry pittance—five and twenty pounds only, you see, for selling out twenty thousand—Get more by one lucky hit than fifty of these would produce.

Tim. Ay!

Scr. Oh yes!—Jobbing—Stock-jobbing, between you and me, is the high road to wealth.

Tim. Lack-a-day, may be so—Well, good day.— (SCRIP *is going, but seeing* SIR HORNET, *stops to listen.*)

Sir Hor. What, old Lack-a-day!

Tim. Ah, Sir Hornet!

Sir Hor. What's the best news with you?

Tim. Ah, lack-a-day, the best news I know is scarce worth relating.

Scr. Beg pardon, sir—(*To* SIR HORNET)—beg pardon—bad news in town, did you say?

Sir Hor. Bad, sir! not that I have heard.

Scr. Exceedingly sorry for it!

Sir Hor. Sir!

Scr. Never was more distressed for bad news!

Sir Hor. Distress'd for bad news!

Scr. Excessively ! The reduction of Gibraltar, the taking of Jamaica, or the destruction of the grand fleet, either of the three would make me a happy man for life.

Sir Hor. The destruction of the grand fleet make you happy for life !

Scr. Completely.

Sir Hor. Here's a precious scoundrel !

Scr. No great reason to complain, to be sure—do more business than any three doctors of the college —Generally of the sure side—Made a large fortune, if this does not give me a twinge—rather overdone it; but any severe stroke—any great national misfortune, would exactly close my account.

Sir Hor. Hark you, sir !

Scr. Sir !

Sir Hor. It is to be hoped——

Scr. Yes, sir, it is to be hoped.

Sir Hor. That a halter will exactly close your account.

Scr. Sir !

Sir Hor. You raven-fac'd rascal ! Rejoice at national misfortunes ! Zounds ! I thought such language was no where to be heard from the mouth of an Englishman, unless he were a member of parliament.

Scr. Lord, sir ! you don't consider that I am a bear for almost half a million.

Sir Hor. You are an impudent villain !—rejoice at the distress of your country !

Scr. Why, Lord, sir, to be sure——when I am a bear—There's not a bear in the Alley but would do the same—Were I a bull, indeed, the case would be altered.

Sir Hor. A bull !

Scr. For instance, at the taking of Charlestown,

no man was merrier, no man more elate, no man in better spirits.

Sir Hor. How so, gentle sir?

Scr. Oh, dear sir, at that time I was a bull to a vast amount, when, very fortunately for me, the news arrived; the guns fired; the bells clattered; the stocks mounted; and I made ten thousand pounds!—— Enough to make a man merry—Never spent a happier night in my life!

Sir Hor. Aha!—then, according to that arithmetic, you would be as merry and as happy to-night, could you accomplish the destruction of this said British fleet.

Scr. Happier! happier by half!—for I should realize at least twice the sum!—twice the sum!

Sir Hor. Twice the sum?

Scr. Ay, twice the sum!—Oh!—that would be a glorious event indeed! Never prayed so earnestly for any thing since I was born—and who knows—who knows what a little time may do for us?

Sir Hor. Zounds! how my elbow aches. (*Aside.*)

Scr. I shall call on some leading people—men of intelligence—of the right stamp.

Sir Hor. You shall!

Scr. Yes, sir.

Sir Hor. Why, then—perhaps you will be able to destroy the British fleet between you.

Scr. I hope so—I hope so—do every thing in my power—Oh! it would be a glorious event.

Sir Hor. Hark you, sir—Do you see that door?

Scr. Sir!

Sir Hor. And this cane?

Scr. Why, but, sir!

Sir Hor. Make your exit, you imp.

Scr. But, sir!

Sir Hor. Get out of the house, you vile rascal, you diabolical——(*Drives* SCRIP *off.*) A son's son of a scoundrel—Who is he? What business had he here?

Tim. Lack-a-day, sir, he is a stock-broker, that Sir Harry employ'd, at his sister's request, to sell out for her; because she chuses to have her fortune in her own possession against to-morrow.—I have been paying him the brokerage, and receiving the money, which I shall deliver to Madam Melissa directly.

Sir Hor. An incomprehensible dog! Pray for the reduction of Gibraltar, the taking of Jamaica, or the destruction of the British fleet!

Tim. Lack-a-day, sir! it is his trade.

Sir Hor. Trade! a nation will never flourish that encourages traders to thrive by her misfortunes.—But come—tell me something of my own affairs—Where is Harry—How does he go on?

Tim. Ah, lack-a-day!

Sir Hor. What—is he a wild young dog—Does he get into thy books?

Tim. Ah, lack-a-day!

Sir Hor. Ay, lack-a-day!—Zounds, don't sigh, man—He won't die in thy debt.

Tim. Ah, lack-a-day, Sir Hornet! he should be welcome to the last farthing I have in the world.

Sir Hor. Should he, old Truepenny!—Then give me thy hand—thou shalt be remembered in my codicil.—But what—he shakes his elbow I suppose, hey?—Seven's the main?

Tim. Ah, lack-a-day, Sir Hornet! what between main and chance he has been sadly nicked.

Sir Hor. Has he?—I'll score his losings upon his pate, a dog—that is, if he will let me—But where is Miss Turnbull?—She'll soon reform him: her angelic smiles will teach him—

Tim. Sir!

Sir Hor. Sir! Zounds, you stare like the wooden heads of the twelve Cæsars—Miss Turnbull's charms, I say, will find employment for all his virtues, and wean him from all his vices.

Tim. Will they, sir?

Sir Hor. Will they, sir! Yes, they will, sir.

Tim. Lack-a-day!

Sir Hor. Lack-a-day!—What ails you?

Tim. Nothing, sir, nothing—only that I am afraid my eyes begin to grow very dim.

Sir Hor. Your head, I believe, begins to grow very thick.

Tim. Ah, lack-a-day, sir, like enough—like enough!

Sir Hor. Be kind enough to answer me a few questions.—Is not Miss Turnbull a beautiful girl?

Tim. May I speak truth?

Sir Hor. May you speak truth! To be sure you *may.*

Tim. Then I answer, no, sir.

Sir Hor. No!

Tim. No.

Sir Hor. Is she not an elegant girl?

Tim. No.

Sir Hor. Nor a witty girl?

Tim. No.

Sir Hor. No!

Tim. No.

Sir Hor. No!!

Tim. No.

Sir Hor. Tol de rol lol!—Tititum!—Pray, what is she in your opinion?

Tim. A silly, ignorant, ill-bred, country girl, and very unfit for Sir Harry's wife.

Sir Hor. Tol de rol lol—laditum—let me look in your face—Yes, yes—he has it—the moon's almost at full. —Poor Lack-a-day!—which is your right hand?— (TIMID *holds it up.*) Indeed! Wonderful!—And are you really in your sober senses?

Tim. Why, indeed, sir, I begin to be rather in doubt—I believe so—but lest I should lose them, I will wish your honour a good morning.　　[*Exit.*

SIR HORNET *alone.*

Lack-a-day—ha! ha!—Not beautiful—nor witty—
nor—tol de rol lol—The old fool has a mind to set up
for a wit, and has begun by bantering *me*—Zounds,
I was neither drunk nor mad—and, to the best of my
knowledge, I am not now in a dream—The brother,
indeed, is a booby, and does not appear to be of
the same family—hardly of the same species—though
he had sense enough to snap at the offer immediately—I remarked he did not stand on ceremony.—
Surely I have made no mistake in the business—
S'blood, if it prove so!—Parson Adams the second—I
shall—Hey!-- Who's this?—No—no, no—it is—'tis
she herself, in propria pers—(*Enter* CLARA.)—Miss
Turnbull, I most heartily rejoice to see you.

Cla. Miss Turnbull!   (*Aside.*)

Sir Hor. Your presence has relieved me from one
of the oddest qualms—But the sight of you has given
me a cordial.

Cla. What do you mean, Sir Hornet?

Sir Hor. Mean, my angel! Why, here has been a
bantering, lying, enigmatical son of a scoundrel, with
a bundle of ironical, diabolical tales, railing at your
beauty and accomplishments, till, egad, I began to
fancy my fine-flavoured pine-apple a crab.

Cla. This is delightful!—-I half suspected this
from the first—But the mistake is so pleasant, that I
cannot find in my heart to undeceive him. (*Aside.*)
There is no answering for the difference of taste, sir.

Sir Hor. True—Asses prefer thistles to nectarines
—But yet he must be an ass indeed, who could not
distinguish St Paul's from the pillory.

Cla. Taste, Sir Hornet, is a sort of shot silk, and
has a variety of shades—a camelion—One says 'tis
blue, another black, and a third is positive 'tis yellow—every body has it, yet nobody can tell what it
is—Like space, it is undescribable, though all al-

low there is such a thing—It would be a vain attempt, therefore, for Miss Turnbull to endeavour to please the whole world.

Sir Hor. An old booby—I would not give a hair of the pope's beard to please him.—But how is it with Sir Harry—Is *he* in raptures ? Is *he* dying for you ?

Cla. No, sir—he eats and drinks as usual, and is, for aught I can discover, in tolerable good health.

Sir Hor. Is he ?——An audacious dog!——In good health '—If I find him in good health, I'll pistol him—But you mistake the matter perhaps—The rascal's proud, and not willing you should see his sufferings—He is a stricken deer, and sheds his tears in solitude and silence mayhap—Do you discover no symptoms of the sighing swain ?—Does he never cut his fingers—or scald himself—or run against a post, and beg its pardon ?

Cla. No, sir.

Sir Hor. I doubt he is a sad dog—But no—no, no—I am certain he adores you—'Tis impossible he should do otherwise—But there is another material point, about which I am not quite so certain.

Cla. What is that, sir ?

Sir Hor. Has he found any place in your affections ?—'Tis true, he's a fine fellow—I don't mean, by that, one that is pickled in cosmetics—preserved in musk and mareschal powder, and that will melt away, like Lot's wife, in the first hard shower—None of your fellows that are too valiant to give a woman the wall, and too witty to let her have the last word—But one that is—In short, his own manner will best describe what he is.

Cla. True, Sir Hornet; but the time has been so short.

Sir Hor. Short !—Ah, madam, if he did not do the business with a *coup d'œil*—at once—I would not give a feather of a goose-wing for all the arrows his Cupid has in his quiver—But come, Miss Turnbull—

I know you are above the silly prejudices that ordinary minds are swayed by—tell me sincerely—Has he made any impression on your heart?—Is he the man?

Cla. To speak ingenuously, Sir Hornet, that is a point entirely undetermined at present.

Sir Hor. Undetermined!—Why!—what!

Cla. Sir Harry's person is engaging—his manners delightful, and his understanding unexceptionable.

Sir Her. Bravo! my dear girl!—you charm me to hear you say so!

Cla. I will say more, Sir Hornet—I find my heart interested in his behalf, and sincerely believe I shall never see another man with whom I could be half so happy.

Sir Hor. My dear Miss Turnbull!

Cia. But yet I have too many reasons to fear it will be impossible we should ever be united.

Sir Hor. Impossible!

Cla. I do most firmly believe Sir Harry possesses a thousand virtues, but they are all tinged, discoloured by a failing, which, if not in its own nature as erroneous as some other vices, is more destructive than any.

Sir Hor. I understand you.

Cla. This will for ever deter a woman who values her own peace and welfare from cherishing a passion that must, in its consequences, be so fatal.

Sir Hor. But you, my angel, will soon cure him of this—It is not a rooted vice.

Cla. Permanently—or my intelligence says false—When he loses, there is no possibility of persuading him to desist— the recollection of his loss preys upon his mind, and had he the Indies, he would set it upon the chance of a card, the turn of a guinea, or the cast of a die.

Sir Hor. Well, but we have hopes that Mr Osborne will find means to reclaim him—he is continually with him, continually warning him, and——

Cla. Subtlety and refined artifice!—Mr Osborne, Sir Hornet, is an interested physician, and would rather encourage than cure the disease.

Sir Hor. Heaven forbid!—But who informs you of this?

Cla. Those who are in the secret, I assure you, sir—I am afraid Mr Osborne is a wicked man—He is—what I dare not speak.

Sir Hor. I confess you alarm me, though I hope without cause—Osborne assumes every appearance of rigid virtue; and if this were true, he would be the worst of villains—However, suspend your opinion a while—I'll soon sift the affair—And, in the mean time, let me beg of you to think as well of Sir Harry as your doubts will permit you.

Cla. I shall do that, Sir Hornet, without an effort.
                                        [*Exit.*

Enter VANDERVELT.

(*Sees* CLARA *going off on the other side of the Stage.*)

Vand. Why, turtle!—Why—Ah! Sir Hornet—I am glad to see you.

Sir Hor. Ah ha—friend Van!—Why, you look tolerably well.

Vand. Tolerably well!——Ay, to be sure—Why should I not?

Sir Hor. Why should you not?——Let me see—There are, as near as I can guess, about seventy reasons why you should not.

Vand. Humph—Oh—what, my age!—No, no—Let me tell you, Sir Hornet, I——I am not an old man.

Sir Hor. No!

Vand. No—nor you neither.

Sir Hor. Indeed!—I am exceedingly glad of that—and pray when did you make this discovery?

Vand. Make it—Why, I have been making it these twenty years and upwards.

Sir Hor. Oh ho!—And how do you prove it?

Vand. By comparison and reflection—I'll tell you —hold—first I'll shew you—what I call *my* list of worthies—There—look at that—(*Gives a common-place book.*)

Sir Hor. What the devil have we here?—(*Reads.*) " *Patrick O'Neal*—married, for the seventh time, at the age of one hundred and thirteen—walks without a cane, never idle—children and great great grand-children, to the number of—one hundred and twenty-three!"

Vand. There's a fellow!—I warrant that man is alive and hearty at this moment.

Sir Hor. Humph!—And pray, do you think to imitate this worthy, as you call him?—Will you be married seven times, and have a hundred and twenty-three children?

Vand. That's more than I can tell.

Sir Hor. Ha!—(*Reads.*) " *Thomas Par*, being aged one hundred and twenty, fell in love with Catherine Milton."

Vand. Ay, and did penance in a white sheet at the church door.

Sir Hor. Humph!—" *Henry Jenkins.*"

Vand. Ay!——There's another!——corrected his great grandson, a youth of seventy, with his own hand, for being idle.

Sir Hor. " *Johannes de Temporibus*, or, JOHN OF TIMES, armour-bearer to the emperor Charlemagne, died, aged three hundred threescore and one years."

Vand. Very well, now tell me—when you compare me to *Johannes de Temporibus*, that is, when you compare sixty-seven to three hundred threescore and one, can you say I am an old man?

Sir Hor. An old man!—By the beard of Methuselah, thou art scarce an infant—it will be perhaps these five years yet before thou art perfectly a child.

Vand. Nay, Sir Hornet, let me beg of you to be serious—you are an old friend, and know the world —I shall be glad of your advice—I ruminate on these things by myself, till I am quite melancholy—Now, if I had but somebody to bear half my griefs, I should suppose—they would be lessened.

Sir Hor. Why, true, as you say, one would imagine so.

Vand. Don't you think then, if I were to take a handsome—young—wife—I should, perhaps, find a cure for all my ills?

Sir Hor. An infallible one.

Vand. And this is seriously your opinion? (*Very gravely.*)

Sir Hor. Seriously. (*Affectedly grave.*)

Vand. Then tell me—You were talking with the young lady that went out as I entered.

Sir Hor. Well, what of her?

Vand. Is she not very beautiful?

Sir Hor. A divinity.

Vand. Finely accomplished?

Sir Hor. Beyond description.

Vand. That's right!—You are a sensible, discerning man, Sir Hornet, and I am delighted to find you approve my choice.

Sir Hor. *Your* choice!

Vand. *My* choice—That is the young lady, you must know, to whom I intend to pay my addresses.

Sir Hor. Your—your—your—your what?

Vand. The lady I mean to marry.

Sir Hor. Ha, ha, ha, ha, ha, ha, ha!

(*Laughs excessively.*)

Vand. Nay, Sir Hornet!

Sir Hor. Ha, ha, ha, ha, ha! all mad—every soul.

Vand. I don't understand!

Sir Hor. Most reverend youth, I beg your pardon; ha, ha, ha, ha, ha!

Vand. You see things in a mighty strange light, Sir Hornet.—Is it any miracle that a man should love a beautiful woman?

Sir Hor. Ha, ha, ha, ha, ha!—Love! Why, thou'rt another Ætna—Cupid's burning mountain.—Your nose has took fire at your fancy, and is become a beacon, to warn all young gentlemen, of threescore and ten, of the rocks and quicksands hid in the sea of amorous desires.

Vand. Upon my word, Sir Hornet, this is exceedingly strange.

Sir Hor. Ha, ha, ha!—You must excuse me—What a rosy youth—Ha, ha, ha!—Hark ye, friend Vandervelt, *(Gravely,)* it's my opinion you have been bantering me rather.

Vand. Odd—that's a good thought. (*Aside.*)—— Bantering you! Why, ay, to be sure I have—ha, ha, ha! (*Forces a laugh.*)

Sir Hor. Oh! you have?

Vand. Certainly; ha, ha, ha!

Sir Hor. Ha, ha, ha, ha! *(With the same tone and manner.)*

Vand. Didn't you perceive that before? Ha, ha, ha!

Sir Hor. No, faith—ha, ha, ha!

Vand. That's a good joke! ha, ha, ha!

Sir Hor. Excellent! ha, ha, ha!

[*The laugh continues some time, during which* SIR HORNET *imitates* VANDERVELT'S *voice and manner exactly, then stops suddenly, and looks very grave.)*

Vand. Ha, ha, ha, ha, ha!

Sir Hor. Ha, ha, ha, ha, ha!

Vand. Ha, ha!——

Sir Hor. Now let us be serious.

Vand. With all my heart.

Sir Hor. And I'll tell you a story.

Vand. Do.

Sir Hor. There was a certain ancient personage of my acquaintance, called Andrew Vandervelt—

Vand. What! Is your story about me?

Sir Hor. Give me leave, young gentleman, and you shall hear—Every body imagined him to be a prudent, sedate, grave person, with a moderate share of common sense.

Vand. Well.

Sir Hor. And as it was evident his beard was grey, his limbs palsied, his skin shrivelled, and his sinews shrunk——

Vand. How, Sir Hornet!

Sir Hor. They naturally concluded he had made his will, wrote his epitaph, and bespoke his coffin.

Vand. Mercy upon me!

Sir Hor. But instead of meditating, like a pious Christian, on the four last things, a crochet takes him in the head, he buys a three-penny fiddle, scrapes a matrimonial jigg, claps a pair of horns upon his head, and curvets through the town, the sport of the mob, derided by the young, pitied by the old, and laughed at by all the world.

Vand. Heaven deliver me! What a picture! But you forget, Sir Hornet—Didn't I explain to you that it was only a joke?

Sir Hor. Oh! true—Ah, witty rogue!—Well—adieu—I'll remember the joke—ha, ha, ha!

Vand. Ay, do—ha, ha, ha!

Sir Hor. Oh for a song to the tune of " Room for Cuckolds !"   [*Exeunt.*

ACT THE FOURTH.

SCENE I.

A Chamber at SIR HARRY'S.

Enter SIR HARRY, *(much agitated.)*

Sir Har. May the everlasting curse of heaven con-
sume those implements of hell—those deceitful, infernal fiends!—I'll never touch, never look on cards
or dice again—If I ever make another bet, may all
the horrors of a ruined fortune haunt me, sleeping
and waking—may I be pointed at by children, and
pitied by sharpers—Distraction! *may* I be—I *am*
already ruined, past redemption.

Enter Servant, and delivers a letter to SIR HARRY.

Sir Har. (*Breaks open the letter hastily.*)—Um
—Um—Stay, sir. (*To the Servant.*)—Damnation!
Is it possible? In league with sharpers!—Who brought
this letter, sir?

Serv. A porter, sir.

Sir Har. Where is he?

Serv. Gone, sir—he ran off round the corner in a
hurry.

Sir Har. You may go, sir.   [*Exit Servant.*

Enter OSBORNE.

Osb. You seem moved, Sir Harry: may I enquire
the cause?

Sir Har. You are the cause, sir.

Osb. I!

Sir Har. Yes, you—There, read, sir.

Osb. (*Reads.*) "Beware of a false friend.—The person who gives you this caution would sacrifice a life to preserve you from the destruction that threatens you—Mr Osborne is in league with Jews and sharpers, and you are a victim to his avarice and duplicity."—So, so—(*Seems chagrined.*)—Well, Sir Harry, do you give any credit to this epistle?

Sir Har. Nay, sir, you are to tell me how much, or how little credit it deserves.

Osb. Why, look you, Sir Harry, I cannot, nor I will not enter into explanations.

Sir Har. Sir!—Cannot, nor will not enter into explanations!

Osb. No, sir.

Sir Har. But I say, sir, you shall.

Osb. Shall!

Sir Har. Yes, sir, shall.

Osb. Ay, sir—Who is he that *shall* make me?

Sir Har. I am he, sir.

Osb. Indeed!

Sir Har. Friendship, honour, honesty ought to make you—but present appearances declare you void of these.

Osb. Present appearances declare you void of reason, sir, otherwise you would remember me for one of those who are not to be terrified by a loud tongue or an angry brow—I repeat it—I will not now enter into explanations—I have played with you: I have staked *my* money, and won *yours*—Would it have been dishonourable had you won mine? I have disposed of that money as I thought proper—no matter whether with Jews or Christians; and I should have supposed your passion and suspicion would have required better proof than the malevolent as-

persion of an anonymous letter, ere they ought to
have incited you to a quarrel with your friend.

Sir Har. I beg your pardon, dear Osborne—I am
to blame—nothing but the severity of my late losses
can plead for me—I know you to be a noble-hearted,
worthy fellow, and explanations, on such an accusation, are as much beneath you to give, as me to demand—Forget my silly warmth ; it is my weakness.

Osb. Do you forget the cause on't, Sir Harry, and
it is forgot.

Sir Har. It was madness—I am above suspicion—
'tis ungenerous—'tis damnable—pray excuse—pray
forgive me.

Osb. Well, well, think no more on't—only guard
against suspicion for the future.   [*Exit* OSBORNE.

Sir Har. No, no—it cannot be—there is an open
fortitude in his manner—a boldness that can only re-
sult from innocence.

Enter MELISSA.

Mel. Oh, brother, I am glad I have found you—
Why did you send these troublesome things to me ?
Why did not you take care of them for me ? Trust
a giddy girl, indeed, with a parcel of bank-bills—
Here, here, here they are—take 'em—take 'em—they
will be safe with you—I have been in a panic ever
since they were in my possession, lest they should
take wing, and fly through the key-hole, or some
other unaccountable way—I am unused to such large
sums, and don't feel happy while they are about me.

Sir Har. But what am I to do with them ?

Mel. Keep them till to-morrow, and then, you
know, when you give my hand to your friend, you
may give them too, to make it the more acceptable
—there are just twenty, of one thousand each.—So
now I am easy—good bye—I am going to purchase
a few knick-knacks.   [*Exit* MELISSA *hastily.*

Sir Har. Well, but, sister Melissa—She's gone

—flown on the light wings of innocence and happiness—while I, depressed by folly, feel a weight upon my heart, that hope itself cannot remove.—What is a ruined gamester?—An idiot—who begins for his amusement, who continues hoping to retrieve, and who is ruined before he can recollect himself—a wretch—deserted, solitary, forlorn—ashamed of society, yet miserable when alone—shunned by the prosperous—despised by the prudent—-deservedly exposed to the poisoned shafts of insolence and envy —a by-word to the vulgar, and a jest to the fortunate—haunted by duns, preyed upon by usurers, persecuted and curs'd by creditors.—Inexplicable infatuation!   [*Exit* SIR HARRY.

SCENE II.

Another Apartment.

Enter CLARA, MELISSA, *and* SQUIRE TURNBULL.

Mel. Mr Turnbull, I must beg, sir, you'll desist.

Sq Dezist—why, to be zure—I'll go and buy license out o' hand—make hay while the zun do zhine —and don't lose the zheep for a ha'perth o' tar— what though—the pepper-box must ha' a lid—a bushel o' words wun't vill a basket—when the owl goes a-hunting, 'tis time to light the candle.

Cla. Ha, ha, ha!—If you'll permit me, my dear, I think I can relieve you from this embarrassment.

Mel. Permit you!—I am sure if you can, you shall be canonized, and have churches erected to your memory.

Cla. I'll talk to him in his own language—he can comprehend no other.

VOL. IV.

Sq. Well, vair lady.

Cla. Well, zir.

Sq. You do zee how the nail do drive—Be you to be one at bridal?

Cla. No.

Sq. No!—Why zo?—You'st be bride-maid.

Cla. No, but I wun't.

Sq. Wun't you?

Cla. No—nor you'st not be bridegroom nother.

Sq. No!

Cla. No.

Sq. How zo?

Cla. Because you've zold the skin avore you've catch'd the vox—You've reckoned your chickens bevore they be hatch'd.

Sq. Nay, nay—stop at the dike—zure I do knaw my own mind—an' miss be agreed.

Cla. But miss ben't agreed.

Sq. No!—That's a good joke—but she be though.

Cla. But she ben't though.

Sq. But I am zure she be.

Cla. But I'm zure she ben't.

Sq. No!—Why, miss—ben't you agreed?

Mel. No, sir.

Sq. (*Astonished.*) No!

Cla. You may gape, but the cherry won't drop—Too much mettle is dangerous in a blind horse—Misreckoning is no payment—John would a' wed, but Mary war na willing.

Mel. You seem surprised, sir—I can only say it is without reason—You have deceived yourself, in supposing such an alliance possible; and I hope your own good sense will inform you that, after this declaration, any renewal of your addresses to me must be considered an insult.

Sq. (*Stares, as if he did not comprehend her, for*

12

some time.) An' zo then—the meaning of all this vine speech, I zuppose, is that you wun't ha' me?

Mel. It is.

Cla. " Make hay while the zun do zhine—Don't lose the sheep for a ha'p'erth of tar—A bushel of words won't vill a basket—When the owl goes a-hunting, 'tis time to light the candle."—Your most obedient, gentle squire—ha, ha, ha!

[*Exeunt* MELISSA *and* CLARA.

Manet Squire.

Zo then—It zeems I a been reckoning without my host here—Well—What tho'—zoon hot zoon cold—zoon got zoon gone—Care's no cure—Zorrow won't pay a man's debts—He wanted a zinging bird that gave a groat for a cuckoo—an' he that loses a wife and zixpence has lost a tester.—*(Enter* MISS TURN-BULL.*)* Why, Barbara! what be's the matter wi' thee? Where has thee been?

Miss Turn. Been!—Why, I a been wildered.

Sq. What, lost!

Miss Turn. Ees—an' if I had na' by good hap met wi' John, who has got direction in written hand, it were vive golden guineas to a brass varthin I'ad been kidnapp'd, an' zent to America, among the Turks.

Sq. Zerve thee right—thee must be gadding—But I a' news vor thee—the cow 'as kick't down th' milk—It's all off 'tween miss and I.

Miss Turn. Zure!—rabbit me, an I didn't guess as much.

Sq. Ees—the nail's clench'd—Zhe and I a' zhook hands an' parted.

Miss Turn. My gracious!—What, won't yo' ha' zhe?

Sq. No—I wun't—Her may whistle, but I zha'n't hear—her may beckon, but I zha'n't come—Catch me an' ha' me—I'm no vool—Zo, do you zee, an'

you be minded to wed, zay grace an' vall too, vor **I**
don't like your London tricks, an zo I'st leave it as
vast as I can.

Miss Turn. An' when be I to be wed?

Sq. Why, I do vind Zir Hornet be come, zo, when
yo' do zee Zir Harry, yo' may zettle't—An', d'ye
hear, Barbara—Don't let me vind yo' at any o' these
skittish off an' on freaks—I a' zeen too much on 'um
lately—Oh, here be Sir Harry coming—An' zo I'st
leave you to make love your own way—I'st not play
my ace o' trumps out yet.   *[Exit Squire.*

Enter SIR HARRY.

Sir Har. So—here's my good whimsical uncle's
Nonpareil, as he calls her—his phœnix—All alone,
Miss Turnbull?

Miss Turn. Ees—Brother be just gone—A's val-
len out wi' miss, an a's plaguily frump'd.

Sir Har. Sure!

Miss Turn. Ees—A zaid, too, at yo' an I be to
make love.

Sir Har. He did!

Miss Turn. Ees—and I do knaw his tricks—a'll
be in a woundy rage, an I don't do as he bids me.

Sir Har. What, will he be surly?

Miss Turn. Zurly!—a'll snarl worser than our
great dog Jowler at a beggar.

Sir Har. He is ill tempered then?

Miss Turn. Oh, a'll zulk vor a vortnight round—
an' when a comes about again, a'll make a believe to
romp—an' then a' lumps—an' gripes—an' pinches—
till I am quite a weary on't.

Sir Har. Well you may, I think——Poor thing.
(*Aside.*)—And which way are we to make love?

Miss Turn. My gracious! don't you knaw?

Sir Har. I believe i can give a guess—You, I
suppose, are to hang down your head and titter.

Miss Turn. Ees—(*Grins.*)

Sir Har. I—hem—and look sheepish.

Miss Turn. Ees.

Sir Har. You gnaw your apron——I twirl my thumbs.

Miss Turn. He, he!—Ees.

Sir Har You say—it's a very fine day, sir; and I answer, yes, ma'am, only it rains.

Miss Turn. He, he, he!—Ees—iveck, that be vor all the world the very moral of our country vashion —Oh! but here be zomebody coming.

Enter Sir Hornet, Clara, *and* Vandervelt.

Sir Hor. Why, Harry, you dog, what, have you hid yourself, because you would not see me?

Sir Har. Dear sir, I am exceedingly glad to see you, but it is not a quarter of an hour since I heard of your being in town; and I suppose, sir, you will scarcely be angry at finding me in this company—— (Vandervelt, Sir Harry, *and* Miss Turnbull *walk up the stage in conversation.*)

Sir Hor. Finding you in—Zounds, what awkward cargo of rusticity has he got there? *(To* Clara.*)*

Cla. A young lady from Somersetshire, with a tolerable good fortune, that Sir Harry, it is thought by some, intends to marry.

Sir Hor. Marry!—He should as soon marry the mummy of Queen Semiramis.

Cla. She has been strongly recommended to the family, sir.

Sir Hor. Recommended!—By whom?

Cla. By one you are very intimate with, and who has very great influence with Sir Harry, as well as with yourself.

Sir Hor. Ay!—Who is that?

Cla. Pardon me there, Sir Hornet.

Sir Hor. Certainly the fellow cannot be foolish enough to admire her—but I shall soon discover that, by what he thinks of you.—Harkee, Harry!

Sir Har. Sir!

Sir Hor. I cannot, upon the whole, tell very well what to make of you—Are you thoroughly convinced that you are at this instant legally capable of making your will?

Sir Har. My will, sir!

Sir Hor. Ay—Are you of sound mind?

Sir Har. I believe so, sir!

Sir Hor. Then pray tell me, now we have you face to face, what is your opinion of Miss Turnbull?

Sir Har. Sir!—That is by no means a question proper to be answered in this company.

Sir Hor. Pshaw!—Damn your delicacy—Make your panegyric, and I'll blush for her and you too.

Sir Har. (*Shrugs up his shoulders.*) Sir, I have no panegyric to make.

Sir Hor. Sir!

Sir Har. Even so.

Sir Hor. Why, you impudent, confounded—Have you the barefaced effrontery, with such a picture before your eyes, to—

Sir Har. You have applied the torture, and my own ease requires confession.

Sir Hor. Humph—And so you—Now pray all be attentive, for Bacon's brazen head is going to utter —So you do not think Miss Turnbull a most engaging—

Sir Har. (*Smiles.*)

Sir Hor. Why, you intolerable—

Sir Har. I am concerned to see you so serious on the subject—I must acknowledge, that in this case, sir, I have either a most perverse or stupid imagination, and cannot, for the soul of me, discover the latent wonders in the young lady, which your better sight has so distinct a view of.

Sir Hor. Ha!

Sir Har. I am, however, exceedingly willing to try the utmost strength of my faith, to believe as

much as I can, and take the rest for granted ; provided you will not inflict the punishment of a wife
upon my superstition.

Sir Hor. Obliging youth !—(*Bows.*)—Inflict the
punishment of a wife upon your superstition—And so
you think, no doubt, a wife a burden, much too heavy for the back of so fine and pretty a town-made
gentleman as yourself ?

Sir Har. With the addition of Miss Turnbull's accomplishments, I most undoubtedly do, sir.

Sir Hor. You do—triumph—Pray, most civil sir—
permit me to ask—perh ps there may be some other
lady in this good company to whom your profound
penetration would give the preference.

Sir Har. If such preference could in the least make
me deserving of her, I have no scruple to say there
is.

Sir Hor. Miracle of modesty !—there is.

Sir Har. Most assuredly—But though to possess
the lady you hint at would make me blest beyond
description, I have never dared to declare so much
before, because I am conscious of being unworthy of
such a profusion of charms and accomplishments.

Cla. Generous diffidence ! (*Aside.*)

Sir Hor. Charms and—What the devil is all this ?
—Where am I—at sea, or on shore—Have I a calen-
ture in my brain, or is this my nose ?—They—they
call you Sir Harry Portland, don't they, sir ?

Sir Har. And your nephew, sir.

Sir Hor. No—that's rather dubious—Well then,
Mr Harry, or Sir Harry, or what you p ease—You
are pretty well convinced, I suppose, that I *have* had
some slight regard for you.

Sir Har. Perfectly, sir, and remember it with gratitude.

Sir Hor. That remains to be proved, friend—Ever
since your father's death, if I don't mistake, I have

been tolerably busy, a little active, or so, in forming
your mind and manners, and moulding you into a
sort of being a man might behold without blushing.

Sir Har. It is impossible, sir, I should ever forget
your goodness, though I am happy to be reminded
of it.

Sir Hor. That's a lie, I believe—However, sir—
among the rest of my cares, I was anxious to find a
woman worthy of you—Nay, so solicitous was I about
adjusting preliminaries, that though the gout had
laid an embargo upon a parcel of my fingers and toes,
I resolved to forego my own ease, and set sail immediately, that I might convoy you safe into the har-
bour of happiness.

Sir Har. I am very sensible of the benevolence of
your intentions, sir, and only wish you had done me
the honour to—

Sir Hor. Well, I have only a word or two more to
say on the subject—I have been an enthusiastic old
blockhead, 'tis true, and was fool enough to think all
men had eyes; however, if you have not either the
complaisance, the wit, or the love to hit upon some
expedient to make your peace with Miss Turnbull, I
will never see, never know, never speak to you again.
And now, sir, you will act as your great wisdom shall
direct.

Sir Har. Indeed, sir, I am distressed to see you
so intent upon this business; I am exceedingly unhappy to do the least thing to incur your displeasure
—at this moment especially—I have a thousand reasons to be dissatisfied with myself, and am grieved to
add your anger to the list—I would do any thing in
my power to preserve your friendship and affection,
but this is too severe a task—I cannot totally forget
common sense—I cannot entirely command so delicate a passion as that of love—A little time will
discover whether I am ever to think of love or hap-

piness again!—Of this, however, I am certain—I never can possess either with Miss Turnbull.

[*Exit* Sir Harry.

Sir Hor. Indeed, youngster! so resolute!

Cla. What a noble fortitude! (*Aside.*)

Sir Hor. We shall see who will first read their recantation——An insensible blind puppy——I'll be a greater torment to him than a beadle to a beggar—a cat to a rat—or a candle to a moth—I'll singe his wings—I'll plague him worse than Moses did the Egyptians.

Cla. Oh! Sir Hornet you'll soon be of another opinion.

Sir Hor. Never—never—never.——(*Enter Squire behind, unperceived.*)—However, let him act as he will, Miss Turnbull shall have no cause to repent her coming to London.

Miss Turn. What! will yo' take me to zee the zights?

Sq. Who the devil bade that goose cackle?

Sir Hor. A curst idiot—or I have no skill in physiognomy.

Sq. What, Barbara!—Ees—that her be—though no vool neather—her do knaw better than to thatch her house wi' pancakes.

Sir Hor. Pshaw—Miss Turnbull! (*To* Clara.)

Miss Turn. Ees—I be here.

Sir Hor. Again!—(*Takes* Clara *by the hand.*) Give me leave, I say, dear Miss Turnbull, to—

Vand. Hey! Sir Hornet!

Cla. Ha, ha, ha, ha, ha!

Sir Hor. Why!—what!

Vand. You don't take my turtle for Miss Turnbull, sure?

Sir Hor. Your turtle!—I don't know what you mean by your turtle; but I take this young lady for Miss Turnbull, sure.

Vand. You do!

Sir Hor. Yes—I do.

Vand. } Ha, ha, ha, ha, ha!
Cla. }

Sir Hor. Why—what the devil—hey—why, sure—

Vand. Ah ha, ha, ha, ha!—This is a good joke.

Sir Hor. A good joke!—Why, madam—Squire—Zounds!

Vand. Ah ha, ha, ha, ha!——I would not have missed this for a thousand pounds in new coined guineas.

Sir Hor. Mr Turnbull—Sir—Is not this your sister, sir?

Sq. Zister!

Sir Hor. Yes.

Sq. What, thic!

Sir Hor. Yes.

Sq Thic Barbara!

Sir Hor. Zounds, yes, I tell you.

Sq. Why, no, to be sure—thic be Barbara.

Cla. Ha, ha, ha!

Vand. Ha, ha, ha!——the biter bit—the fleerer fleer'd—ha, ha, ha!

Sir Hor. (*Whistles.*) Thic be Barbara.

Sq Ees—Thic be Barbara.

Miss Turn. Ees—I be Barbara.

Vand. Why, what a numskull your nephew is, Sir Hornet!

Sir Hor. Do you think so?

Vand A blind, insensible puppy!

Sir Hor. Is he?

Vand. But you'll torment him—you'll singe his wings—you'll plague him worse than Moses did the Egyptians—What a discovery!

Sir Hor. Oh yes—I have made more discoveries!

Vand. Ay, what are they?

Sir Hor. Why, the first is—You're an old fool—

the next is—I am another—and the third is, that we
are not the only two fools in company.

[*Exit, in a passion.*

[*Exeunt* CLARA *and* VANDERVELT, *laughing.*

Manent Squire and MISS TURNBULL—(*they stand
some time.*)

Sq. Barbara.

Miss Turn. Ees.

Sq. How does thee like London?

Miss Turn. I knaw not——It do zeem a strange
place.

Sq. A strange place!

Miss Turn. Ees—I do think it be.

Sq. Thee dost?

Miss Turn. Ees.

Sq. An' zo do I—whereby, dost zee, I'll get out
on't as vast as I can—a pretty chace, as the man zaid
that rode vitty miles a'ter a wild goose.—London!
—an' this be London, the devil take London—Come,
pack up thy ribbands an' vlappets, an' make thyzel
ready.

Miss Turn. Neea, zure—you wun't go zo zoon.

Sq. Wun't I?—an' I stay in thic town to-night,
I'll eat it vor breakvast to-morrow.

Miss Turn. My gracious!

Sq. Come, come—don't stand mauxing and dawd-
ling, but make thyzel ready.

Miss Turn. Lord!—Why, I a' zeen nothing yet.

Sq. No—nor nothing thee zhalt zee—that I promise thee—zo stir thy stumps, I tell thee.

Miss Turn. My gracious!—Mun I go down into
't country again like a vool, an' ha' nothing to say
vor myzel?

Sq. Why, look thee, Barbara—come along—vor
thee have come up like a vool, zo there can be no harm
in thy going down like a vool.   [*Exeunt.*

ACT THE FIFTH.

SCENE I.

A Library in SIR HARRY'S *House.*

SIR HARRY *and* TIMID *discovered.*

Tim. Indeed, sir, you have always been the best of masters to me.

Sir Har. No, Timid, no——I have been a very weak, idle fellow, and have put it out of my power to be a good master to any one.

Tim. Lack-a-day, sir—don't say so—I am afraid I have been a bad servant—a very bad servant.

Sir Har. Never.

Tim. Lack-a-day, sir, you don't know—you don't know—Lack-a-day, I thought all for the best.

Sir Har. You have only done what I commanded.

Tim. To be sure, sir—but, lack-a-day—I wish I durst open my mind to him—I am terrified—he will never believe me innocent. (*Aside.*)

Sir Har. My ruin is all my own work—Here, Mr Timid, take this ring, and remember me—It may be the last present I shall ever make you.

Tim. Pray don't say so, sir—I am terrified.

Sir Har. I am going to Mr Osborne's.

Tim. To Mr Osborne's!

Sir Har. Yes. If you should not see me to-morrow morning——if any accident should happen——

Tim. Lack-a-day!

Sir Har. Give the state of my affairs, which I
ordered you to draw up, to my uncle, and this picture to Clara, the young lady that is with him.

Tim. Sir, what do you mean?

Sir Har. Oh, nothing, nothing—I'm not very well
—I—a slight swimming in my head, that's all; but
there is no knowing what may happen.

Tim. Lack-a-day, sir, you terrify me! You talk
like a dying man making his will.

Sir Har. No, no, not so; I have nothing to leave;
and as to dying, men must die; live as long as they
can, they must all die at last.

Tim. Shall I go for Sir Hornet, or your sister, or
the young lady?

Sir Har. No, no young ladies for——Oh

Tim. Lack-a-day! my heart aches

Sir Har. I am going to Mr Osborne's presently.

Tim. Lack-a-day! I wish he knew——I'll take the
mortgage of the Kentish estate. Mr Osborne ordered
me to bring it. I'll lay it open on Mr Osborne's table. I hope my dear master will see it—I hope he
will discover all.—(*Aside.*)

Sir Har. Heigho!

Tim. Dear sir, don't sigh so; don't look so——
Tell me what I can do to serve you, to oblige you,
to make you happier?

Sir Har. Nothing, nothing. Past hope!—past
cure!—quite, quite——

Tim. Lack-a-day!

Sir Har. A thoughtless, profligate, idle, dissipated
fellow! Oh, my head, my head!

Tim. I cannot bear to see him so. I'll hurry to
Mr Osborne's. I'll try if I can yet persuade him to
be a true friend. I'll beg, I'll pray, I'll go down on
my knees, I'll do any thing.   [*Exit* TIMID.

Sir Har. Clara! an angel! a cherub! And what
am I? Well, well, it will soon be all over!—there
will be a sudden stop, a speedy end!—(*Laughing
without.*) So happy! Heaven, Heaven increase your
joys! Mine are for ever fled!—Light laughter, innocent smiles, and social mirth are fled for ever, for
ever! Oh folly! Oh madness! [*Exit* SIR HARRY.

Enter SIR HORNET, VANDERVELT, *and* CLARA,
(*laughing.*)

Sir Hor. Ay, ay, pray laugh, laugh heartily, I
beseech you.—I deserve and I desire no mercy.

Cla. It is one of the oddest adventures.

Vand. How the deuce could you mistake that
blowzabel, Miss Turnbull, for my turtle?

Sir Hor. Why, true, as you say, friend Van; but
that happens to be a blunder which I never did, nor
ever could make. I should as soon take myself for
a king, or you for a conjuror. I only mistook this
lady to be Miss Turnbull, not Miss Turnbull to be
this lady.

Vand. Mistook Miss Turnbull and this lady, and
—I don't understand it.

Cla. Be kind enough, Sir Hornet, to explain the
matter.

Sir Hor. You remember, madam, I had some conversation with you in the rooms at Bath.

Cla. Perfectly.

Sir Hor. And you could not but perceive how
forcibly I was struck with your wit, beauty, and accomplishments.

Cla. I recollect you were very polite, sir, and were
pleased to say abundance of obliging things.

Sir Hor. Not half so many as I thought, I assure
you, madam.

Vand. Well said, Sir Hornet. My old friend is
quite enamoured with you, turtle.

Sir Hor. Yes, sir, so I am——though I do not intend to marry the lady.

Vand. Hem!

Sir Hor. My grand object, the thing that, of all others, I have most at heart, is to see my nephew, Sir Harry, happy. As for myself, I feel I am growing old apace, and am almost tired of the farce of life.

Vand. Why so, Sir Hornet? I am sure you play your part excellently.

Sir Hor. No, no, I am rolling down hill apace, and as the first steep declivity may precipitate me to the bottom, there are certain affairs I wish to see finished, one of which is the marriage of Sir Harry.

Cla. So the person you asked concerning me, when I went out of the rooms, mistook the question, and thought you meant Miss Turnbull.

Sir Hor. So it appears, madam, and I was too much enraptured to stay to rectify mistakes. When I negociated the affair with 'Squire Turnbull, I studiously avoided an interview with his supposed sister, for fear the business should wear a face of precipitate indelicacy; and I thought if I could once bring you and Sir Harry together, I would leave the contingent possibilities to love, and the superior good qualities and penetration of the parties, which I, rationally enough, concluded could not fail to produce the desired effect.

Cla. But, Sir Hornet, how did it happen that you did not enquire of me myself who I was?

Sir Hor. Why, faith, madam, I had been so particular with you, and had spoken so freely on the subjects of love and matrimony, that I was afraid, if I made those kind of enquiries, you would mistake the matter perhaps, and think I wanted to make love to you in my own proper person. Hey, young Van—— (*Half aside.*)

Vand. Heigho!

Cla. Oh no, Sir Hornet; I assure you I had a better opinion of your understanding.

Vand. Hem!

Sir Hor. Certainly, had I been capable of such a whim, I should have made myself cursed ridiculous. Hey, young Van—(*Half aside.*)

Cla. Beyond dispute!

Vand. Heigho!

Enter TIMID, *looking wild and frighted.*

Sir Hor. Hey-day! What's the matter with you, old Lack-a-day?

Tim. I'm terrified!—I'm terrified!—I'm terrified!

Sir Hor. Terrified! What's the matter? Zounds! why don't you speak?

Tim. Lack-a-day! I can't—I can't speak.

Sir Hor. Make signs then.

Tim. I'm a miserable old man!—I ran all the way to tell you——

Sir Hor. What?

Tim. Mr Osborne——

Sir Hor. Mr Osborne! What of him?

Tim. Lack-a-day!—Sir Harry——

Cla. Heavens!—A duel!

Tim. I have put my trust in man, and am deceived—I have lean'd upon a reed, and am fallen—I have seen the shadow of friendship, and——

Sir Hor. Curse light on your metaphors; come to facts. What of Osborne? What of Sir Harry? Where are they? What have they done? What are they doing?

Tim. Gambling!

Sir Hor. How!

Tim. I was at Mr Osborne's when Sir Harry came, I was there with the mortgage of the Kentish estate.

Sir Hor. Of what?

Tim. It was executed this very day.   I am a miserable old man!—All lost!

Sir Hor. Lost!

Tim. Lack-a-day! That's not at all! I went into the next room, and heard Sir Harry go to gaming with a gang of sharpers that were there on purpose. Sir Harry had lost every thing he had in the world. Mr Osborne has got all—all the mortgages of all his estates—I saw 'em, left 'em all in a box on his table.

Sir Hor. Mortgages of all his estates! Perdition! How did he get them? How came you to know?

Tim. Lack-a-day! I am terrified! I dare not tell!—I am an accomplice!—a wicked, innocent, miserable old man!

Sir Hor. Damnation! Order the coach there.— I'll tear him to atoms—I'll rend him piece-meal!— My poor boy! An intolerable villain! Dear madam, you don't know what I feel.

Cla. Pardon me, Sir Hornet; if you knew my heart, you would not say so. I detest the treachery of Mr Osborne as much as you do, and, woman as I am, would risk my life to see it properly punished.

Sir Hor. A smooth-tongued, hypocritical villain, that owes his life to my boy!

Cla. Dear Sir Hornet, excuse my weakness.—I am in the utmost terror—in dread of consequences still more fatal.

Tim. Lack-a-day, sir, so am I—I am terrified!— Sir Harry gave me this ring for a remembrance, and bade me deliver this picture to you, madam.

Cla. (*Looks at it, and bursts into tears.*) It is his own!

Tim. He look'd so melancholy and so furious.— He had his pistols.

Cla. His pistols!—Oh, for pity's sake, Sir Hornet, let us fly.

Sir Hor. Instantly.

Tim. I am a miserable old man!   [*Exeunt.*

SCENE II.

MR OSBORNE'S *House.*

SIR HARRY *enters excessively agitated, followed by*
OSBORNE, *with a brace of pistols he had wrested
from him.*

Osb. How now, Sir Harry—What is the cause of
this sudden phrenzy? Why expose your want of
temper and fortitude thus to the company? You
have driven them away; they are all going.

Sir Har. Oh! horror!

Osb. If you must wreak vengeance on yourself,
let it be a becoming one at least.

Sir Har. Insupportable horror!

Osb. Fie, fie, recover your temper; be, or seem
to be, a man. What, you knew you were ruined before this event.

Sir Har. Oh, Osborne! Oh, Melissa! I cannot
speak—I cannot utter it—I'm a wretch—a villain—
the meanest—the worst of villains and infamy—
eternal infamy is mine!

Osb. Why, what have you done?

Sir Har. Ruined you—ruined my sister!

Osb. How?

Sir Har. And branded myself everlastingly a villain!

Osb. Ruined me!—ruined your sister! Which
way?

Sir Har. The money I have lost within——

Osb. Well.

Sir Har. Is hers—is yours.

Osb. Mine!

Sir Har. Melissa's——her fortune ; she put it into my hand this very day.

Osb. Damnation!

Sir Har. Have compassion on me.—Give me the pistols ; let me at once put an end to my misery and shame.

Osb. Thoughtless, weak man ! Do you think the momentary pang of death a sufficient punishment for the ruin and destruction you have entailed upon all those who have had the misfortune to love, or to be related to you? Do you think that to *die*, and to forget at once your infamy and crimes, is a compensation for the havoc you have made with the peace and property of those who were dearest to you, who must *live* to feel the effects of your vices, and bear, unjustly, the reproach of your abandoned conduct?

Sir Har. Oh, torture !

Osb. Was it not enough that you had reduced yourself from affluence and honour to contempt and beggary, but you must wantonly, wickedly sport with what was not your own, and involve the innocent and unborn in your wretchedness? Shall not your sister's offspring, whom your intemperance shall have reduced to poverty and misery, detest your memory, and imprecate curses on your name?

Sir Har. Oh, hell !

(SIR HORNET *speaks without, and afterwards enters, followed by* CLARA *and* TIMID.)

Sir Hor. Where are they ? Which is the room ? So, Mr Lucifer, could you decoy your friend to no other place to rob him but your own house ?

Osb. Did you address yourself to me, Sir Hornet?

Sir Hor. Yes, I did, Sir Satan, and if——

Sir Har. Dear sir, forbear ; I alone am the proper object of anger, of vengeance—a wretch!—a despised and miserable outcast : and bitterness and despair are deservedly my portion.

Sir Hor. You are a dupe! a poor fascinated fool! You have beheld the serpent's mouth open, have felt the influence of his poisonous breath, yet stupidly dropt into his ravenous jaws, and sung a *requiem* to your own destruction.

Osb. You are liberal, sir, of your epithets and accusations. What do you mean by them?

Sir Hor. Horrible impudence! Have you not taken a vile, a rascally advantage of the want of temper in the man for whom you professed the most perfect friendship? Have you not stripped him of his estate by the most villainous arts, by plotting with Jews and scoundrels?

Osb. You talk loud, sir.

Sir Har. Osborne!—plotting!—The letter then was true!

Sir Hor. Yes, plotting.—He is the principal, the leader of the hellish gang that has been plundering you.

Osb. Well, sir, suppose it—what then?

Sir Hor. What then?—Halters!

Osb. Why so, sir? He has persisted in bringing destruction upon himself, and must suffer the effects of his obstinacy. What crime was there in my receiving what he was resolved to throw away? He had not been a month returned from his travels, before his passion for play made him the jest of every polite sharper in town; they saw there was an estate to be scrambled for, and every one was industrious to obtain a share. After squandering a part of his fortune among these adventurers, he engaged at play with me, and after losing one sum, was never easy till he had lost another. Am I then to be accountable for his folly?

Sir Har. Infernal treachery! Dares he avow it?

Osb. Dare! Yes, sir, I dare.

Cla. Righteous Heaven! Is there no peculiar, no quick vengeance for ingratitude? (*Aside.*)

Sir Hor. The deeds, the annuities you have granted, the mortgages you have made, are in his possession; he owns he has them all.

Sir Har. He!

Osb. Yes, sir, I.

Sir Har. Madness! Remember and beware!—
remember and tremble!—though I have no longer
the fortune of Sir Harry Portland, I have still Sir
Harry's spirit, and dare chastise insolence and perfidy yet.

Osb. No doubt.—The man who is rash enough to
risk his estate upon the chance of a die, has generally
valour enough to wish to cut the winner's throat.—
Friendship is no protection.

Cla. Friendship!—Monstrous prostitution! Friendship! Deeds, Mr Osborne, are the best proofs of
friendship; and that preacher will gain but little
credit who is a detected villain, while he is describing
the fitness and beauty of moral virtue.

Sir Hor. Friendship! Where are the deeds, the
mortgages?

Osb. There they are, sir.—(*Points to a box.*) They
are mine; the annuities he has granted, and the
mortgages he has made, are mine; his effects are
min , his houses are mine, his estates are mine, his
notes are mine, his *all* is mine, except his poverty
and spirit, which, as he says, are his own.

Sir Har. Heavens! must I bear this?

Sir Hor. Oh! for ratsbane or hemp.

Osb. Nay, more, sir. (*To* SIR HARRY.) I was
not only aware, but certain of my own superior address, or I had not been weak enough to have risked
any part of my fortune.—I have not yet acquired
your heroic contempt for riches. As it was, I used
every art to stimulate and incite you to play, took
every advantage, studied every trick, improved every
lucky chance, and rejoiced at every and all of your
losses, till I had you totally in my power.—I beheld

distress accumulating on your head, and was happy
at it; remarked the agitation of your mind, and increased it; saw the infirmity of your temper, and
aggravated it.

Sir Har. Damnation!—Are you a man?

Osb. Try me.

Sir Har. Dare you give me the satisfaction, the
revenge of a man?

Osb. I'll give it you instantly, sir.

(*As* SIR HARRY *offers to go,* OSBORNE *seizes his
arm, and, before he speaks, his countenance changes from assumed anger and contempt, to the most
tender and expressive friendship.*)

There, there lies your revenge—there is your satisfaction—take them—remember your former folly,
and be happy.

Sir Har. Sir!

Sir Hor. What!

Cla. Astonishment!

Osb. Why do you seem surprised?—My heart is
yours, my life is yours—I owe you every thing—
A debt which never can be repaid, and never will be
forgotten.—When sinking beneath the murderous
hand of villainy, it was the benevolent ardour of your
soul, it was the intrepid valour of your arm that rescued me.

Sir Har. Generous friend!

Osb. In that box is contained all that I have ever
won of you, and almost all you have ever lost—I have
become an associate with sharpers to protect you
from them, and by sacrificing a little, have preserved
the rest. I have worn the mask till it is become too
painful, and now gladly cast it off.—(*To* SIR HORNET
and Company.) If my conduct has yet a dubious appearance—I have a witness that will instantly be
credited. (*Goes to the chamber door and calls* ME-
LISSA; MELISSA *enters, runs to* SIR HARRY, *and
falls upon his neck.*)

Mel. My brother!

Sir Har. Sister! Osborne!

Cla. Oh my heart!

Sir Hor. (*After a pause, and endeavouring to restrain his tears.*) Tol de rol.

Tim. Lack-a-day!—I'm a happy old man!—He's a true friend!—he's a true friend!—I'm a happy old man!

Sir Har. Can you too, sister, forgive my folly? You that I have injured so unpardonably?

Mel. Dear brother, you are not so guilty as you suppose—it was a plot upon you; you were led into it, to shew you what a losing gamester is capable of.

Sir Hor. Hark you, sir. (*To* OSBORNE.) All the mortgages and deeds are there, you say?

Osb. All, sir—together with whatever money else has, at any time, been won of him, since I have been concerned in this transaction.

Sir Hor. All in that box?

Osb. All.

Tim. I'm a happy old man.

Sir Har. My dear uncle!

Sir Hor. Let me alone—Tol de rol—(*Goes up to* OSBORNE, *takes his hand, and wipes his own eyes.*) Will you forgive me, Osborne? Will you? Will you forgive my boy?

Sir Har. (*Takes* OSBORNE'S *other hand.*) Osborne!—I cannot speak.

Cla. Indeed, Mr Osborne, I don't know how to tell you what I think—Esteem—admiration—veneration—are poor expressions to convey my feelings—I have been mistaken, and to blame—I trembled for Sir Harry, I rashly condemned you, and wrote a letter——

Sir Har. Dear madam, was that letter yours?

Cla. It was.

Sir Har. How much obliged am I to you, and to you all!

Cla. I am sorry—I was to blame.

Osb. Nay, madam—Nobody was to blame—Angels are actuated by motives like yours, and if they never err, it is because they have commerce with angels only.—And now, dear Harry, suffer me to say one word—Let this transaction be a powerful, an everlasting memento to you.— Remember the blood that has been spilt in the moment of passion and distress, in consequence of indulging in this shocking vice—Remember the distracted wife and widow's curse, the orphan's tears, the sting of desperation, and the red and impious hand of suicide; despise the folly that made the practice fashionable; oppose its destructive course, and for ever shun, for ever abominate the detestable vice of gaming.

Sir Har. Professions of resolution from me, Osborne, come with an ill grace—I am ashamed of my folly—I despised, even while I practised it ; but the punishment you have inflicted has been so judicious, so severely generous, I think I can safely say, there is no probability of a relapse.

Sir Hor Well, but, Harry, turn about—look at this lady—surely you have not forgot Miss Turnbull —have you ?

Sir Har. Your Miss Turnbull, sir, I shall never forget.

Sir Hor. Oh! what, you have heard the renowned history of my Bath adventure ?

Sir Har. I have, sir.

Sir Hor. Well, and what say *you* to—hey, my cherub—you told me, you know, you had no aversion to the fellow.

Cla. Nay, Sir Hornet, is that the part of a confidant ?

Sir Hor. Why, yes, it is—for, as I take it, a confidant is but a kind of a go-between. to bring the parties together——And here comes the blooming youth—(*Enter* VANDERVELT)—here comes Johannes de Temporibus, to second the motion.

Vand. To second what motion, Sir Hornet?

Sir Hor. A hymeneal motion.

Vand. Can't tell.—Who are the candidates?

Sir Hor. Harry Portland and Clara Forester.

Vand. Hold, hold, Sir Hornet, not so fast!—That lady is my ward.

Sir Hor. Yes, and may, if she pleases, be your wife.

Vand. Nay—I—I did not say so, Sir Hornet.

Sir Hor. No, but I did, young Van.—But hark you—(*Takes him aside*)—resign all your silly pretensions peaceably, throw your worthies into the fire, and give up the lady to her lover; or you shall be held up, *in terrorem,* an object of ridicule, to frighten all the dangling, whining, old fools in Christendom, who are turned of threescore.

Vand. Well, well, speak in a lower key.

Sir Hor. May I be certain of your consent then?

Vand. Why, yes—yes—heigho!

Sir Hor. Dear madam—this worthy old gentleman, your guardian, most humbly implores you would have pity upon Sir Harry.

Cla. Did you say so, papa?

Vand. Me! no.

Sir Hor. How?

Vand. N——not in those exact words, but something very like it, turtle—heigho!

Mel. Come, my dear Clara—let me have the happiness to call you sister.

Osb. Let me intercede, madam.

Cla. Pshaw—here is every body interceding, but him that can intercede most to the purpose.

Sir Har. Forgive me, dearest Clara—My fate is suspended on your lips, and I am so conscious o unworthiness, and so much affected by the fear of a severe sentence, that I have not power to plead for mercy.

Cla. Yes—but you have a partial, tender-hearted judge.

Sir Hor. Ay—and a wise young judge too.

Cla. Well, well!—I cannot dissemble. A generous heart, a noble mind, are seldom met and seldom merited. When happiness like this presents itself, to reject is not to deserve it.   [*Exeunt omnes.*

THE

SCHOOL FOR ARROGANCE;

A

COMEDY,

IN FIVE ACTS.

AS PERFORMED AT THE

THEATRE-ROYAL, COVENT-GARDEN.

BY

THOMAS HOLCROFT.

DRAMATIS PERSONÆ.

COUNT CONNOLLY VILLARS,	*Mr Lewis.*
MR DORIMONT,	*Mr Aickin.*
SIR PAUL PECKHAM,	*Mr Wilson.*
SIR SAMUEL SHEEPY,	*Mr Munden.*
EDMUND,	*Mr Farren.*
MACDERMOT,	*Mr Johnstone.*
PICARD,	*Mr Marshall.*
BUTLER, } *Omitted.*	
COOK, }	
EXEMPT,	*Mr Thompson.*
BAILIFFS,	{ *Mr Cross.*
	{ *Mr Lee.*
FOOTMEN,	{ *Mr Farley.*
	{ *Mr Evatt.*
	{ *Mr Letteny.*
	{ *Mr Blurton.*
LADY PECKHAM,	*Mrs Mattocks.*
LUCY,	*Mrs Wells.*
LYDIA,	*Miss Brunton.*

Scene, London : The House of Sir Paul Peckham and the Apartments of the Count. Time twelve hours.

SCHOOL FOR ARROGANCE.

ACT THE FIRST.

SCENE I.

The House of SIR PAUL PECKHAM.

Enter LYDIA, *followed by* MACDERMOT.

Ly. Once again, Mr MacDermot, have done with this nonsense.

MacDer. Arrah, and why so scoffish? Sure now a little bit of making love—

Ly. Pshaw! Do me the favour to answer my questions. The count, your master, is in love with Miss Lucy Peckham?

MacDer. Faith, and you may say that.

Ly. Is he really well born?

MacDer. Oh! as for that, honey, let him alone. The noblest blood of France, ay, and what is bet-

ter, of Ireland too, trickles to his fingers' ends—the
Villars and the O'Connollies.

Ly. And he wishes to marry into the family of the
Peckhams?

MacDer. The divle a bit, my dear.

Ly. How?

MacDer. He is viry willing to marry the young
lady, but not her family. His pride and his passion
have had many a tough battle about that, d'ye see.
Only think! A direct descindant of the former kings
of Ireland, and collateral cousin to the prisent peer
of France, to besmear and besmoulder his dignity,
by rubbing it against porter butts, vinegar casks, and
beer barrels.

Ly. Miss Lucy is indeed a lovely girl, animated to
excess, and sometimes apparently giddy and flighty;
but she has an excellent understanding, and a noble
heart; and these are superior to birth, which is indeed a thing of mere accident.

MacDer. Faith, and that it is—I, a simple Irishman, as I am—why now, I would have been born a
duke, had they been civil enough to have asked my
consint.

Ly. The count fell in love with her at the convent,
to which she was sent to improve her French.

MacDer. And where I think you first met with
her?

Ly. Yes—she saw me friendless, and conceived a
generous and disinterested affection for me.—He has
followed her to England: has taken apartments in
our neighbourhood, and lives in splendour—yet is
not rich.

MacDer. Um, um.—No—But then he is a colonel
in the Irish brigade, and, beside his pay, has sacrit
supplies.

Ly. From whom?

MacDer. Faith, and I don't believe he knows that
himself.

Ly. That's strange!—His pride is excessive.

MacDer. To spake the truth, that now is his failing.
—An if it was not for that, oh! he would be the
jewel of a master!—He trates his infariors with con-
timpt, keeps his distance with his aquals, and values
the rubbishing dust of his great grandfathers above
diamonds!

Ly. His character is in perfect contrast to that of
his humble rival, Sir Samuel Sheepy; who, even
when he addresses a footman, is all bows and affability; whose chief discourse is, yes, if you please, and,
no, thank you; and who, in the company of his mistress, stammers, blunders, and blushes, like a great
boy.

MacDer. What is it you till me? He the rival of
the count my master! That old——

Ly. A bachelor, and only fifty; rich, of a good family, and a great favourite with **Lady Peckham**, by
never having the courage to contradict her.

MacDer. Why, there now! You talk of the count's
pride! Here is this city lady as proud as ten counts!
Her own coach horses, ready harnessed, don't carry
their heads higher! And then she is as insolent, and
as vulgar, and—Hem!

Enter LADY PECKHAM *and* SIR SAMUEL SHEEPY,
*followed by two Footmen, in very smart morning
jackets.*

L. Peck. Here, fellers—go with these here cards.
*(Footmen receive each a parcel of large cards, and are
going.)* Oh! Tell that there butler to come to me
instantly.—And—Do you hear?—Vhen you comes
back, get those dismal heads of yourn better powder'd; put on your noo liveries, and make yourselves
a little like Christians. These creeters are no better
nur brootes, Sir Samooel! They are all so monstrous
low and wulgar!—I have a party to-night: I hopes
you vill make von?

Sir S. Certainly, my lady.

L. Peck. Vhy, vhere is this butler?

Enter Butler.

But. I am here, my lady!

L. Peck. Is all the furniter rubb'd?

But. All, my lady!

L. Peck. The m'ogany bright?

But. As bees-wax can make it, my lady!

L. Peck. Bow pots in the china jars?

But. Yes, my lady!

L. Peck. The picters on the hall stair-case scoured?

But. Clean, my lady!—But, I—(*Hesitating.*)

L. Peck. You! You vhat?

But. I am afraid their eyes and noses will soon disappear.

L. Peck. Psha!—Feller!——Are the noo prints come home?

But. Yes, my lady!

L. Peck. And the karakatoors hung up in the drawing-room?

But. All, my lady!

L. Peck. You shall come and see 'em, Sir Samooel!

Sir S. Your ladyship has exquisite taste.

L. Peck. Oh! Sir Samooel!—Vell, feller?

But. My lady!

L. Peck. Vhat do you stand gaping at?

But. My lady!

L. Peck. Vill you be gone, feller?

But. Oh!—Yes, my lady, (*Aside,*) and thank you too!   [*Exit.*

L. Peck. So, miss! is Sir Paul come to town?

Ly. I have not seen him, madam.

L. Peck. Sir Paul generally sleeps at our country seat, at Hackney.

Sir S. A pleasant retreat, my lady!

L. Peck. Wastly! A wery paradise!—Vhere is my daughter, miss?

Ly. I don't know, madam.

L. Peck. And vhy don't you know? Please to go and tell her Sir Samooel is here. (*Exit* LYDIA.)—A young purson that my daughter has taken under her purtection.

Sir S. Seems mild and modest, my lady.

L. Peck. Not too much of that, Sir Samooel.— Who—(*Surveying* MACDERMOT)—pray, who are you, young man?

MacDer. I!—Faith, my lady, I—I am—mysilf— MacDermot.

L. Peck. Who?

MacDer. The count's gintleman.

L. Peck. Gentleman! Gentleman, indeed! Count's gentleman!—Ha!—A kind of mungrel count, Sir Samooel; half French, half Irish! As good a gentleman, I suppose, as his footman here! I believes you have seen him though?

Sir S. I think I once had the honour to meet him here, my lady.

L. Peck. An honour, Sir Samooel, not of my seeking, I assure you! Aspires to the hand of Miss Loocy Peckham!—He!—An outlandish French foriner!— I hates 'em all! I looks upon none on 'em as no better nor savages! Vhat do they vant vith us? Vhy, our money, to be sure! A parcel of beggars!—I vishes I vus queen of England for von day only! I vould usher my orders to take and conquer 'em all, and tran port 'em to the plantations, instead of negurs.

Sir S. I have heard, my lady, that the count was my rival.

L. Peck. He your rival, Sir Samooel! He! A half-bred, higglety-pigglety, Irish, French fortin-hunter rival you indeed!—(*Enter* LYDIA.)—Vell, miss! Vhere is my daughter?

Ly. In her own apartment, madam, dressing.

L. Peck. She'll be down presently, Sir Samooel—Gentleman indeed! The count's gentleman! Ha! Pride and poverty!

[*Exeunt* LADY PECKHAM *and* SIR SAMUEL SHEEPY.

MacDer. (*Highly affronted.*) Pride!—By the holy footstool, but your ladyship and Lucifer are a pair!
(*Knocking.*)

Ly. Here comes Sir Paul.

MacDer. Then I will be after going.

Ly. No, no; stay where you are.

Enter SIR PAUL PECKHAM.

Sir P. Ah! My sweet dear Liddy! You are the angel I wished first to meet! Come to my—(*Running up to her*)—Why, how now, hussy? Why so shy?

Ly. Reserve your transports, sir, for Lady Peckham.

Sir P. Lady!—But who have we here?

Ly. Mr MacDermot, sir.

Sir P. Oh! I remember—servant to the count, my intended son-in-law.

MacDer. The viry same, sir. (*Bows.*)

Sir P. I hear an excellent character of your master. They tell me he is a fine, hearty, dauntless, swaggering fellow! If so, he is a man of family, and the very husband for my Lucy.

MacDer. Faith, thin, and he is all that!

Sir P. As for this Sir Samuel Sheepy, he shall decamp—A water-drinker! A bowing, scraping, simpering, ceremonious sir! Never contradicts any body!—Dammee! An old bachelor! And he—he have the impudence to make love to my fine, young, spirited wench!—But he is my lady's choice!—Is she within?

Ly. Yes, sir.

Sir P. I suppose we shall have a fine breeze on

this subject! But what! Am I not the monarch, the grand seignior of this house? Am I not absolute? Shall I not dispose of my daughter as I please? Do you hear, young man? Go, present my compliments to the count, and tell him I mean to give him a call this morning.

(LYDIA *makes signs to* MACDERMOT *to stay.*)

MacDer. I am waiting for him here, sir.

Sir P. Waiting for him here, sir! No, sir! You cannot wait for him here, sir!

MacDer. But, sir—

Sir P. And, sir! Why don't you go?

MacDer. The count bid me, sir—

Sir P. And I bid you, sir—pack! be gone! [*Exit* MACDERMOT.]—Now we're alone, my dear Lydia —Why, where are you going, hussy?

Ly. Didn't you hear my lady call?

Sir P. Call? No.—And if she did, let her call.

Ly. Surely, sir, you would not have me offend her?

Sir P. Offend! Let me see who dare be offended with you in this house! It is my will that you should be the sultana!

Ly. Me, sir!

Sir P. You, my queen of hearts! You! My house, my wealth, my servants, myself, all are yours!

Ly. You talk unintelligibly, sir.

Sir P. Do I? Why, then, I'll speak plainer.—I am in love with you! You are a delicious creature, and I am determined to make your fortune!— I'll take you a house up in Mary-le-bone: a neat snug box; hire you servants, keep you a carriage, buy you rings, clothes, and jewels, and come and sup with you every evening!—Do you understand me now?

Ly. Perfectly, sir!

Sir P. Well, and—hay!—Does not the plan tickle your fancy? Do not your veins tingle, your heart beat, your—hay! What say you?

Ly. I really, sir, don't know what to say—except

that I cannot comply, unless a lady, whom I think it my duty to consult, should give her consent.

Sir P. What lady?—who?

Ly. Lady Peckham, sir.

Sir P. My wife! Zounds! are you mad? Tell my wife!

Ly. I shall further ask the advice of your son and daughter, who will wonder at your charity, in taking a poor orphan like me under your protection; will be happy to see themselves ruined for my sake, and will profit by the example of so venerable a father.

Sir P. Poh!—nonsense!

Ly. A little farther off, if you please, sir.

Sir P. Nearer, angel, nearer.

Ly. I'll raise the house, sir.

Sir P. Pshaw!

Ly. Help!

Sir P. My handkerchief! You sweet——

Enter EDMUND.

Edm. Lydia!—Sir!

Sir P. How now, sir?—(*Aside to* LYDIA.)—Hem! Say it was a mouse.

Edm. What is the matter, sir?

Sir P. What's that to you, sir? What do you want, sir? Who sent for you, sir?

Edm. I perceive you are not well, sir.

Sir P. Sir!

Edm. How were you taken?

Sir P. Taken!—(*Aside.*) Young scoundrel!— Take yourself away, sir.

Edm. Impossible, sir! You tremble!—your looks are disordered!—your eyes wild!

Sir P. (*Aside.*) Here's a dog!

Edm. Be so obliging, Miss Lydia, as to run and inform Lady Peckham how ill my father is.

Sir P. Why, you imp! (*Stopping* LYDIA.) Lydia,

stay where you are. You audacious!—will you be gone?

Edm. That I certainly will not, sir, while I see you in such a way.

Sir P. Way, sir!—Very well, sir, very well.

Edm. I'll reach you a chair, sir.—Pray sit down; pray cool yourself.

Sir P. Oh that I were cooling you in a horsepond!

Edm. You are growing old, sir.

Sir P. You lie, sir!

Edm. You should be more careful of yourself.— Shall I send for a physician?

Sir P. (*Aside.*) Dammee, but I'll physic you! I'll——

Enter a Man Cook.

Cook. Your soup is ready, sir.

Sir P. Sir!

Cook. Knew your worship's hour—never made better in my life—rich and high—just to your worship's palate.

Sir P. Why, fellow, don't you see I'm very ill?

Cook. Ill, Sir Paul!

Sir P. That my eyes are wild, that I tremble, am old, and want a physician?

Cook. Lord, Sir Paul! I have been your physician for these fifteen years.

Sir P. I tell you I'm ill, and want cooling.—Ask that scoundrel else. I'm dying! so serve up your dose.

Cook. Ha, ha, ha! Yes, your worship. [*Exit.*

Sir P. (*Muttering as he goes off.*) A sly, invidious——The demure dog has a mind to her himself. Yes, yes.—Oh, dammee, pitiful Peter, but I'll fit you! [*Exit.*

Ly. You see, sir!

Edm. (*Shrugging.*) I do.

VOL. IV. H

Ly. I must leave this family.

Edm. Leave!—Why, charming Lydia, will you afflict me thus? Have I not declared my purpose?

Ly. Which cannot be accomplished. You promise marriage, but your father will never consent.

Edm. Then we will marry without his consent.

Ly. Oh no; do not hope it. When I marry, it shall be to render both my husband and myself respectable and happy; not to embitter, not to dishonour both.

Enter a Footman.

Foot. A person, who calls himself Mr Dorimont, inquires for you, madam.

Ly. Heavens! can it be? Shew him up instantly.
                                        [*Exit Footman.*

Edm. You seem alarmed.

Ly: No, no; overjoyed.

Edm. Who is it?

Ly. I scarcely can tell you. A gentleman who used to visit me in the convent.

Edm. Have you been long acquainted?

Ly. Little more than two years, during which he was my monitor, consoler, and guide.

Edm. (*Seeing him before he enters.*) His appearance——

Ly. Is poor, but his heart is rich in benevolence. Pray leave us.   [*Exit* EDMUND.

Enter MR DORIMONT.

Ly. (*Running to meet him.*) Ah! sir.

Mr Dor. I am happy to have found you once again.

Ly. What, sir, has brought you to England?

Mr Dor. Business; part of which was to see you.

Ly. You have been always generous and kind.— Yet I am sorry you should see me thus.

Mr Dor. Why? (*Eagerly.*) What are you?

Ly. An humble dependant; a lady's companion.

Mr Dor. Alas! why did you leave the convent without informing me?

Ly. 'Twas unexpected. You had forborne your visits, and I feared death, or some misfortune. At my mother's decease, the young lady with whom I live having an affection for me, and seeing me deserted, offered to take me with her to England, promising I should rather be her friend than her companion.

Mr Dor. And has she kept her word?

Ly. On her part faithfully, tend∘rly.

Mr Dor. That is some consolation.

Ly. But——

Mr Dor. What?

Ly. She has a mother, who does not fail to make inferiority feelingly understand itself.

Mr Dor. (*With some emotion.*) Indeed! (*Collecting himself.*) But with whom were you in such earnest conversation when I entered?

Ly. The brother of my young lady; a gentleman worthy your esteem.

Mr Dor. And worthy yours?—You blush!

Ly. Do you blame me for being just?

Mr Dor. No. He is rich, young, and handsome. —Do you often meet?

Ly. We do.

Mr Dor. You are lovely, inexperienced, and unprotected.

Ly. Fear nothing: I shall not easily forget myself.

Mr Dor. (*Earnestly.*) I hope not. But what does he say?

Ly. That he loves me.

Mr Dor. Is that all?

Ly. No; he offers me secret marriage.

Mr Dor. Secret marriage!

Ly. I see the danger, and wish to shun it.—You may find me some place of refuge in France.

Mr Dor. Can you so easily renounce all the flattering prospects love has raised?

Ly. Yes; and not only them, but love itself, when it is my duty.

Mr Dor. Noble-minded girl! Remain where you are; nay, indulge your hopes; for know, your lover will be honoured by your hand.

Ly. Sir!—honoured!

Mr Dor. Honoured. By birth you are greatly his superior.

Ly. Can you be serious? Oh, trifle not with a too trembling heart! Why did my mother conceal this secret from me? Or, if true, why die and leave it unrevealed?

Mr Dor. There were reasons. She was not your mother.

Ly. Not! Oh, sir, you have conjured up ten thousand busy thoughts! Is my mother living?

Mr Dor. No.

Ly. My father?

Mr Dor. He is.

Ly. Why has he so long forsaken me?

Mr Dor. That must be told hereafter. Be patient; wait the event. You are acquainted, I think, with Count Connolly Villars?

Ly. He visits here.

Mr Dor. I have business with him.

Ly. Ah, sir, I fear you will meet a cool reception. Your humble appearance and his pride will but ill agree.

Mr Dor. Fear not: my business is to lower his pride.

Ly. Sir!—He may insult you.

Mr Dor. Humble though I myself am, I hope to teach him humility. To visit you, and to accomplish this, was the purport of my journey. Adieu for the present. Think on what I have said; and though by birth you are noble, remember virtue alone is true nobility.

(LYDIA *rings. Exit* MR DORIMONT, *and enter* LUCY; *her dress more characteristic of the girl than of the woman, and her manner full of life, but tempered by the most delicate sensibility.*)

Lucy. Well, Lydia, any news for me?

Ly. Mr MacDermot has been here, with the count's compliments, but, in reality, to see if Lady Peckham were at home. You know how much he wishes to avoid her.

Lucy. Yes; and I don't wonder at it. She has just been with me, ushering her orders, as she calls it. "I desires, miss, you vill receive Sir Samooel Sheepy as your intended spouse." And so she has sent me here to be courted; and the inamorato is coming, as soon as he can take breath and courage.

Ly. But why, my dear, do you indulge yourself in mocking your mamma?

Lucy. Lydia, I must either laugh or cry; and though I laugh, I assure you it is often with an aching heart.

Ly. My dear girl!

Lucy. I hope, however, you will own there is no great harm in laughing a little at this charming Adonis, this whimsical lover of mine!

Ly. Perhaps not.

Lucy. What can his reason be for making love to me?

Ly. There's a question! Pray, my dear, do you never look in your glass?

Lucy. Um—yes; but does he never look in his glass too?

Ly. Perhaps his sight begins to decay.—But are not you alarmed?

9

Lucy. No.

Ly. Do not you love the count?

Lucy. Um—yes.

Ly. Well! and you know how violent and preju-
diced Lady Peckham is!

Lucy. Perfectly; but I have Sir Paul on my side;
and as for Sir Samuel, he was dandled so long in the
nursery, and is still so much of the awkward, bashful
boy, that he will never dare to put the question directly to me; and I am determined never to understand him till he does.

Ly. Here he comes.

Lucy. Don't leave me.

Enter SIR SAMUEL.

Sir S. (*Bowing with trepidation.*) Madam—hem!
—madam——

Lucy. (*Curtseying and mimicking.*) Sir—hem!—
sir—(*Aside to* LYDIA.) Count his bows.

Sir S. Madam, I—hem!—I am afraid—I am
troublesome.

Lucy. Sir—hem!—a gentleman of your merit—
hem!

Sir S. (*Continues bowing through most of the scene.*)
Oh, madam, I am afraid—hem!—you are busy.

Lucy. (*Curtseying to all his bows.*) Sir—hem!——

Sir S. Do me the honour to bid me be gone.

Lucy. Surely, sir, you would not have me guilty
of rudeness?

Sir S. (*Aside.*) What a blunder! Madam—hem!
—I ask ten thousand pardons.

Lucy. Good manners require—hem!——

Sir S. That I should be gone without bidding.—
(*Going.*)

Lucy. Sir!

Sir S. (*Aside.*) I suppose I'm wrong again.

Lucy. I didn't say so, sir.

Sir S. (*Turning quick.*) Didn't you, madam?

Lucy. A person of your politeness, breeding, and accomplishments—hem!——

Sir S. (*Aside.*) She's laughing at me.

Lucy. Ought to be treated with all reverence.— (*Curtseying with ironic gravity.*)

Sir S. (*Aside.*) Yes, she's making a fool of me!

Lucy. Sir.—Were you pleased to speak sir?— Hem!

Sir S. Hem!—not a word, madam.

Ly. This will be a witty conversation.

Lucy. I presume, sir—hem!—you have something to communicate.

Sir S. Madam?—Hem!—Yes, madam; I mean no, madam—no, nothing—hem!

Ly. Nothing, Sir Samuel?

Sir S. Hem!—Nothing, nothing.

Lucy. Then may I take the liberty, sir, to inquire —hem!—what the purport of your visit is?—Hem!

Sir S. The—the—the—Hem!—The purport is— Hem!—I—I have really forgotten.

Lucy. Oh, pray, sir, take time to recollect your- self. Hem! I am sure, Sir Samuel—hem!—you have something to say to me.—Hem!

Sir S. Yes—no, no, nothing.

Ly. Fie, Sir Samuel! Nothing to say to a lady!

Sir S. No. Hem! I never had any thing to say to ladies in my life. That is—yes, yes, I own I have something of the—the utmost—Hem!

Lucy. Indeed!

Sir S. A thing which lies at my heart. Hem!

Lucy. Mercy! Sir Samuel! Hem!

Sir S. Which I—hem!—have long——But I will take some other opportunity. (*Offering to go.*)

Lucy. By no means, Sir Samuel. You have quite alarmed me! I am impatient to hear. I am afraid you are troubled in mind. Hem!

Sir S. Why—hem!—yes, madam, rather—hem!

Lucy. I declare I thought so. I am very sorry. Perhaps you are afraid of death?

Sir S. Madam!

Lucy. Yet you are not so very old.

Sir S. Madam!

Lucy. But I would not have you terrify yourself too much. Hem!

Sir S. Madam!

Lucy. I perceive I have guessed it.

Sir S. Madam! Hem! No, madam.

Lucy. No! What then is this important secret? Nay, pray tell me. Hem!

Sir S. Hem! N—n—n—n not at present, madam.

Ly. Nay, Sir Samuel!

Sir S. Some other time, madam. Hem!

Lucy. And can you be so cruel to me? Can you? I declare I shall dream about you—shall think I see you in your winding-sheet, or some such frightful figure, and shall wake all in a tremble. Hem!

Sir S. A tremble indeed, madam!

Lucy. And won't you tell me, Sir Samuel?—won't you?

Sir S. N—n—n—n not at present, madam. Hem!

Lucy. Well, if you won't, Sir Samuel, I must leave you; for what you have said has absolutely given me the vapours. Hem!

Sir S. I, madam! Have I given you the vapours?

Lucy. Yes, you have, Sir Samuel, and shockingly too. You have put such gloomy ideas into my mind!

Sir S. Bless me, madam. Hem!

Lucy. Your salts, Lydia. Hem!

Sir S. I hope, madam, you—you are not *very* ill!

Lucy. Oh, I shall be better in another room. Hem!

Sir S. (*Aside.*) Yes, yes; 'tis my company that has given her the vapours. (*Aloud.*) Shall I—(*Confusedly offering his arm.*)

Lucy. No, no; stay where you are, Sir Samuel.

Sir S. (*Aside.*) She wants to be rid of me. Hem!

Lucy. Only remember you are under a promise to tell me your secret. Hem! If you don't, I shall certainly see your ghost! Remember. Hem!

[*Exit.*

Sir S. Madam, I—(*Not knowing whether to go or stay.*)—(*To* LYDIA.) Miss Lydia—Hem!

Ly. Sir.

Sir S. If you would—hem!—be so civil, I——

Ly. Oh, sir, I have the vapours as bad as Miss Lucy! [*Exit.*

Sir S. Have you? Hem! Bless me! Death, winding-sheets, ghosts! Gloomy ideas indeed. Hem! She was laughing at me; I am sure she was. Hem! All my life long have I been laughed at by young coquettish girls—yet I can't forsake 'em. Then the vapours; my old trick. I always give young ladies the vapours: I make 'em ill: They are always sick of me. Hem! 'Tis very strange that I can't learn to talk without having a word to say. A thing so common too. Why can't I give myself monkey airs; skip here and there; be self-sufficient, impertinent, and behave like a puppy, purposely to please the ladies? What! is there no such thing to be found as a woman who can love a man for his modesty? This foreign count, now, my rival, is quite a different thing. He—(*Mimicking*)—he walks with a straight back, and a cocked-up chin, and a strut, and a stride, and stares, and takes snuff, and——Yes, yes—he's the man for the ladies! [*Exit.*

ACT THE SECOND.

SCENE I.

An Apartment in the House of SIR PAUL PECKHAM.

Ly. I cannot forget it! My father alive! and I of noble descent! 'Tis very strange! Hope, doubt, and apprehension are all in arms. Imagination hurries me beyond all limits of probability.

Enter EDMUND.

Edm. Why do you thus seek solitude?

Ly. To indulge thought.

Edm. Has your friend brought you bad news?

Ly. No.

Edm. What has he said?

Ly. Strange things.

Edm. Heavens! What?

Ly. You would think me a lunatic, were I to repeat them.

Edm. Lydia, I conjure you not to keep me on the rack.

Ly. I was enjoined silence, but I feel my heart has no secrets for you—Yet you will laugh.

Edm. Ungenerous Lydia!

Ly. Yes, you will think me mad.

Edm. Lydia, you are unjust.

Ly. Am I? Well then, I am told—Would you believe it?—I am told that my family is illustrious!

Edm. Good heavens! 'Tis true! I feel it is true! Charming Lydia, (*Kneeling,*) thus let love pay you that homage which the world, blind and malignant, denies.

Ly. Rise, Edmund. Birth can at best but confer imaginary dignity: there is no true grandeur but of mind.

Edm. Some one is coming.

Ly. Ay, ay. Get you gone.

Edm. I am all transport!

Ly. Hush! Away!

Edm. My angel! (*Kisses her hand.*)

[*Exit hastily.*

Enter Footman, introducing MR DORIMONT.

Foot. A gentleman to you, madam.

Ly. This sudden return, sir, is kind.

Mr Dor. I have bethought me. The moment is critical, and what I have to communicate of importance. Are we secure?

Ly. We are. This is my apartment. (LYDIA *goes and bolts the door.*) Have you seen the count, sir?

Mr Dor. No, but I have written to him anonymously.

Ly. And why anonymously?

Mr Dor. To rouse his feelings, wound his vanity, and excite his anger: His slumbering faculties must be awakened. Is he kind to you?

Ly. No; yet I believe him to be generous, benevolent, and noble of heart, though his habitual haughtiness gives him the appearance of qualities the very reverse.

Mr Dor. Worthy, kind girl! You were born for the consolation of a too unfortunate father.

Ly. Again you remind me that I have a father. Why am I not allowed to see him? Why am I not suffered to fly into his arms?

Mr Dor. He dreads lest his wretched and pitiable condition should make you meet him with coldness.

Ly. Oh! how little does he know my heart! Yet speak; tell me what monster was the cause of his misery?

Mr Dor. The monster Pride.

Ly. Pride!

Mr Dor. Your mother's pride, which first squandered his wealth, and next endangered his life.

Ly. How you alarm me!

Mr Dor. A despicable dispute for precedency was the occasion of a duel, in which your father killed his antagonist, whose enraged family, by suborning witnesses, caused him to be convicted of murder, obliged him to fly the kingdom, and with your mother wander under a borrowed name, a fugitive in distant countries.

Ly. Heavens! But why leave me ignorant of my birth?

Mr Dor. That, being unfortunate, you might be humble; that you might not grieve after happiness which you seemed destined not to enjoy. 'Twas the precaution of a fond father, desirous to alleviate, if not succour your distress.

Ly. Oh, how I burn to see him! Is he not in danger? Is his life secure?

Mr Dor. He himself can scarcely say. His enemies have discovered him, are hot in pursuit, and fertile in stratagems and snares: they know that justice is now busied in his behalf; but justice is slow, and revenge is restless. Their activity, I hear, is redoubled.

Ly. Guard, I conjure you, guard my father's safety. Let me fly to seek him. Conduct me to his feet.

Mr Dor. He wished you first to be informed of his true situation, lest, knowing him to be noble, you should expect to see him in all the pomp of affluence, instead of meeting a poor, dejected, forlorn old man.

Ly. His fears are unjust; injurious to every feeling of filial affection and duty. The little I have I will freely partake with him. My clothes, the diamonds which my supposed mother left me, whatever I possess shall instantly be sold for his relief : my life shall be devoted to soften his sorrows. Oh that I could prove myself worthy to be his daughter! Oh that I could pour out my soul to secure his felicity!

Mr Dor. Forbear! Let me breathe! Affection cannot find utterance! Oh, this melting heart! My child !

Ly. Sir !

Mr Dor. My Lydia!

Ly. Heavens !

Mr Dor. My child! My daughter!

Ly. (*Falling at his feet.*) Can it be ? My father! Oh, ecstacy !

Mr Dor. Rise, my child. Suffer me to appease my melting heart. Oh, delight of my eyes! Why is not your brother like you ?

Ly. My brother ! Who ? Have I a brother ?

Mr Dor. The count is your brother.

Ly. 'Tis too much !

Mr Dor. He is not worthy such a sister.

Ly. The sister of the count !—I ! Ah ! Nature, thy instincts are fabulous; for, were they not, his heart would have beaten as warmly toward me, as mine has done for him !

Mr Dor. I will make him blush at his arrogance. You shall witness his confusion, which shall be public, that it may be effectual.

Ly. Would you have me avoid explanation with him ?

Mr Dor Yes, for the present. I mean to see him. Our meeting will be warm, but he shall feel the authority of a father.

Ly. If you are a stranger to him, I fear lest——

Mr Dor. No, no. He knows me, but knows not all his obligations to me. I have secretly supplied him with money, and gained him promotion, which he has vainly attributed to his personal merits. But

I must be gone. My burdened heart is eased.
Once more, dear child of my affections, be prudent.
I have much to apprehend; but, should the present
moment prove benign, my future days will all be
peace !—(*Knocking heard at the chamber door.*)

Ly. (*Alarmed.*) Who's there ?

Sir P. (*Without.*) 'Tis I.   Open the door.

Ly. I am busy, sir.

Sir P. Pshaw ! Open the door, I tell you.

Mr Dor. Who is it ?

Ly. Sir Paul.

Mr Dor. And does he take the liberty to come
into your apartment ?

Ly. Oh, sir, he will take any liberty he can.

Sir P. Why don't you open the door ?

Mr Dor. You are surrounded by danger and
temptation !

Ly. Have no fears for me, sir.

Sir P. Will you open the door, I say ?

Mr Dor. Let him come in.   (LYDIA *unbolts the
door.*)

Enter SIR PAUL.

Sir P. What is the reason, you dear little baggage, that you always shut yourself up so carefully ?

Ly. You are one of the reasons, sir.

Sir P. Pshaw ! You need not be afraid of me.

Ly. I'm *not* afraid of you, sir.

Sir P. Why, that's right. I'm come to talk matters over with you. My lady's out—a-wisiting—(*Mimicking*)—the coast is clear—I have secured my
graceless dog of a son. I suspect !

Ly. What, sir ?

Sir P. But it won't do. Mind ; take the hint.—
I've heard of an excellent house.

Ly. You are running on as usual, sir.

Sir P. With a convenient back door. I'll bespeak
you a carriage : choose your own liveries : keep as

many footmen as you please. Indulge in every thing
your heart can wish—operas, balls, routs, masque-
rades ; Rotten Row of a Sunday ; town house and
country house ; Bath, Bristol, or Buxton ; hot wells
or cold wells :——only—hem !——hay !

Ly. Sir, I must not hear such ribaldry.

Sir P. Indeed but you must, my dear. How will
you help it ? You can't escape me now. I have you
fast. No scapegrace scoundrel of a——(MR DORI-
MONT *comes forward.*) And so——

Mr Dor. (*Sternly.*) And so, sir !

Sir P. Zounds ! (*Pause.*) And so ! (*Looking
round.*) Locked up together ! You were busy !

Mr Dor. Well, sir ?

Sir P. Oh, very, sir. Perhaps you have a house
yourself, sir ?

Mr Dor. Sir ?

Sir P. With a convenient back door ?

Mr Dor. So far from offering the lady such an
insult, sir, I am almost tempted to chastise that impotent effrontery which has been so daring.

Sir P. Hem ! You are very civil, sir ; and, as a
return for your compliment, I am ready to do myself
the pleasure, sir, to wait on you down stairs.

Ly. I'll spare you the trouble, sir.

Mr Dor. Though this lady's residence here will
be but short, I would have you beware, sir, how you
shock her ears again with a proposal so vile.

Sir P. Your caution is kind, sir.

Mr Dor. I am sorry it is necessary, sir. What !
The head of a house ! the father of a family ! Oh !
shame ! He who, tottering on the brink of the grave,
would gratify appetites which he no longer knows,
by reducing the happy to misery, and the innocent
to guilt, deserves to sink into that contempt and
infamy into which he would plunge unwary simplicity. [*Exeunt.*

SCENE II.

The Apartment of the Count, an elegant Room, with Chairs, Sofa, Glasses, Pictures, &c.

MACDERMOT *and* PICARD, *with a Letter in his hand, meeting.*

MacDer. So, Mr Picard, what have you got there?

Pic. Von lettre for Monsieur le Comte.

MacDer. Well, give it me, and go about your business.

Pic. No, I not go about my bisaness. My bisaness is to speaka to you.

MacDer. To me! And what is it you want?

Pic. *Mon argent!* My vage an my *congé!* My dismiss!

MacDer. How, man alive!

Pic. You are dee—dee *factotum* to dee count. He suffare no somebody to speaka to him, so I am come speaka to you.

MacDer. Arrah now, and are you crazy? Quit the sarvice of a count! Your reason, man?

Pic. My raison is, you talka too mosh enough; he no talk at all. I follow him from France: I yet live vid him by and by four month, he no speaka to me four vord!

MacDer. What then?

Pic. Vat den!—*Je suis François, moi!* I ave dee tongue for a dee speaka; I mus speaka; I vila speaka! He not so mosh do me dee *faveur* to scold a me! I ave leave dee best madame in Paris for *Monsieur le Comte—Quelle femme!* Her tongue vas nevare still! Nevare! She scold and she clack, clack, clack, clack,

clack, from all day an all night! Oh! It vas delight
to hear!

MacDer. And so you want to be scolded?

Pic. *Oui*—I love to be scold, I love to scold;
to be fall out, an to be fall in—*C'est mon gout*—Dee
plaisir of my life! *J'irai crever!* If I no speak I
burst!

MacDer. And is it you now, spalpeen, that would
chatter in the prisence of the count?

Pic. Shatter! Shatter! Ha! Vat you mean shatter?

MacDer. Have not you roast beef and plum pud-
ding?

Pic. Vat is roas beef, vat is plom boodin, gotam!
if I no speaka? I ave a dee master in France, dat
starva me, dat pay me no *gage*, dat leave a me *tout
en guenilles*, all rag an tattare; yet I love him better
as mosh! *Pourquoi?* (*Affectionately*.) *Helas! J'étois
son cher ami!* his dear fren! He talka to me, I talka to him! I laugh at his joke, he laugh *aussi;* an I
am both togeder so happy as dee prince! But dee
count! Oh! He as proud!—Ha!—*Comme ça.* (*Mimicking.*)

MacDer. Poh! Now—My good fillow, have patience.

Pic. Patience! *Moi!* I no patience——If I no
speak, I am *enragé*—I am French—I am Picard—
Ven dee heart is full dee tongue mus run! I give
you varn—Let my masta speak, or I shall dismissa
my masta!

MacDer. Here comes the count! Stand back,
man, and hould your tongue!

(*Enter the Count, followed by two Footmen, in handsome liveries. Footmen place themselves in the back
ground.* MACDERMOT *comes a little forward.*)

Count. The more I reflect on my own infatuation,
the more I am astonished!

MacDer. My lord—

Count. (*Traversing the stage.*) A man of my birth!
my rank! so to forget himself!—Still she is an angel!—But the family of a cit!—A brewer's daughter!

MacDer. My lord—

Count. (*Gives him a forbidding look.*) The world
contains not a woman so lovely!—Yet the vulgar,
haughty, disgusting airs of the mother!—the insulting familiarity of the father!—and the free, unceremonious tone of the whole family!—I am fascinated!
—Neither do they condescend to court my alliance!
I must be the humble suitor: I must entreat, must
supplicate permission to degrade my noble ancestors,
who will abjure me, blushing through their winding-sheets!—I must petition, and fawn, and acknowledge
the high honour done.—No! If I do!—Yet 'tis false!
I shall, I feel I shall be thus abject.

MacDer. If—I might be so bould—

Count. Well, sir.

MacDer. A letter for your lordship.

Count. Oh!—What, from the ambassador?

MacDer. No, faith, my lord.

Count. Ha! The duchess?

MacDer. No, my lord, nor the duchess neither.

Count. (*Taking it.*) Who then, sir?

MacDer. Faith, my lord, that is more than I can
say—But perhaps the letter itsilf can tell you.

Count. Sir!—Who brought it?

Pic. *Un pauvre valet* footaman, mee lor—His shoe,
his stocking, his habit, his *chapeau,* vas all patch an
piece.   And he vas—

MacDer. (*Aside, interrupting him.*) Bo!

Count. (*Throwing down the letter, blowing his
fingers, and dusting them with his white handkerchief.*)
Foh!—Open it, and inform me of the contents.

MacDer. Yes, my lord.

Pic. His visage, mee lor—

Count. How now!

Pic. (*In a pitiful tone.*) Mee lor—

MacDer. 'Sblood, man!—*(Stopping his mouth, and pushing him back.)*

Count. (*Makes signs to the footmen, who bring an arm-chair forward, and again submissively retire.*) She is ever uppermost! I cannot banish her my thoughts! Do you hear?—Dismiss those—(*Waving his hand.*)

MacDer. Yes, my lord.—Hark you, spalpeens! (*Waving his hand with the same air as the count.*)

[*Exeunt Footmen.*

Pic. (*Advancing.*) Monsieur le Comte—

Count. (*After a stare.*) Again!

Pic. I ave von requête to beg.

Count. Pay that fellow his wages immediately!

MacDer. I tould you so! (*Pushing him away.*) Hush! silence!

Pic. Silence! I am no English! I hate silence! I——

MacDer. Poh! Bodtheration! Be asy!—I will try now to make your pace! (*Pushes him off, and then returns to examining the letter.*)

Count. Insolent menial!—Well, sir? The contents?

MacDer. Faith, my lord, I am afraid the contints will not plase you!

Count. How so, sir?

MacDer. Why, as for the how so, my lord, if your lordship will but be plased to rade—

Count. Didn't I order you to read?

MacDer. To be sure you did, my lord; but I should take it as a viry particular grate favour, if that your lordship would but be plased to rade for yoursilf.

Count. Why, sir?

MacDer. Your lordship's timper is a little warm; and—

Count. Read!

MacDer. Well—If I must I must!—" The person who thinks proper at present to address you"—

Count. (*Interrupting.*) Sir!

MacDer. My lord.

Count. Be pleased to *begin* the letter, sir!

MacDer. Begin! Sarra the word of beginning is here—before or after—

Count. " The person ?"

MacDer. Yes, my lord.

Count. Mighty odd! (*Throws himself in the arm-chair.*) Proceed, sir.

MacDer. " The person who thinks proper at present to address you, takes the liberty to inform you that your haughtiness, instead of being dignified, is ridiculous."

Count. (*Starting up.*) Sir!

MacDer. Why now, I tould your lordship!

Count. (*Traversing the stage.*) Go on.

MacDer. (*With hesitating fear.*) " The little—merit—you have"—

Count. (*With a look.*) The little merit I have ? The little ?—The little ?—(MacDermot *holds up the letter.*) Go on.

MacDer. " The little merit you have—cannot convince the world that your pride—is not—is not—is not"—

Count. Is not what ? (*Sternly.*)

MacDer. (*Fearful.*) " Impertinent."

Count. (*Striking* MacDermot.) Rascal!

MacDer. Viry well, my lord!—(*Throwing down the letter.*) I humbly thank your lordship!—By Jasus! But I'll remimber the favour.

Count. (*More coolly.*) Read, sir.

MacDer. To the divle I pitch me if I do!

Count. (*Conscious of having done wrong.*) Read, MacDermot.

MacDer. No, my lord!—MacDermot is a man !—an Englishman!—or an Irishman, by Jasus, which is better still! And by the holy poker, if but that your lordship was not a lord now—(*Pulling down his sleeves, and clenching his fist with great agony.*)

Count. (*Carelessly letting his purse fall.*) Pick up that purse, MacDermot.

MacDer. 'Tis viry well!—Oh!—Well!—Well!— Well! (*Lays the purse on the table.*)

Count. You may keep it—MacDermot.

MacDer. What!—I touch it!—No, my lord!— Don't you think it!—I despise your guineas!—An Irishman is not to be paid for a blow!

Count. (*With increasing consciousness of error, and struggling with his feelings.*)—I—I have been hasty.

MacDer. Well, well!—'Tis viry weil!

Count. I am—I—I am sorry, MacDermot.

MacDer. (*Softened.*) My lord!

Count. (*Emphatically.*) Very sorry.

MacDer. My lord!

Count. Pray forget it!—(*Taking him by the hand.*) I cannot forgive myself.

MacDer. By the blessed Mary, then, but I can.— Your lordship is a noble gentleman!—There is many an upstart lord has the courage to strike, whin they know their poor starving depindants hands are chained to their sides, by writchedness and oppression; but few indeed have the courage to own the injury!

Count. I will remember, MacDermot, that I am in your debt.

MacDer. Faith, and if you do, my lord, your mimory will be better than mine!—I have lived with your lordship some years; and though not always a kind, you have always been a ginerous master. To be sure, I niver before had the honour of a blow from your lordship; but then I niver before had the satisfaction to be quite sure that, while you remimbered yoursilf to be a lord, you had not forgotten poor MacDermot was a man.

Count. Well, well! (*Aside, and his pride returning.*) He thinks he has a licence now to prate.—

There is no teaching servants ; nay, indeed, there is
no teaching any body a sense of propriety !

MacDer. Did your lordship spake ? (*Bowing
kindly.*)

Count. Give me that letter.   And—take the money.—It is yours.

MacDer. Your lordship will be plased for to pardon me there.—If you think proper, you may give me
twice as much to-morrow—but the divle a doit I'll
touch for to-day !

Count. Wait within call.

MacDer. (*Going.*) I niver before knew he was
all togedther such a jewel of a master !   ⌐ *Exit.*

Count. 'Tis this infernal letter that caused me to
betray myself thus to my servant !—And who is this
insolent, this rash adviser ? May I perish if I do not
punish the affront !—Here is no name !—A strange
hand too !—(*Reads.*) " The friend who gives you
this useful lesson has disguised his hand, and concealed his name"—Anonymous coward !—" His present intention being to awaken reflection, and make
you blush at your own bloated vanity"—Intolerable !
" Or, if not, to prepare you for a visit from one who
thinks it his duty to lower your arrogance, and who
will undertake the disagreeable task this very day."—
Will he ? Will he ?—MacDermot !

MacDer. (*Entering.*) My lord !

Count. If any stranger inquire for me, inform me
instantly.

MacDer. Yes, my lord.

Enter EDMUND.

Edm. Good morrow, count.

Count. (*Slightly bowing, and with vexation to* MAC-
DERMOT.) Why, where are my fellows ? Nobody
to shew the gentleman up ?

Edm. Oh ! You are too ceremonious by half,
count !

Count. (*With quickness.*) A little ceremony, sir,
is the essence of good breeding.

Edm. Psha!

Count. Psha, sir!

Edm. Ceremony, like fringe hiding a beautiful
face, makes you suspect grace itself of deformity.

Count. Do you hear, MacDermot?

MacDer. My lord!

Count. See that those rascals are more attentive.

Edm. Why, what is the matter with you, count?

Count. (*Muttering and traversing.*) Count, count!

Edm. You seem out of temper!

Count. (*Strongly feeling his own impropriety.*) Oh
dear! No—No—Upon my honour, no!—You totally
mistake—I assure you, you mistake.   I'm very glad
to see you! I am indeed! (*Taking him eagerly by
the hand.*)

Edm. I'm very glad you are—though you have
an odd mode of expressing your joy! But you are
one of the unaccountables! Cast off this formality.

Count. (*Aside.*) Very fine! (*Biting his fingers.*)
Formality, sir!

Edm. Give the heart its genuine flow!—Throw
away constraint, and don't appear as if you were always on the tenter-hooks of imaginary insult.

Count. I! (*Aside.*) This is damn'd impertinent!
(*Struggling to be over-familiar.*) You entirely mis-
conceive me. My character is frank and open! No
man has less constraint! I even study to be, as it
were, spontaneous.

Edm. Ha, ha, ha! I perceive you do.

Count. Really, sir!—(*Aside.*) Does he mean to
insult me?

Edm. I thought to have put you in a good humour.

Count. I am in a good humour, sir—I never was
in a better humour, sir! Never, sir!—'Sdeath! a good
humour, indeed!—Some little regard to propriety,

and such manners as good breeding prescribes to gentlemen.

Edm. Ha, ha, ha! Well, well, count, endeavour to forget the gentleman, and—

Count. Sir—No, sir : however you may think proper to act, that is a character I shall never forget.

Edm. Never, except at such moments as these, I grant, count.

Count. By—

Edm. Well gulped!—I had a sort of a message, but I find I must take some other opportunity, when you are not quite in so good a humour. (*Going.*) I'll tell my sister what——

Count. Sir—Your sister! My divine Lucy!—A message!

Edm. So—th magic chord is touched!

Count. Dear sir, I—I, I, I—I am afraid I am warm.—Your sister, you said !—I doubt I—that is—

Edm. Well, well, make no apologies.

Count. Apologies! No, sir!—I didn't mean—That is—Yes—I—My Lucy! My Lucy! What message?

Edm. Nay, I cannot well say myself. You know the mad-cap. She bade me tell you, if I *happened* (*Significantly*) to see you, that she wanted to give you a lecture.

Count. Indeed! (*Aside.*) I'm lectured by the whole family. (*Aloud.*) On what subject?

Edm. Perhaps you'll take pet again!

Count. I, sir—Take pet!—My sense of propriety, sir—(*Biting his lips.*)

Edm. Why, ay. Your sense of propriety, which, by the by, my flippant sister calls your pride, (*Count in great agitation*,) is always on the watch, to catch the moment when it becomes you to take offence.

Count. You—you are determined I shall not want opportunities.

Edm. You mistake, count—I have a friendship

for you Why, what a forbidding stare is that now!
Ay! A friendship for you.

Count. Sir—I—I am not insensible of the—honour—

Edm. Yes, you are.

Count. (*With over-acted condescension.*) Sir, you
are exceedingly mistaken—Very exceedingly; indeed
you are. As I am a man of honour, there is no gentleman whom I should think it a higher—that is—
Upon my soul—

SIR PAUL *on the stairs.*

Sir P. Is the count at home, young man?

Foot. (*Without.*) Yes, sir.

Edm. I hear my father! We have had a fracas; I
must escape! If you will come and listen to my sister's lecture, so—Good morrow!   [*Exit.*

Count. 'Tis insufferable! Never, sure, did man of
my rank run the gauntlet thus! No respect—No distinction of persons! But with people of this class 'tis
ever so—Hail, fellow, well met!

Enter SIR PAUL.

Sir P. Ay! Hail, fellow, well met!—Hey! You
jolly dog! (*Shaking him heartily by the hand.*)

Count. Hem! Good—good morrow, sir! (*Aside.*)
Here is another family lecturer.

Sir P. Was not that young Mock-modesty that
brushed by me on the stairs?

Count. It was your son, sir.

Sir P. Good morning, sir! (*Mimicking*) said the
scoundrel, when he was out of my reach. Darame!
(*With a kick.*) I would have shewn him the shortest
way to the bottom!—Well—Hey! You have elegant
apartments here!

Count. (*With contempt.*) Very indifferent, sir.

Sir P. I shall remain in town for a fortnight, and
am glad you live so near.—We'll storm the wine-cel-

lar !—I hear you are no flincher !—Hey ! When shall
we have a set-to ? Hey ! When shall we have a rory-
tory ? A catch, and a toast, and a gallon a man—
But, hey ! What's the matter ?—An't you well ?

Count. (*With sudden excess of affability.*) Oh, yes,
Sir Paul ! Exceedingly well, Sir Paul ! Never better,
Sir Paul !

Sir P. Why, that's right—I thought you had been
struck dumb.

Count. Oh, by no means, Sir Paul :—I am very
happy to see you—extremely happy—inexpressibly——

Sir P. I knew you would—What say you to my
Lucy ? Hey !

Count. Say ! That she—She is a phœnix. (*In raptures.*)

Sir P. Damme, so she is ! What is a phœnix ?

Count. I adore her !

Sir P. That's right.

Count. The day that makes her mine, will be the
happiest of my life !

Sir P. So it will—For I'll make you as drunk as
an emperor. Hollo, there ! Get your master's hat—
Come, come ; you shall dine with me. (*Locking him
by the arm.*)

Count. Sir !

Sir P. Damme, I'll make you drunk to-day.

Count. Did you speak to me, sir ?

Sir P. To you ? Why, what the devil ! Do you
think I spoke to your footman ? (*Quitting his arm.*)

Count. (*Again endeavouring to be affable.*) Oh, no,
Sir Paul. No ! I—Pardon me—I—I was absent.

Sir P. Absent !—I smell a rat—Your dignity took
miff !

Count. No, Sir Paul ; by no means—No—I—That
is—I will acknowledge, I am not very much accustomed to such familiarities.

Sir P. Are you not ? Then you soon must be.

11

Count. Sir!

Sir P. Ay, sir! A few lessons from me will cure you.

Count. Sir—I—

Sir P. I am the man to make you throw off! I'll teach you to kick your stateliness down stairs, and toss your pride, as I do my wig, behind the fire.

Count. Good breeding, sir—

Sir P. Good breeding, sir, is a blockhead, sir— None of your formal Don Glums! None of your *grand pas* for me: A friend, good fellowship, and t'other bottle—That's my motto.

Count. People of my rank distinguish——

Sir P. Damn distinctions!

Count. They make it a condition, sir—

Sir P. Indeed!—Look you, my dear count, either unbridle, or you and I are two. You tell me you love my daughter—She is the finest girl in England; and I believe the slut has taken a fancy to you. The match pleases me, because it displeases my wife: and, except when you are riding your high horse, I like you, count.—Dismount, and it's a match. If not, turn the peg, and prance! I'm your humble——

Count. (*Aside.*) I'll not endure it! Racks shall not make me bend to this.

Sir P. Lucy is a wench after my own heart!—No piping, no pining, no sobbing for her! I have a fine fellow in my eye—

Count. Sir! (*Alarmed.*)

Sir P. None of your Sir Ramrod Grumble-gizzards.

Count. By Heavens! I would cut the villain's throat who should dare impede my happiness.

Sir P. Why, ay! Damn me, now you talk!

Count. The loss of my Lucy would render me the most wretched of beings!

Enter MACDERMOT *with the hat.*

Sir P. To be sure—(*Taking him again by the arm.*)
Come, come! (*Claps the Count's hat on his head.*)
Dinner is waiting! I smell the haunch; it perfumes
the whole street! Come along—I hate the shackles
of ceremony. A smoking table, and a replenished
side-board, soon put all men on a level. Your hungry and thirsty souls for me! He that enters my
house always deposites his grandeur, if he has any,
at the door. (*Sings.*)

" This brown jug, my dear Tom, which now foams with
    mild ale."

MacDer. Well said, old Toby—Oh! (*Rubbing his
hands.*)
[*Exeunt. The Count making disconcerted attempts
    to preserve his stateliness, wishing to be familiar,
    scarcely knowing how to behave, and* MACDER-
    MOT *enjoying his embarrassment.*

ACT THE THIRD.

SCENE I.

The Drawing-Room of SIR PAUL PECKHAM *elegantly furnished, but hung all round with prints, chiefly caricatures.*

EDMUND *and* LYDIA.

Edm. I shall never recover from my surprise.

Ly. Hush!

Edm. The count your brother?—My sister, my family must be informed.

Ly. Not on your life, Edmund. So implacable are his enemies, that my father informs me an exempt, bribed by them, has followed him to England.

Edm. Impotent malice! The laws will here protect him.

Ly. Oh! Who can say? The wicked cunning of such life-hunters is dreadful!—I insist therefore upon your promise.

Edm. My angel! Fear nothing! (*Kissing her hand.*)

Enter LUCY *unperceived.*

Lucy. (*Placing herself beside* EDMUND.) Turn about—Now me. (*Holding out her hand.*)

Edm. Oh, sister! I am the happiest of men!

Lucy. And you appear to be very busy too, with your happiness.

Edm. Did you but know!—

Lucy. Oh! I know a great deal more than you suspect—Not but you seem to be taking measures to inform the whole house.

Edm. Of what?

Lucy. (*Placing herself between them.*) That you two are never easy apart.

Edm. Sister—I—I must insist that you speak of this lady with—with every respect.

Lucy. Brother!

Ly. Edmund!

Lucy. (*Looking first at one and then at the other.*) Strange enough this!

Edm. Were I to tell you—

Ly. (*Aside, and making signs.*) Very well!

Lucy. Tell me what?—Why don't you tell me?

Edm. Pshaw! No, no—Nothing—I—I don't know what I am saying.

Lucy. Why, surely you don't imagine your fondness for each other is any secret?

Edm. Sister! I don't understand—Are you narrow-minded enough to suppose this young lady unworthy the hand of—

Lucy. Of my brother?—No—To call my Lydia sister—(*Taking her hand*)—is one of the things on earth I most fervently wish.

Ly. My generous friend!

Edm. My charming girl!

Lucy. But—then—

Edm. There are now no buts! It will be an honour—I say, sister, you—you don't know—In short, I must very earnestly solicit you to treat Miss Lydia with all possible delicacy—I—I—I cannot tell you more at present—But I once again request, I conjure, nay, I—

Ly. Hem!

Lucy. Hem!—Humph!

Edm. You—You understand me, sister.   [*Exit.*

Lucy. Indeed I don't!—There now goes one of

your lord and masters ! Take care of him—he'll make
an excellent grand Turk—(*Humorously burlesquing.*)
Treat Miss Lydia, I say, with all possible delicacy—
And have I, Lydia, have I shewn a want of delicacy
to my friend ?

Ly. Oh, no ! My heart throbs with an oppressive
sense of your generous, your affectionate attention to
me.

Lucy. Oppressive ?—Well ! This is the proudest
world !

Ly. Nay, I didn't mean—

Lucy. Oh ! No matter.

Ly. Have you had any conversation with the count?

Lucy. No—There has been no opportunity yet
to-day—I am really afraid his pride is quite as absurd
as that of my good mamma !

Ly. And your affection begins to cool.

Lucy. Um—I—I can't say that—Heigho ! He has
his faults.

Ly. (*Ardently.*) I hope he has his virtues too !

Lucy. So do I—But how to cure those faults ?

Ly. If incurable, 'twould break my heart.

Lucy. Your ardour surprises me !—But, hush !

Enter Count.

Count. (*Bowing.*) I was afraid, madam, love would
not have found so much as a moment to speak its
anxieties—Nay, even now—(*Looking haughtily toward* LYDIA.)

Ly. (*Pointedly, and almost in tears.*) Sir, I—I am
sensible of my own unworthiness.   [*Exit.*

Lucy. That lady, sir, is my friend.

Count. Madam !

Lucy. Why are you surprised ?

Count. Madam !—No—no, not surprised—There
is a maxim, indeed, which says—Friendship can on
ly subsist between equals.

Lucy. But where is the inferiority ?

Count. Madam !

Lucy. You are above the poor, the pitiful idea, that wealth confers any claims ?

Count. Perhaps it does not, madam. But beauty, understanding, wit—in short, mind, confers ten.thousand ! And in these I never beheld your peer !

Lucy. Very prettily spoken, indeed ! And I am almost persuaded that you love me very dearly.

Count. Madam, I adore you !

Lucy. Yes, you are continually thinking of my good qualities.

Count. Eternally, madam ! I think of nothing else.

Lucy. True—you never remember your own !

Count. Were I totally insensible of my own, madam, I should be unworthy of you.

Lucy. You admire me even in my representatives, my relations and friends ! Affable to all, good-humoured to all, attentive to all ; your politeness, ease, and urbanity extend to every person for whom you think my heart is any way interested ! Your passions are all subservient to love !

Count. Yes, madam ; subservient is the very word ! They are all subservient to love.

Lucy. You never recollect the dignity of your descent, nor accuse mine of meanness : You have too much understanding to plume your thoughts with turgid arrogance ; or to presume on the imaginary merit of an accident, which none but ignorance, prejudice, and folly, are so besotted as to attribute to themselves.

Count. Mankind have agreed, madam, to honour the descendants of the wise and the brave.

Lucy. They have so—But you have too much native merit to arrogate to yourself the worth of others : You are no jay, decked in the peacock's feathers : You are not idiot enough to imagine that a skin of parchment, on which is emblazoned the arms and acts of one wise man, with a long list of succeeding fools, is any honour to you ! Responsible to mankind

for the use or the abuse of such talents as you feel
yourself endowed with, you think only of how you
may deserve greatly ; and disdain to be that second-
ary thing, that insignificant cypher, which is worthless except from situation.

Count. The feelings of injured honour, madam,
perhaps may be too irritable. They shrink from insult, and spurn at contamination ! Yet honour is the
source of a thousand virtues ! The parent of ten thousand glorious deeds ! Honour is generous, sincere,
and magnanimous ! The protector of innocence, the
assertor of right, the avenger of wrong : Yes ! Honour is the patron of arts, the promoter of science,
the bulwark of government, the defender of kings,
and the saviour of nations !—Indulge me then in
cherishing a sentiment so noble.

Lucy. Indulge ?——Applaud, you mean ! Honour
with you never degenerates into ostentation—Is never
presumptuous—Is no boaster.—Is eager to earn, but
scorns to extort pre-eminence ! Your honour is not
that abject inflated phantom which usurps contested
claims, exacts submission which it does not merit, of-
fends, irritates, and incites disgust ; nay, tarnishes
even virtue itself ! You do not, under the word Honour, seek a miserable cobweb covering for exorbi-
tant pride.

Count. Madam, accusation so pointed, so—

Lucy. Nay, now ! Have not I been reading your
panegyric ?

Enter a Footman.

Foot. My lady desires you will come to her immediately, madam.

Lucy. Very well. (*Exit Footman.*)—I am a thoughtless, flighty girl ! What I say can have but little
meaning—Else, indeed, I would have ventured to
have given you a word of advice—But—'Tis no matter.

Count. Madam, you have stung me to the soul! If I am indeed what you describe, 'twere time I should reform.

Lucy. I must be gone.—I have, I own, been wildly picturing something to myself, which I greatly fear I could not love.   [*Exit.*

Count. And is it my likeness?—Surely it cannot be! Could not love?—Excruciating thought!
                                  [*Exit after* LUCY.

Enter EDMUND, *in haste, and* LYDIA *from an inner chamber, meeting.*

Edm. Where is the count?

Ly. This moment gone.

Edm. (*Eagerly.*) Which way?

Ly. Through that door.

Edm. (*Running, stops at the door.*) Ah! 'Tis too late! The footman is telling him.

Ly. Why are you so much alarmed?

Edm. The clouds are collected, and the storm is coming!

Ly. What do you mean?

Edm. Lady Peckham has watched her opportunity: Sir Paul has dropt asleep in his arm-chair; she has ordered your sister to her apartment, and has sent to the count to come and speak with her: that is, to come and be insulted, here in the drawing-room.

Ly. What can be done?

Edm. I know not—I dread her intolerable tongue.

Ly. Perhaps were you to retire, and, when they grow warm, to interrupt them at the proper moment, the presence of a third person might be some restraint on the workings of pride; of the violent ebullitions of which I am in great apprehension.

Edm. Had I but met the count before he had received the message!—

Ly. Here comes Lady Peckham. Be gone!
                                  (*Exit* EDMUND.

Enter LADY PECKHAM, *followed by a Footman.*

Foot. I have delivered your ladyship's message, and the count is coming.

L. Peck. (*Swelling.*) Wery vell '—Go you about your business, feller—(*Exit Footman.*) Your company is not vanted, miss.

[*Exit* LYDIA *after* EDMUND.

Enter Count, bowing.

L. Peck. So, sir! They tells me, sir, that you and my foolish husband are colloguing together, for to marry my daughter! Is this troo, sir?

Count. (*With his usual polite haughtiness.*) If it were, madam?

L. Peck. Do you know who Miss Loocy Peckham is, sir?

Count. Not very well, madam.

L. Peck. Sir!

Count. Except that she is—your daughter.

L. Peck. And do you know who I am, sir?

Count. I have been told, madam—

L. Peck. Told, sir! Told! Vhat have you been told? Vhat have you been told, sir?

Count. That your ladyship was an honest wax-chandler's daughter.

L. Peck. Yes, sir! The debbidy of his vard, sir! A common councilman, and city sword-bearer! Had an aldermand's gownd von year, vus chosen sheriff the next, and died a lord mayor elect.

Count. With all his honours blooming on his brow.

L. Peck. And do you know, sir, that I design Sir Samooel Sheepy, sir, an English knight and barrow-knight, for the spouse of my daughter? A gentleman that is a gentleman! A purson of honour and purtensions, and not a papish Jesubite.

Count. Of his honours and pretensions I am yet to be informed, madam.

L. Peck. Vhat, sir! Do you mean for to say, sir, or to insinivate, sir, that Sir Samooel Sheepy is not your betters?

Count. If Sir Samuel himself, madam, had put such a question to me, I would have replied with my sword; or, more properly, with my cane.

L. Peck. Cane! Wery vell, sir: I'll let Sir Samooel know that you threatens to cane him—i'll take care to report you! Cane quotha! He shall talk to you.

Count. Let him, madam!

L. Peck. Madam! madam! At every vord—Pray, sir, do you know that Sir Paul Peckham has had the honour to be knighted by the king's own hand?

Count. I have heard as much, madam.

L. Peck. Madam, indeed!—And for you for to think for to look up to my daughter.

Count. Up, madam!

L. Peck. Yes, sir—Up, sir!—Pray, sir, vhat are your purtensions?

Count. (*With great agitation.*) Madam!

L. Peck. Who are you, sir? Vhere do you come from? Who knows you? Vhat parish do you belong to?

Count. Madam, I am of a family known to history, known to Europe, known to the whole universe!

L. Peck. Ah! I believes you are better known nur trusted.

Count. The names of Connolly and Villars, madam, never before were so degraded as they have been in my person.

L. Peck. Oh! I makes no doubt but you are a purson that vould degurade any name.

Count. Insult, like what I have received from you, madam, no *man* that breathes should utter, and escape death—But you are—

L. Peck. Vhat, sir? Vhat am I, sir? Vhat am I, sir?

Count. A woman.

L Peck. A voman, indeed! Sir, I vould have you to know, sir, as how I am a lady! A lady, sir, of his majesty's own making! And moreover, sir, don't you go for to flatter yourself that I shall bestow the hand and fortin of Miss Loocy Peckham upon any needy outlandish Count Somebody-nobody!—My daughter, sir, is for your betters!

Count. Madam, though scurril—(*Recollecting himself.*) I say, madam, though such vul—such accusations are beneath all answer—yet I must tell you that, by marrying your daughter, if after this I should sink myself so low—I say, by marrying your daughter, madam, I should confer an honour on your family, as much superior to its expectations, as the splendour of the glorious sun is to the twinkling of the worthless glow-worm.

L. Peck. Vhat! vhat!—

Enter EDMUND.

Marry come up! An Irish French foriner! Not so good as von of our parish porpers! and you—you purtend to compare yourself to the united houses of the Peckhams and the Pringles! Your family indeed!—yourn! Vhere's your settlement? Yourn! Vusn't my great uncle, Mr Peter Pringle, the cheese-monger of Cateaton Street, a major in the Train-Bands before you vus born, or thought of?

Edm. (*Aside.*) So, so! I'm too late! (*Aloud.*) Let me entreat your ladyship——

L. Peck. Vhat! Hasn't I an ownd sister at this day married to Mr Poladore Spragges, the tip-toppest hot-presser in all Crutched Friars? Isn't my maiden aunt, Miss Angelica Pringle, vorth thirty thousand pounds, in the South Sea funds, every day she rises? And doesn't I myself go to bed and get up the greatest lady in this here city? And for to purtend for to talk to me of his family! Hisn!

Edm. (*Very warmly.*) I must tell you, my lady,

VOL. IV.   L

you strangely forget yourself, and expose your family to ridicule.

L. Peck. You must tell me, sir! Vhy, sir, how dare you have the temeracity for to come for to go for to dare for to tell me? Here's fine doings! Henpecked by my own chicken!

Edm. The count, madam, is a man of the first distinction, in his native country.

L. Peck. Vhat country is that, sir? Who ever heard of any country but England? A count among beggars! How much is his countship vorth?

Count. I had determined to be silent, madam, but I find it is impossible. (*With vehement volubility.*) And I must inform you, my family is as ancient, as exalted, and as renowned as you have proved yours to be——what I shall not repeat. That I am the heir to more rich acres than I believe your ladyship ever rode over; that my father's vassals are more numerous than your ladyship's vaunted guineas; that the magnificence in which he has lived, looked with contempt on the petty, paltry strainings of a trader's pride—and that in his hall are daily fed——(*Stops short, and betrays a consciousness of inadvertent falsehood, but suddenly continues with increasing vehemence.*) Yes, madam, are daily fed, now, at this moment, madam, more faithful adherents, with their menials and followers, than all your boasted wealth could for a single year supply.

Edm. Are, at this moment, say you, count?

Count. Sir, I—I have said.

Edm. I know you to be a man of honour, and that you cannot say what is not.

Count. I—I—I have said, sir. (*Walking with great perturbation.*)

L. Peck. You have said more in a minute nur you can prove in a year.

Edm. (*Warmly.*) Madam, I will pledge my life for the count's veracity.

L. Peck. You pledge! Vhat do you know about the matter? I'll pledge that he has been telling a pack of the most monstrous——

Edm. Forbear, madam. Such insult is too gross to be endured almost from an angry woman. Dear count——

L. Peck. Voman again! Wery fine! Wery pretty! Voman quotha! To be called a voman by my own witals!

Count. (*Aside.*) What have I done? (*With agony.*) A lie!

L. Peck. As for you, sir, I doesn't believe von vord you say. I knows the tricks of such sham shevaleers as you too vell!

Count. (*Walking away from her.*) Torture!

L. Peck. But I'll take care to have you prognosticated.

Count. (*Aside.*) Damnation!

L. Peck. I'll have you karakatoored in your troo colours. I'll have you painted in your father's hall; you and your vooden shoe shrug and snuffle scarecrows; your half dozen lank and lean shotten herring shadows, vith the light shining through 'em, like parchment at a vorkshop vinder; grinning hunger over a dish of soup-meegur, with a second course of frogs, and a plate of hedge-berries and crab-apples for the desert! I'll depicture you! I'll not forget your wassals!

Count. (*Aside.*) I can support it no longer. (*Going.*)

Edm. (*Catches him by the hand.*) My dear count.

Count. Sir! I am a dishonoured villain! [*Exit.*

L. Peck. There! there! He tells you himself he is a willin! His conscience flies in his face, and he owns it.

Edm. (*With great ardour and feeling.*) Madam, he is a noble-hearted gentleman. His agonizing mind deems it villainy to suffer insult so gross. Sorry am I, madam, to be obliged to tell you that, humble though your family is, the disgrace with which you have loaded it is indelible. With anguish of heart you force me to repeat, I blush while I listen to you.   [*Exit.*

L. Peck. Vhy, who ever heard the like of this here now? Here's a prodigal son! Here's a regenerate reprobate! Here's a graceless Gogmagog! To purtend as how he's ashamed of me! Me!—a purson of my carriage, connections, and breeding! I!— whose wery entrance of a ball night puts Haberdasher's Hall all in a combustion!

Re-enter the Count, deep in thought, and much agitated.

L. Peck. (*Seeing him.*) Marry my daughter indeed! Faugh!   [*Exit* LADY PECKHAM.

Count. Into what has my impetuous anger hurried me? Guilty of falsehood!—I!—To recede is impossible. What! stand detected before this city madam! whose tongue, itching with the very scrofula of pride, would iterate liar in my ear! No; falsehood itself is not so foul! MacDermot.

Enter MACDERMOT.

MacDer. My lord.

Count. MacDermot, I—you—you have heard of the state which formerly my father held; of his household grandeur, of the hinds and servants whom he daily fed, and the train by which he was attended?

MacDer. To be sure I have, my lord. Here your dukes and your peers know nothing at all of style. Abroad, some hundreds starve that one may ate. But in England they have learned the trick of aich man ating for himself.

Count. Psha! listen. The—the misfortunes that since have befallen us are little known in this country.

MacDer. To be sure they are not, my lord.

Count. Nor—n—hem!—nor would I have them. D—d—d—a—hem!—do you understand me, Mac-Dermot?

MacDer. My lord!

Count. I—I—I would not be exposed to the insolent taunts of upstart wealth.

MacDer. Faith then, my lord, you must not live in this city.

Count. Nay, but attend to me. I—I would—I would have them think——

MacDer. (*After waiting.*) What, my lord?

Count. (*Traversing the stage, striking his forehead, and then returning.*) MacDermot, there are situations——I say, it may sometimes be wise, at least prudent and—and—excusable——Have not you remarked, MacDermot, that Lydia——(*Short pause.*)

MacDer. Oh, to be sure I have remarked, my lord, that she is a sweet crater, that Miss Liddy.

Count. Nay, but—Her influence in the family—

MacDer. Oh yes, my lord!

Count. Now if—if—suppose you were—to take—an opportunity——Is she proud?

MacDer. Mild as mother's milk, my lord.

Count. If she were persuaded, I say——Our family misfortunes—that is—no—no—the family magnificence——Do you comprehend me?

MacDer. My lord!

Count. Psha! Damnation! [*Exit.*

MacDer. (*Stands some time amazed.*) Why, now, am I MacDermot or am I not? The devil! He would have me take an opportunity with Miss Liddy! Faith, and I would very willingly do that, and persuade her——Oh, honey! but she is not so asy to be persuaded. (*Pauses.*) To be sure he must mane something. (*Pauses again.*) Oh! *Hona mon dioul!* but I have it. Ahoo! what a thick-scull have I been all this while. He is a little bit ashamed to be

thought poor among this tribe of Balifarnians, who
have nothing but their dirty guineas to boast of. And
so he would have me persuade——Oh ho! let me
alone. There she goes. I will be after——Bo!—
flustration! There is that Mr Edmund now, close
at her heels. The young royster is always getting
the sweet crater up in a corner. Take an opportunity! Sarra the opportunity there is for me to take.
[*Exit.*

ACT THE FOURTH.

SCENE I.

The Count's Apartment.

Enter MR DORIMONT *and* MACDERMOT.

Mr Dor. Pray, sir, is the count within?

MacDer. The count, sir! And pray why may
you ask?

Mr Dor. I want to speak with him, sir.

MacDer. Spake! Oh! the count is not so asy to
be spoken with. Plase to deliver your message to
me.

Mr Dor. Inform him I am come for an answer to my letter.

MacDer. (*Alarmed.*) Letter, sir! What, the letter brought by a shabby footman?

Mr Dor. Ay, ay. Has he read it?

MacDer. Read it! Faith, and it has been very well read. But pray, sir, now are you the writer?

Mr Dor. I am.

MacDer. (*With dread.*) Then take my advice— make your escape. 'Tis very well for you my master is not at home.

Mr Dor. (*Smiling.*) Why so?

MacDer. Why so? Man alive! have you a mind to be murdered?

Mr Dor. Fear nothing.　　　　[*Knocking heard.*

MacDer. (*With increasing terror.*) By the holy phial! but there he is! Why, will you be gone now?

Mr Dor. No, I will not.

MacDer. Marcy upon my soul! For the Lord's sake, sir! Why, sir, I tell you he'll have your blood! And won't you be gone now?

Mr Dor. No, sir.

MacDer. Lord Jasus! what will I do? If he comes into this room, here will be murder!

Mr Dor. Go, tell him I am waiting for him.

MacDer. Me tell him! I warn you to be gone. Remimber, I wash my hands of your blood. Make off, make off, I tell you, while I go and keep him to his own apartment.　　　　　　　[*Exit.*

Mr Dor. (*To a Footman crossing.*) Hark you, young man. Tell the count, your master, that the stranger who wrote the anonymous letter to him is here, waiting for an answer.

Foot. Yes, sir.　　　　　　　　　[*Exit.*

Mr Dor. The fears of the servant strongly speak the anger of the master: but that was what I partly feared, and partly wished.

Count. (*Enraged without.*) Where is the rash, the audacious,

Enter Count.

the insolent wretch, who—(*Aside.*)—My father!

Mr Dor. I scarcely could have expected so kind a welcome, sir ; 'tis exemplary.

Count. Passion, sir, is sometimes guilty of improprieties. Pray pardon me.

Enter MacDermot *behind, in trepidation.*

Count. I imagined—(*Seeing* MacDermot.) How now, sir? Be gone!

Mr Dor. Why so? Let him stay.

Count. Be gone! or——

Mr Dor. Stay, I say.

Count. And do you hear? I am not at home.

MacDer. (*Aside, and going.*) Oh Lord! Oh Lord! Here will be murder! [*Exit.*

Mr Dor. What should that mean, sir?

Count. Sir! There are reasons. I ought not to expose my father's safety.

Mr Dor. Rather own, you ought not to blush at your father's poverty. Is this my reception? This the warm welcome of a duteous son?

Count. 'Tis so sudden. Yet my heart feels an affection——

Mr Dor. Which is stifled by your vanity. Your father is contemned, because he is unfortunate.

Count. No, sir; I do not merit a reproach so cruel! Contemn my father! You know me not. Tell me, which way can I prove my respect and love.

Mr Dor. By openly acknowledging me; not by concealment; not by disavowing me in the day of my distress.

Count. Think, sir, of your own safety.

Mr Dor. What danger is there with people of honour? Present me to the family of Sir Paul.

Count. Impossible, sir.

Mr Dor. (*Sternly.*) Impossible!

Count. Let me conjure you not to be too precipitate. You know not the vulgar pomp of new-made gentry, whose suffocating pride treats indigent merit, nay, birth itself, with the most imperious disdain.

Mr Dor. Talk not of their pride, but of your own! You complain of others haughtiness!—you! in whom the vice is so intolerable, that you willingly would disown your father!

Count. Sir, you wrong me.

Mr Dor. But, determined to be known for what I am, since you refuse, I'll introduce myself.

Count. For Heaven's sake, sir! I entreat, I supplicate, on my knees I conjure you to forbear!

Mr Dor. Yes, pride, kneeling, conjures a father in poverty to suffer himself to be disclaimed. Your mother's pride was my house's downfal: this she has bequeathed to you.

Count. Sir! (*Starts up at hearing.*)

Sir P. (*Without.*) I tell you I know he is at home.

MacDer. (*Without.*) Upon my soul, Sir Paul——

Sir P. Zounds! why, I saw him from my own window.

Count. (*Alarmed.*) Here is Sir Paul! You know not, sir, how much is at stake. I have not time to tell you now; but let my entreaties——

Mr Dor. Oh, how humble are the proud! But remember, I consent only on condition that you restrain your arrogance. If, while I am present, any symptom——(*Retiring back.*)

Enter SIR PAUL.

Sir P. 'Sblood! I knew you were at home. But to instruct servants how to lie with the most cool,

composed, and barefaced impudence, is one branch
of modern education.

Count. I am sorry, Sir Paul—

Sir P. Pshaw! damn apologies. I have good
news for you.

Count. Sir!

Sir P. I do believe, (God forgive me!) that my
wife is growing reasonable.

Count. Does she consent?

Sir P. Yes, to permit you to ask her pardon.

Count. Sir! Ask pardon?

Mr Dor. (*Advancing.*) Yes, sir, ask pardon.

Sir P. Hem! (*Aside.*) Zounds! again! Why,
what the plague can he do here?

Mr Dor. Your servant, sir.

Sir P. Sir, your very humble.

Count. (*Aside, and alarmed.*) What can this mean?

Mr Dor. You seem surprised, sir.

Sir P. Yes; you have a trick of taking people by
surprise.

Count. (*Aside.*) Does he know him?

Sir P. (*Aside, and then to the Count.*) Odd
enough! Who is this queer old fellow?

Count. (*Aside.*) All is safe. (*Aloud.*) Sir, the—
the gentleman—(*Aside.*) What shall I say? (*To*
Sir Paul.) A gentleman, sir, who——

Sir P. A gentleman!

Count. Yes, that is——

Sir P. What, some poor relation, I suppose?

Count. Yes, sir, a relation. The—the—family
estates have been under his management.

Sir P. Oh! your steward?

Count. No, not absolutely my—my steward—

Sir P. What, your land-bailiff, then?

Count. No, sir, no; that is——

Sir P. Does not seem to have made his fortune
by his office! A little weather-beaten.

Count. He is a man of the strictest probity, sir.

Sir P. Nay, his appearance is the pledge of his honesty.

Mr Dor. (*Aside.*) I can perceive he is practising deceit. Oh vanity! But I will restrain my anger. The moment of open punishment is not yet come.

Count. (*Crossing to his father.*) Let me request you, sir, not to reveal yourself.

Mr Dor. (*Dryly.*) Well, sir.

Count. (*Returning to* SIR PAUL.) His economy and good management are equal to his fidelity.

Sir P. (*Aside.*) Confounded odd all this though. (*Aloud.*) Well, count, I have exerted my whole authority with Lady Peckham ; and her son Edmund, who has more influence over her than any body else, is your friend. So be wary, do your duty, and the day is your own.

Count. My duty, sir!

Mr Dor. Yes, sir, your duty, sir.

Sir P. (*Aside.*) A damned strange fellow. (*Aloud.*) Is it not your duty, count, to serve yourself?

Mr Dor. And would you contend about a word?

Sir P. Very true, sir. You seem a—a plain-spoken —a—hem!

Mr Dor. (*Significantly.*) Yes, I think it *my* duty to tell vice and folly the truth.

Sir P. Hem! You hear, count?

Mr Dor. His punctilious pride is contemptible.

Count. (*Half forgetting himself.*) Sir!

Mr Dor. And sir! I repeat: Do your duty, sir.

Sir P. (*Aside.*) The most unaccountable—hem!

Count. (*Aside.*) I am on the rack! He will betray himself.

Sir P. (*To the Count.*) The old gentleman does not mince matters.

Count. (*Aside to his Father.*) You will ruin me.

Mr Dor. Do as he requires, or I will feign no longer.

Sir P. Lady Peckham is expecting you. Come,

come; try whether you cannot put on a winning submissive air.

Count. (*Aside.*) I shall burst!

Mr Dor. Submissive, sir!—Remember.

Count. I shall not forget, sir.

Sir P. You approve my advice, don't you, sir?

Mr Dor. Entirely.—The lesson you give him, sir, is a useful and a necessary one. I know him!

Count. (*Aside.*) Fiends!

Sir P. What, sir—you—have lived long in the family?

Mr Dor. Sir!

Sir P. Nay, don't be affronted.

Count. (*To* Sir Paul.) Let us be gone, sir. I am ready to attend you.

Sir P. (*Aside.*) The bluntest, drollest——

Count. We are losing time, sir.

Sir P. Well, well; in a moment. (*To* Mr Dorimont.) Pray, under favour, what may be the amount of the count's rent-roll?

Mr Dor. Sir! His rent-roll, sir!

Sir P. Ay, his rent-roll; the nett produce of his estates?

Mr Dor. Why that question to me, sir?

Count. (*Coming between them.*) For Heaven's sake, Sir Paul, let us go.

Sir P. 'Sblood! what a violent hurry you're in all of a sudden.

Count. (*Endeavouring to force him away.*) Lady Peckham is waiting, sir. I beg, I entreat——

Sir P. (*Aside.*) The mystery thickens.

Mr Dor. Pray, sir, has the count——

Count. (*Interrupting.*) For the love of mercy, sir, answer no questions; hear none, ask none. I am frantic!

Mr Dor. (*To the Count.*) Silence, sir. (*To* Sir Paul.) Has the count ever talked of his estates?

Sir P. Oh yes,

Count. (*Aside.*) Damnation!

Mr Dor. And told you the amount?

Sir P. No—no—But, as you—

Count. I must insist, sir, on going. (*To* Sir Paul.)

Mr Dor. I'm not prepared, sir, just now to answer your question, of the rent roll. I have business, and must leave you; but I will shortly give you the information you require. In the mean time, young gentleman, think on what has passed! Observe Sir Paul's advice, and act as becomes you. Put off your vanity—Be humble, and know yourself.

[*Exit.*

Count. (*Aside fervently.*) Thank Heaven he is gone!

Sir P. Your steward is an odd one!

Count. Sir—I—I tell you he is not my steward.

Sir P. No!

Count. No, sir.

Sir P. What is he then?

Count. Sir—I—

Sir P. I thought you taught every body to keep their distance; but he treats you with as little ceremony as—(*Aside*)—as he did me.

Count. Yes, sir; people do take very unaccountable liberties.

Sir P. But what brought him here?

Count. Sir—He—Business, sir.

Sir P. Oh, the family estates.

Count. And pray, sir, what do you know of him?

Sir P. I—Nothing.

Count. You appear to be acquainted.

Sir P. Um—No, no.

Count. You had seen him before.

Sir P. Hem! Yes, I had seen him. Come, let us be going.

Count. But permit me to ask.

Sir P. Pshaw! Come, come—Lady Peckham is waiting.

Count. I must own, Sir Paul, I meet with many mortifications. Your daughter is an angel. But there are certain things to which a man of my rank must not, cannot stoop. Do you, Sir Paul, come to an agreement with your lady, and I am ready.—*(Calls.)* MacDermot!—I'll return in a moment. *(Retires.)*

Sir P. Now, if the demon of ambition did not possess me, I should never truckle to the self-sufficient airs of this man of rank! He has put a spell upon me!—I'll break with him this moment—Yet, if I do that, all is over. My authority is gone! Madam will be triumphant; and then farewel to submission! —Beside, the honour of the alliance! Nobility! Precedence! A family so famous! 'Sblood! Who knows but my grandson may be a marshal of France? *(To the Count, who returns.)* Come, come, count; let us be gone. You must make your peace with my madam.

Count. Solicitation, Sir Paul, does not become me ; it is a thing I have not been accustomed to. Do you speak for me. Say all, say every thing you please. Your mediation will, I presume, be sufficient.

Sir P. (Quite angry.) Damn me if this is not beyond all human patience! After all I have done in your behalf! What! Would you have me and my whole family approach your footstool, there present my daughter, and kneeling beg your highness to accept her? No, my haughty count! Either my daughter is worth asking for, or not worth having. Carry your pomp to a better market; I'll stoop to it no longer. Your servant, sir!   [*Exit.*

Count. (Following.) Nay, Sir Paul—Must I endure this? Must I? I! The descendant of an ancient race! The rightful lord of a thousand vassals! Ought I to cringe in supplicatory baseness, use servile dishonourable adulation, bend to sufflated wealth, act

the parasite to new-fledged pride, and petition where
I should command? No! Earth should hide me rather! But that love, imperious love hurries me forward, with impulse irresistible! What! Wait, and
fawn on madam, and mince, and simper, and act the
skipjack, and chatter to her parrot, and be of her
opinion, and fetch and carry, and praise her taste,
and join her scandal, and laugh when she laughs, and
kiss her monkey!—And to whom?—Oh!   [*Exit.*

SCENE II.

Changes to the House of SIR PAUL PECKHAM.

MACDERMOT *and* LYDIA.

MacDer. Oh, yes! Stabling for a hundred horses!
Open house all the year about! Sarvants five-and-
twinty to the score; all making work for one another!

Ly. Then the count, your master, should be im-
mensely rich.

MacDer. Should be? To be sure he is. Don't I
tell you—

Ly. Yes; you tell me one thing at night, and ano-
other in the morning—You had forgotten the colonel's pay!—And the secret supplies!

MacDer. (*Aside.*) Faith, and so I had!

Ly. And pray was this all your own invention?

MacDer. Why, as to that—And is it me, now,
that you would have to betray my master?

Ly. What, then, he bid you spread this report?

MacDer. Arrah now, did I say that?—Did I say
that?—I tell you he bid me no such thing!—What,
and did you think, now, you could get that out of

me ? By St Patrick, but I would bite off my tongue, if it should dare to blunder out one word against so good a master !—

Ly. (*Aside.*) Honest, affectionate fellow !

MacDer. (*Aside.*) Oh ! Blarney !—She wants to be too cunning for me, the sweet crater ! And so, for fear of—Miss Liddy, your servant.   [*Exit.*

Ly. I almost love him myself, for his love to his master.

Enter SIR PAUL, *followed by* EDMUND.

Sir P. I tell you, I have done with him.   He is a pompous, insolent coxcomb ! The Great Mogul himself is a fool to him !

Edm. All men have their foibles, sir.

Sir P. Damn his foibles.   I have enough to do with my own ! And, do you hear, sir ? (*Significantly.*) Don't let me be troubled with any of your foibles either ! You understand me. (*Looking at both.*) I'll not be trifled with.   [*Exit.*

Ly. What has put him into so ill a humour ?

Edm. The cursed supercilious haughtiness of the count.   He has insulted Sir Samuel Sheepy, too !

Ly. I am sorry for it ; but that's a trifle.

Edm. You are mistaken. Sir Samuel's resentment is very high ; and, notwithstanding the servility of his manner, is more to be apprehended than you imagine.

Ly. Surely you do not expect a challenge?

Edm. Nay, my love, I would not wish to terrify you.

Ly. But you have terrified me !

Enter LUCY.

Lucy. Well, brother, have you succeeded with my mamma ?

Edm. I believe so—I can't tell—Where is the count ?

Lucy. I hear him on the stairs.

Edm. Well, warn him to be careful.

[*Exit, with chagrin.*

Lucy. What's the matter?

Ly. The old story! The count's pride. If he should quarrel again with Lady Peckham, all will then be over!

Lucy. You have put me quite in a tremor!

Enter the Count. Bows.

Lucy. (*Going.*) I will inform my mamma, sir, that you are here; and she will be with you immediately.

Count. May I not, madam, be indulged with one previous word?

Lucy. Yes, sir; one, and but one. Instead of conciliating, I find your manners offend and disgust every one. Either cast away your *hauteur*, regain the affections and consent of my friends, and above all make your peace with Lady Peckham, or this shall be the last meeting of our lives! [*Exit.*

Ly. Are you aware, sir, of your danger? Sir Samuel, Sir Paul, Lady Peckham, all affronted! Nay, your best friend, Edmund, has this moment left the room to avoid you! Oh! Think on that lovely lady! And if you have any affection for her, for yourself, or for your father—recal your reason, discard your folly, and act with a little common sense! [*Exit.*

Count. This is strange!—My father?—She know my father?—And why am I schooled and tutored thus? What have I done? What is it they expect from me?—Do I indeed offend and disgust?—Which way? Has not love induced me to overlook all the high distinctions which honour holds sacred? Nay, am I not now come on the most abject of errands?—Yet, to lose her—The last meeting of our lives!—They will absolutely drive me mad among 'em!

Enter LADY PECKHAM.

Count. Madam—(*Bowing*)—When I last had the honour—of a—an interview with your ladyship, I— I am afraid—I might possibly be inadvertently betrayed into—some warmth.

L. Peck. Vhy, sir, seeing as how my son tells me you are a real nobleman, and not von of the rifraff fortin-hunting fellers, if so be as you thinks fit to make proper 'pologies, vhy, sir, I—i—

Count. To a lady, madam, every apology may be made. Any concessions therefore—

L. Peck. Oh, sir, as for that there, I vants nothing but vat is right and downright. And I supposes, sir, you are wery villin to own that an outlandish foriner must think himself highly honoured, by a connection with an English family of distinction. Because that I am sure you cannot deny. And that it vus a most perumptery purceedin in you, being as you are but a Frenchman, or of an Irish generation at best, to purtend to the hand and fortin of Miss Loocy Peckham, vithout my connivance.

Count. Madam!

L. Peck. As I tells you, sir, I am upright and downright. So do you, or do you not?

Count. Madam!—I am ready to acknowledge that the charms of your daughter's mind, and person, are equal to any rank!

L. Peck. Her mind and purson, indeed! No, sir! Her family and fortin!—And I believes, sir, now you are come to your proper senses, you vill own too that no outlandish lord, vhatever, can uphold any comparagement vith the Peckham family and connections!

Count. (*With great warmth and rapidity.*) Madam, though I am ready to offer every excuse which can reasonably be required, for any former inadvertency; yet, madam, no consideration whatever shall

lead me—I say, madam, my own honour, a sense of
what is due to my ancestors, myself, and to truth—
that is, madam—No! The world, racks, shall not
force me to rank my family with yours.

L. Peck. Vhy, sir? Vhat is it that you are talking
of? Rank my family vith yourn, indeed! Marry come
up! No, to be sure! I say rank! I knows wery vell
vhat is my doo: and that there, sir, is the thing that
I vould have you for to know! And I insist upon it,
sir, that you shall know it; and shall own that you
knows it; or, sir, I rewoke every thing I have condescended to specify vith my son! So do you, sir, or
do you not?

Count. Madam—What, madam?

L. Peck. Do you depose, that outlandish foriners
are all beggars, and slaves; and that von Englishman
is vorth a hundred Frenchmen?

Count. Madam—Whatever you please. (*Bows.*)

L. Peck. Oh! Wery vell!—And do you purdict
that this here city is the first city in the whole
vorld?

Count. I—I believe it is, madam.

L. Peck. Oh! Wery vell!—And that the Moni-
ment, and the Tower, and Lunun bridge, are most
magnanimous and superfluous buildings?

Count. Madam—

L. Peck. I'll have no circumbendibus! Are they,
or are they not?

Count. Your ladyship is pleased to say so. (*Bows.*)

L. Peck. To be sure I does! Because I knows it
to be troo! And that the wretches in forin parts are
all fed upon bran; seeing as how there is no corn!

Count. As your ladyship thinks! (*Bows.*)

L. Peck. And that the whole country could not
purwide von lord mayor's feast!

Count. I—Certainly not, madam: they have few
turtle, and no aldermen.

L. Peck. Ah! A pretty country, indeed! No ale

dermen! And that it vould be the hite of pursumptiou, in you, for to go for to set yourself up as my equal? Do you own that?

Count. (*Passionately.*) No, madam!

L. Peck. Sir!

Count. No force, no temptation shall induce me so to dishonour my great progenitors!

L. Peck. Vhy, sir!

Count. My swelling heart can hold no longer! Honour revolts at such baseness! Patience itself cannot brook a fallacy so glaring! No! Though destruction were to swallow me, I would assert my house's rights, and its superior claims!

L. Peck. Wery vell, sir! Wastly vell, sir! And I vould have you for to know, sir, vhile my name is my Lady Peckham, I vill dissert my house's rights, and claims! That I despises all!—Ha, ha!—Ha! Wery fine, indeed! Am I to be sent here to be hectored, and huffed, and bluffed, and bullied, and bounced, and blustered, and brow-beat, and scoffed, and scouted, and—Ha!

Count. (*Recovering his temper, and interceding.*) Madam—

L. Peck. I a brought my hogs to a fine market! But I'll let 'em know who's at home!

Count. My warmth, madam—

L. Peck. Your honour and glory, indeed! And for to purtend for to send for me here, to palaver me over, as I supposed——

Count. I am ready to own, madam—

L. Peck. But I'll rid the house of you! I'll take good care you shall have no daughter of mine! You may post off to your father's hall, and there starve in state. Varm it with a blaze of dried leaves, and stop up the gaps in the shattered vinders, and old groaning doors, vith clay; then send your shivering wassals, that stand jabbering behind your von-armed vooden chair, to skin the sheep that died of hunger and the rot, to make you a varm vinter surtout!

Count. (*Still interceding.*) Madam—

L. Peck. My daughter, indeed! I'll karakatoor you! [*Exit.*

Count. Flames and fury! (*Following, is met by* Sir Samuel Sheepy, *who shuts the door after him, and will not suffer the Count to pass*) How now, sir!

Sir S. (*Bowing.*) Sir, your humble servant.

Count. What does this mean, sir? Let me pass.

Sir S. A word or two first, if you please, sir.

Count. Let me pass! (*Putting his hand to his sword.*)

Sir S. (*Bowing, but resolutely guarding the door.*) Sir, I must humbly entreat—

Count. Damnation!—What is it you want with me, sir? Who are you, sir?

Sir S. My name is Sheepy, sir. (*Bowing.*)

Count. Sheepy? (*Aside.*) So, so, so! Hell and the devil! At such a moment as this!

Sir S. I am told, sir, I have some obligations to you, which it becomes me to discharge.

Count. Well, sir.

Sir S. Not quite so well, sir, as I could wish. (*Bowing.*)

Count. (*Aside.*) Was ever man so tormented?

Sir S. I am informed, sir, that you have condescended to mention me, in my absence.

Count. And so, sir?

Sir S. You did me an honour, sir. (*Bowing.*)

Count. Either speak your business, and suffer me to pass, or I will nail you to the door!

Sir S. Dear sir, you are so warm! (*Bowing.*)—I have been told you were so good as to threaten to cane me.

Count. Ay, sir! By whom?

Sir S. By Lady Peckham, sir.

Count. Indeed—Well; suppose it.

Sir S. 'Twas kind of you!—Unluckily, I have not

been much used to threatening messages, and am really afraid I shall not be very prompt at submission.

Count. Oh, do not doubt yourself, sir.

Sir S. Humble though I am, I do not find that a swaggering look—(*Bowing.*)

Count. Sir ! (*With his hand to his sword.*)

Sir S. Moderate your anger, kind sir—I have a petition to you. (*Putting on his white gloves.*)

Count. Damn your sneer, sir ! Speak !

Sir S. Bless me, sir ! You are so warm ! It is only that you would kindly do me the favour either to cut my throat, or suffer me to cut yours. (*Draws, and flourishes.*)

Count. (*With his hand to his sword.*) Are you mad, sir ? Do you recollect where you are ? In whose house ?

Sir S. Gadso ! True, sir ! I should be sorry to be interrupted—Luckily, my carriage is at the door; and I know a snug room in a neighbouring tavern, where this business may be effectually settled, as quietly, as coolly, and as privately as possible.

Count. 'Twere well for you, sir, had you chosen another opportunity—But come !

Sir S. Oh! sir, I know my place—After you! (*Bows.*)

Count. Away, sir. [*Exeunt.*

SCENE III.

Changes to the Count's Apartment.

A considerable noise of hasty footsteps without, and voices at some distance calling—" Here! Here!—This way!—Up, up!—Follow!"

Enter MR DORIMONT, *abruptly.*

Mr Dor. I am pursued, beset, and cannot escape!

Enter MACDERMOT.

MacDer. Blood and thunder! Why, what's all this? Oh! and is it you, sir?

Mr Dor. Where is the count?

MacDer. Faith, and that is more than I can tell. (*Noise approaching*—" Here, here, I tell you! This room!") Why, what the divle—

Mr Dor. I am hunted! My liberty, perhaps my life is in danger!

MacDer. Why, sure the count would not—

Mr Dor. Here! Take, hide this packet from the eyes of my pursuers: Don't lose it; but it you have any sense of worth and honesty, deliver it safe into the hands of Sir Paul Peckham!

MacDer. Niver fear me, honey.

Enter an Exempt and two Bailiffs.

Ex. That's the man. Seize him!

First Bail. Sir, you are our prisoner.

Mr Dor. On what authority, sir?

First Bail. Authority, sir! The authority of law, sir.

Mr Dor. For what crime?

First Bail. As to crime, sir, I can't tell; but for a trifling debt of fifty thousand pounds.

Mr Dor. At whose suit

Ex. At mine, sir.

Mr Dor. Yours? Vile wretch! Gentlemen, he is a spy! the creature of a foreign court! I never had dealings with him in my life!

First Bail. We know nothing of that, sir. He has sworn to the debt.

Ex. No parleying; take him away.

First Bail. Ay, ay. Come, sir. (*They all three forcibly drag him out.*)

Mr Dor. (*Going and without.*) Help! Rescue! False imprisonment!

MacDer. Why, what is all this now?—Poor ould gintleman.

(*Noise without at a distance*—" Rescue! Rescue! Help!")

MacDer. Where is my shillalee?—Oh, by St Peter and his crook, but I will be one among you, scoundrels.   [*Exit, running.*

ACT THE FIFTH.

SCENE I.

The House of SIR PAUL PECKHAM.

Enter LYDIA *agitated,* EDMUND *following.*

Edm. Be pacified : you are too much alarmed.

Ly. If Sir Paul should have let them pass, what dreadful consequences may have followed ! Where can he be ?

Edm. He is here !

Enter SIR PAUL.

Ly. Oh, sir !—Where are they ?—Has any thing happened ?

Sir P. Happened !—Damme ! I could not believe my own ears !—A silky Simon !— The count was in a right humour—'Sblood ! I had a great mind to have let him kill the old fool.

Ly. Then they have not fought ? Are they safe, sir ?

Sir P. Yes, yes ; they are safe enough—But do you know the amorous swain, his blood being heated, could only be pacified on condition that he might have another interview with Lucy !—I'm glad on't ! I'll go and give her her lesson.

Edm. Oh, sir, leave him to my sister, she needs no instructions.

VOL. IV.   N

Sir P. No ?—Gad, I believe not ! She's my own girl ! But clear the coast ; he is coming.

Edm. I will go to Lady Peckham ; and do you, Lydia, watch for the count.

Sir P. Ay, ay. He is suddenly grown humble ; apologized to me, and promised to come and plead with my lady. But away.

[*Exeunt* EDMUND *and* LYDIA, *and*

Enter SIR SAMUEL SHEEPY.

Well, Sir Samuel, you are here !

Sir S. Yes, sir. (*Aside.*) And I half wish I was any where else, already.

Sir P. And so you absolutely have the courage to attack my Lucy ? Ha, ha, ha ! Why, you are quite a hero ! You fear neither man nor woman !

Sir S. (*Aside.*) I wish I didn't.

Sir P. Nay, but don't begin to look so pitiful ! She'll be here in a minute. Don't flinch : Stand to your guns ! She'll not easily strike ! Ha, ha, ha ! Die hard, my old boy !   [*Exit.*

Sir S. What is the matter with me ? I declare he has talked me into a tremble ! Why should I be so terrified at a harmless woman ? I can't help it ! A pair of beautiful eyes are flaming swords, which no armour can resist.

Enter LUCY, *cheerfully.*

Lucy. So, Sir Samuel !

Sir S. Bless me !—My heart is in my mouth !

Lucy. You seem taken by surprise.

Sir S. Madam—Hem !—No, madam—Yes, madam. (*With his usual bows.*)

Lucy. My papa informed me you were waiting, purposely to disclose this important secret.

Sir S. Madam—Hem !—Yes, madam—

Lucy. Do you know that I have had you in my mind I don't know how often, since I saw you ?

Sir S. Hem!—Have you, madam?

Lucy. Yes, I have—'Tis a pity, nay indeed a shame, that so famous an English family as that of the Sheepy's should become extinct.

Sir S. Hem!—There is no danger of that, madam.

Lucy. No!—Why, it is too late in life for you to marry, Sir Samuel.

Sir S. Hem!—Yes, madam. No, madam.

Lucy. Indeed! So you—Well! I should like to know your choice—Some staid body, I imagine.

Sir S. Madam—Hem!—

Lucy. But I would not have her too old, and disagreeable.

Sir S. Hem! I can assure you, madam—She— Hem!—She is a very beautiful young lady.

Lucy. You surprise me!—Oh! Then perhaps she is some low-born girl, who has more pride than understanding, and is willing to sacrifice her youth, and beauty, to the silly vanity of riding in a coach?

Sir S. Quite—Hem!—Quite the contrary, madam.

Lucy. Then she must be poor, and must think of marrying you for the sake of your riches, hoping you will die soon.

Sir S. Madam—Hem! She is very rich.

Lucy. Is it possible!

Sir S. And I should flatter myself would not expect me to die soon.

Lucy. Oh, but she will! Young women never marry old men, but with a wish to dance over their graves.

Sir S. Hem!

Lucy. Perhaps the poor girl may—may have made a *faux pas.*

Sir S. Hem! Her virtue is unspotted, madam.

Lucy. You amaze me! Young, rich, beautiful, and virtuous! What can her reason be for making choice of you? Why does not she rather marry some youth, whose rare qualities resemble her own?—Oh! I've found the secret at last! She's an idiot.

Sir S. Hem ! No, madam——No——Hem !——I am afraid she has too much wit !

Lucy. Nay then, Sir Samuel, you are the most fortunate gentleman I ever heard or read of !—But are you sure she is in love with you ?

Sir S. Hem !—N—Not very, madam.

Lucy. No !—Oh ho ! I have unriddled it at last ! You have been bargaining for her with her father, or her mother, or—Ay, ay ! The poor young lady's consent has never been asked !—And would you be so selfish as to seek your own single gratification, and be contented to see her condemned to misery, pining to death for the youth she loves, and justly detesting the sight of you, as the wicked unfeeling author of her wretchedness ?

Sir S. Hem ! (*Looking toward the door.*) Madam, I—Hem !—I wish you a good evening.

Lucy. (*Preventing his going.*) Another word, Sir Samuel. Have you ever talked to the young lady on the subject ?

Sir S. Hem ! I—Hem !—I have and—Hem ! I have not.

Lucy. You never made a direct proposal ?

Sir S. Hem ! No, madam.

Lucy. But why ?

Sir S. I, I—Hem !—I can't very well tell.

Lucy. But I can——With much folly and depravity, there is still some virtue in you.

Sir S. Madam ! (*Looking how to escape.*)

Lucy. Though you could form so unjust a project, you never had the courage to insult the lady by an avowal of your guilt.

Sir S. Hem ! Guilt, madam !

Lucy. Yes, sir, guilt—However, sir, she has perfectly understood your insinuations.

Sir S. Madam !

Lucy. She has infinite respect for filial duties.

But, though she would beware of offending her parents, I know her to be equally determined never to entail misery on herself; nor to accept a husband whom she could neither esteem, admire, nor love.

Sir S. Madam—I—Hem!—Your servant, madam.

Lucy. (*Between him and the door.*) Not till you first promise—

Sir S. (*Forgetting his fear.*) I'll promise any thing, madam.

Lucy. That you will not render yourself more ridiculous, by persevering in so absurd, so unjust a pursuit.

Sir S. No, madam! I'm quite ridiculous enough already!

Lucy. Nay, more, that you will not seek some less friended, more enslaved, or more timid young creature, whom your misapplied wealth might command.

Sir S. Whatever you please, madam!

Lucy. But that you will rather apply your superfluous hoards to the protection of youthful innocence.

Sir S. Suffer me but to depart, madam, and I will bequeath my estates in perpetuity as you shall direct; I'll entail them on the Magdalen; or I'll advertise for marriageable men and maids, and you shall portion out my money among them! I'll—I'll do any thing, except marry, or go a-courting!

Lucy. Why, then, Sir Samuel—(*Kissing his hand*) —There—That be your reward.

Sir S. Madam—Your humble servant.

[*Exit abruptly.*

Lucy. Ha, ha, ha! Poor Sir Samuel: This is the first time he ever forgot his bow.

Enter the Count.

Well, sir! have you effectually made your peace with my mamma?

Count. I have done my endeavour, madam——Would I were at peace with myself!

Lucy. And are you still, sir, under the dominion of prejudice so weak? Do you still repent of what you so long have deemed your condescension?

Count. Far otherwise, madam. There are beings so peculiarly favoured of Heaven, and endowed with such high perfections, both of body and of mind, that they are superior to all the distinctions of men, among whom they walk angels upon earth! You are one of these! And my misery is, I never can deserve you!

Lucy You may have stumbled, but this self-condemnation shews it was but to rise with tenfold strength. Persevere, and we will be severed only by death.

Enter EDMUND.

Edm. At length, my dear count, Lady Peckham is pacified. To stoop to her ill-placed pride, to overlook her prejudice, and to petition as you did, was noble in you. I have seconded your efforts, have pledged myself for your honour, and guaranteed your veracity.

Count. Then, sir, you have struck a dagger to my heart! I have been guilty of falsehood! That very pride, and that exalted, or I fear extravagant, sense of honour, which should have preserved me from a stain so hateful, have dashed me down the precipice!

Edm. You amaze me!

Count. 'Tis true, 'twas inadvertent; but rankling vanity, strengthened by a purer motive, the trembling alarms of love, induced me to persist; nay, a second time to aid deception.

Lucy. You did wrong—But which of us can say they never erred?

Edm. Ay! Who will stand forth and affirm, that, amid the rude whirl, the confused doubts, or the terrors of passion, they never once have been betrayed into your crime? For a crime I own it is; and with consequences so wide, so pernicious, and so fatal, that, when it shall be extirpated from the earth, that moment man will be perfect ! But, in this poor world's present state, it is so far venial, that (painful, humiliating thought !) no—the nobiest, the purest of us all, cannot strike his heart, and say—I never was a liar !

Lucy. Frail as we are, and hourly as the arts of falsehood are practised upon us, to our detriment, and often to our ruin, those only are most free from guilt, who shake contagion soonest from them ; and, by the next sublime effort of truth, scorning to shrink from shame, which is their due, in some sort turn the vice itself to virtue.

Edm. But what have you said that—

Enter SIR PAUL.

Sir P. Come, come ! We must strike while the iron is hot ! We must take my lady while she is in the humour, since she must necessarily be a party in our deeds. And first I have agreed, as you know, count, that my daughter's portion shall be 80,000*l.* The remainder will chiefly rest with you. What settlement do you intend to make ? And on what estates ?

Count. None, sir.

Sir P. None !

Count. I have no estates.

Sir P. Sir !—Why, what !—Zounds ! After the inquiries I made, I cannot be so deceived ! Are not you Count Connolly Villars ?

Count. I am, sir.

Sir P. A colonel in the armies of the Most Christian King ?

Count. I am, sir.

Sir P. Recommended to me by Messieurs Devigny, the great merchants at Marseilles ?

Count. The same, sir.

Sir P. Why, then, what do you mean?

Count. When I first paid my addresses to this lady, I imagined my rank and family were a sufficient counterpoise to wealth.

Sir P. Ha! Gold in one scale, honour in t'other? —Flimsy ware!—No, no—Kick the beam—

Count. But, ardent, violent, and eternal, as my love for your angelic daughter is, and must be, even the loss of her shall not tempt me, any longer, to practise the least imposition.

Sir P. Well, but, 'sblood! The steward! The family estates!

Count. I have told you the truth, sir.

Enter LYDIA.

Lucy. What's the matter, Lydia?

Ly. Poor Mr MacDermot—

Count. What of him?—Any harm?

Ly. He has been in some fray, and is so bruised!

Count. Bruised! Where is he?

Ly. Below, with a packet, which he wants to deliver to Sir Paul.

Sir P. To me?

Ly. Yes, sir. Pray go to him.

Sir P. A packet for me! (*Going.*) I shall never hear the last of this from my lady!

[*Exit* SIR PAUL.

Lucy. Brother, go to my mamma, and endeavour to keep her in temper. (*To the Count.*) Be not dejected! I know my father's affection for me, and do not yet despair.   [*Exit after* SIR PAUL.

Count. Charming, generous girl!—This poor MacDermot—

Ly. He is afraid of seeing you. He says you will never pardon him, for having taken the part of some man, whom you threatened to murder!

Count. I? I threatened to murder no man! Will

you, madam, be so kind as to tell him I am here ; and
that I insist on seeing him ?

Ly. With pleasure.   [*Exit.*

Count. Kingdoms should not tempt me to pass another day like this !

Enter MacDERMOT, *with his left arm in a sling.*

Count. How now, MacDermot ! Where have you
been ? What's the matter with you ?

MacDer. No great matter, my lord—Only a little
bit of a joint here. (*Pointing to his arm.*)

Count. (*Alarmed.*) Broken ?

MacDer. A double tooth or two—Not much, my
lord.

Count. Much !—How ?—What have you been doing ?

MacDer. (*Pitifully.*) I hope your lordship won't
be angry ! (*Enraged.*) But the rascals sazed him
neck and heels !

Count. Seized who ?

MacDer. (*Passionately.*) He was as innocent as
the babe unborn, my lord, and he tould 'em so :
(*Rage*)—the dirty rapscallions !

Count. Who are you talking of ?

MacDer. (*Pitifully.*) To be sure, he—he sent your
lordship a—a viry impartinent letter.

Count. How ? (*The Count's perplexities and passions are here effectually roused, and increase through
the scene.*)

MacDer. There were three of them. Niver did
your lordship set your two good-looking eyes on
such a pair of thieves !

Count. For Heaven's sake, tell your story straight
forward ! What letter do you mean ? Who ?

MacDer. (*With great emotion.*) I hope your lordship will forget and forgive ! It would have moved
the bowels of your compassion, to have seen the ould
gintleman !

Count. Is it possible ? What can he mean ? What old gentleman ?

MacDer. (*Enraged.*) The dirty shaberoons took him by the throat—My viry blood boiled !—Upon my soul, my lord, I could not bear it ! I hope you will forgive me ! By the merciful father, I could not bear it.

Count. Tell me, this moment, who you mean !

MacDer. He came running back, out of breath, and asked for your lordship. And so, my lord, (*Pleading*,)—being a fillow-crater in distress—

Count. Came where ?

MacDer. A couple of as ill-looking Tyburn-turn-pike bum-bailiffs as your lordship could wish ! With a cowardly complotter at their back ! It was he that came behind me with his shillalee, while I was hard at work with them both. But the brave ould gintleman stepped in ; and, by the Virgin's night-cap, but he gave him his dose !

Count. Once more, tell me instantly, what old gentleman ?

MacDer. Considering his age, he is as active, and as brave a fillow, as ever handled a fist.

Count. (*Aside.*) He cannot surely mean my father ! MacDermot, I entreat, I command you to tell me of whom you are talking.

MacDer. If your lordship had but seen the noble ould soul, I'm sure you would have forgiven me.

Count. But what letter—

MacDer. Oh ! The divle burn the letter ! Now, my lord, don't mention it. Pray, don't remimber it, your lordship ! Pray don't ! By my soul, now, my lord, he is a fine ould fillow.—Oh, how he laid about him !

Count. Was it the person who came this afternoon ?

MacDer. My lord—

Count. Fear nothing ! Speak.

MacDer. Why, then, my lord—To be sure—it was he himsilf.

Count. And is he safe? Did you free him from them?

MacDer. Why, my lord, I could not hilp it!— (*Emphatically.*) I could not hilp it! By the holy footstool, but I couldn't!

Count. MacDermot! (*Taking him by the hand.*)

MacDer. My lord!

Count. Well, well! A time will come—

MacDer. My lord!

Count. Are you much hurt, MacDermot?—Here —hollo!—

Enter a Footman.

Call a chair! Run for a surgeon and a physician! The best that can be procured.

MacDer. For me, my lord?

Count. For you, my noble fellow!

MacDer. Spare yourself the labour, young man.

Count. Go! Do as I order you; instantly. (*Exit Footman.*) MacDermot, you must be put to bed!

MacDer. To bed, my lord!

Count. And lose some blood.

MacDer. Faith, my lord, that will be a little too much: I've lost quite blood enough already.

Count. Pray! I request! I must have you do as I desire! I would not have any ill happen to you for the world!

MacDer. Oh! And the divle of ill or harm can happen to MacDermot, the while he has such an a ginerous prince-royal of a master. Though I believe, the best thing that could happen to me just now, would be a good supper, and a hearty tiff of whisky-punch.

Count. Not for the Indies!

MacDer. Faith, my lord, it was hard work; and has given me a very craving kind of a call.

Re-enter Footman.

Foot. The chair is waiting, sir.

Count. Go, my good fellow! Obey me but this once, and I'll never act the master to you more.

MacDer. Well, well, my lord. But I hope your lordship won't quite kill me with kindness.   [*Exit.*

Enter SIR PAUL *and* LUCY.

Sir P. (*With the packet opened.*) So, count, I find, after all your pretended raptures, you never wished to marry my daughter!

Count. Sir!

Sir P. Why did not you retract like a man; and not make a paltry, false excuse of poverty?

Count. Sir, I made no false excuse.

Sir P. How, sir! Shall I not believe my eyes? Have I not bills here in my hand, drawn in your favour, for five hundred thousand crowns?

Count. In mine!

Sir P. In yours. Given me this moment by your own servant.

Count. Impossible, sir!

Sir P. Impossible, is it? Why, look you, here are the bills: and, hollo!

Enter Footman.

Go you, sir, and desire Mr MacDermot to come back.

Count. Stir not for your life, on such an errand! He must not, shall not be disturbed.

Sir P. Nay, my word, it seems, is not to be believed; nor perhaps the bills themselves! But, sir, though you vaunt so highly of being a man of honour, the trick was beneath a man of honesty.

Enter LADY PECKHAM *and* EDMUND.

L. Peck. Here's a komakul kind of an obstrope-

rous person, that says he must speak to the count—
You may come in, mister.

Enter MR DORIMONT *and* LYDIA.

Sir P. Ah! What, my friend the steward! I am
glad you are come! Never was so amazed in my life!
Your master, here, has been telling me he has no
estates!

L. Peck. How!

Mr Dor. My master, sir!

Count. The feelings of man cannot support this
open shame! (*Crossing to go.*)

Mr Dor. Whither now, sir?

Sir P. Ay! Talk to him! I'm in a mist!

Count. Suffer me to pass, sir. (*Crosses to the door.*)
Speak the truth—Render me contemptible! Abhor-
rent! But make me not a witness of my own disgrace!

Mr Dor. Stay, sir!

Count. I cannot.

Mr Dor. Stay! or dread a father's malediction!

Sir P. His father! The plague! Hem!—Lydia!

Ly. Hush!

L. Peck. Father, indeed! Vhat, he! So, so! Here's
a wirago! Here's a chouse!

Sir P. My lady—

L. Peck. I thought vhat vould be the upshot on't!

Edm. Madam—(*Takes her aside for a moment in
dumb shew.*)

Mr Dor. Spurred on by suppositions and conceits
the most absurd, wholly intent upon yourself, con-
temning others, exacting respect you did not merit,
refusing ceremony where 'twas due, protuberant with
pride, yet poorly carping at and holding idiot warfare
with the pride of others, forgetful of the dignity of
reason, but with tenacious grasp clinging to the lu-
dicrous dignity of birth, the heir indeed and first-
born of Folly, ignorance itself has mocked and taunt-
ed at you!

L. Peck. Wery troo.   Give him his own.

Sir P. Zounds! My lady, I wish he would give you your own a little.   Not but it's right enough.

L. Peck. To be sure; I knows wery vell I am right.

Mr Dor. Your father too has been avoided, nay, disowned.   Your father, who for years has lived in indigence, that he might secretly supply your wants, support you in splendour, and preserve you from all the misery of which he made himself the willing victim.

Count. Sir! You?—Was it you? Oh! ingratitude!

Mr Dor. Your father was offensive to your sight. And what was it you despised? Why, this poor garb. You wished no kindred with virtuous poverty.   Had I appeared in all my former state, though knave or fool had been blazoned on my brow, yet, decked in the trappings of magnificence, I had received an open welcome.   But, blest be my penury, since it has been your punishment.

Count. Sir, wrung as my heart is by remorse, and guilty as I know myself, for I have still increase of guilt, no words can mitigate my crimes.   Yet, though I have erred, I feel I have something in me capable of good; and strong propensities to all the tender ties, the filial duties, and the severer virtues which I have seemed to want; a mind which, once convinced, has strength to shun and to subdue its master passion, renounce its folly, and abhor its turpitude. Deep is my offence against you and nature; but let nature plead in my behalf.   Here at your feet, repentant for my faults, I claim that pity which a father so good and so affectionate will not sure refuse.

Mr Dor. Oh, no; for now you speak like the son of my heart, the image of my brightest hopes.   You have stood the fiery trial, and are pure.

L. Peck. Vhy, but hark you me, mister.   Vhy, vhat—you are not a count too, to be sure?

Mr Dor. No, madam.

L. Peck. Vhy then——

Mr Dor. If a title can flatter your ladyship, mine is something higher.

L. Peck. How!

Mr Dor. I am a marquis.

L. Peck. A marquis!—You!—Vell! (*Aside.*) For an outlandish marquis!

Edm. My lady——

Sir P. Well, but the bills? (*Holding them out in his hand.*)

Mr Dor. They are mine.

Count. Yours, sir!

Mr Dor. Remittances for some recovered arrears. But where is my brave protector, my hero?

Count. Safe, sir —Every care is taken of the generous fellow. Is the physician come?

Sir P. Yes, yes. I have taken care of that. I have sent him my own physician. Hem! (*Aside.*) My cook.

Count. You know not half his worth.

Mr Dor. Which shall not go unrewarded.

Count. No, by Heaven.

Mr Dor. We have now the means; we no longer are oppressed and poor.

Count. Yet are you not in present danger?

Mr Dor. No: malice has spent its last effort. Our ambassador has just sent me the final decision of the judges: my sentence is reversed, my whole estates are restored, and the power of my persecutors is at an end.

Count. Oh Fortune! Oh my father! And may I hope it? My Lucy! may I?

Lucy. Yes; hope every thing.

Count. Mine!

Lucy. Yours—heart and soul.

Sir P. She is a brave wench.

L. Peck. Hold a blow, if you please.—Vhat! Am I nobody?

Count. Madam, to you a thousand excuses are due.

L. Peck. To be sure they are.

Count. I am conscious of my past ridicule, and will no more contend with your ladyship, for prejudices so false and weak.

L. Peck. I knoo I vus right. I knoo you made yourself ridicolous. I told you so often enough.

Sir P. Well said, my lady. But hark you, Miss Lydia—(*Significantly.*) And, sir——

Mr Dor. A moment's patience, sir.—Count! How shall I tell him? My son, look at this charming, this virtuous young lady.

Sir P. (*Aside.*) Zounds! what now?

Count. I am conscious of having treated her with proud unkindness, at the very moment too when I perceived she was sincerely my friend.

Mr Dor. Your friend! Look at her! Does not your heart throb? Feel you not sensations more tender? Are you not all doubt, all hope, all fear, all perturbation?

Count. Sir! What?—Who?

Mr Dor. Can you not imagine? Look at her, I say!—Behold her agitation!

Count. Mercy!

Mr Dor. Open your arms, your heart, to receive her——

Count. Sir! Madam! Who?

Mr Dor. Your sister!

Count. My sister!

Ly. My dearest, best of brothers! (*Running into his arms.*)

Lucy. My friend!—my Lydia!

Count. Oh! how culpable have I been!

Sir P. (*Aside.*) 'Sblood! Here's a pretty piece of business!

L. Peck. Vhat's that you say, sir? Miss Liddy the count's sister!

Edm. 'Tis very true, madam.

L. Peck. Troo! Vell, I purtest I'm quite in a quandary!

Mr Dor. (*To* SIR PAUL.) And now, sir——

Sir P. (*Aside.*) Yes, 'tis my turn now!—Yes, sir.

Mr Dor. While labouring to reclaim the follies of youth——

Sir P. Yes, sir.

Mr Dor. We ought not to forget the vices of age.

Sir P. Hem! We'll talk of them after supper, sir. (*Looking round at* LADY PECKHAM *and the Company.*)

Mr Dor. Well, sir, on condition——

Sir P. Oh, any condition you please, sir.

Edm. (*Leading* LYDIA.) My dear father!——

Sir P. My kind son!—(*Aside.*)—Sly rascal!

Ly. (*To* SIR PAUL.) We shall want a house, sir.

Sir P. Hem! Ay, ay!

Ly. Somewhere in Mary-le-bone.

Sir P. Very well.

Ly. With a——

Sir P. Zounds! (*Aside to* LYDIA.) Hush! Don't mention the back door.

Ly. Then we are all friends?

Sir P. To be sure.—But, you may as well not tell Scapegrace!

Ly. Never fear.

Sir P. Not a word of the new liveries!

Ly. Depend upon my honour.

Count. My sister and my friend! Can it be?

Edm. Would you not wish it thus?

Count. Oh! most ardently!

Mr Dor. Chequered are the scenes of life. Pleasure and pain, joy and grief, austerity and laughter, intermingling, weave a motley web. Our prejudices are our punishments: they cling about us, warp our

6

actions, distort our manners, render us the food of
satire, the mockery of fools, and torture us as wail-
ing urchins are tormented to make sport for boys.
Error and folly impede the progress of perfection.
Truth alone can make men wise and happy. Myself
the sacrifice of falsehood and mistake, feebly have I
striven to stem the torrent: and here my task, and
here I hope my troubles end.   [*Exeunt omnes.*

HE'S MUCH TO BLAME;

A

COMEDY,

IN FIVE ACTS.

AS PERFORMED AT THE

THEATRE-ROYAL, COVENT-GARDEN.

LORD VIBRATE,	*Mr Quick.*
SIR GEORGE VERSATILE,	*Mr Lewis.*
MR DELAVAL,	*Mr Pope.*
DR GOSTERMAN,	*Mr Murray.*
THOMPSON,	*Mr Davenport.*
WILLIAMS,	*Mr Clarke.*
HARRY,	*Mr Abbot.*
MASTER OF THE HOTEL,	*Mr Thompson.*
JENKINS,	*Mr Rees.*
WAITER,	*Mr Blurton.*
FOOTMAN,	*Mr Curtis.*
LADY VIBRATE,	*Mrs Mattocks.*
LADY JANE,	*Miss Betterton.*
MARIA,	*Mrs Pope.*
LUCY,	*Mrs Gibbs.*
LADY JANE'S WOMAN,	*Mrs Norton.*

HE'S MUCH TO BLAME.

ACT THE FIRST.

SCENE I.

Ringing heard.—The Hall of a Hotel, with a spacious Staircase.

Enter the Master and Head Waiter, meeting.

Ma. Why, where are all the fellows, Jenkins? Don't you hear the bell No. 9?

Jen. Tom is gone up to answer it, sir.

Ma. Who occupies that apartment?

Jen. The handsome youth and girl that arrived late last night.

Ma. Just as I was going to bed?

Jen. Yes, sir.

Ma. He is quite a boy.

Jen. Razor has never robbed him of a hair.

Ma. Some stripling, perhaps, that has run away with his mother's maid.

Jen. They ordered separate beds.

Ma. Well, see what they want.

Jen. Yes, sir.

Ma. And, hark ye, be attentive the moment you hear Lord and Lady Vibrate, or their daughter, stirring. People of quality must never be neglected.

Jen. Oh no, sir. Here is Dr Gosterman. [*Exit.*

SCENE II.

Enter the Doctor.

Ma. Good morrow, Doctor.

Doc. Coot morgen, my tear friend. Is de Fiprate family fisible to see?

Ma. Not yet.

Doc. My lordtship und my latyship vas sharge me to be mit dem betime.

Ma. You are a great favourite there, Doctor.

Doc. Ya, sair. Dat I am efery vhere.

Ma. You act in a double capacity: physician and privy-counsellor.

Doc. Und I am as better in de von as in de oder.

Ma. Why, ay, Doctor, you have a smooth pleasant manner.

Doc. Ya, sair. Dat is my vay. I mix de syrup mit all my prescription.

Ma. Ay, ay, you are a useful person.

Doc. Ya, sair. Dat is my vay. I leave Yarmany, und I com at Englandt mit little money, und great cunning in de art, und de science. I shall af de essence, und de cream, und de balsam, und de syrup, und de electric, und de magnetic, und de mineral, und de vegetable, und de air, und de earse, und de sea, und all dat vas subject under my command. So

I make de nation benefit, und myself rish.   Dat is
my vay.

Ma. Yes; you can tickle the guineas into your
pocket.

Doc. Ya, sair.   Dat is my vay.

Ma. You have had many patients?

Doc. Ya, sair.   I af cure tousand und tousand!
Dat is my vay.

Ma. And how many have you killed, Doctor?

Doc. Der Teufel, sair!   Kill?   Ven my patient vas
die, dat vas Nature dat vas kill.   Ven dey vas cure,
dat vas Dr Von Gostermans.   Dat is my vay.   No,
sair!   Dr Von Gostermans vas kill himself, dat oder
people may live.

Ma. How do you mean kill yourself, Doctor?

Doc. Der Teufel, sair!   Vas I not be call here?
Vas I not be call dere?   Vas I not be call efery vhere?
I af hundert und tousand patient dat die efery day
till I vas com.   So I vas drive to de city: und dere
I vas meet my besten friend, de gout, de apoplexy,
und de asthmatica: und den I vas drive to de inn of
court, und de lawyer; und dere I vas find more of
my besten friend, de hydropica, de rheumatica, und
de paralytica.

Ma. What, Doctor!   The lawyers and inns of
court paralytic?

Doc. Ya, sair.

Ma. I wish they were, with all my soul!

Doc. Und den I vas drive und make my reverence
mit de lordt, und mit de duke, und mit de grandee;
und dere I vas meet mosh oder of my besten friend;
de hypochondrica, de spasmodica, de hysterica, de
marasma, de morbid affection, de tremor, und de
mist before de eye.

Ma. Morbid affections, tremors, and mists before
the eyes, the diseases of the great?

Doc. Ya, sair.   Und dey vas grow vorse und vorse
efery day.

Ma. Well, well, they have chosen a skilful doctor!

Doc. Ya, sair. I shall do all deir business, efery von. Dat is my vay. I shall af de essence, und de cream, und de balsam, und de syrup, und de electric, und de magnetic, und de mineral, und de vegetable, und de air, und de earse, und de sea, und all dat vas subject under my command. Dat is my vay. Bote dat is as noting at all. Ah sa, my liebste: you vas my besten friend. You make me acquaint myself mit all de patient dat vas come to your house; und so I vas your besten friend, und I vas gif de physic for yourself, und de physic for your shile, und de physic for your vife.

Ma. For which my wife will never more thank you, Doctor.

Doc. No; your vife vas die, und you vas tank me yourself. So now you tell me: Af you any new customer dat vas com?

Ma. Yes; a youth, and a girl that looks like a waiting-maid, arrived late last night.

Doc. Vhich it vas a person of grandeur?

Ma. Oh no; wholly unattended.

Doc. Ah, ah! Vhich it vas a lofing couple, den?

Ma. It seems not.

Doc. A poy und a vaiting-vomans! Dere shall be someting mystery in dat.

Ma. So I think. Here comes the girl.

Doc. Ah, ah! Let me do: I shall talk to her. I shall begin by make acquaintance mit her.

SCENE III.

Enter LUCY *down the staircase.*

Lucy. Pray, sir, desire the waiter to make haste with breakfast.

Ma. Here, Jenkins! Breakfast to No. 9. Be quick!

Jen. (*Without.*) Yes, sir.

Ma. Tea or coffee, madam?

Lucy. Tea.

Doc. How you do, my tear? You vas pretty young frau: fery pretty girl, my tear. Perhaps you vas stranger, my tear?

Lucy. Perhaps I am.

Doc. Ah! Vhat is your name, my tear?

Lucy. That which my godmother gave me.

Doc. Your mastair af made de long journey, my tear.

Lucy. Has he?

Doc. From vat country you com, my tear?

Lucy. Hem!

Doc. I ask, from vat country you com, my tear,

Lucy. Ask again.

Doc. From de town of——Ha!

Lucy. Ay. How do you call it?

Doc. Dat is vat I vant you shall tell?

Lucy. I see you do.

Doc. Your mastair is fery young, my tear.

Lucy. Thank you, sir.

Doc. For vat you tank me?

Lucy. For your news.

Doc. Ah, ah! You are fery vitty und pretty, my tear.

Lucy. More news. Thank you again.

Doc. Vat vas you call de young yentleman's name?

Lucy. I will ask, and send you word.

Doc. How long shall he be stay in town?

Lucy. Till he goes into the country.

Doc. Vat is your capacity, my tear?

Lucy. Like yours, little enough.

Doc. You not understandt me, my tear. Vat is your post, your office?

Lucy. To answer rude questions.

Doc. Your mastair is man of family?

Lucy. Yes. He had a father, and mother, and uncles, and aunts.

Doc. Und tey vas tead?

Lucy. I am not a tomb-stone.

Doc. Com, com, my tear, let you make me answer.

Lucy. Anan?

Enter Waiter.

Wait. Here is the breakfast, madam.

Lucy. Take it up stairs.

    [*Exeunt* LUCY *and Waiter up the staircase.*

Doc. Der Teufel! A cunning yipsey! She has make me raise my curiosity. (*Calls.*) My tear! My tear! Com pack, my tear! (LUCY *returns.*) Do my compliment to your mastair, und I shall make me mosh happy if I shall af de honeur to make me acquaintance mit him. My name is call Dr Von Gostermans. I shall af de essence, und de cream, und de balsam, und de syrup, und de electric, und de magnetic, und de mineral, und de vegetable, und de air, und de earse, und de sea, und all dat vas subject under my command. I shall af de best recommendation for de honest docteur dat vas possible. My lordt und my lady Fiprate vas my besten friend. I vas practice mit all de piggest family in de uniferse. Docteur Von Gostermans vas know efery poty; und efery poty vas know Docteur Von Gostermans. You tell him dat, my tear.

Lucy. Tell him that? I cannot remember half of it! Are you, sir, acquainted with Lord Vibrate's family?

Doc. Ya, my tear. I vas make friendship mit dem more as many year.

Lucy. And do you know where they are?

Ma. To be sure he does. They are in this—

Doc. (*Aside to Master.*) Hush! Silence your tongue! Dere is someting mystery. (*Aloud.*) If you

shall make me introduce to your mastair, my tear, I
shall tell him efery ting und more as dat, my tear.
Vill you, my tear?

Lucy. I will go and inquire.

Doc. Tank you, my tear.   You are fery pretty
girl, my tear : fery vitty pretty—Ah! You are so
sly cunning little yipsey, my tear. Ah, ah! [*Exeunt.*

SCENE IV.

A Chamber. MARIA *in man's clothes with a letter in
her hand and walking with anxiety. The Waiter
enters and leaves the breakfast.   She then reads.*

Mar. " Dear sister, the letter I now write is almost needless, for I shall leave Italy and follow it
immediately ; having at last obtained intelligence of
your faithless lover.   I am sorry to inform you that,
in addition to your unpardonable wrongs, I have my
own to vindicate.   But I have threatened too long.
You have heard of the Earl of Vibrate.   He and his
family are by this arrived in England ; your betrayer
accompanies them, and I am in close pursuit.

PAUL DELAVAL."

In what will this end? Must they meet? Must they
fight? Must one or both of them fall? Oh horror!
Shall I be the cause of murder? And whose blood
is to be spilled? That of the most generous of brothers, or of the man on whom my first and last affections have been fixed! Is there no safety ; no means?

SCENE V.

Enter LUCY.

Lucy. Why, look here now, madam, you are letting the breakfast grow cold! You have been reading that letter again. I do believe I shall never get
you to eat any more. Come now, pray do take some
of this French roll; and I'll pour out the tea. Do!
Pray do! Pray do!

Mar. I cannot eat. Lucy: I am eaten. Terror
and despair are devouring me.

Lucy. Dear! Dear! What will all this come to?
Did not you promise me that, as soon as you had
got safe to London in your disguise, you would be
better?

Mar. Can it be? My kind, my gentle, my true-
hearted George!

Lucy. True-hearted! No, no, madam, he was never true-hearted: or he could not so soon have
changed, because his ill fortune changed to good.
Every body knows true love never changes.

Mar. What have I done? How have I offended?
His caresses, his protestations, his tender endear-
ments! Is then the man in whom my soul was wrapt
a vil—Oh!

Lucy. I declare, madam, if you take on this way,
you will break my heart as well as your own. Beside, you forget all the while what you put on this
dress and came up to London for.

Mar. Oh no. It was if possible to prevent mischief! Murder!——They have never met. They do
not know each other. But how shall I discover Sir
George? Of whom shall I inquire?

Lucy. If you would but eat your breakfast, I do think I could put you in the way.

Mar. You?

Lucy. Yes.

Mar. By what means?

Lucy. Will you eat your breakfast, then?

Mar. I cannot eat. Speak.

Lucy. Why, I have just been talking to an outlandish comical doctor, that says he is acquainted with Lord Vibrate.

Mar. Indeed! Where is this doctor?

Lucy. He is waiting without; for I knew you would wish to speak to him.

Mar. Shew him in immediately.

Lucy. I'll tell him you are not well, which is but too true; though you must remember, madam, you are a man So dry your eyes, forget your misfortunes, and, there, cock your hat, a that fashion, and try to swagger a little, or you will be found out. You stand so like a statue, and look so pitiful! Lord, that's not the way! If you are timorsome, and silent, and bashful, nobody on earth will take you for a youth of fortune and fashion.   [*Exit.*

Mar. (*In revery.*) If they should meet! Heavens! they must not.

SCENE VI.

Re-enter LUCY *and Doctor.*

Lucy. My master is not very well; he eats neither breakfast, dinner, nor supper, and gets no sleep.

Doc. He noder eat, noder drink, noder sleep! Dat is pad! Fery pad! But dat is as noting at all, my tear. Let me do. You shall see presently py and py vat is my vay.

Mar. Your servant, sir.

Doc. Sair, I vas your mosh oblishe fery omple sairfant, sair. My name is call Dr Von Gostermans. I shall af de best recommendation for de honest docteur dat vas possible. I vas practice mit all de piggest family in de uniferse. Docteur Von Gostermans is know efery pody; und efery pody is know Dr Von Gostermans. De pretty coquine yung frau tell me dat you not fery fell. You not eat, you not drink, you not sleep. Dat is pad! Fery pad! Bote dat is as noting at all. You tell me de diagnostic und de prognostic of all vat you vill ail; und I shall make you prescripe for de anodyne, oder de epipastic, oder de balsamic, oder de narcotic, oder de diaphoretic, oder de expectoratic, oder de restoratif, oder de emulsif, oder de incisif; vhich is efery ting so shveet und so delectable as all vat is possible.

Mar. Your pardon, sir, but I wish to see you on business of another nature.

Doc. Ah ah! Someting of de prifate affair! Dat is coot. I shall be as petter for dat as for de oder. I vas know de vorl. I vas know efery pody, und efery pody vas know me. Dat is my vay.

Mar. Perhaps then you happen to know Sir George Versatile?

Doc. Oh, Der Teufel, sair! Ya, ya. Sair Shorge is my besten friend. Vhich it vas six month dat he vas succeed to his title und estate; und den I vas make acquaintance mit him: dat is my vay.

Mar. But he has been abroad since.

Doc. Ya, sair. Ven he vas poor, he vas fall in lofe mit fery pretty yung frau. Bote so soon as he vas pecome rish paronet, dat vas anoder ting. So his relation und his friend vas sent him to make de gran tour.

Mar. And he was easily persuaded.

Doc. Ya, sair.   He vas vat you call fery coot nature : he vas alvay comply.

Mar. Compliance with him is more than a weakness.   I fear it is a vice.

Doc. So he vas make acquaintance mit Lordt und mit Laty Fiprate ; und den he vas tink no more of de pretty yung frau, pecause he vas fall in lofe mit anoder.

Mar. Sir ! Another ! What other ?

Doc. Vat you shall ail, sair ? You shange coleur.

Mar. With whom has he fallen in love ?

Doc. Mit de taughter of Lordt Fiprate.

Mar. With Lady Jane ?

Doc. Ya, sair ; mit Laty Shane—My Cot, sair ! vat you shall ail ? You not make fall in lofe yourself mit Laty Shane ?

Mar. No, no—they are no doubt to be married.

Doc. My Cot, sair ! you so pale as deaths—My Cot, you shall faint !

Lucy. Faint, indeed ! (*Aside.*) Bear up, madam. (*Aloud.*) My master is too much of a man to faint. (*Aside.*) I'll run for a glass of water.   [*Exit.*

SCENE VII.

Mar. The charming Lady Jane ! Where is she ?

Doc. My Lordt und my Laty Fiprate und my Laty Shane vas all in de house here.

Mar. In this house ?

Doc. Ya, sair.

Mar. And is Sir George here too ?

Doc. He is com und go alvay sometime efery tay.

Mar. Are they to be married ?

Doc. My Cot, sair ! you af de ague fit.

Mar. Are they to be married ?

Doc. My Laty Fiprate vas mosh incline to Sair

Shorge, und my lordt vas sometime mosh incline
too; und den he vas sometime not mosh incline; und
den he vas doubt; und den he vas do me de honeur
to consultate mit me.

Mar. And what is your advice?

Doc. My Lordt Fiprate vas my besten friends,
und I vas adfice dat he shall do all as vat he please;
und Sair Shorge vas my besten friends too, und I vas
adfice dat he shall do all as vat he please; und my
Laty Fiprate vas petter as my besten friends, und den
I vas more adfice dat she shall do all as vat she please.

Mar. But Lady Jane had another lover?

Doc. Ya, sair. Mr Delafal vas make lofe mit her.
He vas com from de East Indie, und he vas lofe her
fery mosh; und she vas go mit de family to Italy,
und my Laty Fiprate vas make acquaintance mit Sair
Shorge, pecause he vas so mosh pleasant und coot
humeur, und he say all as vat she say: vhich vas de
vay to alvay make agréable.

Mar. Could you do me the favour to introduce me
to Lady Jane?

Doc. Ya, sair. I shall do all as vat shall make
agréable. Dat is my vay.

SCENE VIII.

Re-enter LUCY *hastily.*

Lucy. (*Aside to her mistress.*) Oh, madam, don't be
terrified, but I declare I have spilled almost all the
water!

Mar. (*Alarmed.*) What is the matter?

Lucy. He is come!

Mar. Who? Sir George?

Lucy. No : don't be frightened : Mr Delaval, from abroad.

Mar. My brother ! Heavens ! Did he see you ?

Lucy. No.   I had a glimpse of him, and whisked away just as he stepped out of the post-chaise.

Mar. Should he meet me in this disguise, what will he say ?

Lucy. Send away the doctor, and let us lock ourselves up.

Mar. (*To the Doctor.*) I must beg you will excuse me, sir, but it is necessary at present I should be alone.   With your permission, I will see you again in the afternoon, and, in the mean time——(*Gives money.*)

Doc. Oh, sair ! I vas your mosh oblishe fery omple sairfant, sair.   I shall make you mosh more fisit, und den you shall tell me de diagnostic und de prognostic of all vat you vill ail.

Lucy. Yes, yes, another time.

Doc. Und I shall af de essence, und de cream, und de balsam, und de syrup, und de electric, und de magnetic, und de mineral, und de vegetable, und de air, und de earse, und de sea, und all dat vas subject under my command.

Lucy. You have told us all that before.

Doc. Und I shall make you prescripe for de anodyne, oder de epipastic, oder de balsamic, oder de soporific, oder de narcotic, oder de diaphoretic, oder de expectoratic, oder de restoratif, oder de emulsif, oder de incisif, vhich is efery ting so shveet und delectable as all vat is possible.

Lucy. (*Aside.*) Was ever any thing so provoking ? —Pray, sir, make haste.

Doc. You shall make remembrance of Dr Von Gostermans.   I am practice mit all de piggest family in de uniferse.   Sair, I vas your mosh oblishe fery omple sairfant, sair. (*The Doctor goes off talking, and* LUCY *locks the door while the scene changes.*)

SCENE IX.

The Hall of the Hotel.

DELAVAL, WILLIAMS, *Master, and* JENKINS.

Del. Is the portmanteau safe?

Wil. Yes, sir.

Del. And the trunks?

Wil. All right.

Del. Have you paid the postillions?

Wil. Yes, sir.

Ma. (*To* DELAVAL.) This way if you please, sir. Jenkins!

Jen. Coming, sir.

Ma. Shew the damask room. What will you please to have for breakfast, sir?

Del. Nothing.

Ma. Sir!

Del. Any thing.

Ma. Bring tea, coffee, and new-laid eggs.

Jen. In a minute, sir.

Del. (*To* WIL.) Observe the directions I gave you. Inquire immediately, and find if the Vibrate family be in town.

Wil. I will be careful, sir.—Hay?—(*To* DEL. *going.*)—Sir! Sir!

Del. Well?

Wil. Look! Here comes Lord Vibrate's secretary!

SCENE X.

Enter THOMPSON.

Del. (*To* THOMPSON.) Mr Thompson!

Thom. Ah! Mr Delaval? I am heartily glad to see you in England!

Del. Thank you, my good friend. But how is this? Where is the family? Where is Lady Jane?

Thom. I thought that would be your question! They are all in this house.

Del. Indeed!

Thom. I knew, when Lady Jane left Italy, your stay there would be short.

Del. Ay, ay! The follies and frenzies of the madman are visible to all eyes, except his own.

Thom. I see you are dissatisfied.

Del. Tortured, till my thoughts and temper are so changed, that I am almost as odious to myself as the world is become hateful to me.

Thom. I own, you have some cause.

Del. Would *my* injuries were all! But there are other and still deeper stabs. It is not yet ten months since I returned from India; my heart how light, my eye how cheerful, and my hand prompt at any commendable act. I could then be moved to joy and sorrow, and every sympathising passion. Smiles and mock courtesy passed current on me, the word of man and woman was taken on trust, and I lived in the sunshine of an open unsuspecting soul. But I am now otherwise taught. I am changed. My better part is brutalized; and the wrongs that lie rankling here have stripped me of human affections, and made me almost savage.

Thom. What can be said? Patience is the—

Del. Talk not of patience: I must act. I may then perhaps inquire whether I have acted rightly. But I must first see Lady Jane and Lord Vibrate.

Thom. Shall I inform his lordship of your arrival?

Del. By no means. Having injured, he may wish not to see me; and I would not afford him time to invent excuses, and avoid giving me a hearing. Though my wrongs must be endured, they shall yet be told.

Thom. I own, they are great.

Del. Those that you know are heavy; yet, severe as the struggle would be, 'tis possible they might be hushed to rest: but there are others which blood only can obliterate, which can only sleep in death! Such is the road I must travel. Not long since nature was jocund, the azure heavens were bright, and pleasure was in every path; but now darkness, fathomless gulphs, guilty terrors, and all the dreadful phantoms of meditated desolation, lie before me.   [*Exeunt.*

ACT THE SECOND.

SCENE I.

LORD VIBRATE *at a Table with a Quarto Volume reading.*

L. Vib. The ancient sceptics doubted of every thing, affirmed nothing, and kept the judgment al-

ways in suspense. All things, said they, are equally
indifferent, uncertain, and indeterminate. The mind
is never to assent to any thing, that it may never be
astonished or disturbed, but enjoy a perfect calm.
(*Rises with important wisdom in his looks.*) Such were
the maxims of Pyrrho and his disciples, those renowned sages of antiquity! Well! And such too have
been my maxims practically. All my life have I been
wavering, uncertain, and indeterminate! A sagacious
sceptic without knowing it, and as it were by instinct!
It was but lately I discovered what a wise man I am!
And yet it seems to me as if I were scarcely half wise
enough, for I am told that I am to doubt of every
thing which I find rather difficult. For example : that
my wife, Lady Vibrate, is an extravagant rackety
rantipole woman of fashion, can I doubt that? No.
That she squanders my money, disturbs my peace,
and contradicts for contradiction's sake, can I doubt
that? No. Then have I not a daughter to marry, a
law-suit to begin, and a thousand perplexing affairs,
so that I do not know which way to turn? Why, all
this appears true to me; but the sceptics teach that
appearances deceive, and that nothing is certain. I
may be Lord Vibrate, or I may be the Grand Turk.
These doctrines are prodigiously deep. (*Considers.*)
But I must think of something else just now. I have
a thousand things to do, and know as little where to
begin as where they will end. Ay! All is uncertainty! (*Rings.*) Harry! Edward!

SCENE II.

Enter JENKINS.

Jen. Did your lordship call?

L. Vib. Where are my servants? I want some of my plagues.

Ien. They are ready at hand, my lord. Here is your lordship's secretary.

SCENE III.

Enter MR THOMPSON, *and exit* JENKINS.

L. Vib. What is the reason, Mr Thompson, that nobody waits? Here am I, fretting myself to a mummy for the good of my family, while every body about me is as drowsy as the court of common council after dinner! Have they taken laudanum? Are they in a lethargy? Are they all dead?

Thom. If they were, your lordship would have the goodness to raise them.

L. Vib. Don't you know how many people I have to see, and places I have to go to?

Thom. No, my lord.

L. Vib. Why, did not I tell you?

Thom. Yes, my lord.

Lord Vib. Then how can you say you don't know?

Thom. Because I venture to presume, my lord, you do not know yourself.

L. Vib. I am distracted with doubts. Harry!

SCENE IV.

Enter Footman.

Har. Did your lordship call?

L. Vib. Where are you all? What are you about?

I think you have lived long enough with me to know my way.

Har. Yes, my lord: we know it very well.

L. Vib. If you are not more attentive, I'll discharge you every one.

Har. Oh no ; (*Half aside ;*) you will not do that.

L. Vib. What are you muttering, sirrah ?

Har. Only, my lord, that we know your way.

L. Vib. Order the coach at eleven.

Har. Yes, my lord.

L. Vib. No; order it at one.

Har. Yes, my lord.

L. Vib. Come back. Order it in ten minutes: and remember I am not at home. Come back. Don't order it at all.

Har. Must visitors be admitted ?

L. Vib. Yes—no—I cannot tell—I will consider. Be within call. Thompson !   [*Exit Footman.*

Thom. My lord.

L. Vib. Step to that picture-dealer. I will have the Guido. Yet—'tis a great sum. No—It is a master-piece ; I must have it. Why don't you go ?

Thom. The picture is sold, my lord.

L. Vib. Sold !—gone ! Have I lost it ? This is always the way ! I am for ever disappointed. Harry !

Re-enter Footman.

Har. My lord.

L. Vib. Did you go with the message to the stable-keeper, last night ?

Har. Yes, my lord.

L. Vib. Let me know when he comes.

Har. He will come no more, my lord.

L. Vib. Come no more !

Har. No, my lord.

L. Vib. Why so ?

Har. He says you never know your own mind, my lord.

L. Vib. Insolent fellow!

Har. Dr Gosterman is below.

L. Vib. Admit him. Stay; I cannot see him yet. In half an hour—in ten minutes—by and by.

[Exit Footman.

SCENE V.

L. Vib. I must not waste any time in these trifles. I must attend to this law business. I wish I could determine. What am I to do, Thompson?

Thom. In what, my lord?

L. Vib. The affair of the ejectment. If I once embroil myself in law, there will be no end; and if I do not, the consequences are still worse.

Thom. Then they are bad indeed, my lord.

L. Vib. 'Tis strange that I can come to no resolution on this subject.

Thom. (*Aside.*) Nor on any other.

L. Vib. I must decide this very day, or the time will be elapsed.

Thom. A lawyer, I should suppose, my lord, would give you the best advice.

L. Vib. How! Are you mad, Thompson? A lawyer give good advice!

Thom. The present possessor has held the estate twenty years.

L. Vib. Not till to-morrow. I have time still to make my claim. How shall I act? Shall I never leave this hotel?——Has the builder been here?

Thom. No, my lord.

L. Vib. I can get nothing done. My whole life long I have been distracted with the multiplicity of my affairs.

Thom. And so am I afraid, my lord, you always will be.

L. Vib. Why so, sir?

Thom. Because your lordship undertakes so much, and does so little.

L. Vib. So he has not been here?

Thom. No, my lord.

L. Vib. Nor the lawyers?

Thom. No, my lord.

L. Vib. Nor my steward?

Thom. No, my lord.

L. Vib. Nor Sir George?

Thom. No, my lord.

L. Vib. Where is Lady Vibrate? Where is Lady Jane? Are they all in their graves? Have none of them shewn signs of life yet?

Thom. Not one. Your lordship is the only person in the family who begin your miseries so soon in a morning.

L. Vib. The crosses and cares that prey upon me are enough to make any man on earth miserable.

Thom. Pardon me, my lord, but if you would care less, both yourself and your servants would sleep the more. My lady cares for nothing; and she can sleep when she is in bed, and sing, and dance, and laugh at your lordship's cares and fears when she is up.

L. Vib. She will drive me mad!

Thom. (*Going.*) Ah, here she is, as it were for the purpose.

L. Vib. Tell Harry to admit the doctor. No— not just yet—yes—in five minutes—I don't know when.   [*Exit* THOMPSON.

SCENE VI.

Enter LADY VIBRATE.

Lady Vib. Upon my honour, my lord, you are the

most insupportable person imaginable. You vocife-
rate worse than the man who calls when my carriage
stops the way. Is any body dying? Is the house
on fire? Is the world at an end?

L. Vib. By the life your ladyship leads, I should
suppose it is pretty near.

Lady Vib. You always give me such shocking
head-aches of a morning.

L. Vib. You always give me such shocking heart-
aches of an evening.

Lady Vib. Did not I send to you last night, to request your lordship would not disturb me?

L. Vib. It has been your ladyship's amusement to
disturb me all your life.

Lady Vib. Your lordship knows I love amusement.

L. Vib. I have not slept a wink since.

Lady Vib. You had slept quite enough before.
Pray how long are we to remain in this hotel? Your
lordship should remember it is degrading for a man
of rank to doze away life in the style of a colonel reduced to half-pay.

L. Vib. Your ladyship should remember, it is degrading for a woman of rank to riot away life, and
reduce her creditors to live without pay.

Lady Vib. Pshaw! that is the old story.

L. Vib. But it is a very true story. It is a great
misfortune that persons so opposite should pair.

Lady Vib. A terrible one indeed. I am all gaiety
and good humour: you are all turmoil and lamenta-
tion. I sing, laugh, and welcome pleasure wherever
I find it: you take your lantern to look for misery,
which the sun itself cannot discover.

L. Vib. I am overwhelmed by crosses and vexa-
tions; and you participate in none of them.

Lady Vib. No; Heaven be praised!

L. Vib. Will you attend to me, my lady, for half
an hour?

Lady Vib. Mercy! attend to you for half an hour! You, my lord, may think proper to be as miserable as Job: but I am not Job's wife.

L. Vib. I insist, Lady Vibrate, on a serious answer. How ought I to act? What should I do, in this law affair?

Lady Vib. I cannot tell what you ought to do; but I know what you will do.

L. Vib. Do you?—What?

Lady Vib. Nothing.

L. Vib. The recovery of this property would enable me to give my daughter a portion suitable to her rank. If it is lost, she will be almost destitute of fortune.

Lady Vib. You should have thought of that before, my lord.

L. Vib. Before!——Why, I have thought of nothing else for years.——I have asked every body's advice.

Lady Vib. And followed nobody's.

L. Vib. It shall be so. The ejectment shall be served: proceedings shall commence.

Lady Vib. Ha, ha, ha!

L. Vib. I say they shall.—I am determined.

Lady Vib. Ha, ha, ha! I know you, my lord.

L. Vib. You know! I say they shall, if it be only to prove that you know nothing of the matter.

Lady Vib. Ha, ha, ha! A pleasant motive: but even that will not be strong enough.

L. Vib. But it will, my lady.

Lady Vib. But it won't, my lord.

SCENE VII.

Enter Doctor.

L. Vib. I say it will, my lady.

Lady Vib. I say it won't, my lord.

Doc. Coot morgen, to my coot lordt und my coot laty.

L. Vib. For Heaven's sake, doctor, stop my lady's tongue.

Lady Vib. For Heaven's sake, doctor, give my lord a quieting draught.

Doc. I shall do efery ting as vat you desire, my coot lordt und my coot laty.

L. Vib. Can nothing silence you, Lady Vibrate? Shall I never have a quiet hearing? I want to talk with you and the doctor on a thousand things.

Lady Vib. Yes; you wish to have all the talk to yourself.

L. Vib. On the marriage of our daughter.

Lady Vib. Oh, with all my heart. A marriage at least begins with music, feasting, and dancing. So say on.

L. Vib. I am not yet determined in favour of Sir George.

Lady Vib. But I am.—(*While they speak, the Doctor gesticulates in favour of each.*)

L. Vib. Mr Delaval is an unobjectionable gentleman; and he was the first suitor.

Lady Vib. Sir George can sing; Sir George can dance; Sir George has air, grace, fashion, and fortune.

L. Vib. Pshaw!—His best qualities are prudence, and attention to his own concerns. Ask the doctor.

Doc. He has fery mosh prudence, my coot lordt.

Lady Vib. Ha, ha, ha! I vow Sir George is the most airy, thoughtless, pleasant person living; except myself.

Doc. Ya; Sair Shorge is fery mosh pleasant; und my latyship is fery mosh more pleasant.

L. Vib. Absurd!—His humour is calm, cold, and serious.

Doc. Fery serious, inteet.

Lady Vib. Whimsical, animated, delightful.

Doc. Fery animate, fery telightful, upon my vordt.

L. Vib. I never met a more disc:eet, sensible man in my life.

Lady Vib. True; for he thinks of nothing but his pleasures.

L. Vib. His affairs, you mean.

Lady Vib. I tell you, my lord, he is exactly what I wish: the very soul of levity, whim, and laughter.

L. Vib. I tell you, my lady, he is exactly like myself: prudent, and full of sage hesitation. He considers before he acts. Does he not, doctor?

Doc. Dat vas all yust as vat you say, my coot lordt.

Lady Vib. He never considers at all. Does he, doctor?

Doc. Dat vas all yust as vat you say, my coot laty.

L. Vib. How so? We cannot both be right.

Doc. You shall please to make me parton, my coot lordt. Sair Shorge vas all as vat you say, und all as vat my coot laty say. Mit my laty, he vas merry; mit my lordt, he vas sad. Mit my laty, he vas laugh, und vas sing, und vas tance; und he vas make melancholy, und misery, und vas do all dat shall make agréable mit my lordt.

L. Vib. Is he so variable?

Doc. Ya, he vas fery mosh comply; fery mosh coot humeur. He vas alvay make agréable. Bote vas my lordtship und my latyship know dat Mr Delafal vas com from Italy?

Lady Vib. Come where?—To England?

Doc. He vas in the house below. I vas see und speak mit his falet.

L. Vib. In this hotel?

Doc. He vas yust arrife, und vas demandt dat he shall see my lordtship, oder my latyship.

Lady Vib. I am very sorry he is here. He is a

dun of the most disagreeable kind, and shall not see
me; and I hope, my lord, you will no longer permit
his addresses to Lady Jane.   My word is given to
Sir George.   Come with me, doctor.

          [*Exeunt* LADY VIBRATE *and Doctor.*

SCENE VIII.

Enter MR DELAVAL.

Del. Pardon me, my lord, if I intrude with too
little ceremony.   Something, I hope, will be allowed
to a mind much disturbed, and a heart deeply wounded, and impatient to ease its pangs.

L. Vib. Which way deeply wounded, Mr Delaval?

Del. Can your lordship ask?   Was it not with
your permission I paid my addresses to Lady Jane?
And was the ardour of my affection, or the extent of
my hopes unknown?

L. Vib. Why, I did permit, and I did not.—I had
my doubts.

Del. My visits were daily, their purpose was declared; and I should imagine I spoke more respectfully to say that you permitted, than that you con-
nived at them.

L. Vib. True; but still I had my doubts.

Del. Those doubts have stung me to the soul;
and I could wish you had expressed them more de-
cidedly.

L. Vib. Impossible!   Doubts here, doubts there,
doubts every where.   No rational man can be decided, on any point whatever.   My doubts are my
continual plagues; my whole life is consumed by
them.

Del. It appears, my lord, you have conquered them on one subject.

L. Vib. Ay, indeed! I wish to Heaven I had! What subject is that?

Del. You have affianced your daughter to Sir George Versatile.

L. Vib. Humph!—Yes, and no. I have, and I have not. I cannot determine. Sir George is a prudent man; his estate is large; and the Versatiles are an ancient race. But your family is ancient; you are prudent; and the wealth left by your uncle is at least equal. What can I say? What can I do? I don't know which to take, nor which to refuse. I am everlastingly in these difficulties. I am harassed night and day by them: they are the night-mare; they sit upon my bosom, oppress me, suffocate me. I cannot act—I cannot move.

Del. This, my lord, may be an apology to yourself, but the consequence to me is misery. Your daughter lived in my heart: with her I had promised myself ages of happiness; and had cherished a passion, impatient, perhaps, but ardent and pure as her own thoughts. This passion your conduct authorized. My fortune, my life, my soul, were devoted to her. Mine was no light or wanton dalliance; nor did I expect a light and wanton conduct from the noble family of which your lordship is the head.

L. Vib. What do you mean, Mr Delaval? I told you I was undecided; and so I am still. My lady, you know, was never much your friend. Sir George is her favourite. And is Lady Jane equally changeable?

Del. And is Lady Jane equally changeable?

L. Vib. I don't know. She is *my* daughter; and, judging by myself, I should suppose she is perplexed and doubtful. She never, I believe, declared in your favour?

Del. Not expressly, my lord: she referred me to time and you. 'Tis true, I flattered myself her af-

fections were wholly mine. Should she prefer Sir
George, or any other man, be my feelings what they
will, I then am silenced. My heart could not be
satisfied with cold compliance.—Oh no! 'tis of a
different stamp. I am told she is not at home. I
hope, however, she will not have the cruelty to deny
me a last interview; till when I take my leave. Only
suffer me to remark that, had you discovered in me
any secret vice, any defects dangerous to the happiness of the woman I adore, you then were justified
in your present conduct. But, if you have no such
accusation to prefer, I must do my feelings the
violence to declare, I cannot but think it highly unworthy of a man of honour. [*Exit.*

SCENE IX.

L. Vib. Mr Delaval!—Insolent! Highly unworthy of a man of honour! I will challenge him. He
shall find whether I am a man of honour or no. I
will challenge him. Harry!

SCENE X.

Enter Footman.

Har. My lord.

L. Vib. Run—tell that Mr Delaval——Hold—
Yes, fly!—tell him——Stay. Get me pen, ink, and
paper. I will teach him to insult——No; I will not
do him the honour to write. Order him back.

Har. Order who, my lord?

L. Vib. He shall give me satisfaction. In that at
least I am determined. He shall give——And yet,

what is satisfaction? Is it to be run through the
body? Shot through the head? A man may then
indeed be said to be satisfied. I had forgotten my
doubts on duelling.—Tell my lady I wish to speak to
her. No——

Har. She is here, my lord.   [*Exit.*

SCENE XI.

Enter LADY VIBRATE *and the Doctor.*

Lady Vib. What is the matter, my lord? You
seem to be even in a worse humour than usual.

L. Vib. Mr Delaval has treated me disrespect-
fully.

Lady Vib. Have not I a thousand times told you
he is a disagreeable, impertinent person?

L. Vib. Why, God forgive me, but I really find
myself of your ladyship's opinion. 'Tis a thing, I
believe, that never happened before.

Lady Vib. And a thing, I believe, that will never
happen again. I hope, my lord, you are now determined in favour of Sir George?

L. Vib. Positively; finally; I pledge my honour.

Lady Vib. You hear, doctor?

Doc. Ya, my coot laty; I vas hear.

L. Vib. I say, I pledge my honour. I authorise
you, my lady, to deliver that message to the baronet;
and that I may not have time to begin to doubt, I
will instantly be gone.   [*Exit.*

SCENE XII.

Lady Vib. This is fortunate.

Doc. Oh, fery mosh fortunate, fery mosh.

Lady Vib. Had Mr Delaval married my daughter, we should have had a continual sermon on reason, common sense, and good order : and these, and such like antediluvian notions must have been introduced to our family.

Doc. Ah, dat shall be pad, fery pad inteet, my coot laty.

Lady Vib. Now that Sir George is the man, the danger is over.

Doc. Dat is creat plessing !

Lady Vib. But what think you are my daughter's thoughts ? I fear she has a kind of esteem for Delaval. He was her first lover.

Doc. Ya ; she vas fery mosh esteem Mr Delafal, my coot laty.

Lady Vib. But I observe she listens with great pleasure to the gay prattle of Sir George.

Doc. Oh, fery creat inteet, my coot laty.

Lady Vib. We must second the rising passion; for we must get rid of that solemn sir.

Doc. Dat vas all yust as vat you say, my coot laty.

Lady Vib. Go to her, doctor ; convince her how intolerable it will be to have a husband whom she cannot quarrel with, nor reproach. Paint in the most lively colours the stupid life she must lead with so reasonable a man.

Doc. I shall do efery ting as vat shall make agré-able, my coot laty. Dat is my vay. My laty, I vas your mosh oblishe fery omple sairfant, my laty.

[*Exeunt.*

ACT THE THIRD.

SCENE I.

The Hall of the Hotel. WILLIAMS *and* HARRY.
LUCY *speaking to the Master of the Hotel.*

Will. All you say is very true, Mr Harry. Our
masters suppose we have neither sense nor feeling,
yet exact every thing that requires the five senses in
perfection. They expect we should know their meaning before they open their lips; yet won't allow we
have common understanding.

Har. More shame for 'em. I warrant, for all that,
we can game, run in debt, get in drink, and be as
proud and domineering as they for their lives.

Will. Yes, yes: let them but change places, and
they would soon find we could rise to their vices,
and they could sink to ours, with all the ease imaginable.

Har. They have no such notion though, Mr Williams.

Will. That is their vanity, Mr Harry. I have
lived with Mr Delaval ever since he returned from
India; and though he is a good—— (*Sees* LUCY.)
Hay!—Surely it must be her! Do you know that
young woman, Mr Harry?

Har. No; but I have heard a strange story about
her.

Will. Ay! It is—what? I am sure it is Lucy!
What strange story have you heard?

Har. Why, that she came here late last night with
a young gentleman, now above, pretending to be his
waiting-maid!

Will. With a gentleman!—(*Aside.*) Oh, the jilt!
Waiting-maid to a man! I never heard of such a
thing!

Har. Nor any body else.

Will. (*Aside.*) The deceitful hussy!

Har. (*Hears a bell.*) That's my lord's bell. I told
you he is never easy. I must go.

Will. (*Aside.*) I am glad of it. By all means,
Mr Harry. Good day.   [*Exit* HARRY.

SCENE II.

Will. Run away with a gentleman! Oh!

Lucy. (*Coming forward.*) I declare there is Mr
Williams.

Will. (*Aside.*) What a fool was I to believe she
loved me!

Lucy. (*Aside.*) How my heart beats! Dear, dear!
I could wish to speak to him—but then if any harm
should come of it?

Will. (*Aside.*) She shall not escape me.

Lucy. (*Aside.*) I should like to ask him how he
does.—But I must not betray my dear lady. (*Going.*)

Will. (*Placing himself in her way.*) I beg pardon,
ma'am.

Lucy. (*Aside.*) Does not he know me?

Will. I thought I had seen you before; but I find
I am mistaken.

Lucy. (*Aside.*) What does he mean?

Will. You are very like a young woman I once knew.

Lucy. (*Aside.*) How angry he looks!

Will. But she was a modest, pretty-behaved person, and not an arrant jilt.

Lucy. Who is a jilt, Mr Williams?

Will. One Lucy Langford, that I courted and promised to marry: but I know better now.

Lucy. You do, Mr Williams?

Will. I do, madam.

Lucy. It is very well, Mr Williams!—it is very well! Pray let me go about my business.

Will. Oh, to be sure! I have no right to stop you.

Lucy. You have no right to speak to me as you do, Mr Williams.

Will. No, no; ha, ha, ha! I dare say I have not.

Lucy. (*Her passions rising.*) No, you have not; and so I beg you will let me pass. My mistress—I mean——

Will. Ay, ay! You mean your master!

Lucy. Do I, sir? Well, since you please to think so, so be it.

Will. All the servants know it is a man! Would you deny it?

Lucy. I deny nothing, Mr Williams; and if you are minded to make this an excuse for being as treacherous as the rest of your sex, (*Keeping down her sobs,*) you are very welcome, Mr Williams.—I shall neither die—nor cry, at parting.

Will. I dare say not. The young gentleman above stairs will comfort you.

Lucy. (*Bursts into tears.*) It is a base false story. I have no young gentleman above stairs, nor below stairs neither, to comfort me!—and you ought to know me better.

Will. Did you, or did you not, come here late last night?

Lucy. What of that?

Will. With a young gentleman?

Lucy. No—yes. Don't ask me such questions.

Will. No!—You are ashamed to answer them.

SCENE III.

MARIA, *from the staircase.*

Mar. (*Calls.*) Lucy!

Lucy. Ma'am—sir—coming, sir.

Will. There!—there! I will see what sort of a spark it is, however.

Lucy. (*Struggling.*) Be quiet, then! Keep away! You sha'n't!

Mar. (*Descending.*) What is the matter? Who is molesting you?

Lucy. (*To* MARIA.) Go back, sir!—go back!

Will. I will see; I am determined.

SCENE IV.

DELAVAL, *from a room door.*

Del. Williams!

Will. I tell you I will. (*Looking at* MARIA.) Hay! Bless me!

Mar. Why, Lucy!—Mr Williams!

Will. My young lady, as I live!

Del. Why do not you answer, Williams?

Will. Coming, sir.

Mar. Mercy! it is my brother's voice! What shall I do?

Lucy. Hide your face with your handkerchief, ma'am. Pull down your hat.

Mar. Pray do not betray me, Mr Williams.

Lucy. If you do, I will never speak to you as long as I have breath to draw.

Will. How betray?

Lucy. Don't say you know us. Mind! Not for the world.

[*Exeunt* MARIA *and* LUCY *up the staircase.*

SCENE V.

Del. What is it you are about, Williams?

Will. Nothing, sir.

Del. What do you mean by nothing? Whom were you wrangling with?

Will. Me, sir? Wrangling, sir?

Del. Why are you so confused?

Will. Why, sir, I—I committed a small mistake. I was asking—asking after a gentleman that—that—that proved not to be a gentleman; that is, not—not *the* gentleman that I supposed.

Del. Why did you not come back with your message? Have you learnt the address of Sir George?

Will. Yes, sir: he lives in Upper Grosvenor Street; his name on the door.

Del. Well, be in the way. The day shall not pass before I see him. My own wrongs I could forgive. He it seems is preferred; and perhaps I have no right to complain: but for his injuries to my sister he shall render me a dear account.   [*Exit.*

Will. What can be the reason of Miss Delaval's disguise?

Lucy. *(Peeping from the top of the stairs.)* Hst! hst! Mr Williams!

Will. Is it you?   Oh! now I shall know.

[*Exit up the staircase.*

SCENE VI.

LADY VIBRATE *and* LADY JANE.

Lady Vib. Really, daughter, I cannot understand you.

L. Jane. No wonder, madam; for I do not half understand myself.

Lady Vib. Is it possible you can hesitate?   The good humour and complaisance of Sir George might captivate any woman.

L. Jane. They are very engaging; but they are dangerous.

Lady Vib. Which way?

L. Jane. His character is too pliant. If others are merry, so is he: if they are sad, he is the same. Their joys and sorrows play upon his countenance; but though they may slightly graze, they do not penetrate his heart. Even while he relieves, he scarcely feels them.

Lady Vib. Pshaw! He is a delightful man.

L. Jane. I grant he does his utmost.   But it is a folly to be the slave even of an endeavour to please.

Lady Vib. Ha, ha, ha! Upon my honour, you are a whimsical young lady!   Afraid of marrying a man because of his assiduous endeavours to please!   As if that were a husband's failing!   You can prefer no such accusation against Mr Delaval.

L. Jane. I own he is of a very different character.

Firm and inflexible, he imagines he makes virtue his rule, and reason his guide.

Lady Vib. Firm indeed! No, no: ferocious, obstinate, perverse. Sir George tries to be agreeable, and is successful: Mr Delaval has no fear of offending, and does not miss his aim.

L. Jane. Heaven help us We all have faults and follies enough.

Lady Vib. Mr Delaval never was approved by me; and this morning he has insulted your father.

L. Jane. Insulted! How do you mean, madam? Mr Delaval is abroad. Has he written?

Lady Vib. No. He is here.

L. Jane. Here! And has he not thought proper to let me know of his arrival?

Lady Vib. No, no. The haughty gentleman has only thought proper to reproach Lord Vibrate for admitting the pretensions of Sir George. He is too proud to endure a competitor.

L. Jane. Indeed! Such pride is the very way to insure his competitor success. Insulted my father!

Lady Vib. I will leave you to judge how deeply, when I tell you that, fluctuating and undecided as Lord Vibrate always is, he was so offended, that he pledged his honour in favour of Sir George.

L. Jane. Insult my father, and not deign to let me know of his arrival!

Lady Vib. I hope, when Sir George comes, you will admit him.

L. Jane. Certainly, madam, certainly.

Lady Vib. And that Mr Delaval will be denied.

L. Jane. It seems I need give myself no concern about that: the gentleman will not even take the trouble to send up his name.

Lady Vib. I am glad you feel it properly.

L. Jane. Pardon me, madam; I will not condescend to feel it in the least. It shall not affect me; no, not for a moment. I had indeed conceived a

very different opinion of Mr Delaval.   I am glad I
have discovered my error, before it was too late.   I
could not have believed it possible!   But it shall not
disturb me.   It shall give me no uneasiness.   I will
keep myself perfectly cool and unconcerned, and—
ungenerous, unfeeling man!   [*Exit.*

SCENE VII.

Lady Vib. She is delightfully piqued, and Sir
George will succeed!

Sir Geo. (*Without.*) Are the ladies above?

Foot. (*Without.*) Yes, sir.

Lady Vib. I hear him! The very sound of his
voice inspires mirth.

Enter SIR GEORGE.

Sir Geo. Ah, my dear lady!

Lady Vib. I am infinitely glad to see you, Sir
George.   You are come at a lucky moment.

Sir Geo. Is then my fate decided?

Lady Vib. It is!—it is!

Sir Geo. Happy tidings!

Lady Vib. But first tell me——

Sir Geo. Any thing!—every thing!   Speak!

Lady Vib. Are you not of my opinion?

Sir Geo. To be sure I am!   What is it?

Lady Vib. That pleasure is the business of life.

Sir Geo. Oh, beyond all doubt!

Lady Vib. That inspecting accounts——

Sir Geo. Is vulgar drudgery!

Lady Vib. And looking after our affairs——

Sir Geo. A vile loss of time!

Lady Vib. That care in the face denotes——

Sir Geo. The owner a fool!!

Lady Vib. And that sorrow is a very ridiculous thing!

Sir Geo. Fit only to excite laughter!

Lady Vib. Why then, Sir George, I am your friend.

Sir Geo. Ten thousand thousand thanks! But what says my lord?

Lady Vib. Would you believe it? He consents, has pledged his honour, and sent the message by me.

Sir Geo. Rapture! Enchantment!

Lady Vib. Yes; the reign of pleasure is about to begin!

Sir Geo. Light, free, and fantastic; dancing an eternal round!

Lady Vib. No domestic troubles!

Sir Geo. No grave looks!

Lady Vib. No serious thoughts!

Sir Geo. We will never think at all!

Lady Vib. No cares, no frowns!

Sir Geo. None, none; by Heavens, none! It shall be spring and sunshine all the year!

Lady Vib. Then our appearance in public!

Sir Geo. Splendid! Dazzling!—Driving to the opera!

Lady Vib. Dressing for Ranelagh!

Sir Geo. A phaeton to-day!

Lady Vib. A curricle to-morrow!

Sir Geo. Dash over the downs of Piccadilly, descend the heights of St James's, make the tour of Pall Mall, coast Whitehall——

Lady Vib. Back again to Bond Street——

Sir Geo. Scour the squares, thunder at the doors!

Lady Vib. How do you do? How do you do? How do you do?

Sir Geo. And away we rattle, till stone walls are but gliding shadows, and the whole world a galanty show.

Lady Vib. You are a charming man, Sir George! and Lady Jane is yours.

Sir Geo. My dear lady, your words inspire me! I am all air, spirit, soul! I tread the milky way, and step upon the stars!

Lady Vib. But you must not, before the marriage, talk thus to Lord Vibrate. Silly man! He and you will never agree.

Sir Geo. Oh yes, but we shall. I—I—I like his humour.

Lady Vib. Do you?

Sir Geo. Prodigiously! Whenever I am in his company, I am as grave as Good Friday.

Lady Vib. Indeed!

Sir Geo. He is full of sage reflection. So am I. Doubtful of every thing. So am I. Anxious for the present, provident for the future. So am I. Overflowing with prudential maxims; sententious, sentimental, and solemn. So am I.

Lady Vib. You sentimental!

Sir Geo. As grace before meat in the mouth of an alderman.

Lady Vib. You solemn!

Sir Geo. As the black patch on a judge's wig.

Lady Vib. I must tell you, Sir George, I hate sentiment.

Sir Geo. Oh! So do I!

Lady Vib. Solemnity is all a farce.

Sir Geo. And those that act it buffoons. I know it!

Lady Vib. I love mirth, pleasantry——

Sir Geo. Humour, whim, wit, feasting, revelry, shout, song, dance, and joke. So do I!—so do I!—so do I!

Lady Vib. The very mention of duties and cares makes me splenetic.

Sir Geo. Curse catch duties! I hate them! Give

me life, the wide world, the fair sun, and the free
air !

Lady Vib. I say, give me midnight, the rattling of
chariot wheels, and the lighted flambeau !

Sir Geo. Ay ! A rout ! A crash of coaches ! A lane
of footmen ! A blazing staircase ! A squeeze through
the anti-chamber ! Card tables ! Wax lights ! Patent
lamps ! Bath stoves and suffocation ! Oh Lord ! Oh
Lord !

Lady Vib. Exquisite ! You are a delightful man !

Sir Geo. Am I ?

Lady Vib. You enter perfectly into all my ideas.

Sir Geo. Do I ?

Lady Vib. And describe them even better than I
myself can.

Sir Geo. Oh, my dear lady !

Lady Vib. Yes, you do.

Sir Geo. No, no.

Lady Vib. But then, ha, ha, ha ! that you should
be able to fall in with my lord's absurdities so readily !

Sir Geo. Nothing more easy. I have one infallible
rule to please all tempers. I learnt it of our friend
the doctor.

Lady Vib. Sure ! What is that ?

Sir Geo. I prove that every body is always in the
right.

Lady Vib. Prove my husband to be in the right !
Do, if you can.

Sir Geo. My lord loves to be restless, and doubtful, and distressed : he delights in teasing and tormenting himself ; and why should I interrupt his
pleasures ?

Lady Vib. Ha, ha, ha ! Very true.

Sir Geo. I fall in with his humour.—I shew him
how rational it is, afford him new arguments for discontent, and encourage him to be miserable.

Lady Vib. Ha, ha, ha ! Oh, you malicious devil !

Sir Geo. My dear lady, you mistake. I do it from pure compassion. It makes him happy. Every child delights in the squeaking of its own trumpet; and shall I have the cruelty to break the toy? A well-bred person is cautious never to contradict. It is become a very essential requisite to say ay and no, in the most complying manner possible.

Lady Vib. Ah, Sir George, you are one of the dear inimitable few.

Sir Geo. Only a copy of your charming self.

Lady Vib. You and I must totally reform our stupid family. Amusement shall be our perpetual occupation.

Sir Geo. Day and night.

Lady Vib. We will commence with your marriage. It shall be splendid!

Sir Geo. A feast, a concert, a ball! The whole town shall ring with it!

Lady Vib. I hate a private wedding. A small select party is my aversion.

Sir Geo. Oh, nothing is so insipid! Pleasure cannot be calm.

Lady Vib. I wish to be seen, and heard——

Sir Geo. And talked of, and paragraphed, and praised, and blamed, and admired, and envied, and laughed at, and imitated!

Lady Vib. I live but in a crowd.

Sir Geo. Give me hurry, noise, embarrassment—

Lady Vib. Confusion, disorder——

Sir Geo. Tumult, tempest, uproar, elbowing, squeezing, pressing, pushing, squeaking, squalling, fainting!

Lady Vib. Exquisite! Transporting!

Sir Geo. You remember I receive masks this evening?

Lady Vib. Can I forget?

Sir Geo. You will be there?

Lady Vib. There? Ay! Though I should come in my coffin.

Sir Geo. Ha, ha, ha! An excellent idea! I never yet saw a mask in the character of a *memento mori.*

Lady Vib. Ah! Turn about, and you will see a *memento mori* without a mask!

Sir Geo. What, my lord?

L. Vib. (*Without.*) I cannot tell. I will consider, and send an answer.

Lady Vib. Here he comes, to interrupt our delightful dreams: a very antidote to mirth and pleasure. He will give you a full dose of the dismals. But you must stay and speak to him. Remember, his honour is pledged : insist upon that. I pity, but cannot relieve you.   [*Exit.*

SCENE VIII.

Enter LORD VIBRATE.

L. Vib. I have been too sudden. I ought not to have pledged my honour. This is the consequence of hasty determination : of not doubting before we decide. Shall I never correct myself of that fault ? (*Sees* SIR GEORGE. *They look full at each other, till* SIR GEORGE *catches the same dismal kind of countenance.*) Ah, Sir George ! Here am I, brimful of anxiety and turmoil !

Sir Geo. Alas! man was born to trouble.

L. Vib. Perplexed on every side ; thwarted in every plan : no domestic comfort, no friend to grieve with me, no creature to share my miseries.

Sir Geo. Melancholy case !

L. Vib. One crossing me, another blaming me, and my wife driving me mad!

Sir Geo. Distressing situation!

L. Vib. My cares laughed at, my vigilance mocked, my sufferings insulted! And why? Because I am cautious! because I doubt! because I am provident! What is man without money?

Sir Geo. A fountain without water.

L. Vib. A clock without a dial.

Sir Geo. (*Warming, and becoming rapid as he proceeds.*) What is it that buys respect, and honour, and power, and privilege, and houses, and lands, and wit, and beauty, and learning, and lords, and commons, and—

L. Vib. Why, money!—Then the manners of this dissipated age!

Sir Geo. They are truly shocking! They, they, they are absurd, ridiculous, odious, abominable.

L. Vib. And to what do they lead?

Sir Geo. To every thing that is horrid! To loss of peace, loss of property, loss of principle, loss of respect, bankruptcy, ruin, contempt, disease, and death!

L. Vib. (*Aside.*) Yes, yes: he's the man! I do not think I repent——Heaven be praised, Sir George, you are a man of understanding; an economist. You will regulate your family and affairs to my heart's content.

Sir Geo. Oh! it shall be my study! my daily practice! my duty! my delight!

L. Vib. You make me happy—and yet I cannot but wonder, being so rational a man, how you and my lady should agree so well.

Sir Geo. Dear, my lord, why so? Women are the most manageable good creatures upon earth.

L. Vib. Women good?

Sir Geo. Indubitably: when they are pleased.

L. Vib. So they say is the devil.

Sir Geo. The sweet angels deserve to be humour-
ed. Their smiles are so enchanting! And should
they frown, who can be angry, when we know the
dear wayward syrens will only look the more bewitching, as soon as they are out of their pouts? It is so
delightful to see the sun breaking from behind a
cloud.

L. Vib. Pshaw! When a woman begins to grow
old—

Sir Geo. Hush! The sun—The sun never grows
old. I grant you that formerly there used to be old
women: but there are none now!

L. Vib. Then you think me a fool for being wretched at my wife's thoughtlessness, caprice, and imper-
tinence?

Sir Geo. No, I don't. Every body tells us that
wives were born to be the plague of their husbands.

L. Vib. And mine is the greatest of plagues!

Sir Geo. What is a wife's duty? To obey her lord
and master. 'Tis her marriage promise, and the law
binds her to it. She is the minister of his pleasures,
the handmaid of his wants, his goods, his chattels, his
vendible property.

L. Vib. Ay: we find the husband may take the
wife to market in a halter.

Sir Geo. In which I should hope he would afterward hang himself!   [*Aside.*

L. Vib. My lady thinks of nothing but revelling,
and racketing, and turning the world upside down!

Sir Geo. 'Tis a great pity.

L. Vib. Her tongue is my torment.

Sir Geo. The perpetual motion! It never ceases!

L. Vib. Then how can you like her company?

Sir Geo. She is not *my* wife.

L. Vib. No, or you would not be such good
friends. Did she say any thing concerning the marriage?

Sir Geo. Oh, yes. She delivered your lordship's kind message.

L. Vib. What, that I had pledged my honour?

Sir Geo. Irrevocably.

L. Vib. I was very rash. Hasty resolutions bring long repentance—She insists that the nuptials shall be public!

Sir Geo. Does she, indeed?

L. Vib. For my part, I hate any display of vanity.

Sir Geo. It is extremely ridiculous! What would our ostentation, pomp, and magnificence be, but advertising ourselves to the world as fools and coxcombs?

L. Vib. Is that a rational use of money?

Sir Geo. Should it not be applied to relieve the aged, comfort the poor, succour the distressed—

L. Vib. What?

Sir Geo. Reward merit, encourage industry, and promote the public good?

L. Vib. Promote a farce!

Sir Geo. Very true : the public good is a farce!

L. Vib. The true use of money is to defend our rights——

Sir Geo. Revenge our wrongs, purchase for the present, provide for the future, secure power, buy friends, bid defiance to enemies, and lead the world in a string!

L. Vib. Ay! Now you talk sense. So, if I should consent, the wedding shall be private.

Sir Geo. Calm : tranquil.

L. Vib. No feasting.

Sir Geo. No dancing: no music: no pantomime pleasures: but all silent, serene, pure, and undisturbed.

L. Vib. We will just invite a select party.

Sir Geo. A chosen few.

L. Vib. None but our real and sincere friends.

Sir Geo. And then we shall be sure the house will hold them.

SCENE IX.

Enter HARRY.

Har. My lord, the builder desires to know if you will see him?

L. Vib. I am coming. I will be with him in five minutes.

Har. He says, he can stay no longer.

L. Vib. Then let him go. I will be with him presently.

Har. The lawyers have sent word they are waiting for your lordship, at Counsellor Demur's chambers.

L. Vib. Very well. There let them wait. The law is slow, and every man ought to be slow who is going to law. Come with me, Sir George. I have some papers to consult you upon.

Har. The trades-people too are below.

L. Vib. Thus it is! I am eternally besieged! I never have a moment to myself!

Har. This is the tenth time they have been here, by your lordship's own appointment.

L. Vib. What of that?

Har. They are become quite surly. They all abuse me; and some of them don't spare your lordship.

L. Vib. Do you hear, Sir George?

Sir Geo. Oh, shocking! Your trades-people are a sad unreasonable set. You cannot convince them that, if we were to keep our appointments, be punc-

7

tual in our payments, and know what we do want and what we do not, we should no longer be persons of fashion.

SCENE X.

Enter THOMPSON.

Thom. I am just come from the lawyers, my lord. The courts are sitting, their clients waiting, and if your lordship do not go immediately, they will be gone.

L. Vib. Very true; and this last opportunity of serving an ejectment will be lost. I have a thousand things to attend to. Would you be kind enough, Sir George, to go and——Hold——No——I don't know what to do! The estate is valuable: but law is damnable. I may lose the cause: it may cost even more than it is worth. Writs of error! Brought into Chancery! Carried up to the lords!

Sir Geo. Then the stupidity of juries, the fictions of law, the chicanery of lawyers, their tricking, twisting, turning, lying, wrangling, brow-beating, cajoling!

L. Vib. Their frauds, collusions, perjuries, robberies!

Sir Geo. Ay! Detinue, replevin, plea, imparlance, replication, rejoinder, rebutter, surrejoinder, surrebutter, demurrer——

L. Vib. Take breath! We ought both to demur; for it is the devil's dance, and both plaintiff and defendant are obliged to pay the piper.   [*Exeunt.*

ACT THE FOURTH.

SCENE I.

The Apartments of LORD VIBRATE.

LADY JANE, *her Woman, the Doctor, and Foot-man.*

L. Jane. (*To Footman.*) Tell the young gentle-man I wait his pleasure. (*Exit Footman.*) It is very singular! Men, I believe, do not often travel attend-ed by waiting-maids!

Doc. Dat is de mystery, my Laty Shane.

L. Jane. What can he want to say to me?

Doc. Dat is de more mystery, my Laty Shane. He vas fery mosh young, und fery mosh handsome, und he vas fery mosh make fall in lofe mit you, my Laty Shane.

L. Jane. Nonsense!

Doc. My Laty Shane vas so full of de beauty dat you vas make sharm efery pody, my Laty Shane! Und as your name vas make mention, my Laty Shane, he vas all so pale as deaths!

L. Jane. (*Aside to her Woman.*) You are sure, you say, Mr Delaval made inquiries; and sent up his name?

Wom. (*To* LADY JANE.) Law, my lady! Could you think he would not? I saw him before ten o'clock; just as you sent me where I was kept so long: and, goodness! had you beheld what a taking he was in!

I warrant you, my lady, he asked a hundred and a
hundred questions in a breath ; and all about you !

L. Jane. Well, go now where I desired you.

Wom. Yes, my lady.   [*Exit.*

SCENE II.

Footman returns, introducing MARIA. *Salute.*

Mar. (*Aside.*) Why do I tremble thus ?

L. Jane. (*To Doctor.*) What a charming countenance !

Doc. Oh ! fery mosh sharming !

L. Jane. How prepossessing his appearance !

Doc. Ya : he vas fery mosh possess.

Re-enter Footman.

Foot. Sir George has sent this domino and mask,
to know if they meet your ladyship's approbation.

L. Jane. Ha, ha, ha ! Italian refinement, copied
after some Venetian Cicisbeo. Put them down.

Mar. (*Aside. Regarding the domino and mask.*)
Here his presents, and here his affections are now
directed ! How shall I support the scene ?

L. Jane. You wish, sir, to speak to me.

Mar. (*Faltering.*) Embarrassed by the—liberty—
I have taken—

L. Jane. Let me request you to waive all apology,
and tell me which way I can oblige or serve you.

Mar. You are acquainted with Sir George—I—
you—Pray pardon me. I am overcome. My spirits
are—so agitated—

L. Jane. (*Eagerly reaching a chair.*) Sit down,
sir. You are unwell ! Bless me ! Doctor !

Doc. (*To* LADY JANE *significantly.*) I vas tell my

Laty Shane vat it vas—Here, sair, you shmell mit dat elixir; und I shall make your neck-bandt tie loose, und— (*Going to loosen her neckcloth.*)

Mar. (*Alarmed, and putting him away.*) Pray forbear!

Doc. (*Aside. Imitating the heaving of the bosom.*) Ah ha! Der Teufel! He vas a vomans!

L. Jane. Are you better?

Mar. A moment's air. (*Goes to the window.*)

Doc. (*Aside.*) Dat vas de someting mystery!

Mar. (*To* LADY JANE.) If you would indulge me a few minutes in private?

L. Jane. By all means.—Doctor—(*Whispers.*)

Doc. Ya, ya, my Laty Shane, I vas unterstandt; und I vas do efery ting as vat shall make agréable. Dat is my vay——Sair, I vas your mosh oblishe fery omple sairfant, sair. I vas unterstandt. My Laty Shane, I vas your mosh oblishe fery omple sairfant, my Laty Shane—(*Aside.*) Ah ha! [*Exit.*

SCENE III.

L. Jane. Take courage, sir.

Mar. I am unequal to the task. This disguise sits ill upon me.

L. Jane. What disguise?

Mar. I am not what I seem. I——

L. Jane. Speak!

Mar. I am a woman.

L. Jane. Heavens!

Mar. Distressed——

L. Jane. By poverty?

Mar. Oh no. I come to claim your counsel.

L. Jane. In what way?

12

Mar. To prevent mischief—the shedding of blood.

L. Jane. The shedding of blood?

Sir Geo. (*Without.*) I will be with you again presently, my lady.

Mar. Mercy! It is Sir George! What shall I do? He must not see me! This way—(*Hurries on the domino and mask.*) Aid me, dear lady, to conceal myself; and excuse conduct which I cannot now explain.

L. Jane. Depend upon me, madam. (*Aside.*) This is as unaccountable as it is alarming!

SCENE IV.

MARIA *in the back ground.* SIR GEORGE *introduced by a Footman.*

Sir Geo. I come, my charming Lady Jane, flying and full of business, to consult you on a thousand important affairs!

L. Jane. Surely! What are they?

Sir Geo. Upon my soul, I don't know!

L. Jane. Hey-day!

Sir Geo. They have every one slipped my memory.

L. Jane. Miraculous!

Sir Geo. Whenever I have the inexpressible pleasure of enjoying your smiles, I can think of nothing else.

Mar. (*Aside.*) Perjured man!

L. Jane. My smiles! Ha, ha, ha! What if I should happen to frown?

Sir Geo. Impossible! No lowering clouds of discontent dare ever shade the heavenly brightness of your brow.

Mar. (*Aside.*) Oh!

L. Jane. Very prettily said, upon my word. Where did you learn it?

Sir Geo. From you! 'Tis pure inspiration, and you are my muse.

L. Jane. No, no; 'tis a flight beyond me. I love plain prose.

Sir Geo. So do I! A mere common-place, matter-of-fact man, I! The weather, the time of day, the history of where I dined last, the names and titles of the company, the dishes brought to table, the health, sickness, deaths, births, and marriages of my acquaintance, and such like tooth-pick topics for me! I am as literal in my narratives as any town-crier; and repeat them as often.

L. Jane. Yet I should wish to talk a little common sense.

Sir Geo. Oh! So should I! I assure you, I am for pros and cons and whys and wherefores. Your Aristotles, and Platos, and Senecas, and Catos are my delight! I honour their precepts, venerate their cogitations, and adore the length of their beards! which luckily reminds me of the masquerade. Is my domino to your taste?

L. Jane. Ha, ha, ha! Ancient sages, dominos, and taste.

Sir Geo. Did you not notice the colour?

L. Jane. Oh! The taste of a domino is in its colour?

Sir Geo. Why, no: but there may be meaning.

L. Jane. Explain.

Sir Geo. Mine is saffron.

L. Jane. What of that?

Sir Geo. Cruel question! Hymen and his robe.

L. Jane. Oh ho!

Mar. (*Aside.*) She is pleased with his perfidy.

L. Jane. A very significant riddle truly!

Mar. (*Advancing.*) Are you so soon to be married, sir?

Sir Geo. Bless me, Lady Jane! What frolicksome gentleman is this? In masquerade so early, and my domino!

Mar. Permit me once more to ask, if you are soon to be married?

Sir Geo. Your question, sir, is improperly addressed. Put it, if you please, to that lady.

Mar. (*Aside to* SIR GEORGE.) Is that the lady to whom the question ought to be put?

Sir Geo. (*Aside.*) What does he mean?—Will you indulge me, sir, by taking off that mask?

Mar. No, sir.

Sir Geo. 'Tis mine; and I am induced to claim it, from the great curiosity I have to see your face.

Mar. Do you not adore this lady?

Sir Geo. (*Aside.*) An odd question!—More than language can express!

Mar. (*Aside.*) Oh, falsehood!—Then I put myself under her protection.

Sir Geo. You know guardian angels when you see them. Pray, however, let us become acquainted.

Mar. For what reason?

Sir Geo. 'Twould gratify me. I should like you.

Mar. Oh, no!

Sir Geo. I certainly should. There is something of pathos and music in your voice, which, which—I never heard but one to equal it.

Mar. And whose voice was that?

Sir Geo. Oh, that—that was a voice so ingenuous, so affectionate, so fascinating!

Mar. But whose voice was it?

L. Jane. (*Aside.*) What does this mean?

Mar. Tell me, and you shall see my face.

L. Jane. (*Aside.*) Astonishing!

Sir Geo. I must not—I dare not—I shall never hear it more!

Mar. (*Aside.*) My feelings so overpower me, I shall betray myself. (*To* LADY JANE.) Permit me to retire.

L. Jane. You have alarmed and strangely moved me! I hope you will return?

Mar. Oh yes; and most happy to have your permission.

Sir Geo. Why do they whisper? (*To* MARIA *going.*) Will you not let me know who you are?

Mar. No.

Sir Geo. Why?

Mar. Because—I am one you do not love. [*Exit.*

Sir Geo. One I do not love!

L. Jane. (*Aside.*) This is incomprehensible!

Re-enter MARIA *hastily.*

Mar. (*To* LADY JANE.) Oh, madam!

L. Jane. What more is the matter?

Mar. For your life, do not mention the names of either of these gentlemen to the other!

L. Jane. What gentlemen?

Mar. He is coming! They do not personally know each other. If they should, there would be murder! I dare not stay. For the love of God, beware!

[*Exit masked, as* DELAVAL *enters.*

SCENE V.

Sir Geo. (*Calling.*) Hark ye, sir, come back! the domino! I shall want it in an hour or so—Who have we here?

Del. (*With much agitation of manner.*) Your ladyship's very humble servant.

L. Jane. Oh! How do you do? How do you do?

(*Aside.*) Who can that lady be? She knows them
both, it seems; and knows their rivalship! Her terror is contagious! Is their hatred so deadly? I shall
certainly betray them to each other.

Del. (*Aside.*) What a strange behaviour she puts
on! Does she affect to overlook me? (*Observing* SIR
GEORGE.) Who is this?

L. Jane. Are you just arrived?

Del. This very morning: sooner I fear than—than
—was desired.

L. Jane. Do you think so? (*To* SIR GEORGE.)
Why don't you go to Lady Vibrate? She is waiting.

Sir Geo. 'Tis the fate of forty.

L. Jane. What?

Sir Geo. To wait.—(*Aside. Eyeing* DELAVAL.)
Who can this spark be, that she wants me gone?—
Pray what is the name of the youth that has made
so free with my domino and mask?

L. Jane. I really don't know.

Sir Geo. Don't know?

L. Jane. I can't answer questions at present. I am
flurried; out of humour.

Del. I fear at my intrusion?

L. Jane. I wish you had come at another time.

Del. I expected my visit would be unwelcome;
let me request, however, to say a few words.

L. Jane. Well, well; another time, I tell you:
when I am alone.

Sir Geo. (*Aside.*) Oh ho!

Del. They were meant for your private ear.

Sir Geo. (*Aside.*) Were they so?

Del. (*Aside.*) By her confusion and his manner, I
suspect this to be the base betrayer of my sister's
peace: the man whose bare image makes my heart
sicken, and my blood recoil.

L. Jane. (*Aside.*) Will they neither of them go?
—Why do you loiter here, Sir Geo—(*Coughs.*)

Sir Geo. I must stay till the gentleman brings
back my domino and mask, you know. (*Aside.*) I'll
not leave them.

Del. (*Aside.*) I am persuaded it is he—Excuse
me, sir; would you indulge me with the favour of
your name?

Sir Geo. My name, sir! My name is—

L. Jane. (*Aside to* SIR GEORGE.) Hush! Don't
tell it!

Sir Geo. (*To* LADY JANE.) Why not?

L. Jane. I insist upon it!

Sir Geo. Nay, then—My name, sir, is a very pretty name. Pray what is yours?

Del. (*Aside.*) Yes, yes, it must be he—Have you
any reason to be ashamed of it?

Sir Geo. Sir! Did you please to speak? Upon my
honour, you are a very polite, pleasant person.

Del. (*Aside.*) If I should be mistaken—I acknowledge, sir, there is but one man, whose name I *do*, but
whose person I do *not* know, to whom that question
would not have been rude in the extreme. Should
you not be that man, I ask your pardon.

Sir Geo. Should I not! Sir, that I may be sure I
am not, allow me to ask his name?

Del. His name is—

L. Jane. (*Screams, and sinks on the chair.*) Oh!

Del. Good Heavens!

Sir Geo. What has happened?

Del. Are you ill?

Sir Geo. Is it cramp, or spasm?

Del. Surely you have not broken a blood-vessel?

Sir Geo. Shall I run for a physician?

L. Jane. Instantly.

Sir Geo. I fly! Yet I must not leave you!

L. Jane. No delay, if you value my life.

Del. Your life! I will go!

L. Jane. (*Detaining him.*) No, no.
Sir Geo. I fly! I fly!   [*Exit.*

SCENE VI.

Enter LADY JANE'S *Woman.*

Wom. Dear! my lady, what is the matter?
L. Jane. Lead me directly to my own room.
Del. Shall I carry you?
L. Jane. No: only give me your arm, and come with me. I want to talk to you. I wish to hear what you have to say. (*Aside to her woman.*) When Sir George comes back, tell him I am partly recovered, but must not be disturbed. It is my positive order.
Del. (*Aside.*) What does she whisper?
L. Jane. Stay—The doctor may come in; but not Sir George. Mind, on your life, not Sir George!—Come, sir.
Del. (*Aside.*) This sudden change is mysterious. Here is concealment.
L. Jane. Come, come.
                              [*Exeunt* DELAVAL *and* LADY JANE

SCENE VII.

Wom. I purtest, it has put me in such a fluster that I am quite all of a twitter!

Enter SIR GEORGE, *followed by* DOCTOR GOSTERMAN.

Sir Geo. Come along, doctor! Make haste. Where
is Lady Jane?

Wom. In her own room.

Sir Geo. Is she worse?

Wom. No, sir; much better: but she must not be
disturbed.

Sir Geo. Nay, nay, I must see her.

Wom. Indeed, sir, I can let nobody in but the
doctor.

Sir Geo. Why so? Is not the gentleman I left
here now with her?

Wom. I suppose so, sir.

Sir Geo. And I not admitted?

Wom. On no account whatever.

Sir Geo. He allowed, and I excluded! Indeed I
shall attend the doctor.

Wom. Upon my honour, sir, you must not.

Sir Geo. Upon my honour, I will! My rival shall
not escape me!

Doc. Ah ha! De rifal! Ha, ha, ha! Dat is coot!
De young fer dat vas mit Laty Shane vas make you
shealousy? Ha, ha, ha! Dat is coot! Bote dat is as
noting at all. I shall tell you de someting mystery.
He vas no yentlemans. Ah ha! He vas a vomans.

Sir Geo. A woman!

Doc. Ya, sair. He vas make acquaintance mit me,
und I vas make acquaintance mit him; und he vas
make faint, und I vas tie loose de neck-bandt, und
den! Ah ha! I vas discober de mans vas a vomans!

Sir Geo. You astonish me!

Doc. Ya, sair. I vas make astonish myself.

Wom. Won't you go to my lady, doctor?

Doc. Ya, my tear. Let me do. Laty Shane is
fery pad; und I shall af de essence, und de cream,
und de balsam, und de syrup, und de electric, und

de magnetic, und de mineral, und de vegetable, und
de air, und de earse, und de sea, und all, &c.

[Exit, gabbling.

SCENE VIII.

Sir Geo. I should never have suspected a woman!
A stout, tall, robust figure! And for what purpose
disguise herself? That may be worth inquiry.   I
will wait, and if possible have another look at the
lady.

SCENE IX.

Enter LORD VIBRATE *and* MR THOMPSON.

L. Vib. Two hundred and forty pounds! 'Tis a
very large sum, Mr Thompson.

Thom. So large, my lord, that I have no means
of paying it. I must languish out my life in a prison.

L. Vib. No, Mr Thompson, no : you shall not do
that.   I will—And yet—Two hundred—A prison—
I don't know what to say.   If I pay this money for
you, I shall but encourage all around me to run in
debt.

Thom. It is a favour too great for me to hope.

L. Vib. You are a worthy man, and a prison is a
bad place—I—you—Pray what is your opinion, Sir
George? Is it not dangerous for a man to have the
character of being charitable?

Sir Geo. No doubt, my lord! It is the very certain way for his house to be besieged by beggars!

L. Vib. The master who pays the debts of one domestic makes himself the debtor of all the rest.

Sir Geo. He changes a set of servants into a set of
duns! He first encourages them to be extravagant,
and then makes it incumbent upon himself to pay
for their follies and vices! He not only bribes them
to be idle and insolent, but to waste his property as
well as their own!

L. Vib. It is, as you say, a very serious case.—I
—I am sorry for your misfortune, Mr Thompson—
very sorry—but—really—

Sir Geo. Misfortune! What misfortune?

L. Vib. He has foolishly been bound for his sister's
husband; and must go to prison for the debt.

Sir Geo. To prison?

L. Vib. You have shewn me how dangerous it
would be for me to interfere.

Sir Geo. Very true: very true.—He has lived with
your lordship several years?

L. Vib. He has; and I esteem him highly.

Sir Geo. A worthy man, whom it would be no disgrace to call your friend?

L. Vib. None. Still, however, consequences must
be weighed. I must take time to consider. 'Tis folly
to act in a hurry.

Sir Geo. Very true—Caution—caution—Is it a
large sum?

L. Vib. No less than two hundred and forty
pounds!

Sir Geo. Caution is a very excellent thing—Two
hundred and forty—A fine virtue—Two—I would
advise your lordship to it by all means—hundred and
forty—(*Looks round.*) Will you permit me just to
write a short memorandum: a bit of a note? (*Goes
to a table.*) I must send to a certain place. (*Writes.*)
Excuse me a moment.

L. Vib. What can be done in this affair, Mr Thompson?

Thom. Nothing, my lord. I am resigned. When
I assisted my brother, I did no more than my duty.
Those who lock me up in a prison may, for aught I
know, do theirs : yet, though they are at liberty, and
I shall be confined, I would neither change duties
nor hearts with them. (*Going.*)

Sir Geo Hark ye! Hark ye! Mr Thompson! Will
you just desire this to be taken as it is directed?
(*Aside to him.*) Don't say a word: 'tis a draft on
my banker. Discharge your debt ; and be silent—
You are very right, my lord: we cannot be too considerate ; lest, by mistaken benevolence, we should
encourage vice.

Thom. Sir George! My lord!

Sir Geo. Why now will you not oblige me, Mr
Thompson? Pray let that be delivered as it is direct-
ed. You surely will not deny me such a favour—
For you know, my lord, if we give—

Thom. Indeed, I—

Sir Geo. Will you be gone? Will you be gone?
(*Pushes him kindly off.*)—If we give without—without—

L. Vib. Poor fellow! I suppose he is afraid of being taken.

Sir Geo Oh! Is that it?—If we give, I say, with
—too—Pshaw! I have lost the thread of my argu-
ment.

L. Vib. I must own, this is a dubious case. Perhaps I ought to pay the money. (*Calls.*) Mr Thompson!—I don't think I ought to let him go to prison.
What shall I do, Sir George?

Sir Geo. Whatever your lordship thinks best.

L. Vib. But there is the difficulty!—Mr Thompson! He is gone. How foolish this is now! (*As he is
going off.*) Harry! Run after Mr Thompson, and
call him back. One would think a man going to
prison would, like me, be wise enough to doubt, and
take time to consider of it.   [*Exit.*

SCENE X.

Enter LADY VIBRATE.

Lady Vib. I assure you, Sir George, I am very angry. I have been waiting an age, expecting you would come and give your opinion on my masquerade dress.

Sir Geo. Why did not your ladyship put it on?

Lady Vib. On, indeed? It has been on and off twenty times: I have sent it to have some alteration. Beside, it is growing late: masks will be calling in on you, in their way to the opera-house, and you not at home to receive them!

Sir Geo. I ask ten thousand pardons, but you know I am the most thoughtless creature on earth.

Lady Vib. So I would have you. Were you like the sober, punctual Mr Delaval, I should hate you. But then—

SCENE XI.

DELAVAL *returning from* LADY JANE'S *apartment.*

Lady Vib. (*Aside.*) Here the wretch comes!

Sir Geo. So, so! Now I shall interrogate the lady. She has a very masculine air! (DELAVAL *bows to* LADY VIBRATE.) A tolerable bow that, for a woman!

Lady Vib. (*Aside.*) He wishes, I suppose, to sermonize me: but I shall not give him an opportunity. —Are you coming, Sir George?

Del. (*Aside.*) Ha!

Sir Geo. I will follow your ladyship in a minute.

Del. (*Aside.*) I was right! It is he!

Sir Geo. (*Aside.*) She eyes me very ferociously!

Lady Vib. I shall just call in upon you : or, if not, we shall meet afterward. I expect you to be very whimsical and satiric upon all my friends; so pray put on your best humour. Grave airs, you know, are my aversion.   [*Exit.*

SCENE XII.

Del. (*Aside.*) That was intended for me. Now for my gentleman.

Sir Geo. (*Aside.*) She really has a very fierce look! A kind of threatening physiognomy; and would make no bad grenadier.

Del. I understand your name is Sir George Versatile?

Sir Geo. (*Aside.*) A bass voice too!—At your service, sir; or madam; I really cannot tell which.

Del. Cannot!

Sir Geo. No, I cannot, upon my soul! (*Aside.*) A devilish black chin!

Del. I have an account to settle with you, sir.

Sir Geo. Have you? (*Aside.*) What the plague can she mean?

Del. When can I find you at leisure, and alone?

Sir Geo. Alone?

Del. Yes, sir; alone.

Sir Geo. Must this account then be privately settled, madam?

Del. Madam!

Sir Geo. I beg your pardon! *Sir,* since you prefer it.

7

Del. If you know me, sir, your insolence is but a confirmation of the baseness of your character!

Sir Geo. I beg a million of pardons! I really do not know you.

Del. Then, sir, when you do, you will find cause to be a little more serious.

Sir Geo. (*Aside.*) What a Joan of Arc it is! There is danger she should knock me down.

Del. Be pleased to name your time.

Sir Geo. (*Aside.*) Zounds! She insists upon a tête-à-tête!—I hope you will be kind enough to excuse me, but I am just now so pressed for time, that I have not a moment to spare. Company is waiting. I must be gone to the masquerade. You, I presume, are for the same place, and are ready dressed. I am your most obedient—

Del. (*Seizing him.*) Sir, I insist upon your naming an hour, to-morrow; and an early one.

Sir Geo. Why, what the plague!—Here must be some mistake! Permit me to ask, do you know Dr Gosterman?

Del. Yes, sir.

Sir Geo. Was you not just now in danger of fainting?

Del. Faint? I faint!

Sir Geo. It would I think be a very extraordinary thing! But so he told me : with other particulars.

Del. Absurd! Dr Gosterman has not seen me for several months.

Sir Geo. He said, sir, you were a woman; and perhaps, from that error, I may have unconsciously provoked you to behaviour which would else have been rather strange. Have I given you any other offence?

Del. Yes, sir; a mortal one.

Sir Geo. Mortal!

Del. And mortal must be the atonement.

Sir Geo. If so, the sooner the better.   Let it be immediately.

Del. No.   I have serious concerns to settle.   So have you!   'Tis time you should think of things very different from masquerading.   Name your hour to-morrow morning ; then, take an enemy's advice, re-tire to your closet, and make your will.

Sir Geo. To whom am I indebted for this high me-nace, and this haughty warning ?   Your name, sir ?

Del. That you shall know when we next meet : not before.

Sir Geo. What age are you, sir ?

Del. Age !

Sir Geo. Such peremptory heroes are not usually long lived.

Del. You are right, sir ; my life is probably doomed to be short.   But this is trifling.   Name your hour.

Sir Geo. At ten to-morrow morning.

Del. The very time I could wish.   I will be with you at your own house, inform you who I am, and then—

Sir Geo. So be it.   [*Exeunt.*

SCENE XIII.

Changes to the House of SIR GEORGE.   *A suite of apartments richly decorated, and numerous Masks : some dancing ; others passing and repassing.*

SIR GEORGE *and* LADY VIBRATE *advance unmasked.*

Lady Vib. What is the matter with you, Sir George ? You are suddenly become as dull and almost as into-lerable as my lord himself.

Sir Geo. I own, I had something on my spirits.

But it is gone.   Your ladyship's vivacity is an antidote to splenetic fits.

Lady Vib. Oh, if you are subject to fits of the spleen,
I renounce you.

Sir Geo. No, no! Heigho! Ha, ha, ha! Let me go
merrily down the dance of life!

Lady Vib. Ay! or I will not be your partner.

Sir Geo. As for recollections, retrospective anxieties, and painful thoughts, I—I—I hate them. They
shall not trouble me. For if a man, you know, were
to be sprung on a mine to-morrow, ha, ha, ha! it were
folly to let that trouble him to-day.

Lady Vib. Sprung on a mine? You talk wildly!

Sir Geo. True. I am a wild unaccountable non-
descript. I am any thing, every thing, and soon may
be—

Lady Vib. What?

Sir Geo. Nothing. Strange events are possible;
and possible events are strange.

Lady Vib. Come, come, cast off this disagreeable
humour, and join the masks.

Sir Geo. With all my heart. A mask is an excellent utensil, and may be worn with a naked face.

Lady Vib. (*Retiring.*) Why don't you come? You
used to be all compliance.

Sir Geo. So I fear I always shall be. 'Tis my worst
virtue. Call it a vice, if you please; and perhaps it
is even then my worst.

Lady Vib. I really do not comprehend you.

Sir Geo. No wonder. Man is an incomprehensible animal! But no matter for that. We will be merry still, say I—at least till to-morrow.

Lady Vib. (*Joins the masks.*) Yonder is Lady Jane.

SCENE XIV.

Sir Geo. Nay then, I am on the wing!

Mar. (*Advancing.*) Whither?

Sir Geo. Ah! Have I found you again? So much the better! I have been thinking of you this half hour.

Mar. Ay! That must have been a prodigious effort!

Sir Geo. What?

Mar. To think of one person for so great a length of time.

Sir Geo. True. Were you my bitterest enemy, you could not have uttered a more galling truth. I am glad I have met with you, however.

Mar. So am I. 'Tis my errand here.

Sir Geo. You now, I hope, will let me see your face?

Mar. I might, perhaps, were it but possible to see your heart.

Sir Geo. No, no : that cannot be. I have no heart.

Mar. I am sorry for it!

Sir Geo. So am I. But come, I wish to be better acquainted with you.

Mar. And I wish you to be better acquainted with yourself. You know not half your own good qualities.

Sir Geo. Ha, ha, ha! My good qualities? Heigho!

Mar. Your fame is gone abroad! Your gallantry, your free humour, your frolics in England and Italy, your—A propos: I am told Lady Jane is captivated by the ardour and delicacy of your passion! Is it true?

Sir Geo. Are you an inquisitor?

Mar. Are you afraid of inquisitors?

Sir Geo. Yes.

Mar. I believe you.

Sir Geo. You may. Keep me no longer in this suspense. Let me know who you are?

Mar. An old acquaintance.

Sir Geo. Of mine?

Mar Of one who was formerly your friend.

Sir Geo. Whom do you mean?

Mar. You must have been a man of uncommon worth; for I have heard him bestow such praises upon you that my heart has palpitated if your name was but mentioned!

Sir Geo. Of whom are you talking?

Mar. Lord! that you should be so forgetful!— That can only have happened since you became a person of fashion : for no man once remembered his friends better. It is true, they were then useful to you.

Sir Geo. Sir, I—Be warned! Pursue this no farther.

Mar. You little suspected at that time you were on the eve of being a wealthy baronet. Oh no! And to see how kind and grateful you were to those who loved you! No one would have believed you could so soon have become a perfect man of the mode; and with so polite and easy an indifference so entirely have forgotten all your old acquaintance! I dare say you scarcely remember the late Colonel Delaval.

Sir Geo. Sir!

Mar. His daughter too has utterly slipped your memory?

Sir Geo. I insist on knowing who you are.

Mar. How different it was when, your merit neglected, your spirits depressed, and your poverty despised, you groaned under the oppression of an unjust and selfish world! How did your drooping spirits revive by the fostering smiles of the man who first noticed you, took you to his house and heart, and adopted you as his son! Poor Maria! Silly girl, to love as she did! Where is she?

Sir Geo. This is not to be endured!

Mar. What was her offence? You became a baronet! Ay! True, that was her crime. Yet, when your fortunes were low, it was not imputed to you as guilt.

Sir Geo. (*Aside.*) Damnation!

Mar. Are your new friends more affectionate than your old? Fortune smiles, and so do they. Poor Maria! Has Lady Jane ever heard her name? Will you invite her to your wedding? (*Her voice continually faltering.*) Do. She should have been your bride: then let her be your bride-maid—She is greatly altered—She will be less beautiful—now—than her fair rival. Her birth is not quite so high—but—if a— heart—a heart—a heart—(*Struggling with her feelings, sinks into* SIR GEORGE'S *arms, and her mask falls off.*)

Sir Geo. Heavens and earth! 'Tis she! Help! 'Tis Maria! Who waits?

SCENE XV.

Enter LADY JANE.

L. Jane. What is the matter?

Sir Geo. Help! Help!—Salts! Hartshorn!—Water! Help!

L. Jane. Bless me! This lady again.

Sir Geo. Is she then known to you?

L. Jane. No! Who is she?

Sir Geo. Quick! Quick!

L. Jane. Nay, but tell me?

Sir Geo. I cannot! Must not!

L. Jane. Must not?

Sir Geo. Dare not!—She revives; and, to my confusion, will soon tell you herself.—Maria! Are you better, Maria?

Mar. I am very faint.

L. Jane. My carriage is at the door. Will you trust yourself to me?

Mar. Oh yes. I am weak—Very weak, and very foolish! But I shall not long disturb your happiness. I hope soon to be past that.

Sir Geo. Past! Oh, Maria!—I—have no utterance —Lady Jane, you will presently know of me what to know of myself is—Oh!—No matter. Not then for my sake, but for pity, for the love of suffering virtue, be careful of this lady; whom, when you know, as soon you must, you will despise and abhor the lunatic, the wretch, that could—Maria—I—I—

[*Exit abruptly.*

SCENE XVI.

Enter DELAVAL.

Del. What is the matter? Any accident? Was not that Sir George?——Good God! My sister!

L. Jane. Your sister!

Del. How comes this? Why this dress? And with that apostate! that wretch! Speak, Maria!

Mar. I cannot.

L. Jane. Mr Delaval, be more temperate. Your sister's spirits and health ought not to be trifled with by your violence. I do not know, though I think I guess, her story. I hope you have a brother's tenderness for her?

Del. That shall be shortly seen. A few hours will shew how dear she is to my heart.

L. Jane. I fear you cherish bad passions: such as I never can love, and never will share.

Del. Well, well, Lady Jane, that is not to be argued now. I am a man, and subject to the mistakes of man. There are feelings which can, and feelings which cannot be subdued. I must run my course, and take all consequences.

Mar. Oh God! in what will they end?

L. Jane. No more of this, Mr Delaval. Come with me: lead your sister to my carriage. She shall be under my care. She can inspire those sympathies which your too stubborn temper seems to despise.

Del. Indeed, indeed, you wrong me.   [*Exeunt.*

ACT THE FIFTH.

SCENE I.

MARIA *in her proper dress,* LADY JANE *and* LUCY, *Footmen waiting. Breakfast equipage on the table.*

L. Jane. Remove those things. We have done.
          [*Exeunt Footmen.*

Mar. What is it o'clock?

Lucy. Just struck ten, ma'am.

L. Jane. Lady Vibrate is a sad rake ! She did not leave the masquerade till five this morning.

Mar. And Sir George not there !

L. Jane. After the discovery of last night, could you suppose he would be seen revelling at such a place ?

Mar. I dread another and more horrible cause! My brother !

L. Jane. Mr Delaval, you know, slept in this house.

Mar. But he has been out these two hours !

Lucy. What then, ma'am ? Is not Mr Williams on the watch ? You know, ma'am, you may trust Mr Williams with your life.

Mar. If all were safe, he would be back.

L. Jane. Pray, calm your spirits.

Mar. Nay, nay, but Mr Williams must have been here before this, if something fatal had not happened !

Lucy. I am sure, ma'am, you frighten me to death !

L. Jane. (*Aside.*) Her terrors are but too well founded !

Mar. (*Footsteps without.*) What noise is that ?

Lucy. Bless me !

L. Jane. See who it is.

Lucy. (*After opening the door.*) Law, ma'am ! I declare it is Mr Williams !

SCENE II.

Enter WILLIAMS.

Lucy. Well, Mr Williams ! Every thing is right ! is not it ? All is as it should be ?

Will. That is more than I know.

Mar. Why, then, the worst is past.

Will. No, ma'am, I can't say that, either.

L. Jane. Nay, but what news do you bring?—
Speak.

Will. Why, you know my master last night made
inquiries how to find the chambers of Counsellor
Demur: so, when he went out this morning, I observed your directions, and followed him. He went
to the counsellor's, in Lincoln's Inn; and there I left
him, and hurried away to Sir George's, to inquire
and hear all I could: though it was rather unlucky
that I was not acquainted in the family.

L. Jane. Did not you make use of my name?

Will. Oh yes, my lady. Beside, servants, your ladyship knows, are not so suspicious as their masters:
they soon become friendly together: so in five minutes Sir George's valet and I were on as intimate a
footing as we could wish.

Mar. And what did he say? Tell me.

Will. Why, ma'am, he said that Sir George did
not leave his own house last night, after the fainting
of the young gentleman.

Lucy That was you, you know, ma'am.

Will. And, what is more, that he did not go to
bed; but walked up and down the room till day-
light in the morning; and then called I don't know
how often to warn the servants that he should not be
at home to any body whatever, except to a strange
gentleman.

Mar. My brother!

Will. Why, yes, ma'am, according to the description, it could be nobody else.

L. Jane. And at what hour was Mr Delaval to be
there?

Will. (*Aside.*) Zooks! I forgot to ask—That, that,
my lady, I did not learn. So, this being all the servants told me, I ran post haste to make my report to
you.

Mar. The worst I foreboded will happen!

L. Jane. What can be done?

Will. Perhaps it will be best for me to go back to Sir George's, wait for the arrival of my master, and, if he should come, hasten away as fast as I can to inform you of it.

Lucy. That is a good thought, Mr Williams! Is not it, madam? A very good thought, indeed! Don't you think it is, my lady?

L. Jane. I know not what we can do better.

Mar. Nay, but while Williams is bringing us the intelligence, every thing we most dread may happen.

Lucy. Dear! So it may!

Will. Suppose then, madam, I should stay at my post, and dispatch Sir George's valet to you with the news?

Lucy. Well, that is the best thought of all! I am sure you will own it is, madam.

Mar. I know not what to think.

L. Jane. We must resolve; or, while we are deliberating—

Mar. Merciful God! Run, Williams! Fly! Save my brother! Save Sir George!

L. Jane. Succeed but in this, and command all we have to give.

Will. I will do my best.

Lucy. That I am sure he will.   [*Exeunt.*

SCENE III.

Changes to the House of SIR GEORGE.—SIR GEORGE *walking in perturbation of mind. After some time he looks at his watch.*

Sir Geo. He will soon be here—Five minutes— but five minutes, and then—(*Walks again, throws himself on a sofa, takes up a book, tosses it away, and rises.*) What is man's first duty? To be happy. Short-sight-

ed fool ! The happiness of this hour is the misery of
the next! (*Again walks and looks at his watch.*)—
What is life? A tissue of follies ! Inconsistencies !
Joys that make reason weep, and sorrows at which
wisdom smiles. Pshaw ! There is not between ape
and oyster so ridiculous or so wretched a creature as
man. (*Walks.*) Oh! Maria ! (*Again consulting his
watch.*) I want but a few seconds. My watch perhaps is too fast. (*Rings.*)

Enter Footman.

Sir Geo. Has nobody yet been here ?
Foot. No, sir.
Sir Geo. 'Tis the time to a minute. (*Loud knock-
ing.*) Fly ! If it be the person I have described, ad-
mit him.   [*Exit Footman.*
Sir Geo. Now let the thunder strike !

SCENE IV.

DELAVAL *introduced. They salute.*

Sir Geo. Good morning, sir !
Del. You recollect me ?
Sir Geo. Perfectly.
Del. 'Tis well.
Sir Geo. I have been anxious for your coming.
Your menace lives in my memory ; and I shall be
glad to know the name of him who has threatened
such mortal enmity.|
Del. A little patience will be necessary. I must
preface my proceedings with a short story.
Sir Geo. I shall be all attention. Please to be seat-
ed. Wave ceremony, and to the subject—(*They sit.*)
Now, sir.

Del. About six years ago, a certain youth came up from college ; poor and unprotected. He was a scholar, pleasing in manner, warm and generous of temper, of a respectable family, and seemed to possess the germ of every virtue.

Sir Geo. Well, sir.

Del. Hear me on : my praises will not be tedious. Chance made him known to a man who desired to cherish his good qualities; and the purse, the experience, and the power of his benefactor, such as they were, he profited by to the utmost. Received as a son, he soon became dear to the family : but most dear to the daughter of his friend : whose tender age and glowing affections made her apt to admire the virtues she heard her father so ardently praise and encourage.—You are uneasy ?

Sir Geo. Be pleased to continue.

Del. The assiduities of the youth to gain her heart were unabating; and his pretensions, poor and unknown as he then was, were not rejected.   The noble nature of his friend scorned to make his poverty his crime.—Why do you bite your lip ? Was it not generous ?

Sir Geo. Sir !

Del. (*Firmly.*) Was it not ?

Sir Geo. Certainly ! Nothing could equal the—generosity.

Del. The health of his benefactor was declining fast ; and the only thing required of the youth was that he should qualify himself for the cares of life, by some profession. He therefore entered a student in the Temple ; and the means were furnished by his protector, till the end was obtained.   Was not this friendship ?

Sir Geo. It was.

Del. The lady, almost a child when first he knew her, increased in grace and beauty faster than in

years. Sweetness and smiles played upon her countenance. She was the delight of her friends, the admiration of the world, and the coveted of every eye.
Lovers of fortune and fashion contended for her
hand : but she had bestowed her heart—had bestowed
it on a—Sit still, sir ; I shall soon have done. I am
coming to the point. Five years elapsed; during which
the youth received every kindness friendship could
afford, and every proof chaste affection had to give.
These he returned with promises and protestations
that seemed too vast for his heart—I would say for
his tongue.—Are you unwell, sir ?

Sir Geo. Go on with your tale.

Del. His benefactor, feeling the hand of death
steal on, was anxious to see the two persons dearest to his heart happy before he expired; and the
marriage was determined on, the day fixed, and the
friends of the family invited. The intended bridegroom appeared half frantic with his approaching
bliss. Now, sir, mark his proceeding. In this short
interval, by sudden and unexpected deaths, he becomes the heir to a title and large estate. Well !
Does he not fly to the arms of his languishing friend?
Does he not pour his new treasures and his transports
into the lap of love ? Coward and monster !

Sir Geo. (Both starting up.) Sir !

Del. Viler than words can paint ! Having robbed
a family of honour, a friend of peace, and an angel
of every human solace, he fled like a thief, and concealed himself from immediate contempt and vengeance in a foreign country. But contempt and vengeance have at length overtaken him : they beset
him : they face him at this instant. The friend he
wronged is dead : but the son of that friend lives, and
I am he !

Sir Geo. 'Tis as I thought !

Del. You are—I will not defile my lips by telling
you what you are.

Sir Geo. I own that what I have done—

Del. Forbear to interrupt me, sir. You have nothing to plead, and much to hear. First say, did my sister, by any improper conduct, levity of behaviour, or fault or vice whatever, give you just cause to abandon her?

Sir Geo. None! None! Her purity is only exceeded by her love.

Del. Then how, barbarian, how had you the heart to disgrace the family, and endanger the life of a woman whose sanctified affection would have embraced you in poverty, pestilence, or death; and who, had she possessed empires, would have bestowed them with an imperial affection?

Sir Geo. Sir, if you ask, Have I committed errors? call them crimes if you will, Yes. If you demand, Will I justify them? No. If you require me to atone for them, here is my heart: you have wrongs to revenge: strike: and, if you can, inflict a pang greater than any it yet has known.

Del. Justice is not to be disarmed by being braved. To the question. It can be no part of your intention, and certainly not of mine, that you should marry my sister. Something very different must be done.

Sir Geo. What? Name it.

Del. You must give me an acknowledgment, written and signed by yourself, that you have basely and most dishonourably injured, insulted, and betrayed Maria Delaval; and this paper, immediately as I leave your house, I shall publish in every possible way: till my sister shall be so appeased, and honour so satiated, that vengeance itself shall cry, Hold!

Sir Geo. Written by me! Published! No. I will sign no such paper.

Del So I supposed; and the alternative follows. Here I am: nor will I quit you, go where you will,

till you shall consent to retire with me to some place
from which one of us must never return. Should I
be the victor, flight, banishment from my native
country, and the bitterest recollections of the vil-
lainies of man, must be the fate of me and my sister.
If I fall, you then may triumph, and she languish and
die unrevenged. This, or the written acknowledgment. Consider, and chuse.

Sir Geo. What can I answer? The paper you
shall not have. My life you are welcome to: take it.

Del. Have you not brought disgrace enough on
my family? Would you make me an assassin? My
sister and my father loved you. Let me, if possible,
feel some little return of respect for you.

Sir Geo. Having wronged the sister, would you
have me murder the brother? Already the most guilty of men, would you make me the worst of fiends?
Though an enemy, be a generous one.

Del. Plausible sophist! The paper, sir: or, man
to man and arm to arm, close the scene of my dishonour, or your own. The written acknowledgment.
Determine. (*Walks away and views the pictures.*)

Sir Geo. (*Apart.*) Why, ay! 'Tis come home!
I have sought it, deserved it; 'tis fallen, and the rock
must crush the reptile!—Then welcome ruin. The
sword must decide. (*Goes to take his sword, but stops.*)
The sword? What! Betray the sister and assassinate
the brother? Oh God! And such a brother! Stern,
but noble-minded: indignant of injury, peerless in affection, and proud of a sister whom the world might
worship; but whom I, worthless wretch, in levity
and pride of heart, have abandoned. (*Aloud.*) Mr
Delaval!

Del. Have you resolved to sign?

Sir Geo. Hear me.

Del. The written acknowledgment!

Sir Geo. My behaviour to your sister is—what I
cannot endure to name—'Tis hateful! 'Tis infamous!

My obligations to your most excellent father, the respect you have inspired me with, and my love for
Maria—

Del. Insolent! Insufferable meanness! The paper,
sir!

Sir Geo. Angry though you are, Mr Delaval, you
must hear me. I say, my love, my adoration of Maria has but increased my guilt. It has made me dread
her contempt. I durst not face the angel whom I
had so deeply injured.

Del. Artifice! Evasion! Cowardice!—Your signature!

Sir Geo. (*Snatching up his sword from the table.*)
You shall have it—Follow me.

Del. Fear me not.

Sir Geo. (*Stopping short.*) Hold, Mr Delaval.—
Justice is on your side. If your firmness be not a savage spirit of revenge, if you do not thirst for blood,
you will feel my only resource will be to fall on your
sword. I cannot lift my arm against you.

Del. Then sign the acknowledgment.

Sir Geo. Can you in the spirit even of an enemy
ask it? Do you not already despise me enough?—
Think for a moment: am I the only man that ever
erred? Is it so wonderful that a giddy youth, whose
habitual failing was compliance, by sudden accident
elevated to the pinnacle of fortune, surrounded by
proud and selfish relations, of whose approbation I
was vain, is it so strange that I should be overpowered
by their dictates, and yield to their entreaties? Your
friendship or my death is now the only alternative.
Suppose the latter: will it honour you among men?
At the man of blood the heart of man revolts! Will it
endear you to Maria? Kind forgiving angel, and
hateful to myself as her affection makes me, I last
night found that affection still as strong, still as pure,
as in the first hour of our infant loves. Lady Jane—

Del. Forbear to name her! 'Tis profanation from

2

your lips! No more casuistry! No subterfuge! The paper!

Sir Geo. Can no motives—

Del. None!

Sir Geo. My future life, my soul, shall be devoted to Maria.

Del. The paper!

Sir Geo. Obdurate man! (*Reflects a moment.*) You shall have it. (*Goes to the table to write, during which* DELAVAL *remains deep in thought and much agitated.*) Here, sir! since *you* will not be generous, let *me* be just. 'Tis proper I remove every taint of suspicion from the deeply-wronged Maria.

Del. (*Reads with a faltering voice.*) " I George Versatile, once poor and dependent, since vain, fickle, and faithless, do under my hand acknowledge I have perfidiously—broken my pledged promise—to the most deserving—lovely—and—(*Begins in much agitation to tear the paper.*)

Sir Geo. Mr Delaval?

Del. Damn it—I can't—I can't speak. Here! Here! (*Striking his bosom.*)

Sir Geo. Mr Delaval?

Del. My brother!

Sir Geo. (*Falls on his neck.*) Can it be? My friend!

Del. This stubborn temper—always in extremes! The tyger, or the child.

Sir Geo. Oh no! 'Twas not to be forgiven! Best of men!

Del. Well, well: we are friends.

Sir Geo. Everlastingly! Brothers!

Del. Yes; brothers.

SCENE V.

Enter WILLIAMS *in great haste.*

Will. Sir!

Del. How now?

Will. I beg your pardon, but Lady Jane and your sister are below. They insist on coming up, and the servants are afraid to—

Sir Geo. Maria! Let us fly!   [*Exeunt.*

SCENE VI.

The *Apartments of* LORD VIBRATE.

LADY VIBRATE *and the Doctor.*

Doc. Ya, my coot laty; dat vas efery vordt so true as vat I say. I vas discober it vas a vomans; und Sair Shorge, und my Laty Shane, und de vaiting-vomans vas discober to me all as vat I say more.

Lady Vib. Ay, ay! That was the reason Sir George was not at the masquerade.

Doc. Ya, my coot laty.

Lady Vib. I observed he was in a strange moody humour.

Doc. My Lordt Fibrate vas fery mosh amazement, ven I vas make him discober all as vat I vas make discober mit my coot laty.

Lady Vib. Sir George has behaved very improperly.

SCENE VII.

Enter LORD VIBRATE.

L. Vib. So, so, so! All I foreboded has come to pass! The day is slipped away, a new one is here, and every possibility of recovering the estate is gone!

Lady Vib. Ha, ha, ha!

L. Vib. Do you laugh?

Lady Vib. Ha, ha, ha! I do, indeed!

L. Vib. Is your daughter's loss the subject of your mirth?

Lady Vib. Ha, ha, ha! No, no; not her loss, but your positive determination to prove I did not know you! Ha, ha, ha! When I told you that even that motive would not be strong enough, how you stormed! " But it will, my lady! But it won't, my lord! I say it will, my lady! I say it won't, my lord!" Ha, ha, ha! Will you believe that I know you now?

L. Vib. What shall I do? Advise me, doctor.

Doc. I vas adfice, my coot lordt, dat you shall do efery ting as vat you please.

Lady Vib. Ay, think! ask advice. Ha, ha, ha!— Now that you can do nothing, the inquiry will be very amusing.

SCENE VIII.

Enter THOMPSON.

L. Vib. Well, Thompson, what says Counsellor Demur? Has the time absolutely elapsed?

Thom. Absolutely, my lord.

Lady Vib. How wisely your lordship doubts, before you decide! Hay, doctor?

Thom. I have good news, nevertheless.

L. Vib. Good news? Speak! Of what kind?

Thom. The honesty of the opposite party.

L. Vib. What, the holder of the land?

Thom. Yes, my lord.

L. Vib. Which way? Explain.

Thom. He has engaged to Mr Demur, I being present, that, if your lordship will only shew the legality of your late title, he will resign the estate.

L. Vib. Is it possible?

Lady Vib. It cannot be ! The last purchaser is in India.

Thom. The last purchaser is dead ; and it has descended to one whom you, my lord and lady, little suspect to be its possessor.

L. Vib. Who ?

Lady Vib. Who ?

Thom. Mr Delaval.

Lady Vib. Mr Delaval !

L. Vib. Mr Delaval resign it on exhibiting the legality of my title ?

Thom. He will, my lord.

L. Vib. Did he make no conditions ?

Thom. None.

L. Vib. What, did he not mention Lady Jane ?

Thom. Her name did escape his lips ; but rising passion, and, if I rightly read his heart, emotions of the most delicate sensibility, immediately closed them : as if he would not endure the love he bore her to be profaned by any the slightest semblance of barter and sale.

L. Vib. What do you say to that, Lady Vibrate ? What do you say to that ?

Lady Vib. The proceeding is honourable, I own.

L. Vib. Did I not always tell you Mr Delaval was a man of honour ?

Lady Vib. You tell me, my lord ? Why, you were going to challenge him yesterday morning !

L. Vib. He is no such weather-cock as your favourite, Sir George.

Lady Vib. You mistake : Sir George is no favourite of mine. Is he, doctor ?

Doc. Dat vas all yust as vat you say, my coot laty.

L. Vib. What, he did not come to make a buffoon of himself, for your diversion, at the masquerade last night ! Hay, doctor ?

Doc. Dat vas all yust as vat you say, my good lordt.

Lady Vib. His perfidious treatment of Miss Delaval is unpardonable.

Doc. Dat vas pad! Fery pad, inteet!

L. Vib. Ay, ay! He has plenty of words, but he
has no heart.

Doc. Dat is pad! Fery pad, inteet!

Thom. Pardon me, my lord: Sir George may have
committed mistakes, but to the goodness of his heart
I am a witness.

Lady Vib. You?

L. Vib. How so?

Thom. By his benevolence I was yesterday relieved from the disgrace and the horrors of a prison.

L. Vib. Indeed!

Lady Vib. Which way?

Thom. He paid a debt, which, had I been confined, I never could have discharged; and, for this unexpected act of humanity, he would not suffer so
much as my thanks.

L. Vib. Did Sir George pay the two hundred and
forty pounds, Mr Thompson?

Thom. The note, which he pretended to write and
send by me, was a draft on his banker for three hundred.

L. Vib. Why, he confirmed all my arguments against
it, and added twice as many of his own.

Doc. Sair Shorge vas alvay make agréable. Dat
vas his vay.

Lady Vib. I own, however, I am still more surprised
at the unexampled generosity of Mr Delaval.

SCENE IX.

Enter WILLIAMS.

Lady Vib. Where is your master, Mr Williams?

Will. They are all coming, my lady.

Lady Vib. Who is coming?

Will. Mr Delaval, Lady Jane, Miss Delaval, and Sir George. There has been sad work! But it is all over, and they are now so happy! Here they are.

SCENE X.

Enter MR DELAVAL, *leading* LADY JANE, *and* SIR GEORGE *with* MARIA, *followed by* LUCY.

L. Vib. Mr Delaval, I have great obligations to you. Thompson has been telling me of your disinterested equity.

Del. The obligation, my lord, was mine. Your lordship well knows that the first of obligations is to be just.

L. Vib. Well, well; but the estate you are so willing to resign will still, I hope, be yours.

Del. Nay, my lord.

L. Vib. Dubious as all things are, that is a subject on which I protest I do not believe I shall ever have any doubts. What say you, Lady Jane? (*Irony.*) But now I have my doubts again.

L. Jane. (*Eagerly.*) What doubts, my lord?

L. Vib. I doubt whether you understand me.

L. Jane. Would your lordship teach me to dissemble?

L. Vib. Um—I doubt whether that would be much for your good.

Del. I hope Lady Vibrate will not oppose our union?

Lady Vib. No, Mr Delaval. Your last generous action has charmed me; and Sir George—

Sir Geo. Has declined in your good opinion. But

you cannot think so ill of me as I do of myself; and if ever again I should recover my own self respect, I shall be indebted for it to this best of men, and to this most incomparable and affectionate of women !

Mar. My present joys are inexpressible!

Del. Which my impetuous indignation threatened for ever to destroy. (*Comes forward.*) How dangerous are extremes ! Sometimes we doubt, and indecision is our bane : at others, hurried away by the sudden impulse of passion, our course is marked with misery. One man is too compliant : another too intractable. Yet happiness is the aim of all. Since, then, all are so liable to be misled, let gentle forbearance, indulgent thoughts, and a mild forgiving spirit, be ever held as the sacred duties of man to man.   [*Exeunt omnes.*

SEDUCTION;

A

COMEDY,

IN FIVE ACTS.

AS PERFORMED AT THE

THEATRE-ROYAL, DRURY-LANE.

BY

THOMAS HOLCROFT.

DRAMATIS PERSONÆ.

SIR FREDERICK FASHION,	*Mr Palmer.*
LORD MORDEN,	*Mr Kemble.*
GENERAL BURLAND,	*Mr Aickin.*
LAPELLE,	*Mr Bates.*
BAILIFF,	*Mr Chaplin.*
MR WILMOT,	*Mr King.*
LADY MORDEN,	*Miss Farren.*
HARRIET,	*Mrs Wilson.*
EMILY,	*Mrs Brereton.*
MRS PINUP,	*Miss Tidswell.*
MRS MODELY,	*Miss Pope.*

*The time within twelve hours. The Scene is the House
of* LORD MORDEN, *and does not change ; and the
Stage is never vacant, but at the end of an Act.
The action is single.*

SEDUCTION.

ACT THE FIRST.

SCENE I.

A superb Drawing-Room in the House of LORD MOR-
DEN, *with several Doors leading to other Apartments.*

LAPELLE, *from* LORD MORDEN'S *dressing-room,
looking at his watch.*

Lap. Twenty minutes past ten !—a shameful time
of the morning for a gentleman's gentleman to be disturbed.——My lord has lost his money, can't sleep
himself, and won't suffer others to take their natural
rest.

SCENE II.

LAPELLE, MRS PINUP, *from* LADY MORDEN'S *dressing-room.*

Mrs Pin. I declare, upon my honour, this is a most
monstrous time of night for a lady's gentlewoman to

be kept up, dosing over a dull novel, or nodding in an anti-chamber and an arm-chair, while others are taking their pleasure, and losing their estates, among their friends.

Lap. Good morrow, Mrs Pinup.

Mrs Pin. Good morrow, Mr Lapelle! Good night, you mean.—I have not been in bed yet!

Lap. No!

Mrs Pin. That vile bed-side bell!—They'll wear me haggard before I am old! Knew I should not rest long, so threw myself down in my clothes; and, just as I was got into a sound sleep, tingle, tingle, tingle; up I must get, to dress my lady, who, for my part, I believe, never sleeps at all.

Lap. Why, yes; your fashionable folks are a kind of ghosts, that walk of nights, and greatly trouble the repose of valets and lady's maids—and late hours, like white paint, are excellent promoters of crack'd complexions.

Mrs Pin. I declare, upon my honour, I am as tired as—as——

Lap. A hackney coach-horse, on a rainy Sunday.

Mrs Pin. Yes—and as drowsy as—

Lap. An alderman at an oratorio.—Your lady had a deal of company at her rout—Was Sir Frederick Fashion there?

Mrs Pin. To be sure.

Lap. He is a prodigious favourite with your lady, I think.

Mrs Pin. Favourite!—There are strange doings in this world!—Staid I know not how long, after every body else was gone!

Lap. What, alone with your lady?

Mrs Pin. Alone with my lady.

Lap. Indeed!—Was Mrs Modely at the rout?

Mrs Pin. Yes—but don't ask me any questions; it's impossible I should say ten words more: I am talking in my sleep now.—When I get up in the morning, that is, about three o'clock in the afternoon, I'll tell you all; so good night.

SCENE III.

Lap. A wonderful change in a short time!—Lady Morden, young, handsome, and full of spirits, was, not a month ago, reserved in her conduct, fond of her husband, contented with home, and, indeed, a miraculous kind of exception among wives of quality—Whereas, now, she has suddenly turned fantastical in dress, capricious in temper, free of speech, and, what we half-bred folks should call, light of carriage. She games with the women, coquettes with the men, and seems, in every respect, ambitious to become—a woman of fashion. As for my lord—why—he is a man of fashion.

SCENE IV.

GENERAL BURLAND, LAPELLE.

Gen. Is your lady up, Mr Lapelle?

Lap. Yes, sir—I believe she has never been in bed.

Gen. Who—what do you mean?

Lap. My lady had a rout last night.

Gen. A rout—and never in bed? Impossible!

Lap. Yes! but it's very true, sir.

Gen. Lady Morden! She whom, but a few weeks since, I left so singular, so eminent an example of simplicity and purity of manners!

Lap. Sir Frederick Fashion was here.

Gen. Sir Frederick Fashion!

Lap. He staid after every body else had retired.

Gen. What! alone with Lady Morden?

Lap. So her ladyship's woman, who is scarcely yet undressed, informed me.

Gen. (*After a pause of astonishment.*) Why, then, all hopes of goodness, in this world, are vanished!— Go—bid my daughter, my Emily, come to me.

Lap. She is not stirring, I fancy, sir.

Gen. But I fancy she is, sir; I am sure she is.— What, sir, she had not a rout, to keep her up all night!

Lap. She was of my lady's party, I believe, sir.

Gen. (*After a pause of great anxiety.*) Go—go— pray, go, and do as I bid you.

SCENE V.

Gen. What will this town, this world come to?— The only perfectly amiable, the only enchantingly virtuous woman I knew, fascinated at last, and sinking into the gulph of depravity!—She will drag down my Emily too!—No! I'll hide her in a forest, seclude her in a cave, rather than suffer her to be infected by the pestiferous breath of this contagious town.—But is she not already tainted?—Of my lady's party!— She that I left her with as a pattern, commanded her to observe, to study, to imitate in all things!

SCENE VI.

GENERAL BURLAND, LAPELLE.

Gen. Well, where is my daughter?

Lap. I have called her woman, and she will call Miss Emily.

Gen. I'll call her myself—and it shall be the most ungentle call she has long heard from me.

SCENE VII.

LAPELLE, HARRIET, *in the dress of a Croat.*

Lap. Who comes here? Some foreign sharper, I dare say—One of my lord's morning duns for last night's debts.

Har. (*With the brogue.*) Hark you, young man; may I be asking you where I will find my lord Morden?

Lap. He is not come down, sir.

Har. Oh, that, I suppose, is becase he is not up.

Lap. My lord told me he expected a gentleman or two would call—but he has had so many calls lately——

Har. That he is a little slow in answering?

Lap. Rather——Riches, regularity, and roast beef, will soon, I fear, take their leave of our house.

Har. Faidth, and that may viry will be; for they are all three become great vagabonds. Riches is turned Amirican pedlar, Regularity a Prussian grenadier, and as for Roast Beef, why, the Frinch are now so fond of good ould English fashions, that poor Roast Beef is transported alive to Paris.

Lap. My lord, I believe, is a little out of cash at present.

Har. Will, now, that is viry prudent of him to put it out; for, whin a man finds he can't keep his cash himself, he is viry right to lit odther people keep it for him.

Lap. Nay, then, I don't know a more careful gentleman.

Har. Careful? Why, sure, always whin a man of spirit begins to take care of his money, 'tis becase he has none.

Lap. Well, sir, if you will please to leave your card, his lordship, I suppose, will know who has called.

Har. Indeed and he won't.

Lap. How so, pray, sir?

Har. Faidth, for a viry good raison—He niver saw me in his life.

Lap. Who then shall I say?—

Har. And is it my name you would know?

Lap. If you please.

Har. Let me see—What the white divle is my name now?—Oh!—Char-les Phelim O'Fire-away; an Irishman by accident, a gentleman by policy, and a captain of Croats, in the Austrian sarvis, by design.—Do you understand that riddle now?

Lap. Not clearly.

Har. I did not intind you should.—What time can I see my lord?

Lap. Most likely about one.

Har. Will, then, give him this litter, and inform his lordship I will take the liberty of calling this afternoon, to bid him a good-morrow.

SCENE VIII.

LAPELLE, LORD MORDEN.

L. Mor. (*In his morning gown and slippers, and calling as he enters.*) Lapelle!

Lap. So! here he comes, already. (*Answering.*) My lord.

L. Mor. What time is it?

Lap. Eleven o'clock, my lord.

L. Mor. What a damn'd night have I passed!—
Is my coffee ready?

Lap. I'll go and see, my lord.

SCENE IX.

L. Mor. (*Throws himself on the sofa.*) This head-
ache!—No rest!—Oh for half an hour's sleep!—A
cursed silly course of life mine!—But there is no
accounting in the morning for the conduct of over-
night.

SCENE X,

LORD MORDEN; LAPELLE *with Coffee.*

L. Mor. This is not half strong enough—get me
some as strong as possible.—Any message? (*Rises.*)

Lap. This letter, my lord.

SCENE XI,

L. Mor. From Lady Westbrook, I see. (*Reads.*)
—" Um—A young lady in disguise!—um—Will relate her own story!—um—um—Rely on your honour

to keep her secret, and serve her cause !——Would
have addressed myself to Lady Morden, but for reasons which you shall know hereafter !"

SCENE XII.

LORD MORDEN ; LAPELLE *with more Coffee.*

L. Mor. Who brought this letter?
Lap. An Irish gentleman, in a foreign dress.
L. Mor. A gentleman !
Lap. Said he would call about one, my lord.
L. Mor. Shew him into my room, and inform me
the instant he comes.
Lap. General Burland is here.
L. Mor. (*Aside.*) General Burland ! Zounds !
Lap. Came to town late last night, my lord.
L. Mor. Tell him I am come down.

SCENE XIII.

L. Mor. Must not let him see the present temper
of my mind—My guardian once, he is determined
never to think me of age—I need not his reproof to
increase my present chagrin ; my own follies and
Lady Morden's unexpected, unaccountable reverse
of conduct are sufficient—He will lay it all to me ;
and, perhaps, with reason !—Heigho ! Here he comes
—Really, one of these very prudent, plain-spoken
friends is a very disagreeable person, in these our

moments of folly.———Well, I must assume a cheerfulness I don't feel, and ward off his wisdom with raillery.

SCENE XIV.

LORD MORDEN, GENERAL BURLAND.

Gen. Good morrow, my lord.

L. Mor. General, good morrow.

Gen. You seem scarcely awake.

L. Mor. (*Stretching.*) Slept ill—troubled with the night-mare.

Gen. Your troubles, I am afraid, are rapidly increasing.

L. Mor. How so, general?

Gen. Lady Morden had a rout last night!

L. Mor. Oh! and forgot to send you a card, I suppose.———Is that my fault?

Gen. You are merry, my lord; but he who drinks poison, out of a frolic, will soon be glad to send for a physician, out of fear; and the chances are, the doctor will come too late.

L. Mor. Trope and figure!

Gen. My lord! My lord! This levity is unseasonable: blushes and shame would better become you.

L. Mor. Pff! They are out of fashion.

Gen. Yes, you leave your friends to blush for your faults.

L. Mor. My friends are very good; nay, indeed, generous; for were they but to spare a single blush for each of their own faults, they would have none to bestow on mine.

Gen. Fie! The mirth of a madman is sport only

13

to boys——I was your guardian; I wished to prove
myself your friend. 'Twas I first discovered that
then angelic woman, who is, now, Lady Morden; I
was the cause of her union with you; and I am,
therefore, accountable to myself, to her, and to society, for her conduct.

L. Mor. That is, you are a kind of second-hand
sponsor——godfather-in-law, as it were.

Gen. Very well, sir! proceed! despise reproof!
ridicule advice!

L. Mor. Nay, good doctor, you really wrong me;
'tis not the advice, but the physic, I hate——At
least, I hate the form under which it is administered
——But, pray, tell me; when last you saw Lady
Morden, did you perceive any symptoms of that de-
generacy in her ladyship you now complain so loudly
of?

Gen. None! I thought it impossible!

L. Mor. And is it not rather extraordinary, then,
that my example should, so suddenly, subdue what,
within this month, seemed so invulnerable?

Gen. (*Great surprise and energy.*) It is extraordinary, my lord! most extraordinary! but not less
true; and had you any sense of your duty to yourself, your family, or society, the truth of it would
make you tremble!

L. Mor. See how differently different people understand things! My acquaintance are, every day,
wishing me joy of her ladyship's reformation, and
telling me how surprisingly she has retrieved her
character in the world.

Gen. (*Sarcastically.*) And Sir Frederick Fashion,
no doubt, among the rest.

L. Mor. (*Endeavouring to conceal his feelings.*)
Hem!—yes—yes. He is one of our very first men,
you know; and he is quite in raptures with her—
swears she was born to lead and outshine us all.

Gen. (*With continued irony.*) The approbation of so great an adept must give you vast pleasure!

L. Mor. Hem!—a—infinite!——Not but this sudden change has rather surprised me.

Gen. How so?

L. Mor. Just as you left town, her ladyship's melancholy seemed increasing—wandering over the house like a perturbed spirit, as the play says, mournfully clanking her chains, and frightening the gentle smiles and pleasures from her, she seemed to waylay me, and, with moving look and melting eye intreat compassion, till, egad, I really at last began to pity her.

Gen. You did!

L. Mor. Yes—But, suddenly forsaking the—*penseroso*, she broke in upon me one morning, and with an air of levity and good humour, and a small tincture of reproach, then and there read me a very pretty, wife-like remonstrance.

Gen. To which you listened with a truly picktooth insensibility.

L. Mor. Yes—You know my way.

Gen. And what was the subject of her discourse?

L. Mor. Why, chapter the first was a recapitulation of my agreeable follies, and her own perverse virtues.—She was no partaker in my pleasures—I had forgot every endearment—She was left to dine, sup, and sleep by herself—I dined, supped, and slept, nobody knew where—She more recluse than the abbess of a convent: I more uncertain than the price of stocks, or the place of prime minister.

Gen. (*With earnest concern.*) And what did you say to this?

L. Mor. (*Aside.*) I must face it out. (*Aloud.*) Say? What could I say to such a simple woman?

Gen. You did not attempt to deny the charge then?

L. Mor. What should I deny? 'Twas every syllable true, and every syllable in my praise.

Gen. (*Sighs.*) Humph!—Then you do not think
the sweets of affection ought sometimes to alleviate
the bitterness of neglect.

L. Mor. Sweets! pshaw! they are too cloying to
the stomach, and ought to be taken sparingly.——I
am fond of sweet music, but too much of it sets me
to sleep.——Besides, a wife, like a barrel organ, can
only play one set of tunes.

Gen. (*Sighs.*) Well, sir, but the conclusion?

L. Mor. A very unexpected one, I assure you.——
I misunderstood this for a declaration of war, and,
with a smile, was very obligingly about to entreat her
ladyship would hatch her melancholy into mischief
her own way, when, turning short upon me, she
curtsied, seemed abashed, began to apologize, applaud my conduct, ridicule the silliness of her own,
and promised to become as fashionable a lady as I,
or any lord in Christendom could wish.

Gen. Your increase of happiness is then prodigious?

L. Mor. Hem!—a—unspeakable.——Lady Morden, I own, was certainly a kind of——demi-angel,
though my wife——but then her—her goodness seemed to throw one at such a distance—so much in the
back ground, that there was only one figure noticed
in the picture!

Gen. 'Tis well, sir, you are so perfectly satisfied.

L. Mor. Nay, general, I will own I have often felt
a kind of inclination, a sort of wish, as it were, to become very prudent and wise, and—and all that—
but, really, one has so much to do, that one does
not know where to begin.—Besides, you very good
kind of people, you—upon my honour, you are, in
many respects, the most queer, precise, particular,
species of beings, and have such strange notions!—
Instead of taking one's pleasure, and doing just what

one likes best, which, you know, is so natural, one must live for the good of one's country, love one's wife and children, pay tradesmen, look over accounts, reward merit, and a thousand other of the—the most ridiculous whims——and what nobody, absolutely, nobody does.

Gen. Intolerable profligacy!—I have listened to you, my lord, with grief, vexation, astonishment, and pity!—Your mind is degraded, and the more dangerously so, because you believe your worst vices to be your greatest merits! You have had honour, happiness, and pleasure, of the most perfect kind, within your power, and you have rejected them, to clasp their shadows! To merit pity by misconduct is humiliating; but by misconduct to incur contempt, is, to a manly spirit, insupportable; and the latter will, I fear, be suddenly your lordship's fate. Did not the remembrance of your noble father affect me, I should look upon your approaching punishment with apathy, because you wilfully have plunged to perdition; but for your lady, if I cannot retrieve, if I cannot save her, I shall mourn indeed!

SCENE XV.

L. Mor. Faith, this good general is, like a cuckoo, always in a tune. (*Sighs.*) He has reason! I have laboured to laugh at my own follies; but the farce is over, the forced jest forgotten, and the sorceress Recollection conjures up the ugly phantom Disgust!— Why, what a child am I!—Oh! Lady Morden—pshaw! —absurd!—I will not make myself the butt and byword of my acquaintance—I—I—I will laugh—ha, ha, ha!—laugh at my lady's gallantries.—I jealous! —I!—that have daily made jealousy a standing jest;

the criterion of an ill-bred, vulgar mind!—No, no, no. (*Sees* LADY MORDEN *and* SIR FREDERICK FASHION *coming, and is seized with a suspicious anxiety, which he endeavours to conceal.*)

SCENE XVI.

LORD MORDEN, LADY MORDEN, in an undress, SIR FREDERICK FASHION.

Lady Mor. (*Entering.*) No, no, Sir Frederick; you are partial.

Sir Fred. Not in the least, madam.

Lady Mor. Yes, you are—good morrow to your lordship—yes, you are.—I feel I still retain a leaven of former silly prejudices ; but a little collision among you people of superior fashion will soon wear these asperities smooth, and bring them to bear a proper polish.

Sir Fred. Ah! madam, you have a leaven of something celestial, which we *inferior* people wonder at, but cannot imitate!

L. Mor. (*Aside.*) So!

Lady Mor. (*Taps* SIR FREDERICK *with her fan.*) Fie! flatterer!—but you are always saying civil things, and that, I fancy, makes you so agreeable.

Sir Fred. (*Serious and ardent.*) No, Lady Morden ; you wrong me—my tongue is forced to give utterance to the effusions of my heart—By Heaven, you are an angel! and I am, involuntarily, obliged to repeat, and repeat, and repeat, that you are an angel!—You must not be angry with me, for I cannot help it.

Lady Mor. No, no—angry! no—Though I really believe I do improve—don't I, my lord?

L. Mor. Certainly, madam, certainly!

Lady Mor. Yes—I have discovered that one of my most capital errors, formerly, was being too sensible of my own defects.—I find that to wear on one's countenance an open and avowed consciousness that one possesses every grace and perfection, is the grand secret of really possessing them; or, at least, of persuading the world one really does, which is the same thing.

Sir Fred. Your ladyship is very right; nothing can put a face of real fashion out of countenance: the placid features are all fixed.

Lady Mor. Oh, immoveable!—Like the owner's names, cut in brass, and nailed to their doors.

Sir Fred. Ha, ha, ha! Charming!

Lady Mor. Do but observe one of our well-bred beaus, at a public assembly, and you will see him enter, plant himself in a spot, elevate his eye-brows, fix his eyes, half open his mouth, and stand like an automaton, with its head turning on a pivot. (*Mimicks the manner.*)

Sir Fred. Ha, ha, ha! Charming! Charming!

L. Mor. (*Smiling.*) But don't you think this a *little* tending to the ridiculous, madam?

Lady Mor. Oh dear, no!—Nothing can be ridiculous that's fashionable.

Sir Fred. Oh, no, impossible!

Lady Mor. Formerly, I should have blushed if stared at; but now, I find, the only way is to stare again—without looking—that is, without betraying the least indication of knowing whether one is looking towards the man or the wall—thus.

L. Mor. (*With forced pleasantry.*) Ha, ha, ha! Your ladyship is very right: modesty—modesty is an obsolete bugbear.

Lady Mor. Yes, and, like the—the ghost in the tragedy, has been stared out of doors.

Sir Fred. Oh, the very quakers despise it at present.

Lady Mor. Yes—'tis a shabby fellow, whose acquaintance every body wishes to drop.—To be sure, I was a most absurd creature : was not I, my lord?

L. Mor. I—upon my honour, madam—I—you—no—no—not absurd—no.

Lady Mor. Oh fie—not absurd—why, do you know, Sir Frederick—ha! ha! ha!—I—ha! ha! ha! I was downright in love with his lordship.

Sir Fred. Ha, ha, ha! in love with his lordship?

Lady Mor. Ha, ha, ha! upon my honour, 'tis true! —is it not, my lord?

L. Mor. Ha, ha, ha!—ye—ye—yes—madam, yes.

Lady Mor. Thought him the most charming man in—in—in the whole world!

Sir Fred. Ha, ha, ha! Is that possible?

Lady Mor. Why, it—it is scarcely credible!—But—but such is the fact—Nay! I doated on him—and continually reproached myself for wanting power and attractions to obtain my lord's affection!—For I never blamed him—Ha, ha, ha!—I—ha, ha, ha! —I used to sit whole nights, while my lord was out, watching and weeping ; and whole days studying which way I could regain his love!

Sir Fred. Regain, Lady Morden!—Why, was his *lordship* ever so unfashionable as—as—

Lady Mor. As to love his wife—Why, yes, really —I—I do believe he was so singular, for—for a whole fortnight.

Sir Fred. Why! ha, ha, ha! Why, were you, Lord Morden?

L. Mor. (*Forcing a laugh.*) Ha, ha, ha!—I—I— (*With a little spleen.*) I don't know, sir, what I was.

Lady Mor. Nay, don't be out of countenance, my lord! You hear I have the justice to relate my own foibles, as well as your lordship's—and mine—mine were infinitely the greatest.—It is exceedingly strange, but so——fascinated——was I, that——ha, ha, ha!—— I——ha, ha, ha!—(*Suddenly becoming very serious*)

——I am verily persuaded I could have died with pleasure, to have insured his affection.

L. Mor. Ha, ha, ha!—(*Aside, and turning away.*) I cannot bear it.

Sir Fred. Ha, ha, ha! These things are unaccountable.

Lady Mor. (*Resuming her levity.*) Ay, one wonders how one could be so weak!—Oh, Sir Frederick! I am going to Christie's. There is a painting I have a mind to purchase. They tell me 'tis very fine.

Sir Fred. What is the story, madam?

Lady Mor. The metamorphosis of Actæon.

Sir Fred. Ha, ha, ha! A fashionable subject.

Lady Mor. Yes—that—that—that is the very reason I wish to have it.—Poor Actæon is taken at the precise moment when the—the change is taking place.

Sir Fred. In his forehead?

Lady Mor. Yes, I am going down there now; will you go with me, Sir Frederick?

Sir Fred. With pleasure, madam—Ha, ha, ha! Poor Actæon!

Lady Mor. Ay, poor Actæon!—Adieu, my lord.

SCENE XVII.

L. Mor. Madam! (*Following, stops short.*) 'Sdeath! what am I about? Shall I at last sink into one of the vulgar, and become jealous?—Wretched about a —Oh, no—Actæon! (*Striking his forehead.*) Sure all men are idiots, and never know the value of that most inestimable jewel, a lovely and a loyal wife, till in danger of having it purloined. (LORD MORDEN *retires into his dressing-room.*)

ACT THE SECOND.

SCENE I.

LAPELLE, (*coming from the door of the anti-chamber,
as if he had been listening.*)

So Mr Irishman, by accident!—a lady, in disguise!
That's the riddle, is it?—But hush!

SCENE II.

LORD MORDEN, *dressed,* HARRIET, (*from the anti-
chamber.*)

L. Mor. (*To* LAPELLE.) Leave the room—I am
sorry we were disturbed: your story, madam, has interested me deeply: though too reprehensible for
the irregularities of my own conduct, I cannot but
condemn the licentious libertinism of this Sir Frederick—Indeed, I—I have reason, perhaps, to dread
it.

Har. A man of honour among men, the ruin of
woman he thinks as necessary to his fame as to his
pleasure; and, like too many others of your cruel
sex, holds it no crime to make war upon those who
cannot defend themselves.

L. Mor. But what do you propose by this disguise, madam?

Har. There is a contract, which I, indeed, refused, but which he forced upon me, to demonstrate, as he said, the purity of his intentions, wherein he bound himself, in a penalty of ten thousand pounds, to marry me within a month: for, in his fictitious raptures, he protested no sum, no proofs, could sufficiently express the ardour and sanctity of his affection.

L. Mor. And have you this contract?

Har. Oh, no! The day preceding that on which it was my good fortune to discover his real designs, he asked to see, and artfully exchanged it, for a counterfeit copy.

L. Mor. This contract you wish to regain?

Har. If possible, or some other unequivocal means of detection.

L. Mor. And force him to marry you?

Har. Oh, no—To own the truth, I have a generous and a constant lover, who, perhaps, has been a little ill used.

L. Mor. As most generous and constant lovers are.

Har. 'Tis too true.—To avenge him, and humble the pride of one who thinks himself too cunning for our whole sex, is my determination.

L. Mor. Well, madam, ours is a common cause—But as we have both been imprudent, and invited misfortune, we must both endeavour to conceal our true feelings, mask our suspicions, and—Hush! here he comes; and with him a lady, whose principles are as free as his own, but who has had the art so well to conceal her intrigues, and preserve appearances, that she is every where received in society.—I will introduce you, in your assumed character.

Har. Not now: let us withdraw—when he is alone.

The fewer eyes are on me, the less liable I shall be
to a discovery.

    (LORD MORDEN *and* HARRIET *return to the anti-*
      chamber, just as MRS MODELY *and* SIR FREDE-
      RICK *appear.*)

SCENE III.

MRS MODELY *and* SIR FREDERICK.

Mrs Mod. Really, Sir Frederick, there is no accounting for the strangeness of your present taste!—
I pity you!—I foresee the downfal of your reputation!—What, you! who have vanquished so many
elegant coquettes, and driven so many happy lovers
mad; you! who were the very soul of our first socie-
ties, and whose presence made palpitate the hearts of
belles and beaux; the first with hope and delight, the
latter with fear and envy; you! sighing at the feet
of a prude, and become the rival of a husband!

Sir Fred. (*Laughing.*) Deplorable!

Mrs Mod. Have not you for this month past buried yourself in Lady Morden's sober society, and
dosed over crown whist with her night after night?
—Nay, have not you attended her even to church,
and, there, with a twang, joined the amen chorus of
charity-children, paupers, and parish clerks; sitting
with your face drawn as long as its shadow at sun-
set, and a look as demure and dismal—

Sir Fred. As poor Doctor Faustus, waiting for the
devil to come and fetch him—Ha, ha, ha!—Granted.

Mrs Mod. And what do you think has been said
of you, meanwhile, in the polite circles you have
abandoned?—Your very best friends have been the
very first to condemn you.

Sir Fred. That's natural—When we are guilty of any folly, our very best friends are always the very first to condemn us, to shew they neither advise nor countenance us.

Mrs Mod. I thought the gay, young beauty, besieged by pleasures, surrounded by flatteries, who believes herself the goddess she is painted, to fix her wandering fancy, to humble and bring her to a sense of frailty, or to supplant the happy, the adored lover, while yet the breath is warm that vows eternal constancy; these, I imagined, were the only achievements worthy Sir Frederick Fashion!

Sir Fred. These have their eclat. But to initiate a youthful, beauteous wife, who, from her childhood, has been accustomed to say her prayers, believe in virtue, and rank conjugal infidelity among the most heinous of the seven deadly sins; to teach her to doubt, fear, wish, tremble, and venture; to be a witness afterward of her repentance, her tears involuntarily falling, her eyes motionless, her form fixed, and the severe saint transformed to a statue of weeping sin; to read her fall in the public papers; be praised, reproached, admired, and curs'd in every family in England; in short, to be for ever immortalized in the annals of gallantry, and the hero of the tea-table for a whole month, for this will be no common vulgar wonder, this were glory equal to my ambition! And this glory I am determined to acquire; nay, it is already within my grasp.—This day, or, rather, this night, this very blessed, ecstatic night, shall I gain the greatest of all my victories!

Mrs Mod. Insulting!

Sir Fred. Nay, my dear Mrs Modely, you know my enthusiasm, and must not take exceptions—Nor can I, surely, be blamed. Lady Morden is a concealed horde of native sweets, that delights the senses; while the made-up beauties we commonly meet, like artificial flowers, are all shew, and no fragrance.

Mrs Mod. Raptures!

Sir Fred. Inferior to her, in form and perfection, as the Venus of a Dutch image-hawker to the genuine Grecian antique!

Mrs Mod. It matters not wasting your rhetoric on this topic; for I will not give my consent to your pursuing this affair any further, Sir Frederick.

Sir Fred. You will not?

Mrs Mod. I will not.

Sir Fred Ha, ha, ha! Don't provoke me, my dear Mrs Modely; don't provoke me.

Mrs Mod. Nay, no threatening.

Sir Fred. Ha, ha, ha!—Well—To arms then— War is the word.

Mrs Mod. The choice remains with you.

Sir Fred. Ha, ha, ha!

Mrs Mod. Lady Morden is my relation; and though I despise prudery, and know the world—

Sir Fred. (*Aside.*) That you do, indeed!

Mrs Mod. Yet—you can hardly suppose I will silently acquiesce in her ruin!

Sir Fred. Ha, ha, ha! You—you forget yourself, dear madam—-These qualms would do vastly well in some places, but to me—

Mrs Mod. And why not to you, sir?—Though I do allow myself a little liberty of conscience—

Sir Fred. Not a little. (*Aside.*)

Mrs Mod. And though you—you—-know I do, must I—In short, I have another favourite project, which I am determined not to give up.

Sir Fred. (*Aside.*) Oh ho! But it will be best to avoid a rupture.—(*Aloud.*) May I ask what this favourite project may be?

Mrs Mod. You know the public affront General Burland gave me last winter, and you cannot suppose I have forgotten it.

Sir Fred. (*Aside.*) No; I know you better.—- (*Aloud.*) Oh! the general is an eccentric mortal,

12

licensed to say any thing; and, instead of being listened to, is laughed at.

Mrs Mod. Yes; but I am determined he shall be
punished.

Sir Fred. Which way?

Mrs Mod. His daughter Emily is a pretty, simple
girl—I mean, untutored in the world.

Sir Fred (*Conceiving her design.*) True!

Mrs Mod. To see her married to a man of fashion
would, at least, break his heart.

Sir Fred. (*Laughs.*) Infallibly!

Mrs Mod. Your fortune, I believe, Sir Frederick,
like your family seat, begins to want repairs: and she
is a rich heiress, with twenty thousand pounds at her
own disposal, beside the general's estate, which must
be hers—Why do you laugh so?

Sir Fred. Oh! the delights of anticipation!

Mrs Mod. An—an—anticipation

Sir Fred. (*Still laughing.*) It is a part of my plan
to carry her off; I mean, to let her carry me off, this
very night.

Mrs Mod Who? Emily?

Sir Fred. Emily.

Mrs Mod. To-night!

Sir Fred. This active, this important, this blissful
night!

Mrs Mod. Lend me your eau de luce, you divle!

Sir Fred. Ha, ha, ha!—This surprise from you,
Mrs Modely, is the supreme of panegyric.

Mrs Mod. And have you made any advances to
Emily?

Sir Fred. Yes, yes—Ha, ha, ha!—I made advances
to her, and she made advances to me—The conquest
was too easy—Were it not for the circumstance of
the elopement, which will give the sauce a flavour the
food wants, it would scarcely invite my appetite.

Mrs Mod. But Lady Morden—

Sir Fred. Is mine, whenever I please to make my

final attack. I am no bad orator in general; but in
company with her I seem inspired—am absolutely
astonished at my own eloquence!—Nay, I have several times spoken with such energy, enthusiasm,
and momentary conviction, in praise of virtue, that I
have actually been in imminent danger of making a
convert of myself!

Mrs Mod. In praise of virtue?

Sir Fred. In praise of virtue. There is no making
one of these virtuous visionaries rational, but by flattering their bigotry, and pretending to adore their
idol; by pursuing which method, I have inured her
to, and made her as familiar with what is prudishly
called vice and vicious sentiments, as she is with her
own thoughts.

Mrs Mod. Yes, yes, vile rake: but remember I'll
have no concern in this affair!—I—

Sir Fred. Oh, poh! Ay, ay, that is understood—
You wink—and know nothing of the matter.

Mrs Mod. Nay, but I here publicly protest against
your proceedings.

Sir Fred. (*Aside.*) And will privately do your utmost to promote them.

Mrs Mod. I exclaim against such licentiousness!

Sir Fred. I know you do—But if you are thus
tender of her ladyship's reputation, you will feel no
repugnance at assisting me to irritate his lordship's
sensibility.

Mrs Mod. What do you mean?

Sir Fred. To confess the truth, I am a little piqued
at Lord Morden's want of feeling—I wish I could
make him jealous.

Mrs Mod. Jealous! Fie! He is too well bred.

Sir Fred. That's unfortunate.—The antics of a jealous husband add highly to the enjoyment, as well as
the reputation of an amour. The poor man is so injured, so enraged, so distressed, so industrious to publish his calamity, and is so sincerely pitied and laugh-

ed at—must positively rouse my lord to a sense of
his misfortune, or it will want poignancy—A turtle
feast without French wines !

Mrs Mod. Well, should I find any opportunity of
aiding you—

Sir Fred. Ay, ay ; I have no doubt of your zeal
in the cause.

Mrs Mod. Nay, but don't mistake me—I only
mean as far as teazing his lordship is concerned.

Sir Fred. Oh! Certainly—certainly.

Mrs Mod. If his lordship had any real cause for
jealousy, I should, for Lady Morden's sake, be the—
the—the—the—the most miserable creature upon
earth.

Sir Fred. To be sure.

Mrs Mod. But you seem mighty secure of your
conquest.

Sir Fred. I am no novice : I can tell when a woman's time is come.—Besides, her ladyship has granted me a rendezvous.

Mrs Mod. When ?

Sir Fred. Why, this very evening, to be sure.

Mrs Mod. Where ?

Sir Fred. Here, in this very house.

Mrs Mod. Since you are so very certain, how came
you not to take advantage of being alone with her
after the rout ?

Sir Fred. I did ; that is, should have done, had we
not been interrupted.

Mrs Mod. By whom ?

Sir Fred. A new footman—an odd kind of—Oh !
here the very fellow comes.

SCENE IV.

MRS MODELY, SIR FREDERICK, GABRIEL, *loitering
and leering.*

Mrs Mod. What does the rude lout peer at?

Sir Fred. Country curiosity.

Gab. (*Attempting to go once or twice, then pausing,
and turning back.*) Did—did—did your ladyship's honour call?

Mrs Mod. No.

Gab. (*Again going and turning.*) I—I thought,
mayhap, you wanted my lord.

Mrs Mod. What should I want your lord for, think
you, friend?

Gab. Nay, marry, that's more nur I can tell.

Sir Fred. What is your name?

Gab. Gabriel, an't please you.—In my last place,
they used to call me the Sly Simpleton.

Mrs Mod. And who did you live with last?

Gab. Why, you an heard of my lady's brother, the
rich nabob, that be just come over fro' th' Eastern
Indies.

Sir Fred. Mr Wilmot?

Gab. Ees.—I do come fro' his estate, out o' Staf-
fordshire.

Sir Fred. You are part of the live stock?

Gab. Anon!

Mrs Mod. Were you in his service?

Gab. (*Hesitates.*) N—E—Ees.

Mrs Mod. How long?

Gab. Better nur a week.

Sir Fred. What sort of a man is he?

Gab. Humph!—A be well enough, when a's plea-

sed——tho' I canno' say as I do like him much for
a measter.

Mrs Mod. Why so?

Gab. Becase a'l neither let a servant tell lies nur
take money.

Sir Fred. Indeed!

Gab. No—A' wonnot—whereof, here, I find I canno' please my lady, if I donna tell lies; and, I am
sure, I canno' please myself, if I donna take money.

Sir Fred. Ha, ha, ha!

Mrs Mod. Ha, ha, ha! So he did not suit you?

Gab. No.—A's too high flown, as 'twere, in's no·
tions——.

Sir Fred. Which way?

Gab. A makes a great case o' what a calls friendship, and honour, and honesty, and such like; and,
you know, if a poor sarvant gis head to that there
sort o' stuff, a's not likely to get rich.

Mrs Mod. Upon my word!

Sir Fred. So Mr Wilmot's head is full of such
nonsense, is it?

Gab. Oh! a's brimful of such nonsense—and so
were I while I lived wi' he; which wur the reason,
as I do suppose, that they called me a simpleton; but
I am not so simple as folk think me.

Sir Fred. (*Aside to* MRS MODELY.) My dear Mrs
Modely, leave me for a moment with this fellow.—
You'll be upon the watch, to throw in any hints or
aids you happen to see necessary and à propos?

Mrs Mod. Yes, yes—that is, for Emily and the
elopement; but be cautious; a defeat would turn the
tables upon us, and make us the jest of the whole
town, friends and enemies.

Sir Fred. How can you fear it?

Mrs Mod. Nay, I do not: I know my sex, and I
know you.

SCENE V.

Sir Frederick, Gabriel.

Sir Fred. Gabriel is your name, you say?

Gab. Ees.

Sir Fred. You seem a sharp kind of fellow, and one that understands his own interest.

Gab. Ees, I understand my own interest.

Sir Fred. Are you, if occasion should offer, willing to do me a piece of service?

Gab. Humph! What will you gi' me?

Sir Fred. I see you are a sensible fellow, and come to the point at once.

Gab. Ees; I love to come to the point.

Sir Fred. And you would not betray me to any body?

Gab. Why—not unless somebody were to pay me better.

Sir Fred. Upon my honour, thou art the honestest rogue I ever met with.

Gab. Ees, that I be.

Sir Fred. Here, here is money for thee; and observe, as thou seemest perfectly to understand a bargain, thou shalt have more in proportion to thy fidelity and capacity: and moreover, canst thou read and write?

Gab. Ees.

Sir Fred. Well, then, be faithful, and I will get thee a place in the excise. And now, observe—I— I have a—very great respect—and friendship for your lady.

Gab. Ees, ees; as we sen i' th' country, you have more nur a month's mind to her.

Sir Fred. How, sirrah! Dare you suppose I have—

Gab. Nay, now, belike *you* think me a simpleton too! Your great folk supposen a sarvant has neither ears nor eyes; but, Lord! they are mistaken!— Ecod, their ears are often plaguy long. What, mun, I wur no' sa fast asleep as you thought me i' the passage this morning.

Sir Fred. (*Aside.*) The rascal!

Gab. Belike, because I be a country lad, you reckon I should think it strange, like, that one gentleman should teak a liking to another gentleman's wife; but, Lord, I know well enough that's nought here—I ha' learned a little o' what's what.

Sir Fred. Nay, friend Gabriel, I am more and more convinced thou art a clever acute fellow.

Gab. Lord, mun, your worship need no' be so shy like. You do know you ha' promised me a place— an places that are no bought one way, mun be bought another.

Sir Fred. Well said, friend Gabriel.

Gab. An as for keeping o' family secrets, donno' you fear me; becase, why, I do find they be a sarvant's best parkizites—For an it wur na for family secrets, how should so many poor country Johns so very soon become gentlemen?

Sir Fred. (*Aside.*) This fellow's thoughts run all in one channel: his ruling passion is money; the love of that sharpens his intellects, and opens his eyes and ears.——Well, Gabriel, you shall find me generous as a prince, provided——Here's somebody coming—-go into the next room: I'll speak with you presently.

Gab. Ees; but I do hope your honour' worship wunna forget the place, like.

Sir Fred. Never fear.

[GABRIEL *goes into* LADY MORDEN'S *dressing-room.*

SCENE VI.

SIR FREDERICK, EMILY.

Sir Fred. My angel ! my life !

Em. Hush ! my papa is coming, and wants to take me away with him home.

Sir Fred. Away !

Em. Yes—hush—take no notice.

SCENE VII.

GENERAL BURLAND, SIR FREDERICK, EMILY.

Gen. Come, Emily, are you ready ?

Em. I am always ready and happy to obey my dear papa ; but surely, sir, you will not let me leave Lady Morden without so much as bidding her adieu ?

Gen. I will write a card of thanks to her ladyship, with your respects, and as many compliments as you please.

Em. Nay, but, dear sir, consider, it will seem too abrupt. Lady Morden is so good, so kind, I would not give her a moment's pain for the world. Besides, I have so many obligations to her ladyship.

Gen. I begin to be afraid, child, lest you should have too many obligations to her ladyship.

Em. Let me only stay to-night, and to-morrow morning I will go with all my heart, and as early as you please, if you desire me.

Sir Fred. (*Aside.*) I protest she is bantering him ! Oh ! the charming malicious little angel.   (*Aloud.*)

Ay, general, let Emily stay to-night; I will answer for her: she will go to-morrow morning, as soon as you please, if you desire her.

Gen. You will answer for her!

Sir Fred. Yes—won't you permit me, Emily?

Em. (*Curtsies.*) My dear papa knows I never attempt to break my word.

Gen. Yes, my child, I do know you have hitherto been unspotted and pure as the morn-blown lily; and my anxiety that you should remain so makes me thus desirous of your quitting this house. When I brought you here, these doors did not so easily fly open at the approach of such fine, such accomplished gentlemen as Sir Frederick Fashion.

Sir Fred. (*With vast pleasure.*) By Heavens! he anticipates his misfortunes! (*Aside.*)

Em. (*Takes the general's hand.*) Do, my dear papa, consent only for to-day; I don't ask any longer.

Sir Fred. (*Aside.*) I could hug the charming hypocrite.

Gen. Well, well, Emmy, you know I never deny you any thing; for indeed you never yet asked any thing that could give the most anxious and affectionate father a moment's pain.

Em (*Kisses his hand.*) I thank you, dear, dear sir: you have made me happy.

Sir Fred. By my life, I shall find this a much more agreeable affair than I hoped!—Yes, general, you—you are a very good papa.

Gen. You think so?

Sir Fred. Yes, I do, upon my soul.

Gen. Then I am what you, I am afraid, will never be.

SCENE VIII.

Sir Fred. Ha, ha, ha! He does not suspect we are so soon to be so nearly related. Ha, ha, ha! I should like to be present when he first hears the news. He—he will foam and bounce like a cork from a bottle of champaigne.

SCENE IX.

LORD MORDEN, *from the anti-chamber.*

L. Mor. Well, Sir Frederick, is her ladyship returned?

Sir Fred. Yes; she is dressing for dinner. She bought the Actæon.

L. Mor. She did?

Sir Fred. Oh yes.—She is a charming woman!—The eyes of the whole room were upon her. There were some smart things said. One observed a likeness between me and Actæon; another thought it bore a far greater resemblance to your lordship.

L. Mor. Ha, ha, ha! About the head, no doubt?

Sir Fred. For my part, I said, I thought the likeness was very capable of being improved.

L. Mor. You were very kind.

Sir Fred. Oh, pray have you heard that Sir Peter Pry is going to sue for a bill of divorce?

L. Mor. No.

Sir Fred. 'Tis very true. I should not have suspected Sir Peter of such vulgar revenge; but I find our married men of fashion are far less liberal in their sentiments than the ladies.

L. Mor. Ha, ha, ha! Yes; they often want a woman's philosophy in these matters.

Sir Fred. Yes, they are wasps, that fly and feed wherever they can find honey, but retain a sting for any marauder that shall approach their nests.

L. Mor. Somewhat selfish, I own.

Sir Fred. Much more liable to be jealous than the women; and jealousy, your lordship knows, is the most ridiculous, ill-bred, contemptible thing in nature!

L. Mor. Ha, ha, ha! Yes, yes—ha, ha, ha!—perfectly despicable.

Sir Fred. Oh, nothing so laughable as the vagaries of a jealous husband: no creature suffers so much, or is pitied so little.

L. Mor. Ha, ha, ha! Ay, the thefts of love are applauded, not punished.

Sir Fred. Yes, and the poor robb'd husband, watchman-like, twirls his rattle, alarms the neighbourhood, and collects assistants, who never fail to aid the thief, and laugh at him and his loss.

L. Mor. Ye— *je*—yes. Ha, ha, ha!—A husband is a very strange, ignominious animal.

Sir Fred. A jealous husband!

L. Mor. A paltry, mechanical——

Sir Fred. Without an idea of life or manners!

L. Mor. Ha, ha, ha! Very true. But come with me; there's a young gentleman in the antichamber, of a good family, who wishes to be introduced to you—A very pretty fellow; has an ambition to do something which shall give him eclat, and is therefore desirous of being known to us men of the world.

Sir Fred. Well, I am yours for a few minutes; but I must attend Lady Morden at her toilette presently.

ACT THE THIRD.

SCENE I.

GENERAL BURLAND, LORD MORDEN, *meeting :* GA-
BRIEL *introduces* GENERAL BURLAND.

Gen. Well, my lord, is Lady Morden to be seen?

Gab. Oh ees, your worship, hur will be, anon ; for
yonder is Sir Frederick, helping the maid to dress
her ladyship.

Gen. Helping to dress her ladyship!

Gab. Ees. They sent me for some milk of roses,
here ; (*Shewing the phial ;*) and, would you believe
it, I wur sich an oaf, I had never heard before that
roses gave milk.

Gen. Ah! you are some half-taught country
booby.

Gab. Why, so I do find ; for in the country the
folk do only clear-starch their aprons and ruffles, but
here, ecod, they clear-starch their faces.

Gen. Well, go carry in your milk, and inform
her ladyship I am waiting her leisure.—(*Laughing
within.*)

Gab. Ecod, here they all come, your honour, and
rare and merry they be. But your Londoneers do
lead a rare ranting life!

SCENE II.

GENERAL BURLAND, LORD MORDEN, SIR FREDE-
RICK, LADY MORDEN, MRS MODELY—*The three
last from* LADY MORDEN'S *dressing-room, laughing.*

Lady Mor. Ha, ha, ha!—Oh! you whimsical toad
you! Ha, ha, ha! You have half killed me!—I am
glad to see you in town, general. We have been
drawing the characters of our acquaintance; and
Mrs Modely and Sir Frederick Fashion have been so
droll and so satirical!

Gen. Ah, no doubt.

Lady Mor. I could not have thought there was so
much satisfaction in remembering the failings of one's
friends.

Mrs Mod. Oh, it makes one so cheerful!

Sir Fred. And keeps one so charmingly in countenance!

Gen. (*Aside.*) Which you stand in very great need
of.

Sir Fred. I assure your ladyship you have an exquisite turn for satire: you cut with excessive keenness, and yet with a dexterity that makes the very
patient tingle with pleasure.

Lady Mor. You are partial: a little more experience will make these things quite familiar, but habit
only can give one perfect ease.

Sir Fred. Oh, habit!—habit is a wonderful thing!
Have you heard the anecdote of the Newmarket
jockey?

Lady Mor. No; what is it?

Sir Fred. Why, a jockey, having had a bad run at
the last October meeting, was willing to correct the

errors of Fortune by turning his lead to gold. Accordingly, on Epping Forest he stopped Major Warboys, and bade him deliver ; to which the major, being one of those singular officers who think it some disgrace to be robb'd, replied by firing his pistol.—— The ball happened to be fatal. The horse set off ; and, to shew the effect of habit, the body of the jockey kept its seat as far as the stable door, and there deliberately tumbled off; nay, some go so far as to assert, it was seen to rise in the stirrups ; but that, I believe, wants confirmation.

L. Mor.   ⎫
Mrs Mod.   ⎬ Ha, ha, ha !

Lady Mor. Pshaw ! you tragi-comic wretch !

L. Mor. I think you had not much company last night.

Lady Mor. Your lordship was so well bred, and made your visit so short, else you would have found a great deal.

Mrs Mod. Oh yes, they poured in from all quarters.

Sir Fred. Sir Nathan Neaptide, the yellow admiral came.

L. Mor. An agreeable guest !

Mrs Mod. Oh, rude as his own boatswain !

Sir Fred. Would teach a starling blasphemy, rather than want good conversation.

Lady Mor. He attempts satire.

L. Mor. But utters abuse.

Mrs Mod. That makes him so much respected.

Lady Mor. Yes : like a chimney-sweeper in a crowd, he makes his way by being dirty.

Sir Fred. I protest your ladyship is prodigiously brilliant to-day

Lady Mor No, no ; though I am a vast admirer of wit. A person of wit has one very peculiar and enviable advantage.

L. Mor. What is that, madam ?

Lady Mor. Long life.

L. Mor. Long life!

Lady Mor. Yes; a wit has more ideas, conse-
quently lives longer in one hour than a fool in seven
years.

Sir Fred. For which reason your ladyship is already three times the age of Old Parr.

Lady Mor. Dear Sir Frederick, that is so gallant.

Mrs Mod. And so new.

Gen. Why, yes; this is the first time I ever heard
a lady told she was old, and receive it as a compliment!

L. Mor. But your visitors—who had you next?

Mrs Mod. There was Sir Jeremy Still-life.

Lady Mor. (*Mimics.*) And his bouquet. He
primmed himself up in one corner, and seemed to
think that, like the image of a saint on a holy-day,
he was powdered and painted on purpose to be
adored.

Mrs Mod. He was not singular in that.

Lady Mor. Oh no: there was a whole row of them
that, like jars and mandarins on a mantle-piece,
look'd vastly ornamental, and served charmingly to
fill up vacancies.

Gen. Every trifle has its use.

Mrs Mod. Lord Index came, and stalk'd round
the rooms as if he had been loaded with the wisdom
of his whole library.

Lady Mor. Yes, he look'd as solemn as a monkey
after mischief.

Sir Fred. (*Mimicking his solemnity.*) And drew
up his face in form, like a writ of inquiry into da-
mages, with a " Take notice" engrossed in front.

L. Mor. He would not stay late, for his lordship
is as careful of his health as he is vain of his understanding.

Lady Mor. And yet he is but a kind of rush-can-

dle ; he may glimmer a long while, but will never
give much light.

L. Mor. It seems strange that your people who
have acquired a little knowledge always think they
possess an infinite deal ; while those who are the best
informed appear continually conscious of wanting
more.

Gen. Not strange at all, my lord.   Amassing
knowledge is like viewing the sun through a tele-
scope ; you enlarge the object, but you destroy the
glare.

Mrs Mod. Did not you observe that, notwithstanding the pearl-powder, my lady Bloom's neck looked
remarkably sallow ?

L. Mor. Oh, as a Jew's face under a green um-
brella.

Sir Fred. The widow Twinkle, as usual, talked a
vast deal about reputation.

Lady Mor. One is apt to admire a thing one wants.

L. Mor. She always takes infinite pains to place
her reput on, like broken china in a beaufet, with the
best side outward.

Lady Mor. She may plaster and cement, but will
never bring it to bear handling.

Mrs Mod. Mr Pensive, the poet, came in too.

Sir Fred. Yes, but as nobody took any notice of
him, he presently went out again.

Gen. A great proof of his good sense.

Sir Fred. Your poets and sheriff's officers are a
kind of people every body has heard of, but that nobody chuses to know.

Lady Mor. Or if you are under the necessity of
receiving a private call from them now and then, it
would be quite disgraceful to be seen with them in
public.

L. Mor. Your ladyship used to be very partial to
Mr Pensive.

Gen. Yes, her ladyship *used* to have many singular partialities. She was once partial to merit and virtue, wherever she found them : she had a partiality for order, economy, and domestic duties, likewise ; nay, she even went so far as to cherish a partiality for your lordship !

Lady Mor. Ha! ha! ha!   Odious partialities !

Sir Fred. } Ha! ha! ha!
Mrs Mod. }

L. Mor. Ma—ma—madam !—Odious !

Lady Mor. Ha! ha! ha!   To—to be sure, sir—is it not odious to be unfashionable ?

Mrs Mod. Certainly. Ha! ha! ha ! ha!

Sir Fred. Ha! ha! ha!   I protest, general, you —Ha! ha! ha!—you are too severe.

Gen. Am I ?

Sir. Fred. Ha! ha! ha! You are
really.

Mrs. Mod. Ha! ha! ha!   Yes,
you are indeed, general.   *(All together.)*

Lady Mor. Ha! ha! ha! Yes,
yes, you absolutely are.

Gen. Humph! Why don't you laugh, my lord ?

L. Mor. I do. Ha! ha! ha!—I—!—I do, general ; though, as to severity, I own I—I don't see it in that light.

Gen. No !

L. Mor. No ; I cannot accuse myself of any fault, unless the love of pleasure be one.

Gen. Hah! (*Sighs.*) And your catalogue of pleasures, I fancy, is pretty extensive.

L. Mor. Not half so extensive as one could wish.

Gen. A dice-box, for instance, is one.

L. Mor. A very principal one.

Lady Mor. My short experience hardly entitles me to venture an opinion ; but I find a wonderful similarity between gaming and a cold bath.—You

have a—a tremor—a—a hesitation at first, but having once plunged in, you are thrown into the most
delightful glow!

L. Mor. Oh, an ardent tingling.

Gen. Beware, sir, that a shivering fit does not
succeed.

Mrs Mod. } Ha, ha, ha!
Lady Mor. }

Sir Fred. Ha, ha, ha! You really have no mercy,
general.—You hit so often and so hard, egad!

L. Mor. I'm vastly—happy—to see you all so
merry, though, upon my honour, I can't find out the
jest.

Gen. That is strange, when you yourself make it.

Lady Mor. Not in the least—There is many a professed joker who does not understand his own wit.

Gen. (*Half aside.*) I am tired, disgusted with this
mixture of folly and wickedness.— (*Aloud.*) May I
intrude so far upon your ladyship as to obtain half an
hour's private conversation?

Lady Mor. Why—upon my word—general—I—
I have so many affairs on hand to-day, that I must
beg you—to excuse me:—To-morrow you may command me for as long as you please.

Sir Fred. Ay, do, general, have the complaisance
to wait till to-morrow, when my lady will be more at
leisure.

Gen. (*Deeply affected.*) Well, madam, I did not
use to be thought an intruder by your ladyship, and
will not begin now—But since I cannot have the
honour to tell you privately, I still think myself bound
to do my duty, and inform you publicly, you are in
the hands of sharpers, " who will filch from you your
good name."—(*With great anxiety.*) Nay, perhaps,
you are on the very eve of destruction!—Oh, guile!
—Can it be?—My heart is full!—I—(*Goes up to her,
and most affectionately takes and presses her hand.*)
Lady Morden, I have no utterance—But if there be

such a thing as sympathy, some small portion of the
horror I now feel will communicate itself to you.

SCENE III.

LORD MORDEN, SIR FREDERICK, LADY MORDEN,
and MRS MODELY.

(LADY MORDEN *seems affected,* LORD MORDEN *deeply so,* SIR FREDERICK *and* MRS MODELY *disconcerted.——A pause.*)

Lady Mor. (*Endeavouring to recover herself.*)—
The—the general—has the—strangest way of—af-
fecting—and—harrowing—Has not he, my lord?

L. Mor. Ye—yes—Upon my honour, he—he—I
don't know how—(*Putting his hand to his heart.*)

Sir Fred. Ha, ha, ha!—The general—the general is a true Don Quixote: He first creates giants,
and then kills them.

Lady Mor. Yes. Ha, ha, ha!—His head is full of
—of windmills, to grind moral sentiments.—But come,
Mrs Modely, you have not seen my new purchase.

Mrs Mod. Oh, what, the Actæon?

Sir Fred. Is it come home?

Lady Mor. Oh yes—I could not rest till I had it.
(*Talking as they are going off.*)

Mrs Mod. Come, my lord—I long to see it!

Lady Mor. The tints are charming.

Mrs Mod. So I hear—the grouping excellent!

Lady Mor. Oh, delightful!

SCENE IV.

HARRIET, *from the anti-chamber*, SIR FREDERICK.

Har. Hist!—Sir Frederick.

Sir Fred. (*Turning back.*) Oh!—Well, sir, how proceeds your amour? I thought you had been busied in schemes about that affair.

Har. Faidth, and I am so—But I don't believe I can succeed without your assistance.

Sir Fred. Perhaps you are a little scrupulous about the means.

Har. Me!—Indeed and you have mistaken your man—Why, you don't think, Sir Frederick, I regard the complaints or tears of women!—You and I, sure, seek our own gratification, not their happiness—For if the love of man sought only the happiness of woman, faidth, there would be nothing but dull marriages, fond husbands, and legitimate children; and we should lose all the satisfaction of seducing wives, ruining daughters, and of bringing so many fine, sweet, innocent craters upon the town!

Sir Fred. Oh, it would strangely reverse the order of things.

Har. Order!—Faidth, and it would occasion a blessed confusion—in Doctor's Commons.

Sir Fred. For my part, present pleasure is my pursuit; I never disturb my imagination with dismal conjectures on future consequences.

Har. Faidth, and you are right—For, as you say, it would be dismal enough to trace these consequences into—into streets, and hospitals, and—places that the imagination sickens at.

Sir Fred. Marriage, you say, is not your object.

Har. Oh no! I don't like that said matrimony music.

Sir Fred. A mortgaged rent-roll only can make it supportable. A wife is like a child's whistle, which every breath can play upon, but which no art can make melodious.

Har. Faidth, and you have viry proper notions about wives. So whin the dare crater gave a marriage hint, why, I told her a dale of boister consarning an old cross fadther, and being under age, and that I could not marry these three months. For you know one does not stand for a good double handful of oaths and lies, whin one wants to ruin a sweet, kind angel, that one loves.

Sir Fred. Ha, ha, ha!—Suppose you were to make a sham marriage.

Har. A sham marriage:— Faidth, and I would make that, if there were not a parcel of low rascals that make halters.

Sir Fred. Pshaw! That's a paltry, mechanical fear.

Har. But you—you were telling me, you know, of—a—scheme—

Sir Fred. Oh! The contract.

Har. Ay, faidth! The contract. You said you would shew it me.

Sir Fred. I will—I have brought it for that purpose. (*Feeling for his pocket-book.*) I lately found it an efficacious expedient.

Har. And successful?

Sir Fred. Would have been, but for an unlucky accident.

Har. But there is one small impediment.

Sir Fred. What is that?

Har. Westminster-Hall.

Sir Fred. Baw! A house of cards.

Har. Oh, and that it is; for 'tis supported by knaves, and full of tricks.

Sir Fred. Here—here is the very contract I myself gave.

Har. Ay! (*Endeavouring to conceal her eagerness.*)

Sir Fred. And here a counterfeit copy, with a few slight, but essential alterations.

Har. I understand—To put the change upon her. (*With an anxious eye continually toward the contract.*)

Sir Fred. Which you may easily take, or make an opportunity to do.

Har. (*With affected indifference.*) Will, thin, lind them both to me, and, faidth, you shall see fine divarsion.

Sir Fred. No—I—I'll have them copied for you. This is signed and sealed.

Har. Arrah, what of that?—Ha, ha, ha! Sure, you are not afraid you would be obliged to marry a man?

Sir Fred. No—The only danger in trusting them to you is, that of losing them; and even then there could be no ill consequence, except by falling into the hands of one who is far enough from London.

Har. Ay, ay, lit me have them—I give you my honour to make a proper use of them.

Sir Fred. Ha, ha, ha! You are a promising youth, and it would be a pity such talents should be baulked—So here—here.

Har. Promising? Oh, faidth, and I hope to surprise even you yourself. You shall presently hear of the succiss of your schaimes.

SCENE V.

SIR FREDERICK, GABRIEL.

Gab. (*Looking after* HARRIET.) There a' goes—

Hop, step, and jump!—(*Pause.*)—Ecod, she does it featly!

Sir Fred. She! What's that you say?

Gab. How a' skipp'd into the carriage!—There! Off it drives! Whur-r-r-r! Rattling away!

Sir Fred. What does the fellow mean?—S'death! —Sure!—Who are you talking of?

Gab. Why, of that Irish gentleman-like lady.

Sir Fred. Lady!

Gab. I wur coming straight to tell you!—There is a plot, mun, against you!

Sir Fred. A plot. (*Runs toward the door.*)

Gab. Nay, you are too late!—A's gone!—Three streets off by this.

Sir Fred. Confusion!

Gab. Ees—She means to breed a confusion.

Sir Fred. Who?

Gab. Miss Harriet.

Sir Fred. Harriet!—By Heavens, 'tis she!

Gab. Ees—'tis she.

Sir Fred. Secure fool! Ineffable idiot!—And yet, in that disguise, Lucifer himself could not have discovered her!—And who told you?

Gab. Why, his worship's gentleman, Mr Lapelle —A' o'erheard her tell my lord aw her plot.

Sir Fred. What course shall I take?

Gab. Suppose I wur to watch, and when she comes back, let your worship know?

Sir Fred. Do so—But be very careful—and be very secret.

Gab. Ees, ees; I remember the place, mun.

Sir Fred. Away—be watchful, and be rewarded.

SCENE VI.

Sir Fred. This is a thunder-stroke!—Lord Morden

in the plot too!—It will come to Lady Morden's ears ; I shall be blown, all my plans disconcerted, myself laughed at, and my reputation eternally ruined ! (*Walks about.*) Ha!—There is one way to prevent the mischief yet—By Heavens, it cannot fail!——I will go to Lady Morden, and, with feigned penitence, tell her every circumstance myself; only making her believe I knew Harriet when I returned the contract. She will admire my candour, think my contrition real, and thus will I turn this seeming disaster to excellent account, by making it an additional proof of sincerity and affection for her ladyship !—Dear Wit, I thank thee; thou never forsakest me at a crisis !—Indeed !—My lord ! And my young lady ! —Ah ha !—But you shall find one, perhaps, who can plot as deeply as yourselves.

ACT THE FOURTH.

SCENE I.

LORD MORDEN, LAPELLE.

L. Mor. Into what an abyss of evils have I plunged, through inexperience, want of reflection, and an absurd imitation of fashionable follies !—Lapelle.

Lap. My lord.

L. Mor. Is the young—young gentleman returned?

3

Lap. (*Significantly.*) No, my lord.

L. Mor. I am on the rack!—The liberties in which Lady Morden permits this Sir Frederick are insupportable!—Unable to be silent, and ashamed to complain, I am tortured by contending passions.—Lapelle—let me know the instant—the—the young gentleman comes back.

Lap. (*Going.*) Yes, my lord.

L. Mor. Stay—(*To himself.*) What if I were to inform Lady Morden of this affair?——Surely she could not shut her eyes against such a palpable, such an unprincipled attempt at seduction!—(*Aloud.*) Go, and tell your lady I beg to speak with her a moment.

SCENE II.

L. Mor. What an absurd being is man!—Not a fortnight ago, Lady Morden was totally indifferent to me, and now I am in danger of losing her. I find I love her—to distraction love her!—Yet to sink into a civil, sober, domestic man—to become the standing jest of all those high-spirited companions whose society I have courted, whose maxims I have pretended to admire——

SCENE III.

LORD MORDEN, LADY MORDEN.

Lady Mor. So, my lord, in melancholy contemplation; and at home too!

L. Mor. Yes, madam.

Lady Mor. Lud! I wonder how your lordship

can endure home ! Of all places in the world, home
is certainly the most disagreeable.

L. Mor. Did not your ladyship meet Lapelle ?

Lady Mor. Lapelle ! no.

L. Mor. I—I wished to see your ladyship.

Lady Mor. To see me ! What can your lordship
possibly want with me ?

L. Mor. To speak to you.

Lady Mor. Speak to me !—You perfectly surprise
me.

L. Mor. On a subject which—I—I scarcely know
how to begin.

Lady Mor. Ha, ha, ha ! What can have made your
lordship so serious ? Ha, ha, ha ! I declare I never
saw you look so grave before !—This must be some
very important secret, that can occasion your lordship to look so very dismal !—I vow I am quite impatient—Come, my lord—Why don't you proceed ?

L. Mor. I—I begin to find—I have been very
foolish.

Lady Mor. Ha, ha, ha ! Is that the secret ?

L. Mor. I—I feel I have been to blame.

Lady Mor. To blame, my lord ! How ? Which
way ?—Or, if you have, how does it concern me ?

L. Mor. Your ladyship used to think our interests
inseparable.

Lady Mor. For which your lordship always laughed at me. And I freely own I was a very silly—out-
of-the-way woman.

L. Mor. Perhaps not, madam.

Lady Mor. How, my lord !—Not ?—Your lordship
is very polite, but you know very well I was.

L. Mor. Lady Morden, you once loved me—You
yourself, not long since, kindly owned you did.

Lady Mor. Very true, my lord ; but why—why
now should *you* reproach me with my follies ?

L. Mor. I feel the severity of your reproof—It is
no more than I merit !

Lady Mor. (*With affected surprise.*) I really don't understand your lordship!—I—I meant no reproof—We loved each other as long as it was agreeable to us, and if my passion happened to outlast your lordship's, that was none of your fault. These are the principles of—of all rational people, you know, my lord.

L. Mor. They are principles, madam, that, from my soul, I wish I had never heard!

Lady Mor. Upon my honour, you astonish me! —Have not I learnt them from you yourself?

L. Mor. Unjustifiable, madam, as my conduct may have been, I never carried them to the same excess as Sir Frederick Fashion.

Lady Mor. (*With an air of pique.*) Sir Frederick Fashion may perhaps be as capable of reformation as your lordship.

L. Mor. Your ladyship may—may be partial.

Lady Mor. Partial!

L. Mor. Who so great a libertine as this Sir Frederick?

Lady Mor. Has been——He has candour enough to confess it.

L. Mor. Has been!——Madam, there exists a present proof of deliberate seduction!——An injured lady——

Lady Mor. (*Smiling.*) Oh! What, the—the—the Croat.

L. Mor. Madam!

Lady Mor. What's your surprise, my lord? Don't I tell you he has confessed all his follies to me?

L. Mor. But, madam, did he mention the contract?

Lady Mor. To be sure! And the—the counterfeit copy—with the generous manner in which he just now returned Harriet the original, though she thought he did not know her.

L. Mor. I am petrified!—Lady Morden—I perceive I have lost your affections.

Lady Mor. My lord—I am above dissimulation.—
Yes—I own I have a passion, too permanent to be
shaken, and the satisfaction of a self-assurance that
he who at present possesses my heart will not so soon
be weary of me as he who who had it before.

L. Mor. You cut me to the soul!—Did you know
what I feel!

Lady Mor. Feel, my lord! Ha, ha, ha! Oh fie!—
Your lordship is a man of fashion, not of feeling.

L. Mor. Hovering mischief, madam, has quicken-
ed benumbed nature in me. (*Kneels, and takes her
hand.*) Oh! let me conjure you, Lady Morden, to
reflect on your present situation! I have conducted
you to the horrid precipice of guilt and destruction!
Oh! suffer me to save, to snatch you from danger!

Lady Mor. Ha, ha, ha!

SCENE IV.

LORD MORDEN, LADY MORDEN, SIR FREDERICK.

Sir Fred. Ha, ha, ha! How now, my lord! Ha,
ha, ha! Making love to your wife?

Lady Mor. Ha, ha, ha! Oh! Sir Frederick, if you
had but come a little sooner, you would have heard
the most delightful morality!

Sir Fred. Ha, ha, ha! Morality from my lord?

L. Mor. Yes, sir, morality from my lord!

Lady Mor. Ha, ha, ha! Nay, I assure you, he is
quite serious. (*Retires, coquetting with* SIR FREDE-
RICK.)

L. Mor. Rejected! Ridiculed! Despised! Their
sport! Their scorn! Their subject for open sarcasm,

laughter, and contempt ! Oh ! insupportable. (LORᴮ
MORDEN *retires into his own room.*)

SCENE V.

LADY MORᴅEN, SIR FREDERICK.

Lady Mor. Ha, ha, ha! My lord has a mind to
fall in love with me once more.

Sir Fred. Nobody but my lord, madam, would ever
have ceased a moment to love you !

L. Mor. Well, Sir Frederick, and may I then at
last flatter myself I have found that sympathy of soul
for which I so long have sighed ?

Sir Fred. Alas, madam, I dare not rank myself
your equal !—No, I dare not !—There is such infini-
tude of perfection in your every thought, look, and
expression, that to merit you were to be, as you are,
something celestial !—Yet such virtue as mere humanity may arrive at, I will exhaust nature with endeavours, and weary Heaven with prayers to acquire !

Lady Mor. There is surely some secret charm in
our words.

Sir Fred. Did I think the gratification of any sinis-
ter passion influenced my present conduct ; were it
not my hope to remove you from the cold embrace of
satiated apathy, to the sweet and endless transports
of love, founded on, permit me to say, on a congeni-
ality of soul and sentiment; did I not feel an innate
conviction that there already subsists between us a tie
of the most indissoluble nature, an immaculate tie, a
marriage of the mind, superior infinitely to all human
institutions ; did I not think and feel thus, I would
instantly, dreadful as the image is to thought, re-

nounce that heaven which I have had the presumption to contemplate, nay, aspire to possess !

Lady Mor. And if, after all this, you should prove
false, Sir Frederick !

Sir Fred. False, madam !—Oh ! Let me conjure
you to inflict any punishment on me, rather than that
of suspecting my sincerity !—Thus, kneeling, on this
angelic hand I vow——

SCENE VI.

LADY MORDEN, SIR FREDERICK, LORD MORDEN.

L. Mor. I cannot resist the impulse which—How !
—Sir Frederick !

Sir Fred. (*Rising.*) My lord. (*With perfect indifference.*)

L. Mor. So, madam.

Lady Mor. So, sir.

L. Mor. You can listen to *morality* from others,
madam, if not from me !

Lady Mor. Oh ! I—I have no dislike to a sermon,
when I—admire the preacher.

L. Mor. Madam, if you have no respect for my
honour, you might have some for my feelings, and—

Lady Mor. (*Interrupting him.*) A, a—Hold, hold,
my lord—You are beginning your *discourse* again,
but I am in a hurry, and will hear you draw your
conclusions some other opportunity.

L. Mor. Madam——

Lady Mor. Nay, I will, upon my honour.

SCENE VII.

LORD MORDEN, SIR FREDERICK.

L. Mor. Hold, sir ; a word with you, if you please.

Sir Fred. With me, my lord?

L. Mor. With you.

Sir Fred. Willingly. Your lordship seems in so pleasant a humour——

L. Mor. Sir, I am in a humour neither to be trifled with nor sneered at.

Sir Fred. Ha, ha, ha! I can assure your—ha, ha, ha!—your lordship, no man is happier to see you in your present temper than I am.

L. Mor. Look you, Sir Frederick, you and I have been too long of the same school, for me to be ignorant of your principles. But I begin to detest them!

Sir Fred. Ha, ha, ha!

L. Mor. They are now, at this very moment, rending my heart : they have planted a nest of adders in my bosom.—In short, sir—you must forbear your visits to Lady Morden.

Sir Fred. My lord—

L. Mor. I am serious—determined.

Sir Fred. Ha, ha, ha! When her *ladyship* gives me this advice, it may—perhaps—be followed.

L. Mor. It must and shall be followed, sir, when I give it.

Sir Fred. Ha, ha, ha!

L. Mor. Ridiculous as it may appear to you, and such as you, I feel and will assert a husband's rights.

Sir Fred. Ha, ha, ha! I congratulate your lordship on the keenness and delicacy of your feelings ; they give me great pleasure, infinite pleasure, upon my soul. Ha, ha, ha!—As to—a husband's rights, I—

have no doubt you will—very shortly—be in full possession of them all.

L. Mor. Sir, I will have you know I am at present
in *full* possession of them all.

Sir Fred. May be so, egad !

L. Mor. And can no longer forbear telling you, I
believe you to be a villain.

Sir Fred. Ah, now your lordship is perfectly explicit, (*Draw, and fight.*)

SCENE VIII.

LORD MORDEN, SIR FREDERICK, GABRIEL, *who
runs fearless between them, and looks first at one,
then at the other.*

L. Mor. How now, sirrah ! How dare you take
this liberty ?

Gab. Nay, ecod, there do seem to be some danger
in it ; an I had not dared to dare, but that I thought
that your lordship wou'd na stick I.

L. Mor. Be gone, sirrah !

Gab. Nay, but my lady sent me, and would be
glad to speak wi' your honour's worship.

L. Mor. With me ?

Gab. Oh no ! Not wi' your lordship's honour's
worship ; but wi' his worship's honour, Sir Frederick
Fashion.

Sir Fred. This is no place, my lord ; we'll settle
this business to-morrow—To-morrow, my lord—To-
morrow——

SCENE IX.

LORD MORDEN, GABRIEL.

L. Mor. Damnation!—Torture!—To-morrow?—
He has some concealed meaning—A thousand little
circumstances tell me some mischief is brooding—I
could not have believed Lady Morden so confirmed,
so far gone in guilt.—The behaviour of them all, their
dark illusions, their sarcasms pointed at me, convince
me they are acting in conjunction to hold me up.—
How now, sirrah! What do you stand gaping at?—
How durst you come between us?

Gab. Why, ecod, I knew that, wi' us, i' th' country,
murder would have been against the commandements;
and I had forgot that here in town you have no commandements.

L. Mor. This fool can see the excesses of passion
in their true light.

Gab. I'm sorry 'at I angered your lordship's worship; becase as why I wur determined to do like the
rest of my neighbours; for, sartinly, wur a body to
keep the commandements, while every body else is
breaking them—a'd be a poor devil, indeed. (LORD
MORDEN *walks about.*) Belike, your lordship be a
bit jealousy like?

L. Mor. How, sirrah?

Gab. Nay, I should no' a' wondered an you wur—
An I had no' been told that your Londoneers be never jealousy like.

L. Mor. Should not have wondered!—Why not,
sirrah?

Gab. Nay, ecod, I munna tell!

L. Mor. Tell what?

Gab. Nay, that's it—As I said, I munna tell !

L. Mor. (*Puts his hand to his sword.*) Speak all you know instantly, or——

Gab. (*With half serious, half sulky reproof.*) Nay, nay, donna be in a passion, your worship—I be no goose : you munna spit me.

L. Mor. Speak, I say—I'll have your secret or your soul.

Gab. Ecod, I believe your worship will be puzzled to find either—Though that Sir Frederick be an old fox—A's used to steal chicken.

L. Mor. Be explicit. What has he done ?

Gab. Done—Oh—A's—

L. Mor. What ?

Gab. Promised me a place !

L. Mor. Zounds !

Gab. And, moreover, a' ga' me a purse, which is better still ; for your worship's grace do know that an egg in hand is better nur a hen in expectation.

L. Mor. Suppose, sirrah, I give you my purse too.

Gab. Nay, ecod, an you gi' it me—I believe I shall—I shall take it.

L. Mor. There, sir.

Gab. Thank your worship's lordship.—(GABRIEL *puts up the purse, and walks leisurely into* LADY MOR-DEN'S *dressing-room.*)

SCENE X.

LORD MORDEN, HARRIET.

L. Mor. (*Following* GABRIEL.) Why, hark you, sirrah !—Come back !—Why, rascal !

Har. (*Calling.*) St ! My lord ! My lord !

L. Mor. (*Looking back to* HARRIET, *and then re-collecting* GABRIEL.) Astonishing effrontery!

Har. My lord!

L. Mor. (*Returning.*) Oh! madam, I am distracted.

Har. Have patience but for one quarter of an hour, and I hope to rid you of all your fears, and inflict that punishment on the author of them which he dreads most.

L. Mor. How, madam?

Har. By exposing him; making him what he delights to make others—a subject of laughter and contempt.

L. Mor. Which way, madam?

Har. We may be overheard: step with me into the anti-chamber, and I'll inform you.

SCENE XI.

GABRIEL, SIR FREDERICK.

Gab. (*Peeping after* LORD MORDEN *and* HARRIET, *and then calling.*) Sir Frederick!—Sir Frederick!

Sir Fred. Well, what's the matter? How camest thou off with his lordship?

Gab. Off? Ecod, I—I wish you may come off as well.

Sir Fred. I!

Gab. Ees—Why, mun, there be the bailiffs below!

Sir Fred. Bailiffs!

Gab. Ees—Sent by the Irish gentleman, lady I mean, a'ter your worship!—Ecod, hur is determined to ha' you safe!

Sir Fred. The devil! What's to be done?—Is she
with them?

Gab. No; hur be come back, and is gone into the
anti-chamber wi' my lord.

Sir Fred. And has not seen them?

Gab. Likely not.

Sir Fred. Here, quick, change clothes with me,
and tell them you are Sir Frederick Fashion.

Gab. Me!—Ecod, thank you for that—No, no—
I would na' be in your coat for fifty pounds!

Sir Fred. Fool! they durst not detain *you.*

Gab. I'll take care they sha'n't.

Sir Fred. S'death! What's to be done?

Gab. Ecod—Suppose—Suppose I wur to go and
tell the Irish gentleman somebody wanted *hur,* and
so make 'em arrest she?

Sir Fred. Ha! Exquisite fellow! I conceive—
Away: send her instantly!

SCENE XII.

SIR FREDERICK, *two Bailiffs.*

Bail. Is your name Sir Frederick Fashion, sir?

Sir Fred. No, sir; but Sir Frederick will be here
directly, if you have any business with him.

Bail. (*Aside to his companion.*) Have your handkerchief ready, should he make any noise, for fear
of a rescue.—This is a very serious affair. (*To* SIR
FREDERICK.) Pray, sir, what kind of person is Sir
Frederick.

Sir Fred. Um—a handsome—agreeable little gentleman, and very young.

Bail. May I ask, sir, how he is dressed?

Sir Fred. (*Aside.*) Gad! well remember'd.—(*To the*

Bailiffs.) Dressed! Oh! he is dressed for—for the masquerade—Here he comes. (*The Bailiffs retire a little upon the watch.*)

SCENE XIII.

SIR FREDERICK, *Bailiffs*, HARRIET.

Sir Fred. (*To* HARRIET.) Well, Sir Frederick! Ha, ha, ha! How goes your scheme.

Har. Oh ho!—Faidth, and are you so jocular?

Sir Fred. I have been thinking this is a dangerous business, and would advise you not to give the girl that contract—It may bring you into trouble.

Bail. (*Aside to his companion.*) You hear!

Har. Oh! Faidth, and she has it safe enough.

Bail. (*Advances.*) Sir Frederick Fashion, (*Touches* HARRIET *on the shoulder,*) you are my prisoner, sir —I have a special writ against you.

Har. Ha, ha, ha! Against me!—Arrah, friend, but you are making a bit of a bull here.

Bail. We know what we are about, sir. My carriage is below: you shall be treated like a gentleman; but we must beg you to go with us instantly, and without noise.

Har. (*Alarmed, and forgetting the brogue.*) I tell you, friend, you mistake the person.

SCENE XIV.

Sir Frederick, Harriet, *Bailiffs*, Gabriel.

Gab. (*Goes up to* Harriet.) Here, Sir Frederick, here be a card from Colonel Castoff, wi' his compliments.

Har. Sirrah ! me !

Gab. (*With pretended astonishment.*) Ees, to be sure !

Bail. Sir, we must be gone.

Har. This is a concerted trick.—Here—(*As soon as* Harriet *begins to call, the Bailiffs clap the handkerchief over her mouth, and hurry off with her.*)

SCENE XV.

Gabriel, Sir Frederick.

Gab. Did not I do it rarely ?

Sir Fred. Do !—I could wonder and worship thee ! In half a year thou wouldst make an ass of Machiavel !—Oh that I could but retrieve that cursed contract.

Gab. I do think I could get it.

Sir Fred. Ay !—Nay, I do almost begin to believe in miracles ! Which way ?

Gab. No matter for that—What will you gie me ?

Sir Fred. Whatever thou canst wish—A hundred guineas——

Gab. And the place in the excise ?

Sir Fred. Any thing, every thing !—Run, try, fly !
—Think, succeed, and I'll make an emperor of thee !

Gab. Ees—I'll be emperor of excise-men.

SCENE XVI.

SIR FREDERICK, MRS MODELY, EMILY.

Sir Fred. The shrewdness and abilities of this fellow are amazing !

Mrs Mod. (*Entering.*) Yes, my sweet little Emily,
the greatest beauty in London would be envied, had
she made such a conquest.

Em. Ah !—you say so.

Mrs Mod. Say ! Why, to-morrow morning the
whole town will be in a flame !

Em. Well, that will be pure.

Mrs Mod. Oh, Sir Frederick !

Sir Fred. (*Runs to* EMILY.) My life ! my soul !
my transport !

Em. (*To* MRS MODELY.) What sweet words !

Mrs Mod. You are very much obliged to me, I
assure you. I have been speaking to my sweet, dear
little Emily here in your behalf.

Sir Fred. Then, madam, I am inexpressibly obliged
to you.

Em. Yes, Mrs Modely is very much your friend,
and very much my friend.—A'n't you, Mrs Modely ?

Mrs Mod. Yes, my little dear, I am, indeed, *very*
much your friend ; and if I had not the best opinion
in the world of Sir Frederick, would not have spoken
as I have.

Em. Well, Sir Frederick, have you ordered the
chaise and four ?

Sir Fred. (*Pretending to be afraid* MRS MODELY *should overhear.*) Yes!—Hush!

Em. Nay, you may say any thing before Mrs Modely.—I have told her all; for you know she is my friend.

Mrs Mod. Yes, yes, Sir Frederick, be assured I will not betray any secret, the keeping of which will make my dear Emily so happy.

Em. Yes, we shall be so happy!—You know, Sir Frederick, you swear to marry me.

Sir Fred. Solemnly! (*All through the scene he looks anxiously round at intervals, fearful of being surprised.*)

Em. Well, but swear it again now, before Mrs Modely.

Sir Fred. By all the saints!

Em. Saints! Pshaw! you should swear by—by my bright eyes, that dim the stars.

Sir Fred. Oh! by those bright eyes, that dim the blazing sun.

Em. And—and my beauties, that eclipse the blushing moon.

Sir Fred. Ay, by those, and all your burning charms, I swear

Em. To marry me the moment we come to Scotland.

Sir Fred. The moment we come to Scotland.

Em. And if we are pursued——

Sir Fred. To fight for you!—die for you!

Em. Oh! that will be delightful!

Sir Fred. (*Aside.*) The devil it will!

Em. Come, let us set off. My band-box is ready.

Sir Fred. That is impossible, my angel.

Em. Impossible!

Sir Fred. I have not ordered the chaise till ten o'clock.

Em. Oh dear! what, two whole hours longer!

Sir Fred. They are two ages, I grant. (*Looking*

round.) Forgive my fears, my dearest Emily, but
though the pleasure of your company is the most
precious thing on earth, a—a—yet——

Em. What, you want me gone ?

Sir Fred. Rather than you should think so un-
kindly, I will run the hazard of being surprised, and
eternally separated from you.

Em. Will you ? I am sure you don't love me then.
However, I'll go.   You will be sure to be ready the
moment the clock strikes ten.

SCENE XVII.

SIR FREDERICK, MRS MODELY.

Sir Fred. Time is precious. Here have been such
plots against me !

Mrs Mod. Plots !

Sir Fred. Oh ! I have escaped Scylla and Charyb-
dis ! But wind and tide are now both with me. Lady
Morden is to meet me here in half an hour. Through
that door is her chamber.

Mrs Mod. Oh, you vile creature !

Sir Fred. What prude, to-morrow, will dare pretend that woman and education are a match for man
and nature ?

Mrs Mod. And so you will persist in your wickedness, in spite of my persuasions ?

Sir Fred. Lady Morden has still all the rhodo-
montade of love in her brain ; thinks of nothing but
cooing constancy and eternal raptures !

Mrs Mod. Simple woman !

Sir Fred. Except, indeed, tormenting her husband, which seems to give the sin a double sweetness.

Mrs Mod. Or she would be no wife.

Sir Fred. So, as soon as I am gone off with Emily,
I will have a consolatory epistle delivered to her.

Mrs Mod. Compassionate toad!

Sir Fred. Here it is ready written, and, if I don't
flatter myself, a master-piece.

Mrs Mod. Let me see, let me see.

Sir Fred. No; you shall hear. (*Reads.*) " Dear
madam, though you are an angel, if there are other
angels, am I to blame?"

Mrs Mod. Certainly not.

Sir Fred. (*Reads.*) " If man is naturally incon-
stant, and if I am a man, am I to blame?"

Mrs Mod. Certainly not.

Sir Fred. (*Reads.*) " If nature has made variety
the highest enjoyment, am I to blame?"

Mrs Mod· Certainly not.

Sir Fred. (*Reads.*) " If, since happiness is the pursuit of us all, I am happy as often as I can, am I to
blame?"

Mrs Mod. Certainly not.

Sir Fred. (*Reads.*) " Farewell, madam: circumstances, as you will find, force me thus suddenly from
your arms, in which, I own, I found heaven center-
ed : but if you should call me cruel, perjured, and
ungrateful, because I act naturally, and therefore
rationally, am I to blame?"

Mrs Mod. Certainly not.—Well, as I live, this is
a master-stroke! Perfectly, as I thought I knew you,
you have astonished me!

Sir Fred. Yes, 'tis the true Socratic mode.   But
now, my dear Mrs Modely, go you to Emily; prevent her disturbing us, and keep her in readiness.

Mrs Mod. Well, remember every thing is at stake,
and be yourself.

Sir Fred. Fear me not: that prescience which
they say is the forerunner of all great events gives
me a happy assurance of success; a confidence that
makes success certain.

ACT THE FIFTH.

SCENE I.

GENERAL BURLAND.

Gen. I cannot keep from this house!—There is a foreboding of mischief, which haunts and perturbs my imagination!—And I fear with reason!—The malignant joy, the smothered exult, the obscure, ironical satire which ran through the discourse of that Sir Frederick, were not without a meaning.—I wish I had not consented to let Emily stay—He sneered, I remember, at the moment; nay, it seemed the sneer of triumph!—I wish she were safe at my own house.—Poor Lady Morden!—And is it possible?—Such rectitude of heart!—Such purity of sentiment!—I wish Emily were at home—Should my child, my darling fall, I were a wretch indeed!

SCENE II.

GENERAL BURLAND, LORD MORDEN.

L. Mor. (*Wildly.*) I am miserable! distracted! racked!—The thunderbolt has struck before I heard it!—Oh that its exterminating power had been final! But it has maimed, and deformed, and left a full feeling of wretchedness!

Gen. How now, my lord?

L. Mor. General, I am a wretch!—an irretrieveable, eternal wretch!

Gen. What, and are you come to a sense of this, now it is too late ?

L. Mor. There's the misery!—The curse is accomplished, and hope is fled !

Gen. Why, ay ! Such is the infatuation of folly and vice, they will not believe vengeance has an arm, till its fatal gripe is felt !

L. Mor. I cannot support these tortures !—Oh that it were possible !

Gen. What ?

L. Mor. To reclaim Lady Morden.

Gen. What then ? Another month, and Sir Frederick Fashion, or any other libertine of fashion might take her.

L. Mor. Never !—Never !—Were her affections once again mine, the stroke of death only should separate us !

Gen. (*With deep compassion.*) Well, my lord, if you are at last convinced of the immensity of your loss—I pity you !

L. Mor. Oh ! would you could relieve !

Gen. Would I could !—But you were a witness how ineffectual my endeavours were. However, walk with me into the anti-chamber, and let us consult what is best to be done.—Her principles I fear are shaken ; the only rock on which virtue can stand secure.

L. Mor. Sapped, destroyed !—She avows her intents !—unblushingly avows them ! And, recapitulating my errors, my crimes, dares me to complain of, or notice hers ! Scorns and contemns me, and justly too, that such a thing as I should pretend to repeat or respect the word virtue !

Gen. It is what every husband, every father of a family must expect ! His smallest foibles will stand as precedents for a swarm of follies ; and if he has any vices, they will propagate a hideous brood, that shall extirpate his name from the earth, or overwhelm it with obloquy !

SCENE III.

GABRIEL, SIR FREDERICK.

Gab. (*Peeping after* LORD MORDEN *and the General.*) Come, mun!—Your worship, come!

Sir Fred. Are they gone?

Gab. Ees.

Sir Fred. Well, what hast thou done?—Where is Harriet?

Gab. Oh, I ha' her safe.

Sir Fred. Thou!

Gab. Ees, mun—For when the bailiffs found out a wur a woman, they wur partitly ravenous!

Sir Fred. And let her go?

Gab. Ees.

Sir Fred. S'death!

Gab. But I secured her.

Sir Fred. Secured! Impossible. How?

Gab. Nay, never do you mind how—I tell'ee, I ha' her safe.

Sir Fred. But where are the bailiffs?

Gab. In this house.

Sir Fred. The devil they are!

Gab. Ees, they be—waiting for your worship.

Sir Fred. Death and destruction!

Gab. But what o' that? I a' got the contract, mun.

Sir Fred. Hast thou?

Gab. Ees, here it is.

Sir Fred. Precious fellow! I cou'd worship thee Give it me.

Gab. (*Putting his hand behind him.*) Nay, hold there '—I wunna do that.

Sir Fred. Won't!

Gab. No—I wunna.

Sir Fred. Pshaw! Make no words, but deliver it
—and here—here is—

Gab. Nay, put up your paper, for I wunna part
wi' mine.

Sir Fred. S'death, fellow!

Gab. Nay, be mild tempered—stand where you
be; for an you stir another step, I'll call the bailiffs.

Sir Fred. (*Aside.*) Cunning scoundrel!—He has
me in his power, and time presses.—Well, Gabriel,
be faithful, and, depend on't, I'll make thee a clever
fellow.

Gab. Why, ecod, I think I am like a Monmouth-
street coat—ready made.

Sir Fred. Thou rememberest the instructions I
gave thee?

Gab. Parfitly.

Sir Fred. The chaise is to wait at the corner of
the street.

Gab. Ees.

Sir Fred. Thou art to convey Emily's band-box
away privately, and, if any questions are asked, to
say it is Lord Morden's.

Gab. Ees.

Sir Fred. Hast thou taken care of the letter I
gave thee?

Gab. Care! Ees, ees: I a' ta'en good care on't.

Sir Fred. Observe, thou art to deliver it to Lady
Morden, half an hour after we are departed.

Gab. Half an hour before you are departed.

Sir Fred. Zounds! No, half an hour after, man.

Gab. Oh! Ees, ees: half an hour after.

Sir Fred. Now be gone.

Gab. But—but how will your worship get by the
bailiffs?

Sir Fred. S'death, that's true!—Is there no disguise?

Gab. Why—ees—there be a long great coat i' th'
hall.

Sir Fred. Ay, true!—Bring it me.

Gab. Nay, nay—I'll put it on first, and let 'em see me—so, then, when they see you, they'll think it be I.

Sir Fred. Excellent! Where are Lord Morden and the general?

Gab. I' th' t'other chamber.

Sir Fred. Unlucky! I wish they were any where else.

Gab. Oh!—an that be all, I'll soon make 'em budge.

Sir Fred. How?

Gab. Nay!—Lord, you're so quisitive!—I tell you I'll do't—I'll saunter through this door, lock it, and send 'em packing through t'other.

Sir Fred. Thou art the prince of plotters.—Away: be vigilant.

Gab. Oh! never do you fear me.

[*Goes into the anti-chamber.*

SCENE IV.

SIR FREDERICK, LADY MORDEN.

Sir Fred. This fellow would outwit a whole conclave of cardinals!

Lady Mor. Well, Sir Frederick! here I am, you see, punctual to my promise.

Sir Fred. (*With vast insinuation, seeming sincerity, and humble rapture, all through the scene.*) Oh, madam, how can I repay this bounty—this condescension?—Never.—My life were a poor sacrifice to such sweetness and such charms!

Lady Mor. Sir Frederick, this is a trying, a decisive moment! I am going to be either the most happy or

9

the most wretched of women ! You tell me it is your wish, your resolution, to be no longer that general lover, that man of the world you have hitherto been thought.

Sir Fred. Say not, dear lady, it is either my wish or resolution ! Heaven can testify, I have not the power to be any thing but what it shall please you to make me !

Lady Mor. I have owned to you that the levity I have lately affected is not natural to me; that my heart sighs for an acquaintance, a mate, that like itself is subject to all the sweet emotions of sensibility !—Yes, it was the first wish of my soul to find this correspondent heart !—a heart beating with the same ardour, vibrating to the same sensations, panting for the same pleasures, shrinking from the same pangs ; pliant, yet firm ; gentle, yet aspiring ; passionate, yet pure !—Such I once thought Lord Morden's—Should I a second time be deceived !

Sir Fred. I am poor in proofs of sincerity ! I have none to offer !—My former errors are present punishments ! To deny, or even palliate them would imply intentional deceit ; and this is a moment in which I would wish for men and gods to be witnesses of my truth !—I have had, I own, most libertine opinions of your gentle sex ; but these I now solemnly renounce ! —Had I before met with a Lady Morden, I should before have made this renunciation !—But perhaps the women it has been my misfortune to know deserve in part the light esteem in which I held them. Never till now did I find one who could mutually inspire such passion and respect ! Such agitated, burning hopes ! Such excruciating fears, or thoughts so sanctified as those I this moment feel !

Lady Mor. Yet, Sir Frederick, I cannot help observing your conversation in society seems still tinged with the impurity of your former libertine principles.

Sir Fred. I own, Lady Morden, with confusion

own, I have not hitherto had the courage, or perhaps
I have wanted strength to stem the torrent; but, aided
by you, I feel I dare promise any thing!

Lady Mor. I confess, Sir Frederick, the mind finds
some difficulty in rooting out fears planted in it by
reiterated accusations. The stories the world tells of
you are dreadful! And yet there is such heartfelt
conviction attends your present words, that to me it
is impossible to listen, and retain a doubt.

Sir Fred. This generous confidence transports me,
fills me with gratitude, and inspires rapturous hope!
(*Clasps her round the waist.*) Oh, gently suffer me to
conduct you where love lies in panting, breathless
ecstasy——

SCENE V.

To them GABRIEL, *abruptly, in a Great-coat; stands
fixed, staring.*

Sir Fred. (*Sternly.*) How now!

Gab. (*Deliberately.*) Belike——you dunna want
company?

Sir Fred. No, sir.

Gab. I thought as much.

Sir Fred. (*Laying hold of him.*) Be gone, instantly!

Gab. Nay! Hands off! (*Throws him from him.*) I
sha'n't stir till I have delivered my message.

Sir Fred. What message? What have you to say?

Gab. (*Aloud.*) Why, the chaise and four be come.

Sir Fred. How?

Gab. (*Still louder.*) The band-box ready.

Sir Fred. Infernal booby!

Gab. Miss Emily waiting.

Sir Fred. (*Violently.*) Be gone, I say.

Gab. Gone!—Nay, sartinly you would no' ha' I run away wi' her.

Lady Mor. (*With contempt.*) Ha, ha, ha!

Sir Fred. Lady Morden!

Lady Mor. Ha, ha, ha!—Why, surely you! the never-failing victor! the fertile-brained Sir Frederick Fashion! who knows not defeat, and who never yet was at a loss for stratagems! though you are taken somewhat unawares, you cannot want invention!

Sir Fred. You'll pardon me, madam, if I want understanding to comprehend your meaning.

Lady Mor. Indeed!—Well, if you are so very dull of apprehension—am I to blame?

Sir Fred. Madam!

Lady Mor. Oh!—Do you recollect—this letter?

Sir Fred. How!—Faithless fiend! (*Goes to assault* GABRIEL, *who throws back his great-coat, and appears dressed as a gentleman.*)

Gab. Keep off, or dread the chastisement I am prompted instantaneously to inflict!

Sir Fred. Chastisement!—What is this?—Who are you?

Gab. A man!—You are—

Lady Mor. For Heaven's sake, brother—

Sir Fred. Brother!

Gab. Gabriel Wilmot; whose head is so full of the nonsense of friendship, honour, and honesty.

Sir Fred. I'll be revenged, however. (*Attacks* MR WILMOT *again.*)

SCENE VI.

To them LORD MORDEN *and General.*

L. Mor. Turn, wretch, and receive your punish-

ment from this arm ! (SIR FREDERICK *turns on* LORD
MORDEN.)

Gen. (*Beating down their swords.*) Oh, for shame !
—Look to the lady.

Lady Mor. Oh, general !—Oh, my lord ! (*Runs
to* LORD MORDEN, *and falls on his neck.*)

L. Mor. My life ! My ecstasy ! My saviour !

SCENE VII.

To them MRS MODELY *and* EMILY.

Mrs Mod. Bless me, what uproar !—Hey-dey !—
(*Aside.*) So, so ! Here is a very pretty *denouement*
to our plot, indeed !—(*Aloud.*) I see, good folks, you
are all embroiled here ; and as it is a very disagreeable thing to be present at family disputes, I'll—(*Is
going ; the General plants himself against the door.*)

Gen. Pray, madam, stay, and receive the compliments of the company—mine and your friend Emily's
in particular.

Mrs Mod. Oh, with pleasure !

L. Mor. Mr Wilmot ! My best brother !—Though
you have in part acquainted me with what is past,
yet it is so sudden—And you ! my dearest lady ! To
find you still the same is joy unspeakable !

Lady Mor. The task of making you suppose I had
effectually become what I seemed, was indeed most
painful ; but the loss of your affections were not pain !
'Twere horror !—I told you my passion was too permanent to be shaken—Ah ! how could you imagine
I meant another ? Or think it possible I ever could
forget that chaste, that ardent, that eternal love I
have so repeatedly vowed ?

L. Mor. Oh for words !—I am all love ! gratitude! rapture ! and amazement !

Gen. And so is Sir Frederick, apparently—Nay, even you, madam, seem a little surprised.

Mrs Mod. Me ! Oh dear, no.

Lady Mor. (*To* SIR FREDERICK.) Dear sir, though you are a deep and excellent plotter, if there have been counterplots—am I to blame ? (*Curtsies.*)

Mrs Mod. (*With affected candour.*) Certainly not.

Lady Mor. If man is sometimes vain, presumptuous, and unprincipled, and if you are a man—am I to blame ?

Mrs Mod. Certainly not.

Mr Wil. If I assumed a mean disguise, that I might aid a sister to detect and expose the mean machinations of Seduction—am I to blame ?

Mrs Mod. Certainly not.

Em. If, following the advice of this dear lady, (*To* LADY MORDEN,) simplicity has made cunning outwit itself—am I to blame ? (*Curtseying first to* SIR FREDERICK, *and then to* MRS MODELY.)

Gen. (*With vast pleasure*) Certainly not.

Lady Mor. If, since happiness is the pursuit of us all, I wish to be as happy as possible—(*Most affectionately taking* LORD MORDEN's *hand*)—am I to blame ?

Omnes. Certainly not.

Sir Fred. (*With affected ease.*) Certainly not.—So the catechism being ended, the scholars may depart.

Mr Wil. Certainly not.

Sir Fred. Sir !

Mr Wil. You forget the bailiffs.

Lady Mor. Besides, Sir Frederick, before you go, you must give me leave to introduce you to—

SCENE VIII.

To them HARRIET, *in Woman's Clothes, presented by*
LADY MORDEN.

—This lady.

Sir Fred. Harriet!

Har. Yes, sir—that Harriet, whom, hearing she
had happiness in view, and proportioning your ideal
triumph to the weight of misery you might entail,
you raised heaven and earth to bring to wretchedness and ruin.

Mrs Mod. Upon my honour, you—you are a sad
man, Sir Frederick!—A very sad man!

(*The Company by their looks shew they understand*
MRS MODELY's *real character.*)

Har. But your vanity is humbled—you now stand
detected; and, instead of envied, you will be sneered
at by the depraved, pitied by the good, and hence-
forth avoided by the credulous young creatures you
so manfully have delighted to involve in guilt and
destruction!

Mrs Mod. A very dangerous man, indeed, Sir
Frederick!

Gen. (*Ironically.*) Ay; beware of him, madam.

Mrs Mod. Oh! I—I will!

Har. Yes, sir, the finger of scorn points where it
ought; you are exposed, and my resentment is appeased.

Sir Fred. Then, madam—the—the contract—

Har. There it is, sir. (*Returns it.*) I never meant
to make any other use of it than what has been better
effected by different means. (*Curtseying to* LADY
MORDEN *and* MR WILMOT.)

Sir Fred. Madam—

Har. No thanks, sir.

Gen. No ; they would sit a little awkwardly.

Lady Mor. And now, Sir Frederick, if, after this lesson, you should still retain your former principles and practices, and hereafter receive a still severer punishment, I hope you will acknowledge—we are not to blame.   [*Exeunt omnes.*

THE

SCHOOL FOR PREJUDICE ;

A

COMEDY,

IN FIVE ACTS.

AS PERFORMED AT THE

THEATRE-ROYAL, COVENT-GARDEN.

BY

THOMAS DIBDIN.

DRAMATIS PERSONÆ.

OLD LIBERAL,	*Mr Munden.*
FRANK LIBERAL,	*Mr Lewis.*
EPHRAIM,	*Mr Fawcett.*
COUNSELLOR FRIENDLY,	*Mr Murray.*
MILDMAY,	*Mr H. Johnston.*
JOHN GROUSE,	*Mr Emery.*
CHEVY CHACE,	*Mr Farley.*
PARCHMENT,	*Mr Simmons.*
LANDLORD,	*Mr Davenport.*
TOUCH,	*Mr Atkins.*
TAP, } Bailiffs,	*Mr Abbot.*
TAKE,	*Mr Wilde.*
SERVANT to Old Liberal,	*Mr Curties.*
1st SERVANT } to Squire	{ *Mr Platt.*
2d SERVANT } Chace,	{ *Mr Blurton.*
WAITER.	*Mr Seaton.*
MRS HOWARD,	*Miss Chapman.*
MARIAN,	*Miss Murray.*
MISS LIBERAL,	*Mrs Davenport.*
FANNY LIBERAL,	*Mrs Mills.*
JENNY,	*Miss Simms.*
RACHEL,	*Mrs Whitmore.*

THE

SCHOOL FOR PREJUDICE.

ACT THE FIRST

SCENE I.

A Hall at OLD LIBERAL'S.

Enter MISS LIBERAL, *followed by* JENNY.

Miss Lib. Now don't talk to me, Jenny, for it's in
vain. Am I not about to make his fortune? Haven't
I sacrificed my tender years, passions, and inclinations, to raise my cousin's consequence, treble his
estate, and perhaps to grace the family tree with a
coronet? And sha'n't I do what I please?

Jen. Certainly, madam—and if I was a lady of
your quality and fortin, by gosh, I wou'd.

Miss Lib. And so I will, Jenny—I'll have that
man, Grouse, the game-keeper, discharged immediately—that base-born son of my cousin's shall be

instantly dismissed the house; and without the girl is suffered to marry as I please, I'll throw the whole estate into Chancery, and see if all my cousin's knowledge of the law will help him to get it out again.

Jen. Why, dear me, ma'am, the more Mr Liberal has studied the law, the more he knows as how it would be impossible.

Miss Lib. True; but he studies nothing except how to cross my wishes and intentions. I endeavour to set an example of rigid propriety to the whole hamlet; but he, if a girl in it demeans herself with any of his servants or tenants, instead of clearing the parish of them, as a man of strict virtue ought to do, he pays a portion, truly, to marry them out of harm's way, as he calls it.

Jen. It's a shame, madam, so it is, that such wicked doings should be encouraged, while we poor vartuous girls are not taken the least notice of.

Miss Lib. Yes; and I must leave my money to be employed in settling other people's love affairs, forsooth! But I shall do no such thing, I promise you.

Jen. I'm sure if you do, ma'am, you're very much to be pitied.

Miss Lib. What! pitied! There again—after all my exertions, do I live to be pitied? No, thank Heaven, Miss Lucretia Liberal was never pitied in her life.

Jen. I'm sure, ma'am, I meant no offence; and for matter of that, though the neighbours do all pity old master very much, I don't think one of them would take such a liberty with your ladyship upon any account whatever.

Miss Lib. The neighbours are a set of meddling busy bodies; and the tenants, in consequence of my cousin's indulgence, are so familiar, that they do not even scruple sometimes to shake him by the hand— the children are suffered to feel in his pockets for ginger-bread, and a common farmer's man, the other day, was actually disrespectful enough, behind his back, to call him a hearty good creature.

Jen. It's all his own fault. If he was but to carry himself like your ladyship, not a soul in the place wou'd say any such thing of him.

Miss Lib. How unlike is his conduct to that of my late friend, Mr Rackrent, from whom I have received so handsome a bequest! He never lowered his consequence among children and tenants—he kept them at awful distance, and the respect inspired by his presence was almost insupportable.

(OLD LIBERAL *without.*)

Old Lib. There, now, can't you be quiet? It's all settled, I tell you. Hold your tongue, for if my cousin was once to know—

OLD LIBERAL *enters, followed by* JOHN GROUSE.

Old Lib. Why, zounds! there she is.—Go about your business; you're a bad man, and I have nothing to say to you.

John. Why, but your worship said just now—

Old Lib. I didn't say a word—it's no such thing, I tell you.

Miss Lib. Mr Liberal, if you haven't entirely relinquished all respect for me, never let that John Grouse come into my presence. I have heard of his scandalous reports.—A chattering, tattling brute, that ought to be minding his family, instead of troubling his head with his betters.

Old Lib. So he ought, cousin—he ought to be minding his family.—And a fine family it is.—Seven as beautiful, healthy, chubby, dirty, little fellows—Why, the youngest has three teeth already, hasn't he?

John. 'Twife says he has four, and twea mear coming.

Old Lib. There, cousin, there! And then his brother begins to run about charmingly. I dare say—I like that boy, he's so mischievous.

Miss Lib. This is beyond bearing—Listen to me, sir—Will you dismiss that man?

Old Lib. Certainly, my dear cousin, by all means. Hark ye, sir, never presume to come into this house again—till I send for you. (*Apart.*)

John. Why, it makes na odds about coming to t'house; your worship—you'll be taking a walk, I warrant, aboon t'brig, and our Mary and I shall be vast glad to see you.—And as to the tales old Doublechalk war telling o' me, why, he's a chattering windy chap, and likes to have all the talk till himself; but as I wou'dn't fratch wi' him, why, I shall say nought on't; howiver, I shall have some talk with him, before I've done.

Miss Lib. Leave the room, sirrah! If my cousin will put up with it, I won't.

John. Well, but now do call, your worship—you need not to heed putting us in a muddle. We are frightful enough o' maist maks o' quality; but your worship we mind na mair than a post.

Old Lib. Well, well; get out, I say.

John. And the bairns will so chuckle, and laugh at your worship.

Old Lib. Pretty creatures! but get along, I tell you. (*Forces* JOHN *out.*) Impudent blockhead! But come, my dear Lucretia, don't look so angry. In future, I'm determined to do every thing upon your own plan.

Miss Lib. And so you ought, to be sure. Jenny, leave the room.   [*Exit* JENNY. You know very well, cousin, that I do all for your good—and if I wasn't to interfere, things would be very different in this house.

Old Lib. They would—they would be very different, and I have often thought so.

Miss Lib. In the first place, you are too good natured. Your benevolence, as you call it, is extravagance: Where is the use of having a great estate, only to spend it?

Old Lib. Where, indeed? For my part, I was foolish enough to think that the only utility of a great estate proceeded from its being in the hands of those who *would* spend it.

Miss Lib. Then, sir, your intended provision for that boy of yours, Frank, whom you are so fond of, is infinitely too much. Have you considered his situation? What can be lower in the estimation of propriety, than the character of a natural son?

Old Lib. Why, that of an unnatural father.

Miss Lib. Perhaps so: but you have not been unnatural. You have already done every thing for him a father could do.

Old Lib. Have I? Well, now, that is kind of you —It's the first compliment you ever paid me, and if you were to study till doomsday, you cou'dn't pay me a greater.

Miss Lib. But you pervert my meaning. Was it at all proper that the son of a kitchen wench—

Old Lib. No, no—housekeeper, you mean. No, hang it, I never descended so low as the kitchen, neither.

Miss Lib. No matter—was it necessary, I ask, to give such a child the education of a gentleman, and that he should be qualified to appear in the most fashionable circles?

Old Lib. To qualify a man for appearing in the circles of modern fashion, requires little or no education at all. I have brought him up very differently from the plan of *your* men of fashion. I have taught him, that no one is honourable, who is not of use—And if ever I find him inactive when an opportunity of doing good presents itself, I'll cut the dog off with a shilling.

Miss Lib. You have raised his notions too high—
Had he been left to me—

Old Lib. You would have made a grocer or a chandler of him. Every bason of bohea I drank would have brought former follies to my remembrance, or I must have done penance before every wax candle in my drawing-room.

Miss Lib. And let me tell you, cousin, that to be an industrious tradesman, and to make a fortune by perseverance and integrity, is to acquire one of the highest ranks society can boast.

Old Lib. Yes, and let me tell *you*, cousin, that the man who is rich himself, and leaves his child, legal or illegal, no other materials than perseverance and industry for the formation of his fortune, justly deserves to be reckoned in the *lowest* ranks of society.

Miss Lib. Nonsense, I tell you   There is, and ought to be a medium in ev'ry thing.

Old Lib. I know it; but I, like a stupid old blockhead, could never find any medium in a father's affection. I love my boy, and I love my girls; I love ev'ry body's boys and girls, and if you had a dozen, I should only like you the better for it.

Miss Lib. Me! Mercy forbid! Did you ever hear poor dear Mr Rackrent say so—O' my conscience, I believe you carry your romantic notions so far, that, if your fortune permitted, you would be a father to all the children in the parish.

Old Lib. O, I wish I could—I'd make 'em all so happy—odsbobs, I'd—

Miss Lib. Stop, sir—I've no more leisure to give good advice to so little purpose. I am now going to fetch home your daughter, who this day bids adieu to school.—And I leave you to consider how far it may be worth while to prefer your own narrow system to the direction of a relation, who has fifty thousand pounds, to place in or out of the family, as she pleases.   [*Exit.*

Old Lib. Fifty thousand pounds! Ay, there's the rub. Fifty thousand pounds! In addition to my present estate, how useful it would enable a man to be! The interest of it would provide soup and Sunday schools for all the country.

Enter PARCHMENT, *a decrepid old Servant.*

Well, my gay old fellow, what's the news with you?

Parch. I have done every thing you have ordered, sir, and every thing Miss Lucretia ordered, so that I have been taking great pains for nothing at all; for what I had first done by your commands, was completely neutralized by what I afterwards did by hers.

Old Lib. Never mind.—We'll set all to rights again.—Tell that fellow who snared the hares in my grounds, that if I catch him, I'll make an example of him. Be very particular in looking out for him; and if he should be seen poaching again, why, tell the park-keeper to walk another way, and say nothing about it.

Parch. And what's to be done with old Cropley's cow? The bailiff has taken it for the rent of his cottage and garden.

Old Lib. Has he? a dog! That's quite right, you know; the law must be satisfied—It's a fine cow, so, d'ye hear, purchase it for me. Be sure to give as much money as he wants to make up, and when the cow's my own, why, I'll make old Cropley a present of it.

Enter a Servant.

Serv. Counsellor Friendly, sir.

Old Lib. Counsellor Friendly! What, my old friend and fellow-student? Admit him directly.

[*Exit Servant.*

Parchment, go and do as I have told you—And if

my cousin should ask any thing about it, you may say——

Parch. The truth. I was forty years in your father's service, and never told one lie the whole time.

Enter FRIENDLY.

Friend. Mr Liberal, I rejoice to see you. Friend Parchment, how is it? [PARCHMENT *bows, and exit.*] An old servant that, and almost past his labour.

Old Lib. But he is so independent, he wou'dn't accept the least acknowledgment of long services, if I were not to allow him some employ; and he executes the trifling commissions I entrust to him, with as much pride as if he was a secretary of state. But to what do I owe the pleasure of this unexpected visit?

Friend. Business, business. I am executor to the will of one friend, who died in this neighbourhood, and am come to administer some solid comfort to another friend, who lies on the bed of sickness.

Old Lib. Has he any children?

Friend. The person I speak of is a female—She is a relict, and has one daughter.

Old Lib. You don't mean the widow Howard?

Friend. I certainly do.

Old Lib. She's very bad—I send every day to inquire about her health, and, as usual, yonder comes her dear, dutiful daughter to inform me of it.

Friend. (*Looking out.*) Truly a well-looking girl! Cou'dn't you leave us together a few moments.

Old Lib. Together! Eh!—Oh, I've no objection. I've some directions to give within, and will desire her to walk in here the while—But you mustn't make any pecuniary offers.—They are as proud as they are poor, and that I fear is saying a great deal. I rather wonder at it; for if the pleasure of receiving assistance does but half equal the glorious satisfaction of giving, they must possess the greatest degree of self-denial who can refuse the enjoyment of it.

[*Exit.*

Friend. My friend is in the right—Those to whom we give may create compassion; but the man who possesses means to relieve, and adds will to the ability, is, indeed, an object highly to be envied.

Enter MARIAN.

Mar. Sir, I ask pardon; but Mr Liberal told me——

Friend. And he has told me too that your mother is sick, and you are kind to her.

Mar. What wou'd my heart be, if I were *not* kind to her?

Friend. Your heart wou'd be to blame; for if there is any thing which truly pictures to the mind the semblance of angels, it is, when we see the children of filial virtue ministering with affection to the necessities of a parent.

Mar. But I fear, sir, what little attentions I have been able to pay my mother will not long avail her. She has had, in vain, every medical aid the country can afford; were she but in London——

Friend. Even here she may recover—Providence is every where.

Mar. But, sir, she dwells so fervently on the idea that a physician who formerly knew her could effect her release from pain, that, were he present, imagination alone might do much in favour of his prescriptions.

Friend. And this you formerly mentioned to a friend of mine, who met you in a fearful storm, fetching medicines for your mother, when the virtuous warmth of your heart preserved you from a tempest, which, to many of your sex, would have proved fatal.

Mar. And your friend—Ah, sir, he made me a promise, which I fear——

6

Friend. I am come to answer for the goodness of his intentions. Return to your mother, and say, that a friend from town, who is the messenger of good news, will shortly wait on her.

Mar. A friend! Pardon me; but should it—should it be the friend she wishes for—

Friend. If it should, it were dangerous to tell her so at first.

Mar. You are right, sir—I will be cautious. Yet do not be angry with me, if I say my mother's circumstances are not as when you might have known her formerly—And fearful of lessening the little she has to leave me, she would even deny herself the relief which might incur expence. Had I but the means to pay what your attendance may demand——

Friend. You mistake—I am no doctor; if I were, I would not deprive you of contributing thus nobly to a mother's welfare. And were I able, I wou'd give a sum to be placed at interest, for the relief of indigent fathers and mothers, who maintain their own offspring, and of children like thee, who are dutiful to their parents. [*Exeunt.*

SCENE II.

A plain and neat Apartment.

Mrs Howard *enters.*

Mrs How. How tediously do the moments creep along when Time carries Pain upon his wings! The hours of happiness, which have fled in rapid succession, seem now to look back and reproach the little account they were made of; so true it is that no good

appears in its real garb till we have suffered it to
escape us.

Enter RACHEL, *an old Domestic.*

Rach. Ma'am, ma'am, he's coming. (*In a half
whisper.*)

Mrs How. I thought your stay was long, Rachel.
I hope we shall accomplish our aim before the return of my dear daughter. I wou'd'nt for worlds her
tender solicitude should be augmented by a knowledge of our real situation.

Rach. Ah, madam, you are both so good, and it
does so go to my heart, that you can't think the
pleasure it gives me to see you weeping over one
another.

Mrs How. Surely some of the vast fortune my
uncle has heaped on others might have been left to
us. For me, I am bending to my parent earth; but
my sweet girl, rising like a beauteous flower, will
catch each worldly eye, unguarded by a mother or
a friend.

Rach. O, here's Mr Ephraim, madam.

Enter EPHRAIM.

Eph. (*To* MRS H.) I'm glad to see you can walk
apoud, madam : I hope de young gentlewomans is
well—I hope you are well, ma tear. (*To* RACHEL.)

Mrs How. I sent for you, sir, on business. The
only property I acquired by the death of my uncle,
Mr Rackrent, is what you see about me.

Eph. Ah ! I knowed de old gentleman well enough.
He was de besht at a pargain I ever met. He tried
von time mit all his m'ght to get de better of me ;
but some how or other von of us vas sheated, meder
it vas him, or meder it vas myself, it vou'dn't be vorth
ma vile to tell you.

Mrs How. As he left me all the moveables in a
particular part of his house, those chests became mine

among the rest. (RACHEL *opens a door, discovering two boxes in a recess.*) I thought them worthless, as containing nothing but his clothes; but there are some suits among them so richly laced, that——

Eph. (*Examining them.*) Bless ma! it is very rich indeed. He never cou'dn't wear dese clothes himself. I never saw a coat a top of his back vorth twopence in ma life, except von, which I sould him maself for sevan shillans.

Mrs How. If you will fetch them away immediately, you can look over them at your leisure. I do not wish my daughter to be acquainted with this circumstance. In the evening bring me what you can best afford in return.

Eph. You forget I am a Jew. If you make it vorth ma vile, I shall buy dem; but if de pargain isn't made before your face, I cou'dn't give ma vord dat I shou'dn't have de best share of it.

Mrs How. You have the reputation of being honest.

Eph. So much de vorse—it's de ruin of all pusiness. I lose twenty per cent. by it every day.

Mrs How. If you are *not* honest, you can deceive me as easily here as by taking them away. I know their number, but not their value—And if you would serve me——

Eph. You take away my power to sheat you, because you put confidence a top of me. But why mus'n't your daughter know apoud it?

Mrs How. It wou'd wound her feelings to see me thus reduc'd. She often thinks she deceives me, by putting on a cheerful countenance when her heart is in an agony. I wou'd do any thing to avoid adding to what she feels.

Eph. (*Apart.*) And so de moder and de daughter do all dey can to sheat von anoder. I didn't tink nobody but a Jew could be guilty of such a ting.

Mrs How. Your fair dealing in the disposal of my

other property entitles you to my good opinion. But will you examine those articles now?

Eph. I won't examine; I can guess pretty vell vat I can do. I will give you de moniesh now, and I shall come ven your daughter is out, and fetch something vat I can put 'em in. Bless me, de young lady is coming—put dem avay—put dem avay!

Enter MARIAN.

Mar. My dear mother, you look quite well to-day. Ah! Mr Ephraim!

Eph. How d'ye do, miss? I vas only doing some pusiness mit your mamma, my dear. Here, ma good madam, it wou'dn't be vorth ma vile to give no more as dis. (*Apart to* MRS HOWARD, *offering a bank-note.*)

Mrs How. This! 'tis a mistake—here is too much, sir.

Eph. Keep it, I tell you. If you speak anoder vord, I'll tell all apoud it.—Good day, ma good ladies. Dear, dear, vat a pity dese people shou'dn't be Jews—it wou'd den be vorth ma vile to love dem dearly; but, as it is, none but a Christian moder wou'd tink of sheating her own shild. (*Aside.*) [*Exit.*

Rach. Well-a-daisy! that's a good-natur'd old soul! Ah! if he was but one of us.

Mar. Why, is he *not* one of us?

Rach. What, he? A Jew! Why, miss, they are not, no, not even Christians.

Mrs How. Certainly not, Rachel; but they are men.

Rach. True, ma'am; but not like us. My poor, dear husband used to say they were fit for nothing, but to lend money, wear long beards, and buy bad shillings.

Mrs How. But, Rachel, you shou'd recollect, that if the Christians didn't furnish, by their extravagance, the ground of Jewish usury, the sons of Israel wou'd be more respected.

Rach. Ah, I dare say what you tell me is right.—

Dear me ! a Jew one of us ! Bless us, how a body
may live and learn !   [*Exit muttering.*

Mar. I am truly happy to see you in such spirits.
You were yesterday so low.

Mrs How. Rest and sweet dreams have made the
alteration. But you have watch'd me without inter-
mission, so long, that shou'd your own health be the
sacrifice, the restoration of mine wou'd make poor
amends.

Mar. But, mother, since I saw you, I have found
a friend.

Mrs How. A friend, child !

Mar. Yes; he will be here presently. He is a delightful man, and if ever I could think of loving any
body besides you, it would be—dear, dear, I never
thought of asking his name—But he says he has such
good news——

Mrs How. Good news! What can it be? For thy
sake, my child, the bare idea gives me pleasure.

Mar. And, indeed, you cannot conceive the pleasure I feel at seeing your eyes sparkle once more
with their wonted lustre.

Mrs How. Nor can any but a mother experience
the rapture which causes these eyes to flow with love,
gratitude, and pride, at the attentions of a dutiful and
virtuous daughter.   [*Exit, led in by* MARIAN.

ACT THE SECOND.

SCENE I.

An Apartment at an Inn.

FRANK LIBERAL *and* MILDMAY.

F. Lib. My dear Charles, welcome most sincerely to my native village—The obligations you could so ill afford to lay me under when in town, shall here be as far repaid as the intrinsic worth of mere coin will admit; for their *real* value, I must ever be your debtor.

Mild. You are determined not to be outdone on the score of acknowledgment.

F. Lib. Nor you on that of diffidence. And yet, when, through my foolish extravagance, my companions derided and forsook me, you stood boldly forward, and forfeited your pretensions to it for ever, for daring to countenance a poor devil, cut by the rest of his acquaintance.

Mild. You speak of this too often, forgetting that *you* stood *my* friend on many occasions, and now mean, by introducing me to your father, to lay the foundation of my future prospects.

F. Lib. And a worthy old gentleman you'll find him—if he has one foible, it takes its rise from a most amiable source; for the future good of his children, he submits rather too implicitly to the caprice of a female cousin and counsellor, who is more absolute than the master of a full ferry-boat, or the landlord of the only inn in a village.—But why so melancholy, Charles?

Mild. I am uneasy on account of the sweet girl I so happily protected from the rustic violence of that booby squire.—She refuses to write to or see me; and, what is more extraordinary, I have met the squire himself, since my arrival here.

F. Lib. What fear of him?

Mild. Exasperated at my interfering between him and his brutal gallantry, I learn that he has purchased a bond of mine; and his following me here sufficiently explains his intentions.

F. Lib. Believe me you are among friends, who will study to provide a remedy.

Enter Landlord.

Aha! My worthy host, how fares it?

Land. My *young* squire, and *old* friend, welcome home, and welcome to my house, an hundred, ay, a thousand times!

F. Lib. Thank you—This is Mr Mildmay, who, as a friend of mine, must expect every attention from you.

Land. And he shall have it too.—Sir, I'm proud to see you under my roof. Mr Liberal there has been my benefactor—I'm not asham'd to say it.—He lent me money when I was poor—helped me up when I was down—and when it slips my memory——

F. Lib. Spare your professions, and tell us the news —Is all right at the Hall? Any thing pleasant? Is my father quite well, or has the old lady got the gout?

Land. Your good father is as well as ever, and I believe the old lady has more command than ever, for she has sent for a sweetheart from London for your sister Miss Fanny; one Squire Chace—I'm sure it's none of the old gentleman's doing.

3

Mild. Squire Chace!

Land. Chevy Chace, esquire, of Hunter's Hall; he's just arrived with a whole bevy of grooms, and now lodges in my house.

F. Lib. So, so! I wish my sister joy of her bargain.

Land. He's rather noisy, or so.

Mild. A troublesome, boisterous fellow, fond of giving the view-holla, to prove what strength of sound his lungs derive from the emptiness of his head!

Land. The very man, I'm sure, your honour. But though his head may be empty, his pockets are full, brimful, Mr Liberal, and that's every thing, you know.

F. Lib. Not with me. Egad! if this is the case, we must lose no time. Come, Charles, let us prepare to visit the mansion—And if I can help it, neither the squire's pockets nor his head shall find their way into our family, depend on't. [*Exeunt.*

Land. (*Calling* FRANK *back.*) Mr Liberal, I beg pardon, but you know there is a small matter of cash between you and me—Two hundred pounds, I think —I didn't expect your return so suddenly, and am rather unprovided.

F. Lib. No apology—I confess I had some hopes of your being able to return it. I shou'd blush to intrude on my father's liberality, when the carelessness of my past conduct has so little claim to it.

Land. Ah! you're a worthy—a good young man —You talk exactly like your father—You're the very moral of him.

F. Lib. I know nothing about that, Mr Doublechalk; but I know, that if there are two characters worse than the generality, they are, the debtor who possesses means of payment and withholds them, and the creditor who tears the blessings of liberty from an honest man, only because his inclination to do justice outweighs his ability. [*Exit.*

Land. (*Obsequiously bowing, and following him to the door.*) There goes one we may safely set down for a blockhead. His father is so fond of him, he may do just whatever he pleases, and instead of making his advantage, he gets more and more out of favour every day, by doing and saying what is right and honest, as he calls it—It would be an ill action for me to refund money to one who so little knows the value of it.

Enter Waiter.

Wait. The young lady from the cottage wants to see you, sir.

Land. Young lady! Oh, what—Bid her come in.
[*Exit Waiter.*

Young lady indeed! Miss Marian, I suppose, as they call her. I wonder what poor people have to do with pretty names! More excuses about money, I warrant.

Enter MARIAN.

So—I'm glad to see you—You've kept your word at last; you've brought the rent, of course, and here's the receipt. You see I expected you.

Mar. Your kindness, in waiting so long, has, indeed, been great, and I come——

Land. To pay me, of course.

Mar. Ah! no—to entreat a little further patience —My mother's returning health——

Land. If my money depends on that, I may wait till doomsday.

Mar. She is much better, sir—Do not, by your impatience, occasion a relapse;—had you a parent rising gradually from the brink of death, what wou'd you think of those, who, with unfeeling hand, wou'd plunge her down into the opening grave!

Land. Why, as to that, it's——but what signifies talking to *you?* I'll go to your mother—hear the true state of the case, and learn what I have to trust to.

Mar. Stay, sir; whatever may be your determination, do not acquaint my mother with it—To quiet

her mind, I have been obliged to keep her in ignorance of what passes—To this I owe the amendment
of her health—As that increases, she will have more
power to endure and to arrange every thing.

Land. That's very clever—and so she knows nothing at all about this business?

Mar. To what end shou'd I have added to her sufferings, by relating what I have happily conceal'd?
Heaven knows, nothing could have supported *me*, but
the delightful pride of standing a willing shield between the arrows of calamity and an honour'd parent.

Land. I tell you I will go—I won't say any thing
harsh to the old lady. You know I'm good natur'd
enough when people pay me as they ought.

Mar. Pray, sir, for pity's sake, forbear! (*Seizes
his hand passionately.*)

Re-enter FRANK.

F. Lib. My old friend, I forgot to say that—Hey!
by Heavens, the very charming girl I saw once before—in tears too! May I venture to inquire——

Land. You'd better not—it's a trifle—the young
woman only—there, there, go home.—I'll consider
on't. (*To* MARIAN.)

Mar. And you will spare my mother?

F. Lib. (*Respectfully.*) You may not immediately
recollect me, madam, but you once entrusted me
with a commission, which I hope was executed to
your satisfaction. If I can now be of use to you, pray
command me.—I only regret that so much sweetness
and beauty in distress will take away all pretensions
to merit, in my best efforts to do you service.

Land. No occasion——no occasion, squire——it's
only——

Mar. Sir, we are poor, but not dishonest. This
gentleman is our landlord—he fears our intentions to
do him justice, and—pardon me, I had forgot, that,
to a stranger, this cannot be interesting.

Land. True, you're right—I'll tell the story myself.

F. Lib. (*Stopping his mouth.*) No, you won't, while there's one present who can tell it so much better. Pray, madam, do me the honour to proceed—This gentleman is my particular friend—We are on such familiar terms, that, should he interrupt you any more, I'm sure he'll not be offended if I keep his mouth shut in spite of his teeth.

Mar. I have made him a request, which his humanity will incline him to attend to. And it is more proper I shou'd owe his compliance to the influence of that virtue, than to that of any gentleman, however kindly meant, or generously exerted.   [*Exit.*

F. Lib. Did you hear her, old Icicle? I begin to comprehend this business.

Land. Why, I'm sure your honour's not angry. I am hurt at not having money to pay you; and, if I was a little severe, it was all on your account.

F. Lib. I understand—You mean to say your heart is naturally soft, and my patience impressed it with so much gratitude, that you was uneasy till you repaid me.

Land. Exactly so—you see how it was.—But you have so much penetration—I thought it my duty to get my own, entirely out of justice to you.

F. Lib. A good example. Now, sir, I think it *my* duty to get *my* own, entirely out of justice to *you.* So, d'ye hear, pay me instantly down the two hundred pounds I lent *you* in your necessity, or take the consequence.

Land. Why, surely you wou'dn't expect——

F. Lib. I didn't expect that any one bearing the form of man wou'd experience the offices of liberality, without learning at the same time to bestow them on others. Benevolence is not our own—'tis lent from Heaven, on the condition of extending its effects to our neighbours, and he who spreads it widest, does most honour to his commission.

Land. Umph!—As to the two hundred pounds, I shall speak to your father. I don't think he will be much pleased at your parting with so large a sum; nor will he be angry with me for taking it, to prevent a worse use being made of it, had it remained with you.

F. Lib. That's your *real* opinion?

Land. It is, *upon my honour.*

F. Lib. Now you shall know mine——upon *my* honour. With regard to myself, I expect my money— I must be paid; and that you may not complain for want of time, I give you a quarter of an hour to get it ready in. As to my father, I know him so well, that were you only to go to him, and tell the simple truth, he'd kick *you* out of the house, for daring to come into it, and *me* after you, for having befriended such a miserly old hypocrite.   [*Exit.*

Land. Mighty pretty! how am I to raise the ready?—The money from the cottage I will have, if it's only to vex the young squire—That will go but a little way; and for the rest, let me see, there's Ephraim the Jew, perhaps he would—A sad old rogue too— but never mind; money I want—and for money there's so many who wou'dn't mind going to old Harry himself, that——(*Turning round, sees* EPHRAIM, *who enters a little before.*)

Eph. Did you vant me, ma good sir?—I heard you talk apoud ma name just now.

Land. Yes; I was speaking of the devil, just as you enter'd.

Eph. I hope I didn't interrupt you mit none of your friends?

Land. No, no—You call'd in the old way, I suppose—on the look-out for business?

Eph. I can't help it, Mr Doublechalk; I was born so, and I cou'dn't live if I had no pusiness in the world.

Land. Ay, ay ; you drank in trade with your mother's milk.

Eph. Na, ma friend, I never had a drop of it—Ma
poor moder died when I washn't a month old; and
brother Moses carried me apoud in his pasket, along
mit de rest of de shleeve puttons and shealing wax,
vat he sould among the people.

Land. Indeed !

Eph. It's true, indeed—and venever I cried out
mit a noise, he gave me the cushtomers' money to
play mid, becaush he knowed vat I cou'dn't never be
quiet mitout it.

Land. So, so—you learnt the art of multiplication
without going to school, I warrant ?

Eph. I vent to school a top of de Change, and St
Paul's, and Leicester Fields—Ma task vas to get all
vat I cou'd, and I never vas out in ma life.

Land. But you did'nt get all your money by slippers and candied lemon-peel ?

Eph. I began mit little, but I took care of it—'Tis
de great secret in ma trade ; and dere's many of ma
tribe keeps a coach, vat was first set a running upon
rollers.

Land. The country-folks say you are a good, civil,
kind-hearted man, and have been known to give money
to the poor : You couldn't learn that among your
own people—I don't mean to affront you ; but you
know there's a great many rogues among them, nobody denies that.

Eph. Vell—you vou'dn't keep all de rogueries to
yourself, vou'd you, Mr Doublechalk ? If I have any
goodness apoud me, I didn't learn it out of de Jews,
noder out of de Christians—It was part of de shtock
in trade given me from a better world, and if I don't
put it out to lawful interest, I shall wrong the property of my employer.

Land. Well, then, suppose I wanted two hundred
pounds, wou'd you lend them me ?

Eph. Two hundred pounds! why, it's worth a shillan a-piece to see such a sum.

Land. Come, no joking—My note, interest, and premium are all you want, I'm sure—I know I must come down a little—so, wait a moment, and you shall have my terms upon a stamp immediately.   [*Exit.*

Eph. Shtop—shtop! Dear, dear, de people dink vat a Jew is made of money—Besides, I don't like him a bit, and I von't lend him a farthing.

Sq. (*Sings without.*) Old Towler—-dash way! Yoecks!

Eph. Pless ma heart! Who is Old Towler, vat de gentleman is making so much noise apoud, I wonder?

Enter SQUIRE CHACE.

Sq. Yoicks! Doublechalk! Waiter! Where the devil are ye all? And what sort of game have you got here? What sport, eh, old gentleman?

Eph. I hav'n't got no shport, sir—I only minds ma pusiness.

Sq. Well, clear the road—I expect a gentleman here, and mus'n't be seen in such company.

Eph. Ven you came in, I expected a gentleman myself, but I vas disappointed.

Sq. If you dare open your lips to me, I'll call my hounds, grooms, and whippers-in, to teach you the respect due from such reptiles as you to their betters.

Eph. Don't, ma dear sir—I'm frighten'd out of ma senses at a *puppy*, and if you bring de whole pack—

Sq. (*Smacking his whip.*) What, you old badger, did you call me a puppy? (*Drives him up into a corner.*)

Eph. Dear me, you hurt ma—Murder! if you knock me mid your whip, I can't bear it, I tell you. —Mr Doublechalk! de gentleman will kill ma.

Enter MILDMAY.

Mild. I've lost Frank somewhere—-What's the

matter here ? For shame, sir ! I beg pardon : but you
are really degrading yourself by such conduct.

Sq. (*Turns round to* MILDMAY.) And, pray, who
are you ? What, my bully from town, the saucy champion of boarding-school misses !

Mild. I wou'dn't offend, but I believe you know,
sir, that when once angry, I endeavour to supply my
want of words with more effective arguments. (*Shaking his cane.*)

Eph. Py cod, I vish he'd knock him down.——
(*Aside.*)

Sq. You cane a gentleman !

Mild. When a man, born to the inheritance and
opportunities of a gentleman, is afflicted with the mania
of imitating helpers and stable-boys, it is only in unison with his assumed plan he *can* be chastised, and a
cane or a horse-whip are the most appropriate implements.

Sq. I gave you credit for your looking big when a
pretty girl was in the case ; because you might cast a
sheep's eye at a fine woman and a fortune ; but there's
nothing to be got here, unless you'd borrow money
at fifty per *shent.*

Eph. (*Coming out of the corner.*) Well, if he did,
I'd lend it him without any per *shent* at all.

(*Squire threatens ;* EPHRAIM *runs back again.*)

Mild. You are unworthy my notice ; but, as we
may probably meet in a family where I am as solicitous to deserve as to obtain patronage, I wou'd advise you to keep some guard upon your insolence,
and spare me from degrading myself in the presence
of my friends, so far as to enforce my opinions with
the weight of an arm you are already acquainted
with.   [*Exit.*

Sq. Was ever any gentleman of landed property
treated in this manner ? Stables and dog-kennels, truly ! I'll do for him : he forgets I have his bond.——

And you, Mr Black Muzzle, your friend will get
little by you, I believe.

Eph. I don't vant nobody to get any thing by *me.*

Sq. I've a bit of paper here in my pocket shall send
him to the county jail—Tell him that—And what's
more, it shall too, I promise him.   [*Exit.*

Eph. (*Calling after him.*) Well, and I've got a bit
of paper in my pocket, vat can pull him out again, if
I like it.

Sq. (*Returning.*) What say you, mongrel?

Eph. Noting at all, sir—I only shpeak to de landlord—Dear, I wish de oder gentlemans wou'd come
back, and talk to him a little more. I never was fond
of fighting maself, and de only reason vat I can give
is, dat whoever gets most by it is always de greatest
loser in de end.   [*Exit.*

Sq. A gentleman to be treated in this manner indeed!

Enter JOHN GROUSE.

John. I ax pardon, sir—but did you see ought of
old Doublechalk?

Sq. No, sir, I did not see *ought* of him—I want
him myself—Go you, and look for him.

John. Nay, nay, I moant do that—I've gotten t'rent
to pay o' my little farm, ready for him—'tweant do
to run after folk wi' money at these times—It's here
all ready, and he may look for me, an' he likes.

Sq. What, you are a tenant of his?

John. I am, sir, because he's my landlord.

Sq. And a precious landlord he is!—He seems to
be as attentive to his guests as his tenants.

John. Why, sir, it's 'tway wi' these chaps, I reckon.
He was but waiter here a bit since—he war civil
enough then; but now he's gain'd a deal of brass,
and lost all his good manners, he sets himsel up for a
gentleman.

Sq. By the by, who was that pretty girl I saw

with him a little while ago—Do you know of any sly little fair one he has in his eye?

John. It cou'dn't, for sure, be Black Betty, t' chamber-maid, you mean?

Sq. Black Betty! I tell you it was an angel.

John. An angel! I ne'er saw one at this house. Yet Miss Marian, fra'twood cottage, comes here sometimes when she lacks wine for her sick mother, and that makes her look more like one, than even that bonny face of her'n.

Sq. Ah! It's she I mean—I see you understand a beautiful face.

John. Why, as to that, sir, we Yorkshiremen are reckoned pratty good judges of women and horses.

Sq. This girl is without friends, you say?

John. She mut ha' plenty an she wou'd—but they ax nought of nobody. Squire Liberal, at the Hall, wou'd do a great deal for 'em, if the ou'd lady, his cousin, wou'd let him; but shew's a cross-grained toad, and ould Doublechalk told her that I said so, and Ise turn'd off from being game-keeper—but I know the squire's my friend at bottom, so I never heed it.

Sq. Could you put me in a way to see this girl?

John. Why, if you doant keep your eyes shut, you may put *yoursel* i' 'tway.

Sq. Ay; but I mean, you cou'd take a letter?

John. Nay, I know nought about letters—they na but bring a poor man into trouble; besides, I can't read 'em when they're written.

Enter Landlord.

Land. There is a stamp'd receipt for the money, friend Ephraim, and a premium of——

John. (*Taking it.*) Vary well—Four pounds three shillings and two-pence; it's all right to a halfpenny. (*Giving money.*)

Land. Right!—What's right? Why, that receipt is for two hundred and twenty pounds.

John. Why, is't?

Land. Yes; and an obligation to return it.

John. Nay, there's no obligation to return it, as I know on. (*Reading.*) Why, 'tis two hundred and twenty pounds, sure enough.

Sq. I thought you cou'dn't read.

John. Why, not much; but I understand grammar a bit.

Sq. You, grammar!

John. Why, yees, sir: I pay my rent, and that's grammar, an't it? There be three parts of speech, pounds, shillings, and pence, and he that knows how to get 'em is no bad scholar at last.

Land. Yes; but there's no scholarship in keeping my property.

John. I want none o' thy property—give me my own receipt, and here's thine again. You went tattling o' what I said up to t' Hall; you made me lose my place; and you may take back your dirty bit of a farm for your pains.—Squire has given me a better; so there's grammar for *thee*. [*Exit.*

Land. Why, but, John, John Grouse, I say——

Sq. Never mind him, but get me a bailiff directly; I must have that Mildmay arrested in the first place, and then I've a commission to entrust you with, shall be the making of you; for I've game in view will admit of no lost time, and is worth spending a fortune in pursuit of. [*Exeunt.*

ACT THE THIRD.

SCENE I.

The Inside of JOHN GROUSE'S *Cottage. The Door opens towards a Wood.*

Enter JOHN *and* PARCHMENT.

John. What, and so he says he'll always be good to me, in spite of the old lady? Why, now, that's vary kind on him. I like him so well, that I think I cou'd go all over t'world to do ought for him. Well, but thou'll ha' a drop o' drink? a sup o' yeal, ou'd lad, weant thee?

Parch. No, no, I thank ye. I have business in hand. Besides, there seems to be a storm brewing. —Fare thee well.

John. I mun away to work too. I ha' gotten a foine pig to kill.—I hope his worship will accept of some puddings. Bless his heart! he can eat a homely meal as well as a poorer man.

Parch. And so he can; ha! ha! ha! I've seen him, after a long ride, take away the children's bread and butter, on purpose to give them something for it; ha! ha! ha!

John. Ha! ha! ha! only think now, that of all trades, so good a man should have been bred a law-

yer, and thee his clerk! Thou moant mind my
jokes; but I've oft been puzzled to account for it—
You lawyer folks are so cunning.

Parch. Very cunning; and hardly one of them
that isn't as keen as a Yorkshireman.—You mus'n't
mind my jokes, you know, ha! ha! ha!   [*Exit.*

John. Ha! ha! ha! Well, go thy ways—thou'rt
a funny ould man, ha! ha! ha! It gets very dark
and cloudy; I think there'll be some thunner flashes
come down afore long. My dame, I warrant, has
gotten into some house on t' road. I wonder where
shew's put my great knife: t' pig will never get
kill'd an' I doant find it.

Enter FRIENDLY, *through door.*

Friend. Pardon my intrusion, friend. I'm looking
for the house of the widow Howard, and I have
missed the way.   [*Rain and hail heard.*

John. Why, when 'trains a bit o'er I'll go wi' you,
sir. I' th' mean time, if you'll sit you down till the
weather's fairer, you'll be heart'ly welcome. My
mistress, shew's gone to market, childer are all at
school, and there's nobody left but mysel to take
care o' the house.

Friend. Thank ye, thank ye, friend. Your cottage
is pleasant, though lonely.

John. Yees, sir; we live tolerably well. We have
no folk but our ownselves and a lodger, who is sometimes here, and sometimes there, and sometimes—
nowhere.—I should like the man vary well, but he's
a Jew; and one don't care to have o'er much to do
wi' such folk, thou knows.

Friend. (*Aside.*) A Jew and a Yorkshireman—
pretty companions!   [*Rain heard again.*

John. How 'train comes down! And see thee,
here comes ould Ephraim, like a soak'd sop in a
pint o' yeal.

Enter EPHRAIM.

Eph. Pless ma heart! it rains all the vorld so as
de flood vas come again. Sir, your sarvant. How
do you do, sir? Dere me, who is dis? Dere is monish
up stairs. De gentleman looks like a lawyer, and
I never cou'd like dose people in all my life.——
(*Aside.*)

John. Pray sit you down, sir. Mr Ephraim, you'd
better doff your wet clothes, while I get some drink
for you and stranger.

Friend (*Sits close to the door.*) I will sit near the
door; for though the rain falls heavy, it is sweet to
snuff up the scent of the newly-refreshed herbs and
flowers.

Eph. (*Apart to* JOHN.) Pless me, Mr Grouse,
dere is your pig so fright'ned at de storms, and is
running apoud, and grunting mit his nose, for all
de vorld so he vas out of his senses.

John. O, true; I'd forgot him. I'll be wi' you
again directly.   [*Exit.*

Eph. De gentlemans is sleepy. Dere's nothing I
dislike my landlord for but his being so fond of pork.
I always buy it of him when I can, that it may not be
eat in de house, and because I get great deal monish
by selling it some where else. Pless ma! I stand
talking here ven I'm so vet, that if I catch cold, it
vill ruin me to buy a doctor for making me yell again.
                                    [*Exit up a staircase.*

Friend. (*Looking at his watch.*) I shall be too late
at the widow's. I don't much like the appearance of
my host; but to seem suspicious, is to court danger.
(*Rains.*) The storm increases.—The trees, which
bend before it, and are washed by the rain, may apt-
ly be compared to man, who bows to misfortune,
while the tears bedew his cheeks; but, possessing patience, he bows but to rise again, and the tears he

lets fall serve to enliven the spring of happiness which
follows.

(*During the above speech he is playing with his watch,
which he involuntarily lays on the table near him.*)

Enter JOHN.

John. Eh! my guest ha' dropt in a nap, I think—
I moant waken him. I ha' catched that plaguy pig
at last, however. (*Calls at the foot of the staircase.*)
Maister Ephraim! Maister Ephraim!

(FRIENDLY *attentively listening, and occasionally
assuming the appearance of sleep.*)

Eph. (*Above.*) I come, ma friend.

John. Speak softly—wisht, lad! wisht!

Eph. (*Coming down in another coat.*) Pless ma!
vat is it you vant?

John. Why, the ou'd one's safe at last. Thou mun
come and help me to hould him, or I shall never be
able to kill him quietly.   (FRIENDLY *starts.*

Eph. Dear me, you know I don't like it; it goes
against ma conscience.

John. Nay, then, I'll do it mysel. I gotten a rare
knife here, (*Whets it;*) if you'll no but just come,
and——

Eph. I tell you vat, Mr Grouse, I vill go your
half in de profit, but I vill not have a hand in the
death of him—It is against my laws, I tell you.

(FRIENDLY, *much agitated, gradually gets the door
open, and steals softly out, unobserved.*)

John. Well, happen the gentleman will for once
lend a hand. (*Turns round, and misses* FRIENDLY.)
Why, he's gone.—He mought ha' staid to say thank
ye for your shelter, afore he stole out o' the house.

Eph. Stole! Dear me, I hope he didn't shteal noting out of de house.

John. Steal! Noa; I don't think he wou'd do that,

nowther.—He said he was in a hurry; and see, he
has left his watch behind him.

Eph. Dear me, the gentleman must not lose his
vatch. Vhich vay did he go? You must run after
him—'tis a good vatch—make haste. (*Exit* JOHN.)
Now I'll go up stairs, and see dat all is right. It is
de only day vat I have put my monish here. De house
used to be safe. I have been here often, and stayed
very long, but I never saw any more rogues in de
place than my landlord and myself in all my life.

[*Exit up the staircase.*

SCENE II.

A Landscape.

Enter MARIAN.

Mar. The storm has abated. What can have kept
the gentleman? My poor mother will relapse into
low spirits again, and I shall be so unhappy. Ah,
thank Heaven, here he comes! Good man! conscious of his delay, and unwilling to give pain, I declare
he is running to meet me!

Enter FRIENDLY, *out of breath.*

My dear sir, why fatigue yourself thus?—Were not
the happiness of my mother so precious to me, I had
rather you had staid where you were, than thus endanger your health.

Friend. Had I staid any longer where I was, the
safety of my life would have been more uncertain
than even that of your mother.

Mar. Your life, sir?

Friend. Figure to yourself a Jew of most vile aspect, and a tall raw-bon'd Yorkshireman, with a knife in his hand, ready to——Let us be gone, for he is even following me!

Mar. (*Looking out.*) Why, that, my dear sir, is only——

John. (*Without.*) Stop, sir, stop.

Friend. If I do, I'll be hang'd.   [*Exeunt.*

Enter JOHN, *running, with the watch in one hand and the knife in the other.*

John. Whew! what a run!—He'll neither stop nor listen. I'll e'en gi' it up; and yet if I had a hare in view, I shou'dn't be so easily flung out.—Dom, I'll have t'other try; for a good-natured action is better worth following than all the game i' th' county—so here goes.

SCENE III.

An Apartment in OLD LIBERAL'S *House.*

Enter MISS LIBERAL *and* FANNY.

Miss Lib. Well, child, I protest I think you have improv'd vastly. Had my cousin's notions been indulg'd, he'd have made you as unfit for fashionable life as he is himself.

Fan. Nay, now, ma'am, you mustn't speak against my papa; he may be a little old-fashion'd, but he's always so good to me, that I can't find in my heart to think otherwise than well of him.

Miss Lib. Good to you!—Yes, he has been so— he confided you to my care, and that alone shou'd

certainly entitle him to your regards. In other respects, he has been more indulgent to the young man
you call your brother.—He has suffer'd him to gal-
lop about, Heaven knows where, and throw away
money in learning to be useful, as he styles it.

Fan. Lud! I hope Frank is well. When I was
here at our last vacation, we had the reputation of
being the best players at battledore and shuttlecock
in the whole county.

Miss Lib. Indeed!—and are these the accomplishments you study to acquire? Is this to be the fruit
of my care and your education? Is this your attention to that grandeur of manner and dignified deport-
ment which were always so dearly affected by the
late Mr Rackrent?

Fan. Dear madam, why, where's the harm? Is
not exercise both fashionable and healthy? Or wou'd
you have me do nothing, but sit demure as Miss Prim-
rose, who wou'dn't play at blind man's buff for the
universe, abominates a reel or a lively dance, and never skips but when she's reading?

Enter OLD LIBERAL.

Old Lib. Fanny, my girl, how goes it? Why, you
are grown as tall, and look as cheerful—Come, cousin, if all your plans succeed as well as your management of Frances, I may give you joy of 'em. I shall
have Frank home to-day, to give an account of the
last three months. I found him so clever in knowledge
and management of the world, that, after permitting
him to figure away in great style for the quarter before, I sent him this time to see how he cou'd make
his way *without* money, as the best method of teaching him what to do *with* it.

Miss Lib. And who wou'd be so imprudent as to
send youth into the world without money? Such a
want is the prompter of all evil.

Old Lib. And money is the root of it.

Miss Lib. But, sir, a young man in London without money——

Old Lib. Is like a coach without horses, a watch without wheels, a ship without water, or a woman without a tongue.

Miss Lib. It would require a hundred tongues to preach sense into that miserable head of yours. Hav'n't I repeatedly told you, that to keep young people poor, is to make them mean-spirited and mischievous?

Old Lib. Yes, you did tell me so, for which reason I let Frank have *plenty* of money ; then you were angry, call'd the lad extravagant, me an old fool, and money a passport to all manner of wickedness.

Miss Lib. I did so, sir ; and now——

Old Lib. And now, because I kept him a little while without it, you're as bad t'other way. You make riches the *summum bonum*, and youth the only time for possessing them.

Fan. Nay, my dear father, and my dear madam, I'm sure, after all, you are very often of the same opinion.

Old Lib. Yes, but, unfortunately, it's never at the same time.

Enter FRANK LIBERAL.

F. Lib. My dear sir, I pay my duty with respect and gratitude. I hope I have lost nothing, in my absence, of your good opinion, ma'am. And as for you, Miss Fanny, you look so well, and smile so sweetly, that, were I not kindly permitted to call you sister, I should be over head and ears in love in less time than it takes to tell you so.

Old Lib. Well said, Frank : want of money has taught you how to flatter.

Miss Lib. If it has render'd him a little more polite, 'tis less an evil than I imagined.

F. Lib. I hope most sincerely that the want of it

will never make me forget my own worth, nor the possession of it degrade me to overlook superior merit in another.

Old Lib. Frank, I have often told you that knowledge of the world was only to be acquired by practice—sent you into it well stock'd with money and advice, and then—what was the consequence?

F. Lib. To speak honestly, sir, the advice went further than the money. Indeed, till one was gone, I had no opportunity of putting the other in practice.

Old Lib. What, you found your way pleasant and easy? It's ever so with the rich : all manner of folly can be covered with a piece of thin paper ; and nothing is better calculated to smooth the way than a rough guinea.

F. Lib. Faith, sir, I found it so exactly. But it was impossible to think myself wrong, while I had so many friends to tell me I was right. The balance was, however, quickly struck between wisdom and folly, and I soon found myself considerably *minus* to the former.

Miss Lib. When your money was all gone, what follow'd ?

F. Lib. My friends, madam, of course. However, as it isn't my way to despond, I took heart of grace, and determined to shew the world how much I was above it, by returning to my father on the top of the heavy coach.

Old Lib. So you did ; you told me you had lost all your money, and I bid you go back and look for it.

Miss Lib. Cousin, that was very wrong.

F. Lib. It has, however, madam, brought me to the knowledge of three persons, with each of whom an acquaintance is absolutely necessary to support life tolerably.

Fan. Lord, Frank! who are they ?

1

F. Lib. You shall hear. Being without cash, and in want of better company, a very short time introduced me to myself; a gentleman I was mighty fond of at first; but a little observation convinced me he was such a giddy, rattle-brain'd, eccentric animal, that I must ask pardon for having made him the theme of so much conversation.

Miss Lib. And to whom next did your poverty lead you?

F. Lib. To a wonder—a man of merit, modesty, and friendship: of merit sufficient to become the object of envy; of modesty enough to think it no more than his desert; of friendship to contradict me when I was rich, and take me by the hand when I was poor, and all others had forsaken me.

Old Lib. Where is he, Frank? How I do like that man, whoever he is! If he has a family, I'll bring up all his children; the boys shall go to India, the girls to boarding-school, and the little ones——

Miss Lib. (*Stopping his mouth.*) Cousin! cousin! you get worse and worse; I am impatient of your folly.

Fan. And I to hear who the third personage can be that Frank has to tell us of.

F. Lib. The third—yes, every way the third, positively, comparatively, and superlatively so. I have told you of myself, and no small favourite of mine, with all my oddities; I have told you of my friend— a man who would probably die for me; but there is yet another——

Fan. For whom, perhaps, you are dying at this moment.

F. Lib. But with whom I cou'd live till Time shou'd break his glass, lose every feather of his wings, and yield his scythe to the more powerful arms of Cupid.

Old Lib. Curse me if I didn't think so.

Miss Lib. And can you encourage such romantic nonsense ?

Old Lib. I order'd him to speak freely.   Come, sir, let us hear.   But no love, no raptures, no descriptions of brilliant eyes, cherry lips, taper fingers, rosy cheeks, lily complexions, for I can't bear 'em, they put me into such a——Zounds ! why don't you go on with your story ?

F. Lib. Since I am not to describe her person, look around you, sir : you, madam, will forgive my saying that one beauty may sometimes put us in mind of another.

Miss Lib. (*Bridling.*) Go on, child; I am all attention.

Fan. And so am I.

F. Lib. Figure to yourself, sir——

Old Lib. I do ; I see all you would say ; I see——

Miss Lib. Silence, cousin.   What can you possibly see worth talking of?

Old Lib. (*Bowing to her.*) Nothing at present.— But go on, Frank.

F. Lib. Figure to yourself, sir, one of the most tremendous storms of hail, rain, thunder, and lightning that ever rattled over our heads—the storm of this morning was nothing to it.

Old Lib. Why, I was thinking of a woman, and you tell me of a thunder-storm.—That's no allusion to my cousin, I hope.

F. Lib. It was a day, sir, in which, as Shakespeare says, I wou'dn't have turn'd my enemy's dog into the street.   I, among others, took shelter in a cottage by the road-side, where I beheld a straw hat, and under it such a face !——Put sensibility into a pair of eyes, virtue into the tears which moisten'd two lovely cheeks, and if it doesn't put your hearts into a flutter, never believe me.

Old Lib. I do believe you, I do, so go on.

F. Lib. Her mother was ill. In this storm, so violent that no one, for money or entreaties, would venture out, did she at length sally from the door, to go three miles for a cooling medicine. I had most need of it, for my heart was in a flame. I had the pleasure to be her messenger. That done, I set off for London, and have appriz'd a worthy friend of hers of her mother's situation.

Old Lib. Why, it's the widow Howard you're telling us of. She has but lately come into our neighbourhood. Her uncle has left his fortune unaccountably away from her; and my cousin there has a principal share of it.

F. Lib. Indeed! I met with her again this morning.—Whereabouts did you say she lives?

Miss Lib. Wherever she lives, she can be no match for you. Her uncle was my particular friend. Disobedience to him, from both mother and daughter, occasion'd their loss of that fortune which is justly added to mine.

F. Lib. Nay, but, madam——

Miss Lib. If you and my cousin do not follow their example, you also will be gainers. Miss Fanny, come with me. I have something of particular moment to say to you, and a proposal to make, which it will be for the interest of you all to comply with.
[*Exit.*

F. Lib. Madam, I have already heard of this proposal.

Old Lib. Don't follow her, Frank; it will be of no use—After all, she means us well. But where is this friend of yours? I should like to see him.

F. Lib. I guess'd as much, sir, and took the liberty to invite him so far, that he is now in the next room, waiting the issue of my reception.—He is, however, so modest, so very diffident, that you must not form a judgment of his worth from a short interview.

Old Lib. I understand you: we'll not alarm him.

Modesty is like a rose, and the world is the weather
to it—An unkind blight in the bud often turns its
sweetness to——Zounds! come along, Frank; I was
always a blockhead at a simile.   [*Exeunt.*

SCENE IV.

Another Apartment in the same House.

MILDMAY *discovered writing at a table.*

Mild. I have taken advantage of these waiting
moments to write to my dear Fanny; and, after all,
where is the use of it? She is, in point of fortune,
so much above me; and this enemy of mine, this intolerable timidity, which I cannot shake off, is of itself enough to prevent my rising in the world. What
is to be done? Perhaps Frank's introduction of me
to his father, for the trifling services I have rendered
him, may assist me, in spite of myself. My dress, I
fear, will not recommend me. It will be thought a
liberty, perhaps, that I have us'd these writing materials on so elegant a table. (*Goes to move them, and
overturns the standish.*) 'Sdeath! how unfortunate!
Some one is coming! How shall I extricate myself?
I am ever in the wrong! (*Wipes up the ink with his
white handkerchief, which he immediately returns into
his pocket.*)

Enter FANNY.

Fan. Ah! there, it's all out!—An odious proposal
of marriage has blighted all my hopes, and now——
(*Sees* MILDMAY, *and screams.*) Ah!
Mild. (*Turns.*) My Fanny! why, how is it possible that I see you here; you, whom I left so distant?

Fan. Dear, dear, how my heart does flutter, and ——Reach me a chair, or I shall faint; or, stay, your arm will do as well.

Mild. But tell me by what strange accident do I behold you?

Fan. By an unaccountable circumstance, which happens to all boarding-school misses : they are sent to school, taught a great many pretty things, and then return home again : just so has it happened to Frances Liberal.

Mild. Why, Frank Liberal is my friend, and has brought me here on a visit to his father.

Fan. And Frances Liberal is his sister. He has given you such a character, and my father is so impatient to see you, that if you offer to tell him that you knew me at the boarding-school, that you sav'd me from that brutal country squire, and that I, fearful of consequences, refused to see you, conceal'd my name, and gave you the slip, he'd be so angry with me, or both of us, that perhaps we shou'd never see each other again.

Mild. But what consequences could you fear from the affection of a man who wou'd sacrifice life to be of service to you? It was accident brought us acquainted; but I owed to that accident so complete an insight to your heart and disposition, that though to lose you would be worse than death, yet never wou'd I accept that hand, if your real interest demanded its resignation.

Fan. Why, Charles, I have a female relation, on whom my father greatly depends. Whether my governess discovered any thing to inform her of, I know not, but she has just proposed the very man to me as a match, from whose insolence you generously released me.

Mild. How unfortunate! Can nothing be done? Your father will be more generous : he will never permit such a sacrifice. Were it for your good, I wou'dn't hesitate; but to give you to such a wretch ——Sooner than it shall happen, I swear upon this hand—(*Kneels, kisses her hand, just as* OLD LIBE-RAL, FRANK, *and* MISS LIBERAL *enter.*)

Old Lib. Why, zounds! if this be modesty, the devil's in't.

F. Lib. Mildmay! my friend! why, how, in the name of wonder, came this about?

Miss Lib. I am perfectly astonished! This, then, is the reason of your reluctance, madam?

Fan. Now do only let me explain.

Mild. Nay, 'tis I who ought to explain. Mr Li-beral, there is no man can feel more on such an oc-casion, or——

Miss Lib. Or express his feelings with more un-becoming warmth to a young lady. Miss Liberal, go to your room; go, I say, and thank my clemency if I deign to speak to you when you quit it, which, till you are married, you shall never do. [*Exit* FANNY.] Cousin, I leave the dismission of that gentleman to you. A man of merit, modesty, and friendship, ha! ha! ha!   [*Exit.*

Old Lib. (*To* MILDMAY.) Ay, sir, my son de-scrib'd you as an auctioneer does an estate—all ex-cellence and utility, and I find you only fit to be knock'd down.

F. Lib. Pardon me, sir; it is to me he owes an ex-planation, which, I hope, for both our sakes, will not turn out to his dishonour. I have been proud of you, Charles, as my friend; have reported you in glowing colours to a parent it wou'd be infamy to deceive, and if you don't make good every tittle of my asser-tion, I'll—I'll——Zounds, Charles! why don't you speak?

Old Lib. His modesty won't let him.

Mild. (*With great hesitation.*) Appearances, gen-tlemen, nay, more than appearances, at present con-demn me. Were I to relate the commencement of my acquaintance with Miss Liberal, it wou'd look too much like speaking in my own behalf. But tho' no possible circumstance cou'd add to my present embarrassment, yet this I will say, (*Pulls out the inky handkerchief, and incautiously wipes his forehead with it,*) that tho' my conduct may wear the blackest appearance——

Old Lib. And this I will say, that if you talk till you are *black* in the face, I wou'dn't believe but what——Why, Frank, what the devil is he at now?

Mild. Sir, I owe myself at least thus much in justification, that notwithstanding the opinion you may have been pleas'd to form, my own reflections assure me——(FRANK *holds a pocket-glass to* MILDMAY'S *face ; he looks astonished, recurs to his handkerchief, attempts in vain to speak, and runs out.*)

Old Lib. Why, he's out of his senses—stark staring mad! What the devil did he mean by that pyeball'd pocket-handkerchief? I suppose it was to give proof of his insanity in black and white.

F. Lib. Ha! ha! ha!

Old Lib. Why then, if this is modesty, I'll be content to pass for the most impudent old fellow in existence. Get along, you puppy! What are you laughing at? I suppose you call that modesty.

[*Exeunt.*

ACT THE FOURTH.

SCENE I.

The Widow HOWARD'S.

Enter COUNSELLOR FRIENDLY *and* JOHN.

Friend. Well, my good fellow, for the care and trouble my whimsical mistake has given, perhaps this money will make amends. (*Gives silver.*)

John. Well, sir, I'll tak'd brass, to shew I bear no malice; but I hope another time you weant think so ill of a Yorkshireman. There be honest folk in all places; and though some be born i' Yorkshire, we munna be look'd on like Jews.

Enter EPHRAIM *and* RACHEL.

Eph. Vell, vat you talk apoud Jews? The Jews are mighty good sort of peoples, yet they are treated all de vorld so dey vas Turks and Mussulmans.

Rach. (*Shewing the trunks.*) There are the things, Mr Ephraim. You must make haste, for young mistress is coming.

Eph. Mr Grouse, be so goot as help ma to come out mit dis bundle of clothes. Dear me, dere's de gentlemans vat run away from his vatch. How cou'd you be so frighten'd, sir?

Friend. I had evil thoughts, which I now repent of. But what is it you are removing, friend?

Eph. Some of de dead gentleman's clothes, vat I pought of de laty of de house. You don't dink vat I wou'd take away nobody's property but ma own?

Friend. Who was the dead gentleman, as you call him?

Eph. I believe it vas old Squire Rackrent. But I don't trouble myself mit noting but puying de clothes. I shou'd be happy if you vas dead, and I shou'd puy your clothes, if you like to sell it.

John. Come, ould Ephraim, I think thou'st gotten all right.—(*During the above speeches they have been taking the clothes from the trunk, and placing them in a large green bag, brought by* EPHRAIM *for the purpose.*)

Rach. Ay, ay, they are all right. This way out, Mr Jew gentleman.

(JOHN *and* EPHRAIM *take the bag between them.*)

Eph. Take care you don't break de bag, Mr Grouse. I wish you good bye, sir. You're very welcome to puy some of de clothes back again, if you like it.

[*Exeunt* JOHN *and* EPHRAIM, RACHEL *assisting.*

Friend. I am sorry the widow shou'd thus hastily part with her uncle's property. I have seen and conversed with her, and am perhaps to blame for not having yet open'd my commission. But she comes, and by this time may be better prepar'd for it.

Enter MRS HOWARD *and* MARIAN.

My good Mrs Howard, I fear there has been some mistake with regard to your uncle's will. Did he leave no token of his once having been a friend to you?

Mrs How. He left me only the furniture you see.

Friend. And those chests among it.

Mrs How. He did.

Friend. He left *me* a letter, which, till this day, I was not to open, and which I will now read, as a art of his will.

Mar. Indeed!—Oh, sir, may I hear?

Friend. You may. (*Takes out a letter and reads.*) " As a further punishment to my niece, for the sin of disobedience, in marrying against my inclination, I have only left her some furniture and wearing apparel; but she will be punish'd no longer than till this informs her, that in the lining of the left hand pocket of my old drab-colour'd coat there is a reward for her past sufferings, and a token of my forgiveness."

Mrs How. Gracious Heaven! my daughter will be rewarded. (*Runs to the chest, opens it, misses the things, and, after a short pause, recollects herself.*) Oh! my child! can you forgive me? (*Sits down on the chest, and hides her face with her hands.*)

Mar. Mother! dear mother! why do you look so wildly?

Friend. I recollect : I may perhaps recover the loss. I'll go to the Jew's, and purchase back the clothes, which he cannot already have parted with, and which, but now, he offer'd to sell me.   [*Exit.*

Mrs How. My child! my love! wou'd I had strength to second our friend's exertions. The Jew, I believe, is honest; if not, the impatience of a mother will be the ruin of a child dearer to her than life.

Mar. And do you think Providence will forsake us? Oh no! a mother and a daughter, who love virtue and each other, will never be in want of a father and a friend.   [*Exeunt.*

SCENE II.

OLD LIBERAL'S.

Enter MISS LIBERAL *and* SQUIRE CHACE.

Miss Lib. But why despair, sir? In this house I am absolute. Her father has no objection; and the girl must have you.

Sq. So far we are on the right scent; but if we are to be cross'd by that hound Mildmay, we shall be thrown out at last.

Miss Lib. Why need you fear him? Didn't you tell me you had his bond for a thousand pounds? Isn't he poor, and hasn't he insulted you?

Sq. He has, a cur; but I've sent the staunch lads after him—the whippers-in. But what of that?—where's the odds? Lock him up in one prison, and miss in another, they come together at last.

Miss Lib. Indeed! but how?

Sq. How! You may as well ask a hare why it runs, or a harrier why it follows the hare: it's the nature on 'em, to be sure: why, I cou'dn't keep 'em apart myself. He knock'd me down like a calf, and ran off with the girl like a leveret.

Miss Lib. Well, well, she's coming: and till she consents, these apartments will be her prison.

Enter FANNY.

Sq. Ah! my dear miss, you know I love you. Say but you'll have me, and Chevy Chace, esquire, with all his goods, chattels, hunters, and hounds, are yours into the bargain.

Fan. I don't like hounds, and I'll have nothing to say to *you.*

Sq. No!—Only think of being mistress over one of the first manors in the world, patroness of the first hunt, toast of the first sportsmen, ranger of the first parks, and lady to the first squire in the county.

Miss Lib. Yes, or else think of living in this room, and your bed-chamber, which adjoins it; no liberty, and not a soul to talk to.

Sq. Ay, not a soul to talk to!—If that isn't enough to punish a woman, the devil's in't.

Miss Lib. Speak, miss: what's your determination?

Fan. I shall appeal to my father. I am sure he doesn't know of this; and if you offer to—to—lock me up, I'll run away as soon as ever I can, I will— (*Sobbing.*)

Miss Lib. We'll try that. Come, sir, leave her to herself; a little solitude will bring her to reason.

Sq. Nay, but, hang it, I don't much like to see the tears of a stag at the death, much more those of a pretty girl. Now, come, miss, I tell you what— if you take *me*, you may expect——(*Goes coaxingly to her; she slaps his face.*)

Fan. And if you take me, you may expect—*that !* —I won't have you—that's once for all.—And the man that's mean enough to plague a poor girl so un mercifully, deserves nothing better for his pains.

Sq. It's very well.—Odrotten ! why, she hits like a hammer. And so I be to be knock'd down by one, and box'd by t'other, be I ? I can't say much to you, seeing you are but a woman ; but if I don't ferret out that Mr Mildmay, never trust me : I'll teach folk to strike their betters.

Miss Lib. I'm quite ashamed !—But I'll go to your father directly, and if he don't punish this insolence, I and my fortune are lost to him for ever. In the mean time, this key shall be your security. [*Exit.*

Fan. (*Jeeringly.*) Won't *you* stay with me, squire ?

Sq. No, I won't; and if you don't learn to behave better next time, I don't know that I'll come again at all or no; so think well of it. My face do burn all one as a fire-brand. [*Exit.*

Fan. I wonder who the deuce wou'd have a rich cousin in a family? Here am I to be lock'd up, and us'd ill, because a cross old woman has a great deal of money. What shall I do? The windows are too high to jump from. Is there no way to escape— no kind fairy, like those I us'd to read of at school, to whisper means for my release?

Jen. (*From a closet.*) Ma'am! miss!

Fan. Mercy on me! how cou'd I have such wicked thoughts?

Jen. (*Comes forward.*) Don't be alarmed; it's only Jenny.

Fan. Jenny! what, Jenny! my dear Jenny! how did you come here?

Jen. Why, ma'am, I heard Miss Lucretia threaten to lock you up in this room; and as vou have always been so good to me, I came up before her, unseen by any one, with this key in my pocket, which will open the door. I hid myself in the closet, and over- heard all that pass'd, and will do any thing to help you out of the way till old master can be brought to reason; and I'm sure it won't be long first.

Fan. What a kind, charming girl! I wish Frank was here; I'm sure he'd assist us. O dear! do you know they talk of arresting poor Mr Mildmay?

Jen. Suppose you go to your father—and yet, if the old lady should have been with him, that would only discover us, and spoil all.

Fan. So it wou'd, Jenny. But, Jenny, I'll tell you what we'll do.—My brother has some uniform coats, that were made for a club, or society, or some such thing; they lie in the back room with his other clothes. Do you fetch 'em, and, for a frolic's sake,

we'll slip out into the village, merely to see what
effect our absence will have on the old lady.

Jen. But I have a better thought still.

Fan. Ay, what is it?

Jen. My cousin is a volunteer: I'll borrow his
dress, make him get me another, and in these we
may march boldly off, without danger of suspicion.

Fan. No; do as I bid you at first.—Your plan will
never do.

Jen. No, miss! why not?

Fan. Why not? I should never be able to respect
myself, or any one else, who could put on the dress
of a volunteer with an intention of running away in
it.   [*Exeunt.*

SCENE III.

The Inn.

Enter Landlord and SQUIRE CHACE.

Land. Well, sir, the bailiffs are on the look-out.
Mildmay will soon be in your power.

Sq. Ay, but I'm thinking of a better prize. Miss
Fanny is rather too strong in the wrist for *me.* I've
seen one I like better too.—Such a girl! poor and
pretty—the two most accommodating qualities in
the world.

Land. But who, sir, who? You are so changeable and headstrong. You were quite taken a while
ago with Miss Marian of the cottage, whom you saw
here.

Sq. Why, that's the very girl I mean. As beautiful as an angel, but scornful as Lucifer. I've

laid a plan—you shall see the success of it, you dog.
—I came down for a wife, and if I can't get *her*, I
will have a mistress at any rate.

Land. But why carry her off, your honour?

Sq. Because she'll not go without. Marriage,
where there's no money, will never do, and without
marriage she'll never consent—So she must e'en be
compelled to her own good.

Land. That's very considerate, your worship:—
But what will the family at the Hall say to all this?

Sq. What care I what they say? It's my way to
act first and think afterwards.—If the point turns out
wrong, I try to think of something better—if right,
it saves farther trouble, by being ready done to one's
hands.

Enter Squire's Servant.

Serv. Every thing's as you ordered, sir—we only
wait for you.

Sq. You sha'n't wait long then; I'll go with you
—And hark ye, landlord, when they bring Mildmay,
my lawyer will settle with you. [*Exit with Servant.*

Land. Very well, your honour.

Enter Bailiff.

Well, have you got him?

Bail. Not yet; our lads are on the look-out though,
and I shall join them presently.

Land. You're so long about business. Why do
you lose so much time, my friend?

Bail. Me! Lord, I never lose a moment. Just
lay my hand so—(*Touching Landlord's shoulder*)—
shew the writ, and—by the by, did you ever see one
of our warrants?

Land. Plenty—often enough.

Bail. But not with your own name in it, mayhap.

Land. My own name indeed! What d'ye mean?

Bail. I mean that you're down here for the sum of two hundred pounds. You see I don't lose my time so much as you imagine.

Land. (*Reads.*) " At the suit of Francis Liberal, esquire :"—A villain !

Bail. That's always the way. Creditors are good fellows enough till they want their money, and then nothing's too bad for them. So, come—if you can't find bail among some of your customers, I must lock you up in your own bar, till Mildmay comes to keep you company.

Land. Nay, but listen with a little patience.

Bail. I tell you what, Master Doublechalk ; I know you never listened in your life with patience to a poor debtor ; so you must e'en take up with the same fare you gave to others.

Land. Vastly civil ! But what can one expect from a bailiff ?

Bail. That he does his duty—if every one else did the same, there wouldn't be half so much occasion for us.

[*Exeunt.*

SCENE IV.

An Apartment at OLD LIBERAL'S.

OLD LIBERAL *and* PARCHMENT, *meeting.*

Parch. Sir, your lady cousin is looking for you in a great passion. Something has made her angry, and every body is getting out of her way. Adod, I believe she's coming here.

Old Lib. Is she ? Why then, stay a bit : I don't much care to be left alone with her—If it wasn't for the young ones, I would not put up with her temper

—But a good father is his children's steward, and shouldn't mind a little inconvenience, when it's for their good.

Enter Miss Liberal.

Miss Lib. Well, cousin, here are fine doings in the house ; there has been neither peace, quietness, or satisfaction from the moment I set foot in it.

Old Lib. No more there has—I perfectly agree with you.

Miss Lib. And I, sir, as perfectly understand your sneer : But I shall not stay to be thus derided—Your daughter follows your example; your servants join in it ; and I shouldn't wonder next if old Parchment there was ordered to make me his laughing-stock.

Parch. I never refused to do what I was ordered in my life, madam, so you needn't be angry with me ; and I will not stay to be wrongfully entreated. [*Exit.*

Old Lib. Well, but tell me, cousin, what has my daughter done ?

Miss Lib. She has refused to marry Squire Chace, one of the first matches in the county.

Old Lib. Has she ? Why, who the devil asked her to have him ?

Miss Lib. Who, sir ? Why, I asked her—nay, I commanded her; and he begged, prayed, and entreated to no effect.

Old Lib. That was mighty condescending! And what did she say to him ?

Miss Lib. Say ! Why, she struck him—absolutely boxed his ears.

Old Lib. The devil she did ! What a desperate baggage—My daughter box'd the squire—Oh ! the spirited little hussy !

Miss Lib. Do you laugh, sir ? I think it a very serious matter.

Old Lib. So do I, upon my soul.

Miss Lib. And what satisfaction is to be given the squire for such treatment ?

Old Lib. Why, hasn't she given him enough already ?

Miss Lib. Have the goodness, sir, to let me know what I am to understand by this kind of conversation ?

Old Lib. If you don't know, I'll tell you. You have always confessed that your money was the reason why your will should be a law in this family— My children were to benefit by it—And for their sakes I permitted a foolish old woman to have her way.

Miss Lib. Sir, I will not stay another moment in the house.

Old Lib. Then you may go out of it. If you chuse to stay and make *me* the butt of your ill-natured whims, you've free leave ; do it, and welcome ; but my children are my own ; they are my existence, my every thing, and their happiness shall not be made a sacrifice, for twenty times the paltry cash in your possession.

Miss Lib. I shall expire with rage.

Old Lib. Why don't you then ? You may do what you please with me, only behave well to the young ones.

Miss Lib. And is it not behaving well, to endeavour to open their eyes to their own good ?

Old Lib. But you should consider what is truly, and not seemingly for their good.—What's your quarrel with my daughter ? Why, she won't *love* where you bid her ; and how should she ? The very request, much more a command, is as unreasonable as to bid a Laplander wear furs in the West Indies.

Miss Lib. So, so ; I have given my time and anxiety to a fine purpose ; but your ingratitude shall be paid with interest. Haven't I dedicated half my life to serve you ?

Old Lib. And who asked you ? But come, send

for my daughter. Let me hear her story, and I'll give fair judgment between you.

Miss Lib. No, sir. I shall submit to no such arbitration. Here is the key of her rooms, and with it I render up all further intentions for the good of a family so blind to its own interest.

Re-enter PARCHMENT.

Parch. Sir! Sir! Miss Fanny has run away, and left this letter for you.

Miss Lib. There, cousin, what say you now?

Old Lib. What do I say? Why, confound your system. Come along, old Parchment; muster the servants, and let us seek her directly.

Miss Lib. Hear me, sir!—If the late Mr Rackrent——

Old Lib. Rat Mr Rackrent—I hate his memory, and abhor his doctrines; his ill got property is as ill bequeathed—And I'll no more suffer my family to be in future imposed on by its influence, than I'll squeeze my tenants as he did, or debase their honest natures to fear a landlord, who, by kinder treatment, would merit and receive their gratitude. Out upon 't! Why do I stand talking to you all this while? Here, John! Gregory! [*Exit, followed by* PARCHMENT.

Miss Lib. I haven't patience—but no matter— I'll be even with them all. What is it to me what they do? I have no reason to be concerned—To be sure, there is some pleasure in governing; but for my part, I've so little desire for it, that—Oh! Oh! Oh! if they don't let me have my way I shall break my heart. (*As she is going,*)

Re-enter PARCHMENT.

Parch. Madam, I forgot to say that there is a report in the village that the Jew Ephraim, who bought some of the old squire's furniture, has found money concealed among it to a considerable amount.

[MISS LIBERAL, *who, at the beginning of* PARCH-
MENT'S *speech, has continued to cry, suddenly
brightens up.*]

Miss Lib. What, money! It belongs to me—every
guinea belongs to me—I'll go to the Jew's this instant—he shall refund, and my half-witted cousin, till
he comes to his senses, sha'n't be a penny the better
for it.   [*Exit.*

Parch. Bless my heart, what a vexatious thing it
seems to be rich!—Now, money never troubles me;
and if old Parchment was to live till he fretted about
who was to be his heir, I verily believe he'd never
die at all; ha, ha, ha!   [*Exit, hobbling.*

SCENE V.

EPHRAIM'S *Apartment.*

EPHRAIM *discovered sitting with all the Clothes scat-
tered loose about him, holding the Drab Coat in one
hand, and a number of Bank-Notes in the other.*

Eph. No, no, I have looked all over, and dere is
noting more to be found. These bills are vorth
more as ten thousand pounds. Dear, dear, what a
fine purchase! Let ma see—Vat vill it be vorth ma
vile to do mit dem? It vill take a great deal of consideration.

F. Lib. (*Without.*) I'll find the way, I warrant.

Eph. Bless ma! somebody is coming: I must hide
'em all in a minute.

(*Puts the notes in his pocket, and throws all the
clothes behind a curtain across a part of the
room.*)

Enter FRANK.

F. Lib. Ah, old Benjamite, how is it with you, eh, my fine fellow?

Eph. It is petter mit me now than it was a little while ago. But hadn't you petter walk down stairs?

F. Lib. No, not I—my business won't detain me a moment. I know that, notwithstanding you occasionally lodge in this cottage, and are a very shabby looking sort of a gentleman, you have more money than most folks think.

Eph. I hope he doesn't suspect. (*Aside.*) Me moniesh! dear me, I'm so poor as nobody else in de parish. I haven't got a guinea in all de vorldt.

F. Lib. Very likely—but I want a thousand.

Eph. A thousand guineas!

F. Lib. Yes; or, what's of more consequence, a friend of mine wants them—is on the point of being arrested by a rascal; so let me have it, how, and upon what terms you like—only it must be directly.

Eph. Dear me, your father has plenty moniesh.

F. Lib. Yes, he has; and so much good nature, that I can't bear to be troublesome to him. If he was a little more crabbed, I should no more mind teazing him, than I shall kicking you down stairs, if you don't let me have the money this instant.

Eph. I'd better get rid of him before somebody comes to get de clothes again—Here, here, fill up dis bond—I always have one ready—Here is de money, and——

Miss Lib. (*Without.*) What a horrid staircase.

F. Lib. The old governess of my father and all his family. What can she want? If she sees me here, she'll ruin me.—Where can you put me? I'll hide in here. (*Goes to the curtain.*)

Eph. No, no—dere is someting.

F. Lib. Hold your tongue—don't speak of me for your ears—I must contrive to get away in spite of her

immediately, or I shall be too late with the money.
(*Hides in the recess behind the curtain.*)

Eph. Vat de devil de people all vant, I vonder. I
vish dey were at de devil.

Enter MISS LIBERAL.

How d'ye do, ma'am ? I'm glad to see you.

Miss Lib. Mr Ephraim, I wait upon you, upon a
business so particular——

Eph. Vell, madam, I have some pusiness myself.

Miss Lib. Sir, I shall not detain you. I have heard
it reported that Mr Rackrent, who generously left
me so much money, died possessed of much more,
which was supposed to be concealed in some of his
furniture.

Eph. Pless mà heart ! I can't think he vou'd hide
avay his money—And if he did, how could I help it,
you know ?

Miss Lib. True ; but I believe you bought part of
his furniture.

Eph. Yes ; I bought all vat I could ; but I hope
dere vas none of de moniesh left among it.

Miss Lib. Why not ?

Eph. Because vat I happened to sell it all again.
Is dat all you please to vant ?

Miss Lib. No, sir ; I must make further inquiries
—Besides, I understand it has been reported, through
you, that I persuaded him to desert his niece, and
forget her in his will.

Eph. Vell, I don't doubt it.

Miss Lib. Sir !

Eph. I don't doubt the report—I can say noting
about the truth of it.

Miss Lib. But, sir, the old gentleman left me his
money for the care I took of him, and the anxiety
with which I watched the moment of his departure.

Eph. Yes, you vas mighty anxious apoud his departure.

Miss Lib. Poor dear man ! were he here himself,

he would acknowledge it.—Never shall I forget him
in his fine out drab coloured suit and flowing wig ; a
respectable remnant of the old court—the grace
with which he walked into and out of a room—and
then the style with which his picture was drawn, with
his left hand elegantly placed on his hip, and the
other in his bosom—Ah ! were I once again to see
him—I should expire with——Ah !

(*During the above speech,* FRANK *comes from be-*
hind the curtain, dress'd in the drab-coloured suit,
as described, and stalks off, after making a formal
bow to MISS LIBERAL, *who screams, and falls on*
EPHRAIM.)

Miss Lib. (*Recovering.*) It was his ghost—Did you
not see him ?

Eph. See him ! Vy—vhat !—it's only ma friend,
Mr——Dear me ! I very near let all de cat come out
of de bag at once.

Miss Lib. 'Twas he himself! What can it fore-
bode ? There is, there must be money concealed.
Perhaps he is now going to point out the spot.

Eph. It vill be more petter if I follow him. I had
not quite done mit de coat. (*Aside.*)

Miss Lib. Follow him ! What, and leave me here
alone. (*Pulls him back.*)—You sha'n't stir a foot without——

Enter COUNSELLOR FRIENDLY, *who stops* EPHRAIM.

Friend. No, you shall not stir till you sell me the
drab-coloured suit you just purchased of my friend's
widow.

Eph. Vell, let me go fetch it, I tell you.

Friend. You have it here ; and but for the wind-
ings of this labyrinth you live in, I should have been
here before you.

Eph. I tell you, ma friend, it is not here. You
may look among de rest of 'em, and you vill not
find it.

Miss Lib. Oh, Mr Friendly, such an alarming circumstance!

Eph. Yes, mighty alarming! Von man runs avay mit ma goods, and de oder says vat I must stay behind, to sell it him.

Friend. If you do not produce the property, I would not be in your coat for a trifle.

Eph. Vell, but dere is a man in my coat already, and vat can I do?

Miss Lib. Did you meet no one on the stairs?

Friend. I *saw* nobody, for it is dark; but I was nearly overturned by some one who passed.

Eph. Vell, it vas Mr Frank, I tell you, mit ma coat.

Miss Lib. Mr Frank! Hark ye, Mr Ephraim, I shall make further inquiry into your conduct—And in the mean time I'll see what my hopeful cousin will say to his children now. To be made a jest of, truly!
                                                   [*Exit.*

Eph. He has made a jest of me, I think.

Friend. You know, Ephraim, that there is money concealed in that suit, which I shall make you restore.

Eph. I tell you I pought de tings; and if dere is money, it is ma own.—Let ma go, sir—I am no dief —De law is mine as vell as yours—and if you dink it impossible a Jew can be honest, it may be because you find it a hard matter to be so yourself.

Friend. Would you withhold what belongs to the fatherless?

Eph. I have had children myself, and though dey never lived to be fatherless, dey taught me in deir life-time to respect de children of anoder.

Friend. And will you not listen to the widow?

Eph. You are no widow, and I will not listen— Ven you come to make me do good meder I vill or not, you take avay de merit of it. Go avay den—If dere is money to be found, I shall see vat is vorth ma

vile to do mit it. Ask your own conscience vat a
lawyer vou'd call his duty.

Friend. Every honest lawyer knows that to perform
his duty is his true interest.

Eph. And a Jew knows his interest as vell as a
lawyer, or else the devil's in it!   [*Exeunt.*

ACT THE FIFTH.

SCENE I.

A Landscape, with a House at a little distance.

Enter MILDMAY.

Mild. Was ever an unfortunate being thus persecuted? The victim of suspicion on one side, and an
implacable creditor on the other. I overheard the
sheriff's officers inquiring for me, and which way to
avoid them, without giving up all hopes of explanation with Frank Liberal and his father, I see at present no sort of prospect.

Enter FRANK, *in the old man's dress.*

F. Lib. Mildmay! Charles! What the deuce do
you run for? I'm no sheriff's officer—Here, I've
brought the means of quieting your fears.

Mild. Frank! Why, what masquerade frolic is
this?

F. Lib. Never you mind.   I have been to my old banker, borrowed a thousand, and—Yes, I have—I certainly have—(*Feeling in his pockets.*)

Mild. What, my dear friend?

F. Lib. Left it behind me.   The devil fly away with all antiquated cousins, say I—I put on this coat to avoid her, and left my own in its place, with all the notes, which in my hurry I had stuffed into the pocket of it.

Mild. But surely you couldn't have meant so much generosity for me.

F. Lib. It's no matter what was meant, for now all's over, without some contrivance.   Here—I have it—Take this coat and waistcoat, give me yours in exchange—I'll run back to the Jew's.—The bailiffs will never suspect you in that disguise.

Mild. There are some people now crossing that inclosure.

F. Lib. Then step here, behind these trees.   The shade will make a pleasant dressing-room; and we sha'n't be the first who have taken umbrage at the sight of a sheriff's officer.   [*Exeunt.*

Enter FANNY *and* JENNY *in men's clothes, dress'd alike, in blue coats with red collars.*

Fan. Well, Jenny, and what are we to do now?

Jen. Why, ma'am, we must make the best of our way to my mother's cottage : brother John shall run and see how things go on in our absence—And I'm sure when my old master finds that his cousin has forced you to run away, he'll give you your own terms to come back again.

Fan. Come then—Ah, we are watched.   There are two men lurking behind those trees.

Jen. Yes, ma'am, and three more running down the hill on that side.   Do you step into this house.

Fan. But upon what pretence?

Jen. Why, Lord, ma'am, a'n't you a woman in distress? And isn't that sufficient?

Fan. You forget that at present we pretend to be men.

Jen. Well then, we are men in distress, fearful of being arrested—Any thing

Fan. And that will do purely ; for when a poor fellow is trying to preserve his liberty, there are very few Englishmen would refuse to afford him shelter and assistance.   [*Exit into house.*

Enter Bailiff and two Followers.

Bail. I've locked up the landlord, and now for Charles Mildmay, gent., at the suit of Chevy Chace, esquire.—Why, I'm sure I saw him but this moment —A blue coat and a red collar—What's to be done, lads?

1 Fol. Each go a different way, and let whoever catches him first give a whistle.

2 Fol. Then that will be I—I was always lucky at finding a shy bird.

1 Fol. You don't find him first, for a tankard with you.

Bail. I say, for a crown bowl of punch, the two losers to pay it between 'em.

1 Fol. Done ! Done !

Bail. You take the lower road—*You* go that way, and I'll remain hereabout—And, d'ye hear, look out sharp, for it's a very little way to the next county.

1 Fol. What a thing it is, Master Touch, we can't follow a defendant if once he carries his shoulder in- to another shire ! For my part, I'm an advocate for liberty, and thinks every bailiff ought to follow his profession wherever he can.

Bail. True : In some places there's nothing at all said about carrying a man to prison ; but in this coun- try they make such a fuss, that if a gentleman offi-

cer doesn't mind what he's at, ecod, he stands no bad
chance of being clapt there himself.

[*Exit up the stage, the two followers on
opposite sides.*

Enter FRANK, *in* MILDMAY'S *coat and waistcoat.*

F. Lib. (*As he enters.*) Stay where you are, my
friend; I'll return in a few seconds, and then you will
have no more fear of the bailiffs. (*Going.*)

Bail. (*Comes forward and interrupts him.*) Not so
fast—I must keep you company.

F. Lib. I don't like keeping company, my friend.
Nobody gets any thing by it.

Bail. Except gemmen of our profession. But
come, I've nabbed you, and won the wager. I know
you well enough—Squire Chace shewed you to me
from the castle windows—And as sure as your name
is Charles Mildmay, you must go with me. (*Whistles.*)

F. Lib. (*Stops him.*) Don't whistle—I shall make
no resistance. I'm walking this way for the benefit
of the air—It does me good.

Bail. Psha! nonsense! It will do you more good
to pay your debts. Come along. (*Pulling him.*)

F. Lib. Now don't do that—It will bring on my
old complaint.

Bail. Your old complaint!

F. Lib. Yes. You must know there are periods
when I can't, for the life of me, resist an inclination
to kick any body that says I must do what I don't
like.

Bail. What! Will *you* kick *me?*

F. Lib. I can't help it—particularly, as it's your request. (*Kicks him; he whistles.*) Vastly well, friend!
If a burr will stick to me, why, you know I must get
rid of it.

Bail. Here, William! Fellows! Rescue!

[*Exit, kick'd off by* FRANK.

Enter MILDMAY, *in the old drab suit.*

Mild. I hope Frank won't stay long. These habiliments will at least secure me from being known till his return.

Enter FRIENDLY.

Friend. No where can I find the man who has taken the drab suit from Ephraim. Aha! Stop, friend; I must speak to you.

Mild. (*As an old man.*) Sir, what did you say? I'm rather deaf.

Friend. You can't impose on me, friend. That coat I remember to have been worn by a deceased friend of mine, and I know your design in putting it on.

Mild. The deuce you do! Then I have nothing but flight for it at last. [*Exit.*

Friend. And I have nothing to do but to follow.
[*Exit.*

SCENE II.

A Landscape, with a Road leading to a Wood.

Enter JOHN GROUSE.

John. There's some mischief a-foot, I reckon, wi' that Squire Chace—There war he and his gentleman, as they call him; they were talking of a chaise, and a nice job, and Miss Marian—Ecod, if they war to do any thing wrong to her, they mun be bad ones sure enough—I don't know what the law would say to me for leathering a squire, but as to his gentleman, I'd pay him enough; and if the squire was but

a gentleman, I'd knock one head against the t'other
—Eh! marry, she's coming.

Enter MARIAN.

Mar. Ah, John! I'm glad to see you.

John. And so am I glad—And your mother will
be glad, and Mr Frank, and the lawyer gentleman,
and every body else but the squire.

Mar. Indeed! How so, John? (*Crossing him.*)

John. You moant go that way—there's plots upon
your precious vartue—I'll be shot if there isn't.
There be squires and gentlemen, and horses and
chaises, all ready to devour you.

Mar. For Heaven's sake!—You alarm me.

John. That's what I want—and I'll alarm the whole
place; for I know vary well thou'rt a good girl to thy
dutiful mother, and wou'dn't like to be run away with
against your will, though it were even by a squire.

Mar. Indeed you judge rightly. Hark! I hear
footsteps—Will you protect me?

John. Whya—I don't know if it be manners for a
poor man, like me, to protect a young lady; but I'll
wage half a guinea, if ony squire touches you without
leave, I'll bang his head for him.

Mar. I believe you; but there's no necessity to
meet the danger—Shew me to my mother's—Ah,
bless me, who are these?

John. Houd your noise—There's a little bit of a
by-path i' t'wood—I made it myself last nutting-
time.

Mar. I thank ye, my good fellow—my mother shall
thank you too.

John. Come, come—never mind thy mother, but
take care o' thy sen.

(*They retire;* JOHN *keeps in sight.*)

Enter two of the Squire's Servants.

1 *Serv.* (*As he enters.*) Wait there with the car-

riage. I wish the job were well over—It may prove more pleasant to master than to us.

2 Serv. Somebody watches us——Young man! young man! Why the plague don't you answer? (*To* JOHN.)

John. Why, there be more young men than me hereabouts—My name's John Grouse.

1 Serv. But did you see a young woman?

John. Yees, I seed a many.

2 Serv. Ay; but a young, handsome——

John. Why, Lord, I know—I'm in the secret. You belong to Squire Chace—Whisht! Whisht! I ha' gotten summit to tell you. (*Takes an arm of each, and brings 'em to the front.*) You're come to take Miss Marian to yonder chaise.

1 Serv. You suspect a little roguery, do you?

John. No, I suspect a great deal of roguery—I war sent by t' squire to lend a bit of a hand, and you were to give ma a guinea to drink his health.

1 Serv. He said he wou'd send more assistance. But while we stand chattering, she may be far enough off.

John. No, shew isn't far enough off yet—So hand out a guinea, or I won't help a bit.

2 Serv. I shall give no guinea without orders—Here's the squire himself; let him give it you.

Enter Squire.

Sq. Well, lads, is the game started? Stand close.

John. Under favour, sir, I did offer to help Miss Marian off, and these chaps refused to pay ma—You spoke to me about her to-day—I no' but axed a guinea, and I've a pretty good guess where shew is.

Sq. Here's a guinea, my boy—Well, where is she?

John. Why, I do think by this time, sir, shew's at whoame.

Sq. At home! No such thing—Why should you think so, booby?

John. Why, sir, because I showed her t' nearest road, that's all.

Sq. You shew'd her—Return my money, and make amends, or——

John. Mends! Nay, there's no mends now, you know. I've gotn't a guinea, and things are well enough as they be—As to t' brass, I've earn'd it—And if a bad action deserves a guinea, a *good* one does at any rate.   (*Goes up stage.*

Enter MISS LIBERAL.

Miss Lib. Squire, why do you loiter here? your mistress has eloped; but I've discovered her retreat, and if you make haste, may intercept her—I saw your chaise at the corner—Come, it will just do to put her into it—Your bringing her back to her father will do all his objections away at once.

Sq. I began to think I was thrown out at all quarters. But come, madam, shew me the game, and if I lose sight of it again, may my best hunter bring me in last at the death.

                    [*Exeunt Squire and* MISS LIBERAL.

John. Why, how the deuce can *she* know ought of Miss Marian?—They'll never find her that way, however—I'll just watch 'em though.—(*Steals off.*)

Enter OLD LIBERAL.

Old Lib. (*Agitated.*) No news of her! No tidings! —Who wou'd be plagu'd with *young* women that are pretty—*old* ones that are rich—or *any* that will have their own way?—I'm out of breath!—How angry shall I be when I find—No—-Ha, ha, ha!—Find her!—I shall be so pleas'd, that I'll forgive her directly—I'll forgive every body but the squire, and my cousin, and——She didn't run away from *me*—'twas from them—And how do I know but it's all a trick, and that she has been *forced* to go?—Why was I born to love my children so well?—There's so much misery,

so much plague———I'll have no more, I'm determined.

Re-enter JOHN.

John. (*Looking back as he enters.*) They're gone
t'wrong road—That oud woman's a fool, and t'squire's
no better.

Old Lib. (*Turning short upon him.*) Squire! what!
who!—Has he got her?

John. No, not yet—He hasn't gone t' right road to
get her.

Old Lib. Is she out of his clutches?—If you know,
tell me this instant.

John. Lend your ear—Shoo's at whoame.

Old Lib. At *whoame!*—Are you sure of it—Is she
indeed?

John. On the word of an honest man.

Old Lib. (*Gives him money.*) Here, drink my health
—A hussy! I knew she'd find her way home at last.

John. Shoo wou'dn't ha' found t'way, if I hadn't
shewn her.

Old Lib. Indeed! and was that necessary to make
her return?—Well, well, (*Hurt,*) she may go again
if she likes. It wasn't I that lock'd her up—I was
too fond of her, like a blockhead—I own it, and
I'm ashamed of it.

John. Ay, ay, I thought you were too good a
gentleman to be ashamed o' being fond of poor folk.

Old Lib. Poor!—Fellow, how dare you take such
a liberty?—I'll leave her half my estate, and till then
she shall live like a duchess.

John. Why, you must be fond indeed, to do so at
your time o' life—You should be thinking of other
matters—Consider your poor children.

Old Lib. What! (*Astonished.*)—What did you say?

John. Your worship has been kind to me, and I
respect you—I should be sorry to see you lose your
good name.

Old Lib. Why, you impudent vagabond—Lose my good name!—If you hadn't been the means of restoring my——but I won't believe it till I see her—I'll go and ask her directly. (*Going.*)

John. This way, your worship—you may soon be convinced.

Old Lib. Didn't you say she was at home?

John. To be sure I did, and I say so again.

Enter PARCHMENT.

Parch. Sir! sir! I have found her. Come with me—She is now waiting your pardon for her frolic.

Old Lib. Well, I'm going home to her—I know it.

Parch. She's not at home—She's afraid to go till she has seen you, which she expects to do at the widow Howard's.

John. I told him so—I told him she was at the widow Howard's.

Old Lib. *You* told me!—Mercy on us! You repeatedly assured me you had seen my daughter Fanny safe home, and called me an old fool for being fond of her. Did you, or did you not?

John. I'll take my Bible oath I never said a word on't.

Old Lib. Parchment, run for a constable, and while I go to the widow Howard's, do you take this fellow up for perjury.

John. Why then, I'll be shot if I've seen your daughter since she went to school—I was talking o' Miss Marian, and you said you'd give her half your estate, out of pure love and fondness.

Old Lib. Only let him come within reach of my cane—Don't speak, you Yorkshire jackanapes.— Hark ye, Parchment: are you quite sure my daughter is where you say?

Parch. Quite sure, your worship.

Old Lib. Come along then—if I'm deceived, you shall all mourn with me—I'll put that impudent rogue in the stocks—give you nothing to do for a month, and shut myself from ye all!—But if I find her, she shall have a good husband directly—you both shall caper at her wedding—and not a poor man in the village but shall have cause to join in the nuptial benediction. [*Exeunt.*

SCENE III.

A Room in the Inn—Three Doors in the Room.

Enter BAILIFF *and* FRANK.

Bail. Well, well, if you are sorry for your resistance, and have a mind to come down handsomely, we'll say no more about it. So step in here while I order a chaise.

F. Lib. Why, you wou'dn't lock me up—But no matter—You'll find your mistake out presently, and then it will be my turn.

Bail. Walk in, sir.—I'll just examine the windows though, for fear of accidents.

[*Goes into the first apartment with* FRANK.

Enter First Follower, with FANNY.

1 Fol. It's no use saying a word—You called yourself Mildmay, and the man of the house said you were in fear of being seen.—As you've sent to the gemman that's to bail you, you've only to wait in this room with me till he comes.

Fan. I shall expect civil treatment.

1 Fol. Yes—And we shall expect to be paid for it.

Fan. Have a care, friend!—When the law places an unfortunate man in the power of its agents, it also places him under its most immediate protection.

[*Exit into second apartment.*

Enter Second Follower and JENNY.

Jen. Upon my word, sir, you're wrong.—I'm not the person you mean——I'm not indeed——I'm only a——

MISS LIBERAL *speaks behind.*

Miss Lib. I know she's somewhere in the house.

Jen. Dear, dear, there's old mistress!—Where shall I run?—Ah, sir, don't tell 'em I'm in this room, and I'll go where you please.

(*Runs into the third apartment.*

2 Fol. And for fear of an escape, I'll lock the door. —Lord, how vex'd they'll both be to pay share of the punch!

Enter Bailiff, from First Apartment.

Bail. Now for the sport. (*Locks door.*) Ah! what, Snap, are you there?—I give you joy.

2 Fol. True—I've got him safe enough.

Bail. What, the punch-bowl, I suppose?

2 Fol. No, the prisoner, I tell you.

Bail. Ay, where?

2 Fol. Why, here, here—Can't you believe a man?

Re-enter First Follower, from Second Apartment.

1 Fol. Ah! what, you're both come back.

Bail. Yes; and he wants to persuade me as how he's made the caption.

1 Fol. He must be cunning indeed. I know better than that.

Bail. That's honest now—It was I made the caption.

Followers. You!

Bail. And why not? (*Opens the door.*)—Pray, Mr Mildmay, come and speak for yourself.

1 Fol. Oh, if you want proofs——(*Opens second door.*)

3

2 *Fol.* Sir, I summonses you to appear. (*Opens third door.*)

        (FRANK, JENNY, *and* FANNY *appear at the same moment ; the three Officers stand astonished.*)

F. Lib. Three Mildmays, and neither of them genuine.—Gentlemen, I give you joy of your errors.

Bail. Why, I'll be upon oath you said———(*To* FRANK.)

F. Lib. I said I was subject to fits—They're coming on again, so you'd better take care.

1 *Fol.* (*To* FANNY.) And didn't you say, sir, that you was Mr Mildmay ?

Fan. Why, yes, I did say so—but I am only Fanny Liberal ! (*Runs to* FRANK.)

2 *Fol.* Why, I think *you must* be the right man— (*To* JENNY)—for you are the only one that said you was *not.*

Jen. But I am not the right man, sir : I'm only Jenny ! (*Runs to* FRANK.)

F. Lib. And pray, Master Fanny, and Miss Jenny, how came all this about ?

Fan. Why, Lord, brother, I dare say the reason is known all over the village by this time—I've sent to entreat my father to meet and forgive me at the widow Howard's. If you'll accompany me, we'll soon convince these gentlemen of their error—And you shall hear my story by the way.

F. Lib. Well, my lads, what say you ?

Bail. Why, if the gemman will promise to have no more of his fits———

F. Lib. This way, then—and as the rogues have been civil, we'll settle matters amicably.

Fan. No, my dear brother—I heard my cousin's voice that way. Here seems to be another staircase. —Jenny, stay behind a moment; and as soon as she leaves the house, come to the widow Howard's, and tell me what has passed. [*Exeunt all but* JENNY.

Jen. I can't say I much like to be left behind—I may get out of this scrape into a worse—I declare the old lady and the squire are coming.—I'm sure I never shall be able to look at 'em. (*Hides her face with her hat.*)

Enter MISS LIBERAL *and* SQUIRE CHACE.

Miss Lib. So, so, hussy, your pretty frolic's at an end.—This gentleman's affection is willing to over-look your imprudence; and with *him* you must go to your father immediately.

Jen. (*Aside.*) Ecod, perhaps I may come in for a husband instead of my mistress! (*Pretends to sob.*)

Sq. Nay, don't cry, miss—Rabbit it, I ben't so ugly, nor so ill natur'd, but what you might as 'twere fancy a much worse man. So come along kindly, and say no more about it.

Miss Lib. Ay, you may well hide your face.—But, child, if you repent your folly, it's all as it should be. My influence with your father will set all to rights. So come, come—I knew this would be the case at last.

[*Exeunt the Squire and* MISS LIBERAL, *leading* JENNY *between them.*

SCENE IV.

The Widow HOWARD'S.

Enter MARIAN *and* RACHAEL.

Mar. Thank Heaven, I have escaped!—Rachael, go watch my mother—A little rest may dissipate her uneasiness.   [*Exit* RACHAEL.
How cruel this anxiety!—Neither the counsellor nor

the Jew are to be found.—At any rate she must not
as yet be informed of the danger I have been in.

Enter FRANK *and* FANNY.

F. Lib. Miss Howard, my knowledge of your goodness induces me to ask shelter for a stray sister of
mine, who, having displeased her father by a girlish
elopement, wishes to meet him here, and make your
hospitable roof the scene of her reconciliation.

Mar. With pleasure, sir.—The interest you took
in the happiness of my mother entitles you to it.—
But we are under anxieties, which will for the moment lessen our power to attend this lady as we
wish.

Fan. Is there any thing, Miss Marian, we can do
to remove that anxiety?—I am giddy, and have just
now let that giddiness get the better of my duty.—
But, believe me, I have a heart which wou'd beat
with transport at the performance of any act, to convince you how much I revere the possession of virtue and prudence in another.

Enter OLD LIBERAL *and* JOHN GROUSE.

Old Lib. Where is she—where is she?—My dear,
disobedient, darling girl!—So, so, I'm made a fool
of, and she's not here after all.—Miss Marian, I beg
ten thousand pardons! (*Keeps looking about.*)—Frank,
why, what are you doing here?—And who the devil's
that fellow that looks so impudently at me?

Fan. Ah, if that impudent fellow could but prevail to be taken into favour once more——

Old Lib. Taken into favour!—What, you?—Why,
who, and——Eh!—ah, ah, ah! it's herself!—it's my
saucy good-for-nothing——Come and give your old
father a kiss; and if ever you play me such a trick
again——

F. Lib. Let my friend Mildmay have her, sir,
and then you needn't fear.

Old Lib. What, keep her to myself, by giving her
to another?—A pretty mode of security that!—
What, and so John Grouse here really did see you
safe!

Mar. No, sir; it is *I* who am so much indebted
to our Yorkshire neighbour, that the obligation, I fear,
can never be repaid.

Old Lib. I'll repay him—I'll repay you all, though
I think to have serv'd so fine a young woman is ample recompence in itself.

John. I think it be, sir—and if I could but ha'
manag'd to ha' bang'd squire a bit, I should ha'
been quite satisfied.

Enter FRIENDLY.

Friend. I have found the coat, but the treasure is
stolen. Friend Liberal, there has been much roguery
transacted in this village of yours.

Enter MRS HOWARD.

Mrs How. Ah, sir, have you succeeded—are the
papers found?

Mar. (*Who has been watching at the window.*) No,
my dear madam; but I see Ephraim hastening towards us—doubtless he brings good news.

Friend. I don't like that Ephraim; but we must
wait his determination.

Enter EPHRAIM.

Hark ye, sir; why wou'd you not deliver me the
papers which you have taken from the lining of this
coat?

Eph. Because, ma friend, I don't know meder a
lawyer is more honest as a Jew; and because dis lady
is de person vat has de most right to receive dem.
(*Gives notes to* MRS HOWARD.)

Mrs How. Honest Ephraim! Daughter, friends,
look here—Ten thousand pounds.

Eph. Yes, it's a mighty snug sum.

Old Lib. A snug sum indeed. What, a Jew refuse to keep ten thousand pounds, when he had it in his power?

Eph. It wou'dn't be worth ma vile to keep it.

Friend. Not worth your while?

Eph. No; to an honest man, ten thousand pounds is no more recompence for de loss of a good conscience, than if it was a dwopenny bank-note.

Friend. Let me shake him by the hand—And if ever I look coolly upon your tribe in future, may I never plead the cause of an honest man again.

Mrs How. Mr Friendly, be kind enough to read this paper which accompanies the notes, while I endeavour to acknowledge the generosity of this worthy man.

Eph. If dere is any ting vat you vou'd say to me apoud pusiness, or have any more of de dead gentleman's clothes vat you can sell, I vill talk to you; but I can't afford my time for noting.

Mrs How. Nor shall you. A part of this will justly recompence your probity.

Eph. So, after I've been so honest vatever I can, you vant to pay me for it, and make a rogue of me; but I sha'n't let you do noting of de kind.

Friend. This paper contains a revocation of that part of my friend's will which left twenty thousand pounds to Lucretia Liberal, and gives that sum to Marian Howard.

Old Lib. And I will give the like sum to Frank Liberal, if Marian Howard will accept him for a husband.

F. Lib. If I may hope to render my father's proposal likely to be accepted, my gratitude to him, and affection to you, (*To* MARIAN,) will end but with my being.

Mar. My sentiments must ever depend on those of the best of mothers.

Old Lib. But what the devil will Lucretia say to all this?

Fan. Why, sir, she'll be so angry, that if you don't marry me to somebody, she'll make Squire Chace run away with me, out of mere spite.

Enter MILDMAY.

Old Lib. Well, then, the knight of the sable countenance here shall be your protector.—No thanks—I have been governed so long to the prejudice of my family, that I do but make proper amends in thus contributing to its happiness.

Enter MISS LIBERAL.

(FANNY *runs up the stage.*)

Miss Lib. Well, cousin, for all your opposition, Fanny is by this time happy with the squire.

Old Lib. Squire Mildmay you mean, I suppose.

Miss Lib. Squire Blockhead! I put her into the chaise with Squire Chace; and so humbled, she was ashamed to shew her face.

(OLD LIBERAL *brings* FANNY *forward.*)

Miss Lib. Why, what wonder is this? Was it not you I left with the squire?

Enter JENNY.

Jen. No, ma'am, it was *me.* And the moment the gentleman found it, he jumpt out at the opposite door, left me to myself, mounted his horse, and was out of sight in an instant.

Miss Lib. What, and am I fooled then?—My rage shall know no bounds.—My heart is so full—

Old Lib. But we can make it twenty thousand pounds lighter. Remain with us—Lose sight of prejudice, cherish liberal opinions, endeavour to make others happy, and you cannot fail of being so yourself. May good nature and benevolence unite to banish prejudice from us all ! Or, if any shou'd remain in the bosoms of our patrons, let us hope it will be in favour of our respectful efforts to contribute to their amusement.

END OF VOLUME FOURTH.